THE ARDEN RESEARCH HANDBOOK OF SHAKESPEARE AND ADAPTATION

THE ARDEN SHAKESPEARE HANDBOOKS

The Arden Research Handbook of Contemporary Shakespeare Criticism
Edited by Evelyn Gajowski
ISBN 978-1-3500-9322-5

The Arden Research Handbook of Shakespeare and Social Justice
Edited by David Ruiter
ISBN 978-1-3501-4036-3

The Arden Research Handbook of Shakespeare and Contemporary Performance
Edited by Peter Kirwan and Kathryn Prince
ISBN 978-1-3500-8067-6

The Arden Research Handbook of Shakespeare and Textual Studies
Edited by Lukas Erne
ISBN 978-1-3500-8063-8

FORTHCOMING TITLES
The Arden Handbook of Shakespeare and Early Modern Drama
Edited by Michelle Dowd and Tom Rutter
ISBN 978-1-3501-6185-6

THE ARDEN RESEARCH HANDBOOK OF SHAKESPEARE AND ADAPTATION

Edited by Diana E. Henderson and Stephen O'Neill

THE ARDEN SHAKESPEARE

LONDON • NEW YORK • OXFORD • NEW DELHI • SYDNEY

THE ARDEN SHAKESPEARE
Bloomsbury Publishing Plc
50 Bedford Square, London, WC1B 3DP, UK
1385 Broadway, New York, NY 10018, USA
29 Earlsfort Terrace, Dublin 2, Ireland

BLOOMSBURY, THE ARDEN SHAKESPEARE and the Arden Shakespeare logo
are trademarks of Bloomsbury Publishing Plc

First published in Great Britain 2022

Series design by Charlotte Daniels
Cover image © Dinga/Shutterstock

A catalogue record for this book is available from the British Library.

A catalog record for this book is available from the Library of Congress.

ISBN: HB: 978-1-3501-1030-4
         ePDF: 978-1-3501-1032-8
         ePUB: 978-1-3501-1031-1

Series: The Arden Shakespeare Handbooks

Typeset by Integra Software Services Pvt. Ltd.
Printed and bound in Great Britain

To find out more about our authors and books visit www.bloomsbury.com
and sign up for our newsletters.

CONTENTS

MEDIA LENSES AND DIGITAL CULTURES

PART THREE: NEW DIRECTIONS

LIST OF FIGURES

NOTES ON CONTRIBUTORS

Anna Blackwell is the Programme Leader for the BA English Literature and Institute Head of Research Students for English at De Montfort University, Leicester, UK. Anna has published widely on the topic of the contemporary Shakespearean actor, popular cultural and digital adaptations of Shakespeare. Her first monograph on this topic, *Shakespearean Celebrity in the Digital Age: Fan Cultures and Remediations* was published in 2018. She is currently working on a new research project that examines the intersections of craft adaptations of literature, 'bookishness' and the digital maker economy.

Katherine Steele Brokaw is Associate Professor of English at University of California, Merced, USA, and co-founding artistic director of Shakespeare in Yosemite. She authored *Staging Harmony: Music and Religious Change in Late Medieval and Early English Drama* (2016) and has published articles and reviews in several journals and essay collections. With Jay Zysk she co-edited *Sacred and Secular Transactions in the Age of Shakespeare* (2019), and she edited *Macbeth* for the Arden Performance Editions series (2019). Her next book is 'Shakespeare and Community Performance.

William C. Carroll is Professor of English Emeritus at Boston University, USA. Among his publications are *The Great Feast of Language in Love's Labour's Lost* (1976), *The Metamorphoses of Shakespearean Comedy* (1985) and *Fat King, Lean Beggar: Representations of Poverty in the Age of Shakespeare* (1996). He has also published editions of Middleton, *Women Beware Women* (New Mermaids, 1994), Shakespeare, *Macbeth: Texts and Contexts* (1999), Shakespeare, *The Two Gentlemen of Verona* (Arden Third Series, 2004), Shakespeare, *Love's Labour's Lost* (2009) and *Thomas Middleton: Four Plays* (New Mermaids, 2012). His book, *Adapting Macbeth: A Cultural History*, is forthcoming from The Arden Shakespeare. He is Co-General Editor of the New Mermaids Drama Series.

Vanessa I. Corredera is Associate Professor and Chair of the Department of English at Andrews University, Michigan, USA. Her scholarship examines race, gender and representation in both early modern literature and in modern re-imaginings of the premodern across adaptations/appropriations, performance and popular culture. This work has appeared in *Borrowers and Lenders, Shakespeare Quarterly, The Journal of American Studies, Literature/Film Quarterly* and *Shakespeare*, and is forthcoming in *Literature Compass*. Her forthcoming monograph, '*Speak of Me As I Am*': *Othello in Post-racial America*, examines how antiblack and antiracist engagements with *Othello* across media (comic books, podcasts, performances, television and film) advance or challenge America's post-racial imaginary.

Melissa Croteau is Professor of Film Studies and Literature and the Film Program Director at California Baptist University, USA. Her research, teaching and publications centre on global cinema, media adaptation, film theory and early modern British literature. She has published in *Shakespeare Survey*, *Cahiers Élisabéthains* and several other journals and edited volumes. Her books include the monograph *Re-forming Shakespeare: Adaptations and Appropriations of the Bard in Millennial Film and Popular Culture* (2013) and co-edited volume *Apocalyptic Shakespeare: Essays on Visions of Chaos and Revelation in Recent Film Adaptations* (2009). Her book *The Expression of Spiritual and Human Transcendence in Japanese Cinema* is forthcoming in 2022.

Annie Dorsen is a director and writer whose works explore the intersection of algorithms and live performance. Her most recent project, *Infinite Sun* (2019), is an algorithmic sound installation commissioned by the Sharjah Biennial 14. Previous performance projects, including *The Great Outdoors* (2017), *Yesterday Tomorrow* (2015), *A Piece of Work* (2013) and *Hello Hi There* (2010), have been widely presented in the US and internationally. The script for *A Piece of Work* was published by Ugly Duckling Presse, and she has contributed essays for *The Drama Review*, *Theatre Magazine*, *Etcetera*, *Frakcija* and *Performing Arts Journal*. She is the co-creator of the 2008 Broadway musical *Passing Strange*, which she also directed. In addition to awards for *Passing Strange*, Dorsen received a 2019 MacArthur Fellowship, a 2018 Guggenheim Fellowship, the 2018 Spalding Gray Award, a 2016 Foundation for Contemporary Arts Grant to Artists Award and the 2014 Herb Alpert Award for the Arts in Theatre.

Valerie M. Fazel currently teaches in the Department of English at Arizona State University, USA, where she earned her PhD. She is co-author (with Louise Geddes) of *The Shakespeare Multiverse: Fandom as a Literary Praxis* (2021), and co-editor of *The Shakespeare User: Creative and Critical Appropriations in a Networked Culture* (2017) and *Variable Objects: Speculative Shakespeare Appropriation* (2021). Her essay work on Shakespeare and popular appropriation appears in several edited collections, as well as *Borrowers and Lenders: A Journal of Shakespeare Appropriation*, *The Arizona Center for Medieval and Renaissance Studies Sundial* and *Shakespeare*.

Miriam Felton-Dansky is Associate Professor of Theater and Performance at Bard College, New York, and Director of the Undergraduate Theater and Performance Program. She teaches courses on modern and contemporary theatre and performance, political and socially engaged performance, performance spectatorship, and performance in the digital world. She is the author of *Viral Performance: Contagious Theaters from Modernism to the Digital Age* (2018), as well as articles in numerous theatre and performance studies journals and publications for general readership such as Artforum.com and the *Village Voice*. She is currently writing a book about spectatorship in contemporary performance.

Ailsa Grant Ferguson is Principal Lecturer in Literature at the University of Brighton, UK. Her research interests focus on Shakespeare and Early Modern Literature and their afterlives, particularly in relation to cultural memory, adaptation and appropriation, heritage and gender. She is the author of two monographs, *The Shakespeare Hut* (2019, The Arden Shakespeare) and *Shakespeare, Cinema, Counterculture* (2016) and co-author, with Kate Aughterson, of *Shakespeare and Gender*, a major new textbook for the Arden Shakespeare (2020, The Arden Shakespeare). Her current research explores Susanna Hall (nee Shakespeare) and the representation of early modern women in contemporary heritage, literary and performance settings.

Kavita Mudan Finn has taught literature, history and gender studies at MIT, Georgetown, George Washington University, the University of Maryland College Park and Simmons University, all USA. Her first book, *The Last Plantagenet Consorts: Gender, Genre, and Historiography 1440–1627*, was published in 2012 and her work has appeared in *Viator*, *Shakespeare*, *Medieval & Renaissance Drama in England*, *Critical Survey*, *The Journal of Fandom Studies*, *Quarterly Review of Film and Video* and a range of edited volumes. When not managing a two-child, three-dog circus, she is working on a biography of the fifteenth-century queen Elizabeth Woodville.

Louise Geddes is an Associate Professor of English at Adelphi University, New York. She received her PhD in English from the CUNY Graduate Center, New York. She is the author of *Appropriating Shakespeare: A Cultural History of Pyramus and Thisbe* (2017). She is co-author (with Valerie M. Fazel) of *The Shakespeare Multiverse: Fandom as a Literary Praxis* (2021), and co-editor of *The Shakespeare User: Creative and Critical Appropriations in a Networked Culture* (2017) and *Variable Objects: Speculative Shakespeare Appropriation* (2021). Her work has been published in *Shakespeare Bulletin*, *Shakespeare Survey*, *Medieval and Renaissance Studies in Drama* and *Interdisciplinary Literary Studies*. She is one of the General Editors of *Borrowers and Lenders: A Journal of Shakespeare Appropriation*.

Susanne Greenhalgh is an Honorary Research Fellow at the University of Roehampton, UK, where she taught in the Department of Drama, Theatre and Performance for many years. Her publications include special issues of *Shakespeare* and *Shakespeare Bulletin*, *Shakespeare and Childhood* (with Kate Chedgzoy and Robert Shaughnessy, 2009), *Shakespeare and the 'Live' Theatre Broadcast Experience* (with Pascale Aebischer and Laurie Osborne, The Arden Shakespeare, 2018) and many essays on Shakespeare and his contemporaries in radio, television and digital media.

Diana E. Henderson, Arthur J. Conner Professor of Literature at MIT, USA, is author of *Collaborations with the Past: Reshaping Shakespeare Across Time and Media* (2006), *Passion Made Public: Elizabethan Lyric, Gender, and Performance* (1995) and many scholarly essays. She edited Routledge's *Alternative Shakespeares 3* (2008), Blackwell's *Concise Companion to Shakespeare on Screen* (2005) and (with

Kyle Vitale) The Arden Shakespeare's *Shakespeare and Digital Pedagogy: Case Studies and Strategies* (2022). With James R. Siemon, she co-edits the annual *Shakespeare Studies*. She works as a dramaturg in professional theatre, co-directs MIT's Global Shakespeares Curriculum Initiative and served as PI creating the open-access course 'Global Shakespeare: Re-creating *The Merchant of Venice*'.

Rui Carvalho Homem is Professor of English at the University of Porto (Oporto), Portugal. He has published widely, in a variety of formats, on early modern English culture (with a particular focus on drama), Irish literature, translation and intermediality. As a literary translator, his publications include annotated versions of Shakespeare, Christopher Marlowe, Seamus Heaney and Philip Larkin. He was the Chair of ESRA, the European Shakespeare Research Association, for the period 2013–21.

Douglas M. Lanier is Professor of English and Coordinator of the Literature program at the University of New Hampshire, USA, as well as the current chair of the Adaptation Studies forum of the MLA. He has written widely on Shakespeare and modern adaptation, with a special interest in Shakespeare and mass media. His book *Shakespeare and Modern Popular Culture* appeared in 2002; he has recently published an edition of *Timon of Athens* and the book *The Merchant of Venice: Language & Writing*. He is currently working on two projects, one on *Othello* on screen, the other on reparative uses of Shakespeare.

Joyce Green MacDonald is Professor of English at the University of Kentucky, USA. She is the author of *Shakespearean Adaptation, Race, and Memory in the New World* (2020) which explores how race appears in early modern drama and how it can function in post-Renaissance responses to Shakespeare's plays and poems. She is a member of the editorial boards of the journals *Shakespeare Studies, Borrowers and Lenders: The Journal of Shakespeare and Appropriation* and the Research Board for the Royal Shakespeare Company. She is editing *Antony and Cleopatra* for the new Cambridge Shakespeare Editions series.

Stephen O'Neill is Associate Professor in English at Maynooth University, Ireland. He is the author of *Shakespeare and YouTube* (The Arden Shakespeare, 2014), *Staging Ireland: Representations in Shakespeare and Renaissance Drama* (Four Courts, 2007), editor of *Broadcast Your Shakespeare* (The Arden Shakespeare, 2018) and co-editor of *Shakespeare and the Irish Writer* (2010). He has published widely on adapted Shakespeare, especially in digital cultures. Recent work includes articles on HBO's *Westworld* in *Cahiers Élisabéthains* and Maggie O'Farrell's award-winning novel *Hamnet* in *Shakespeare*. His new work is focused on eco-critical approaches to literature, with a project on the literary life of trees in early modern Ireland.

Varsha Panjwani's research focuses on the way in which Shakespeare can be deployed for intersectional feminism and how this approach, in turn, invigorates Shakespeare. Her forthcoming book, *Podcasts and Feminist Shakespeare Pedagogy* is under contract with Cambridge University Press and she is the creator of the podcast series, 'Women & Shakespeare' (www.womenandshakespeare.com). Her articles have been published in international journals such as *Shakespeare Survey* and *Shakespeare Studies*, and in pioneering edited collections such as *Shakespeare: Race and Performance*, *Shakespeare and Indian Cinema* and *Eating Shakespeare*.

Paul Prescott is Professor of English and Theatre at the University of California, Merced, USA. He has acted, adapted and taught Shakespeare in a range of countries and contexts and published widely on Shakespeare in performance. As a dramaturg and adaptor, he has collaborated with a number of companies including the National Theatre of Great Britain, and is co-founder of Shakespeare in Yosemite. He is the author of *Reviewing Shakespeare* (2013), the editor of *Othello* (Arden Performance Editions, 2018) and co-editor of the books *A Year of Shakespeare: Re-living the World Shakespeare Festival* (2013), *Shakespeare on the Global Stage* (2015) and *Shakespeare on European Festival Stages* (forthcoming 2022) (all Arden).

Julie Sanders is Professor of English Literature and Drama and currently Deputy Vice-Chancellor and Provost at Newcastle University, UK. She has published widely on topics ranging from Shakespeare, Ben Jonson, early modern literature and adaptation studies, including *Adaptation and Appropriation* (2006, updated second edition, 2016), and has produced scholarly editions of plays by Jonson, James Shirley and Richard Brome. Her current research focuses on Global Shakespeares and social justice and geopolitical contexts for adaptations of his work as well as early modern literary geographies. She co-edits a series on the latter with Garrett A. Sullivan Jr.

Sabine Schülting is Professor of English at Freie Universität Berlin, Germany. Her research focuses on early modern and nineteenth-century literatures and cultures, Shakespeare, Gender Studies, and transcultural encounters. She is the editor of *Shakespeare Jahrbuch*, and her book publications include a co-edited collection *Early Modern Encounters with the Islamic East: Performing Cultures* (2012), and two monographs: *Dirt in Victorian Literature and Culture: Writing Materiality* (2016), and a book co-authored with Zeno Ackermann, *Precarious Figurations: Shylock on the German Stage, 1920–2010* (De Gruyter, 2019).

Emma Smith is Professor of Shakespeare Studies and Tutorial Fellow at Hertford College, University of Oxford, UK. She has published widely on Shakespeare's reception in print, performance and criticism. Her *Shakespeare's First Folio: Four Centuries of an Iconic Book* (2016) combined aspects of the history of the book, histories of reading and the interpretation of Shakespeare on the page to produce a biography of the book. Her *This Is Shakespeare* (2019) invited readers to see the plays as incomplete, ambiguous texts to think with. She edits the international journal *Shakespeare Survey*. She is currently working on a new edition of *Twelfth Night*.

Preti Taneja is a writer and activist. Her novel *We That Are Young* won the 2018 Desmond Elliott Prize for the UK's best debut of the year, and was listed for awards including the Folio Prize, the Shakti Bhatt First Book Prize (India), Republic of Consciousness Prize (UK) and Europe's premier award for a work of world literature, the Prix Jan Michalski. It has been translated into several languages and is published in the USA by AA Knopf. Preti is a Contributing Editor at The White Review, and at the independent press, And Other Stories. She is Professor of World Literature and Creative Writing at Newcastle University, UK.

Yong Li Lan is Associate Professor of Theatre Studies in the Department of English at the National University of Singapore, and the Director and Editor-in-Chief at Asian Shakespeare Intercultural Archive (A|S|I|A). She co-edited (with Dennis Kennedy) *Shakespeare in Asia: Contemporary Performance* (2010) and edited *Macbeth* (1999). She has published widely on Shakespeare and intercultural performance, translation in performance, Asian theatre, and digital archiving, both as book chapters and in journals such as *Shakespeare Survey*, *Theatre Journal*, *Literature/Film Quarterly* and *Shakespeare Jahrbuch*.

Yukari Yoshihara is an associate professor at the University of Tsukuba, Japan. Her publications include 'Bardolators and Bardoclasts: Shakespeare in Manga/Anime and Cosplay' in *Asian Interventions in Global Shakespeare* (2021), 'Postwar American Studies in Asia and Its Pre-History: George Kerr and Taiwan as an American Frontier' in *American Quarterly* 73 (2) (2021), 'Ophelia and Her Magical Daughters: the Afterlives of Ophelia in Japanese Pop Culture' in *Shakespeare and the Supernatural* (2020) and '"Raw-Savage" Othello: The First Staged Japanese Adaptation of *Othello* (1903) and Japanese Colonialism' in *Shakespeare and the Ethics of Appropriation* (2014).

ACKNOWLEDGEMENTS

The editors would like to thank Maynooth University Department of English and the Literature Faculty at MIT for their support, and the Arden Shakespeare team at Bloomsbury Publishing (especially Mark Dudgeon and Lara Bateman) for their guidance and assistance through an especially challenging number of years. Our additional thanks to Kavita Mudan Finn for creating the volume's index. More generally, this volume is enriched by the international community of Shakespeare scholars, by conversations at meetings of the Shakespeare Association of America and conferences in Europe and Asia, and by creative and critical adaptations of Shakespeare's works from around the world.

Introduction

DIANA E. HENDERSON AND STEPHEN O'NEILL

PLUGGING INTO ADAPTATION

Reflecting on his adaptation of Aeschylus' *Oresteia* (*c*. 450 BCE), theatre director Robert Icke offers a description that resonates with the contents of *The Arden Research Handbook of Shakespeare and Adaptation*:

> I think of adaptation as like using a foreign plug. You are in a country where your hairdryer won't work when you plug it straight in. You have to find the adaptor which will let the electricity of now flow into the old thing and make it function. That's the long job.

> (qtd. in Clapp 2015)

If we plug into Icke's simile, Shakespeare is the familiar mechanism or object, the 'old thing', that requires another energizing object to flow, to link into circuits and locations and take on new meanings in these contexts. That granted, from the perspective of many potential audiences, Shakespeare itself is the 'new thing' or indeed the 'foreign' thing, requiring more familiar tools – be they contemporary media, genres or other forms of recognizable categorization – to help them participate in whatever pleasure and usefulness that circuit might afford. The catalyzing Shakespeare object, as this volume attests, operates in a myriad of forms, from theatrical performance, poetry and film to the novel, television and digital media, across the centuries and a wide range of locations. Adapting is, as Icke suggests, a 'long job'. It is also one of immense scale since Shakespeare is the most quoted (Maxwell and Rumbold 2018: 1) and most adapted (Elliott 2020: 25) of any writer in literary history. Adapting Shakespeare is a process at once creative, contextual, ethical and political. There are the individual writers, performers, fans and practitioners who engage with the text, initiating a dialogue with it, and there are companies and collaborators who enlist the man and his works to add texture or authority to their own projects, for both pragmatic and idealistic reasons. These entities of adaptation have their own complex, often fascinating environments and histories. Discrete media, all with their own frame effects and affordances that occur in and from particular cultural contexts, carrying their own histories and politics, likewise shape what Shakespeare adaptations are and how audiences respond to them. And their makers themselves demonstrate an intense adaptability to circumstance, be it joyous or painful: during the first year of the COVID-19 pandemic, for instance, actor and director Rob Myles produced *The Show Must Go Online*, a series of all thirty-seven of Shakespeare's plays shown on Zoom and archived on YouTube (Myles 2021). In prisons, concentration camps, under state surveillance and confined to asylums as well as in schools, community parks and artists colonies, adaptors have found in Shakespeare a spark as well as a tool to illuminate their worlds.

ADAPTED/ADAPTING SHAKESPEARE

Shakespeare himself already knew about the adaptational process, turning to a variety of texts in his own time to produce plays for the early modern stage. This is not to negate his achievements as a playwright but rather to recognize that, as Emma Smith emphasizes in the opening chapter of this volume, part of his immense skill was adaptive creative practice: he worked with materials – or 'originals' as he and other Renaissance writers would have understood them – to create a new text for production as a performance. In this way, Shakespeare adaptation begins with Shakespeare's own hand – the author's pen, if you will, as one medium – that quickly becomes part of other media, from the actor's voice (see Weimann 2000) to the space of the stage itself. Shakespeare adaptation has, then, long constituted a transmedia process. But the process of adaptation is more complex still than the trajectory from authoring hand to page and to stage just sketched. There are those prior authoring hands and a set of texts, palimpsests and collaborations that invite us to regard adaptation – and literary and artistic expression more broadly – as a writing over of prior stories. In this way too, Shakespeare's plays, and those of his contemporaries, can be understood as layers, the play text and the world it conjures through performance enabled by prior texts and the stories they contain.

Such terms as layers and palimpsests highlight how, in describing and theorizing adaptation, critics and scholars turn to metaphors. The word, palimpsest, derives from manuscript culture. It comes, via Latin, from Greek *palimpsēstos*, from *palin* 'again' + *psēstos* 'rubbed smooth', to denote a piece of writing material on which later writing has been superimposed or layered over earlier writing. Christine Geraghty notes how 'adaptations are deemed to borrow, transform, translate, hold a conversation with, and provide a reading of' (2007: 194) earlier texts. The metaphors we employ to describe adaptation in turn draw on theories of writing as ghostly, the effect of past voices or texts reappearing, a phenomenon noted in relation to Shakespeare's own ghostly resurfacing in modern culture as the 'return of the expressed' (Garber 2008: xvii). Indeed, the metaphors we use to theorize adaptation are themselves haunted by past voices of such theorists as Gérard Genette, Richard Schechner and Jacques Derrida. Adaptation, Geraghty argues, is a 'layering process [that] involves an accretion of deposits over time, a recognition of ghostly presences, and a shadowing or doubling of what is on the surface by what is glimpsed behind' (2007: 195).

The idea of adaptation as a doubling is elaborated in Linda Hutcheon's *A Theory of Adaptation* (2013), to date the most cited book-length study in the field (Elliott 2020: 156). The adapting work, Hutcheon argues, is a repetition of a prior work, but, in a now oft-cited phrase, crucially it is 'repetition with variation' (2013: 4), with the adaptive faculty characterized by its ability 'to repeat without copying, to embed difference in similarity, to be at once both self and Other' (174). This dialogic of 'both and' rather than a binary of 'either/or' licenses an appreciation of adaptation as 'the doubled pleasure of the palimpsest' (116). Contemporary novelist Jeanette Winterson's *The Gap of Time* (2015) invokes this process in announcing itself as a 'cover story' of *The Winter's Tale* that imprints itself on the play and prompts a reconsideration of it. The cover of Shakespeare's late romance invites the reader into a both-and relational dynamic between adaptation and Shakespeare.

This dialogic emphasis has proved crucial to studies of Shakespeare adaptation and in no small way has liberated the field. 'The evaluative cry "not as good as the original" is now fading' (Bickley and Stevens 2021: 2). Douglas Lanier, writing in this volume, goes further: 'Now in academe (and in popular culture), adaptation is newly ascendant as a cultural force, no longer carrying (quite) the stigma of secondarity and parasitism.' These assertions speak to deeper debates within literary criticism and theory as to the value of adaptation both as a creative practice and critical field of study.

Adaptation studies is now well established as an international field, one which Shakespeare scholars have profited from and also influenced. At some points in its history, however, adaptation studies has operated in defensive mode, arguing the case for its legitimacy and that of the texts and cultures it analyses. Debates within the field have often centred on what precisely adaptation is and the potential taxonomies that might be suggested to arrive at a definition. For the student and researcher seeking an answer to the question, 'What is an adaptation?', the considerable scholarship available does not always deliver conclusively. Related questions include 'What is Shakespeare?' and, as Julie Sanders and Douglas Lanier both ask in this volume, 'What is Shakespeare adaptation?'. With the first question, the degree of indecision and the blurring of categories are appealing. Adaptation theorist Thomas Leitch, having surveyed methodological problems and suggested pliable definitions of adaptation, concludes with this observation:

> After reviewing the problems involved in organizing the discipline more rigorously, adaptation scholars may well decide to defer the question of what isn't an adaptation indefinitely. After all, no matter how they answer that question, they will be imposing new disciplinary constraints on a field that may well flourish more successfully when a thousand flowers bloom.
>
> (2012: 103)

Adaptation's openness may be its defining and enabling characteristic. We come to another metaphor to describe the adaptational process: Leitch's botanical imagery resonates with theorizations of adaptation that draw analogies with biology (Bortolotti and Hutcheon 2007: 443–58; Hutcheon 2013: 176–7). Adaptation resembles a plant in its capacity to replicate, to change and even to blur origin and offshoots, if one follows Poonam Trivedi's suggestion of the banyan tree as a fresh metaphor for adapted Shakespeare. The tree 'develops a dense, weblike canopy of branches, roots and trunks, intermeshing and supporting each other' (Trivedi 2021). In this arboreal model of adaptation, overstory and understory, branches and roots, are interdependent, their functions metamorphosing in time and melding into a vast, fertile canopy of related multiplicity. To Shakespeare and the early moderns, horticultural imagery conveyed the act of writing itself: Ben Jonson cited Seneca's image of the writer as a worker bee, pollinating many flowers 'to draw forth out of the best and choicest flowers, with the bee, and turn all into honey' (Jonson 2012: 583). Or a new piece of writing might be as a child to parent and suggestive of a symbolic desire to overwrite the authority of an older literary tradition: these metaphors converge in the famous 'engrafting' arguments within *The Winter's Tale*'s Act 4 and *The Sonnets*. As Emma Smith argues in her chapter in this volume, such 'governing composition metaphors confirm the abiding sense of writing as construction rather than, or as well as, invention'. They may also speak to a negative perception of adaptation – and the field's already noted paranoia about its legitimacy – as secondary or belated, a following on from other writers, sources and texts. Challenging 'the subtle and not so subtle denigration of adaptation in our (late Romantic, capitalist) culture that still tends to value the "original"' (Hutcheon 2013: xx) has and continues to be a key motivation for scholars of adaptation as they make the argument for the 'longevity of adaptation as a mode of retelling our favourite stories' (xx).

But perhaps we need to reframe the debate around adaptation: Kamilla Elliott, in a detailed study of adaptation's history and theoretical (mis)fortunes, challenges its status as a 'bad theoretical object' (2020: 171). The problem is not with adaptation per se, she argues, but with a presumed hierarchy of theory to adaptation and its effect on theorizations of adaptation which internalize adaptation's putative secondariness (Elliott 2020: 187). While recognizing theories of adaptation, Elliott urges us not to 'treat theorization as a governing discourse of adaptation but one of its many environments' (2020: 238) and to ask how attending to the adaptational process might 'retheorize' the very critical frameworks we might bring to it. Flipping critical hierarchies in this way, Elliott argues that we 'need to see and theorize adaptation as adaptation' (2020: 231).

Adaptation as adaptation: this has a clarity but also a tautological structure that might lead to some frustration in the student and scholar trying to map the relation between Shakespeare and adapted Shakespeare. And so, those questions regarding the boundaries of what constitutes Shakespeare in the first place return. As Maurizio Calbi and Stephen O'Neill note, 'the indicative scare quotes around "Shakespeare" often function as a performative gesture, [the] field's way of differentiating the historical figure from a wider cultural phenomenon, which encompasses adaptations across a range of genres and media as well as citations and appropriations in popular culture' (2016: n.p.). Bruce Smith uses a series of acronyms to suggest the phenomenon of multiple Shakespeares across history: WSA for 'William Shakespeare as Author', referring to the 'supposed all-knowing all controlling mind-in-charge that readers often assume is immanent in a text'; THWS for 'The Historical William Shakespeare', who 'may have entertained thoughts quite different from those registered' in his plays; and WSCI for 'William Shakespeare as Cultural Icon', a figure 'whose identity has changed radically across four centuries' (2009: xi). Smith uses these seemingly stable taxonomies playfully to suggest that it's by noticing what is happening in-between the various iterations of Shakespeare that we come close to why his works 'remain phenomenal in our own time and place' (xvi). Adaptation brings this sense of relation to the fore: it's the bleed between these entities, without one gaining or presuming supremacy, that gets us to the nature of adaptation. Granted, mention of primacy and firstness is especially vexing in the context of a writer like Shakespeare, traditionally associated with ideas of artistic genius and originality, Smith's 'WSA'. Chronologically, of course, plays such as *Hamlet* or *King Lear*, prized in the Western literary canon as exemplars of great literature, do come before their adaptations, yet, the very existence and awareness of those adaptations changes how we think about them as 'originals', inviting us to see the plays themselves as pollinators of earlier works and to discover a web of connections not just between the adapting text and the adapted text but other texts and contexts too, so that what we experience is 'diachronic collaboration' (Henderson 2006: 1). Holly Dugan captures this dynamic when she notes that each iteration of a Shakespearean play 'adds new kinds of metaphoric and material meanings' to its sensory world (2009: 729). But we can return to Elliott to provide a further sense of the to and fro that adaptation entails:

> Adaptation is the ultimate form of the uncanny – that disconcerting merger of the (un)familiar, the varied, and the repeated. Adaptation never completely lets go of the past or entirely embraces the new: it refuses to forget, even as it moves on. It never allows anything to die completely or to be completely reborn. It is always holding us back at the same time that it is pushing us forward. It does not allow us to discard anything finally and yet never allows us to remain the same: something old always comes with something new; something borrowed is always made new.
>
> (2020: 306)

The adaptational process, therefore, does something odd to our sense of temporality – at once reinforcing a sense of history, with the adaptation perhaps motivated by bringing Shakespeare into our own times, and also teasing out connections across timeframes and our larger awareness of spacetime itself. 'Adapting Shakespeare is a looking back to look again', as Katie Brokaw and Paul Prescott put it in this volume. And the adaptational process involves not just the artists who undertake the act of adapting Shakespeare, but also the recipients, the readers and viewers, of these works: we each become actors in the process as we feel and interpret that bleed between texts. You are doing so now, as a reader of this volume, and contributing to the making and remaking of Shakespeare. Indeed, experiencing an interplay of familiarity and fresh recognition is part of adaptation's particular cognitive and affective pleasures as texts enable 'acts of endless (re)creativity' (Sanders 2016: 34).

Adaptation is no longer simply a facet of Shakespeare or the field of study based on his works and their afterlives but is, rather, a key driver of Shakespeare's ongoing vitality in the contemporary world. Indeed, adaptation may be said to be the hallmark of Shakespeare: 'much of the credit for his global reach and historical longevity must go to adaptation – both his adaptations of prior works and others' adaptation of his' (Elliott 2020: 45). Pamela Bickley and Jenny Stevens, surveying the terms employed to describe creative engagements with Shakespeare, highlight how 'reimagining, reinvention, revision, and remediation' tellingly share in common the prefix 're' which, they write, 'implies a revisionist activity, revisiting and reinterpreting - taking an original source with the active intention of making it new, of recontextualizing it' (2021: 1). That sense of intentionality might seem odd in the context of postmodern understandings of the death of the author. However, adaptors' 'deeply personal as well as culturally and historically conditioned reasons for selecting a certain work to adapt and the particular way to do so should be considered seriously by adaptation theory' (Hutcheon 2013: 94–5). Here, the most benign interpretation of 'appropriation' might capture the intensity of engagement with Shakespeare: to 'appropriate' is to draw something near to oneself and 'to make [Shakespeare] part of one's own mental furniture as well as to extend the solitary self out towards the broader world of Shakespeare and what Shakespeare touches' (Desmet and Iyengar 2015: 14). Conversely, some writers may not want to disclose such motivations: 'We make the work; we don't always *want* to critically understand why or how we did it; in the end it has to stand alone to honour the compact of trust between writers and readers', explains Preti Taneja, author of the *King Lear* adaptation *We That Are Young*, in this volume. The history of adapted Shakespeare shows, especially from the 1960s on, that creative borrowers often arrived at their chosen 'hypotext' (Genette 1997, cited here by Lanier) through lived experience enmeshed with broader politically inflected agendas. Women writers, as several scholars have highlighted (see Erickson 1991; Novy 1994, 2000), engaged in what Adrienne Rich described as 'acts of revision' to imagine out of Shakespeare's plays more expansive or different stories for his female characters, stories that could model new possibilities for modern cultural representations and understandings of women. Postcolonial writers, too, mobilized Shakespeare to examine and contest discourses of colonialism and empire focusing particularly on *The Tempest* (see Zabus 2002). In Aimé Césaire's *Une Tempête* (1969), a new Caliban takes centre stage, his utterance of the Swahili word for 'freedom' announcing the play's use of Shakespeare as a weapon against the sense of inferiority imposed by centuries of white colonial domination. Adapted Shakespeare can be a mode of political resistance and historical revision, the encounter with the canonical author a step toward forging new stories. Kate Chedgzoy's work on 'Shakespeare's queer children' (1995: 1–7) demonstrates how through creative adaptation and ideological appropriation, artists such as Derek Jarman mobilized the paternal and patriarchal Shakespeare for a queer aesthetics and politics. Adapted Shakespeare continues to pressure the normative and the dominant: as Julie Sanders writes in this volume, 'Shakespeare adaptation studies has emerged as a powerfully connective and importantly disruptive sub-field within international Shakespeare studies, as performances, interpretations and scholarship emerging from Global South and postcolonial contexts offer radical challenge to dominant Western paradigms'.

It would be misguided, however, to assume that the adaptational process is necessarily progressive or that it can easily contemporize Shakespeare. Netflix's *The King* (2019), an adaptation of Shakespeare's Henriad starring actor of the moment Timothée Chalamet, has been critiqued for privileging the 'interpretive ability and authority of men invested in hypermasculinity, compulsive heterosexuality, the erasure of women, the eschewing of difference, and the overwhelming power of whiteness' (Adams 2020). David Michôd and Joel Edgerton's film highlights how adaptations of Shakespeare may recycle existing exclusions or produce their own troubling blind spots. Neither Shakespeare nor adapted Shakespeare are neutral spaces. Ayanna Thompson, writing about the intersections between modern American constructions of Shakespeare and American constructions of race, asserts that adapted Shakespeare may not be conducive to contemporary race relations (2013: 6); indeed, the cultural capital associated with 'the Bard' may overshadow what adapted Shakespeare can achieve. Thompson returns to this argument when it comes to Toni Morrison's *Desdemona*, a collaborative adaptation with Malian singer-songwriter Raoki Traoré and director Peter Sellars, suggesting that, tethered to *Othello*, this creative production confines its own radical potentiality (2016: 505). Yet this reading overlooks *Desdemona*'s status as an adaptation: it is precisely as an adaptation of *Othello*, i.e. a text that enacts a particular relationship with another text and transforms it through that encounter, that Morrison and her collaborators produce a new artistic production that connects an ethics of reading the past to the present and to the future.

Adapted Shakespeare can be catalyzing and a contested figure, sometimes simultaneously. The Eritrean poet Reesom Haile articulates an overt resistance to literary tradition in his poem 'Shakespeare, Enough', translated into English by Charles Cantalupo, calling out assumptions that Shakespeare is still contemporary:

> Shakespeare said,
> Aren't my poems great?
> How about that love story
> Of Romeo and Juliet?
> But I replied,
> Shakespeare, enough.
> Who wants old stuff
> Like that?
> Why not
> A new kind of love?
> A love of Eritreans
> For green Eritrea,
> Not yet found in words,
> Unheard –
> A fearless story
> The angels sing.
>
> (Haile 2016)

The poem's call and response imagines a dialogue with Shakespeare, at once the man himself and a spectral thing that does not so much appear as reappear in literature – as if always there – only to then exorcize the ghostly presence as unwelcome. Romeo and Juliet exit, giving way to 'a new kind of love', perhaps something less heteronormative and European than Shakespeare's quintessential star-crossed lovers. There are, asserts the poem through its lyricism, voices and stories seeking their claim for the visibility traditionally conferred on Shakespeare. Even as Haile's title implies 'enough' of Shakespeare, however, the work and effect of adaptations, including Haile's own imagined exchange with the dead Bard, is to remember him anew: to quote another modern poet, H.D., 'Remembering Shakespeare always, but remembering him differently' (qtd. in Bickley and Stevens 2021: 2). It's in this sense that we can understand adaptation not (always) as a form of solemn commemoration, the literary equivalent of a statue or monument to Shakespeare, but as 'the art of democratization, a "freeing" of a text from the confined territory of its author and of its readers' (Cartmell 2012: 8). What we might ultimately value about Shakespeare adaptations is how, building on what prior adaptations have made possible and intelligible, each one sets out its own terms to reframe the Shakespeare we thought we knew.

USING THIS HANDBOOK

The Arden Research Handbook of Shakespeare and Adaptation does not expound a singular definition of adapted Shakespeare but rather the chapters that follow combine to offer our readers multiple entry points into a dynamic site of cultural production. Shakespeare adaptation emerges as:

- A theory of the relation between Shakespeare and other texts.
- Dialogical rather than a binary, suggesting the simultaneity of the adapted and adapting texts.
- A creative process and a product.
- A form of historicizing and also remembering Shakespeare.
- Dehierarchizing through contesting and revising, especially with regard to ideologies of gender, race and nation in Shakespeare.
- An aesthetic and an affect generating readerly pleasure and a sense of play in the move between adapted and adapting text.
- A network comprising texts, individuals and media.
- A collaboration among texts, individuals and media, and across spacetime too.
- Medium-specific or at least medium-inflected, in that adaptation transposes a text from one predominating medium to another; these particular forms shape the end process of adaptation and its end product, yet also operate within linked citational environments.
- A transmedia phenomenon that occurs in media forms that intersect.
- Additive, in that the adapting text contributes to and becomes entangled with the hermeneutics of the adapted Shakespearean text.
- A micro-history of adaptation as a need within human culture to return to and to retell stories.

This list is not presented as definitive but rather gestures to the nature and scope of adapted Shakespeare. Individual contributors elaborate on these and other ways to think about and examine closely Shakespeare and adaptation. The volume follows the structure of Bloomsbury's research handbooks, with an opening section

'Research methods and problems' containing three chapters – by Emma Smith, Douglas M. Lanier, and Julie Sanders – that each offer their own respective insights but also work in aggregate to provide a detailed picture of Shakespeare as adaptor and adapted.

We begin with Emma Smith's 'Shakespeare as adaptor' – though Smith complicates the very idea of any definitive beginning point for artistic creativity by exploring Shakespeare as deeply adaptive of his own writing as well as that of others. Adaptation is the very condition of his playwrighting, she argues. Understanding Shakespeare in these terms involves situating his process within early modern understandings of writing, which as Smith demonstrates was an allusive and imitative tradition, but she also establishes how the critical insights of modern adaptation studies can illuminate the ways Shakespearean plots and scenes are 'self-exploring allegories of adaptive writing'. One of the most iconic dramatic moments in *King Lear* – Edgar, in the guise of Poor Tom, encountering his blinded father Gloucester – reuses a motif that the playwright had previously explored in *The Merchant of Venice* and *Twelfth Night*. In these moments, Shakespearean drama is a memory machine that recalls or remembers past texts and past performances and adapts them to a new context: the art of playwrighting emerges as the art of ongoing adaptation. Attending to *King Lear*'s adaptive energies complicates the traditional creative teleology of source to text and of text to adaptation, and reveals Shakespeare's own practice as multi-directional and deeply adaptational. Smith delves further into how *King Lear* both synthesizes and is also reimagined from a range of prior texts, including his own and the 1605 play *The True Chronicle History of King Leir*, with the relationship between the two Lears anticipating the adaptational impetus of modern creative reworkings of Shakespeare's tragedy: in their focus on the women marginalized in Shakespeare's *Lear*, Smith argues, works such as the Women's Theatre Group's *Lear's Daughters* (1987), Jane Smiley's *A Thousand Acres* (1992) and Emily St John Mandel's *Station Eleven* (2014) are as much in dialogue with the play's suppressed textual predecessors as with *King Lear* itself. Adaptations thus remember, perhaps indirectly or inadvertently, Shakespeare's own adaptive playwrighting.

Douglas M. Lanier's chapter on 'Shakespeare and adaptation theory' pursues this emphasis on the dialectical interplay between texts as fundamental to adaptation. There is unfinished business in the relation between his two titular entities, Lanier suggests, as he urges Shakespeare adaptation studies to further engage with adaptation's foundational principles and issues. Moving through classificational, intermedial and appropriative theories of adaptation, Lanier provides readers with a state of the field and elaborates on the benefits for critical analyses of adapted Shakespeare in moving back and forth across disciplinary boundaries, including greater engagement from Shakespeare studies with developments in adaptation and media studies to theorize Shakespeare's fundamentally mediated nature. Much work on adaptation has been concerned with the difference of adapting to adapted text but Lanier proposes that we consider similarity too, noting that 'without some element or principle of fidelity at work, there can be no adaptation'. His 'some element or principle' formulation invites a recognition of how an adaptation strikes 'a relation of similarity to some quality of the source that the adaptation identifies as essentially or distinctively Shakespearean', be it an aspect of language, plot, character, setting, motif, tone or social register. In selectively (re)essentializing Shakespeare, adaptations demonstrate how fidelity is an aesthetic effect of the adaptational process.

Julie Sanders's chapter 'What is Shakespeare adaptation?' examines how an adaptation identifies and then expands a quality in the Shakespearean text. First and foremost, adaptation is both process and practice, Sanders argues, a combination that helps clarify how the adapting text comes to be and how it changes over time. Attentive to the interlinking of aesthetics and politics in adapted Shakespeare, as well as the interplay between source and adaptation, Sanders considers Ali Smith's *Spring* (2019) and Mark Haddon's *The Porpoise* (2019), two Anglophone novels that turn to *Pericles,* which Shakespeare and George Wilkins themselves co-adapted from the medieval poet John Gower's *Confessio Amantis* (1393), itself a re-telling of the life story of Apollonius of Tyre. Why this lesser-known Shakespearean work, one that lacks the name recognition of say *Lear* or *Othello*, should figure in these novels is a question Sanders addresses, as she explores how a play full of sea journeys and migrations becomes an especially resonant text for twenty-first-century artists grappling with such issues as migration, climate action and the politics of division. Smith makes deep use of *Pericles* and its themes of shipwreck, famine, war, sexual violence, biological and affective families, fathers and daughters, youth and redemption but remakes them in a context unmistakably of the novel's own time and place. As retold through *Spring*, *Pericles* is a story of and for the twenty-first century, one both troubling and hopeful; indeed, this might be the novel's fidelity to Shakespeare in Lanier's terms, its identification or fashioning of a Shakespearean quality. Similarly contributing to the modern visibility of *Pericles* is Haddon's *The Porpoise* but, as Sanders shows, this novel takes an even deeper dive (if you will) into the play. Haddon's title, drawn from a comparison of Pericles's capacity for survival to the porpoise's capacity to ride the waves ('I saw the porpoise, how he bounced and tumbled'), suggests that this novel is porpoise-like in its narrative fluidity and movements. Exploring the novel's form and Haddon's distinctive style, Sanders demonstrates how the process of adaptation leads to an active-reader narrative that quite deliberately puts female experiences at its heart. Haddon's is a creative and ethical engagement with the play. Both *Spring* and *The Porpoise* in turn emphasize Shakespeare's availability for, and usefulness as, adaptation to urgent cultural and political contexts.

The second and largest section, 'Current research and issues', provides readers with a series of case studies that move across a variegated landscape of genres, media forms, locations and approaches to ask not only how Shakespeare is multifariously transfigured, hybridized and valorized through adaptational play, but also how adaptations produce interpretive communities and new priorities, out of which emerge new literacies, modes of engagement, sensory pleasures and research opportunities.

William C. Carroll initiates its first cluster of chapters with a capacious example of how the time-honoured critical method of focusing on a single play can allow attention to a wide range of cultures and topical uses. 'Politics, adaptation, *Macbeth*' emphasizes the interpretative diversity of performance adaptations, from those upholding the (biblically allusive) 'Authorized' version of Shakespeare's text as endorsing monarchic orthodoxy to those mining the more subversive, indeed radically disruptive possibilities within that drama. Carroll moves in time from Davenant's Restoration-era revision through Ducis's translation for Napoleonic France, the post-Second World War absurdism of Ionesco and the anti-totalitarianism of Müller onward to Greig's truly 'Scottish play', *Dunsinane* (2011). For late-eighteenth-century French audiences, the play needed to be de-royalized and its politics domesticated; by contrast, for more recent writers dealing with their own Bonaparte-tyrants, appropriations and adaptations recognize and often enhance its terror. Jan Kott, famous for making Shakespeare 'our contemporary', believed *Macbeth* had reached 'the Auschwitz experience' and that at essence, 'The new king will be the man who has killed a king' (Kott 1964: 92, 87). Going even further in foregrounding the adaptor's moment (and anticipating Thompson's concern cited earlier), Müller claims, 'We haven't arrived at ourselves as long as Shakespeare is writing our plays' (Weber 1990: 33, 32), while in the wake of postmodernity and postcolonialism Greig's play seeks to disrupt the linearity of time itself, creating a 'temporal palimpsest' that allows *Macbeth* to address the UK's involvement in Iraq and Afghanistan.

Sharing this awareness of adaptation's potential through its temporal complexity to disrupt and remake the nightmares of historical injustice and tyranny, Joyce Green MacDonald shifts the focus westward from Europe and recentres attention on a particular set of audiences and their cultural experiences. 'Animating an archive of Black performance: swing, William Alexander Brown and *The African Company Presents "Richard III"*' reveals Shakespeare as a 'launching point and place of inspiration, but whose presence ultimately recedes before the power of a newly and specifically Americanized performance'. She emphasizes 'how race – specifically, blackness in early nineteenth-century Manhattan' where Brown's company performed – 'can affect the reception and reproduction of Shakespeare', in turn becoming a creative spur: more than a century and a half later, Carlyle Brown's 1988 play *The African Company Presents 'Richard III'* reanimates that earlier dramaturg's creative ambition in order to map and memorialize the resources and values of Black performance. MacDonald situates her case study within the broader debates among thinkers such as Stuart Hall and Césaire who wrestled with the legacies of slavery and institutionalized racism; she turns to the potential of an experimental, even playful hybridity reaching beyond revolutionary defiance alone, finding in both of the Browns' Shakespeare adaptations (as in many jazz adaptations) a Black subject who swings, generating a 'creative ruckus'.

The strength and endurance of those expressing such creative subjectivity in the wake of the mass human trafficking that forced Africans across the Atlantic provides a powerful inspiration, including for those artists and scholars addressing more recently initiated acts of systemic violence and migratory displacement that have transformed Asia, the contemporary Middle East and Europe. Sabine Schülting analyses how twenty-first-century adaptations on the German-speaking stage have turned most frequently to *Othello* to explore meta-dramatically the history of representing Blackness and to comment on the situation of immigrants. Invoking

Shermin Langhoff's coinage 'post-migratory' (*postmigrantisch*) – itself that rare term that has circulated beyond its origins in artistic culture to permeate German politics and the social sciences – she explores how these adaptations deploy 'a polyphony of dissenting and differing voices', 'linguistic diversity, translations into non-standard varieties and sociolects', and 'art forms... associated with post-migratory youth subcultures'. Drawing on Christy Desmet's model of adaptation as dialogic, showing us a previously unacknowledged resemblance between two texts or persons, Schülting emphasizes (amidst quite divergent approaches to the play and its tragic hero) their 'irreverent revision of the cultural signification of Shakespeare in Germany'.

The final chapter in this cluster emphasizing the 'History and politics of adaptation' travels further east to reveal a very different set of cultural associations with adaptation in Japan's *hon'an* tradition. Light years from the obsession with 'fidelity' characterizing much Anglophone Shakespeare (itself arguably a symptom of repressing England's belated status within early modern culture and imperial politics), this island nation dealt with the cultural inheritance from its ancient continental neighbours and their source scripts quite differently, regarding *hon'an* (transforming the original) as a positive opportunity for conscious refinement befitting the occasion. As Yukari Yoshihara outlines, this less hierarchical framework could itself be adapted when modernization first brought Shakespeare to Japan, but increased Westernization then gave way to more literal translations on stage; as a result, for much of the twentieth century the creative impulses of *hon'an* migrated across media to prose fiction, and later film, anime and manga. Yoshihara focuses on the many novelizations of *Hamlet* (and, through Murakami's *Kafka on the Shore* [2002], considers *Macbeth* as well), attending to the ways *hon'an* encourages writers to explore anxieties about modern male power and female sexuality, particularly in relation to the Japanese imperial nation, international politics and post-war occupation.

Since the final decades of the twentieth century in the work of Yukio Ninegawa and in many bold twenty-first-century productions, *hon'an* has returned to the Japanese stage when producing Shakespeare plays, just as freer adaptive practices have come to dominate the study of Global (including but no longer prioritizing Anglophone) Shakespeares. Even in these chapters anchored by a particular named play by William Shakespeare, the importance of adaptation in every theatrical performance emerges, whether the playtexts be attributed to that author, a subsequent writer, a conceptual director, or a combination thereof. In all instances, multilingualism and multimedial affordances as well as the immediate cultural context crucially shape the sociopolitical import of what is (or is not) presented onstage, suggesting the relevance of both media studies and translation studies in providing further analytic tools for historically grounded inquiry. The following chapters pursue those emphases as they move further away from dramatic representation to examine 'Shakespeare in parts'.

Ailsa Grant Ferguson finds Daniel Fischlin and Mark Fortier's 'wide-lens view of adaptation' helpful for analysing the commemorative gala revue, both as a multimedia genre and in the particular instance of *Shakespeare Live!* (dir. Doran, RSC, 2016). She locates this major televised event within the long history of festivities reaching back to David Garrick, with particular emphasis on the 1916 Tricentenary with which

2016 commemorations shared the peculiar labour, within a complex sociopolitical context, of taking the anniversary of a death and spinning it as celebratory. As the example of Garrick's 1769 Jubilee makes vivid, these galas often have a much larger role in shaping cultural memory than the event itself might seem to promise. In the 2016 show, short extracts from performances in various media (dance, song, film, rap, etc.) were interspersed with live and recorded skits composed for the occasion, 'in a liminal space… transgressing the boundaries of "high" and "low" theatre'; as is typical, the commemorative gala then constructs from 'a collection of parts of Shakespearean texts, adapted, often truncated or fragmented' a 'cohesive show… that "remembers" Shakespeare festively'. Ferguson notes that it is only through the rhetorical devices of 'adaptation, synecdoche and metonymy' and what performance studies describes as the 'ghostly predecessors' haunting any stage production that 'Shakespeare (man and text) exists' – much less becomes so emphatically '*Live!*'

Her case study of one privileged event set in Stratford-upon-Avon recalls as well a larger history of recontextualized Shakespeare quotation and citation in part or whole, including its role as rhetorical training within British imperial education – often within a notorious framework (modelled on Macauley's 'Note on Indian Education'), at other times redeployed as a tool to speak back to Empire and to imagine beyond (as in repurposings by Caribbean writers like Caryl Philips, African Presidents such as Julius Nyerere or the famous collective annotations in the 'Robbin Island Bible'). The 2016 gala's 'Shakespeare', Ferguson observes, 'was mediated as both quintessentially English *and* global, representing both the long-established status of the RSC as a "national treasure" *and* its vision as a champion for inclusion and diversity'. Its script for the occasion had actor-comedian Catherine Tate announcing from the outset that there would be 'something for everybody', and used intertextuality and international representation in an attempt to realize this hope. Yet ultimately, perhaps such an event instead and less debatably 'reveals the instability of the cultural memory of Shakespeare we perform'.

That very instability becomes a source for more diverse creative approaches to the Shakespeare text itself, including the non-dramatic poetry to which the next chapter turns. Closely analysing adaptations of the *Sonnets* in two single-authored volumes and two edited collections published in the same decade as the 2016 gala, Rui Carvalho Homem similarly emphasizes '[w]hat burgeons in the memory… ': the tension between tribute and iconoclasm in a diverse set of works that nonetheless commonly illustrate the postmodern premise that 'all writing… be construed as *re*writing'. Applying insights from translation studies to these '*intra*lingual (English to English) transits' between Shakespeare's collection and contemporary writing, he also emphasizes the critical frameworks (especially Hutcheon's) of adaptation, parody and intertextuality which contribute to a 'historicized understanding of the literary canon and to creative breakthroughs that prove the continued currency of the sonnet form'. Erik Didriksen's *Pop Sonnets: Shakespearean Spins on Your Favourite Songs* do so by presuming the lyrics of Britney Spears, Bruno Mars and Frank Sinatra are more specifically recognizable than the vaguely 'Shakespearean' diction into which they are parodically translated – thereby challenging the canonical centrality of the earlier texts. By contrast, James Anthony's *Shakespeare's Sonnets, Retold* modernizes the entire sequence 'highlighting the rewriter's virtuosity'. Sharmila Cohen and Paul Legault's *The Sonnets: Translating and Rewriting Shakespeare* makes space for formal variety and even visual media, 'severing the derivative bond' to such an extent that these contributors create 'not so much rewritings as *after*-writings, reflections and aesthetic gestures that come in the wake of the *Sonnets*, adversarially or otherwise'. *On Shakespeare's Sonnets: A Poets' Celebration*, edited by Hannah Crawforth and Elizabeth Scott-Baumann, is less formally radical, more homage than challenge with an impressive line-up of established poets whose work merits the method of nuanced, deeply attentive close reading that Homem's chapter demonstrates – a core literary practice that helps illuminate how the juxtaposition of Shakespeare and adaptation is a two-way exchange, enhancing our poetic appreciation of both.

While the *Sonnets* as a collection hover at the boundary between lyric and narrative, parts and whole, the meme takes the 'little room' of the stanza to its digital extreme. In '"Play on", or the memeing of Shakespeare: adaptation and internet culture', Anna Blackwell explores the born-digital meme among the rich 'spectrum of potential internet Shakespeare texts' that provide research opportunities. Helpfully surveying current theoretical work on Shakespeare's online fragmentation as well as the variety of meme patterns and uses, she ultimately homes in on one 'previously overlooked node within Shakespeare's ghostly network', the GIF (graphic interchange format), as 'a dynamic adaptive form'. Addressing the ephemerality and idiosyncrasies of search engines and algorithmic results alongside the pleasures and appropriative problems of remediated fragments, her examples range from parodic verbal jokes based on remixing hiphop-derived vernacular with early modern formality ('shooketh') to disturbing reiterations of 'what Lauren Michele Jackson defines as "digital blackface"' to the recuperative juxtaposition of an image from children's animation (*My Little Pony*) alongside a quotation of *Hamlet*.

Drawing fruitfully on criticism by (among others) Kirk Hendershott-Kraetzer and Christy Desmet, Blackwell notes how the necessary fragmentation of the digital text can either reinscribe or deconstruct Shakespeare as author as well as the ideological biases of his plays, while the compulsive repurposing and indiscriminate circulation of internet-native forms creates alternative routes for engagement – with other user communities, the sometimes daunting, abstracted figure of Shakespeare and the huge online archive of adaptations. The looping of the GIF's moving image suggests an alternative dynamic to the emphases of much performance theory and practice, its 'sensation and the recycling of an apparently endless sameness' contrasting with 'liveness' and the shape of an event, which 'can be used to anatomize performance in a productive manner'. Furthermore, given 'so much cultural anxiety about understanding [Shakespeare] correctly', she concludes that the GIF may 'prove a more indicative example of the way that Shakespeare continues to exist in popular and digital culture than more conventional, self-contained adaptations'.

The 'Shakespeare in parts' cluster concludes by expanding this emphasis on multimedia screen Shakespeares as a site of cultural remixing and widening audiences as it turns to the artform that for the past century arguably has introduced more people to Shakespeare's narratives than has any other: film. In 'Bollywood Gertrudes and

Global Shakespeares', Varsha Panjwani takes the 'part' of Hamlet's mother, in two senses: advocating for attention to her underwritten role in Shakespeare's text(s), and emphasizing how Indian artists have enriched that part through representational and cross-media adaptation. Noting especially the role of the camera alongside narrative changes in making Tabu's performance as Ghazala (Gertrude) so powerful in Vishal Bhardwaj's *Haider*, Panjwani reveals its prehistory by focusing on the Gertrudes of earlier Bollywood adaptations. One of her wider goals in so doing is to reveal how 'studying Indian avatars of Shakespeare's women characters can contribute fresh insights to Feminist Shakespeare studies'. Moreover, she models the value of archival research that considers lost, low-quality and fragmentary prints as contributing to important claims – in this instance, that 'serious, analytical engagement with Shakespeare has a long history in Bollywood', which in turn 'contributes to Global Shakespeares's project of decentring Anglophone Shakespeare'. The lost silent film titled *Khoon-e-Nahak* (Murder Most Foul; 1928), sharing its name with a Parsi theatre adaptation in which the Gertrude character instigates the regicide, builds parallels with another famous part, Lady Macbeth; Panjwani calls attention to several actors' awareness of this connection, then and subsequently. Her discussion of the lost *Khoon-ka-Khoon* (Blood's Murder; 1935 – and thus likely the world's first full-length *Hamlet* talkie) reveals the importance of celebrity casting in shaping which relationships come to the fore – in this instance, providing the precedent for a closer bond between Gertrude and Ophelia. Panjwani's analysis of the first surviving *Hamlet* (1954) emphasizes how adaptation gives added texture to Gertrude's part through addition of a backstory which emphasizes her political circumscription, thereby altering her relationship with Polonius as well.

The feature-length film, Panjwani's focus, provided the first major impetus for academic Shakespeare studies to consider cross-media adaptation seriously, the camera lens prompting those not actively engaged with the stage to rethink their literary critical biases. 'Media lenses and digital cultures', the third cluster of chapters, begins by shifting location from Bollywood to Hollywood, as Melissa Croteau brings her film studies training to bear in interpreting Casey Wilder Mott's *A Midsummer Night's Dream* (2018). Its setting in a magical version of the world's other dominant movie industry obviously lends itself to a metafilmic – converging with a metatheatrical – reinterpretation. Noting the role of an earlier film of this play, Max Reinhardt and William Dieterle's 1935 spectacular, in having contributed to the US studio system's aversion to direct Shakespeare adaptations (as distinct from those remediated via Broadway musicals), Croteau positions Mott more in the model of Orson Welles as indie outsider, even as he works with the established film genres of the screwball comedy and LA film. Such 'cinematic genres beyond the pale of literary adaptation', she argues, 'provide a rich vein of semantic material that is often ignored' by scholars viewing only through the lens of the 'Shakespeare film' subgenre. Drawing on her interview with the director and on press kit materials as well as her own analysis of shot selections, Croteau makes a space for artistic intention as part of her research method, and provides a rich reading of the functions of film genres more generally. Mott's film builds in its own consciousness of the digital process of twenty-first-century 'filmmaking' as part of its frame, in ways true as well to Shakespeare's metadramatic precedent; working with concepts of generic hybridity and media convergence applied to film Shakespeares by Michael Anderegg and Katherine Rowe, among others, Croteau's case study demonstrates how deeper understanding of cinematic research illuminates both adaptation and Shakespeare.

Susanne Greenhalgh similarly illuminates the artistic conditions and cultural functions of a fundamental screen medium for adaptation of Shakespeare's plays: television. She does so through a rich historical survey that reaches into our current 'multi-platform age'. One major thread of televisual adaptations involves the heritage and remediation of theatre, divisible into three categories: the recording of live performances in the theatre, studio-based restagings of theatre productions and made-for-television versions shot in studios or on location. The media turn of recent decades has transformed the status and availability of works available, including both those designed for serial scheduling and newer digitized forms of allusive and intertextual televisuality. The longer history of Anglophone Shakespeare's televisual origins, remediating radio as well, reminds us that the affordances of sound recording were crucial to the creation, and now to our understanding, of such adaptations, alongside dynamic changes in the representation of on- and offscreen space. Greenhalgh illuminates differences from cinematic shooting and cutting, the intermixture of live broadcast and what John Wyver calls the 'doubled adaptation' of televised stage productions, and 'new forms of socially distanced, intermedial adaptation' prompted by the COVID-19 pandemic. In comparing UK, Canadian and US 'made-for-TV Shakespeare', she notes the key role not only of the director and script adaptor but of the producer, of 'event television' scheduling, celebrity casting and changes in the media environment. Increased self-reflexivity and freer adaptations, less constraint regarding episode lengths and on-demand viewing have all radically altered the conventions of twenty-first-century televisual adaptations – just as the global turn in scholarly research has begun to widen the range of forms and sociopolitical contexts featured in televisual Shakespeare studies.

Yong Li Lan's 'On location in Asian Shakespeare stage adaptations' extends this cluster in a closely related direction. Given the generational shifts that have many consumers now watching their television through streaming services on computer, boundaries between once-discrete media have all but disappeared for many of those 'born digital' (Henderson 2020: 319–21, 344–6). Video recordings conceived as feature-length films, past television series repackaged for binge-watching, amateur videos uploaded on YouTube (O'Neill 2014) and high-end professional theatre events all cohabit within browsers and digital archives. As the co-founder and driving force behind *The Asian Shakespeare Intercultural Archive* (A|S|I|A), Yong is well situated to consider these formal and temporal layerings in media and performance, creation and reception. She provides richly contextualized readings of diverse stage productions now archived in particular online instantiations, also demonstrating how several nations' diverse artistic and political pasts (Korean, Chinese and Japanese in particular) undermine any simple present sense of 'realist Shakespeares'. Clarifying that the 'imaginary category' 'Asian Shakespeares' cannot 'unify as a set the diverse languages, performance cultures and socio-political histories that have transformed Shakespeare's plays' differently across a continent over time, and situating Rustom Bharucha's criticism of the term as 'a neo-colonialist appropriation of the cultural capital of Asian theatres', she nonetheless observes that the twenty-first century has 'altered the sense of authentic place that Bharucha's argument assumes and champions' as 'international networks among theatre industries expanded' – requiring researchers to recognize now 'how a local theatre culture is a well-travelled one' even before the overlay of its digital recording. She contrasts the use of location in Yohangza Theatre Company's *Pericles* (2015) with its director Yang Jung-Ung's earlier *Midsummer Night's Dream*, thereby destabilizing assumptions about a prior 'English Shakespeare' as well. Furthermore, she illuminates how theories of 'intercultural performance' premised on an 'encounter' between indigenous traditions and Anglophone culture are always already informed by a prior, complicating history. Her comparative description of both the Yohangza and other stage productions recast as digital artifacts – especially Ryutopia's *Othello* (2006) and Wu Hsing-kuo's *Li Er Zai Ci* (Lear is Here) – adds even more layering of media perspectives, requiring awareness of their importance and variety. These case studies recall the pertinence of Thomas Cartelli and Katherine Rowe's observation that '[a]ll adaptations' – to which encyclopedic category we may now add digitally archived reproductions – 'make their habitations not only in specific geographic milieu and media but also in *citational environments*, generic and cultural fields that incorporate specific stances towards source materials and rules for handling them' (2007: 29).

Without doubt, social media and digital affordances have increasingly widened – and challenged – the inclusiveness and visibility of those 'cultural fields', perhaps first and foremost through the practices that have fuelled fan studies. Valerie M. Fazel and Louise Geddes champion this approach while rightly remembering that 'fandoms have always been part of the Shakespeare legacy'; indeed, the long history of reception 'has always been a weave of creative and critical work'. The testimonials and scholarly studies of previous centuries' performers, writers, amateur companies and burlesques, as well as more recent phenomenologically oriented reflections (such as Barbara Hodgdon's on her own material and affective involvement in 'the Shakespeare Trade') certainly confirm this generalization. They provide a pre-history for Fazel and Geddes's focus on 'fanworks' in this concluding chapter of Part Two's 'Current research and issues'. Noting that Shakespeare is represented in the online *Archive of Our Own* (*AO3*) in more than twelve thousand fan-crafted narratives, they call attention to the different interplay across media these stories and their audiences produce: indeed, they even 'have the power to impact dominant media forces such as broadcast serial television'. They do so not only through 'an ever-increasing archive of texts' but through a recursive conversation, as Kavita Mudan Finn has demonstrated, 'between fan authors, fan artists and those who consume their works' (2017: 212). Fazel and Geddes emphasize two major differences from traditional scholarly conventions regarding adaptations: one, that fanwork openly acknowledges its affective investment in Shakespeare; and secondly, that it emphasizes process over product. Predicated 'on a presentist understanding of Shakespeare that insists on the importance of our current moment', it shifts attention to the fan's relationships rather than limiting its horizon to a 'study of objects'.

Online 'user-generated cultural artifacts' – mash-ups, re-mixes, interactivity in all its facets: each instance is 'as dependent on the interaction of its reading community as it is on the appropriating author's intentions'. If ephemeral, these fanworks nevertheless blur and challenge categories of publication, professions and professionalism, expertise and value. Recognizing Shakespeare scholarship itself as a form of fandom (produced by acafans) alongside the deep investments of performers and those outside the academy (by choice or through precarity), Fazel and Geddes respect the multiplicity of perspectives among 'archontic' curators, their examples illustrating how the process Henderson (2006) calls 'Shake-shifting' can create a more diverse space for queer relationships, indigeneity, exposure of white-fan bias, ShaK-pop and more – while also raising questions regarding 'the role of fan art in the dissemination of political and economic subtexts'.

This 'big tent' vision of Shakespeare adaptation studies demonstrates how swiftly research has advanced recently beyond what Leitch identifies as a struggle within adaptation studies 'to emerge from the disciplinary umbrella of film studies and the still more tenacious grip of literary studies' – at least in their more traditional medium-specific forms (2008: 68). Indeed, the possibilities are so capacious now that even our diverse chapter clusters can only selectively represent them, and there are necessarily gaps here – in explicit attention to earlier eras' forms of popular parody and spoof; in the rich history of Shakespeare across the visual arts including illustration, painting, sculpture and installation art; across musical forms including opera, rap, symphonies, jazz and song; in dance, from jukebox musicals to hiphop to ballet; in representing adaptations created across vast regions of the Americas and Global South; in sorting by dramatic subgenre or certain social categories or address to special audiences. We have balanced capaciousness with clarity, hoping not to overwhelm while providing a multiplicity of lenses through which students can begin to discover their own critical dispositions and priorities when pursuing research within such a diverse field of study.

In charting 'New directions', we again provide a few particularly rich strands among many possibilities that we hope will inspire the next generation to engage in transformative social praxis through, as well as study of, Shakespeare and adaptation. Our contributors to this section both build further on a range of topics and approaches introduced in earlier chapters and also complement and expand the priorities of academic discourse through their direct public engagement as artistic practitioners. They emphasize crucial directions in which the field of Shakespeare adaptation is now moving, and the urgent need to represent and engage with wider publics in addressing creatively as well as critically the core life-and-death issues of our time: the survival of the planet, the consequences of the digital revolution and the societal inequities that prevent justice for all.

In 'Reduce, rewrite, recycle: adapting *A Midsummer Night's Dream* for Yosemite', Katherine Steele Brokaw and Paul Prescott call attention to the belatedness of Shakespeare adaptation in addressing the global ecological crisis, even as they have taken up that challenge to 'make the thing we love a thing that matters'. Co-founding an annual mini-festival of 'free, outdoor, site-specific adaptations' for visitors to California's Yosemite National Park, timed to celebrate both the playwright's birthday and Earth Day, they, their company and audiences have found in the comedies renewable resources. Brokaw and Prescott detail their eco-theatre's adaptive principles and practices, working at the 'intersection of Environmental Communications, eco-criticism, and Applied Theatre', and learning from performance-based Practice as Research. Finding that both a progressive use of Shakespeare's canonical authority and the realization of their primary mission of inspiring ecological awareness and action 'depends on adaptive mediation to reach wider audiences', they foreground collaborative practices: in working with the National Park Service and their university; in developing their 90-minute version to fit the location and challenge inherited hierarchies; as participants in the international 'Cymbeline in the Anthropocene' project led by Randall Martin; in 'ignoring – indeed flouting – the hegemony of established performance traditions'; and by 'responding to and theatrically manifesting eco-critical Shakespeare scholarship'. Brokaw and Prescott document the effects of process and product on their diverse cast and attendees, who are often surprised to discover Shakespeare's adaptive potential; indeed, based on their audience survey, 'for many, the re-fitting of Shakespeare to new purposes was the most revelatory aspect of the experience'. Ultimately, they assert that 'eco-adapted Shakespearean theatre has a role to play in the cultural revolution that is necessary to save life on Earth, and that – much less crucially – these adaptive processes also ensure the continued relevance of the plays'.

A different form of collaborative theatre-making informs writer-director Annie Dorsen's *A Piece of Work* (2013), which interviewer Miriam Felton-Dansky calls a 'digital *Hamlet* for a post-humanist age', 'a swirl of connections amongst memory, language and technology, implicating both the past and future of theatre itself'. Dorsen, co-creator of the 2008 Broadway musical *Passing Strange*, produced a piece for a single actor as Hamlet (The Wooster Group's Hamlet Scott Shepherd and The Performance Group's co-founder Joan MacIntosh, in rotation) performing alongside computers using Markov chains 'to generate a new production of the play nightly'. Working with computer programmers and the input of Shepherd on Northwestern's xml text of *Hamlet* – including stage directions – as well as a range of computer voices (some repurposed by the sound designer from Mac[intosh] computers' standard offerings), Dorsen was interested in what the algorithmic reconstructions and absence of bodies could reveal. Taking cues from Harold Bloom's reading of Hamlet as 'inventing' human subjectivity and John Barton's vocal techniques for acting Shakespeare as an 'ideological reversal, that the language tells you how to speak it', she notes that the uncanniness of computer voicing derives from the fact that 'there's no breath', and thus using them was 'a revealing provocation about a lot of assumptions around Shakespearean performance'. Using screens to project text and a wood set that deconstructed basic elements of the Globe Theatre, selected stage effects were similarly meant 'to amplify the absence of bodies'. Discussing steps in the creative process – remixing Hamlet and Ophelia's scenes, tagging emotions and running Gertrude's monologue 'through the algorithmic wringer' – Dorsen makes visible both the remarkable potential of digital humanities practices to enrich critical analysis and artistic production but also the huge gap between 'endless amounts of twenty-first-century, computer-generated hamletishness' and the fully embodied play. Prompted by Felton-Dansky to reflect on *Hamlet*'s genre, Dorsen bracingly clarifies the work ahead that Shakespeareans attuned to digital realities might help articulate and try to avoid:

> Maybe the tragedy of *A Piece of Work* is that we humans are not going to be able to help ourselves from getting more and more entranced by and dependent on these digital technologies that are ultimately only going to be bad news for us. It's the tragedy of technology… It's Prometheus. It's about not being able to stop ourselves from giving these tools incredible amounts of power over us.

Destructive power is also at the tragic heart of Preti Taneja's compelling transposition and reinterpretation of *King Lear*'s essence to contemporary India in her award-winning novel *We That Are Young*. In 'A *King Lear* sutra', she reflects upon her narrative creation and the personal journey to its completion – which, from a writer's perspective, can be (as her words quoted earlier make clear) a daunting, even inhospitable task. Nonetheless, Taneja delves honestly and profoundly into her book's origins, confirming Hutcheon's point that adaptors' 'deeply personal as well as culturally and historically conditioned reasons' for choosing certain texts deserve serious attention – and here, reward it. To this autobiographical reflection Taneja brings the same urgent sense of purpose that drives her novel's exposure of societal injustice and that informs her work to create more diversely collaborative representation in all areas, paying particular attention to women of colour and those with multiple cultural inheritances, and re-creating her 'hybrid lived experience' as 'an insider/outsider'. This work includes making space for linguistic innovation ('a polyvocal, intertextual and multilingual style' enacting 'hybridity at the sentence level') and refusing containment through familiar narrative patterns and genres (such as the 'debut immigrant bildungsroman'). She describes *We That Are Young* as instead, like *King Lear*, working in the 'epic hyperreal', a register befitting the novel's devastating portrayal of the damage done by persisting patriarchal structures, neoliberal corporate rapaciousness, Kashmir's brutal occupation and Hindu nationalism's fascist manifestations. Closely reading the final lines of Shakespeare's tragedy, which also furnish her title, Taneja offers one among several possible interpretations that resonates as well with her adaptation's effects: 'this encounter with art might prompt us to counter systemic harms in our own times'. Yet the play's 'refusal to offer any way forward' and its 'generational damage' also led her as an intersectional feminist to read against the grain of its narrative focus on men's authority, using the interplay between source story and her own to create vivid new perspectives and call attention to what is missing.

Like her novel, her concluding chapter for our volume 'has a poetic register, a syntactical variation from the academic voice, and a sense of structure as a circular journey rather than a linear argument': we as editors likewise hope that among the new directions in our field will be more such experimentation and expansion of what 'counts' as scholarly publication, so that similar layering, stylistic self-consciousness, diversity of approach and such a sense of serious play – all characteristics of the adaptive, collaborative works we study – help critical research not only befit its objects of inquiry, but also perhaps reach and resonate with more diverse audiences as well.

Supplementing its chapter-length models, this handbook assists our readers through the list of sites and tools compiled and described by Vanessa I. Corredera as useful resources for researchers, and the thoughtfully constructed annotated bibliography by Kavita Mudan Finn. Each of these compendia is necessarily selective, again negotiating between the desire for clarity and coverage given the ever-increasing capaciousness of our topic. We hope this balance, as well as the deep analysis and energetic creativity of our contributors, will encourage the next generation's bold advances beyond what we can as yet imagine. If the varied approaches, artistic and sociopolitical awareness, and profound commitment contained herein reach and inspire you, the electric circuitry of Shakespeare and Adaptation will continue to flow, growing ever more illuminating and consequential in the decades ahead.

REFERENCES

Adams, Brandi K. (2020), 'The King, and not I: Refusing neutrality', The Sundial, 9 June. Available online: https://medium.com/the-sundial-acmrs/the-king-and-not-i-refusing-neutrality-dbab4239e8a9 (accessed 21 July 2021).

Bickley, P. and J. Stevens (2021), Studying Shakespeare Adaptation: From Restoration Theatre to YouTube, London: The Arden Shakespeare.

Bortolotti, G. R. and L. Hutcheon (2007), 'On the Origin of Adaptations: Rethinking Fidelity Discourse and "Success: Biologically"', New Literary History 38 (3): 443–58.

Calbi, M. and S.O'Neill (2016), 'Introduction: #SocialmediaShakespeares', Borrowers and Lenders 10 (1). Available online: https://openjournals.libs.uga.edu/borrowers/issue/view/223 (accessed 21 July 2021).

Cartelli, T. and K. Rowe (2007), New Wave Shakespeare on Screen, Cambridge, MA: Polity Press.

Cartmell, D. (2012), '100+ Years of Adaptations, or, Adaptation as the Art Form of Democracy', in D. Cartmell (ed.), A Companion to Literature, Film, and Adaptation, 1–13, Hoboken, NJ: John Wiley.

Chedgzoy, K. (1995), Shakespeare's Queer Children: Sexual Politics and Contemporary Culture. Manchester: Manchester University Press.

Clapp, S. (2015), 'Interview: Robert Icke, theatre director: "Oresteia? It's quite like The Sopranos"', Observer, 23 August. Available online: https://www.theguardian.com/stage/2015/aug/23/robert-icke-director-oresteia-1984-interview (accessed 21 July 2021).

Desmet, C. and S. Iyengar (2015), 'Adaptation, Appropriation, or What You Will', Shakespeare 11 (1): 10–9.

Elliott, K. (2020), Theorizing Adaptation, Oxford: Oxford University Press.

Erickson, P. (1991), Rewriting Shakespeare, Rewriting Ourselves, Berkeley, CA: University of California Press.

Finn, K. M. (2017), 'History Play: Critical and Creative Engagement with Shakespeare's Tetralogies in Transformative Fanworks', Shakespeare 13 (3): 210–25.

Garber, M. (2008), *Shakespeare and Modern Culture*, New York, NY: Anchor.

Geraghty, C. (2007), *Now a Major Motion Picture: Film Adaptations of Literature and Drama*, Washington DC: Rowman & Littlefield.

Genette, G. (1997), *Palimpsests: Literature in the Second Degree*, trans. C. Newman and C. Doubinsky, Lincoln, NE: University of Nebraska Press.

Haile, R. (2016), 'Shakespeare, Enough', trans. C. Cantalupo, *Modern Poetry in Translation*. Available online: https://modernpoetryintranslation.com/magazine/no-2-2016-one-thousand-suns/ (accessed 21 July 2021).

Henderson, D. E. (2006), *Collaborations with the Past: Reshaping Shakespeare Across Time and Media*, Ithaca, NY: Cornell University Press.

Henderson, D. E. (2020), 'Parted eyes and generation gaps in twenty-first-century perceptions of screen Shakespeare', in S. Smith (ed.), *Shakespeare/Sense: Contemporary Readings in Sensory Culture*, 319–51, London: The Arden Shakespeare.

Hutcheon, L. (2013), *A Theory of Adaptation*, 2nd edn, London: Routledge.

Jonson, B. (2012), *Discoveries*, L. Hutson in D. Bevington, M. Butler, and I. Donaldson (eds), *The Cambridge Edition of the Works of Ben Jonson*, vol. 7, Cambridge: Cambridge University Press.

Kott, J. (1964), *Shakespeare, Our Contemporary*, New York, NY: Doubleday.

Leitch, T. (2012), 'Adaptation and Intertextuality, or, What isn't an Adaptation, and What Does it Matter?', in D. Cartmell (ed.), *A Companion to Literature, Film, and Adaptation*, 88–104, Hoboken, NJ: John Wiley.

Maxwell, J. and K. Rumbold, eds. (2018), *Shakespeare and Quotation*, Cambridge: Cambridge University Press.

Myles, R. (2021), *The Show Must Go Online*, YouTube, https://www.youtube.com/watch?v=KTnWmFZevu8 (accessed 21 July 2021).

Novy, M. (1994), *Engaging with Shakespeare: Responses of George Eliot and Other Women Novelists*, Iowa City, IA: University of Iowa Press.

Novy, M. (2000), *Transforming Shakespeare: Contemporary Women's Re-Visions in Literature and Performance*, New York, NY: Palgrave.

O'Neill, S. (2014), *Shakespeare and YouTube: New Media Forms of the Bard*, London: Bloomsbury/Arden Shakespeare.

Sanders, J. (2016), *Adaptation and Appropriation*, 2nd edn, London: Routledge.

Smith, B. R. (2009), *Phenomenal Shakespeare*, Hoboken, NJ: John Wiley.

Thompson, A. (2013), *Passing Strange: Shakespeare, Race, and Contemporary Performance*, Oxford: Oxford University Press.

Thompson, A. (2016), '*Desdemona*: Toni Morrison's response to *Othello*', in D. Callaghan (ed.), *A Feminist Companion to Shakespeare*, 494–506, Chichester: Wiley.

Trivedi, P. (2021), 'Criticae Ficus Indica, or a Banyan Tree View of Shakespeare Film and Indian Cinematic Adaptation', World Shakespeare Congress, Singapore, 18–24 July.

Weber, C. (1990), 'Heiner Müller in East Berlin', *Performing Arts Journal* 12 (2/3): 29–35.

Weimann, R. (2000), *Author's Pen and Actor's Voice: Playing and Writing in Shakespeare's Theatre*, Cambridge: Cambridge University Press.

Zabus, C. (2002), *Tempests after Shakespeare*, New York, NY: Palgrave.

PART ONE

Research methods and problems

Shakespeare as adaptor

EMMA SMITH

IMITATIO AND ADAPTATION

To be a writer in the early modern period was to be an adaptor: '*Othello* was "based on a story by Giovanni Battista Giraldi, or Cinzio, adapted by William Shakespeare." *Julius Caesar, Antony and Cleopatra,* and *Coriolanus* were "based on Plutarch's *Lives*, translated by Thomas North, adapted by Shakespeare"; *Henry V* and most of the other history plays were "based on Raphael Holinshed's *Chronicles*, adapted by Shakespeare"' (Taylor 2016: 144). Every guide and protocol, every schoolroom exercise, every expectation from readers, aligned in anticipating the postmodernist axiom that all writing is rewriting. As Gary Taylor's playful echo of modern movie credits attests, few early modern plays would have been eligible for the Bankside equivalent of the Oscar category for best original screenplay. The task of the writer was to take the materials from prior texts and reshape them to current tastes and requirements: whereas a modern author might be advised to write about her experiences, her early modern counterpart wrote about her reading. The term 'playwright', initially satirical when coined in the early seventeenth century, followed the semantic model of words like cartwright and wainwright, suggesting not the lofty inspiration of the muses but rather artisanal labour and manufacture of new commodities out of raw materials.

Other governing composition metaphors confirm the abiding sense of writing as construction rather than, or as well as, invention. Ben Jonson likened a sentence to 'stones well squared, which will rise strong a great way without mortar' (2012: 565); for Seneca, he observed, the writer was a bee, collecting nectar from different flowers and blending them into something sweetly distinct 'to draw forth out of the best and choicest flowers, with the bee, and turn all into honey' (583). In a less idealizing idiom, Tiffany Stern has traced the early modern vocabularies of 'patching' and associated words from cobbling and shoemaking for thinking about plays as textual assemblages (Stern 2004). The different hands in the manuscript of *The Book of Sir Thomas More*, including the interventions attributed to Shakespeare, make this concept of the patched play visible (Jowett 2011). These theories and practices of imitation and adaptation give the early modern literary text some of the qualities of the twentieth-century 'found poem', an artifice recycled from parts of other texts.

Almost all Shakespeare's works conform to this humanist pattern. They revise or adapt a major source, as well as incorporating allusions or more local borrowings from a range of texts, including previous works by Shakespeare. They thus demonstrate the different vectors of 'adaptation as quotation, as allusion, as embedding, as appropriation, and as palimpsest' (Corrigan 2017: 26). Reviewing changing meanings of the word 'original' across the period, John Kerrigan identifies that Shakespeare 'does new things with and adds extensively to what he draws from pre-existing texts, but his originality is partly original-ity, a drawing upon originals'. He suggests that Shakespeare would not understand the prior texts from which he works as his 'sources', as is now conventional, but rather his 'originals' (2018: 2). That Shakespeare drew extensively on reading in creating his works was always understood, and part of the appreciation of his writing and stagecraft was the pleasure of spotting what was being imitated. Imitatio, the art of imitation, was a sign of the shared sophistication of both writer and reader: the author's allegiances were intended to be visible. One contemporary authority on imitation recommended that the author 'woulde have it knowne whom he imitateth, although he would not have it spyed, how and after what sort he doth it' (Sturm 1570: sig. H1v). Imitation always invited 'comparison between the new text and the earlier one' (Burrow 2019: 17). Linda Hutcheon calls this appreciation of the adaptation 'the doubled pleasure of the palimpsest' (2013: 116). For later adaptations of Shakespeare, the pleasure of recognition is also the pleasure of participation in the elite cultural register signified by Shakespeare's works (Teague 2011; Maxwell and Rumbold 2018); for Shakespeare's first consumers, that shared elite pleasure attached not to contemporary vernacular plays but rather to an educated familiarity with their classical antecedents.

Early appreciations of Shakespeare understood his works within this larger allusive and imitative tradition. Francis Meres drew on the classical trope of metempsychosis: 'as the soule of *Euphorbus* was thought to live in *Pythagoras*: so the sweete wittie soule of *Ovid* lives in mellifluous & hony-tongued *Shakespeare*' (1598: 281v); attending a performance of *Twelfth Night* at the Middle Temple, John Manningham began by describing his enjoyment of its borrowings: 'much like the Commedy of Errores, or Menechmi in Plautus, but most like and neere to that in Italian called *Iganni*' (Manningham 1868: 18). Meres and Manningham articulate Hutcheon's 'doubled pleasure' by acknowledging both the current work and the prior texts they each recognize it adapting.

This chapter discusses adaptation as intrinsic to Shakespeare's poetry and dramaturgy: to the texture of his writing as well as the construction of his plays. Works by Shakespeare that are now considered originary and original were in fact always adaptations. Further, the forms of Shakespeare's collaborative encounter with a range of prior material pre-empt some of the ways later adaptation theory has understood the relationship between an adaptation and the work it is understood to adapt. These foundational collaborations alter the interpretative order of priority: because Shakespeare's own adaptations have taken on the status of originals, they invert the evaluative assumption that the adaptation must always be secondary, derivative or otherwise lesser. Revisiting common metaphors for thinking about an imitating author's relation to his literary predecessors – imagery of digestion, haunting, grafting and parentage – enables us to understand some Shakespearean plots and scenes as self-exploring allegories of adaptive writing. The example of *King Lear*, a play taken from a range of sources including the close relative *King Leir*, enables us to explore in more detail the ways in which Shakespeare adapts his own, as well as others', work. There are suggestive relationships between these initial acts of adaptation by Shakespeare, and the strategies employed by later adaptors of his work.

SHAKESPEARE AND ADAPTATION THEORY

In her book *Adaptation and Appropriation* (2016), Julie Sanders identifies a number of adaptive practices, drawn from her analysis of later reworkings of literary texts. Each of these can be traced in Shakespeare's own engagement with his source materials, establishing his own works as adaptations. Adaptations of prose chronicle material gathered together by Raphael Holinshed into single and serial historical dramas are a Shakespearean example of what Sanders calls 'transpositional' adaptation, or 'casting a specific genre into another generic mode' (2016: 26). 'Trimming and pruning' is part of Shakespeare's adaptive method, as in his habitual condensation of long time spans into shorter, more immediate plots (combining the historical Richard II's two wives from the historical record in *Richard II*, for example), and so too is 'expansion, accretion, and interpolation' (23). *Lucrece* develops almost two thousand lines of poetry out of just seventy-three lines in Ovid's *Fasti*. Shakespearean works which offer 'commentary' via a 'revised point of view on a source text' (61) include *Romeo and Juliet*'s more indulgent take on its transgressive lovers compared with the cautionary moral tale Shakespeare found in Arthur Brooke's poem *Romeus and Juliet*, or the post-heroic retelling of Virgilian epic in the sardonic *Troilus and Cressida*. Sanders's 'processes of proximation and updating' (23) are involved in *Macbeth*'s transformation of violent Scottish history via James I's commitment to the divine right of kings, or in *Measure for Measure*'s urban plague-scape, drawing on a recent serious outbreak of pestilence in 1603–4. And, there were always 'economic rationales' (23) for adaptation in the commercial theatre environment that shaped Shakespeare's writing career. The theatre's appetite for new plays demanded the review of classical and contemporary texts with an eye to appropriate storylines for adaptation (Hutcheon 2013: 6–7): Cinthio's *Hecatommithi*, for *Othello* and *Measure for Measure*, Chaucer's 'The Knight's Tale' for *A Midsummer Night's Dream* and *The Two Noble Kinsmen*, Plutarch's *Lives of the Noble Grecians and Romans* for *Antony and Cleopatra* and *Timon of Athens*. Shakespeare's own relation to his source material, that is to say, can be helpfully understood through the framework of later adaptation theory.

We can also see Shakespeare's reuse of his own material as an adaptive strategy recognizable in later theories of the genre. One small example: in *The Merchant of Venice*, the servant Lancelot Gobbo encounters his blind father who has come to Venice to look for his son, and vows to 'try confusions with him' (2.2.22). Lancelot speaks to his father as if he were a stranger, directing him through the imaginary streets of the city, informing him his son is dead with the proverbial 'it is a wise father that knows his own child' (2.2.49–50). He then reveals his true identity, only for the tables to be turned: his father 'cannot think you are my son', and requires proof. Lancelot shares the name of his mother, Margery, and the two are finally introduced. The encounter between son and father shadows the other parental relationships in the play, between Shylock and Jessica, and Portia and her dead father. The prose exchange in *Merchant* lasts for some fifty lines, and seems to be a virtuoso opportunity for the comedian Lancelot, perhaps acted by Will Kemp, to play off the other actor as stooge.

Shakespeare adapts this scene in two later plays. The first is the recognition scene between estranged family members in *Twelfth Night*, where blood ties are again reinstated through the shared memory of absent relations. Viola and her twin Sebastian meet, and in a lengthy exchange, confirm their bond by reference to their father (5.1.228). This adaptation modifies tone (it is full of pathos rather than humour) and genre (verse rather than prose). The second takes up the dramaturgy of the son and his blind father with more profound adaptive energy. In *King Lear*, Edgar, in the guise of Poor Tom, encounters his father Gloucester: ''Tis the time's plague, when madmen lead the blind' (4.1.54). They are together across three scenes until the climax, when Edgar coaches Gloucester to jump from an imaginary cliff: 'Why I do trifle thus with his despair / Is done to cure it' (4.5.40–1). The transformation of Lancelot's jest with his father is complete as Shakespeare adapts his own earlier scene through amplification, transposition and commentary.

But the scene of the blind father and the disguised son also carries with it the hidden, allusive contours of the earlier iteration. The adaptation is always bound to its generative prior text, and always understood relationally: it is intrinsic to the status of adaptation that it bears what Hutcheon calls a 'double nature' (Hutcheon 2013: 6). The Dover Cliff sequence in *King Lear* has long been seen as the high point of the play's bleak epistemology, but it might also be a chance for the Edgar actor, whose performance was particularly highlighted on the title page of the first edition of the play as 'the sullen and assumed humor of Tom of Bedlam' (Shakespeare 1608), to perform a bravura comic turn rather like that of Lancelot Gobbo. Thinking of shared themes and moments across Shakespeare's plays through the lens of adaptation gives a new way to identify their creative transformations, and to recognize the traces of their previous lives. For example, Shakespeare adapts Jonson's character Thorello from *Every Man In His Humour*, and Cinthio's story of the Moor of Venice, to produce Othello, but he also adapts his own comic jealous lover plot from *The Merry Wives of Windsor* and *Much Ado About Nothing* (and will adapt these and *Othello* again for *The Winter's Tale*). The uneasily comic aspects of *Othello* (Snyder 1979; Teague 1986) are one legacy of this adaptive itinerary: the adaptation cannot – perhaps *would* not – entirely forget its predecessors. As a form of remembering, the adaptation carries within it its own past.

ADAPTATION AND ITS METAPHORS

Shakespeare rarely draws direct attention to his own participation in the humanist hide and seek of imitatio and adaptation. But bringing his source onstage as a prop is a knowing nod to this form of audience recognition – it has its equivalents in later Shakespearean adaptations such as the use of Shakespeare's sonnets as a classroom exercise in *10 Things I Hate About You* (dir. Gil Junger, 1999), or the statue of Shakespeare in *Gnomeo and Juliet* (dir. Kelly Asbury, 2011). In *Titus Andronicus*, author, characters and the audience who also know their grammar school texts, are all complicit in a brutal adaptation of Ovid's *Metamorphoses*, using this text as 'pattern' and 'precedent' (5.3.44) – or, in Kerrigan's terms, an 'original' – for acts of savage violence. The story of the rape of Philomel by Tereus is explicitly invoked by the rapists Chiron and Demetrius, and they attempt to forestall Philomel's recourse to justice through embroidery by cutting off their victim's hands. Rather as Chiron and Demetrius revel in their adaptive inhumanity, so the play too delights in its explicit engagement with the artistic predecessor: Young Lucius, 'with his Bookes under his Arme', as the quarto stage direction designates (Shakespeare 1594: sig. F3v), is chased by his mutilated aunt Lavinia, who uses his school copy of Ovid to reveal her wrongs.

Elsewhere the theme of imitation is less explicit, but still present. Many of the operating metaphors for imitation are thematized in Shakespeare's works, making their indebtedness as adaptations part of the narrative motor of plot. Some books, wrote Francis Bacon, should be 'chewed and digested thoroughly', drawing on classical images from Seneca and Quintilian onwards of imitation and adaptation as digestive (Burrow 2019: 85, 95). When Tamora is fed her sons in 'pasties' (5.2.189), the monstrous banquet literalizes *Titus Andronicus*'s own cannibalistic adaptive practices. The pastried sons, taken from Seneca's *Thyestes*, conclude Titus's revenge by casting it as a form of perverse adaptation, in which the prior texts need to be absorbed bodily, even unwillingly, as part of the work of dynamic transformation. Tamora's horrified revulsion at this enforced meal is a parable of the play's disorderly digestion of its own antecedents. Her horror is a conceptual parallel with stagings that allow Lavinia, too, to express resistance to the play's adaptive logic. Titus kills his daughter following the 'precedent and lively warrant' of 'rash Virginius', and gains Saturninus's agreement that 'the girl should not survive her shame, / And by her presence still renew his sorrows' (5.3.36–43). No stage direction indicates Lavinia's response. The common staging is to have her submit, lovingly and gratefully, graciously transforming murder into mercy killing. Occasionally, however, directors allow her to attempt an escape from her father's grim teleology, to challenge the coercive narrative of the classical past and make a doomed claim to her own autonomy and originality (Aebischer 2004: 56–63). Women's resistance to oppressive classical narratives in the play foreshadows the later, explicitly feminist, revisions of Shakespeare's works (Novy 2000).

That Tamora is fed her children in the frenzy which concludes *Titus Andronicus* is symbolically relevant for this progeny of the English grammar school curriculum (Bate 1995: 91). Another prominent Renaissance metaphor for adaptive imitation was parental: according to Petrarch, the new work should resemble its progenitor text as the child its father (Burrow 2019: 148–9). A play narratively preoccupied with this likeness is *The Winter's Tale*. Questions of parentage hang over the play from the outset. The tyrannical king Leontes repeatedly doubts that his children are his own, asking Mamilius 'art thou my calf?' (1.2.153), branding the baby Perdita 'a bastard, / So sure as this beard's grey' (2.3.190–1) and telling Florizel approvingly: 'your mother was most true to wedlock, prince. / For she did print your royal father off, / Conceiving you' (5.1.152–4). Seeing this theme of damaged, guilty or suspicious parentage as also a kind of allegory or personification of the displaced or potentially illegitimate relationship between *The Winter's Tale* and its 'parent' text, Robert Greene's *Pandosto, or the Triumphs of Time* (1588), helps us move beyond simple source study. Viewers of the play might well have been expecting Greene's tragic conclusion, in which the Leontes character Pandosto 'slewe himselfe' 'to close up the Comedie with a Tragicall stratageme' (Greene 1588: G4). In ending differently, the wayward adaptation or child, *The Winter's Tale*, defies its parent or source, *Pandosto*. 'Have you a father?' the disguised Polixenes asks his loved-up son in Bohemia. 'I have, but what of him?' (4.4.390–1) is the cheerfully unfilial reply. Harold Bloom's Freudian theory of poetic influence suggested that the poetic successor was always in a death wrestle with his strong predecessors: 'battle between strong equals, father and son as mighty opposites, Laius and Oedipus at the crossroads' (1997: 11). But that agonistic parental metaphor is complicated here, and so too, in the various agencies of Paulina, Perdita and Hermione, is the unremitting masculinism of its model of literary and familial struggle (Chedgzoy 1995). Within Greene's paternal fiction, Pandosto dies; in Shakespeare's adaptation it is a son, Mamillius, not a father, who perishes. Mamillius's death represents the adaptation's stunted futurity, both within its fiction, and in its relationship to its predecessor. Just as Sicilian patriarchal succession is thwarted by the death of the prince, so adaptive genealogy is interrupted. Editions of *Pandosto* continue alongside the life of the play *The Winter's Tale* rather as the play's romance conclusion dramatizes not the transition between generations but their queasy simultaneity: the prior text is not consumed, cancelled or otherwise taken over by the adaptation. An additional relevant metaphor turning *The Winter's Tale* into a theory of adaptation comes from Perdita's conversation with Polixenes. Their discussion about art and nature and the grafting of plants as 'an art / Which does mend nature, change it rather' (4.4.110–1) has no equivalent in *Pandosto*, and is therefore, paradoxically, an original conversation about the inevitability of adaptation, both horticulturally and culturally. Gérard Genette makes grafting an image of adaptation within a larger creative economy: 'any text is a hypertext, grafting itself onto a hypotext that it imitates or transforms' (Genette 1997: ix). Perdita draws her lover's disguised father into a conversation that is as much about Shakespeare's relation to Greene's romance as it is about 'nature's bastards' the 'streaked gillyvors' (4.4.113–4).

One final image from theories of adaptation that is suggestively thematized by Shakespeare is the trope of the ghost. Marvin Carlson's book *The Haunted Stage* elaborates how theatre, in particular, prompts us to use 'the memory of previous encounters to understand and interpret encounters with new and somewhat different material' – a good description of meeting an adaptation – and describes this process as 'ghosting' (Carlson 2001: 6–7). Summarizing a long critical tradition, Sanders characterizes the adaptation as spectrally inhabited by 'textual ghosts and hauntings' (Sanders 2016: 15). The prior text returns, unbidden, like a revenant. Burrow establishes ghostly imagery from Lucretius and suggests that 'making a ghost out of an old story is one way of avoiding the peril of being stuck in one's own literary past' (Burrow 2019: 129). Perhaps it is not always so easy. Shakespeare's most famously haunted play, *Hamlet*, seems to dramatize precisely being stuck in a past that is literary as well as familial or psychic. As father and ghost, Old Hamlet does double representational duty in the play's thematization of its own adaptive status. His haunting presence in the play suggests not only the uncanny family drama of the fictive Denmark, but the intertextual and adaptive relationship with the play's famous progenitor, Thomas Kyd's revenge play *The Spanish Tragedy*.

Kyd's play dominated the cultural landscape of the early modern theatre, with scores of performances and editions and allusions across the period (Smith 1998: 133–59). When Shakespeare came to write his own revenge play, therefore, he found that cultural territory decisively occupied by Kyd. Even as *Hamlet* recalls the themes of this earlier play – in the shared figure of Horatio, the murder in a garden, the choric Senecan ghost, the multiple murders, the agony of parent–child relations, the suicide of a young woman – it summons up their uncanny power. *Hamlet* does not dethrone *The Spanish Tragedy*, which continues to be popular in performance and in print, and to be widely cited, imitated and parodied. Rather, Kyd's play is itself like a revenge tragedy ghost: the father of the genre that ought to be dead and buried but still has something to say to the living and so won't lie down. As Bloom's Oedipal formulation allows, adaptations may entertain violent feelings towards their predecessors. But those antecedents too may feel unwilling to be ransacked, quieted or dethroned by ambitious adaptations (Henderson 2006: 13–15).

Study of Shakespeare's sources used to assume that his genius transformed the dross of prior literature, leaving nothing of value behind. The very term 'sources' has seemed to confine these texts in negative relation to their celebrated successors. But in fact Shakespeare's adaptations often coexist with the ongoing print life of these prior texts, in a relationship that is synchronous rather than teleological, intertextual rather than patrilinear. By exploring the widespread metaphors for the relation between the writer and his sources, we can read Shakespeare's own plays as playful and knowing engagements with their own status as indebted adaptations.

KING LEIR AND *KING LEAR*

Nahum Tate's famous 'happy ending' *King Lear* in the seventeenth century has become one of the key exhibits in the long history of post-Shakespearean adaptation. It functions in accounts as a cautionary tale of adaptive success – Tate's play entirely eclipsed Shakespeare's version on the stage for more than 150 years – and failure – its apparent aesthetic inferiority has become axiomatic. Part of the rhetorical work often undertaken by Tate's adaptation is to corroborate the autonomy of Shakespeare's *Lear*, that's to say, even as the existence of the adaptation undermines that creative self-sufficiency. Contemporary versions of *King Lear* from Howard Barker's play *Seven Lears* (1989) to Preti Taneja's novel *We That Are Young* (2017) and HBO's drama *Succession* (2018–) also acknowledge Shakespeare's tragedy as their original: the work of adaptation consolidates the primacy of the prior inspiration. But Shakespeare's play is also itself an adaptation. The eighteenth-century construction of Shakespeare's works as originals paradoxically went hand in hand with the scholarship uncovering the texts on which his plays were built (Kerrigan 2019: 10–11). Identifying Shakespeare's sources has been a standard critical procedure since Edmond Malone traced the outlines of modern documentary scholarship (de Grazia 1991). Modern editions of the plays routinely include source material in appendices, but this method rarely draws on the critical resources of adaptation. Analysis of Shakespeare's sources typically downplays their intrinsic interest or qualities better to reveal – or construct – Shakespeare's own artistry. As such, source study presents as a kind of obverse of adaptation theories. Both critical methods present asymmetric textual relationships, but source study prioritizes the destination text, whereas the study of adaptations until recently tended to prioritize the prior text as original (Leitch 2017). Or, at least, in studies of Shakespeare, where the hyperbolic cultural value attached to the works means an internally inconsistent attempt to assert priority in both directions: whether as adaptor or adaptee, Shakespeare always tries to claim precedence.

The critical emphasis on the Shakespearean text as creative endpoint means that sources tend to be conceptualized as raw material rather than autonomous literary works. In the standard compilation of Shakespeare's source material, Geoffrey Bullough's multi-volume *Narrative and Dramatic Sources of Shakespeare* (1957–75), for example, only those parts of the source texts judged directly comparable to Shakespeare's own works are reprinted, suggesting that the source is an identifiable narrative or linguistic borrowing rather than some more general inspiration to produce a new, related text. Source study has tended to service author-centred critical approaches focusing on Shakespeare's own writing processes and creative intentions: it is one part of the legacy of the codification of modern Shakespearean scholarship around the New Bibliography of the early twentieth century that has not yet been thoroughly critically reframed (Maguire and Smith 2015: 15–17). By contrast, theories of adaptation have developed from initial 'fidelity criticism' (Leitch 2017: 7), which prioritizes the originals, to something more engaged with notions of translation, transmediation, collaboration and intertextuality (Henderson 2006; Corrigan 2017). Revisiting Shakespeare's own originals for *King Lear* shows how combining two textual itineraries – between source and text, and between text and adaptation – can reinvigorate what Stephen Greenblatt memorably called (albeit as a provocation his chapter proceeded to disavow) the 'elephants' graveyard of literary history' (1985: 163).

Shakespeare draws on a range of pre-existing texts to write *King Lear*. As the example of the son and the blind father in *The Merchant of Venice* has already suggested, some of these texts are his own: iterations of the father–daughter motif can be traced in *Titus Andronicus* and, in a different genre, in *As You Like It*, the usurped or alienated king comes from *Richard II* and the *Henry VI* plays, the fool from *Twelfth Night* and the son feigning madness from *Hamlet*. Importantly, though, the play takes up material from other writers' texts as well. Bullough's list of sources includes historical material from Geoffrey of Monmouth, *The Mirror for Magistrates* and Holinshed's *Chronicles*; literary material from Sidney's *Arcadia* and Spenser's *The Faerie Queene*; contemporary philosophy in Samuel Harsnett's *A Declaration of Egregious Popish Impostures* (1603); and documents from court gossip about Bryan

Annesley, a sick elderly man whom his daughter attempted to have certified mad, while her sister, the suggestively named Cordell, fought to preserve her father's household (Bullough 1973: 309–422). Bullough also notes the play's affinities with folkloric material later fixed in print by Grimm and Perrault, including the story of Cinderella and her ugly sisters, and the Goosegirl Princess who told her unknowing father that she 'loved him like salt' (1973: 271). As Thomas Leitch points out in relation to modern film versions, the idea that 'adaptations are adapting exactly one text apiece' is clearly inadequate to the range of precursors, within and outside the canon, for any Shakespeare play (2003: 165; Bladen, Hatcheul and Vienne-Guerrin 2019); Shakespeare's *King Lear* adaptation synthesizes, cherry-picks and is reimagined from a range of prior texts.

The most significant prior text for *Lear* is the anonymous play published in 1605 as *The True Chronicle History of King Leir and his three daughters, Gonorill, Ragan, and Cordella*. The British Library copy has a handwritten attribution to 'Wm Shakespear' on the title page. Although this has been later struck out and the 'anonymous' neatly inscribed instead, it is nevertheless metonymic of the ways source study tends to cancel the prior text and overwrite it retrospectively with the interest and presumed superiority of the later one. Adaptation theory offers a different heuristic. The fact that the *Leir* text, unlike the other sources across different genres gathered by Bullough, belongs to the world of the theatre makes it more likely that Shakespeare's playhouse audiences might well have known it: that's to say, they would have experienced that 'double pleasure' described by Hutcheon as crucial to the understanding of an adaptation *as* adaptation.

The differences between the *Leir* play and Shakespeare's adaptation of it are familiar. In *Leir*, Gonorill and Ragan plot to murder their father, but a happy ending is brought about by Cordella's triumph in battle and the restoration of Leir as king. Shakespeare's subplot, with Gloucester, Edmund and Edgar does not feature: this he adapts from other material. (Why, asked Stephen Dedalus in Joyce's *Ulysses*, 'is the underplot of *King Lear* in which Edmund figures lifted out of Sidney's *Arcadia* and spatchcocked onto a Celtic legend older than history?' [Joyce 1992: 203].) *Leir* is more interested in the women in the story than is Shakespeare, as is evident from its first two scenes. It begins with a long speech by the King about his grief at the death of 'our (too late) deceast and dearest Queen' and the consequences this will have for 'the disposing of our princely daughters' now that they have lost their 'mothers counsell' (Anon 1605: sig. A2). Leir explains to his courtiers Skalliger and Perilus that he will use 'a sudden strategem' (sig. A3) to marry off his daughters, revealing that he proposes to manipulate Cordella into accepting the King of Brittany as her husband. *Leir* then moves to a scene between Gonorill and Ragan, who talk about their 'proud pert' younger sister who attempts to outshine them in all things, particularly with her 'severall choyce of Suters' (sigs A3–A3v). This scene constructs the absent Cordella as something more akin to Shakespeare's own version of the annoying younger sister, Bianca in *The Taming of the Shrew*, rather than the saintly character often projected onto Shakespeare's Cordelia. It also creates sympathy for the sisters by giving their side of the story first. It allows Gonerill and Ragan independent voices before they are drawn into their father's marital schemings.

Shakespeare begins instead with rumblings about 'the division of the kingdoms' (1.1.4), the casual misogyny of Gloucester's description of Edmund's conception, and then shifts to the apparently unmotivated, capricious regal and paternal demand 'which of you shall we say doth love us most' (1.1.50). This is clearly a world in which men dominate and women respond within highly circumscribed sexual and verbal forms.

The adaptive relationship between *Leir* and *Lear* thus patterns and anticipates some of the ways Shakespeare's *Lear* itself has been adapted. Seeing adaptation practices as a combination of collaboration with and rejection of the originary text is helpful (Bradley 2010: 10), or as what Diana Henderson calls 'diachronic collaboration' (2006: 1). Shakespeare transposes the genre of the comic-historical play by turning his drama towards tragedy, rather as Christopher Pye traces in his adjacent analysis of Shakespeare's aesthetic and ideological shift between *As You Like It* and *King Lear* (2015: 19–24). Kent's horrified response to the tableau of the dead king and his youngest daughter, 'Is this the promised end?' (5.3.237) becomes, within the mode of fidelity criticism, a knowingly metafictional remark. But that new promised end – the deaths of Lear and Cordelia, contrary to prior versions of the story – is itself contingent and subject to adaptation. Tate's *The History of King Lear* (1681) ends with the marriage of Cordelia and Edgar blessed by the grateful patriarch, who ends the play by promising – again – to retire and enjoy 'calm Reflections on our Fortunes past. / Cheer'd with the relation of the prosperous Reign / Of this celestial Pair' (Tate 1681: 67). As Henderson has explored in mapping Tate's version in its Restoration context, this is not simply Shakespeare's play 'Reviv'd, with Alterations', as the title page claims (2008: 243–63). Rather, Tate's play adapts *King Lear* backwards towards the *Leir* play that Shakespeare himself adapted, situating the play within a range of textual relationships that is no longer the creative teleology of source to text, nor of text to adaptation, but rather multi-directional, mobile and reciprocal.

We can see something similar if we look at recent feminist adaptations of *King Lear* that attempt, in Sanders' terms, to shift the point of view and to imagine adaptation as commentary. In their focus on the women marginalized in Shakespeare's play, works such as the Women's Theatre Group's *Lear's Daughters* (1987), Taneja's *We That Are Young* (2017) or Emily St John Mandel's *Station Eleven* (2014) are as much in dialogue with the play's suppressed textual predecessors as with *King Lear* itself. Adaptation returns the play to its prior state even as it reimagines a new future. Jane Smiley's *A Thousand Acres* (1992), set on a family farm in Iowa in the 1970s and told from the perspective of Ginny, the equivalent of the play's Goneril, exemplifies what Elizabeth Rivlin has called 'traumatic adaptation'. The recovery of repressed memories within the Cook family in Smiley's novel has its metafictional equivalence in the adaptation's traumatic and repressed memory of the prior text (Rivlin 2014: 74). *A Thousand Acres* is thus structured around 'two recovery movements' that are implicitly aligned: 'that of women's voices and histories, which occurs in adapting Shakespeare, and that of memories, which occurs in coping with trauma (78). Smiley herself described the process as a 'wrestling match with Mr Shakespeare' and suggested her novel might be read in advance of *King Lear*, to protect young women from Shakespeare's own misogyny and 'the guilt about proper daughterhood that I knew *King Lear* could induce' (2014: 659–60). She later acknowledged the parallels between adapted and adapting text: 'I thought of [Shakespeare] doing just what I had done – wresting with old material, given material, that is in some way malleable and in other ways resistant. I thought about how all material, whether inherited or observed, has integrity'. In the end she saw 'an image of literary history, two mirrors facing each other in the present moment, reflecting infinitely backward into the present and infinitely forward into the future (660). In the Epilogue to the novel, Ginny also reflects on the past, drawing on tropes of memory, mortgage, infertility, inheritance, genealogy, DNA, trauma and echo. It is a meditation and commentary on the palimpsestic reciprocity of the adaptation (Smiley 1992: 368–71).

Perhaps the idea of adaptation has been unhelpfully shackled to the purposive notion of authorial and readerly agency – the writer explicitly intends to adapt a prior text, the reader registers the act of adaptation and assesses it in relation to that prior text – and perhaps we might see texts adapting other texts within a larger creative economy not circumscribed by authorial intention. To put it another way, *A Thousand Acres* might still be, in part, an adaptation of *King Leir* even if Smiley had never read that anonymous late Elizabethan play, but only caught a glimpse of it in the reflecting mirrors of literary influence, adaptation and memory. Courtney Lehmann's analysis of the ways in which Baz Luhrmann's film *William Shakespeare's Romeo + Juliet* (1996) recalls the watery imagery of Brooke's source poem is a parallel here. Lehmann identifies how Luhrmann is 'not only faced with the sedimentary literary heritage of the legend [of doomed young lovers] but also with the legendary status of Shakespeare's own play in contemporary popular culture' (Lehmann 2018: 140). Colin Burrow usefully suggests an adaptive category of authorial 'inspired misremembering' (Burrow 2004: 14), but there might also be a kind of non-remembering: a more expansive sense of the forgotten, repressed, unread or unconscious relation of the text to its predecessors within the larger scope of contemporary adaptation theories.

CONCLUSION: SHAKESPEARE AS ADAPTOR

This chapter has explored Shakespeare as adapter: of the work of others, and of his own work. While his works have prompted centuries of adaptations, they are themselves as much adaptation as original. Revisiting the old discipline of source study with some of the new interpretative affordances of adaptation theory complicates notions of the stable or original text, inverts orders of historical and aesthetic priority, and inscribes adaptation as ongoing critical process rather than occasional reified product (Kidnie 2009: 32). Listing 'Twelve Fallacies in Contemporary Adaptation Theory', Thomas Leitch includes the mistaken assumption that 'source texts are more original than adaptations' (2003: 166). Shakespeare's own authorial practices encapsulate this paradox of the original as adaptation. His work already pre-empts and encodes many of the techniques and approaches of later adaptors and their theorizations. Understanding the Shakespeare canon as itself 'a derivation that is not derivative – a work that is second without being secondary' (Hutcheon 2013: 9), helps finally to lay to rest some old ideas about fidelity that have shaped theories of adaptation. Establishing Shakespeare as adapter is an important historical corrective to the common idea that adaptation is always and inevitably post-authorial and post-hoc. Rather, adaptation is the very condition of playwrighting.

REFERENCES

Aebischer, P. (2004), *Shakespeare's Violated Bodies: Stage and Screen Performance*, Cambridge: Cambridge University Press.

Bate, J., ed. (1995), *Titus Andronicus*, London: Routledge.

Bladen V., S. Hatcheul and N. Vienne-Guerrin, eds (2019), *Shakespeare on Screen: King Lear*, Cambridge: Cambridge University Press.

Bloom, H. (1997), *The Anxiety of Influence: A Theory of Poetry*, 2nd edn, Oxford: Oxford University Press.

Bradley, L. (2010), *Adapting 'King Lear' for the Stage*, Farnham: Ashgate.

Bullough, G. (1957–75), *Narrative and Dramatic Sources of Shakespeare*, 8 vols, London: Routledge and Kegan Paul.

Bullough, G. (1973), *Narrative and Dramatic Sources of Shakespeare Volume VII Major Tragedies: Hamlet, Othello, King Lear, Macbeth*, London: Routledge and Kegan Paul.

Burrow, C. (2004), 'Shakespeare and Humanist Culture', in C. Martindale and T. B. Taylor (eds), *Shakespeare and the Classsics*, 9–27, Cambridge: Cambridge University Press.

Burrow, C. (2019), *Imitating Authors: Plato to Futurity*, Oxford: Oxford University Press.

Carlson, M. A. (2001), *The Haunted Stage: the Theater as Memory Machine*, Ann Arbor, MI: University of Michigan Press.

Chedgzoy, K. (1995), *Shakespeare's Queer Children: Sexual Politics and Contemporary Culture*, Manchester: Manchester University Press.

Corrigan, T. (2017), 'Defining Adaptation', in T. M. Leitch (ed.), *The Oxford Handbook of Adaptation Studies*, 23–35, Oxford: Oxford University Press.

De Grazia, M. (1991), *Shakespeare Verbatim: the Reproduction of Authenticity and the 1790 Apparatus*, Oxford: Oxford University Press.

Genette, G. (1997), *Palimpsests: Literature in the Second Degree*, trans. C. Newman and C. Doubinsky, Lincoln, NE: University of Nebraska Press.

Greenblatt, S. (1985), 'Shakespeare and the Exorcists', in G. H. Hartman and P. Parker (eds), *Shakespeare and the Question of Theory*, 163–86, London: Methuen.

Henderson, D. E. (2006), *Collaborations with the Past: Reshaping Shakespeare Across Time and Media*, Ithaca and London: Cornell University Press.

Henderson, D. E. (2008), 'Alternative Collaboration: Shakespeare, Nahum Tate, Our Academy, and the Science of Probability', in D. E. Henderson (ed.), *Alternative Shakespeares 3*, 243–63, Abingdon and New York, NY: Routledge.

Henderson, D. E. (2019), 'Romancing King Lear: *Hobson's Choice*, *Life Goes On* and Beyond' in Bladen, Hatcheul and Vienne-Guerrin, 125–39.

Hutcheon, L. (2013), *A Theory of Adaptation*, 2nd edn, London: Routledge.

Jonson, B. (2012), *Discoveries*, L. Hutson in D. Bevington, M. Butler, and I. Donaldson (eds), *The Cambridge Edition of the Works of Ben Jonson*, vol. 7, Cambridge: Cambridge University Press.

Jowett, J. ed. (2011), *Sir Thomas More*, London: Arden/Bloomsbury.

Joyce, J. ([1922] 1992), *Ulysses*, ed. J. Johnson, Oxford: Oxford World's Classics.

Kerrigan, J. (2019), *Shakespeare's Originality*, Oxford: Oxford University Press.

Kidnie, M. J. (2009), *Shakespeare and the Problem of Adaptation*, London: Routledge.

Lehmann, C. (2018), *Shakespeare Remains: Theater to Film, Early Modern to Postmodern*, Ithaca, NY: Cornell University Press.

Leitch, T. (2003), 'Twelve Fallacies in Contemporary Adaptation Theory', *Criticism* 45: 149–71.

Leitch, T. (2017), 'Introduction', in T. M. Leitch (ed.), *The Oxford Handbook of Adaptation Studies*, 1–19, Oxford: Oxford University Press.

Maguire, L. and E. Smith (2015), 'What is a Source? Or, How Shakespeare Read His Marlowe', *Shakespeare Survey* 68: 15–31.

Manningham, J. (1868), *Diary of John Manningham* ed. J. Bruce, London: Camden Society.

Maxwell, J. and K. Rumbold, eds (2018), *Shakespeare and Quotation*, Cambridge: Cambridge University Press.

Meres, F. (1598), *Palladis Tamia. Wits treasury Being the Second Part of Wits Common weath*, London.

Novy, M. (2000), *Transforming Shakespeare: Contemporary Women's Re-visions in Literature and Performance*, New York, NY: Palgrave.

Pye, C. (2015), *The Storm at Sea: Political Aesthetics in the Time of Shakespeare*, New York, NY: Fordham University Press.

Rivlin, Elizabeth (2014), 'Adaptation Revoked: Knowledge, Ethics and Trauma in Jane Smiley's *A Thousand Acres*', in A. Huang and E. Rivlin (eds), *Shakespeare and the Ethics of Appropriation*, 73–87, London and New York, NY: Palgrave Macmillan.

Sanders, J. (2016), *Adaptation and Appropriation* 2nd edn, London: Routledge.

Shakespeare, W. (1594), *The most lamentable Romaine tragedie of Titus Andronicus*, London.

Smiley, J. (1992), *A Thousand Acres*, London: Flamingo.

Smiley, J. (2014) 'Shakespeare in Iceland (1996)', in J. Shapiro (ed.), *Shakespeare in America: An Anthology from the Revolution to Now*, 640–64, New York, NY: Library of America.

Smith, E., ed. (1998), *The Spanish Tragedie*, Harmondsworth: Penguin

Snyder, S. (1979), *The Comic Matrix of Shakespeare's Tragedies: 'Romeo and Juliet', 'Hamlet', 'Othello', and 'King Lear'*, Princeton, NJ: Princeton University Press.

Stern, T. (2004), 'Repatching the Play', in P. Holland and S. Orgel (eds), *From Script to Stage in Early Modern England*, 151–77, London: Palgrave.

Sturm, J. (1570), *A Ritch Storehouse or Treasury for Nobilitye and Gentlemen*, London.

Tate, N. (1681), *The History of King Lear*, London.

Taylor, G. (2016), 'Collaboration 2016', in S. Gossett and D. Callaghan (eds), *Shakespeare in our Time: A Shakespeare Association of America Collection*, 141–8, London: Arden.

Teague, F. (1986), '*Othello* and New Comedy', *Comparative Drama* 20: 54–64.

Teague, F. (2011), 'Using Shakespeare with Memes, Remixes and Fanfic', *Shakespeare Survey* 64: 74–82.

Shakespeare and adaptation theory: unfinished business

DOUGLAS M. LANIER

It is a curious paradox that the study of Shakespeare adaptation has been so lively an area of scholarship for the past quarter-century, and yet much of that study has taken rather little explicit notice of the history of adaptation theory. This is not to say that analyses of Shakespeare adaptation have been uninformed by theory. On the contrary, it has now become routine to examine a Shakespeare adaptation from a theoretical perspective: we have queer takes on Shakespeare on film (for example, Patricia 2016), feminist takes on Shakespeare television series (for example, Wray 2006), postcolonial takes on Shakespearean novels and plays (for example, Cartelli 1999), cultural economist takes on Shakespeare in advertisements (for example, Holderness and Loughrey 2016). And, to be sure, several Shakespeareans have waded into the deeper theoretical conundrums posed by adaptation as a cultural phenomenon and artistic practice – to name just a few of many examples, Mary Jane Kidnie (2008) has addressed the question of potentiality and possibility as regards the relationship between source and adaptation; Zoltán Márkus (2019) has discussed reciprocality as a key effect in the relation between source and adaptation; Christy Desmet reconsidered the usefulness of fidelity and recognition as governing concepts in assessing adaptations (2014: 41–57); and from different angles Katherine Rowe (2007: 34–53) and W. B. Worthen (2007: 54–77) have addressed the pressures of modern media upon the nature of Shakespeare adaptation. That said, much of the scholarship on Shakespeare adaptation, in its zeal to get to the work of close reading, has not engaged in a sustained way with the foundational issues that have animated debates among scholars in the emerging discipline of adaptation studies. Those issues include:

- how to define adaptation and distinguish it from allied phenomena like imitation, intertextuality and allusion (that is to say, what is *not* adaptation?);
- how to address the persistent issue of fidelity to a source;

- how to assess the validity and relevance of the media specificity hypothesis, and with it the relationship between form and content;
- how to specify which contexts – media historical, social, political, commercial – drive adaptation as a phenomenon, and within those contexts, whether adaptation functions as a progressive or regressive force;
- how to conceptualize the dual nature of adaptation as both process and product;
- how to think through the issue of adaptational authorship (and the attribution of authorial/adaptorial intent), especially for collectively or industrially produced media;
- how to conceptualize an audience's recognition and reception of adaptations (the underlying question being, if the source isn't recognized in the adaptation, in what sense *is* it an adaptation?);
- how should adaptation critics understand their brief: to trace a intertextual or intermedial connection between a particular source and its adaptation? to articulate how an adaptation changes our shared perception of its source? to provide a reading of an adaptation that moves beyond its relationship to a particular source? to examine adaptational trends across a corpus of works? to highlight the oppressive or liberatory force of an adaptation? to suggest how a given adaptation extends or challenges received wisdom about the nature of adaptation more generally?

It has become easy to move quickly to the project of reading an Shakespearean adaptation without stepping back to consider the nature of adaptation, the ways in which different theories of adaptation might complicate the interpretive concerns we bring to Shakespeare and his afterlife. The purpose of this chapter is to offer a very brief and highly schematic overview of adaptation theory, in hopes of encouraging a more robust dialogue between the scholarship on Shakespeare adaptation and theoretical accounts of adaptation.

Not so long ago, adaptation studies focused primarily on the adaptation of literature to film. Indeed, it is there too that the modern Shakespeare adaptation studies had its birth, with skepticism about whether the Shakespearean text could be adequately 'realized' in cinematic form. So defined, adaptation studies struggled to find a disciplinary fit. For literature departments, adaptation critics were too concerned with film, not properly concerned with the primacy of the written word, even suspiciously allied with forces dumbing down the achievements of literary classics. For film departments, adaptation critics were too literary, not properly concerned with the fundamentally visual nature of the medium, too enamoured of what Francois Truffaut derisively called the cinematic 'tradition of quality' (2014: 138). For media studies departments, adaptation critics were too little focused on the sociology and politics of media systems, too interested in producing readings of specific adaptations, too engaged with the relative aesthetic virtues and limitations of the novel, play and film as rival formats.

The last few decades have seen a clear change to all that, and for a variety of reasons. Postmodernism has placed many forms of adaptation – pastiche, remixing, sampling, recontextualization, collages, mash-ups, memes, prequels and sequels – at the centre of artistic practice. Critiques of received notions of originality and the individual author have chipped away at our notions of the aura of some inimitable, un-paraphrasable original 'source'. Digital culture has trumpeted how digitization has enabled the effortlessly smooth movement between media platforms, so that content has now become readily available for intermedial and multimedial adaptation. Performance studies has also pushed adaptation to the foreground of cultural production by inverting the long-standing primacy of text over its performance(s), insisting that, in what became a disciplinary mantra, Shakespeare writes for the stage, not the page, though as the exemplary work of W. B. Worthen suggests (1997, 2003), the question of the relationship between script and performance, particularly vexed in Shakespeare's case, refuses to go away. And the dominance of comic book and videogame film adaptations – that is to say, cross-medial franchises – have now normalized public ideas about cinematic adaptations of pop forms, with long-form television serials now also trading on this trend. We have come a long way from debates about the propriety of adapting novels and plays into films, the place where modern adaptation studies got its start. Now in academe (and in popular culture), adaptation is newly ascendant as a cultural force, no longer carrying (quite) the stigma of secondarity and parasitism. Indeed, because adaptation is now widely accepted, even embraced as a mode of cultural production by many Shakespeareans, routinely integrated into our teaching and research, it has become a bit too easy to sidestep the challenges that adaptation theory might make to longstanding axioms of Shakespearean critical practice.

CLASSIFICATIONAL THEORY

Speaking in the broadest terms, we might identify three major strands of adaptational theory: classificational, intermedial and appropriative. The classificational strand is the oldest, stretching back into the classical rhetoric of Quintilian. It is primarily descriptive, concerned with the definition of adaptation and the classification or categorization of its many different types, the literary equivalent of identifying phyla and species in the natural world. It seeks to establish a basic analytic vocabulary and taxonomy for the practical work of charting the relationship between source and adaptation. It also identifies affiliations in adaptational technique between otherwise disparate examples. For modern adaptation studies, the landmark work, still unmatched in its precision and scope, remains Gérard Genette's *Palimpsests: Literature in the Second Degree* (1982), a structuralist classic. Genette's ambition is to lay out a comprehensive taxonomy of all the permutations of relation between sources and adaptations. One of the great strengths of his study is that he recognizes the ways in which taxonomies can encode perceptual and theoretical predispositions. Genette limits himself to literary adaptation, that is to say, relations between literary works, and so he does not engage with cross-medial adaptation, one of the overarching concerns of twentieth- and twenty-first-century adaptation theory.

In many ways, Linda Hutcheon's *A Theory of Adaptation* (2006) seeks to do for a much wider range of adaptations what Genette does for literary adaptation. Her study surveys adaptations of all sorts and with all kinds of sources, moving well beyond traditional literature to consider also film, television, digital and visual culture, music, theme parks and much more. She takes a theoretically ecumenical approach to her myriad materials, preferring to proceed inductively rather than deductively with her materials and eschewing the tight taxonomic structure preferred by Genette. Instead, her study is organized around a series of broad theoretical questions, 'what?' (transposition between forms and media specificity), 'who?' and 'why?' (adaptors and their motivations), 'how?' (audiences for and reception of adaptations), and 'when' and 'where' (temporal, spatial and cultural contexts for adaptation). What Hutcheon offers is not a single theory of adaptation so much as a loose organizational structure – a poststructuralist structure, as it were – for considering the kinds of theoretical problems posed by adaptation as the postmodern phenomenon par excellence. A third example of the field's continuing concern with taxonomy is Julie Sanders's *Adaptation and Appropriation* (2006; 2nd edn 2015), in which she distinguishes adaptation from appropriation in this way: 'an adaptation signals a relationship with an informing sourcetext or original … on the other hand, appropriation frequently affects a more decisive journey away from the informing source into a wholly new cultural product and domain' (2006: 26). Sanders's influential formulation stresses, in essence, that adaptations tend toward similarity to their sources whereas appropriations tend toward difference and so veer in the direction of originality, 'a *wholly new* cultural product and domain' (emphasis added). So formulated, appropriations reward the kinds of interpretive techniques and assumptions which critics have traditionally brought to 'original' works. This may account for the fact that by and large recent Shakespeare scholarship has been much focused on the appropriation of Shakespeare than in his adaptation.

These three works, and many others concerned with classification of adaptations, demonstrate the challenge of taxonomy in this ever-expanding field. In particular, they suggest the ongoing difficulty of defining adaptation as an object of study and the ways in which nomenclatures are themselves vehicles for models, metaphors and theories of adaptation. (For an illuminating discussion of different metaphorical models of adaptation, see Leitch 2011.) To take one prominent example, the term 'source' carries with it connotations of a single origin and a one-way vector of influence, what we might call an arboreal model (root and branch) of the relationship between originating text and adaptation. The term tends to occlude our seeing an adaptation as multiply influenced or as a collaborative or dialogic relation between works, each interpretively shaping the other. I have proposed, for example, a Deleuzian rhizomatic model for understanding the relationship between sources and adaptations (Lanier 2014); drawing upon object-oriented ontology and the work of Bruno Latour, Christy Desmet has outlined a different network model that stresses the wide range of agents – human, formal, computational, systemic and otherwise – involved the process of adaptation (Desmet 2017); Diana Henderson has proposed a collaborative model for adaptation, one that focuses less on the agon against the source, imagining Shakespeare less as 'the Law of the Father, the inevitable test, or the stony monument', and more like 'an imaginary friend' (2006: 9). More recently, Reto Winckler has proposed hacking as an appropriate master-metaphor for adaptation, with the Shakespearean source understood as something of an algorithm (2020: 1–22). And a fascinating new collection on intercultural Shakespeare (Refskou et al. 2019) embraces the metaphor of cannibalism for adaptation first introduced by Oswald de Andrade in his 1928 essay 'Manifesto Antropófago'.

None of these (and other) reconceptualized models of Shakespearean adaptation, however, entirely abandon the traditional terminology of 'source' and 'adaptation'. In order to avoid the theoretical pitfalls posed by those terms, Genette gives us the terms 'hypertext' for adaptation and 'hypotext' for what is conventionally called the source (1997: 5). The very similarity between '*hypo*text' and '*hyper*text' tends phonically to minimize the traditional hierarchy of source and adaptation and avoids the imputation of special originary status to the source, though the Greek prefixes *hypo-* ('under') and *hyper-* ('over') still retains residue of the arboreal model. The hypertext in some way transforms the hypotext, which 'it consequently evokes more or less perceptibly without necessarily speaking of it or citing it' (Genette 1997: 5). The fact that 'hypertext' gained widespread currency as a software term also worked against its wide adoption as a term of art by adaptation scholars. My general point here is that taxonomical terms within Shakespeare adaptation studies, difficult though they may be to change, are nevertheless bearers of theoretical models, and so should demand close, critical examination.

The difficulty of defining adaptation and its related terms opens a second question, one that Genette's discussion potentially puts in motion: what counts as a Shakespeare adaptation? For Genette, the grounding condition for an adaptation is that it 'evokes more or less perceptibly' its source without explicitly quoting or naming it. If legibility of the Shakespearean hypotext is the condition for a Shakespeare adaptation to be recognized as such, what are the horizons of that legibility? What sort of 'tell' marks a work as a Shakespearean adaptation? Certainly, suggests Genette, it is not some citation of Shakespearean dialogue, a character name, the name of a setting. But if this is not the case, it follows that what makes a Shakespearean adaptation Shakespearean is not the Shakespearean text, what has become *the* defining feature of Shakespeare for academics for the past century. The question of defining Shakespeare adaptation, then, raises a much larger issue of what Shakespeare is or has come to be in the cultural imagination. The identification of a work as a Shakespeare adaptation, then, turns upon the perceptual predispositions of reading and viewing communities who bring with them very different understandings of what is quintessentially or distinctively Shakespearean. To put this another way, a work's status as an adaptation is by its nature a social perception rather than an objective fact, and so Shakespeare adaptation studies must needs also address the perceptual proclivities, social and educational differences, and unequal distributions of cultural capital that accompany our identification of a work as a Shakespeare adaptation. This is a particularly urgent issue given the ever-expanding scope of Shakespeare adaptation studies, where we scholars, armed with critical hammers, are predisposed to see every text as a potential Shakespearean nail. To put the matter simply, scholars of Shakespeare adaptation need to think through theoretically what is not-Shakespeare (see Desmet et al. 2017: 1–24), lest we become critical imperialists intent on ever extending our professional territory. That said, at the same time we need to recognize the ways in which the designation 'not Shakespeare' has been deployed historically as a means to denigrate or disempower adaptations produced outside various cultural, linguistic, national, political, racial, gender and class boundaries, lest in our effort to resist making everything about Shakespeare we unwittingly reproduce those old boundaries and erect new ones. This question, of how scholars conceptualize the distinction between Shakespeare and not Shakespeare, strikes me as one of the more challenging facing a discipline newly awake to the global scope of Shakespeare adaptation, particularly adaptations in those cultural arenas outside the Anglo-American and European spheres.

INTERMEDIAL THEORY

Intermedial theory is the second family of adaptational theory, and here we enter the realm of something that actually looks like theory. Intermedial critics are interested in conceptualizing how a body of content can move from one medium to another. This branch of adaptation studies has its origins in the novel-to-film debates of the twentieth century, where critics worried over the relative virtues of literary and cinematic media and their adequacy to certain forms of storytelling. But under the pressure of proliferating forms of adaptation in the past fifty years, intermedial studies have since branched into broader consideration of the mobility of content across all manner of media. Intermedial studies have affiliations with structuralist semiotics and its ambition to create a unified, overarching theory of relationships between media. One particularly interesting approach has been multimodality theory, what one might call 'atomic' adaptation studies. Multimodality studies suggest that acts of communication depend upon different sensory channels or 'modes' – visual, auditory, tactile (by virtue of the body) and others – the basic building blocks or 'atoms' of communication. Every individual medium consists of a distinctive, characteristic bundle of these modes in different emphases and relations, though certainly many media use combinations of these basic building blocks. Film, for example, uses primarily the visual mode, though it includes secondary elements of the aural mode and even the tactile through its use of motion; classical theatre uses primarily the auditory and tactile modes, the tactile evoked through our experience of the body and space, though it certainly includes the visual as a secondary element. Adaptation then involves moving a message from one mode to another, with potential gains and losses in the message's content or potency. The virtue of this approach is that it returns our attention to the phenomenological and material particularities of media and to adaptors' attempt to find modal equivalencies as one moves content from one communicative channel to another. Lars Elleström's edited collection *Media Borders, Multimodality and Intermediality* (2010) and his monograph *Media Transformation* (2014) has done much to establish multimodal theory as a new, exciting approach to adaptation studies.

Medium specificity has been a central tenet and recurring problem for intermedial adaptation studies. The medium specificity hypothesis can be simply stated: each medium has a set of qualities and forms of reception specific to itself, and that those distinctive set of qualities offer well-defined affordances and limitations. The novel, for example, appeals to the reader's imagination through the qualities of language, a form that is particularly adept at communicating interior states and layered levels of perception; the cinema, by contrast, is a visual form, specifically a photographic form, and so it excels at communicating narrative and exteriors and tends to default to realist modes of representation. As is suggested above, much recent scholarship in intermediality has tended to conceptualize media specificity through the notion of the sensorium, that is, the idea that each medium operates through different constellations of basic senses – film and painting primarily through sight, music through hearing, dance and sculpture through touch, cooking through taste and smell.[1] (In such a formulation, language – the primary vehicle for literature, and to some extent theatre – is capable of vicariously evoking several senses at once.) It follows then that to transpose a work created for one medium into another medium is to run up against the essential formal differences between the two. The problem faced in adaptation, then, is akin to that faced in translation from one language to another, which explains the family resemblance between many aspects of intermedial theory and translation theory. Given these assumptions, cross-medial adaptation inevitably involves loss in the translation, and for much of the first half of the twentieth century, there was considerable debate about whether certain media were simply better vehicles for certain kinds of content than others. One can easily see how, then, the adaptation of literature to film might be regarded as particularly fraught, since it would, so the argument went, lead to the dilution or even destruction of literature's aesthetic or cultural power. (Without doubt, such arguments often suffer from unexamined associations of particular media with certain social classes or communities. What is also left out is the possibility that content might be enriched in the course of transfer from medium to medium, a possibility that has been also been debated in translation studies.) In the case of Shakespeare, the transposition of his work, material encoded in metaphorically rich and allusive language, was especially 'lossy' when shifted over to a photorealistic medium like film, not to mention other media like music, dance or painting, all of which in different ways struggled to communicate Shakespearean content.

The strong version of the media specificity hypothesis suggests that, strictly speaking, content is specific to the media form in which it was originally encoded. To transfer that content to a new medium is necessarily to change that content's meaning, and there will always be elements of the original that are utterly untransposable to another medium. This is the media version of the heresy of paraphrase, and it also underlies the notion of the 'unfilmable book'. Seymour Chatman's article, 'What Novels Can Do That Films Can't (and Vice Versa)', is a classic statement of the strong version of the media specificity principle, for Chatman argues that film has no way of communicating tone, non-direct narrative discourse or unspecificity, effects central to novelistic discourse (1980: 121–40). This sort of strong formulation conveniently forgets that works come to us often, perhaps even typically, in multiple media at once, rarely in some 'pure' media form, something stressed in the multimodal theories of Gunter Kress and Theo van Leeuwen.[2] Novels contain illustrations and ornamental typefaces; films contain subtitles and photographed texts; Shakespearean theatre combines elements of language, bodily movement, architecture, visual arts and music. What is more, in practice our experience of media often involves what one might call synaesthetic perception, in which one sort of sensory experience might evoke an allied experience of a different sense. An insistent musical rhythm can, for example, evoke bodily movement and so the sense of touch; a sour taste might be associated with bright colour or dissonant tones. The composer Aaron Copland was able to evoke the visual and tactile experience of the open spaces of the American West with open fifths, suspended chords, long sustained notes and contrasts between strings in high and low registers. Such sensory affiliations suggest that different media may not be so fully locked into native formal distinctions than it might first appear. In the case of Shakespeare, this opens up the possibility of generating equivalent effects to those of the Shakespeare text by other, non-textual means. The notion of sensory affiliations also draws the debate into discussions of cultural context, for the association of, say, sour taste with bright colour or musical dissonance is likely to be culturally determined, not a formal universal.

Recent accounts of media in the digital age have tended to push strongly against the media specificity hypothesis. The reigning attitude toward media difference is epitomized by the terms 'spreadable media' or 'convergence culture', terms from two influential works, Henry Jenkins's *Convergence Culture* (2006), and the follow-up *Spreadable Media*, co-authored by Jenkins, Sam Ford and Joshua Green. Because, so the story goes, the reduction of content to ones and zeros allows for its relatively seamless transfer between media platforms, the 'same' content can travel easily across media without appreciable loss of content or shift in meaning. Indeed, in an effort to maximize profits from a single property, it is now routine practice for commercial media outlets to provide the 'same' or closely related content across multiple platforms at once. We can, for instance, view Baz Luhrmann's *Shakespeare's Romeo + Juliet* on the big screen or home video, read the illustrated screenplay, listen to the CD soundtrack and peruse production photos online. What is more, once converted to digital form, media content becomes far more readily available for sampling and creative reconfiguring (that is to say, adaptation), so that with a little ingenuity consumers can become producers of adaptations in their own right, adaptations that can extend or contest the meaning of the source.[3] It is in this sense that digital content becomes 'spreadable', empowering the end user as never before and eluding complete control by the producer. The theory of spreadable content tends to downplay the specificity of digital media – since the 'same' content can be easily migrated to another digital platform – and to minimize the ways in which the specific qualities of digital platforms (their interfaces, their scale, their typical sites of consumption) might shape one's experience of content. Is Luhrmann's *Romeo + Juliet* the same film on the big screen and on an iPhone? In what sense the 'same'? In their zeal to embrace the laudable principle of maximal, democratic access and availability for appropriation, a zeal encapsulated in the slogan, 'if it doesn't spread, it's dead', some adaptation theorists may underestimate the extent to which different media platforms might enable or hinder forms of communal experience. Because digitality is the ultimate condition for spreadability, the spreadable content theory also tends to assume that all media are or can be digitally encoded, an assumption that leaves out media like live theatre or dance where their analogue nature may be crucial to their power.[4]

That said, digital media have rightly prompted adaptation theorists to reconsider the media specificity hypothesis. One possibility might be a weaker, less deterministic formulation of the hypothesis: rather than suggesting that different media have immutable, mutually exclusive qualities that definitively shape their content, one might conceptualize those differences in terms of native orientations that can be changed or modified by sufficiently ingenious adaptors.[5] It might be especially challenging to film *Finnegan's Wake* given the dominant orientation of cinema as a medium, but it is not per se impossible. Such a conception would allow for closer consideration of the experiential implications of different media platforms for the 'same' content without suggesting that media are utterly deterministic in what they can communicate.

Zoom Shakespeare, the predominant live performance format for Shakespeare during the 2020–1 COVID-19 pandemic, provides an instructive example.[6] Zoom is designed for facial close-ups, and so as a medium for Shakespeare performance it tends to heighten the importance of the voice and the text at the expense of the body; the frontality of the actors – they speak to the viewer, not to each other – and their isolation from one another into separate boxes means that the evocation of a fictional community is particularly difficult to achieve; the sense that the characters speak from separate worlds to the viewer is all the more heightened by the glimpses we get of the private living spaces we typically see behind the actors, something that also hinders our ability to suspend disbelief in the performance. To put this in extreme terms, Zoom is a medium for soliloquies rather than dialogue, textual recitation rather than stage performance. That is not to say, however, that it's impossible to address Zoom's native orientation as a medium. Performers have experimented, for example, with using virtual backgrounds to suggest that the characters they present are occupying the same fictional space, and with clever blocking it is even possible for those characters to seem to pass objects between Zoom boxes or fight or kiss one another.[7] Where Zoom excels is in communicating a kind of improvised live communalism between the actors and their viewers. The very glitchiness of Zoom, its DIY qualities and its capacity for accommodating live chat, proclaims the actors' determination to create a version of the close relationship between performer and spectator that occurs in live stage performance. The fact that the actors speak directly to us tends to enhance that quality, though of course it is palpably not the same as in the theatre, since we are not visible to the actors. My larger point is that though digital media certainly afford new opportunities for access and creative appropriation, those affordances do not negate analysis of their distinctive formal and sensory natures.

We might note that intermedial theory often has at its heart an unspoken ideal of fidelity, the ideal that content might move across media seamlessly. Indeed, the fact that content can move across media at all is what intermedial theorists seek to explain. In practice, these critics typically acknowledge that this ideal of fidelity isn't always or even often achieved – they chart losses and gains in content in the adaptational process – but intermedial criticism implicitly measures adaptation against an (impossible) ideal of intermedial transposition. What is more, intermedial studies tends to conceptualize adaptation primarily as a problem of translation or transfer between media forms. Indeed, there is often a paucity of human agency in its accounts of adaptation, as if the media, not media practitioners, were the primary forces at work in adaptational processes. Intermedial theory is not so powerful in explaining a creator's willful changes in content as they engage in adapting a source.

APPROPRIATIVE THEORY

The third strand of adaptation theory, appropriative theory, has its roots in Marxist-inflected literary criticism and sociology, in particular the cultural materialism of the 1980s and 1990s. Rather than focusing on adaptation as a matter of translation between media or forms, appropriative critics focus on changes in content that occur during the adaptational process, a process typically conceived as agonistic. The grounding assumption is that the source is allied with oppressive or conservative ideologies. In the case of Shakespeare, the emphasis falls upon his work's imbrication with retrogressive cultural forces – classism, racism, heterosexism, colonialism, capitalism. Adaptation, then, involves some element of struggle against the source (or the source's latter-day uses), struggle over the source's ideological orientation and cultural capital which the adaptor then recasts, demystifies, reorients, in a word, changes to suit some new, more contemporary or politically progressive purpose. The term 'appropriation' thus bears two meanings: the notion of co-opting the property of the author (or those cultural forces which lay claim to that property) into the hands of another user; and the notion of reallocating or redistributing the source's content or cultural capital more equitably.[8] Whereas intermedial theory focuses on form, appropriative theory focuses primarily on content; whereas intermedial theorists work from an implicit model of fidelity of content between source and adaptation, appropriative critics highlight the differences in content that result from adaptational processes, for it is in those differences that ideological transformation might occur. This model of adaptation involves the adaptor consciously co-opting the source's content, repurposing for his or her own ends, assimilating it to the adaptor's artistic enterprise. It is, in other words, an author- or agent-driven conception of adaptation, one where the adaptor asserts his or her originality by changing source material that might threaten or overwhelm, either because of the nature of its content, or because of the source's superior or oppressive position in the artistic canon. Harold Bloom's theory of 'the anxiety of influence' (1973) falls into this category of adaptation theory, with his idea that every strong poet must confront and defeat his most powerful literary forebear. So too in quite different ways does Terence Hawkes's view that 'we mean by Shakespeare' (1992: 3), which is to say, the texts of Shakespeare have meaning only within a never-ending dynamic of appropriation and counter-appropriation. Because Shakespeare's work carries such cultural force, it is a particularly vexed site for the ideological struggle for meaning and power among various artistic and critical constituencies.

For several reasons, appropriative theory has been the dominant force in adaptational criticism for the past two decades. It is especially amenable to the individual case study, in which a critic can trace the ideological relations of an adaptation to its source. This format, akin to the close reading for the New Critics, produces article-length studies that accord well with the institutional needs of academics and it lines up nicely with ideological critique, the dominant practice in contemporary cultural criticism. Appropriative theory accords particularly well with critical concerns about identity politics, globalization and inclusiveness, since adaptations can serve as vehicles for recasting sources to accommodate cultural contexts and concerns well beyond those sources' original scope or orientation. Indeed, Gary Bortolotti and Linda Hutcheon (2007) have gone so far as to suggest that adaptation might be understood in terms of natural selection, as a means for stories to adapt to cultural environments which have become inhospitable to their survival in their original forms. One might point, for example, to the ways in which Shakespeare adaptation has enabled writers to confront the long legacy of using Shakespeare in the service of white supremacy, through works such as Djanet Sears's *Harlem Duet* (1998), Toni Morrison's *Desdemona* (2012) and Keith Hamilton Cobb's *American Moor* (2020) which engage with *Othello*'s racial dynamics. In all of these works, key elements of Shakespeare's play survive, but in transmuted form and in very different contexts that highlight the racial misrepresentations and exclusions of the source, and critique the totemic power of Shakespeare's work in perpetuating racial stereotypes and validating toxic social systems.[9]

That said, appropriative theory depends upon ideological motivations and so an implicit theory of human (or at least institutional) agency at work in the adaptational process. One weakness of the theory lies in its underestimation of the ways in which in practice the process of adaptation might be dispersed across a variety of different creators whose motives and interests may be in conflict or require complicated tradeoffs. In film, for example, the notion of the director as sole 'authorial' agent in creating an adaptation requires one to ignore (or at least homogenize) the agency of others in the adaptational process – producers, actors, designers, editors, marketers and the like. Since adapting a source is often a corporate or communal process, there is a need for better accounts of the industrial and commercial conditions under which sources are adapted, with greater emphasis on charting the adaptational process rather than on reading the adaptational product. Questioning the familiar compare-and-contrast close ideological reading of a source and adaptation, Simone Murray has long called for greater attention to industrial practices and multiple institutional agencies involved in the making of adaptations. In Shakespeare adaptation studies, Russell Jackson's *Shakespeare Films in the Making* (2007) and Emma French's *Selling Shakespeare to Hollywood* (2006), to take two examples, suggest fruitful ways of heeding Murray's call.

The appropriative model of adaptation also rests upon a potentially worrisome paradox. In this model, an adaptation positions itself against its source by virtue of what it changes in the source, but at the same time by its nature an adaptation conserves and transmits at least part of that source in the act of adapting it. Necessarily adaptation perpetuates, at least partly, the memory of the source it modifies; whatever act of transgression it might perform occurs in the long, dark shadow of the source. Because appropriative criticism tends to stress difference from the source, it tends to downplay an adaptation's simultaneous and potentially problematic effect of preserving the source and even adding to its cultural prestige. This paradoxical effect is especially pronounced with already well-established cultural icons like Shakespeare, even if adaptations might shift the ideological valence of Shakespeare over time.[10] The case of Shakespeare and world cinema provides an apt example. As Mark Thornton Burnett (2012) and Craig Dionne and Parmita Karpadia (2014) have amply documented, filmmakers across the globe have reshaped Shakespeare to address cultural conditions well outside his original cultural sphere. By so doing, they have implicitly (and in some cases explicitly) resisted the association of Shakespeare with Anglo-American culture. But of course at the same time those filmmakers have extended the cultural reach of Shakespeare and added to his worldwide cultural capital. Indeed, this dual process raises questions about the changing ideological valence of Shakespeare's work. In the case of global Shakespeare cinema, does the postcolonial model of 'writing back to the empire' still quite fit, and if not, in what ways is the deployment of Shakespeare transgressive? As a world author, has Shakespeare become post-postcolonial, his cultural capital no longer quite so firmly allied with Anglo-American political and cultural dominance? Are certain appropriations of Shakespeare in recent global cinema, to use Richard Burt's terminology, politically 'posthermeneutic' (1998: xxx), which is to say, does Shakespeare now function for some merely as widely familiar tales on which to project one's own stories rather than works always already bearing an ideological charge? In posing these questions in this way, however, is there a risk of suggesting that with this globalized mutation of Shakespeare's cultural capital his work has finally achieved an incarnation that heralds, *pace* Francis Fukuyama, an end to history, a Shakespeare shorn of imbrication with the cultural and political forces that fuelled his worldwide spread?

As I've suggested above, appropriative theory is particularly interested in difference, both difference as a sociopolitical category and differences between adaptations and their sources. It is a mark of the ascendancy of appropriative theory, then, that fidelity to the original has become a denigrated mode of analysis. Indeed, in her magisterial survey of adaptation theory Kamilla Elliott observes that now professional adaptation critics habitually begin by denouncing fidelity, engaging in a ritual stoning of the repressive father before moving on to consider how the adaptation differs from its source (2020: 15–18). To be sure, fidelity discourse, many have observed, has historically carried with it an implicit moral imperative – fidelity too often quickly moves from description to a prescription to respect the source. As Robert Stam has amply documented, historically the discourse of fidelity has carried with it the implication that adaptation is at some level a bastardized, derivative, parasitic, inferior reproduction of the source (2005: 1–52). Appropriative theory tends to reverse this priority of fidelity over difference. Faithful adaptations are linked to repressive conformity, preservation of heritage, political regressiveness and unoriginality, whereas unfaithful adaptations (that is, appropriations), are associated with resistance to oppressive regimes and ideology, liberation, progressiveness and creativity. Whether these critical associations stand up to scrutiny seems worthy of debate. For one thing, as Jacques Derrida repeatedly suggests, to reiterate a work is to introduce a gap in contexts that by its nature introduces difference, the politics of which are not so easily or univocally determined. The lesson of Borges's Menard is that even a word-for-word repetition of a text occurs over a gap in time or cultural context that unsettles or reroutes its original meaning. Strictly speaking, there is no such thing as a faithful adaptation.

In any case, the privileging of differences between source and adaptation, what is the reigning trope of much adaptation criticism, risks losing the dialectical interplay that is fundamental to adaptation as a mode. Without some element or principle of fidelity at work, there can be no adaptation. The 'some element or principle' in my formulation is crucial and suggests the need for a more thoroughgoing, nuanced theorizing of fidelity as an aesthetic effect. Accordingly, there have been several recent attempts to reconceptualize fidelity as a non-prescriptive critical category (see, for example, McCabe et al. 2011; DiCecco 2015: 161–75; Hermansson 2015: 147–60). To be faithful to some element of the original is not to duplicate it in its entirety, but rather to strike a relation of similarity to some quality of the source that the adaptation identifies as essentially or distinctively Shakespearean. Fidelity always involves some element of selectivity – in the case of Shakespeare, fidelity to some quality of his language, some quality of the plots, the characters, the modes of characterization, the distinctive settings (balcony, graveyard), modes of address (soliloquy), motifs, characteristic metaphors, tone, evocation of the theatrical medium, social register or something else – while at the same time adaptors discard or change what they regard as inessential in the source, what is peripheral, accidental, unimportant. Fidelity, then, is not an all-or-nothing matter, but a selective, strategic act, an implicit identification of the essential 'spirit' of the Shakespearean source. For that reason, we need a more finely tuned understanding of fidelity as it functions in practice (which is to say a theory of fidelity). And precisely because every adaptation – as a condition of it being an adaptation – evokes the memory of its source, adaptations have the power retrospectively to revise our perceptions of the source, to suggest that this element is quintessentially Shakespearean and that element is not, by virtue of the adaptation's principles of fidelity. For that reason adaptation does not leave its source interpretively untouched. Any particular relation of fidelity in adaptation is, in effect, a theory of the Shakespearean source, a hypothesis about what constitutes Shakespeare's 'spirit' or the ground of Shakespeare's cultural power. Because adaptations so often locate that essence in some element of Shakespeare other than the text, they pose a potent challenge to long-standing critical axioms of professional Shakespeareans who have, for at least a century, assumed that the essential Shakespeare is or ought to be located in his language, over which they have professional dominion.

IN CONCLUSION

Shakespeare adaptation studies has often been its own little world within Shakespeare studies as a whole, standing somewhat apart from the cross-currents and debates that have animated the field of adaptation studies. There are understandable institutional reasons for this, given that research into Shakespeare adaptation, its roots in scholarship on Shakespeare film, came of age under the ever-widening umbrella of Shakespeare studies and, less widely acknowledged, because Shakespeare adaptation has served the needs of contemporary pedagogy. Accordingly, too many of us at work on Shakespeare adaptation have been content to remain in dialogue with developments in Shakespeare studies, rather than engaging with conversations with developments in adaptation and media studies and considering the radical implications of various adaptation theories and adaptation as a disciplinary paradigm. One of the great benefits of engaging with adaptation studies and theory writ large is that doing so prompts our reconsideration of Shakespeare's place in the dynamics of cultural production, a place that is not as central as we Shakespeareans might be tempted to think it is. To be sure, this places a greater obligation upon the individual critic to move back and forth across disciplinary boundaries and to make Shakespeare's fundamentally mediated, adaptational nature front and centre in our theoretical ruminations. As I hope I've suggested by this admittedly reductive overview, adaptation theory does more than provide models for reading the latest Shakespeare-themed graphic novel or web series. Adaptation theory opens up foundational questions about the objects in our critical gaze and the assumptions that fuel our critical practice. They open broad issues that deserve more vigorous and rigorous debate: what is an adaptation (and what is not)? What does 'Shakespeare' mean when we speak of a Shakespeare adaptation? What are the relations between form, medium and content in the adaptational process? How are we conceiving of the political force or efficacy of adaptation? Is there anything special about Shakespeare adaptation when it is set alongside other kinds of adaptation? What is (or ought to be) the aims of Shakespeare adaptation criticism beyond the generation of close readings? And how might Shakespeare adaptation studies contribute to debates about adaptation outside the charmed circle of Shakespeare studies? In a world in which adaptation (of Shakespeare and otherwise) is one of the most robust modes of global cultural production, engaging with these kinds of theoretical questions more explicitly seems overdue.

NOTES

1   Of course, in some ways our experiences of all media potentially involve all the senses. One might respond to the smells of live stage performance or a book; one might find the ambient noises of a gallery instrumental to one's response to a painting. But these are, in most cases, not the primary vehicles of content from the artwork to the audience. This set of theories turns upon the notion of relative prioritization of sensory modes in a given medium – a painting prioritizes sight, even though it also involves tactility because of its vicarious evocation of space. Equally important is the issue of address: dance, for example, involves tactility in its creation (because the primary instrument of the medium is the dancer's body), but when we experience a dance as a viewer, that tactility is coupled with visuality, since the viewer experiences most dance performances via sight. In other words, tactility is evoked in different ways for the producer and the consumer of dance, though tactility is dance's primary mode. My 'in most cases' in the formulation above opens up the possibility

for artists to innovate within the modal characteristics of a medium, reprioritizing the relationships between its basic modes.

2   In Shakespeare studies, several scholars have stressed the fundamental multimodality of Shakespeare's works – see, for examples, Rowe (2007, 2010), Worthen (2003, 2007) and Smith (2016).

3   For application of this concept to Shakespeare adaptations, see *The Shakespeare User* (Fazel and Geddes 2017) and Blackwell (2018).

4   The relationship of theatre to digital media (and more generally to recorded media) has recently been a lively area of interest to Shakespeareans. Worthen's most recent work (2020) addresses the technological apparatuses engaged by modern theatrical performances of Shakespeare. *Shakespeare and the 'Live' Theatre Broadcast Experience* (2018) offers a range of perspectives on theatrical broadcasts of Shakespeare performances, increasingly a means by which audiences experience Shakespeare on stage. Of some interest is the collection's implicit emphasis on the phenomenology of this performance medium. The scare quotes around the word 'live' identifies the quality of theatrical experience put under pressure by this format, for 'live' broadcast, as Osborne notes in her epilogue to the collection, pushes hard against theatre's long-standing claims to 'liveness' and 'presence' as its defining characteristics.

5   The debates about transfer of content from one medium to another has a very long history, stretching back at least as far as the early roots of European Romanticism. For a good overview of these debates, see chapter 2 of Elliott (2020), esp. 50–88.

6   For representative examples, see the YouTube series by *Shakespeare Happy Hours*, *The Show Must Go Online* and *Zenith Players*.

7   An example might be the Creation Theatre Company's Zoom performance of *The Tempest* in April and May 2020, where Ferdinand and Miranda were able to simulate a kiss through clever blocking, despite filming their parts in separate venues. Though this performance is not available in recorded form, Benjamin Broadribb's review (2020) offers a detailed account.

8   For an incisive overview of how the terms 'adaptation' and 'appropriation' have been used in practice in Shakespeare studies, see Desmet and Igenyar (2015).

9   MacDonald (2020) provides an exemplary example of this line of inquiry.

10 Here one senses a potential gap between academic criticism and artistic practice. Recent academic criticism, with its focus on ideological critique, has tended to be especially attentive to artistic strategies that are potentially self-compromising or unwittingly complicit, whereas artists who employ appropriation as a technique may be more willing to embrace the apparent paradox that appropriation entails.

REFERENCES

Aebischer, P., S. Greenhalgh and L. Osborne, eds (2018), *Shakespeare and the Live Theatre Broadcast Experience*, London: Bloomsbury/Arden Shakespeare.

Blackwell, A. (2018), *Shakespearean Celebrity in the Digital Age: Fan Cultures and Remediation*, New York, NY: Palgrave Macmillan.

Bloom, H. (1973), *The Anxiety of Influence: A Theory of Poetry*, Oxford: Oxford University Press.

Bortolotti, G. R. and L. Hutcheon (2007), 'On the Origin of Adaptations: Rethinking Fidelity Discourse and "Success": Biologically', *New Literary History* 38 (3): 443–58.

Broadribb, B. (2020), '"A vision of the Island": Immersion meets Isolation in Creation Theatre's *The Tempest*', *'Action is Eloquence': Rethinking Shakespeare*, 21 April. Available online: https://medium.com/action-is-eloquence-re-thinking-shakespeare/a-vision-of-the-island-immersion-meets-isolation-in-creation-theatre-s-the-tempest-935bb01a44fa (accessed 21 July 2021).

Burnett, M. T. (2012), *Shakespeare and World Cinema*, Cambridge: Cambridge University Press.

Burt, R. (1998), *Unspeakable ShaXXXspeares: Queer Theory and American Kiddie Culture*, New York, NY: St. Martins.

Cartelli, T. (1999), *Repositioning Shakespeare: National Formations, Postcolonial Appropriations*, New York, NY: Routledge.

Chatman, S. (1980), 'What Novels Can Do That Films Can't (and Vice Versa)', *Critical Inquiry* 7 (1): 121–40.

Cobb, K. H. (2020), *American Moor*, London: Methuen.

Desmet, C. (2014), 'Recognizing Shakespeare, Rethinking Fidelity: A Rhetoric and Ethics of Appropriation', in A. Huang and E. Rivlin (eds), *Shakespeare and the Ethics of Appropriation*, 41–57, New York, NY: Palgrave Macmillan.

Desmet, C. (2017), 'Alien Shakespeares 2.0', *Actes des congrès de la Société française Shakespeare* 35. Available online: doi.org/10.4000/shakespeare.3877 (accessed 21 July 2021).

Desmet, C., N. Loper and J. Casey, eds (2017), *Shakespeare / Not Shakespeare*, New York, NY: Palgrave Macmillan.

Desmet, C. and S. Igenyar (2015), 'Adaptation, appropriation, or What You Will', *Shakespeare* 11 (1): 10–19.

Dicecco, N. (2015), 'State of the Conversation: The Obscene Underside of Fidelity', *Adaptation* 8 (2): 161–75.

Dionne, C. and P. Karpadia, eds (2014), *Bollywood Shakespeares*, New York, NY: Palgrave Macmillan.

Elleström, L., ed. (2010), *Media Borders, Multimodality and Intermediality*, New York, NY: Palgrave Macmillan.

Elleström, L. (2014), *Media Transformation: The Transfer of Media Characteristics Among Media*, New York, NY: Palgrave Pivot.

Elliott, K. (2020), *Theorizing Adaptation*. Oxford: Oxford University Press.

Fazel, V. and L. Geddes, eds (2017), *The Shakespeare User: Critical and Creative Appropriations in a Networked Culture*, New York, NY: Palgrave Macmillan.

French, E. (2006), *Selling Shakespeare to Hollywood: The Marketing of Filmed Shakespeare Adaptations from 1989 into the New Millennium*, Hatfield: University of Hertfordshire Press.

Genette, G. (1997), *Palimpsests: Literature in the Second Degree*, trans. C. Newman and C. Doubinsky, Lincoln, NE: University of Nebraska Press.

Hawkes, T. (1992), *Meaning by Shakespeare*, London: Routledge.

Henderson, D. E. (2006), *Collaborations with the Past: Reshaping Shakespeare Across Time and Media*, Ithaca, NY: Cornell University Press.

Hermansson, C. (2015), 'Flogging Fidelity: In Defense of the (Un)Dead Horse', *Adaptation* 8 (2): 147–60.

Holderness, G. and B. Loughrey (2016), 'Ales, Beers, Shakespeares', in D. Shellard and S. Keenan (eds), *Shakespeare's Cultural Capital: His Economic Impact from the Sixteenth to the Twenty-first Century*, 99–125, New York, NY: Palgrave Macmillan.

Hutcheon, L. (2013), *A Theory of Adaptation*, London: Routledge.

Jackson, R. (2007), *Shakespeare Films in the Making: Vision, Production and Reception*, Cambridge: Cambridge University Press.

Jenkins, H. (2006), *Convergence Culture: Where Old and New Media Collide*, New York, NY: New York University Press.

Jenkins, H., S. Ford and J. Green (2013), *Spreadable Media: Creating Value and Meaning in a Networked Culture*, New York, NY: New York University Press.

Kress, G. R. (2009), *Multimodality: A Social Semiotic Approach to Contemporary Communication*, London: Routledge.

Kidnie, M. J. (2008), *Shakespeare and the Problem of Adaptation: Forms of Possibility*, London: Routledge.

Lanier, D. (2014), 'Shakespearean Rhizomatics', in A. Huang and E. Rivlin (eds), *Shakespeare and the Ethics of Appropriation*, 21–40, New York, NY: Palgrave Macmillan.

Leitch, T. (2011), 'Jekyll, Hyde, Jekyll, Hyde, Jekyll, Hyde, Jekyll, Hyde: Four Models of Intertextuality', in A. Burnham Bloom and M. Sanders Pollock (eds), *Victorian Literature and Film Adaptation*, 27–49, Amherst: Cambria.

Leitch, T. (2009), 'To Adapt or to Adapt to? Consequences of Approaching Film Adaptation Intransitively', *Studia Filmoznawcze* 30: 91–103.

MacCabe, C., K. Murray and R. Warner (2011), *True to the Spirit: Film Adaptation and the Question of Fidelity*, New York, NY: Oxford University Press.

MacDonald Green, J. (2020), *Shakespearean Adaptation, Race and Memory in the New World*, New York, NY: Palgrave Macmillan.

Márkus, Z. (2019), 'Historicizing Appropriability: Hybrid Shakespeare and the Challenges of History', *Cahiers Élisabéthains* 99 (1): 56–65.

Morrison, T. (2012), *Desdemona*, London: Oberon Books.

Murray, S. (2011), *The Adaptation Industry: The Cultural Economy of Contemporary Literary Adaptation*, London: Routledge.

Patricia, A. G. (2016), *Queering the Shakespeare Film: Gender Trouble, Gay Spectatorship and Male Homoeroticism*, London: Bloomsbury/Arden Shakespeare.

Refskou, A. S., M. A. De Amorim and V. M. De Carvalho, eds (2019), *Eating Shakespeare: Cultural Anthropophagy as Global Methodology*, London: Bloomsbury/Arden.

Rowe, K. (2007), 'Medium-Specificity and Other Critical Scripts for Screen Shakespeare', in D. E. Henderson (ed.), *Alternative Shakespeares 3*, 34–53, London: Routledge.

Rowe, K. (2010), 'Shakespeare and Media History', in M. DeGrazia and S. Wells (eds), *The New Cambridge Companion to Shakespeare*, 303–24, Cambridge: Cambridge University Press

Sanders, J. (2016), *Adaptation and Appropriation*, The New Critical Idiom series, London: Routledge.

Sears, D. (1998), *Harlem Duet*, Winnipeg: Scirocco Drama.

Shakespeare Happy Hours (2020–1), YouTube series. Available online: https://www.youtube.com/c/ShakespeareHappyHours/videos (accessed 11 October 2021).

The Show Must Go Online (2020–1), YouTube series. Available online: https://www.youtube.com/c/RobMyles/videos (accessed 11 October 2021).

Smith, B. (2016), *Shakespeare / Cut: Rethinking Cutwork in an Age of Distraction*, Oxford: Oxford University Press.

Stam, R. (2005), 'Introduction: The Theory and Practice of Adaptation', in R. Stam and A. Raengo (eds), *Literature and Film: A Guide to the Theory and Practice of Adaptation*, 1–52, New York, NY: Blackwell.

Truffaut, F. (2014), 'A Certain Tendency in French Cinema (France, 1954)', in E. S. MacKenzie (ed.), *Film Manifestos and Global Cinema Cultures: A Critical Anthology*, 133–44, Berkeley, CA: University of California Press.

Van Leeuwen, T. (2012), 'Multimodality and Multimodal Research', in E. Margolis and L. Pauwels (eds), *The Sage Handbook of Visual Research Methods*, 168–77, London: Sage.

Winckler, R. (2021), 'Hacking Adaptation: Updating, Porting, and Forking the Shakespearean Source Code', *Adaptation* 14 (1): 1–22.

Worthen, W. B. (1997), *Shakespeare and the Authority of Performance*, Cambridge: Cambridge University Press.

Worthen, W. B. (2003), *Shakespeare and the Force of Modern Performance*, Cambridge: Cambridge University Press.

Worthen, W. B. (2007), 'Shakespeare 3.0: Or Text vs. Performance, the Remix', in D. Henderson (ed.), *Alternative Shakespeares 3*, 54–77, London: Routledge.

Worthen, W. B. (2020), *Shakespeare, Technicity, Theatre*, Cambridge: Cambridge University Press.

Wray, R. (2006), 'Shakespeare and the Singletons, or, Beatrice meets Bridget Jones: Post-Feminism, Popular Culture and *Shakespeare (Re)-Told*', in M. T. Burnett and R. Wray (eds), *Screening Shakespeare in the Twenty-First Century*, 185–205, Edinburgh: Edinburgh University Press.

Zenith Players (2020–1), YouTube series. Available online: https://www.youtube.com/channel/UCYwyqqhPiKV18i1r2vltnbg (accessed 11 October 2021).

What is Shakespeare adaptation?: Why *Pericles*? Why Cloud? Why now?

JULIE SANDERS

What is Shakespeare adaptation? It is many and various, and the path is strewn with failed attempts to provide a singular definition of something that is best understood as process and practice. As Margaret Jane Kidnie notes, 'adaptation as an evolving category is closely tied to how the work modifies over time and from one reception space to another' (2009: 5). Seen from this vantage point, we might describe the history and process of Shakespeare adaptation via metaphors of travel, best imagined through a widening motion, with a starting point at what might be viewed as the oldest and narrowest form of adaptation, in theatre itself, the medium in which Shakespeare worked, expanding from there to cross-media adaptations (for example, novel, film, music, animation) and ultimately widening out to the recasting of the material to entirely new ends (referred to here as both cultural studies and appropriation studies).

Shakespeare adaptation, we can argue, takes place every time a theatre group stages their particular production of a play, making collective choices about text, costume, casting, setting, venue and handing it over to different audiences on different days to fashion their own meanings. Sign languages and the fierce embodied storytelling they create onstage bring yet another adaptive and interpretative frame into the picture (Rumbold 2013: 227–36). And transcultural or intercultural performance studies have long made the point that adaptation theory is sometimes dangerously Anglophone, missing the multiple cross-cultural exchanges and new constructions of meaning that take place when Shakespeare is re-made for Chinese, Japanese, Indian, Mexican, Italian, Romanian and many more languages, cultures and contexts (Massai 2005; Trivedi and Minami 2010; Bennett and Carson 2013; Lei, Ick and Trivedi 2016; Desmet, Iyengar and Jacobson 2019; Trivedi and Chakravarti 2020). 'Global Shakespeares' is therefore an increasingly vibrant, polyphonic and often activist area of adaptation scholarship, engaging with his work, as Sandra Young has demonstrated, from a context of 'diasporic mobilities' (2019: loc. 87): 'In travelling across the globe, traditional Shakespeare has been dismantled and reimagined, and the result is illuminating for cultural studies' (loc. 73).[1] All of this *is* Shakespeare adaptation and yet there is still more to come. From here we can expand yet further to the cross-generic, intermedial transformation, or, to use Jay David Bolter and Richard Grusin's much deployed term 're-mediation', that takes place when canonical texts such as *Hamlet* or *Romeo and Juliet* are re-thought as film, game, music, musical, dance or graphic novel (Bolter and Grusin 2000). While this chapter will in its latter sections of close analysis focus on two contemporary Anglophone novels based on Shakespeare's late co-authored play *Pericles,* the selection is both highly particular – asking why adapt this Shakespeare play at this time and in these ways? – and highly applicable to broader point-making beyond specific examples or example genres. My focus novels, by British authors Ali Smith and Mark Haddon, and their at times allusive and slippery engagement with Shakespeare's late play *Pericles, Prince of Tyre* (itself probably co-authored with George Wilkins) as a so-called 'source text' are one means, my chosen means, of making manifest the recurring compulsion since the time of the first performances of his plays to rework and adapt Shakespeare.[2] This adaptive impulse occurs in a range of formats and on a variety of platforms in the context of and with reference to the issues – social, geographic, political – of a given culture and time.

WHAT IS SHAKESPEARE ADAPTATION?

Adaptation studies has burgeoned as an interdisciplinary field in recent decades and in the process made accommodations with cognate domains such as film studies, performance studies, cultural and media studies and translation studies (Leitch 2017). With that plurality comes a challenge around limits: is everything in the end an adaptation and, if adaptation as a concept has no clearly defined parameters, does it cease to be a cohesive focus of study with identifiable research methodologies? How far do objects of study have to travel from their 'source' to cease to be in a meaningful relationship with them? Does a glancing use of a Shakespeare play or line in a television advertisement carry the same intellectual weight and aesthetic pleasure as a full-length film? Can an adaptation, regardless of scale or context, bear the same level of analysis as a Shakespearean text or, to re-frame the question, what new challenges – and indeed opportunities – might adaptive tendencies pose for Shakespearean scholars, and what new research questions might they generate? What *is* Shakespeare adaptation, then, but also what could it *be* and *do*?

A version of this chapter might have provided a critical survey of these different but overlapping areas of Shakespearean adaptation. The handbooks for this certainly exist. If Linda Hutcheon and I have attempted to send a pluralistic set of working definitions of adaptation out into the world, both in turn refining and updating to keep pace with the digital revolution and the sociocultural changes it is enabling, then Shakespeare scholars have responded in turn with collections and overviews of their own (Hutcheon 2006; Hutcheon and O'Flynn 2013; Sanders 2016; Henderson 2006; O'Neill 2014). And, as already noted with reference to 'Global Shakespeares', Shakespeare adaptation studies has emerged as a powerfully connective and importantly disruptive sub-field within international Shakespeare studies, as performances, interpretations and scholarship emerging from Global South and postcolonial contexts offer radical challenge to dominant Western paradigms.

A consideration of Global Shakespeares as adaptation pulls what I am defining here as 'appropriation studies', a now recognized sub-field of cultural studies, even more fully into the discussion (Desmet, Iyengar and Jacobson 2019; Sanders 2019). Acts of adaptation that involve a conscious writing back to Shakespeare and to the Western cultural precepts that first prescribed his cultural 'value' and therefore fostered the ongoing study and circulation of his texts are often described as a step on from adaptation. Shakespearean appropriation might alternatively be described as the umbrella term for works, responses and versions that actively make visible post-colonialism, feminism, LGBTQ+ positionalities, critical race studies (sometimes captured in the social media shorthand of #Shakesrace), gender and transgender studies, and ecocritical and social justice frameworks for understanding Shakespeare.[3]

Adaptations, and in particular Shakespearean adaptations and appropriations, are strongly informed by the critical positions circulating at a given time (DiPietro and Grady 2013). For example, work in critical race studies has brought new focus to adaptations of Shakespeare as memory acts that interrogate race in the plays themselves but that also diversify the stories they tell (MacDonald 2020). In this way, adaptations may also work contrapuntally to challenge the givens of what has come before: writing more generally about literary studies rather than from a specifically Shakespearean vantage point, Peter Widdowson observes how texts are 'revised and re-visioned as part of the process of restoring a voice, a history or an identity to those hitherto exploited, marginalized and silenced by dominant interests and ideologies' (2006: 505–6). If Widdowson's resonant account operates in terms of restoration, supplementing the historical balance sheet as it were with recovered voices or positions, Shakespearean adaptation (and appropriation) studies increasingly orientate us towards forward-looking agendas, situating Shakespeare as a potent vehicle for engaging with presentist global issues and challenges from migration to climate to identity politics, all of which I will suggest render *Pericles* a peculiarly resonant play in the present moment. Thinking about *what* Shakespeare adaptation is produces in part a teleology of the discipline of English literature and its porous edges in globally networked, intercultural as well academic, contexts. And through this kind of critical lens, adapted Shakespeare offers insight into literature's temporal and cultural ebbs and flows.

The cross-disciplinary focus of recent adaptation studies and the proliferation of Shakespeare in multimodal and multilingual contexts has focused attention on process and practice and on the very act of doing and making as actions inflected by identity politics and intersectionality, and by cultural, national and transnational contexts (Lei, Ick and Trivedi 2016). To zoom in on just two examples from the Shakespearean canon (and even that is not a stable entity, as this chapter's focus on the perhaps less predictable choice of *Pericles* will seek to unpack), *Hamlet* and *Romeo and Juliet*, is to register that these plays, these stories, are now so adapted, in print as well as performance contexts, so available in multiple forms and media that their own histories, their multiple 'versions' and the intertexts of those in turn, now form part of their interpretive frames (Lanier 2002; Voigts 2017).

As well as trying to determine the 'what' of adaptation, though, we need to understand the question of 'why': why is Shakespeare adapted in so many different forms by different cultures and in different moments? Sometimes the peculiar charge of the singular case study can be made to bear too much in analyses; nevertheless, an outright rejection of case study approaches is only valid if the mode of study remains hermetically sealed against the questions of practice and praxis, usefulness and utility, raised above. When is Shakespeare adapted and put to use, and what might thinking about those uses generate in terms of research questions and social and political change?[4] The role of *Pericles* in this chapter is to mobilize one set of possibilities for exploring this question of Shakespeare's availability for, and usefulness as, adaptation to different cultural contexts and times. By working with *Pericles* as the focus, a less canonical and less frequently reworked play in that wide motion of Shakespearean adaptation drawn at the start, and by looking through the lens of two very specific contemporary Anglophone long narrative form novel adaptations of that play – Mark Haddon's *The Porpoise* and Ali Smith's *Spring*, both published in 2019 – my aim is to demonstrate the ways in which consideration of Shakespeare adaptation might liberate research methods, allowing us to debate complex topical issues through an intermedial framework, one that places Shakespeare in the context of a complex web of influences and issues and not necessarily at the centre of those.

What follows, then, is a worked example of this thinking about multiple circulations of a play both as performance and allusion, as remediation and remaking, across stage, page and screen (the chapter will close by widening its own referential net to briefly discuss an Italian language film adaptation of *Pericles* which shares some of its compositional drivers with our focus novels). By taking a less frequently adapted Shakespeare play like *Pericles* and by identifying a deep contemporary strain of interest in its adaptation, in ostensibly European contexts for reasons I will also interrogate, this enables a focus on the question: *why now?*[5] Why do certain plays come into sharper focus for adaptation in particular moments, and how might that new resonance inspire recirculation? What new things might a Shakespearean adaptation or cluster of adaptations tell us both about the originating source text and about specific cultural contexts and values at a given point in time?

'ENTER MARINA WITH BASKET OF FLOWERS': *PERICLES*, MIGRATION, ALI SMITH'S *SPRING* AND THE SHAPE OF THE TELLING

British Museum, The Lampedusa Cross

2015.8039.1

Description: Wooden cross of Latin type made from pieces of a boat that was wrecked off the coast of Lampedusa, Italy on 11 October 2013. The vertical and horizontal pieces are joined with a cross halved joint. The cross piece retains scuffed blue paint on the front, upper and lower surface. The front of the vertical section has layers of damaged paint. The base coat is dark green...

I begin this section not with a play or a novel or even the material stage property of a basket of flowers, but with a distinctly different signifying object: the Lampedusa Cross. It was made by Francesco Tuccio, a carpenter, who in October 2013 painstakingly retrieved fragments of a boat from the coastline of the island of Lampedusa in southern Italy. The boat, which had been carrying hundreds of migrants from Eritrea, sank, killing 366 of those on board. Tuccio fashioned these maritime fragments into crosses to mark the lives lost. The singular object of the Lampedusa cross recorded via its catalogue entry in the British Museum in London 'stands as witness to the kindness of the people of the small island of Lampedusa who have done what they can for the refugees and migrants who arrive on their shores'.[6] Acquired in 2015, the cross offers a poignant connection for visitors to one of the major issues of our age: mass migration, much of it conducted across oceans in perilous small boats and undertaken in the face of climate-based and conflict-induced hardships. Many art-forms, including film and fiction, aimed at predominantly Global North readerships and audiences, have sought to engage with the ongoing crisis of migrants, refugees and asylum-seekers.[7] In 2016 artist Ai Weiwei set up a studio on the Greek island of Lesbos where hundreds of thousands of Syrian refugees were arriving by boat after life-risking sea-crossings on an almost daily basis, a human tragedy still ongoing at the time of writing. He created an artwork from over fourteen thousand life jackets discarded on the Lesbos beaches which was exhibited in major European museums and venues, including Berlin's Konzerthaus in 2016, and he went on to release a film called *Human Flow* the following year which explored the global refugee crisis. Migration is a pressing issue of our time shaping as it has the course of elections in numerous European and North American contexts.

Sandra Young has spoken to the significance of Diasporic Studies in this wider context: 'Diasporic Studies offer a lexicon with which to probe a world rendered more complicated through the increased mobilities of people who have been displaced through the disruptions of civil war, regional instability, economic uncertainty or the opportunities that have come with globalization' (2019: loc. 1834). In turn she demonstrates how the adapted and 'travelling' Shakespeare I have attempted to describe above becomes both available to and 'unmoored' (loc. 1811) by these new world circumstances. The scholarship of Ruben Espinosa and David Ruiter, among others, has indicated that themes of migration and immigration can be identified across the Shakespearean canon, amplifying the potential for Shakespeare to be adapted for these new debates and discussions (Espinosa and Ruiter 2016; Young 2019).[8] My purpose here then is to ask why increasingly in the first two decades of the twenty-first century theatre directors, artists, novelists and filmmakers are turning not just to Shakespeare but to the particular Shakespearean play of *Pericles* to undertake this cultural work. And from there my objective is to extrapolate outwards again to consider what that might tell us about Shakespearean adaptation as process and practice and the research methodologies that might be galvanized to explore it further.

Pericles, Prince of Tyre, first staged in 1608 and which enjoyed both public Globe Theatre and court performances in its own time, is a play steeped in the romance genre. Its dramaturgic movements are shaped by various acts of migration, relocation, by sea-crossings and storms, and by family formations, partings and reunions. Shakespeare adapted the life-story of Apollonius of Tyre via the earlier retellings of medieval poet John Gower in his *Confessio Amantis* (1393) (Gower appears as the onstage narrator of events in the play) and the late-sixteenth-century prose reworking by Lawrence Twine. The play's complicated, episodic plotline sees Pericles embark on a quest to find a bride, a venture that ends in a life-threatening discovery of incest at the heart of the Antioch kingdom. Subsequently hailed as a hero for rescuing the people of Tarsus from famine, he is then shipwrecked in the first of two life-changing storms only to be rescued by fishermen off the coast of Pentapolis, and falls in love there with the king's daughter, Thaisa. Thaisa gives birth to their baby daughter in the second of the play's sea-storms but (seemingly) loses her life in the process and Pericles has barely a moment to grieve his lost wife as, adhering to maritime tradition, her body is immediately cast overboard. The grief-stricken Pericles leaves his baby daughter in the care of her nurse with the same ruling family he had earlier rescued from famine in Tarsus, little realizing the new dangers in which he has placed his child Marina (her name indicating her birth at sea) since as she grows to adulthood the jealous Dionyza plots her murder. Marina survives but in true romance tradition is abducted by pirates and sold onto the owners of a brothel in Mytilene who attempt to sell her virginity to the highest bidder. The play witnesses a further series of rolling movements and maritime wanderings between different but interrelated geographies and life courses (ones that have also seen the presumed-dead Thaisa washed up on the shore of Ephesus, an ancient Greek city on the coast of Ionia) only to reunite Pericles with both his wife and daughter in the closing scenes. The sea-tossed trajectories of the characters – 'Alas, the seas hath cast me on the rocks, / Washed me from shore to shore … ' (*Pericles,* 2.1.5–6) says Pericles as early as Act 2 – and the specific Mediterranean geographies of this play find particular resonance in the modern migratory and diasporic contexts conjured for our imaginations by the Lampedusa cross or the work of Ai Weiwei in Lesbos.[9] Tyre itself is in the Lebanon; Antioch where Pericles's problems begin is in Syria; Marina is abducted in Tarsus now in Turkey and sold into prostitution in Mytilene on the Greek island of Lesbos; Thaisa comes from Pentapolis in modern-day Libya and is washed up, coffin-encased, on the shores of Ephesus formerly located in ancient Greece but now 3 km southwest of modern-day Izmir province in Turkey. As Adam Smyth (2019) has noted:

> *Pericles* is a play about migration, about storm-tossed passengers who risk their lives travelling across the Mediterranean and Aegean sea between Turkey, Lebanon, Libya and Greece, the geography of the play is the geography of our migration crisis; the medium of hope and tragedy is the sea…

The multiple storms and weather events of *Pericles* also render this a 'drama of climate' says Smyth and this is certainly relevant for reading Ali Smith's novel as we shall see, as is the undertow of sexual abuse in the play evident in plotlines from Antiochus's incestuous abuse of his unnamed daughter to Marina's subjugations at the hands of men seeking sexual gratification in the Myteline marketplace and the brothel. The play subtly links the two women by ensuring their first descriptions to us are that they 'come appareled like the spring' (1.1.13; the quotation is Pericles's description of Antiochus's daughter in the first act but links subliminally to the flower-bearing entrance of his own daughter Marina at 4.1.11SD). The line links the women in Pericles's mind and our own troubled imaginary. We can read a connectivity to Smith's title and her decision to scaffold her novel with *Pericles* among other intertexts in order to explore the global refugee crisis (large parts of the novel focus around refugee detention centres) and the climate emergency. Issues of sexual abuse that thread through the play's action are also reworked in intriguing and in some respects challenging ways in her novel as we shall see. Certainly, the linked plotlines of Antiochus's unnamed daughter and Marina come strongly to the fore in the second of our focus novel adaptations, Haddon's *The Porpoise*.

Spring, our first focus novel, is a resonant 'spooling, associative' (Smyth 2019) and self-consciously European text, an intervention into issues of migration, environment and belonging, and, at least from an intertextual vantage point, a partial *Pericles* adaptation, giving a certain 'shape' to things in Adam Smyth's terms if a shape only fully discernible to those readers familiar with the play (Smyth 2019).[10] *Spring* is the third in Ali Smith's quartet of seasonally based novels. Each novel responds to the contemporary moment and was written at pace, riffing on Britain's unravelling politics around the question of European status and the so-called Brexit referendum, Trump's America and activist protest movements including #BlackLivesMatter (highlighting issues of systemic racism around the world), #MeToo (campaigning against endemic sexual violence and harassment of women), XR or Extinction Rebellion (addressing the climate emergency) and much more. Each novel in the quartet uses as a scaffold the work of specific female visual artists and the informing intertexts of the Shakespearean late plays.[11]

Spring rethinks *Pericles*'s Marina as a basis for the character of twelve-year-old Florence. That name fashions Florence as a mythic figure linked to the goddess of spring, Flora, presiding deity of the novel, and plays self-consciously on Marina's initial spring-like entrance as a young adult carrying that aforementioned basket of flowers (4.1.11SD). As readers, we first witness Florence rescuing a suicidal man on a railway platform. That man, filmmaker Richard Lease, has already been jokingly compared to Pericles 'of Tired' due to his disheveled appearance (A. Smith 2019: 31). The introduction here of the significance of (quasi) father–daughter relationships, so important to Shakespeare's late plays as a whole and to Smith's quartet, has clearly begun.[12] It is in his own disheveled state in Act 5 that Pericles is reunited with his daughter. Towards the end of *Spring,* we learn that Florence's school bag carries a motto '*Vivunt spe*', or 'In hope they live' (325). This subtly links Florence to Pericles: as a stranger-knight, he wooed Marina's mother Thaisa in the rusty armour bequeathed him by his own father, and retrieved, like Pericles himself, by local fishermen from the sea. The armour functions in the play as a resonant object that, like the Lampedusa Cross, carries traces of maritime trauma and hardship. In this guise, Pericles carries the simple motto: '*In hac spec vivo*', 'In this hope I live' (2.2.43). While Smith's reading of *Pericles* as mobilized in *Spring* is not closed to the darker undertows of the play, as with her novel quartet as a whole, despite the desperate global circumstances they respond to, from political division to global pandemic, the connection with art and culture they perform is also a conscious (re)activation of hope.

We quickly learn that Florence, like her Shakespearean precedent, despite entering dehumanized spaces including brothels and detention centres, brings something redemptive, regenerative, and essentially 'good' into the room (A. Smith 2019: 314). This is a direct parallel with, or adaptation of, Marina's fate in *Pericles*. Detention centres were the spaces in which huge numbers of refugees and asylum seekers in Britain but also in the US and Australia at the time of Smith's writing were being interned. The brothel space in the novel in turn draws attention to the human traffic in sex work to which thousands of others, especially women, were being subjected (both injustices persist on a global scale).

In Marina's case, in Shakespeare's play, having survived attempted murder by her guardian and abduction by pirates, she threatens to put out of business the Bawd to whom she has been sold into prostitution: 'She's able to freeze the god Priapus and undo a whole generation' (4.5.12–13). In Smith's novel, Florence has a similar transformative impact on behaviour in the detention centre that she enters, leading hardened employees to suddenly commission a deep clean:

> The story went, said Sandra under her breath in the Ladies, that this girl had been visiting several other IRCs [Immigration Removal Centres] and persuading people to do all sorts of unorthodox things like cleaning toilets properly.
>
> (A. Smith 2019: 140)

This focus via Florence's almost angelic intervention on the unsanitary conditions of the detention/removal centre – even these different titles signifying an implicit contradiction in the treatment of residents – brings to mind comparable stories that were circulating in the contemporary news media at the time of *Spring*'s publication, highlighting conditions and maltreatment in equivalent holding centres around the world.[13]

Rumours fly around about Florence's provenance. There are claims she arrived from Greece in a dinghy, that she crossed the world dressed in a Manchester United football shirt and that her mother drowned in a boat off Italy (A. Smith 2019: 141–2) for, in a further connection with the play, we learn she is searching for her own mother who has refugee status. Florence becomes a composite of the multiple migrant stories and images circulating in the world press and on social media including the Lampedusa and Lesbos examples referred to earlier which serve as unnamed but clearly perceptible frames of reference. Perilous boat crossings from Syria and Eritrea to Europe provide modern analogues to the tragic experiences at sea of Pericles, Thaisa and Marina in the Shakespearean source. Although Shakespeare's characters are noble-born and therefore possess a different level of power and agency to the modern-day migrants whose stories Smith seeks to articulate, there remains a resonance in the restless arc of sea-borne mobilities the play depicts. Florence's actions in *Spring* in turn invite us as readers to question the criminalization of those seeking sanctuary in the modern era for reasons of economic or personal security.[14]

In one particular retelling of Florence's presence and dramatic intervention in the detention centre, she becomes a direct reincarnation of Marina in the Myteline brothel of the play:

BAWD:

> When she should do for clients her fitment, and do me the kindness of our profession, she has me her quirks, her reasons, her master reasons, her prayers, her knees, that she would make a puritan of the devil if he should cheapen a kiss of her.

(*Pericles*, 4.5.14–18)

The story went that the [...] police had been called in by the pimps [...] Because she'd got in there and in the space of a half an hour had gone through several rooms persuading clients out of doing what they were in the middle of doing [...]

(A. Smith 2019: 137)

For all of her disruptive impact in the institutional spaces of the novel, Florence is resolutely a young girl. Her favourite colour is turquoise; if she were an animal, we are told, it would be a pink fairy armadillo (276) and her favourite day of the week is Friday ('Friday's child is full of grace' a line from a nursery rhyme mnemonic that Smith may well be recalling). With her customary narrative skill and sleight of hand, Smith quietly connects her redemptive young female protagonist not only with the sixteen-year-old Marina of Shakespeare's play but in turn with the climate emergency protests 'Fridays for Future' that had been initiated by the then sixteen-year-old Greta Thunberg in Sweden in 2018 and which, by the time of the novel's publication, had grown to be a global youth protest movement. Florence's wish to travel to Scotland 'with no footprint' (173) accrues double meaning in the context of a climate emergency: 'Even a twelve-year-old girl can see through a lot of what is happening in the world right now' (199); 'Given that I am twelve years old and there are just twelve years left to stop the world being ruined by climate change [...]' (233–4). As already observed, Smith's novel makes deep use of *Pericles* and its themes of shipwreck, famine, war, sexual violence, biological and affective families, fathers and daughters, youth and redemption, but remakes them in a context unmistakably of its own time and place, speaking to now as in the way of so much adaptational endeavour.

Pericles is, as noted, far from the only intertext in *Spring*, with its important allusions to Katherine Mansfield and Rilke as well as the work of other significant artists, an allusiveness that has led Adam Smyth among others to conclude that while the novel is 'patterned with references... It isn't an adaptation because *Pericles* is only the loudest in a chorus of voices from the past' (Smyth 2019). In my view, however, the scaffold that the Shakespearean playtext provides for the emotional and political impact of the novel is pivotal because it mobilizes the core themes of migration, climate and identity albeit in newly conceived global and local contexts.

Pericles furthermore connects readers and the concerns of the novel very directly to one of the other major informing artworks and intertexts for *Spring*: the cloud and mountain chalk-based sequences of Tacita Dean which had been the focus of three major exhibitions in London in 2018. Richard goes to see the Royal Academy of Arts installations and, as well as being struck by the sublime impact of one particular mountain landscape, he is viscerally and conceptually moved by a series of cloud images with which it is juxtaposed. We can see the issues of climate justice re-emerging here with the subliminal reference to air pollution as well as wider societal needs to find breathing space:

> They'd made space to breathe possible, up against something breath-taking. After them, the real clouds of London looked different, like them they were something you could read as breathing space.
>
> (A. Smith 2019: 30)

In an unsettling but powerful example of how literature can accrue additional meanings through time, Smith's own references have taken on further resonance with the publication of her final novel in the quartet, *Summer*. That novel attends to the impact in 2020 of the global pandemic, COVID-19, which impacted on sufferers' lungs and respiratory capacities, but also connects the importance of breath to the protests which followed the brutal murder of George Floyd in Minneapolis by a police officer who knelt on his neck and blocked his airpaths. 'I can't breathe' became a new term of protest in 2020 in ways that *Summer* riffs on but which also loop back in disquieting ways to the above passage from *Spring* and the use of Tacita Dean's artworks.

Though Smith never explicitly tells us this, Dean's collection of cloud drawings was originally gathered in exhibition under the title *A Complete Concordance of Fifty American Clouds,* inspired by finding her father's *Complete Concordance to Shakespeare* when clearing his belongings following his death (Dean 2018: 258–72). As well as bringing the sub-Shakespearean father–daughter relationship into view once again – Richard even attends the exhibition with his 'imaginary daughter' – many of Dean's individual images bear titles that are direct quotations from Shakespeare plays, connecting either to clouds or ideas of Europe and sometimes both. These lifted lines, some might say wrested from context, debate ideas of belonging and nationhood as well as the quality of the elemental: for example, 'My English Breath in Foreign Clouds' (*Richard II*), 'Yond same cloud' (*The Tempest*) and 'Why Cloud?', this last a direct quotation from *Pericles*, an aside delivered by the eponymous protagonist in the context of the riddling and incestuous Antioch scenes early in the play. A reproduction of this specific Dean image forms the endpaper to Smith's novel and invites us to find the fuller reference in the Shakespearean text:

> But, O, you powers
> That gives heaven countless eyes to view men's acts
> Why cloud they not their sights perpetually
> If this be true, which makes me pale to read it?
>
> (*Pericles*, 1.1.73–6)

The choice of this particular framing quotation from Shakespeare is not without its own unsettling impacts on our response to both image and novel as a whole. In the play, Pericles questions the gods as to why humans who see such great injustices done to others – as he is clearly party to in the case of Antiochus's daughter – and who do nothing are not blinded on the spot, as if not to see anymore is the only way to survive, to carry on living. It might be felt that this bitter complaint undoes the regenerative hopefulness that I have suggested otherwise exists in *Spring*; in some ways, it does ask that we resist the romance ending of *Pericles* and return instead to the scene of moral corruption where its action began. Our failure to act in the face of global ethical challenges such as the refugee crisis or indeed the climate emergency are surely being held up to the light here. Yet Smith's novel and her own sustained efforts to ascribe agency to refugee stories and storytelling holds out to the end a glimmer of hope for renewal and positive change. Smith re-makes *Pericles* as a tale of now, one of migration and climate action, and of the politics of division. The play as retold in modern contexts remains troubling and unsettling, with many uncomfortable subtexts, and yet, through her reimagining of Marina as Florence (and as Greta Thunberg), Smith retains the possibility at least of a narrative of hope and forgiveness as the overriding human impulse.

'THE FAINTEST OF SHADOWS': MARK HADDON'S *THE PORPOISE* AND READING BETWEEN THE GAPS

If Smith (re)locates *Pericles* at the heart of contemporary debates about migration and climate, and defiantly finds youthful female agency possible in the face of both, then Haddon's *The Porpoise* is a novel written in the depths of the storms blowing around decades of institutionally endorsed sexual harassment and the silencing of women, sometimes referred to in shorthand as the #MeToo movement.[15] Storms and weathering are a tangible feature of the plot in *The Porpoise* and, in an intriguing alignment to Smith's *Spring*, there is threaded through the narrator's descriptions of the material world a profound awareness of clouds. Clouds in Haddon's novel are meteorological happenings but also metaphors for the hidden, obscured or clouded. They are repeatedly harbingers of bad weather, and portents of tragic action to follow; as at the very outset of the novel when the air accident that will take Maja's life is described as being the result of thickening cloud cover and obscured vision (Haddon 2019: 7–8). Clouds are seemingly noticed most at threshold moments in the narrative:

A single white cloud sits on the far hill like a snow-white tree. Everything hangs in the balance. So many things could happen now, so many things which cannot be undone. Mother and daughter, complete strangers to one another. What if Emilia tells her story? What if Marina learns that her mother knew of her existence but never came to find her?

(294)

and they hover over Philippe's mansion throughout those sections of the novel that feature his abusive relationship with his daughter Angelica:

Clouds like swansdown pulled from a torn pillow by a bored child. They would be beautiful if they did not float above those trees and this house.

(84)

At the novel's close a 'three miles high' (301) *cumulus* forming will also be the sign of the storm that will destroy that riven family home along with its troubled inhabitants. In this tragic framework, *Pericles*, and in particular the complex fate of its female characters, becomes for Haddon a means to explore highly troubling contemporary issues through a complex revisiting of the ancient and early modern pasts and a melding of these with an all-too-resonant present. Shakespeare is once again being adapted to speak to present times; remade, repurposed and reimagined for a very particular version of 'now'. At multiple points in *The Porpoise* we are asked to consider fate and (in)action and, as in Shakespeare's play, to ask, as it were, 'Why cloud?' in a myriad versions.

Suzanne Gossett, an Arden editor of *Pericles*, has observed that when other early modern dramatists turned to the play as raw material 'they concentrated not on the archaic flavor, episodic sweep, fabulous events or Gower's language. Instead, they noticed the unplayful sexuality in the incest and brothel scenes; the social commentary, and the moments of powerful emotion [...]' (2007: 109). The direct line to Smith and Haddon feels more immediate from this vantage point and might seem to negate the case for a hopeful reading of the play made above but for both authors I think there remains a sense, albeit derived from the romance genre, albeit romantic, of potential in female agency and in the younger generation despite all the horrific situations and events their novels describe.

The Porpoise is, on the surface, invested in even greater detail with the playtext of *Pericles* and its compositional context than Smith's *Spring*. The title is a direct allusion to 2.1 of the play where the fishermen of Pentapolis respond to the shipwreck they have just witnessed. That maritime event has cast Pericles up on their shores and they compare his art of survival with the ability of porpoises to ride the waves:

THIRD FISHERMAN:
> [...] said not I as much when I saw the porpoise, how he bounced and tumbled? They say they're half fish, half flesh.

> (*Pericles*, 2.1.23–5)

As well as noting this interest in creatures who seem to challenge easy taxonomy as a parallel to the way that romance as a form, and as a result Haddon's adaptive novel, resists simple categorization and defies normative temporal frames, the astute reader may further recall that for the early modern cultural imaginary the sighting of porpoises was thought to predict oncoming storms. Just as with the recurring descriptions of clouds in Haddon's narrative, the idea of tragic portent, and by association of predictive texts and textuality, is present from the beginning.[16]

The novel also brings Shakespeare's disreputable co-author and collaborator, London publican and pimp, George Wilkins, directly into view; indeed, he even makes a ghostly appearance in the novel. In his 'Author's Note', Haddon observes: 'Wilkins and Shakespeare weren't resurrecting a lost tale when they collaborated on the play *Pericles, Prince of Tyre*, they were ringing changes on a well-known theme' (2019: 307). This paratext reveals the process of adaptation and the contemporary novelist's collaboration with Shakespeare across time. There are fascinating discussions to be had on *Pericles* as itself an adaptive text – a tissue of reworkings, as already noted, from Gower's *Confessio Amantis* to works by Wilkins himself, including *The Paineful Adventures of Pericles* (1608), and Twine's *The Pattern of Paineful Adventures* (1576, 1607) – and as an experimental tragicomedy that was much referenced even within the early modern period.[17] My specific interests here, however, are the contemporary issues which Haddon deploys *Pericles* to shine light upon, using a close reading of *The Porpoise* as another key to unlocking the wider workings of Shakespearean adaptation as process and practice.

Pericles, as already noted, is a play haunted by sexual abuse. As well as the fate of Marina, abducted and sex trafficked, Pericles's narrative journey, but also his moral restlessness, begins when he solves the incestuous riddle of the King of Antioch and his unnamed daughter; the very act of solution proves his unmooring. Several modern commentators on the play have observed the seeming blame laid at the feet of the largely silent daughter in Gower's description that 'the father liking took / And her to incest did provoke' (*Pericles*, 1.0.25–6); 'Bad child, worse father' he continues (1.0.27). The tendency of the novel (and many critics before this) to attribute the more negative treatments of women in the play to the writing of the physically abusive Wilkins can and should be debated as an example of bardolatry. Haddon draws attention to this wish to absolve Shakespeare from blame by allocating authorial responsibility for certain scenes to the morally reprehensible Wilkins: 'Perhaps it was Wilkins who gave the abused princess no name and two empty lines welcoming Pericles. Perhaps it was Wilkins who called her father's crime "incest" and insisted she was equally to blame' (2019: 107). Certainly, biographical and archival work on Wilkins has confirmed that he appeared regularly in the early modern courts charged with abusive and violent treatment of women (Nicholl 2008: 200–4).[18] Yet, as noted in the discussion of *Spring*, through its evocation of spring-like associations in relation to both, the play plants the seed of a link between the abused daughter of Antioch and Marina. Descriptive vocabulary directly aligns the fate of these subjected and sexualized young women; if when we first see Antiochus's daughter she 'comes apparell'd like the spring' (1.1.13), audience members surely actively recall this later when they witness Marina entering onstage with her flowers. This doubling effectively builds into the play a questioning of those earlier acts of silencing, but also perilously links Marina with the Antioch storyline complicating in the process Marina's relationship with her estranged and grieving father (Antiochus we are told turns his sexual attentions to his daughter after the loss of his wife).

Haddon's novel intentionally gives voice, narrative and a name to the King of Antioch's daughter. By means of a tour de force opening in which a plane crash provides a modern First World alternative to a Shakespearean shipwreck, Haddon deliberately blurs the adaptive lines and ensures an active reader: who is Pericles in this story? Who is Marina or Thaisa? Who is the Antioch patriarch? Maja, a film and television star, who dies in the plane crash while her unborn child survives, both is and isn't Thaisa and, in the same way, Angelica, the surviving baby daughter, contains aspects of both Marina and the ill-fated daughter of Antiochus. Angelica will be raised by her disturbingly attentive millionaire father Philippe in the mansion of 'Antioch', a place of hidden horrors and unsolved riddles. To escape her grim reality, Angelica retreats into books – 'Her favourite stories are the old ones…' (38) – and the story of Pericles in particular. When Darius, a suitor for her hand, is seemingly murdered by her father (such is the deliberate instability of story in this text that Darius will reappear as a sub-Pericles figure in another time), she takes control of her body in the only way she feels within her agency, which is to starve herself slowly to death. Hallucinating, she reimagines or revives her suitor as Pericles, and escapes into his world of ocean-bound adventure. Haddon draws attention throughout his vivacious narrative of sea battles and maritime labour to the silenced women of history and the gaps in every narrative, not least those of *Pericles*. This is touchingly evident not only in Angelica's story but also in the less-told narrative of Marina's nurse Lychorida. In this version she actively sacrifices her retirement and an imagined future to stay on with Marina in Tarsus (the play pays no heed to her choice in this issue):

> She is rarely asked her opinion about anything. She is fifty years old. She earned her freedom in Pentapolis. One more year and she would have been sharing a smallholding with her sister and her brother-in-law. She was looking forward to an old age in which she learns how to please herself, how to use time and make friends, sewing her own clothes, growing walnuts and figs, keeping chickens, watching whole sunsets and sleeping past dawn. It will not happen now.
>
> (Haddon 2019: 191)

Elsewhere, we read the story of Chloe as the novel's second version of Thaisa. Her narrative is told in shocking detail as readers join her inside the coffin in which she is thrown overboard from a storm-tossed ship, presumed dead from childbirth and an ill-omen into the bargain, in ways that directly equate her to the Thaisa of Shakespeare's play. As readers we are frighteningly alive – or half-dead – with her in that repurposed box, broken, bloodied and petrified in a way we never are in the play. Haddon's narrative puts us quite deliberately at the heart of female experiences in his rewriting of *Pericles*, filling in the gaps, the 'offstage' moments as it were of performed drama, with often shocking detail, to make this story of the ancient past an inescapably modern retelling but also one attentive to the particular format and possibilities of long-form fiction.[19] Adaptation is creative not only in its acts of retelling over time and across geographical and cultural borders but in the way it explores the different potentials of alternative modes, media and platforms for expression.

CODA: TRAVELLING STORIES, ADAPTATION AND HOPE

The introduction to this chapter mentioned the significance of the emergence of fields such as film studies in the critical history of Shakespearean adaptation and in the expansion of the catalogue of intertexts and influences available to adaptors. *Pericles* has a less extensive filmic afterlife (as yet) than *Hamlet* and *Romeo and Juliet*, but it is not without its own cinematic retellings (White 2018). One of these films is particularly pertinent to the topics under discussion here: Roberto Quagliano's *Pericles by Shakespeare on the Road* is an Italian production made in the direct context of the escalating 2014–15 European migration crisis and which therefore responds to the same real-life events as the two novels discussed in this chapter. Like them, the film finds a compelling impetus to turn and return to Shakespeare's own drama of migration and belonging, *Pericles*.

The film tells the story of an itinerant group, travelling on foot through desolate areas (the language of the film is predominantly modern Italian though it retains some original Shakespearean textual references). Sequences move between endless highways against the background of surveillance helicopters. The focus is on a young girl and her father. The girl dreams the *Pericles* story (a fascinating overlap with the inset narrative in *The Porpoise*). In her dream her fellow travellers appear still dressed in their modern attire so not fully incorporated into the ancient story, and thereby deliberately confusing for spectators and dreamer alike what is past and what is present. The dream is like the film itself an act of adaptation and appropriation melding ancient tale with contemporary images, objects and issues. As one character who is herself a writer notes in Ali Smith's *Spring* of the adaptational principle: 'There's ways to survive these times [...] and I think one way is the shape the telling takes' (A. Smith 2019: 21). Through meldings of ancient narrative with issues of migration, climate justice and sexual abuse, *Pericles* has become a play that is finding new visibility and present purpose in our contemporary moment: theatre productions of the play have certainly demonstrated a parallel interest in the topics of sexual violence, sex trafficking, homelessness and unsettled status, migration and the climate crisis, and may in turn be part of the source material for Smith, Haddon and Quagliano.[20] As one cluster of examples these adaptations make the case that Shakespeare is as often adapted in the twenty-first century for what his texts can say about the present times or contexts as for what his plays staged or responded to in their original moment of performance. How present then is the actual work of Shakespeare in any of this? How far has adaptation travelled from its source and to what extent is a knowledge of Shakespeare and Wilkins's *Pericles* needed or even necessary for a full experience of these novel and filmic appropriations? As I hope the comparative analysis here suggests, there is mutual purpose in studying these contemporary works *as* Shakespeare adaptations: for the Shakespeare student or scholar there is much to discover and be challenged by in the remakings and reimaginings of contemporary adaptors and in turn for those whose point of entry might be the work of fiction, film or other creative format the links to Shakespeare can prove both enriching and empowering.

In the summer of 2019 as I was dreaming this chapter, the climate campaigner Greta Thunberg took two weeks to sail to New York to attend United Nations Climate Summits. On her arrival into harbour she was greeted by a series of sailing boats each depicting one of the United Nations Sustainable Development Goals which serve to focus our collective attention on the global social issues of our times: the right to clean water and sanitation, to education, to gender equality and to peace. Many of these issues correspond directly with the themes and concerns of the novel and film adaptations of *Pericles* that I have been exploring here, but perhaps what this discussion has also evidenced is that these emphases have been there all along in the play – they are not simply ascribed to it by a modern age and by modern adaptors, rather those adaptors find ways to draw these aspects of the play out in fresh ways to tell new stories.

As well as engaging in sea battles and oceanic adventures, in *Pericles* the protagonist is also a bringer of aid, of food and of well-being to places of famine, and of liberation to incarcerated women. The play is, despite its sometimes-dark heart, still hopeful about the values of 'harbourage' (*Pericles*, 1.4.98), and the importance of hospitality. The creative and ethical engagement with the play that adaptations like the novels of Smith and Haddon perform therefore share, evolve and augment these profound investigations of what constitutes humanity in complex circumstances. Adaptation demands active makers, readers, spectators and researchers who travel with the Shakespearean text through and across times, cultures and contexts, and who continue to ask probing questions even in the most difficult or unsettling times.

Hope springs eternal: *'Enter Marina with a basket of flowers'*.

NOTES

1   See Section 3 'The Performance of Shakespeare and Social Justice' in Ruiter (2020), which considers productions grounded in the politics of Mexico, India, South Africa and China.

2   The very concept of a 'source text' is helpfully analysed and critiqued by Douglas Lanier's chapter in this volume.

3   It is important to indicate the longevity of work in these critical spaces as well as current scholarship. See for example, the three volumes of *Alternative Shakespeares* (Drakakis 1985; Hawkes 1996; Henderson 2008); Hendricks and Parker (1994); Chedgzoy (1996); Loomba (1998); Desmet and Sawyer (2013); Martin (2015).

4   See Ruiter (2020) and also the work of Jeffrey Wilson on 'Public Shakespeares', #PublicShax https://wilson.fas.harvard.edu/public-shakespeare (last accessed 15 November 2020).

5   Parallel questions are explored in relation to *Pericles* by Katharine A. Craik and Ewan Fernie in their account of the co-creation of *Marina* at The Other Place in Stratford-upon-Avon in 2016 (Craik and Fernie 2018).

6   The British Museum Collection: Item description, https://www.britishmuseum.org/ research/collection_online/collection_object_details.aspx?objectId=3691920&page= 1&partId=1&searchText=cross+lampedusa (accessed 11 October 2021).

7   For example, *Fuocoammare* or *Fire at Sea* is a 2016 Italian documentary film directed by Gianfranco Rosi shot on Lampedusa during the height of the migrant crisis there. Also, in 2016, Olafur Eliasson's 'Green Light' project sought both to respond artistically to the crisis and to offer very practical social justice employment and training opportunities in his own workshops (Eliasson, Zyman and Ebersberger 2017).

8   See also a forthcoming edition of *The International Shakespeare Yearbook* on 'Shakespeare and Refugees'.

9   As this chapter was being completed, the *Guardian* newspaper in the UK ran an article about the retrieval of a rucksack containing two wedding rings inscribed Ahmed and Doudou. Presumed to be material traces of another tragic loss of life at sea they were ultimately traced with the help of Doctors without Borders to an

Algerian couple staying in a reception centre in Sicily having survived a shipwreck off Lampedusa on 21 October 2020 in which five other people died. The connection across time to the romance plotlines of *Pericles* is both moving and startling (Tondo 2020).

10 On the interplay of familiarity and recognition with the particular cognitive pleasures of adaptation, see Sanders (2016: 34).

11 In *Autumn*, the life of artist Pauline Boty features alongside *The Tempest*; *Winter* brings together the sculpture and drawings of Barbara Hepworth with *Cymbeline;* and *Summer* deploys *The Winter's Tale* as one of a series of intertexts alongside the films and artwork of Lorenza Mazzetti. As explored in this chapter the informing female artist for *Spring* is Tacita Dean and a specific series of her works themselves partially inspired by Shakespeare.

12 On the late plays as a cluster, see Richards and Knowles (1999) and Power and Loughnane (2012).

13 See for example a report from a Papua New Guinea 'Regional Processing Centre' in *The Guardian*, 14 January 2015; Kirk Semple, 'Overflowing toilets, bedbugs and high heat: inside Mexico's migrant detention centres', *The New York Times*, 3 August 2019.

14 In his acceptance speech for the Golden Bear award for *Fuocoammare* or 'Fire at Sea' director Gianfranco Rosi stated: 'It's not acceptable that people die crossing the sea to escape from tragedies' (Merelli 2017).

15 The phrase 'MeToo' was first used on social media in the USA in 2006 by survivor and activist Tarana Burke but by 2017 had become a global movement. The movement had and continues to have the expressed aim of breaking silences and holding assailants to account. One of the most high-profile legal cases that has taken place in relation to this was that of the Hollywood film producer Harvey Weinstein who was found guilty on several charges in 2020 and sentenced to twenty-three years in prison. Haddon's association of the sexual abuse in his play with the media industry is presumably quite intentional in the wake of the Weinstein case which was still ongoing at the time of the novel's composition.

16 My thanks to Stephen O'Neill for discussion of these points.

17 Suzanne Gossett evidences that there were six quarto publications before 1635 and that the play was performed in commercial and court contexts throughout the Jacobean and Caroline periods. Its influence can be traced in allusions in a number of poems and plays from the period, including the 1611 *A Wife for a Month* which reworks the throwing overboard at sea of a wife amid grim jokes that she will 'spoyle the fishing on the coast for ever' (5.2.12), as well as Marina's abduction by pirates and her marketplace sale into prostitution (Gossett 2007: 105).

18 Nicholl offers a shocking catalogue of Wilkins's court appearances for acts of slander, sex trafficking, kicking a pregnant woman, beatings and many more acts of aggression.

19 Emma Smith has written brilliantly about the 'gappiness' of Shakespeare enabling his usefulness for us through the ages (2019: 2, 3, 322).

20 UK theatre productions of *Pericles* that took place around the time of the two novels being considered here included an inclusive community-performed musical directed by Emily Lin for the National Theatre Public Arts programme, a Cheek by Jowl French language production which was staged as an embattled imagining taking place in Pericles's mind at the Barbican and a climate-change conscious outdoors production by the Willow Globe in Wales.

REFERENCES

Bennett, S. and C. Carson, eds (2013), *Shakespeare Beyond English: A Global Experiment*, Cambridge: Cambridge University Press.

Bolter, J. and R. Grusin, eds (2000), *Remediation: Understanding New Media*, Boston, MA: MIT Press.

Chedgzoy, K. (1996), *Shakespeare's Queer Children: Sexual Politics and Contemporary Culture*, Manchester: Manchester University Press.

Craik, K. A. and E. Fernie (2018), 'The *Marina* Project', in P. Edmondson and E. Fernie (eds), *New Places: Shakespeare and Civic Creativity*, 109–25, London: Bloomsbury/ Arden Shakespeare.

Dean, T. (2018), *Complete Works and Filmography*, London: Royal Academy Publications.

Desmet, C. and R. Sawyer (2013), *Shakespeare and Appropriation*, London: Routledge.

Desmet, C., S. Iyengar and M. Jacobson, eds (2019) *The Routledge Handbook to Shakespeare and Global Appropriation*, London: Routledge.

Di Pietro, C. and H. Grady, eds (2013), *Shakespeare and the Urgency of Now: Criticism and Theory in the 21st Century*, London and New York, NY: Palgrave Macmillan.

Drakakis, J., ed. (1985), *Alternative Shakespeares*, London: Methuen.

Eliasson, O., D. Zyman and E. Ebersberger (2017), *Green Light – An Artistic Workshop*, Berlin: Sternberg Press.

Espinosa, R. and D. Ruiter, eds (2016), *Shakespeare and Immigration*, London: Routledge.

Gossett, S. (2007), 'Taking *Pericles* Seriously', in S. Mukherji and R. Lyne (eds), *Early Modern Tragicomedy*, 101–14, London: Boydell and Brewer.

Haddon, M. (2019), *The Porpoise*, London: Vintage/Chatto and Windus.

Hawkes, T., ed. (1996), *Alternative Shakespeares 2*, London: Routledge.

Henderson, D. E., ed. (2008), *Alternative Shakespeares 3*, London: Routledge.

Henderson, D. E. (2006), *Collaborations with the Past: Reshaping Shakespeare Across Time and Media*, New York, NY: Cornell University Press.

Hendricks, M. and P. Parker, eds (1994), *Women, 'Race' and Writing in the Early Modern Period*, London: Routledge.

Hutcheon, L. (2006), *A Theory of Adaptation*, London: Routledge.

Hutcheon, L. and S. O'Flynn (2013), *A Theory of Adaptation*, 2nd edn, London: Routledge.

Kidnie, M. J. (2009), *Shakespeare and the Problem of Adaptation*, London: Routledge.

Lanier, D. (2002), *Shakespeare and Modern Popular Culture*, Oxford: Oxford University Press.

Lei, B., J. C. Ick and P. Trivedi, eds (2016), *Shakespeare's Asian Journeys: Critical Journeys, Cultural Geographies and the Politics of Travel*, London: Routledge.

Leitch, T., ed. (2017), *The Oxford Handbook of Adaptation Studies*, Oxford: Oxford University Press.

Loomba, A. (1998), *Shakespeare, Race, and Colonialism*, Oxford: Oxford University Press.

MacDonald, J. G. (2020), *Shakespearean Adaptation, Race and Memory in the New World*, New York, NY: Palgrave Macmillan.

Martin, R. (2015), *Shakespeare and Ecology*, Oxford: Oxford University Press.

Massai, S., ed. (2005), *World-Wide Shakespeares: Local Appropriations in Film and Performance*, London: Routledge.

Merelli, A. (2017), '*Fuocoammare*: Rescuing refugees is a matter of common sense on the paradisiacal island of Lampedusa', *Quartz qz.com*, 3 February. Available online: https://qz.com/678164/in-the-mediterranean-paradise-of-lampedusa-rescuing-refugees-and-migrants-is-a-matter-of-common-sense/ (accessed 20 May 2021).

Nicholl, C. (2008), *The Lodger: Shakespeare on Silver* Street, London: Penguin.

O'Neill, S. (2014), *Shakespeare and YouTube: New Media Forms of the Bard*, London: Bloomsbury/Arden.

Pericles di Shakespeare sulla strada/Pericles by Shakespeare on the Road (2016), [Film] Dir.R. Quagliano, Bologna: Kamel Film.

Power, A. J. and R. Loughnane, eds (2012), *Late Shakespeare, 1608–1613*, Cambridge: Cambridge University Press.

Richards, J. and J. Knowles, eds (1999), *Shakespeare's Late Plays: New Readings*, Edinburgh: Edinburgh University Press.

Ruiter, D., ed. (2020) *The Arden Research Handbook to Shakespeare and Social Justice*, London: Bloomsbury/Arden Shakespeare.

Rumbold, K. (2013), '"No words!": *Love's Labour's Lost* in British Sign Language', in S. Bennett and C. Carson (eds), *Shakespeare Beyond English: A Global Experiment*, 227–36, Cambridge: Cambridge University Press.

Sanders, J. (1996), *Adaptation and Appropriation*, London: Routledge.

Sanders, J. (2002), *Novel Shakespeares: Twentieth-Century Women Novelists and Appropriation*, Manchester: Manchester University Press.

Sanders, J. (2016), *Adaptation and Appropriation*, 2nd edn, London: Routledge.

Sanders, J. (2019), 'Appropriation', *The Oxford Research Encyclopedia to Literary Theory*, Oxford: Oxford University Press.

Shakespeare, W. ([2004] 2014), *Pericles* ed. Suzanne Gossett, London: Bloomsbury/Arden Shakespeare.

Smith, A. (2019), *Spring*, London: Hamish Hamilton.

Smith, A. (2020), *Summer*, London: Hamish Hamilton.

Smith, E. (2019), *This is Shakespeare*, London: Penguin.

Smyth, A. (2019), 'Play for Today', *LRB*, 24 October.

Tondo, L. (2020), 'Rescuers recover migrants' wedding rings lost at sea', *Guardian*, 24 November. Available online: https://www.theguardian.com/world/2020/nov/24/rescuers-recover-migrants-wedding-rings-lost-at-sea?CMP=Share_iOSApp_Other (accessed 25 November 2020).

Trivedi, P. and P. Chakravarti, eds (2020), *Shakespeare and Indian Cinemas: 'Local Habitations'*, London: Routledge.

Trivedi, P. and M. Ryuta, eds (2010), *Re-Playing Shakespeare in Asia*, London: Routledge.

Voigts, E. (2017), 'Memes and Recombinant Appropriations: Remix, Mashup, Parody', in T. Leitch (ed.), *The Oxford Handbook to Adaptation Studies*, 285–302, Oxford: Oxford University Press.

White, R. S. (2018), 'Rivers of Story: Some Filmic Afterlives of *Pericles*', *Borrowers and Lenders* 12 (1). Available online: https://openjournals.libs.uga.edu/borrowers/article/view/2391 (accessed 25 November 2020).

Widdowson, P. (2006), '"Writing Back": Contemporary Revisionary Fiction', *Textual Practice* 20 (3): 491–507.

Young, S. (2019), *Shakespeare in the Global South: Stories of Oceans Crossed in Contemporary Adaptation*, London: Bloomsbury/Arden Shakespeare. Kindle edn.

PART TWO

Current research and issues

Histories and politics
of adaptation

Politics, adaptation, *Macbeth*

WILLIAM C. CARROLL

Writing to David Garrick in 1774 about his difficulties in adapting Macbeth for French audiences, Jean-François Ducis complained that 'I am dealing with a nation which demands no end of accommodating adjustments when one wants to lead them along the blood-drenched roads of terror' (Golder 1992: 163). Two centuries later, Heiner Müller commented that 'One can say a lot of things about Stalin with a production of Macbeth' (Weber and Young 2012: 4). It would be difficult to find writers more dissimilar than the ones quoted above, but both Ducis and Müller, otherwise so different, sought to counter what has been called the royalist interpretation of Macbeth – also known as the 'King James' or 'Authorized' version – in which the political ideologies embedded and enacted in the play are read as a defense of monarchical power and dynastic succession.[1] Such contrasting interpretations of *Macbeth* reflect larger arguments about Shakespeare's own politics, his affinity for republicanism on the one hand (Hadfield 2005), or his royalist inclinations (as one of the King's Men) on the other (see Paul 1950; Kernan 1995). The earliest adaptors of *Macbeth* generally reinforced the royalist interpretation.

Both Ducis and Müller, like other adaptors, rewrote the play to reflect their political readings of it. But what does the word 'political' mean in such a context? Either: (1) the play's costume/setting/scenery have been updated to suggest or allegorize other time periods or political events; (2) the director/editor has emphasized some textual elements and suppressed others to make a particular point; (3) the play's plot and/or characters have been substantially rewritten to form a different 'message'; or (4) even the most traditional production, depending on its historical context, becomes 'political' simply for being performed. If one play could represent all of these categories, it is certainly *Macbeth*.

Here I analyse how certain influential stage adaptations revised and modified the Folio text to support or undermine political structures and regimes outside the play. This survey is admittedly limited in various ways and does not analyse individual actors' performances – Mrs Siddons's famed Lady Macbeth in the 1780s, for example. Rather, I consider how a given version revised the play's structure, plot or characterization to support or resist a particular political position, with a special focus on how Macbeth's moral condition and Malcolm's succession are represented.[2]

Michael Hattaway has noted the dangers of the plot itself – its representations of tyranny and regicide – in its first production *c.* 1606: 'The very fact of placing a tragic action at court was, because of the particular decorum of English tragedy, likely to demystify the authority of prince and courtiers' (2013: 111). The demystification of state power through representations of regicide on the early modern stage may well have prepared the king's way to the scaffold, as Franco Moretti (1982) has argued. For later royalist adaptors, the depictions of regicide might provide an unpleasant reminder of Charles I's execution. Yet even when Macbeth's murder is justified as tyrannicide, the play seemed equally dangerous. In many post-1945 countries, totalitarian authorities condemned certain plays which, in their interpretation, reflected all too closely the critiques of their rule as authoritarian, or failed to portray 'progressive ideas' of the dominant ideology. If the plays (they feared) mirrored their own actions, then they could not be staged or seen; such censorship is premised on simple and unambiguous interpretations of the plays themselves.[3]

Macbeth himself, over the centuries, eventually transformed from a violent warrior in a near-savage feudal society – the apex of masculine action – into an anguished, increasingly weak husband dominated by his wife, full of guilt and remorse over his misguided ambition. Some modern adaptations enhance this version by making Macbeth the product, even the victim, of an oppressive social system, and, as we will see, attention refocuses away from Macbeth's character to larger conceptions of political-historical process. Yet although the play's politics may *seem* infinitely malleable, at the centre there is always murder.

ENGLAND: DAVENANT, GARRICK AND ROYAL SUCCESSION

The principle of royal succession in *Macbeth* – the 'line of kings' in 4.1 – has seemed self-evident to many readers (see Carroll 2014b), especially to those invested in the Authorized Version: Malcolm is the rightful king, and his crowning at the end represents a restitution of the legitimate line that Macbeth has interrupted (Calderwood 1986: 72; McLuskie 2009: 47). Certainly most directors deployed this interpretation of the play in the first three centuries of the play's afterlife. Davenant's version of 1664 – the first full adaptation – produced a more conventional and patriotic final scene than the First Folio provided. Macduff enters not with Macbeth's head but 'with *Macbeths* Sword' (signifying Macduff as a minister of Justice), heralds Malcolm as King and presents him with

The Tyrants Sword, to shew that Heaven appointed
Me to take Revenge for you, and all
That suffered by his Power.

...

Now *Scotland*, thou shalt see bright Day again,
That Cloud's remov'd that did Ecclipse thy Sun,
And Rain down Blood upon thee. As your Arms
Did all contribute to this Victory;

So let your Voices all concur to give
One joyful Acclamation.
Long Live Malcolm, King of Scotland.

(1674: 66; Klv)

In Malcolm's invented response, Davenant enhances the principles of royalty and succession:

And may they [the titles of 'Earl'] still Flourish
On your Families; though like the Laurels
You have Won to Day, they Spring from a Field of Blood.
Drag his Body hence, and let it Hang upon
A Pinnacle in *Dunsinane*, to shew
To shew [sic] to future Ages what to those is due,
Who others Right, by Lawless Power pursue.

(66; Klv)

The new titles, like the kingship itself, should follow through lineal descent, and there is no question about 'Right' and legitimacy; the unnamed Macbeth's body will become an exemplary semiotic spectacle, like the regicides in Foucault's *Discipline and Punish*.[4]

Most strikingly, the final words of the play are now some freshly written moralizing spoken by Macduff:

So may kind Fortune Crown your Raign with Peace,
As it has Crown'd your Armies with Success;
And may the Peoples Prayers still wait on you,
As all their Curses did *Macbeth* pursue:
His Vice shall make your Virtue shine more Bright,
As a Fair Day succeeds a Stormy Night.

(66; Klv)

Now a morality fable, the play becomes a binary struggle between the 'Crown' and Macbeth, between 'Virtue' and 'Vice', between crowning and cursing, with the 'Fair Day' inevitably following (as in Polonius's platitude)[5] the 'Stormy Night'. Loaded with royalist buzz-words (crown, reign, crowned, prayers, virtue, succeeds), the speech rhetorically sweeps away both the unpleasant violence that has produced this moment but more importantly any conceivable doubts about the legitimacy and moral authority of Malcolm's reign. Earlier, in the 'show of kings' scene in 4.1, Davenant's revisions of the Folio enhanced the racial and blood-lineal aspects of what he saw to be the play's ideological framework, for after asking if Banquo's 'Issue' will 'succeed / Each other still till Dooms-day?', Davenant's Macbeth sees Banquo smiling, as seeming 'to say / That they are all Successors of his race' (48, 49; G3v, G4r); the Folio reads, more ambiguously, '*Banquo* smiles vpon me, / And points at them for his' (TLN 1616–17). The 'race' of future kings will 'succeed' in a naturalized progression that reveals no gaps or fissures. Still, even Davenant's version rests on unstable ideological legs: as Lois Potter has shown, the substance of Davenant's revisions is that the play now 'justifies both those who act and those who merely wait for the prophecies to be fulfilled. What it does *not* justify is Divine Right; Macbeth... is not a fiend from hell, but a man who has pursued "others Right, by Lawless power"' (1989: 207).

Davenant had also added a dying moralizing line for Macbeth, whose Folio death comes silently in a stage direction; by contrast, Davenant's Macbeth gasps out 'Farewell vain World, and what's most vain in it, / *Ambition*' (65). A century later, when David Garrick prepared his version of the play, he kept some of Davenant's changes, and amplified Macbeth's dying final speech into full melodrama:

> 'Tis done—The scene of life will quickly close,
> Ambition's vain delusive dreams are fled,
> And now I wake to darkness, guilt, and horror—
> I cannot bear it—Let me shake it off—
> It wo'not be—My soul is clog'd with blood,
> And cannot rise—I dare not ask for mercy!—
> It is too late—Hell drags me down—I sink—
> I sink—Oh! my soul's lost for ever. [*Dies*]
>
> (1753: 86)

Garrick followed Davenant, too, in depicting subservience to monarchical authority with his stage direction: '*Enter* Macduff *with* Macbeth's *sword, which kneeling he presents to* Malcolm' (87). Garrick (and the many who followed his lead) normalized Macbeth's death into a cautionary tale of misplaced 'Ambition', followed, in a moral chain, by 'guilt' and what seems to be a Faustus-like eternal damnation (Stone 1941). The punishment for treasonous 'Ambition' is clearly acknowledged by the now-beaten Macbeth. Davenant and Garrick thus began the process of correcting what they perceived as *Macbeth*'s flawed aesthetic-political themes and structure, especially its ending, and bolstering what they interpreted as the play's support of kingship and succession.

Garrick's alterations also led, in both stage performances and contemporary scholarship, to an increasing attention centred on the character of Macbeth and the relative amount of sympathy an audience might feel for him (see Bartholomeusz 1969; Rosenberg 1978). The character/psychological emphasis inversely relates to the play's political issues: thus in Garrick's version, Macbeth was dominated 'mentally and physically by his wife', hence 'divested of responsibility for instigating evil .... [Macbeth] reiterate[d] ideals of masculine nobility through the expression of sensitive remorse', as seen in the new final death speech (Prescott 2004: 85). The drive for political power thus devolved into the story of a sensitive soul's personal ambition and punishment.

FRANCE: BONAPARTISM AND ROYALTY

On 22 April 1798 – his last evening in Paris before departing to lead the invasion of Egypt – Napoleon Bonaparte attended a performance of Shakespeare's *Macbeth* (Golder 1992: 218). But it wasn't a play by 'Shakespeare' so much as one by Jean-François Ducis, who had freely adapted the play from earlier translations by de la Place (1746) and Letourneur (1776). Ducis struggled with *Macbeth* for years, writing to David Garrick in 1774 about his frustrations in preparing *Macbeth* for a French audience (see the first epigraph [Golder 1992: 163]). Finding a way to present 'the blood-drenched roads of terror' within a decorum suitable for his age wasn't easy: Ducis continued rewriting the play for years following the inaugural 1784 production's failure after only seven performances.[6] The three versions I will refer to here – 1784, 1789, 1798 – reflect Ducis's evolving aesthetics and his complex relations to royal power.

No matter how earnestly Ducis excised the play's considerable bloodshed and revised the play – deleting the Lady Macduff scenes, for example, and pushing violent scenes into descriptions or even mere summaries – he could not eliminate the play's central action of regicide, although the murder of Duncan 'is always referred to as parricide, never regicide' (Golder 1992: 204). Ducis's transformations of the plot circled closely around issues of sovereignty and rule. Frédégonde (=Lady Macbeth), for example, has a son Clotaire, for whom she will do anything. In the final act of the 1789 revision, Frédégonde enters the play's sleepwalking scene carrying a taper and dagger, walking 'blindly into the wings to stab her sons [now two of them] to death as they lie asleep' (214), in a morally symmetrical punishment for having deprived the kingdom of a father. The rightful son and heir, Malcôme, is crowned in both the 1784 and 1789 versions, and Macbeth is somewhat rehabilitated, stabbing himself after hailing Malcôme as rightful king in 1784, and even dying while defending Malcôme from hired assassins in 1789 (171, 214).

For the 1789 production, Ducis had transformed the play's banquet scene into a coronation scene, and replaced Banquo's ghost with Duncan's. In Ducis's original 1784 version, Duncan's ghost appeared three times during the coronation ceremony, pushing Macbeth away as he tried to sit on the throne. The stage direction reads:

> [Macbeth] sees the spectre or shadow of King Duncan… standing and bloody before the door and on the level of the chamber where this Sovereign and the Prince Glamis have been massacred. From the top of this stage the spectre reveals itself in the eyes of Macbeth and the spectators, but the theater is arranged in such a way… [that] only Macbeth… can see it.[7]

In the 1789 production, however, the coronation scene was cut, and as Macbeth 'reaches for the crown, Duncan's ghost reappears in his mind's eye' (Golder 1992: 212).

When Ducis revised the play for the 1798 performance before Napoleon, however, he had to attack the text once again, removing as many references to royalist discourse as possible – kings, princes, crown, scepter – all in all a considerable percentage of a play that contains three kings, refers to a fourth (the offstage English king Edward the Confessor), and includes two regicides. Moreover, the coronation scene was back, though Ducis had scrubbed the text and turned the scene about as far from Divine Right theory as possible. In earlier versions, the character Loclin (a man of the people) had offered the crown to Macbeth, but now in 1798, 'instead of offering Macbeth a crown, Loclin lifts an impressive folio volume from an ornate cushion, and holds it out to him':

> Macbeth, Duncan is no longer, I bring before you
> This sign of power, the book of the law.

If it assures you that it gives you the empire,
Of your sacred duties it must also instruct you.[8]

Displacing the crown, 'the book of the law' signals Ducis's resistance to potential tyranny.

In all of Ducis's versions, Macbeth suffers from an extraordinary, crippling guilt which eventually leads to his partial redemption; one of the actors in the initial version had taken to referring to the play as the 'Traité du Remords' (Golder 1992: 165). In the 1798 version, Loclin, in handing the 'book of laws' to Macbeth, had commanded him to swear 'That your heart will be sensitive to the good of the state, / That you are nothing here but a first citizen, / Who will do all by law, who without the law is nothing'.[9] Turning the 'dead butcher' into a man of law, a *premier citoyen*, would be a neat trick if it could be done. But it couldn't, neither for Macbeth or Napoleon.[10] (The reaction of Napoleon – no stranger to blood or terror himself – is not known.) For this eighteenth-century French audience, the play needed to be de-royalized and its politics domesticated; by contrast, for twenty-first–century audiences, dealing with their own Bonaparte-tyrants, appropriations and adaptations recognize and often enhance its terror.

For earlier directors, the question had been whether it was possible to generate any kind of sympathy for Macbeth, while still upholding a royalist stance; hence, the sentimentalization of Macbeth as (almost) a victim (of Lady Macbeth, the witches or fate). But in the latter half of the twentieth century, the interpretation of tyranny and power in *Macbeth* pivoted and the perception would become, for many, that the play's violence really reflected or explained the political violence of the culture around it. No longer an individual responsible for the evil in the play (or even merely a conduit for the witches' power), Macbeth would become the product of a corrupt and evil socio-political culture, with the corollary result that figures such as Duncan and Malcolm were not just de-royalized, but became much more complex, even malevolent. At the same time, the settings for many post-Second World War productions became dystopian or fascist worlds of the sort just seen throughout Europe.[11]

BRECHT/MÜLLER/IONESCO

In terms of a conceptual shift in political productions of *Macbeth*, indeed of all of Shakespeare's plays, the importance of Bertolt Brecht cannot be exaggerated, even though little of Brecht's writing on *Macbeth* survives. Brecht produced a radio play version for Berliner Rundfunk in 1927. The performance script has been lost, and only a summary of the production's elements exists in a 1938 book by Erich Schuhmacher. The account describes a revolutionary approach for the time, with Brecht's 'alienation' techniques such as scene titles:

> From the noise of a modern battle could be heard the voices of the 'Field Preachers', the 'Pacifist', a 'Stage [or Dashing] Hero', the 'Dashing Officers', the 'Traitors', 'Cowards', an 'Occultist', and a 'Dying Man'… The noise merged with the nagging of the witches. The text is always very freely and arbitrarily compressed from the original.[12]

The object of these transformations was to deliver the battle scenes from the traditional staging – to 'deface' (or disfigure: *verunstaltete*) them (Schuhmacher 1938: 254). 'Music' (by Edmund Meisel; Brecht 1997: 1160) was used to emphasize important monologue or dialogue parts, and 'as in a film', one scene often faded into another. After the second act of the original text, the Announcer reminded the audience of the king's murder and then explained the content of the entire third act. Brecht replaced the Ghost with a description spoken by the narrator. Brecht's dramaturgy thus defamiliarized the play's plot and characters, as one might expect, and so overturned conventional assumptions about the play and how it should be staged.

Paired with Brecht's revolutionary influence and the ravages of the Second World War, the 1962 publication of Jan Kott's *Shakespeare, Our Contemporary* (English translation, 1964) produced the greatest shift toward a new politics of *Macbeth*, though some productions had anticipated Kott's views. Kott's conception of Shakespeare has been so completely absorbed into contemporary theatrical practice that it is easy to forget how revolutionary it was (Worthen 2010). Kott read Shakespeare's plays in the light of apocalypse and Auschwitz. His most famous and influential chapter may have been 'King Lear or Endgame', but his thoughts on *Macbeth* – in a chapter ominously named 'Macbeth or Death-Infected' – completely changed, for many, their view of the play. For Kott, *Macbeth* was 'a nightmare… which paralyses and terrifies' (1964: 85–6): 'A production of *Macbeth* not evoking a picture of the world flooded with blood, would inevitably be false' (87). Kott saw only one theme in the play – not 'ambition', not 'terror', but 'murder': 'History has been reduced to its simplest form, to one image and one division: those who kill and those who are killed' (87). Long before historicist investigations into Scottish history and its tangled theories of royal succession, Kott understood its essence: 'The new king will be the man who has killed a king' (87). Macbeth, Kott says, has reached 'the Auschwitz experience' (92). All Macbeth can do is murder, and the end of the play 'produces no catharsis… Macbeth does not feel guilty, and there is nothing for him to protest about. All he can do before he dies is to drag with him into nothingness as many living beings as possible… Macbeth is still unable to blow the world up. But he can go on murdering till the end' (97). This view of the play and its relation to twentieth-century history is about as far from Garrick's invented final speech as can be imagined; understandably, many readers and directors have not warmed to Kott's dark vision, and some others have offered critiques from the left (Sinfield 1985) while many ostensibly 'modern' productions still reproduce the traditional thematics of the Authorized Version. But Kott made possible a worldwide shift in conceiving the play. Recent scholars have documented at length how Kott's readings of the plays revolutionized the staging and interpretation in post-Second World War Europe (Fayard 2006: 55–7; Gregor 2010; Rayner 2014; Bassi 2016).

Shakespeare's importance in central Europe is hardly recent – the transcultural traffic between English and European actors dates from the 1590s (Limon 1985) – but since the world war generations of Brecht and Kott, and arguably all the more so since 1989, 'more than anywhere else, Shakespeare's plays have… been appropriated for political interpretations' (Střibrný 2000: 1). Perhaps the best-known version of *Macbeth* from a central European author (via Singapore, India and the UK) is Tom Stoppard's *Cahoot's Macbeth*, designed to be performed after *Dogg's Hamlet* (1979). Stoppard's popular play may not be particularly representative of Czech politics,[13] but in his two-part construction the playwright certainly understands the various artistic and linguistic forms that political resistance can take.

Hamlet has always been *the* Shakespearean play in German culture, but the nation's association with *Macbeth* has been nearly as strong (Pfister 1986; Pfister 1994; Zimmerman 1994; Höfele 2016a). As early as the First World War, the English playwright Henry Arthur Jones wondered, 'What evil angel of their destiny tempted the Germans to choose Macbeth for their anniversary [i.e. 1916] offering to Shakespeare, in this year of all others? It is the very picture of their own character marching to its ruin' (Höfele 2016a: 3). Later, throughout the Nazi regime, the GDR regime and post-1989 politics, *Macbeth* proved an irresistible paradigm, depending on how the play was read, for both the legitimacy of State power and resistance to it.[14]

'[A]s a "Nordic ballad" about a hero tragically overwhelmed while fighting the English', as Werner Habicht (2012: 29–30) has noted, '*Macbeth* enjoyed Nazi favour to the very last'.[15] One functionary proposed, in 1940, that the play 'should be exploited for its propaganda value as an instrument for revealing the perfidy of the English' (Symington 2005: 253–4). Nazi defenders of Shakespeare had argued that Shakespeare 'advocated the submission of the individual person to higher public values (the state in the tragedies and histories, social structures in the comedies), and that many protagonists of his tragedies and histories were, indeed, Germanic heroes and epitomes of strong leadership, commanding and enforcing their subjects' (Habicht 2012: 23). In the post-war period, Höfele notes, the perception of Shakespeare's tragedies reflected the Cold War division of the country: in the East, a focus 'on the dialectics of class struggle', while in the West, 'the timeless dilemmas of the human condition' (2016b: 722). Perhaps the ultimate dismantling of Shakespearean tragedy – Höfele calls it 'the zero point of tragedy' – is Müller's *Die Hamletmaschine*. But his *Macbeth: nach Shakespeare* is nearly as powerful and disruptive.

'One can say a lot of things about Stalin with a production of *Macbeth*' (Weber 2012: 4); so Müller's 1972 adaptation of *Macbeth* proved. The play also reflects his more general indebtedness to, and critique of, Brecht (see Case 1983; Kalb 2001).[16] Müller had a career-long interest in Shakespeare, from an early translation of *As You Like It* to the later, enormous adaptation of *Titus Andronicus*. But more critically, in April 1988 Müller gave a speech – 'Shakespeare A Difference' – to scholars at the Shakespeare Tage in Weimar, in which he commented on the contradictory stature of Shakespeare in the two Germanies at that moment in history, and in his own heritage: 'Shakespeare had no philosophy, no understanding of history: his Romans are of London'. He argued, polemically, 'We haven't arrived at ourselves as long as Shakespeare is writing our plays' (Weber 1990: 33, 32).

While Müller takes the basic structure of *Macbeth* as a starting point, he strongly resisted Shakespeare's text and the entire tradition of the Authorized Version: '*Macbeth* was the Shakespeare play I liked least. Earlier I had translated *As You*

Like It as faithfully as possible. In *Macbeth* I wanted to alter Shakespeare, line by line' (Cohn 1976: 88). Müller realized that the first scene of the play presented a significant problem: to keep it, 'I would have to fully accept this idea of predestination, that the chain of events is programmed by supernatural forces. Therefore I first eliminated that scene, and this resulted in an increasing number of changes' (Weber 2012: 3). Still, Müller recognized another aspect of the witches that was crucial: 'In *Macbeth* there is an optimistic element of history, the witches. Every revolution needs a destructive element, and in my play that is the witches, they destroy without exception all those who possess power' (3). So the play begins with a version of 1.2, roughly following the Folio plot, with the prophecies roughly the same as well. But then there is the stage direction for scene 3 – '*Duncan, seated on corpses that have been stacked to create a throne*' (19) – and the play spirals into violence and abjection: peasants are introduced in order to be slain, Macduff cuts out a servant's tongue (36), the murderers cut off Banquo's penis ('A love-token for our master', 49), a Prisoner is flayed (64) and so on. Duncan, Malcolm and Macduff, in a total inversion of the Authorized Version, are all as cruel and murderous as Macbeth. When Macbeth is killed and his head brought in on a spear, Rosse and Lenox greet Malcolm

> Hail Malcolm, King
> Of Scotland. See how high he once has climbed
> Who was it before you. Learn from his case,

to which Malcolm replies, 'Know, you can't fool around with the boy Malcolm. / For your head is a place here on my spear.' This stage direction follows: '*Malcolm laughs. Rosse and Lenox point at Macduff. Soldiers kill him*'. The play ends with an entrance of the witches, whose choric greeting – 'Hail Malcolm Hail King of Scotland Hail' (75) – is chilling enough even before one recognizes that in German the word is '*Heil*'. Müller's adaptation says something about Hitler as well as Stalin.

Müller also decentralizes character and agency. For his production ten years later in East Berlin in 1982, Müller split the character of Macbeth into three different actors to emphasize not the individual but the systemic structures of power and corruption, while the set 'represented the inner court of a typical Berlin working class apartment building, with a telephone booth… and trash heaps' (Weber 2012: 4). Müller's changes, even from his own text, produced criticism by some East German reviewers for its 'pessimism' and anti-humanistic effect (Mahlke 1999: 40). As Thomas Sorge wrote, 'The desired historical perspective… (Duncan=feudalism; Macbeth=dissolution of feudalism/advent of early bourgeois egotism; Malcolm=socially relatively unspecified promise of an area [sic] of peace and prosperity), was efficiently deflated by the adaptation, especially with regard to Malcolm as a bearer of hopes for better times' (1994: 72). Müller's rewriting of *Macbeth* parallels other twentieth-century revisions in that Malcolm's legitimate succession, a hallmark of the Authorized Version, is inverted: Müller couldn't stomach him (or any part of the play) as 'a bearer of hopes for better times'.

Eugène Ionesco's darkly comic *Macbett* (also 1972) also strongly resists the perceived traditional politics of the Folio text: thus, Ionesco's Malcolm figure is a monster, and murder is the principle of succession, there are two not three witches and so on. Like many before him, Ionesco critiqued Shakespeare for having placed Duncan's murder offstage: 'You think that I, myself, I do not hesitate to put the slaying on the stage'.[17] Perry observes that Ionesco 'ties up some of Shakespeare's loose ends' (2000: 95) by revealing that Macol [=Malcolm] is really Banco's biological son – hence in effect redressing a common complaint about the failure of the witches' prophecy to come good. Brecht's influence is also evident in such estranging techniques as the introduction of the Butterfly Hunter, the Lemonade Seller and the '*life-size dolls [that] represent the other* GUESTS' in the final banquet (Ionesco 1973: 87SD).[18] Ionesco's clear debt to Alfred Jarry's *Ubu roi* is marked most specifically by Macbett's final word, 'Shit!' which in the French ('*Merde*') echoes the first word of Jarry's play ('*Merdre*').[19]

Ionesco's ideological reinterpretation of Shakespeare's text is comprehensive, and he freely acknowledged his debt to Kott:

> I got the idea from my friend Jan Kott, the author of "Shakespeare, Our Contemporary"... There is a king, a tyrant, vicious and criminal. Then comes a young prince, handsome, brave and pure, who kills the tyrant and takes his place. He in turn becomes a tyrant. Another young prince – handsome, brave and pure – kills the tyrant and becomes king. And so on.
>
> (Hess 1972)

Ionesco added, in a later interview, that Kott 'thought of Stalin' and inspired his own piece, in which he tried 'to show once more that every politician is paranoid and that all politics leads to crime'.[20] Ionesco offered that *Macbett* is still a comedy: 'I hope people will laugh' (Hess 1972) – though perhaps not at the '*forest of guillotines*' (31SD) that dispatches enemies of the state.

Ionesco's sardonic plot summary of the 'handsome' young prince who succeeds a tyrant and then turns into a tyrant himself ad infinitum is a dark parody of the play's 'line of kings'. It reorients Duncan and his supposed legitimacy from the weak king of Shakespeare's play, to the lecherous, vicious and cowardly tyrant who stays so far away from the danger of battle that he can only see the front 'through my telescope' (23). In Ionesco's most brilliant irony, Duncan's onstage murder comes through the ritual most designed, historically, to illustrate the monarch's 'sovereign power' (71): the 'heavenly gift' (70) of the Royal Touch. After the Monk (Banco in disguise) blesses the royal scepter, Duncan begins to heal the sick (suffering from leprosy, scrofula, bodily agony) with divine invocations ('By the grace of our Lord Jesus Christ, by the gift of the power vested in me this day' etc., 73), only to be murdered by the unholy triumvirate of Banco, Macbett and Lady Duncan. I doubt that Ionesco knew of King James's own skepticism about the ceremony he inherited from Queen Elizabeth, and his cynical embrace of the ritual as a technique of legitimating his reign, but Ionesco foregrounds a key element of Shakespeare's play. The result doesn't just undermine the ritual, but hollows it out altogether, as the 'divine' blessings are given by Banco, who '*strikes the first blow*' (77SD).

Like Müller, Ionesco also refuses to see Macbeth's as a tragedy of character or 'ambition'. Macbett's characterization, like others in the play, is flat and robotic, as indicated by the technique of parallels and exact verbal repetitions first with Banco, then with Duncan, and by the unoriginality of his language; moreover, there is no 'tomorrow' speech or any other of the Shakespearean soliloquies that produce such a profound illusion of interiority. Instead, there are repetitive cycles of violence, treason and murder. Perry describes this cycle in Kottian terms: 'All who want the crown are conspirators; all conspirators want the crown because the crown is what is wanted' (2000: 93).

If Ionesco's Duncan is a tyrant and Banco a conspirator (as he was, prior to Shakespeare's play, in the chronicles), Ionesco's greatest act of reinterpretation comes in the figure of Macol. Macbett scoffs, after the witches' prophecy that he himself will become king: 'It's impossible. Duncan has a son, Macol, who's studying at Carthage. He is the natural and legitimate heir to the throne' (38; Banco says almost the identical thing, 43). When Macol finally enters the play in the last scene, Lady Duncan announces, in a parody of romantic 'lost child' narratives, that he isn't her son, but was adopted by Duncan: 'Banco was his father, his mother was a gazelle that a witch transformed into a woman' (99). There's nothing magical about Macol's defeat of Macbett however: 'MACOL *stabs* MACBETT *in the back.* MACBETT *falls*' (101SD). As the people herald Macol as their new king, he orders them: 'Quiet, I say. Don't all talk at once. I'm going to make an announcement. Nobody move. Nobody breathe. Now get this into your heads. Our country sank beneath the yoke, each day a new gash was added to her wounds. But I have trod upon the tyrant's head and now wear it on my sword' and a man then '*comes in with Macbett's head on the end of a pike*' (102SD). As the people curse the head, the '*forest of guillotines*' reappears '*as in the First Scene*' (103SD). At this point, Macol ends the play with an almost verbatim quotation of Malcolm's 'test' speech to Macduff in 4.3 of the Folio; in this context the speech becomes a chilling promise rather than a 'test' of Macduff's loyalty. Beginning 'In me I know / All the particulars of vice so grafted', Macol speaks for thirty-seven uninterrupted lines, while the crowd dissipates and at last the Bishop '*goes dejectedly out right*' (105SD). The play ends with Macol pledging to 'Pour the sweet milk of concord into Hell, / Uproar the universal peace, confound / All unity on earth', and finally, 'First I'll make this Archduchy a kingdom—and me the king. An empire—and me the emperor. Super-highness, super-king, super-majesty, emperor of emperors' (105), after which '*He disappears in the mist*' (105SD) and the Butterfly Hunter once more crosses the stage. We are a long way from the reading of Shakespeare's play as authorizing, in Malcolm's ascent to the throne, a lawful and 'righteous' renewal.

SCOTLAND: DAVID GREIG'S *DUNSINANE*

No play, it is safe to say, is more 'Scottish' than *Macbeth*, and the Scottish playwright David Greig took it on in *Dunsinane* (2011). Any casual reader of Greig's drama quickly recognizes the influence of Brecht (see Wallace 2013: 31–6). As Greig does not feel he himself has a 'Scottish voice' (Billingham 2007: 78), with the example of 'Brecht in particular… it occurred to me that if I wrote a play *as if it was in translation*, it would allow two things: a certain sort of formal poetic language because it wouldn't be pretending to be naturalistic as it was obviously translated, and the freedom to write working-class characters as I required them to speak' (Whitney 2010). In *Dunsinane*, Greig responds 'to Shakespeare's Macbeth in a way which is not dissimilar from [Howard] Barker responding to Thomas Middleton in his version of *Women Beware Women*' (Brown 2011). A few years before *Dunsinane*, Greig had warmed up by adapting Jarry's *King Ubu* (2005), now set in an old people's home.

Dunsinane begins approximately where *Macbeth* ends, with the defeat of Macbeth and the triumph of Malcolm, led to apparent victory by the English general Siward and his invading force. But in a radical departure, Lady Macbeth has not perished after all – not only has she survived, but she now has a name (Gruach) and a son (Lulach), neither of which Shakespeare had granted her, though the son existed in Holinshed's *Chronicles of England, Scotland, and Ireland*, Shakespeare's chief source for the story. Greig's transformation of Lady Macbeth into Gruach and the fact of her survival after Macbeth's death follows several other writers, from the late nineteenth century but particularly since 2000, who have turned to Scottish historical sources (unavailable to Shakespeare in 1605–6) to recover, and recuperate, the 'real' Lady Macbeth (see Carroll 2014a). Where Shakespeare's Lady Macbeth had no name and seemed to have little independent agency, imploding with guilt after the murder of Duncan, Greig's Gruach is by contrast a strong-willed, charismatic figure, the dynamic centre of the play. Where Lady Macbeth called on the 'spirits / That tend on mortal thoughts' to 'unsex me here' (1.5.40–1), Gruach deploys her sexuality as needed to survive, and to dominate, men like Siward and Malcolm. Her character, Greig said, 'emerged very suddenly with a single line… Siward finds this woman hiding. He says to her, "Woman, what is your place here?"; and she says, "My place? My place here is queen."'[21] Greig's Gruach 'has a number of very powerful aims, which are rational. She believes that her clan, her faction, should be in charge, and it is her right to be queen' (Brown 2011). Greig's revisionist history results in a powerful, mysterious character who, more or less, represents 'Scotland' against Siward's 'England' (Siward actually introduces himself to Gruach, 'I am Siward. / I am England' [27].) Most Scots, Greig claims, know that the real King Macbeth

> probably wasn't a tyrant, he was probably quite a good king. He ruled for about 15 years at a time in Scottish history when the turnover in kings was something like one in every six months, so he must have been doing something right… So the cheeky bit of me thought, 'What if the stories of Macbeth being a tyrant turned out to be propaganda, a bit like the weapons of mass destruction?'
>
> (Whitney 2010)

– i.e. a pretext for invading a country. Macbeth himself never appears in the play, just an account of his offstage death by Macduff: 'I cut his throat. / His head's on a stick in the castle yard', to which Siward's 'It's over', is answered by Macduff: 'Yes' (25). But of course it's not over at all, it's only beginning. The English attempt to bring order to Scotland lurches into catastrophe.

Siward is, Greig has said, genuinely 'a good man who is trying to do the right thing. It's just that every single action he takes in pursuit of the right thing leads to more and more bloodshed' (Brown 2011). Siward enters the play after his soldiers have routed Macbeth, and his confidence is clear: 'We'll set a new king in Dunsinane and then summer will come and then a harvest and by next spring it'll be as if there never was a fight here. You'll be amazed how quickly a battle can disappear' (24). But then Siward meets Gruach and from that point on nothing that follows makes any sense to him. When he challenges what Malcolm had told him about the situation, Malcolm's reply invokes the Scots' very different understanding of language and truth: 'are you going to continue with this insistent literalness? "You said" – "He said" – you sound like a child' (29).

Siward is undaunted in the beginning, telling Gruach 'My job is to build a new kingdom – not to settle old grudges. So I have to clear away the past now. I have to uproot now and clear away all past claims and – That way there is a chance that we can establish a fair peace in Scotland in which every clan can flourish – including yours' (33), and he instructs his soldiers to conduct themselves morally with the Scots: that way, 'We will make them to trust us' (44). He refuses to kill a farmer Malcolm wants out of the way because 'I will not kill a man for doing a reasonable thing' (52), but after Siward leaves, Malcolm orders others to kill the man and his family. Eventually, Siward begins to order and commit increasingly violent acts himself. Even his chief aide Egham is taken aback when Siward orders the burning of a village and all the people in it: 'It's a bit Scandinavian, isn't it?', but Siward, chillingly rational, says 'If we make a threat we have to follow it through' (94). Even the sinister Malcolm asks Siward to hold back, but Siward responds: 'You don't restrain a dog when he's chasing a deer' (107). The link between Siward's rationality – 'I'm a soldier. I like clarity' (108) – and his violence becomes ever stronger, and he himself ultimately kills the Scottish Boy (who has confessed to being Lulach) after an initial hesitation (123). As with most of Siward's actions, however, the result is the opposite of what he had intended. Siward imagines that 'A knife is a knife, a neck is a neck. / He's dead', but Malcolm sees the Scottish reality: 'I think it's more likely that by killing this boy you have given him eternal life' (125), and in the final scene, Gruach confirms that Siward has brought upon himself and England an endless line of resistance: 'For as long as I reign I'll torment you and when I die I'll leave instructions in my will to every Scottish Queen that comes after me to tell her King to take up arms and torment England again and again and again until the end of time' (136). Siward's defense resounds with irony: 'Everything I did, I did because I thought that doing it was for the best' (132).

Greig never names 'Iraq' or 'Afghanistan' in the play, but at some point audiences realize that the play is a temporal palimpsest, that Siward's actions refract current political issues regarding the extended occupation of these countries. Greig's 'starting point' for the play, he said, was the question '"What happens after the dictator falls?" Macbeth is a play about the toppling of a dictator; we would see in it a mirror of Ceausescu or Gaddafi … However, as we're living in an Afghanistan/Iraq world … [the play is] about an English garrison trying to survive in hostile territory' (Brown 2011). The parallels go beyond Siward's own actions to such incidents as that of the Hen Girl, seemingly modelled on the idea of a suicide bomber. After suffering abuse and humiliation from the English soldiers, she stabs one of them, tries to free the prisoners and then stabs herself. Egham then comments: 'We have got to get out of this fucking country' (119). Indeed, but somehow they can't.

Like Müller, Ionesco and others before him, Greig inverts the traditional reading of Malcolm. The Stuart triumphalism in which Malcolm is not only the 'rightful' successor to Duncan but also a righteous man, like the sainted Edward the Confessor who has taken him in, has given way to a depraved and murderous sociopath. Not to be outdone by Ionesco's or Müller's vicious Malcolms, Greig gives us a Malcolm without human feelings at all – ordering the murder of innocent families, the burning of villages and worse. Greig's Malcolm, promising 'total honesty', tells his nation:

> In that spirit I offer you the following. I will govern entirely in the interests of me. In so far as I give consideration to you it will be to calibrate exactly how much I can take from you before you decide to attempt violence against me. I will periodically and arbitrarily commit acts of violence against some or other of you – in order that I can maintain a more general order in the country. I will not dispose my mind to the improvement of the country or to the conditions of its ordinary people. I will not improve trade. I will maintain an army only in order to submit you to my will. As far as foreign powers are concerned I will submit to any humiliation in order to keep the friendship of England... And, most important of all, you need not waste even a minute of your long cold nights wondering about whether you are in or out of my favour. You are out of my favour. Now and always.
>
> (80–1)

After this astonishing speech, the politics of the Scottish court, usually so murky, clarify in a hopeless image of tyranny: not Macbeth's tyranny, but that of the supposedly righteous successor, Malcolm.

Political adaptations of *Macbeth* thus began immediately after the Restoration, and continue to the present. These revisions add up to far more than just tying 'up some of Shakespeare's loose ends', as one critic said of Ionesco's version; rather, they constitute often radical rethinkings of the play's representations of sovereignty, succession theory, regime change and, especially, Malcolm's 'righteous' claim to the throne, as well as the play's relation to the political worlds around it. What's done can, apparently, be re-done.

NOTES

1   For counters to this reading, see Goldberg (1987). A more extensive version of the current essay appears in *Adapting Macbeth: A Cultural History*, forthcoming from Bloomsbury/Arden Shakespeare (2022).

2   This chapter also does not examine the extraordinary globalization of *Macbeth*. See the MIT Global Shakespeare website: http://globalshakespeares.mit. edu/#play%5B%5D=Macbeth</URI> (accessed 15 July 2019).

3   On Eastern European productions post-Second World War, see Shurbanov (1998); Stříbrný (2000); Makaryk (2006, 2012); Matei-Chesnoiu (2006); Drábek (2014, 2016).

4   Such spectacles, Foucault notes, invariably failed to produce the anticipated
    obedience, as did Malcolm's, historically.

5   'This above all: to thine own self be true / And it must follow as the night the day /
    Thou canst not then be false to any man' (1.3.77–9).

6   Gregor shows that there were as many as 'nine distinct manuscript versions…
    between mid-1782 (or even as early as 1778) and January, 1784' (2014: 62). See
    Dargan (1912) for an overview of Ducis's several adaptations of Shakespeare's plays
    (with brief references to *Macbeth* (28–32).

7   My translation; French text at Golder (1992: 185).

8   My translation; French text at Golder (1992: 219). Golder suggests that this
    scene might have been inspired by Louis XVI's promise, in 1791, to uphold the
    Constitution and act as first citizen under the law (220).

9   My translation; French text at Golder (1992: 219–20).

10 For accounts of *Macbeth*'s later adaptations in France, see Fayard (2006) and Pemble
    (2005). Ducis's pleasure at Napoleon's attendance in 1798 would eventually turn into
    embittered criticism after Napoleon was crowned Emperor in 1804.

11 These modernizing impulses still ran in parallel with more traditional staging, often
    set in an imagined eleventh-century Scotland, ranging from Orson Welles's 1948 film
    to Justin Kurzel's 2015 film.

12 My translation; German text at Schumacher (1938: 254).

13 The play is dedicated to Pavel Kohout, who had been banned from working in the
    theatre after he had drafted the original document founding 'Charter 77'; Kohout
    adapted *Macbeth* to be performed in living rooms. Drábek (2017: 8) describes
    Cahoot's Macbeth as 'a Westernised imaginative impression' of Kohout's *Play
    Macbeth*.

14 Shakespeare's reception in Germany is too large a topic to undertake here; see
    Höfele's excellent brief overview and bibliography (2016b).

15 *Macbeth* was clustered as 'Nordic' alongside *Hamlet, King Lear* and *Richard II* (23).
    One writer (in 1940) found that the play was 'a myth of Nordic winter', but also an
    expression of the 'yearning for salvation' (Höfele 2016a: 205n.46).

16 Thus Müller (Weber 1984: 18): 'It's treason to use Brecht without criticizing him'.

17 My translation; French text at Kamenish (1991: 15).

18 See Kern (1974) on the links to Brecht. Kern's otherwise astute comments on the play
    are partly undermined by her unquestioned acceptance of the 'Authorized' reading of
    Shakespeare's play; for her, Malcolm's deceit in 4.3 is a 'humble misrepresentation
    of himself' (13). Similarly, for Lamont (1973), Shakespeare's Duncan is a 'gracious
    sovereign', while Ionesco's is 'Ubu-Stalin-Hitler-Mao-Castro rolled into one'.

19 *Ubu Roi* was performed (only once) on 19 December 1896 in Paris. Its plot (if that is
    the right term) features a usurper, tempted by his wife, who kills the king and then is
    himself deposed by the king's son. See Kern (1974); Cohn (1976); Perry (2000); and
    Morse (2004) on the links to Jarry.

20 My translation; French text at (Bonnefoy 1966 and 1977: 161, 162).

21 The actual lines in the printed text are 'SIWARD. What is your place here? GRUACH. My place here is Queen' (27).

REFERENCES

Bartholomeusz, D. (1969), *Macbeth and the Players*, Cambridge: Cambridge University Press.

Bassi, S. (2016), 'The Tragedies in Italy', in M. Neill and D. Schalkwyk (eds), *The Oxford Handbook of Shakespearean Tragedy*, 691–705, Oxford: Oxford University Press.

Billingham, P. (2007), *At the Sharp End: Uncovering the Work of Five Contemporary Dramatists*, London: Methuen.

Bonnefoy, C. (1966 and 1977), *Eugène Ionesco: Entre La Vie et Le Rêve: Entretiens*, Paris: Pierre Belfond.

Brecht, B. (1997), *Bertolt Brecht Stücke 10*, Frankfurt: Suhrkamp Verlag.

Brown, M. (2011), 'David Greig pushes beyond Macbeth with Dunsinane', *Herald Scotland*, 8 May. Available online: https://www.chicagoshakes.com/plays_and_events/dunsinane/dunsinaneplaywright (accessed 17 October 2021).

Calderwood, J. L. (1986), *If It Were Done: Macbeth and Tragic Action*, Amherst, MA: University of Massachusetts Press.

Carroll, W. C. (2014a), 'The Fiendlike Queen: Recuperating Lady Macbeth in Contemporary Adaptations of *Macbeth*', *Borrowers and Lenders: The Journal of Shakespeare and Appropriation* 8 (2). Available online: https://openjournals.libs.uga.edu/borrowers/article/view/2213/2118 (accessed 17 October 2021).

Carroll, W. C. (2014b), 'Fleance in the Final Scene of *Macbeth*: The Return of the Repressed', in S. Hatchuel and N. Vienne-Guerrin (eds), *Shakespeare on Screen: Macbeth*, 261–78, Rouen: Publications des Universités de Rouen et du Havre.

Carroll, W. C. (2014c), 'Spectacle, Representation, and Lineage in *Macbeth* 4.1', *Shakespeare Survey* 67: 345–71.

Case, S. (1983), 'From Bertolt Brecht to Heiner Müller', *Performing Arts Journal* 7 (1): 94–102.

Cohn, R. (1976), *Modern Shakespeare Offshoots*, Princeton, NJ: Princeton University Press.

Dargan, E. P. (1912), 'Shakespeare and Ducis', *Modern Philology* 10 (2): 1–42.

Davenant, W. (1674), *Macbeth, A Tragaedy. With all the Alterations, Amendments, Additions, and New Songs*, London.

Drábek, P. (2014), 'From the *General of the Scottish Army* to a Fattish Beer-Drinker: A Short History of Czech Translations of *Macbeth*', in J. Bžochová-Wild (ed.), *'In Double trust': Shakespeare in Central Europe*, 52–72, Bratislava: VŠMU.

Drábek, P. (2016), 'Shakespearean Tragedy in Eastern Europe', in M. Neill and D. Schalkwyk (eds), *The Oxford Handbook of Shakespearean Tragedy*, 746–60, Oxford: Oxford University Press.

Drábek, Pavel (2017), '"Spirit, fine spirit, Ile free thee": Shakespeare's Spaces of Freedom on the Czech Stage', Shakespeare in Prague Conference, Ohio State University, 3–4 March, 1–42.

Fayard, N. (2006), *The Performance of Shakespeare in France since the Second World War: Re-Imagining Shakespeare*, Lewiston, NY: Edwin Mellen Press.

Garrick, D. (1753), *The Historical Tragedy of Macbeth*, Edinburgh.

Goldberg, J. (1987), 'Speculations: *Macbeth* and source', in J. E. Howard and M. F. O'Connor (eds), *Shakespeare Reproduced: The Text in History and Ideology*, 242–64, London: Methuen.

Golder, J. (1992), *Shakespeare for the Age of Reason: The Earliest Stage Adaptations of Jean-François Ducis, 1769–1792*, Oxford: The Voltaire Foundation.

Gregor, K. (2010), *Shakespeare in the Spanish Theatre: 1772 to the Present*, London: Continuum.

Gregor, K. (2014), 'When the Tyrant is a Despot: Jean-François Ducis's Adaptations of Shakespeare', in K. Gregor (ed.), *Shakespeare and Tyranny: Regimes of Reading in Europe and Beyond*, 57–75, Cambridge: Cambridge Scholars.

Greig, D. (2010), *Dunsinane*, London: Faber & Faber.

Habicht, W. (2012), 'German Shakespeare, the Third Reich, and the War', in I. R. Makaryk and M. McHugh (eds), *Shakespeare and the Second World War: Memory, Culture, Identity*, 22–34, Toronto: University of Toronto Press.

Hadfield, A. (2005), *Shakespeare and Republicanism*, Cambridge: Cambridge University Press.

Hattaway, M. (2013), 'Tragedy and political authority', in C. McEachern (ed.), *The Cambridge Companion to Shakespearean Tragedy*, 2nd edn, 110–31, Cambridge: Cambridge University Press.

Hess, J. L. (1972), 'Ionesco Talks of His Latest, "Macbett"', *The New York Times*, 18 January.

Höfele, A. (2016a), *No Hamlets: German Shakespeare from Nietzsche to Carl Schmitt*, Oxford: Oxford University Press.

Höfele, A. (2016b), 'The Tragedies in Germany', in M. Neill and D. Schalkwyk (eds), *The Oxford Handbook of Shakespearean Tragedy*, 706–25, Oxford: Oxford University Press.

Ionesco, E. (1973), *Macbett*, trans. Charles Marowitz, New York, NY: Grove Press.

Jarry, A. (1961), *Ubu Roi*, trans. Barbara Wright, New York, NY: New Directions.

Kalb, Jonathan (2001), *The Theater of Heiner Müller*, rev. edn, New York, NY: Limelight.

Kamenish, P. K. (1991), 'Ionesco's Own *Ubu*', *Postscript*, Spring: 9–16.

Kern, E. (1974), 'Ionesco and Shakespeare: "Macbeth" on the Modern Stage', *South Atlantic Bulletin* 39 (1): 3–16.

Kernan, A. (1995), *Shakespeare, the King's Playwright*, New Haven, CT: Yale University Press.

Kott, J. (1964), *Shakespeare, Our Contemporary*, New York, NY: Doubleday.

Lamont, R. C. (1973), 'Ionesco, Eugène. *Macbett*', *The French Review* 46 (4): 858.

Limon, J. (1985), *Gentlemen of a Company: English Players in Central and Eastern Europe, 1590–1660*, Cambridge: Cambridge University Press.

Mahlke, S. (1999), 'Brecht ± Müller: German-German Brecht Images before and after 1989', *TDR* 43(4): 40–9.

Makaryk, I. R. and J. G. Price, eds (2006), *Shakespeare in the Worlds of Communism and Socialism*, Toronto: University of Toronto Press.

Makaryk, I. R. and M. McHugh, eds (2012), *Shakespeare and the Second World War: Memory, Culture, Identity*, Toronto: University of Toronto Press.

Matei-Chesnoiu, M. (2006), *Shakespeare in the Romanian Cultural Memory*, Madison, NJ: Fairleigh Dickinson University Press.

McLuskie, K. E. (2009), *William Shakespeare: Macbeth*, Horndon, UK: Northcote House.

Moretti, F. (1982), '"A Huge Eclipse": Tragic Form and the Deconsecration of Sovereignty', in S. Greenblatt (ed.), *The Forms of Power and the Power of Forms in the Renaissance*, 7–40, Norman, OK: Pilgrim Books.

Morse, R. (2004), 'Monsieur Macbeth: From Jarry to Ionesco', *Shakespeare Survey* 57: 112–25.

Paul, H. N. (1950), *The Royal Play of 'Macbeth'*, New York, NY: Macmillan.

Pemble, J. (2005), *Shakespeare Goes to Paris: How the Bard Conquered France*, London: Bloomsbury.

Perry, C. (2000), 'Vaulting Ambitions and Killing Machines: Shakespeare, Jarry, Ionesco and the Senecan Absurd', in D. Hedrick and B. Reynolds (eds), *Shakespeare Without Class*, 85–106, New York, NY: Palgrave.

Pfister, M. (1986), 'Germany is Hamlet: The History of a Political Interpretation', *New Comparison* 2: 106–26.

Pfister, M. (1994), 'Hamlets made in Germany, East and West', in M. Hattaway, B. Sokolova and D. Roper (eds), *Shakespeare in the New Europe*, 76–91, Sheffield: Sheffield Academic Press.

Potter, L. (1989), *Secret Rites and Secret Writing*, Cambridge: Cambridge University Press.

Prescott, P. (2004), 'Doing All that Becomes A Man: The Reception and Afterlife of the Macbeth Actor, 1744–1889', *Shakespeare Survey* 57: 81–95.

Rayner, F. (2014), 'From the Snares of Watchful Tyranny to Post-Human Dictators: *Macbeth* Under the Portugese Dictatorship and in Democracy', in K. Gregor (ed.), *Shakespeare and Tyranny: Regimes of Reading in Europe and Beyond*, 127–44, Newcastle-upon-Tyne: Cambridge Scholars.

Rosenberg, M. (1978), *The Masks of Macbeth*, Berkeley, CA: University of California Press.

Schuhmacher, Erich (1938), *Shakespeares Macbeth auf der deutschen Bühne*, Emsdetten: Verlags-Anstalt Heinr. & J. Lechte.

Shurbanov, A. (1998), 'Politicized with a Vengeance: East European Uses of Shakespeare's Great Tragedies', in J. Bate, J. L. Levenson and D. Mehl (eds), *Shakespeare and the Twentieth Century*, 137–47, Newark, DE: University of Delaware Press.

Sinfield, A. (1985), 'Introduction: Reproductions, Interventions', in J. Dollimore and Sinfield (eds), *Political Shakespeare: New Essays in Cultural Materialism*, 130–3, Ithaca, NY: Cornell University Press.

Sorge, T. (1994), 'Buridan's Ass Between Two Performances of *A Midsummer Night's Dream*, or Bottom's *Telos* in the GDR and After', in M. Hattaway, B. Sokolova and D. Roper (eds), *Shakespeare in the New Europe*, 54–74, Sheffield: Sheffield Academic Press.

Stone, G. W. Jr. (1941), 'Garrick's Handling of "Macbeth"', *Studies in Philology* 38 (4): 609–28.

Stříbrný, Z. (2000), *Shakespeare and Eastern Europe*, Oxford: Oxford University Press.

Symington, R. T. K. (1968), 'Brecht und Shakespeare', PhD diss., McGill University.

Symington, R. (2005), *The Nazi Appropriation of Shakespeare: Cultural Politics in the Third Reich*, Lewiston, NY: Edwin Mellen Press.

Wallace, C. (2013), *The Theatre of David Greig*, London: Bloomsbury.

Weber, C., ed. (1984), *Hamletmachine and Other Texts for the Stage*, New York, NY: Performing Arts Journal Publications.

Weber, C. (1990), 'Heiner Müller in East Berlin', *Performing Arts Journal* 12 (2/3): 29–35.

Weber, C. and P. D. Young, eds and trans. (2012), *Heiner Müller: After Shakespeare*, New York, NY: PAJ.

Whitney, H. (2010), 'Interview', *theartsdesk Q&A: Playwright David Greig*, 6 February. Available online: https://theartsdesk.com/theatre/theartsdesk-qa-playwright-david-greig (accessed 7 July 2021).

Worthen, W. B. (2010), 'Jan Kott, Shakespeare Our Contemporary', *Forum Modernes Theater* 25 (2): 91–7.

Zimmerman, H. O. (1994), 'Is Hamlet Germany? On the Political Reception of *Hamlet*', in M. T. Burnett and J. Manning (eds), *New Essays on Hamlet*, 293–318, New York, NY: AMS Press.

Animating an archive of Black performance: swing, William Alexander Brown and *The African Company Presents 'Richard III'*

JOYCE GREEN MACDONALD

By now, we are familiar with the notion of Shakespeare as an avatar of universal value, whose cultural centrality can be measured by his works' translation and performance in countries around the world. We are equally aware of how Shakespeare's universality can be reappropriated to the purposes of the metropolitan centre, as in the case of the 2012 Globe to Globe Festival, in which Shakespeare's Globe Theatre produced thirty-seven plays in thirty-seven languages as part of the Cultural Olympiad accompanying London's hosting of the Olympic and Paralympic Games. One way or another, the institution of Shakespeare asserts its continuing value and relevance, even if, as Douglas Lanier notes, such massive projects as Globe to Globe accomplish this assertion through silently acknowledging the degree to which 'Shakespeare' is now understood to include adapted texts as well as what we find in the First Folio (2014: 22–3). As conditions of reception and interpretation change, Shakespeare keeps enlarging itself so as to maintain a place at the centre of new conversations.

In this chapter, I set aside inquiries into Shakespeare's protean reinventiveness – questions whose answers tend to keep us circling back to Shakespeare himself – to put both a particular set of audiences and their cultural experiences and especially practitioners at the centre of questions about how he maintains his value. Demonstrating the creative impact of global theatres' work with and on Shakespeare was, of course, one of the goals of the London Cultural Olympiad; London, England and Shakespeare himself, fused into a single entity, were emphasized as the generative origin of the festival's global adaptations even as audiences feasted on the performances themselves. By contrast here, in looking at how race – specifically,

Blackness in early-nineteenth-century Manhattan and William Alexander Brown's African Company's Shakespearean performances – can affect the reception and reproduction of Shakespeare, both in the theatre and in an emerging Black urban culture, I want to help imagine a playwright who may serve as a launching point and place of inspiration, but whose presence ultimately recedes before the power of a newly and specifically Americanized performance. The chapter contextualizes William Alexander Brown's work with Shakespeare in the nineteenth century before exploring how, in the twentieth century, Carlyle Brown's play *The African Company Presents 'Richard III'* (1988) memorializes the ambition and creativity of the earlier dramaturg to map out the resources and values of Black performance.

PERFORMING BLACKNESS, ADAPTING SHAKESPEARE

We can trace one strand of Black response to Shakespeare and the colonial authority for which he stood in the work of such Caribbean intellectuals as George Lamming, for whom the 'sacred gang' of British canonical authors had embodied 'something called culture' in their island educations:

> Since the cultural negotiation was strictly between England and the [colonized] natives, and England had acquired, somehow, the divine right to organize the native's reading, it is to be expected that England's export of literature would be English. Deliberately and exclusively English. And the further back in time England went for these treasures, the safer was the English commodity. So the examinations, which would determine [a] Trinidadian's future in the Civil Service, imposed Shakespeare, and Wordsworth, and Jane Austen and George Eliot and the whole tabernacle of dead names, now come alive at the world's greatest summit of literary expression.
>
> ([1960] 1992: 27)

This stifling power over the Caribbean natives' own creativity could only be broken by leaving home. Yet ironically, going to London – the capital of the former empire which had controlled Lamming's home island of Barbados – only exacerbated the problem of learning how to write and speak in their own voices for these Caribbean writers. Lamming's 1971 novel *Water With Berries* explores the experiences of three Caribbean artists who emigrate to London in hopes of finding greater creative freedom, but who instead discover that they are still trapped within the nightmarish afterlife of colonial power.

The title of Lamming's novel echoes Caliban's bitter memory of how Prospero softened him up for conquest – 'wouldst give me / Water with berries in't' (1.2.399–400) – and points to how other postcolonial memories of *The Tempest* reject a sentimental reading of the play as the triumphal final affirmation of Shakespeare's genius, seeking instead to expose and undermine its standing as a document that justifies European domination of the Americas. The emblematic figure in such anti-colonialist American Shakespeares is perhaps Aimé Césaire's new Caliban in 1968's *Une Tempête* (*A Tempest*), who enters the play shouting the Swahili word for 'freedom' and orders Prospero to 'Call me X… Like a man without a name.

Or, to be more precise, a man whose name has been stolen' ([1968] 2002: 20). *Une Tempête* was the third in Césaire's series of pan-Africanist plays from the 1960s, and its place at the end of this series suggests that for Césaire, not only is Shakespeare a colonial property that can be seized and reappropriated, but also that undoing the hold of European high culture can be as much an act of rebellion as political struggle in the streets.[1]

Nonetheless, the idea of an essential Africanity – *négritude* – promulgated by Césaire and his contemporaries as a weapon against the sense of inferiority imposed by centuries of white colonial domination has been criticized for both its political and aesthetic shortcomings.[2] Poet-critic Edward Brathwaite wondered if pan-African revivals, even if they were politically valuable, were not also historically blind to the difficulty of uprooting the deep shame and self-loathing surrounding the Caribbean's African past, a shame that he insisted was not only colonialism's poisonous detritus, but one of its deliberately chosen methods of domination (1974: 73–8).[3] As balefully as such mental barriers to embracing the African part of African American identity may have operated, the sheer facts of time and distance also affected the effort. There could be no straight line back to an uncomplicated embrace of a generative African identity, if the very presence of Black people in the new world is the result of traumatic separation from their homelands (more than one place of origin, instead of an undifferentiated 'Africa'), of forced transportation across unknown oceans, of displacement, rupture and deliberate dispersion of people from the same place. The idealized 'Africa' from which slaves were transported was no longer there, itself as marked and changed by the effects of colonialism as were her far-flung sons and daughters.

A later generation of postcolonial critics has embraced this history of fragmentation and displacement as the fertile origin of modern Black identities. For Stuart Hall, for example, the new world of the Americas is 'the beginning of diaspora, of diversity, of hybridity and difference' (1990: 235). Accepting the trauma of the Middle Passage as a necessary starting point for the generation of modern Black identities in the New World, Hall advocates for a diasporic identity that embraces its origins in division, 'defined … not by essence or purity, but by the recognition of a necessary heterogeneity and diversity; by a conception of "identity" which lives with and through, not despite, difference' (1990: 235). In this chapter, I follow Hall by acknowledging the significance a specifically African American identity can have as the generator of a self-authorized sense of Blackness, broadly construing 'American' to include the Caribbean and South America as well as the continental US.

Many Black Shakespeares produced within the United States in particular have argued for a relationship to the early modern text based on the possibility of an experimental, even playful hybridity rather than on revolutionary defiance. Such productions as the Chicago-based Ethiopian Art Players' 1923 staging of a circus-themed *Comedy of Errors* accompanied by a live jazz band, the 1939 Broadway *Swingin' the Dream* with the Dandridge Sisters as brown-skinned fairies and Louis Armstrong as Bottom, or 1997s *Play On!* – *Twelfth Night* transposed to Harlem with a Duke Ellington score – share a vision of Black culture as the depository of glamour, energy and syncopated fun. All are set to a jazz soundtrack, counterbalancing Shakespeare's creative authority with that of the most distinctively American contribution to world culture. All also offer an alternative to Césaire's sense of an international Black time that imagines Shakespeare only as an initial act whose repudiation can lead to a revolutionary present. And all underscore how the work of adapting Shakespeare is also a form of historicizing: these modern musical revisions focus their sense of Black history around the history of Black people in the United States as they rewrite Shakespeare to produce another kind of black subject than Césaire's – instead of one who rebels, one who swings (Corrigan 2005).

The phenomenon of swing as a factor in Black American adaptations of Shakespeare is less important here as a musical category than as an aesthetic and performative one. One might think, for example, of the work Louis Armstrong did in Chicago and New York in the mid-1920s as a live accompanist for showings of silent movies and tap dancers and at dance clubs at the same time he was more permanently defining the role of improvisation in jazz on pioneering records like 'Heebie Jeebies' and 'West End Blues'. Those records announce and preserve Armstrong's genius as a soloist, but the live work was just as important an articulation of the communal and improvisatory nature of jazz, as dancers' rhythms bounced off the rhythm of the musicians' playing and as musicians and dancers egged each other on (Harker 2008: 67–121).[4] Such performances went beyond mere recitals into the realm of what Diana Taylor calls the 'animative', which she defines as 'part movement; part identity, being, or soul, as in anima or life' (2007: 1417). While the performative might adequately describe the rituals of refereeing a football match and determining a winner, she explains, the animative 'points to the ruckus that breaks out in the stadium' (1417). This sense of joyful, mutually creative ruckus marks the Black musical Shakespeares I note above. A surviving script for *Swingin' the Dream*'s version of *A Midsummer Night's Dream*'s Pyramus and Thisbe scene notes how the show used a jazz animative to supplement and open up its Shakespeare. Peter Quince's introduction of his unpromising actors was accompanied by a version of 'St. Louis Blues', while the lovers' declaration of their passion comes over 'I Can't Give You Anything But Love'. Armstrong played a trumpet version of 'Ain't Misbehavin' as Pyramus realizes Thisbe is late to their meeting and wonders where she is.[5]

AT THE GROVE THEATRE: WILLIAM ALEXANDER BROWN'S AFRICAN COMPANY

I read the sense of creative ruckus that Taylor prizes in the records of William Alexander Brown's African Company's performances before racially integrated audiences in lower Manhattan, in the second decade of the nineteenth century. This group of Black actors not only performed Shakespeare but also worked in such other popular modes as pantomime, broad urban comedy and adventure melodramas, some with Black protagonists – such as James Hewlett's 1821 *Othello* and a dramatization of William Earle's 1800 novel *Obi: or, The History of Three-Fingered Jack* – and some without. Their 1823 *Richard III* at the Grove Theatre was their last production, shut down by the combined power of racial animus, class anxiety and economic competition marshalled by Stephen Price, manager of the rival Park

Theatre. Brown and his actors were arrested and jailed, released only on the promise never to perform Shakespeare again.[6]

William Brown first operated an outdoor pleasure garden in the Five Points district that attracted a racially mixed working-class crowd of Irish immigrants and free Blacks. He then opened indoor theatres on Thomas Street and Mercer Street north of Houston and briefly on Park Row, and finally built a new theatre near the corner of Bleecker and Mercer Street. His entertainment spaces were open to both Blacks and whites, planted in poor neighbourhoods whose residents were nevertheless willing to pay for fun. Both Brown and Hewlett, his leading man, were early products of Paul Gilroy's Black Atlantic, serving as stewards on ships sailing between England and the United States and around the Caribbean before settling in New York. There is something intriguingly modern about Brown's international formation and his African Theatre's admittance of racially integrated audiences (whites were seated in the balcony, the place reserved for Blacks in most white theatres) to watch Black people performing. The African Grove expressed the cultural vitality of working-class New York, as Black people and white people gathered to drink, learn new dances from each other and entertain themselves as citizens of their post-revolutionary generation (White 2007: 7–67). Although the African Theatre welcomed white people, Brown mounted productions that specifically spoke to the memories and knowledge of his Black audience. He added a new scene of a slave auction in Charleston to William Moncrieff's popular musical *Tom and Jerry; or, Life in London*, and staged *Obi*, a play about a runaway Jamaican slave who flees to his island's mountains to continue his revolt (with the aid of *obeah*, a shamanistic practice connected to voudou) but is finally defeated by an army of slaves still loyal to their masters.[7]

Slavery's appearance in the African Theatre's repertory spoke to Brown's emerging Black audience, and articulated a Black response to the slave revolts that marked the first decades of the nineteenth century.[8] Whites' fear of slave uprisings was perhaps exacerbated by the approaching end of slavery in New York. As late as 1790 four out of every ten households within a fifteen-mile radius of New York City had owned at least one slave, a rate of slave ownership higher than could be found in Virginia or most of South Carolina, and the rate of slave ownership would increase 33 per cent by 1800 (White 2007: 12–13). Even though full abolition would not come to New York until 4 July 1827, the first decades of the century often saw city slaves engaged in legal negotiation, and outright resistance directly challenged the institution's authority long before then. The African Grove can be seen as part of an increasing process of community-building and civic and cultural self-assertion. Freedom was coming, and the audiences of the African Theatre gathered there as much to remember – or imagine – an heroic past as to celebrate their place at the edge of a bright future.

Stories in New York's *National Advocate* newspaper in the 1820s reflect how frightening the idea of free blacks was to the city's white majority. In these fevered accounts, New York seems to be swarming with Africans: Black people wearing fancy clothes and accessories, speaking rudely to white people, shoving them off the sidewalks. One white man, Isaiah Kip, reported to the police that he was walking along Broadway at about 10.00 pm in the evening in May of 1812, when he was accosted by four Black women, who 'spoke to him in a very vulgar obscene manner calling him Blue Bollocks' (qtd. in White 2007: 57), then pushed him to the ground and continued to hurl abuse at him. A Black man elbowed a white woman out of his way on the sidewalk, exclaiming, 'Damn these white people, there's no getting along for them' (qtd. in White 2007: 58). The African Company's Shakespeare bust came during this period of increasing white anxiety, in the looming shadow of abolition, when the only social order people had ever known was about to be completely overturned.

The idea of Black people playing Shakespeare before integrated audiences struck the authorities in early-nineteenth-century New York as so threatening and inappropriate that they criminalized it. Shakespeare seemed worth it to both sides, perhaps especially to a threatened white majority that felt it necessary to let the city's Black citizens know they were under surveillance, and that the ways in which they could make their presence in the city known were going to be sharply limited. Locking up Black people for playing Shakespeare was a way of asserting white control over public space and of policing access to what Simon Gikandi calls the 'culture of taste' (2011: xiii), markers of civility that were deemed off-limits to Black people, who had been socially defined only through bondage. Gikandi argues that such markers in fact depended on the abjection and ugliness associated with slaves and slavery to make themselves legible. Black people approaching self-expression freely, openly, and even joyfully, instead of only on the margins and in what small private corners of slave culture they could claim for themselves under a regime of white supremacy, was unthinkable even when white New Yorkers came face to face with it.

But as I noted, Shakespeare was only part of the African Theatre's repertory. Plays like *Obi* or the new slave auction scene in *Tom and Jerry* solicited an audience response that was only made possible through the past trauma of enslavement, experienced through Black people's shared history and their communal memories. We know that Brown was the first Black American dramatist. His *The Drama of King Shotaway* was about the black Carib leader Joseph Chatoyer who led a rebellion against the British governors of the island of St Vincent in 1769 as they attempted to push Chatoyer's people off their territory and seize their land. Chatoyer fought the British garrison and reserves sent from England to a standstill, and four years of conflict ended with a partition of the island between the British and the Caribs. As New York entered the last stages of its life as slave territory, William Brown produced a play about Black people fighting back and holding their own against the power of a white empire. Unfortunately, the play is lost; no copy of *The Drama of King Shotaway* survives.

What we do have from the theatre's papers is the tantalizing 'Soliloquy of a Maroon Chief in Jamaica' from 1821, whose headnote describes it as being 'Lately Spoken at the African Theatre'.[9] Probably designed to be spoken from the stage before or after a regular performance, it directly engages with the charged racial consciousness of the day, as New York struggled with the social and civic implications of abolition. The speaker of the piece is a maroon, a slave who escaped to the often mountainous interiors of the Caribbean's slave territories, sometimes intermarrying with indigenous tribes, and who established free armed communities that existed in uneasy truce with colonial authorities. He scornfully rejects the emerging scientific racism of the day:

Are we the links 'twixt men and monkeys then?
Or are we all baboons? or not all men?
O lily-tinctured liars! o'er whom terror
Hangs her white flag! why need I prove your error?

(2)

Instead, he proclaims pride in the physiognomy that a racist order deemed a sign of inferiority: 'If our lips are thicker, be it known, / That nature, anxious for her children's bliss, / Vowchsafed them for a more capacious kiss' (4).

More than pride in his physical features, the speaker also proclaims his possession of a passionate moral consciousness that slaveholders' culture denied that he was capable of experiencing:

And if to feel, till feeling is no more,
A wrong, and wear it in the vital core,—
If this be godlike, even in chains, and rods,
And slavery, we assimilate the gods!

(4)

The author of the piece has his rebel chieftain speak in a poetic vocabulary that refers scornfully to the arts of European culture, which – as Lamming was to argue in the mid-twentieth century – whites have used as cultural weapons to enforce their political and economic power over Blacks: 'What can those *nine* gods teach, whom ye adore?' Africans may lack access to Europeans' 'learning, priestcraft, medicine, wit, or wealth', but such artifacts of their civilization are ultimately meaningless, since they cannot '[w]het appetite, or give immortal health… / Man, in himself content, alone is blest, / Smoke, shadows, bubbles, wind, is all the rest!'. Using whites' own cultural referents to deny the inherent superiority of European ways, the speaker here inverts the rhetorical device James Mulholland has observed in eighteenth-century British poetry that had its nonwhite characters speak in classical tropes and forms in order to indicate their secure containment within colonial culture, whatever opposition or resistance they might be expressing (2013: 156–66). Instead, the maroon chieftain speaks in European voice in order to reject white supremacy. A rebellious subject of slaveholding culture, he nevertheless maintains a subjectivity that cannot be defined by it.

The Maroon Chief draws from and speaks from within a completely different cultural archive from the one white New York used to derive its historical understanding of what Black people were or could be. We don't know when or even if the 'Soliloquy' was actually performed, and *The Drama of King Shotaway* is completely lost. No matter. Both texts nevertheless survive as part of a repertoire of Black 'embodied memory… performances, gestures, orality, movement, dance, singing' (Taylor 2007: 20) that worked to preserve and transmit Black actors' and audiences' sense of what it meant to be Black and free in the city. In contrast to the compulsory obeisance to the 'sacred gang' of canonical British writers Lamming describes, his colonial contemporaries as being trapped within even as they struggled to write themselves into their own histories and cultures, we can see Brown's actors improvising themselves away from any notion of the sanctity of the literary text. They borrowed Moncrieff's *Tom and Jerry*, a lighthearted comedy with songs about two young men loose in the big city, but made it portray Africans being sold on the block as part of the play's portrait of urban experience. As the city quailed before increasing numbers of Black people daring to behave as if they too were arrogant free New Yorkers (at least as the *National Advocate* had it), they revised received white social texts about Black presumption by putting on a play about a slave revolt. They created an oration wherein a rebellious slave demolished whites' assertions of Black inferiority and difference, even as he proclaimed his formation by standards that did not belong to white people: '[W]e can dream – O yes! – of Afric's plains' (4). And in addition to helping to make a new urban working-class culture as they exchanged new dances and new ways of bearing themselves among the mixed-race entertainment seekers at the African Grove, they demonstrated their response to the dominant culture trying to close itself to their acts of regeneration and recreation by appropriating Shakespeare.

'SAY YA SHAKESPEARE LIKE YA WANT': CARLYLE BROWN'S *THE AFRICAN COMPANY PRESENTS 'RICHARD III'*

Carlyle Brown's 1988 *The African Company Presents 'Richard III'* sets out to resurrect and memorialize the ambition and creativity of William Brown's enterprise. But Carlyle Brown's play is also, and more largely, interested in exploring a Black animative's appropriation of Shakespearean texts and characters. How, he asks, does Shakespeare or anything else achieve meaning within the resources and values of Black performance? How can the ghost of a specifically Black animative manifest in the Shakespearean text?

In *Cities of the Dead: Circum-Atlantic Performance*, Joseph Roach suggests to us that when bodies in motion remember and performatively reproduce history – and here I am especially thinking of the history of Shakespeare's reception and ideological utility in the early republic – they not only mount a distant event for consumption in the present, but also make claims about the meaning of that event (1996: 25–6). This claiming and re-enactment proceeds almost in defiance of the difficulties that postcolonial critics like Stuart Hall note in recovering the past. When animated bodies were raced as Black, as they were in the African Company, the transmission of meaning is complicated by the status of Black bodies as symbols and vehicles of strictly limited meanings. For William Alexander Brown, anything was possible in the crucible of early Manhattan, an outpost in Roach's 'circum-Atlantic', which hosted the cultural inventions born of the interactions of multiple races, nations and peoples. But William Brown's dramatic work also took place in a city struggling to define and stabilize its social hierarchies in the face of such mixture, and the pressing new claims to national, racial and civic identities it engendered. Brown's choice to play Shakespeare, and especially the Colley Cibber *Richard III* then dominating American and British stages, with its extra-deceitful and wicked Gloucester, managed to aggravate all those urban anxieties at once.[10] What meanings could audiences in a socially tense city take away from the sight of a scheming, seductive, murderous – and now *Black* – antihero? The record of the African Company's suppression and dispersal suggests that the performance generated unbearable anxiety for the white majority.

In Carlyle Brown's play, which draws us into the performance history of Black Shakespeare, we hear early about the Africanist creative ruckus that William Brown's company celebrated and that the forces of an official New York sought to suppress when Ann Johnson, one of the company's part-time actors, tells her friend Sarah about a wild episode the night before in the African Grove: 'Folks was out strollin' as usual. Walkin' all sadity like. Sashayin' up and down the African Grove, like them negros thought they was kings and queens, dukes and duchesses or somethin'. But Shakespeare come and make 'em step out them Sunday attitudes. Poundin' that drum a his'.[11] Within the play, 'Shakespeare' is a neighbourhood character known as Papa Shakespeare, mostly unremarkable but capable of creating irresistible popular disturbances through the power of his drumming:

> No he wasn't drunk. But he was a reelin' honey. Had his neck down and his head cocked to the side with his shoulders rolled up like so…. Eye-whites was red as cow peas. Eyeballs rolled back up into his head and he was a swayin'…. It was like he had stepped right out a life itself and was looking around at it, like it was a dream he was dreamin'. Them Negroes who before was prancin' up and down the African Grove like a flock a peacocks, start to trip and stumble. And it seem like the only thing that kept 'em all from fallin' down was the sound a Shakespeare's drum. Ka-boom, ka-boom, ka-boom. And just like that, folks start to dancin'. Dancin' like they was runnin' from death.
>
> (9–10)

'Negroes… prancin' up and down the African Grove' is an apt descriptor for the kind of social anxiety the formation of communities of free Black in the United States' great northern and western cities provoked among white observers in the years before the Civil War. 'Prancin'' also captures a certain kind of performative style of showing off and self-display called up by the act of these residents' walking out together on Sundays, when they were off from work and free to associate and play and create together. Yet Ann Johnson's characterization of the promenaders as 'sadity' suggests that she sees the showy way her neighbours present themselves as still in fact defined by white rules of comportment. If white people thought Black ones should be meek and submissive, then they would choose instead to be flashy and elegant, promenading like 'dukes and 'duchesses' more to upset white expectation than to satisfy their own expressive desires. But the quiet, polite, modest behaviour white people thought appropriate for them as well as the fancy demeanour they adopted for themselves are both revealed to be shams. When Papa Shakespeare pounds that drum, by contrast, an Africanist swing is going to move them, whether they want to be moved or not.

The phenomenon of free Blacks on weekend self-display struck many white observers in antebellum cities as simultaneously ridiculous and unsettling. Blackface minstrelsy, on the rise in the decades after the African Company was run out of business, would work at least in part to relieve white anxiety about the places Black people would occupy in the developing republic through racist caricatures of Black performance (Lott 2013: 66–91). However, the spectacle of real Black men and women, choosing to make themselves undeniably visible through their weekend choices of clothes, accessories and bodily carriage, emphatically dismissed the subordinate places they had been assigned by white society, and directly challenged white authority to name and confine them. Black people wearing elaborate clothing, hairdos and accessories, 'like all other Dandies who measure their importance by their Dress' acted as though they had 'entirely forgotten' who they actually were, and the 'grade and station' they really occupied (qtd. in White and White 1998: 5). The possibility that would truly unsettle American cities in the years before the civil war was not only that festive Sunday demonstrations announced that Black participants had forgotten who they were, but that they were remembering and expressing themselves in ways that ran directly counter to white productions of Black identities.

Carlyle Brown's imagining of Papa Shakespeare's personal history illustrates the layering of African and American identities that helped to produce Blackness in antebellum New York. When he was a slave in the Caribbean, before he came to New York, he functioned as a kind of translator of all the different languages slaves arrived speaking on his plantation, making it possible for them to understand the demands of the whites and more importantly to understand each other. Keeping slaves who couldn't yet speak English from communicating with each other in their own language was a common method slaveowners used to minimize the possibility of their chattel's planning rebellion. His former master derisively started calling him 'Papa Shakespeare' in mockery of the nonsense he presumed the old slave was speaking. What he was actually doing was translating 'what the white man is saying' for other slaves, as well as helping them understand each other's languages. More importantly, he preserved and reproduced the sounds of their speech: 'Even now, I hear them. They mouths and they tongues, they go knockin' and rollin'… I hear them. They're in my head and will stay there so long as I remember' (32).

The creative power and pleasure summoned by Papa Shakespeare's drumming – its improvisatory swing – affirms the existence of a Black public sphere in a moment of primal joy that transcends the various pretensions and disguises individual freedmen and freedwomen must assume in order to make themselves new in the crucible of their city. *The African Company Presents* imagines William Brown's actors summoning the same kind of power as they shuttle messages from Shakespeare to the audiences of poor working people of both races, hungry for entertainment and sensation, who come to hear them. For Brown's actors, Shakespeare is only another kind of booming drum for activating the expressive power they already possess: 'Forgets what them fancy-full people think, them high-blowin' elitists', Brown tells actor James Hewlett, his Richard III, 'and say ya Shakespeare like ya want. "Now is de winter of our discontentment made de glorious summer by dis son a New

York." They gonna love it' (43). Such claiming of Shakespeare for a Black urban animative, full of flash and self-authorizing, self-reflecting pleasure – 'dis son a New York' – presents itself as a powerful alternative to Césaire's revolutionary defiance. I would argue that Carlyle Brown is not interested merely in asserting Black people's right to play Shakespeare, but much more largely in asserting their right to play *with* him. Indeed, *The African Company Presents* suggests that William Brown's Black actors could mount their generative interchange with Shakespeare precisely because of the tragedy and grandeur of their lives as they moved from slavery to freedom and made themselves new in New York. At the beginning of the twentieth century, Adrienne Herndon began directing an annual Shakespeare production at Atlanta University, which had been founded in 1867 to educate former slaves. She believed that her students had a particular affinity for Shakespeare. 'To interpret the depth of the human heart and bring it into another consciousness', she wrote, 'one must have lived and suffered… and who among the Negro race has not received this sympathetic touch as a birthright? A more dramatic life than the one given the American Negro can hardly be imagined' (qtd. in Henderson 2016: 86).

Carlyle Brown's characters intuit that Shakespeare can be a means of authorizing personal experience and thus of writing themselves into the American cultural record, but some of them turn away from the realization. At first, Ann, who joins the company to play Lady Anne, complains that she finds the scene where her character succumbs to Richard over her husband's casket too unbelievable to play. Finally, however, she reveals that the scene's juxtaposition of implicit violence and sexual submission feels so real to her that she can't treat it as only make-believe:

> I don't have a husband. I don't know who my father is, nor my mother. There's just me. Every colored child come into this world is in a little basket on somebody's door step. And if she's a girl, when she gets older where she starts lookin' like a woman, there is always some King Richard who wants to lie with her. And like it say in that play, they'll have us, but they won't keep us long.
>
> (24)

Such personal identification with Shakespeare's characters is, of course, precisely what *Une Tempête* rejects; Césaire's Caliban scorns Ariel's 'Uncle Tom patience' (39) for putting up with what he sees as Prospero's tyranny in the hopes of eventual freedom. But in *The African Company*, characters' identification with the Shakespearean stories William Brown wants them to stage is normalized by their struggles to recreate themselves as free citizens, since to a greater or lesser degree they must pretend to be someone they are not in order to survive in the city after they escape slavery.

In the play, William Brown reminds his leading man James Hewlett of the time he discovered him, sneaking off a ship from the West Indies in New York harbour in an attempt to escape his life as a slave on a sugar plantation. At first, Hewlett was incompetent at performing his new role: 'I said to myself, now there's a Negro tryin' to escape… Had to teach him how to walk. Walk like a sailor. With big, beamy strides and short sturdy steps like the ground might swell up underneath ya like a giant rollin' sea and knock ya down' (16). He notes how readily Hewlett took to his new disguise, as 'Jimmy become a kind of a playwrighter. A playwrighter creatin' the character of James Hewlett. Free Negro, born in Rockaway Island, New York City. Singer, Shakespearean imitator, disguised as a man-servant and as a waiter' (16). As Hewlett himself remarks, 'Colored folk act all the time.... We all charade the great role of the happy, obedient Negros advancin'. What is that, if it ain't actin'?' (13). Papa Shakespeare, once enslaved with William Brown in the Caribbean, agrees: 'And de whole world is de stage' (13).

Despite their skills in improvisation and translation, at the end of the play, William Brown and his actors are all in jail, effectively accused of performative defiance of white privilege. Unlike a postcolonial Shakespeare that posits an antagonistic relationship between the power of the canonical text and the culture of the colonized, resisting the degree to which the status of colonial subjects is dictated by the linguistic authority of the colonizer *The African Company Presents* holds out the possibility that however stringently the verbal and performative power of its Black characters is policed, they will inevitably act out. Perfectly willing to give up performing Shakespeare – 'What, we got to do Shakespeare like his mouth the only mouth what speak? ... Taste just as good sayin' words comin' from one who knows who you are, than one who don't know ya a'tall' (53) – the imprisoned Brown ends the play reciting a passage from his original drama about Joseph Chatoyer, thus underlining the play's concern with history, memory and performance. More than merely remembering Shakespeare, reproducing, re-enacting and re-framing his works for a Black audience underlines the significance of performance in making culture—and identifies it as a stepping-stone toward liberation.

NOTES

1   The two earlier plays were *La tragédie du roi Christophe* (1963), about the general who declared himself king of Haiti in 1811, and *Un saison au Congo* (1966), on the assassination of Patrice Lumumba, first prime minister of the Independent Democratic Republic of the Congo after that nation ended Belgium's colonial rule.

2   In *The Wretched of the Earth*, Frantz Fanon offers an extended critique of *négritude* which rejects what he saw as its apolitical nature (1963: 210–24). Doris Garraway (2010: 74–6) reviews more of these critiques.

3   Fanon remarked of this deeply inculcated sense of shame that 'Colonialism is not satisfied merely with holding a people in its grip and emptying the native's brain of all form and content. By a kind of perverted logic, it turns to the past of the oppressed people, and distorts, disfigures, and destroys it' (1963: 209).

4   Shortly after Armstrong arrived in New York to join Fletcher Henderson's house band at the Roseland ballroom, the dancers loved his work on 'Shanghai Shuffle' so much that they made him play ten choruses and one dancer ended the performance by coming to the bandstand to lift Armstrong up on his shoulders (Teachout 2009: 85).

5   The notated script is included in Corrigan (2005).

6   For discussion of the African Grove Theatre, see Marvin McAllister (2003). On
     Brown's career and repertory, which included scenes from *Julius Caesar* and *Macbeth*
     as well as full Shakespeare plays and other works, see Hill and Hatch (2003: 27–36).
     On Hewlett's career, see Hill (1984: 12–16).

7   William Earle's epistolary novel, *Obi; or The History of Three-Fingered Jack*, loosely
     based on the life of Black Jamaican outlaw Jack Mansong, was published in London
     in 1800; John Fawcett's pantomime *Obi, or Three Finger'd Jack*, followed later that
     year and Earle's novel was republished in Worcester, Massachusetts in 1804. These
     movements into different media and across the Atlantic support my observation of the
     multiple social formations that drove William Brown's work at the African Theatre.

8   In the wake of the Haitian Revolution of 1791, slave revolts broke out across the
     Caribbean and the southern United States, including Louisiana's Pointe Coupée
     Conspiracy in 1795, Gabriel Prosser's Rebellion in Virginia in 1800, Barbados'
     Bussa's Rebellion in 1816 and Denmark Vesey's thwarted Charleston uprising in
     1821.

9   The soliloquy and a critical discussion appear in Warner (2001). I provide page
     references to the soliloquy parenthetically in my text.

10   Cibber's version of the play premiered in 1699 and was performed until the mid-
     nineteenth century. His changes to the Shakespearean text made the play more
     violent – the young princes in the Tower are murdered onstage – and its main
     character more sensationally evil. On body and spectacle in this adaptation, see
     Fawcett (2011).

11   *The African Company Presents 'Richard III'* (New York, NY: Dramatists Play Service,
     1994), 9. I provide subsequent references parenthetically.

REFERENCES

Brathwaite, E. (1974), 'The African Presence in Caribbean Literature', *Daedalus* 103 (2):
     73–109.
Brown, C. (1994), *The African Company Presents 'Richard III'*, New York, NY: Dramatists
     Play Service.
Césaire, A. ([1968] 2002), *A Tempest*, trans. Richard Miller, New York, NY: TCG
     Translations.
Corrigan, A. (2005), 'Jazz, Shakespeare, and Hybridity: A Script Excerpt from *Swingin'
     the Dream*',', *Borrowers and Lenders* 1 (1). Available online: https://openjournals.libs.
     uga.edu/borrowers/article/view/2252 (accessed 27 July 2020).
Fanon, F. (1963), *The Wretched of the Earth*, trans. C. Farrington, New York, NY: Grove
     Weidenfeld.
Fawcett, J. H. (2011), 'The Overexpressive Celebrity and the Deformed King: Recasting
     the Spectacle as Subject in Colley Cibber's *Richard III*', *PMLA* 126 (4): 950–65.
Garraway, D. (2010), '"What is Mine": Césairean Negritude Between the Particular and
     the Universal', *Research in African Literatures* 41 (1): 74–6.
Gikandi, S. (2011), *Slavery and the Culture of Taste*, Princeton, NJ: Princeton University
     Press.

Hall, S. (1990), 'Cultural Identity and Diaspora', in J. Rutherford (ed.), *Identity: Community, Culture, Difference*, 231–42, London: Lawrence and Wishart.

Harker, B. (2008), 'Louis Armstrong, Eccentric Dancing, and the Evolution of Jazz on the Eve of Swing', *Journal of the American Musicological Society* 61 (1): 67–121.

Henderson, A. B. (2016), 'The Work and Legacy of Adrienne Elizabeth McNeil Herndon at Atlanta University, 1895–1910', *Phylon* 53 (1): 80–101.

Hill, E. and J. Hatch, (2003), *A History of African American Theatre*, Cambridge: Cambridge University Press.

Hill, E. (1984), *Shakespeare in Sable: A History of Black Shakespearean Actors*, Amherst, MA: University of Massachusetts Press.

Lamming, G. ([1960] 1992), *The Pleasures of Exile*, Ann Arbor, MI: University of Michigan Press.

Lanier, D. (2014), 'Shakespearean Rhizomatics: Adaptation, Ethics, Value', in A. Huang and E. Rivlin (eds), *Shakespeare and the Ethics of Appropriation*, 22–3, New York, NY: Palgrave Macmillan.

Lott, E. ([1993]; 2013), *Love and Theft: Blackface Minstrelsy and the American Working Class*, New York, NY: Oxford University Press.

McAllister, M. (2003), *White People Do Not Know How to Behave at Entertainments Designed for Ladies and Gentlemen of Colour: William Brown's African and American Theatre*, Chapel Hill, NC: University of North Carolina Press.

Mulholland, J. (2013), *Sounding Imperial: Poetic Voice and the Politics of Empire, 1730–1820*, Baltimore, NJ: Johns Hopkins University Press.

Powell, R. J. (2001), '*Sartor Africanus*', in S. Fillin-Yeh (ed.), *Dandies: Fashion and Finesse in Art and Culture*, 220–4, New York, NY: New York University Press.

Roach, J. (1996), *Cities of the Dead: Circum-Atlantic Performance*, New York, NY: Columbia University Press.

Taylor, D. (2003), *The Archive and the Repertoire: Performing Cultural Memory in the Americas*, Durham: Duke University Press.

Taylor, D. (2007), 'Remapping Genre Through Performance: From "American" to "Hemispheric" Studies', *PMLA* 122 (5): 1416–30.

Teachout, T. (2009), *Pops: A Life of Louis Armstrong*, Boston: Houghton Mifflin.

Warner, M. et al. (2001), 'A Soliloquy "Lately Spoken at the African Theatre": Race and the Public Sphere in New York City, 1821', *American Literature* 73 (1): 1–46.

White, S. (2007), *Stories of Freedom in Black New York*, Cambridge, MA: Harvard University Press.

White, S. and G. White (1998), *Stylin': African American Expressive Culture from its Beginnings to the Zoot Suit*, Ithaca, NY: Cornell University Press.

'Does anyone know another text?': Post-migratory *Othello* adaptations on the German-speaking stage

SABINE SCHÜLTING

In Germany, unlike in the UK or France, it is not a matter of course to be acknowledged as a member of public life if your ancestors were not born in the country. Theatre artists with a so-called 'background of migration' are still the exception. [...] There are hardly any dramatic texts that offer narrativizations or an ideology critique of the stories, experiences and discourses in this field. [...] In those contexts where the theme of migration is not excluded from the start, there is often a sensationalist exploitation of clichés. The figure of the migrant is represented, in an act of quasi-ventriloquism, by white 'bio-German' speakers; at best it is authenticated by actors with the 'correct' ethnic background.

(Langhoff 2011)[1]

These are Shermin Langhoff's words in an interview published in March 2011, in which she discussed the policy of Ballhaus Naunynstraße, a small publicly funded theatre in Berlin, Germany. Her critique of the theatre scene in Germany shall serve as my point of departure for a discussion of *Othello* adaptations that were produced in the last two decades for stages in Germany, Austria and Switzerland. What unites their divergent approaches to the tragedy and its eponymous hero is that they all defamiliarize and alter the canonical Shakespeare in order to gauge the potential (and the limits) of classical drama in general, and Shakespeare in particular, for an exploration of a society shaped by migration.

Langhoff served as the artistic director of Ballhaus Naunynstraße from 2008 until 2013 when she became director of the prestigious Maxim Gorki Theater in Berlin.

She is credited with having coined the term 'post-migratory' (*postmigrantisch*) to characterize the policy of the Ballhaus and now also the Gorki. In the last decade, the term has slowly moved from the cultural scene into German politics and the social sciences. Not unlike the term 'postcolonial', 'post-migratory' is not a strictly temporal concept, but refers more expansively to the impact of migration on a large part of the population – as either biographical fact, family narrative or collective experience[2] – as well as to the political and cultural consequences of, and critical responses to, a history and present of migration. Migration is understood to constitute a major point of reference in conflict-ridden processes of personal and collective identification as well as social classification; it shapes power relations and transforms cultural arenas and institutions (Foroutan 2016: 231). A post-migratory agenda in the theatres, however, does not merely focus on migrants and migration in a narrow sense. Instead, it offers a forum to explore the complex societal and cultural transformations brought about by migration. It is therefore a project that requires the revision of both theatre repertoires and the composition of theatre ensembles.

How does Shakespeare fit in? Contemporary authors, translators and directors, often with their own personal or family histories of migration, have (in addition to writing and staging new plays) reworked Shakespeare for the demands of the post-migratory stage. Shakespeare adaptations written and/or produced by Feridun Zaimoğlu, Nuran David Calis, Asli Kişlal or the Gintersdorfer/Klaßen theatre group are characterized by a polyphony of dissenting and differing voices, by linguistic diversity, translations into non-standard varieties and sociolects, quotations from current political and cultural debates, and the inclusion of art forms (such as rap, for example) that in Germany tend to be associated with post-migratory youth subcultures. Othello functions as an ambiguous figure, alternating between a metaphor of cultural difference and a role model for identification, both adopted and rejected by immigrants, Black and People of Colour in Germany. Post-migratory Shakespeare adaptations thus differ considerably from 'globalized Shakespeares', which often imply a 'homogenous global culture dictated by the interests of transnational capital emanating (usually) from the United States and northern Europe', as William B. Worthen (2003: 123) has put it. Instead of celebrating multiculturalism, the adaptations that I call 'post-migratory Shakespeares' are often disturbing in their exploration of the sharp conflicts in a society shaped by migration as well as in their focus on racist violence and strategies of social exclusion. Moreover, the focus of these adaptations on the ongoing public debate about migration is frequently combined with an irreverent revision of the cultural signification of Shakespeare in Germany. Shakespeare on German-speaking stages is a kind of 'post-migrant' himself, because he is and is not German. His 'foreign' origin has not been completely effaced, despite the fact that since the nineteenth century, he has been considered 'the third German classical author' (alongside Goethe and Schiller) whose poetry and plays have been translated innumerable times into German, for every new generation. It is the 'assimilated' Shakespeare of bourgeois German bardolatry that post-migratory theatre defamiliarizes, in the course transforming the plays into a kind of cultural laboratory.

Othello is the Shakespeare play that in the last decade has most often been adapted to the post-migratory stage. This is of course due to the play's concern with migration and racial differences, but many recent adaptations have also used the play meta-dramatically to explore the history of representing Blackness on the German-speaking stage and comment on the situation of immigrants in the theatres. In 2002, Christopher Balme polemically asked: 'How black must Othello be?' Balme argues that representations of Othello metonymically refer to a larger problem, namely the representation of cultural and racial differences on the German stage. He draws attention to the absence of ethnically diverse theatre ensembles and a general tendency to avoid intercultural topics or productions (2002: 106; see also Kolesch 2016). Until very recently, German theatres generally cast White actors in the role of Othello, sometimes in blackface. It was only in 2012 that the practice of blackfacing triggered a massive public controversy (cf. Sieg 2015), which indicated a new awareness of racial representation. In the two decades since the publication of Balme's essay, the composition of theatre ensembles has also slowly changed, but multi-ethnic ensembles such as the one at the Maxim Gorki Theater are still the exception.

The *Othello* adaptations discussed in this chapter all address these problems by combining the thematic exploration of post-migratory identities with a meta-dramatic reflection of the possibilities and the problems that Shakespeare's *Othello* poses for the post-migratory stage as well as for theatre ensembles, be they either White or multi-ethnic. I will focus in particular on the following adaptations (and their original stage productions):[3]

- Luk Perceval's *Othello* (translated/adapted by Feridun Zaimoğlu and Günter Senkel; Munich, Kammerspiele, 2003);
- Gintersdorfer/Klaßen's *Othello, c'est qui?* (Hamburg, Kampnagel, 2008);
- Asli Kişlal's *How to Kill an Othello* (adapted by Blair Darby and daskunst; Vienna, Theater Nestroyhof Hamakom, 2012);
- Christian Weise's *Othello* (adapted by Soeren Voima; Berlin, Gorki Theater, 2016); and
- Nuran Calis's *Othello X* (Theater Basel, 2018).

As Linda Hutcheon has reminded us, the term 'adaptation' does not merely refer to 'an announced and extensive transposition of a particular work or works' but also to '*a process of creation*' (2006: 7–8, emphasis in the original). My chapter will concentrate in particular on this second aspect. Nevertheless, I discuss the five adaptations/productions less as independent works of art in their own right (which they certainly are) than as occasions to consider the various practices and strategies employed to adapt Shakespeare to the contemporary stage. Rather than analysing the plays in their chronological order in which they are listed above, the analysis will proceed thematically and pay particular attention to the strategies they share: the reflection on and deviation from stage traditions, a marked intertextuality and intermediality and a dynamic engagement with language.

The radical innovations that these adaptations bring to German-speaking theatres should not be underestimated. They add to the debates on what has been called German 'directors' theatre' (*Regietheater*), criticized by those who demand faithfulness to the 'original'. In his history of *Shakespeare on the German Stage: The Twentieth Century* (1998), Wilhelm Hortmann has described the experimental adaptations of Shakespeare by prominent directors such as Frank Castorf, Christoph Marthaler and others as iconoclastic 'antitheater', which radically and violently deconstructed the classics. 'Many of these and other experiments', Hortmann writes, 'had little to do with Shakespeare. His plays were ready to hand, apparently indestructible, infinitely malleable: the proper stuff on which directors young and old could vent their spleen' (Hortmann 1998: 453). Hortmann's assessment of modern German Shakespeare adaptations/productions builds on the idea of an 'original' Shakespeare that should be preserved. The general problematic of such a demand for fidelity becomes even more obvious when the play in question has been translated. What is the original that should be brought onto the stage? Until the second half of the twentieth century, canonical translations (in particular the Schlegel-Tieck Shakespeare) used to fulfil this function. Any deviation from this norm was considered an appropriation, in 'the interests of the writer or group doing the appropriating' (Cartelli 1999: 15), but against the supposed intention of the 'original' author.

Christy Desmet has suggested a different perspective on adaptation. Rejecting the approach that sees adaptation/appropriation as 'a one-way transaction with clear winners and losers' (2014: 42), Desmet favours a dialogic model that 'is based on the act of *recognizing* Shakespeare in another writer or text' (41, emphasis in the original). This recognition, for her, 'is an ethical gesture rooted in both technical fidelity and fealty, or responsibility to and for another, either text or person' (41). She insists that '[t]he value of appropriations lies in showing us a different connection, a previously unacknowledged resemblance, between two texts or persons', and that for this acknowledgement, or recognition, the process of reception is fundamental (55). In the case of German stage adaptations of Shakespeare, reception is multilayered because it involves the author's/translator's rendering of the Shakespearean play, the production created by both director and actors, as well as the audience's and critics' reaction to a particular performance. Based on these considerations, I want to suggest a reading of post-migratory Shakespeare adaptations on the German-speaking stage as multi-faceted dialogues in which – perhaps surprisingly – the recognition of Shakespeare in the adapted play involves a recognition of post-migratory subjects.

TRADAPTING A CLASSICAL AUTHOR

Crucially, any engagement with Shakespeare on the German-speaking stage starts with the selection of the playtext. Directors have at their disposal a large number of Shakespeare translations into German – from the classical Schlegel-Tieck versions to contemporary renderings by Thomas Brasch, Frank Günther, Maik Hamburger, Elisabeth Plessen, Klaus Reichert and others. It is perhaps not surprising that more often than not the directors of post-migratory productions, rather than work with one of the established translations, choose to translate Shakespeare's text anew and adapt the play in the process.[4] Michel Garneau's term 'tradaptation' lends itself to describe this process, even though he coined it for his Shakespeare reworkings in francophone Canada. For Denis Salter, Garneau's combination of translation and adaptation was 'a sustained exercise in linguistic preservation of a kind peculiar to minority cultures struggling for autonomy on many different front(ier)s at once' (1993: 63). Acknowledging the alleged universality and transhistoricity of Shakespeare, Garneau's projects of the 1970s and 1980s also responded to their own historical moment and offered 'a case study in how differing voices – dissenting, contradictory, paradoxical, and anachronistic – can be enabled to speak concurrently within the self-imposed borders of a single text' (Salter 1993: 63). Admittedly, the German situation is markedly different from Garneau's, who adapted the most canonical author of the English language to the francophone stage within the predominantly English culture of Canada. However, his attempt to open up the plays to a polyphony of voices is comparable to the agenda of post-migratory German Shakespeare adaptations. Their characters speak standard German but also the sociolect of urban youths with a background of migration, and these different varieties of German are complemented by other languages – French in Gintersdorfer/ Klaßen's *Othello, c'est qui?* (2008) and English in Asli Kişlal and Blair Darby's *How to Kill an Othello* (2012). These linguistic differences underscore cultural and/or racial differences; indeed, in both productions, the Othello figure was played by a Black actor – one from Côte d'Ivoire, and the other from the UK. The polyphony also implies a deviation from the monolingual paradigm so central for the nation-state (cf. Yildiz 2012: 3) – a paradigm which has remained the norm on German stages until the present day. Post-migratory Shakespeare adaptations thus participate in what Yasemin Yildiz describes as a 'postmonolingual' moment, which is characterized by the 'ongoing dominance of the monolingual as well as the incipient moves to overcome it' (2012a: 4).

As 'classical' texts, Shakespeare's plays pose further linguistic challenges for authors and directors 'with a background of migration'. Nuran David Calis, who has worked as a playwright and director since 2003, has adapted and directed two Shakespeare plays: *Romeo & Julia (Death Is Sure – Life Is Not)* (2009) and *Othello X* (2018). He has admitted that he has always felt challenged by Shakespeare and Shakespeare's language. In adapting Shakespeare, he enters into an imaginary communication with him, which may produce something new beyond traditional translation, namely an 'overwriting' or 'over-painting' of the Shakespearean text with his (i.e. Calis's) own language. Calis insists that he wants his adaptations to be 'wild, not politically correct, sexist, unfair and merciless. Just as "my" world is' (2012b: 499; see also Calis 2018). In his introduction to *Othello X* in Basel, delivered on stage at the opening night (26 October 2018) and projected on a screen in subsequent performances, Calis related how he 'recognized' his autobiographical experience in Othello's story. In 1976, Calis was born in Bielefeld (a town in North Rhine-Westphalia, Germany) as the son of Jewish-Armenian immigrants from Turkey. He describes his adolescence as one of non-belonging, being accepted by neither the German majority culture nor the (post-)migrant youth subcultures in Germany but facing racism from both sides. He therefore reconstructed his (imaginary) identity as that of a Turkish Muslim, only spoke Turkish and Arabic (neither of which is his mother tongue), prayed at the mosque, worked as a bouncer and literally fought for street credibility. He suggests that in adopting such a 'mask', as an outsider in a majority society, he resembled Othello. Shakespeare's hero invited identification because he could be read as a metaphor of cultural otherness. To 'overwrite' Shakespeare's language with the German spoken by youth subcultures thus becomes a means of appropriation. Highlighting these strategies, Calis transforms the play into a 'parable' about identification, racial stigmatization and the powerlessness of the racialized outsider in the German majority society (cf. Calis 2018: 9).

Feridun Zaimoğlu, a German author of Turkish origin, has admitted that he, too, has felt related to Othello, 'his naïve pathos, his egomania that sometimes drifts into poetry, his invocation of Love [...]. This story is simply true, and it has a high recognition value' (Zaimoğlu and Senkel 2004: 127). Zaimoğlu describes such an autobiographically inflected approach to the original classical author as 'partisanship': 'We cannot dissimulate and write about something that is not part of us' (125). For both Calis and Zaimoğlu, then, the process of adaptation takes the form of a dialogue and mutual recognition as Desmet has described it. Their adaptations proceed, first of all, from the discovery of familiar narratives or even parallels to their own biography in the Shakespearean text, which in turn serves as a template to explore the general situation of minorities in a majority society, the experience of migration or the difficulties of love relations across cultural and racial divides.

Zaimoğlu first became known to a wider audience as the author of *Kanak Sprak* (1995), a collection of fictionalized autobiographies of German Turks speaking the German sociolect for which Zaimoğlu coined his titular term.[5] This sociolect resembles 'a Creole language or an argot with secret codes and symbols'. Like 'the free-style sermon of rap music' (Zaimoğlu 1998: 12–13), it is closely related to the masculinist pose and aggressive self-stylization of urban male youths, and it is also performative in its improvisational character and its neologisms. 'Kanak Sprak' empowers its speakers by 'challeng[ing] the cultural icon of the Turkish migrant whose powers of speech fail him in Germany' (Adelson 2005: 97). It is important to note that 'Kanak Sprak' is not 'bad' or 'incorrect' German; instead, as Yildiz stresses, it is a 'synthetic vernacular' (Matthew Hart, qtd. in Yildiz 2012: 173), whose influences include German, Turkish, hip-hop English and even Germanized Yiddish. This sociolect is the vernacular of an 'ethnoscape' co-inhabited by a variety of ethnic groups – Germans (with or without a background of migration), German Turks and migrants from other cultures (cf. Adelson 2005: 98). It thus 'conjoins the local and the global' through 'a new transnational code that is both rooted and not rooted, that affirms and challenges the link between language and ethnicity' (Yildiz 2012: 173). To insist upon the hybridity of both this language and the cultural sphere in which it is spoken is crucial, because it shows the inadequacy of critical approaches presupposing a binary opposition between self and other, natives and migrants, majority and minority, German and foreign languages (see also Adelson 2005: 5).

Together with Günter Senkel, Zaimoğlu has translated Shakespeare for the stage, including *Romeo and Juliet* for a production at the theatre of Kiel in 2006, and *Othello* for Luk Perceval's celebrated production at Kammerspiele

Munich in 2003. Their translations had a double agenda – an engagement with the Shakespearean text and, simultaneously, a response to classical German Shakespeare. In an interview, Zaimoğlu explained that those earlier translations' quasi-religious reverence for the 'original' had always tempted him to violently attack the text (Zaimoğlu and Senkel 2004: 123). His aim was to reclaim the humour, the bawdy and also the racial vocabulary of the Shakespearean text, which had been erased in the 'sanitized' nineteenth-century translation by Wolf Heinrich von Baudissin for the Schlegel-Tieck Shakespeare (2004: 121–2). Zaimoğlu and Senkel's *Othello*-project was achieved by rendering larger parts of the text in a sociolect that shares many features with 'Kanak Sprak'. For Calis, who adopted a similar strategy for his *Romeo & Julia* at Maxim Gorki Theater Berlin (2009), such a linguistic adaptation contributes to giving Shakespeare 'street credibility' (2012b: 499). It is important to note that both the Munich *Othello* and the Berlin *Romeo & Julia* did not merely include a few words of slang or youth language, as all German Shakespeare productions do nowadays. Instead, large parts of the plays were 'translated' into a non-normative German sociolect that was aggressive, obscene, homophobic and misogynistic.[6] In the Munich *Othello*, it was not associated with or spoken by young people at all. It was consciously employed by Iago in his dialogues with Roderigo, Cassio and Emilia, but not when he spoke to the Duke, and it was increasingly adopted by Othello when he fell for Iago's intrigue. Language reproduced social and gendered power relations; it was a means of strategic self-fashioning against women, homosexuals and/or cultural others, but also of disidentification with the norms of the majority society. Desdemona called Othello 'Schoko' (Chocco), thus linguistically racializing him. But when Othello, played by the White actor Thomas Thieme, eventually adopted this eroticized fantasy of Blackness, she rebuked him and reminded him that he was not Black but 'Whiter than most of the Whites'.

Through this particular form of tradaptation, both Zaimoğlu/Senkel's and Calis's productions differed considerably from mainstream modernizations of Shakespeare such as Tim Blake Nelson's *O* (2001) or Baz Luhrmann's *Romeo + Juliet* (1996), whose tribute to youth (pop) culture has been imitated in many recent German productions. This is true despite the fact that Calis's *Romeo & Julia* was clearly inspired by Luhrmann's film: the play started with a video sequence, which – like the TV news report in *Romeo + Juliet* – replaced the Chorus in the Prologue and 'fragment[ed] into a cacophony of sound and image' (Anderegg 2003: 59), with fast cuts and recognizable pictures of Berlin. However, if according to Michael Anderegg Luhrmann's film was stylistically informed by opera and rock video (cf. 2003: 59), the black-and-white video sequence in *Romeo & Julia* looked like an amateur film noir in split-screen mode. The sites that were shown – Kottbusser Tor in Berlin Kreuzberg, bleak tower block areas and walls covered with graffiti – evoked the poorer parts of the city as well as those neighbourhoods where many immigrants live. From the very beginning, the production avoided aestheticization, and its rough character would have disappointed a mainstream audience expecting to see a straightforward rendering of Shakespeare's romantic love tragedy. The setting was supposed to evoke the street gangs and the hip-hop scene of contemporary Berlin; accordingly, the music was (too) loud and violent, including rap songs such as Ludacris' 'Get Back' and Lil Wayne's 'You Ain't Got Nuthin'. This anti-bourgeois gesture was supported by the costumes (the Montagues were wearing hoodies and sweatpants to the Capulets' gangster style suits) and the inclusion of amateurs (with a background of migration) as rappers, dancers and gang members. They were students from the Rütli Oberschule, a (formerly infamous) secondary school in the poor neighbourhood of Neukölln, the part of Berlin with the highest percentage of inhabitants with a background of migration.[7] Most importantly, the characters reproduced the obscenities and the linguistic violence of rap lyrics and urban vernaculars, acknowledging them as a literary language.

In both Zaimoğlu/Senkel's and Calis's adaptations, classical drama, as well as the stage, was appropriated through and for writers, directors, actors and audiences that have traditionally been excluded from the theatre. These adaptations were not joyful celebrations of a colourful multiculturalism nor iterations of a canonical German Shakespeare that is truthful to the 'original' of the Schlegel-Tieck translation. Instead, they were disturbing in their inclusion of both the racism of the majority society and the physical violence, homophobia and sexism prevailing in some (post-migratory) subcultures.

REPETITION WITH A DIFFERENCE

Monika Gintersdorfer's approach to adapting and 'translating' Shakespeare differs considerably from Calis's and Zaimoğlu and Senkel's adaptations. Gintersdorfer is a Berlin-based director, who since 2005 has collaborated with Knut Klaßen and a German-Ivorian team of actors.[8] Early productions such as *Wahlen und Besessenheit* (Elections and Obsession; Volksbühne Berlin, 2005), dealing with the presidential elections in Côte d'Ivoire, turned out to be too 'foreign' for a German audience who did not find in them much to which they could relate. Gintersdorfer/Klaßen then turned to Shakespeare (as well as to other classical writers) as a means to address new topics, exactly because their audience was familiar with the canonical plays and their stage histories.[9] To date, Gintersdorfer/Klaßen have adapted three Shakespeare tragedies: *Othello, c'est qui?* (Othello, that's who?; Kampnagel, Hamburg, 2008), *7% Hamlet* (Deutsches Theater, Berlin, 2009) and *Die Gesellschaft des Bösen/La société du mal* (The Society of Evil), based on *Macbeth* (Festival Rue Princesse, Haus der Kulturen der Welt, Berlin, 2010). Although all three productions were inspired by Shakespearean drama, they almost completely dispensed with Shakespeare's lines, most of the characters and large parts of the plot – the title of *7% Hamlet* ironically commenting on the limited amount of the 'original' that the adaptation preserved. The casts were equally minimalistic. Four actors performed in *Die Gesellschaft des Bösen*: Gotta Depri and Franck Edmond Yao from Côte d'Ivoire, Hauke Heumann from Germany, and the US artist Melissa Logan. In both *Othello, c'st qui?* and *7% Hamlet*, a Black actor, Yao, paired with a White one: Cornelia Dörr in the *Othello* adaptation, and Bernd Moss in *7% Hamlet*. All three productions revolved around cross-cultural encounters, stereotyping and misunderstandings, and explored parallels and differences between African/Ivorian and Western European/German cultures, with regard to gender relations and sexuality, superstition, politics and power relations, but also artistic traditions.

In order to break away from the conventions of the traditional stage, Gintersdorfer/ Klaßen do not work with fixed scripts in their productions, even though in all three adaptations, the themes and the general structure of the performance had been agreed upon and rehearsed before. Each performance took the form of an improvised dialogue, in which the Shakespearean text functioned as the point of departure for the actors on stage, who commented on their knowledge of the play (or lack of it), their respective responses to Shakespeare, shaped by their biographical experiences and cultural imprint, as well as different stage traditions. These dialogues about the 'translation' of cultures also involved linguistic translation but of a different kind than Calis's or Zaimoğlu and Senkel's adaptations.

Othello, c'est qui? began with Yao telling Dörr that he had been offered a role by Monika Gintersdorfer: Othello.[10] But whereas in Germany everyone seemed to know the character, Yao first asked: 'Othello, c'est qui?' – Who is Othello? Why should he, as an African artist working in Europe, be interested in a role that is hardly known in Africa? He thus questioned the problematic assumption that Black and People of Colour automatically identify with Othello or see themselves as metonymically represented by this character.[11] In response to Yao's further question, why the play had been restaged again and again for four hundred years, Dörr replied with a reference to the classics and the symbolic capital that they afforded both actors and theatres. Even though the lines of the characters might not change, she insisted, it was interesting to compare the different interpretations of roles. But where Dörr found variation, Yao could only see an endless reiteration of the same lines by a 'robot-cassette' (tape-cassette robot): the director puts the same tape into the actor-robot who then repeats the very same text, over and over again, but with different mechanical movements. Yao illustrated this view by speaking Othello's line from Act 5 – 'For nought did I in hate, but all in honour' (5.2.288) – in French, with different intonations, and Dörr followed suit, in German. They commented on several German productions of the play, before they moved on to topics suggested by the tragic plot of *Othello*: gender relations, honour and jealousy, and relations between Black men and White women. Their initially harmless banter gradually turned into a violent quarrel, which resembled the relationship between Othello and Desdemona. Yao and Dörr, too, had turned into 'robot-cassettes', re-enacting the prescribed roles.

Othello, c'est qui? appears to echo a well-known Shakespeare adaptation that equally sought to explore a figure that 'has haunted western imagination for 400 years' (Billington 2008): Peter Brook's *Hamlet* adaptation *Qui est là?* (Who is there?), first staged at the Théâtre des Bouffes du Nord (Paris) in 1995. Brook also had an international cast, which included two African actors alongside Japanese, German, Italian and British actors. Looking at the play through the perspective of major theatre theorists of the twentieth century (Stanislavsky, Meyerhold, Craig, Brecht and Artaud), Brook's adaptation was concerned with the rehearsal process and the interaction between actors and directors. But even if *Othello, c'est qui?* may have been inspired by Brook's adaptation, it moved in a different direction.

The production highlighted adaptation as a multi-levelled process, indeed as an improvised performance rather than a finished product. More importantly, it explored the very 'adaptability' of the play, its characters, language and stage history, in different cultures and in intercultural encounters. Dörr always spoke German to the audience and French to Yao. She translated Yao's (Ivorian) French into German and thereby repeated his words. But although she tried to remain neutral, she sometimes smiled, commented on his statements, criticized them or asked when she had not understood his words. Her part thus oscillated between echo of and counterpoint to Yao's. But frequently the relation between the two shifted, and then it was Yao who echoed her. In one scene, for instance, she commented on a successful production of *Othello* at the Hamburg Schauspielhaus in 2004, directed by Stefan Pucher and featuring Alexander Scheer in blackface as Othello. In this production, Scheer's Othello, convinced of Iago's story about the handkerchief, had frantically run across the stage and jumped up against the back wall, moaning 'Taschentuch' (handkerchief). Dörr re-enacted this scene and explained to Yao in French: 'c'est une danse' (this is a dance). 'Why does he dance like this? This is his way to express emotions.' Yao then imitated her performance and echoed her words, also saying, in German, 'Taschentuch'. But rather than reconfirming Dörr's re-enactment of Scheer's Othello, Yao's mechanical and unemotional acting challenged this interpretation and introduced a moment of alienation. Repeatedly, through Yao's 'foreign' gaze, and reinforced through translation and repetition, the Shakespeare productions of the major German stages were defamiliarized – or appeared simply ludicrous.

The performative character of this tradaptation was emphasized by the physicality of the two actors on stage, who took turns in imitating – or 'translating' – the body movement of the respective other. In this way, their acting was rhythmically connected, both on a linguistic and a physical level, but this interaction constantly shifted from a harmonious *pas de deux* to an aggressive confrontation. Sometimes their voices and bodies were in sync before they parted ways or attacked each other. The performance can be described with Homi Bhabha's notion of 'mimicry' in that it was characterized by a replication '*that [was] almost the same, but not quite*' (1994: 86, emphasis in the original). In contrast to the colonial situation, however, the respective roles of 'original' and 'imitation' were not fixed, and the positions of both Dörr and Yao were deconstructed in the dialogic process. Furthermore, neither did the production show how an African actor was introduced to Western bardolatry, nor did it offer a simple postcolonial appropriation of the play for an Ivorian context. Most importantly perhaps, and in contrast to the adaptations by Calis and Zaimoğlu as well as to a large number of postcolonial adaptations of *Othello*, Yao *dis*identified with Shakespeare's hero while at the same time being gradually forced into this role. The production therefore did not offer its audience a stable position from which to 'judge' the debate. Instead, spectators were continuously encouraged to rethink their own cultural stereotypes, both about Africa/Côte d'Ivoire and Germany, and to look at Shakespeare's *Othello* alternately through the eyes of Dörr and Yao, who respectively defended and ridiculed 'classical' Shakespeare productions.

PLAY IT AGAIN …

Both Soeren Voima's *Othello*, directed by Christian Weise at the Gorki Theater in Berlin in 2016, and Blair Darby's/Asli Kişlal's *How to Kill an Othello*, performed by the post-migratory ensemble 'daskunst' for the Theater Nestroyhof Hamakom[12] in Vienna in 2012, addressed the problem as to how a post-migratory and ethnically diverse theatre ensemble can approach Shakespeare's tragedy and its racist stage history. Kişlal said that one of her initial questions was how Othello's position as a Black general in the White Venetian society could convincingly be adapted to the contemporary moment.[13] Her decision to turn Othello into a successful boxer highlighted one of the fields of Black public presence in Austria (and Germany): sports. In *How to Kill an Othello*, the White majority society of Austria appropriates Othello's fame, turns him into the new President of the Austrian Olympic Committee and instrumentalizes him – and the racial diversity he represents – for the bid campaign to host the Olympic Games. It was a fortunate coincidence for the production, Kişlal commented, when a week before the premiere it was announced that Vienna did indeed intend to bid to host the 2028 Olympic Games.[14] In this adaptation, the Iagos multiplied (Eri Bakali, Oktay Güneş, Ulrike Hübl, Alev Irmak, Bernhard Mrak, Susanne Rietz and Christian Strasser all played an 'Iago') and they represented the immense cultural power of the mass media. They first established Othello (played by the London actor and dancer Blair Darby) as an iconic figure and then destroyed him – without any obvious motive. The different stages of their campaign were videoprojected on to the rear stage wall; these included the slogan (in English) 'A New Star is Born: Othello' under the Olympic rings, and a picture of Othello and Desdemona with the headline: 'Liebe in Schwarz-Weiß: Neues Traumpaar Österreichs' (Love in Black and White: Austria's New Dream Couple). At no point in this process did Othello have the slightest chance to change the plot that was being written by others. Indeed, he could only break out of the text in five short monologues, rendered in English, in which he reflected on his role.[15] He was forced to dismiss his assistant Cassio, who in this production was the son of Turkish immigrants and whom the Iagos accused of collaborating with Turkey, the main competitor for Austria's Olympic ambition. Unsuccessfully, Cassio reminded Othello that he had been born in Austria and spoke German as a native language, compared to Othello's poor command of the language. Having sent Cassio away, Darby's Othello then remained alone onstage and shouted his accusation into the audience: 'I am a travelled man, seasoned, despised / The colour of my complexion may ratify your need for confrontation / So I will confront you / Personal appearances not necessary / My very being / Is the horned thorn that crucifies your soul / Wrench it from your innards / And start anew […].'[16] The shift in language – from German to English and from prose to verse – marked a moment of empowerment that, however, did not last.

Desdemona's part (played by Jaschka Lämmert) was also heteronomous, a role written by someone else. Shortly before she was killed, she had an encounter – presumably in a nightmare – with Shakespeare, who told her that her only function in the play was to be murdered, a sacrifice that would be accompanied by a moral apotheosis. In the next scene Othello acted out his role and smothered Desdemona.

But the play ended surprisingly, with a discussion between Desdemona and the Iagos (or, by implication, their actors), in which one of the latter admitted that in the end she had almost pitied Othello. Desdemona was praised for having died terrifically, but she insisted: 'Ja aber das nächste Mal möchte ich echt einen anderen Part übernehmen. Jahrhundertelange Erfahrung, aber trotzdem, immer das Opfer... ' (Yes, but next time, I would really like to play another part. Centuries of experience, but still, always the victim...). The tragedy of *Othello* turned out to be a play-within-a-play that had been performed over and over again, with everyone except for Othello being aware that they were 'merely' playing a cruel game with him. The ending of *How to Kill an Othello* suggested that it had finally become possible for the White woman to challenge the traditional script that had envisaged her in the role of the passive female victim.[17] However, Othello was not similarly able to emancipate himself from his role in the racist plot.

At the Maxim Gorki Theater, Voima's/Weise's *Othello* proceeded from an investigation of the stage history of the play, which was highlighted through costumes from the *commedia dell'arte* and appeared as a mere ossification. Not unlike Yao's 'robot-cassettes', the members of the all-male cast moved like marionettes; they wore garish make-up and were dressed in extravagant clowns' and harlequins' costumes. Taner Şahintürk's Othello, initially dressed in jeans and a tracksuit jacket, appeared as the only exception in this farcical ensemble. This Othello was not Black but a North African, the son of a Tunisian slave. He did not belong, as he admitted in the third scene when he introduced himself: 'Ich weiß, ich bin für manchen hier zu Schwarz; für andere nicht Schwarz genug' ('I know that some have deemed me either "too Black" or "not Black enough"'), thus referring to the ongoing problem of how to represent Othello through a quotation from Barack Obama's 'A more perfect union' speech, given in Philadelphia on 18 March 2008.[18] Like the former President of the United States, Othello invoked the vision of a republic (and perhaps, by implication, a theatre) in which skin colour no longer plays a role. He reminded his soldiers that whosoever derogatively commented on 'skin pigmentation' would be immediately dismissed. But just as the contemporary United States is not a post-racial society, the post-migratory Venice on the stage of the Berlin Gorki Theater had also not moved beyond racist discrimination. Indeed, the second scene showed Thomas Wodianka's Iago and Falilou Seck's Brabantio (who was not Desdemona's father in this adaptation) in dialogue, gossiping about the love affair between Othello and Desdemona (played by a male actor, Aram Tafreshian). Similar to the Shakespearean text, Brabantio mused that Othello must have used magic to make Desdemona fall in love with him. He insisted on his right to use the N-word and compared Othello's sexual potency to that of a gorilla – words for which he was indeed dismissed by Othello.

In addition to the Obama quote, Voima's *Othello* opened up a veritable echo chamber of citations that served to highlight different facets of the play and its tragic hero. A similar strategy can be found in Djanet Sears's *Othello* adaptation *Harlem Duet* (1997), in which several scenes are introduced with recordings of speeches by Martin Luther King, Malcom X, Langston Hughes, Paul Robeson and other famous Black politicians or artists. In Voima's *Othello*, though, the quote is spoken by the character; it is unmarked and is complemented by a number of further passages from other plays by Shakespeare (*Julius Caesar, Hamlet, The Merchant of*

Venice), from current political debates (e.g. on the wars in the Middle East or on political correctness) and from postcolonial theory. Slowly succumbing to Iago's insinuations, Othello is given a long monologue (of which I am only translating a short fragment), in which he reflects on his place in a White society:

> Is she not a human being? Doesn't she see and hear anything, doesn't she have senses? Doesn't she taste sweet, bitter and sour like I do? [...] Has she deceived me? I can't believe it, not she! Not this one! Not Desdemona. [...] The same old story, once again, from the very beginning. But why, why, if I know it, does it unsettle me so much? I entered the world smooth and young, but from the very beginning, their gazes oppressed me. From the very beginning, their gazes contested my being in the world. What did they see? What did they see in me that I didn't see? 'Look, the darky!' A nudge on the nose, in passing. And another one. [...] 'Look, the monkey!' Right, this was me, they were referring to me. [...] 'Mama, I am afraid!' Fear. They were afraid of me. Why were they afraid? [...] And some day, eventually, after a thousand anecdotes, proverbs, narratives and nursery rhymes, my skin had indeed become brown, almost black, and my body was fragmented, patched, animalistic, evil, ugly. [...] I had been born into this world smooth and young, but this world amputated me. [...] But I would teach it a lesson! I checked my incisors and felt that they were strong! [...] You will get to know me! A new man appears, a new human species: I, Othello. 'Look, this Black man is beautiful!' Oh. [...] the white strangled me with his sudden embracement. [...] I suffered from my body, caught between colours and prejudices, marked as if I was damned, and without the prospect of ever escaping my skin [...].
>
> (Voima 2016: 48–51, scene 25)

Whereas at the beginning, Othello's lines echo Shylock's monologue from *Merchant* (3.1), he then adopts – in almost verbatim paraphrase – the famous passage from Frantz Fanon's *Peau Noir, Masques Blancs* (*Black Skin, White Masks*), first published in 1952, in which Fanon describes the psychological impact of White supremacy on Black and People of Colour (2008: 85–7). In this passage, Fanon prepared the ground for a basic tenet of postcolonial theory, which sees the Black subject in a White society as always already constructed by a White gaze: 'I subjected myself to an objective examination, I discovered my blackness, my ethnic characteristics; and I was battered down by tom-toms, cannibalism, intellectual deficiency, fetishism, racial defects, slave-ships, and above all else, above all: "Sho' good eatin"' (2008: 84–5). On the post-migratory stage, Othello has become aware of these discourses and turns into his own analyst. But in order to achieve this position, he has to step out of the Shakespearean text and adopt/adapt the voices of twentieth- and twenty-first-century Black theorists and politicians. Voima's adaptation therefore confirms what Ayanna Thompson has argued for the American context: even if '*Othello* has traditionally provided one of the few classical plays that invites and enables discussions about race in performance' (2011: 175), the outcome of such a performance can never be certain, and there is no reason to believe that it will be 'race-neutral or even race-progressive' (117). Thompson concludes with a quote from Sujata Iyengar: 'For that, we might have to leave Shakespeare behind' (116).

A comparable process of racial inscription and self-awareness could be witnessed in Calis's *Othello X* at Basel. As in other examples I have discussed above, this Othello (played by Simon Zagermann) was also not Black. At the beginning of the play, racist swearwords were literally written onto Othello's/Zagermann's body by the other characters/actors, who thus transformed him into a visual metaphor of racialized Otherness. In addition, his wish to belong was indicated by a silver mask he was wearing – another (albeit unmarked) reference to Fanon's 'white masks'. In an interview, Calis suggested a further association, drawing a connection to the masks worn by Haitian Bocor dancers (cf. 2018: 10). From the beginning, this Othello also showed awareness of his split identity. He expressed his yearning for a life without the mask, which he recognized as his second skin, but without which he would be a nobody, a mere 'guest worker', the term for the work migrants from Southern Europe, who had responded to the recruitment programmes of the German, Austrian or Swiss governments from the mid-1950s to the 1970s. Calis's Othello did not represent People of Colour, but functioned as a symbolic figure metaphorically evoking racial and ethnic differences in general: the gesture to European work migration in the second half of the twentieth century was combined with a reference to Fanon's pan-Africanism, the Haitian Revolution of 1791–1804, and the twentieth-century history of Black emancipation in the US, the latter by setting the play in a 1970s New York record label[19] and by implicitly referencing Malcolm X in the title.

And yet, even if the heroes' familiarity with postcolonial theory enabled them to analyse the interconnected strategies of inclusion and exclusion, as well as the respective identity effects, they were not empowered to break out of the tragedy, which repeated itself: once again, both Voima's/Weise's and Calis's Othellos fell victim to Iago's intrigue. At the Maxim Gorki Theater, Othello lost his natural acting and became a puppet, like the others, and exchanged his jacket for a long coat. Eventually Iago brought a paint pot and coloured his face – with golden paint, thus producing a visual metaphor for racializing strategies that simultaneously evoked the history of blackfacing. In Basel, Othello took off the silver mask and turned indeed, as he had anticipated, into a stereotypical Other, driven by his passions. The production ended with Othello violently battering Desdemona (played by Liliane Amuat) to death when she announced that she would leave him and 'get herself fucked' by the first man she would meet in the street. By thus insisting on the causal interconnection, and mutual reinforcement, of racial and gendered violence, *Othello X* reiterated the tragic ending of Shakespeare's play. This may have been a final bow to the authority of Shakespeare, which prohibits an omission or alteration of the tragic ending. But in this way the adaptation ran the danger of inadvertently reproducing its racist logic by playing racism off against sexual violence.

In contrast, neither *Othello, c'est qui?* nor Voima's/Weise's *Othello* concluded with Desdemona's and Othello's death but with metatheatrical comments on the force of tradition and related audience expectations. With a clear awareness of the ideological pitfalls that the tragic ending almost inevitably entails, Yao confronted the audience with their secret desire to see Desdemona killed, which – as he stressed – he was unwilling to act out. The Berlin *Othello* ended with a long monologue of the chorus (made up of the Cypriots/the extras), who sought to break out of the text:

> We will to say something. Eventually. But what? We only know this one play. THEIR play, about envy and jealousy, gold and greed and aggression. We have seen it, so many times. And we have always been there in the background. Their words were our flesh and blood. And now? How to proceed? [...] Does anyone know another text?
>
> (Voima 2016: 74, scene 42)

The answer was unanimous. 'I don't.'

As with *How to Kill an Othello*, *Othello, c'est qui?* and *Othello X*, Voima's/ Weise's *Othello* developed a meta-theatrical comment on the possibilities that Shakespeare adaptations on German-speaking stages afford, but also highlighted the constraints. Shakespeare's play invites adaptation for the post-migratory moment and an exploration of the tensions between identification and difference, belonging and exclusion, openness to alterity and racist stereotyping, love and lethal violence. Significantly, none of the adaptations offered conciliatory resolutions, and there were no happy endings. A comparative perspective on these productions demonstrates that the post-migratory stage lends itself to playing through different versions of this precarious narrative. Such a multiplication of adaptations may eventually destabilize the cultural power of the Shakespearean plot, from which, as the *Othellos* show, it is still difficult to break free, particularly for Black and People of Colour. In addition, these *Othello* adaptations were written, directed, performed and watched by people who had previously been excluded from the predominantly bourgeois institution that the theatre is. They therefore developed alternatives to earlier plays about migration that, as Shermin Langhoff has argued, have reproduced the stereotypical figure of the migrant played by White German actors. Paradoxically, this visibility of the post-migratory theatre is enhanced by the cultural capital of the 'classical' Shakespeare. Even though (German) bardolatry is deconstructed in the process, it still attracts large audiences and procures critical reviews in mainstream media. Adapting Shakespeare for the post-migratory stage therefore constitutes a powerful act of cultural and political intervention, which in turn radically transform the stages and their 'classical' authors. And yet, the events of the year 2020, in which this article was written – from the murders of Breonna Taylor and George Floyd to the right-wing terrorist attack on a shisha bar in Hanau near Frankfurt, in which nine people with an immigrant background were killed – pose the question whether Shakespeare's tragedy about a murderous Black man is really the right play for the moment.

NOTES

I would like to thank Bettina Boecker from the Munich Shakespeare Library, Monika Gintersdorfer and Knut Klaßen, Asli Kişlal, the Maxim Gorki Theater and the Theater Basel for supporting me in the research for this article with the video recordings, the playtexts, theatre programmes (as well as further material and information on the adaptations and their productions.

1   If not indicated otherwise, all translations from the German are mine.

2   According to official statistics, in 2019 26 per cent of the German population had 'a background of migration', which means that at the moment of birth, either the person themselves or at least one of their parents did not hold German citizenship (cf. Statistisches Bundesamt 2020).

3   I have discussed Perceval's and Gintersdorfer/Klaßen's productions in a previous article (Schülting 2018).

4   Economic considerations may of course also play a role because for a new translation, a theatre does not have to pay royalties.

5   'Kanak language': the spelling 'Sprak' (rather than *Sprache* = language) imitates Turkish-German pronunciation. *'Kanake'* is a derogatory German term for people of southern origin, but like other instances of hate speech it has been appropriated and resignified by second- and third-generation immigrants as a term of self-identification.

6   On the shocked reactions to the guest performance of Perceval's *Othello* at the RSC in Stratford-upon-Avon in 2006, see Rutter (2007) and Cheesman (2010: 207–9).

7   In 2006, the school had been in the national news when teachers complained of the excessive youth violence. This triggered a public debate on violence at schools and the integration of immigrants. Since then, the situation at the Rütli school has changed thoroughly, through material support and a variety of reform projects, including a cooperation with the Maxim Gorki Theater since 2007.

8   See also Gintersdorfer/Klaßen's website at https://www.gintersdorferklassen.org/ (accessed 11 October 2021).

9   Monika Gintersdorfer in a personal conversation, 19 August 2019.

10 My discussion refers to a video recording of the production at Kampnagel, Hamburg, on 29 February 2008.

11 Hugh Quarshie (1999: 5) famously challenged this assumption by stressing that Othello might be the 'one' role 'which should most definitely not be played by a black actor'.

12 *Ha makom* is Hebrew and means 'the place'. The name refers, on the one hand, to the relation between enclosure and expansion and, on the other, to the Jewish tradition of the Theater Nestroyhof. On its website, the theatre stresses its thematic concern with forms of exclusion, racism, migration and diaspora. See the theatre website at https://www.hamakom.at/der-ort (accessed 3 October 2020).

13 Kişlal in a personal conversation, 31 October 2019.

14 In a referendum, held in March 2013, more than 70 per cent of Vienna's citizens rejected the plans.

15 According to Kişlal, they were added by Blair Darby because he felt that Othello does not have a voice in the play.

16 I am quoting from an unpublished manuscript generously provided by Kişlal.

17 In this respect, *How to Kill an Othello* can be read alongside feminist adaptations of *Othello* such as Paula Vogel's *Desdemona: A Play about a Handkerchief* (1993) and

Toni Morrison and Rokia Traore's *Desdemona* (2011). A production of Morrison and Traore's adaptation, directed by Peter Sellars, was first shown at the Vienna theatre festival 'Festwochen' in May 2011, i.e. in the year preceding Darby and Kişlal's production.

18 The Gorki *Othello* premiered on 19 February 2016, nine months before the Presidential Elections in the US.

19 Originally, Calis had intended Othello to be a White musician in a predominantly Black context, until he realized that this would indeed be impossible to realize with the all-White cast at the theatre of Basel.

REFERENCES

Adelson, L. A. (2005), *The Turkish Turn in Contemporary German Literature: Toward a New Critical Grammar of Migration*, New York, NY: Palgrave.

Anderegg, M. (2003), 'James Dean Meets the Pirate's Daughter: Passion and Parody in *William Shakespeare's Romeo + Juliet* and *Shakespeare in Love*', in R. Burt and L. E. Boose (eds), *Shakespeare, The Movie, II: Popularizing the Plays om Film, TV, Video and DVD*, 56–71, London and New York, NY: Routledge.

Balme, C. (2002), 'Wie schwarz muss Othello sein? Polemische Überlegungen zur Repräsentation kultureller Fremdheit im Theater', in C. Balme and J. Schläder (eds), *Inszenierungen: Theorie – Ästhethik – Medialität*, 105–16, Stuttgart/Weimar: J. B. Metzler.

Bhabha, H. K. (1994), 'Of Mimicry and Man: The Ambivalence of Colonial Discourse', in *The Location of Culture*, 85–92, London and New York, NY: Routledge.

Billington, M. (2008), 'Archive Theatre Review: Who Is Hamlet anyway?', *The Guardian*, 18 December. Available online: https://www.theguardian.com/stage/2000/dec/02/peter-brook-hamlet-theatre (accessed 3 October 2020).

Calis, N. D. (2012a), *Romeo & Julia (Death Is Sure – Life Is Not)*, in U. B. Carstensen, S. Von Lieven and B. Walther (eds), *Shakespeare Variationen*, 449–98, Frankfurt am Main: Fischer.

Calis, N. D. (2012b), 'Street Credibility', in U. B. Carstensen, S. Von Lieven and B. Walther (eds), *Shakespeare Variationen*, 499, Frankfurt am Main: Fischer.

Calis, N. D. (2018), 'Ausbruch aus dem phänotypischen Bild des "Fremden"', Interview, in *Othello X*, abridged theatre programme, 6–12, Theater Basel.

Cartelli, T. (1999), *Repositioning Shakespeare: National Formations, Postcolonial Appropriations*, London and New York, NY: Routledge.

Cheesman, T. (2010), 'Shakespeare and Othello in Filthy Hell: Zaimoglu and Senkel's Politico-Religious Tradaptation', *Forum for Modern Language Studies* 46 (2): 207–20.

Desmet, C. (2014), 'Recognizing Shakespeare, Rethinking Fidelity: A Rhetoric and Ethics of Appropriation', in A. Huang and E. Rivlin (eds), *Shakespeare and the Ethics of Appropriation*, 41–57, New York, NY: Palgrave Macmillan.

Fanon, F. (2008), *Black Skin, White Masks*, trans. C. Lam Markmann (1986), London: Pluto Press.

Foroutan, N. (2016), 'Postmigrantische Gesellschaften', in H.U. Brinkmann and M. Sauer (eds), *Einwanderungsgesellschaft Deutschland*, 227–54, Wiesbaden: Springer.

Hortmann, W. (1998), *Shakespeare on the German Stage: The Twentieth Century*, Cambridge: Cambridge University Press.

Hutcheon, L. (2006), *A Theory of Adaptation*, New York, NY: Routledge.

Kolesch, D. (2016), 'Wie Othello spielen', *Shakespeare Jahrbuch* 152: 87–103.

Langhoff, S. (2011), 'Die Herkunft spielt keine Rolle – "Postmigrantisches" Theater im Ballhaus Naunynstraße', interview with Katharina Donath, Bundeszentrale für politische Bildung, 10 March. Available online: http://www.bpb.de/gesellschaft/ bildung/kulturelle-bildung/60135/interview-mit-shermin-langhoff?p=all (accessed 3 October 2020).

Obama, B. (2008), 'A more perfect union' speech, 18 March. Available online: http:// www.youtube.com/watch?v=pWe7wTVbLUU (accessed 3 October 2020).

Quarshie, H. (1999), *Second Thoughts about Othello*, Chipping Campden: Clouds Hill Printers.

Rutter, C. C. (2007), 'Watching Ourselves Watching Shakespeare – Or – How Am I Supposed to Look?', *Shakespeare Bulletin* 25 (4): 47–68.

Salter, D. (1993), 'Between Wor(l)ds: Lepage's Shakespeare Cycle', *Theatre* 24 (3): 61–70.

Schülting, S. (2018), 'German Shakespeare in Translation: Discords from the Margins', *Shakespeare Studies* 46: 48–58.

Shakespeare, W. (2004), *Othello*, trans. and adap. F. Zaimoğlu and G. Senkel, Münster: Monsenstein und Vannerdat.

Sieg, K. (2015), 'Race, Guilt and *Innocence*: Facing Blackfacing in Contemporary German Theater', *German Studies Review* 38 (1): 117–34.

Statistisches Bundesamt (2020), Press release no. 279, 28 July. Available online: https:// www.destatis.de/DE/Presse/Pressemitteilungen/2020/07/PD20_279_12511.html (accessed 3 October 2020).

Thompson, A. (2011), *Passing Strange: Shakespeare, Race, and Contemporary America*, Oxford: Oxford University Press.

Voima, S. (2016), *Othello. Nach William Shakespeare*, Berlin: Henschel Schauspiel Theaterverlag.

Worthen, W. B. (2003), *Shakespeare and the Force of Modern Performance*, Cambridge: Cambridge University Press.

Yildiz, Y. (2012), *Beyond the Mother Tongue: The Postmonolingual Condition*, New York, NY: Fordham University Press.

Zaimoğlu, F. (1998), *Kanak Sprak: 24 Mißtöne vom Rande der Gesellschaft* (1995), Hamburg: Rotbuch Verlag.

Zaimoğlu, F. and G. Senkel (2004), 'Die Flammen der wahren Hölle', interview with Marion Tiedtke, in W. Shakespeare, *Othello*, trans. and adapt. F. Zaimoğlu and G. Senkel, 121–35, Münster: Monsenstein und Vannerdat.

Japanese novelizations of Shakespeare's *Hamlet* and *Macbeth*: the culture of *hon'an* as adaptational practice

YUKARI YOSHIHARA

This chapter discusses Japanese narrative adaptations of Shakespeare's *Hamlet* and *Macbeth*. To arrive at a historically and culturally contextualized analysis, it is first necessary to understand the definition of adaptation in the Japanese context. A rough equivalent of 'adaptation' in Japanese would be *hon'an* (transforming the original), but *hon'an* is different from the traditional biases of Western adaptations, in that the relationship between the original and the *hon'an* was not necessarily hierarchical. With a history of adapting Chinese literature or older Japanese literature, *hon'an* was regarded as a legitimate and respected literary convention that gives a richer afterlife to the older literature by adding, updating and expanding the originals. One of the oldest Japanese narrative fictions, the *Tale of Genji* (eleventh century) by Lady Murasaki, contains some episodes coming from Chinese or older Japanese sources, which can be regarded as *hon'an* of the existing literature. Nineteenth-century Japan has a fictional travel narrative, *Musobyoe* (1810) by Bakin Takizawa (1767–1848), which has remarkable resemblances to *Gulliver's Travels*. One theory is that Musobyoe is an adaptation of a Dutch translation of *Gulliver's Travels* (Japan had commerce only with the Netherlands among European countries during its isolation); another is that they share the same Chinese or Japanese sources (Harada forthcoming 2021). The former defines *Musobyoe* as a *hon'an* of *Gulliver's Travels*, and the latter defines both as *hon'ans* of the unknown original.

A CULTURE OF *HON'AN*

When Japan was undergoing rapid modernization through Westernization in the late nineteenth century, after opening its doors to the West in 1854, *hon'an* proved to be a useful tool to overcome the tremendous cultural difference between the West and Japan, to make things Western look familiar, relatable and understandable. J. Scott Miller dispels 'the notion that hon'an translations were necessarily seen as inferior by their contemporary readers' (2001: 13) and adds that *hon'an* adaptations can be seen as 'a method by which Japanese writers took the literary artifacts of the Other and appropriated them, reinvented them, as something Japanese' (20). As Joseph Anderson notes, *hon'an* was considered as a 'thoroughly genuine creative endeavor that was different from original composition and from direct translation into Japanese but inferior to neither' (2011: 279). Furthermore, as in the case of the first stage *hon'an* of *The Merchant of Venice* (1885), set in the feudal period but anachronistically advocating for the spirit of capitalism (Yoshihara 2001), *hon'an* became a means to assimilate Western thoughts into a Japanese context. *Hon'an* of Western literature was bold in adapting the original 'in ways that obscured and often left few traces of the original' (Anderson 2011: 279). More generally, *hon'an* were more important to the development of modern Japanese literature than a direct translation of foreign originals. *Hon'an* became the aesthetic manifestation of the philosophy in Japan under rapid modernization through Westernization: *wakon yosai* (Japanese *spirit/values* governing the application of Western *science/ learning*).

With the further development of Japan's modernization through Westernization, *hon'an* became obsolete on the early-twentieth-century stage. Productions of Shakespeare's works up until the 1910s were mostly *hon'an*, but as higher importance came to be placed on fidelity to the original in stage performance, the novel became a more accommodating means for transfiguring Shakespeare's works in the fashion of *hon'an*. Around that time, perhaps not coincidentally, Shakespeare's plays came to be regarded as something to be 'read and studied rather than staged' (Gallimore and Minami 2016: 487). Those stage performances using direct translation of the original in imitation of Western realist performance style were considered authentic, authoritative and highbrow. *Hon'an* onstage came to be regarded as appropriate only for middle-to-lowbrow entertainments. In 1955, Tsuneari Fukuda's production of *Hamlet* staged in close imitation of an Old Vic production (1953) set the standard for the latter half of the twentieth century. Nevertheless, *hon'an* of Shakespeare came back in a new medium, film: Akira Kurosawa's *Kumonosu jo* (*Throne of Blood*, 1957), given in imitation of Noh performance style, transforms *Macbeth* into a samurai drama. On stage, too, Yukio Ninagawa explored new possibilities of *hon'an* in his Shakespearean productions such as *Macbeth* (1980) and *Kabuki Twelfth Night* (2007). Bold adaptation or fantastic *hon'an* of Shakespeare now thrives on stage (Hidenori Inoue's 2006 *Metal Macbeth*), in animation (Gonzo's 2007 *Romeo x Juliet*) and in manga comics (Aya Sugano's *Barao no soretsu* [*Funeral of the Rose King*; based on *Richard III*], 2013–).

This chapter focuses primarily on adaptation/*hon'an* of Shakespeare's *Hamlet* and *Macbeth* in the novel from 1906 (Soseki Natsume, *Kusamakura*) to 2002 (Haruki Murakami, *Kafka on the Shore*). Among novel adaptations/*hon'an*, *Hamlet* stands out in number, ranging from the esteemed novels examined in this chapter to formulaic detective fictions. In Japan, perhaps as elsewhere, Hamlet is considered an embodiment of modern Western male subjecthood in agony. Hypothetically, this could be one reason why there are numerous *hon'an* of *Hamlet* in Western-style Japanese novels. I shall pay particular attention to the theme of anxiety over modern male subjecthood and female sexuality. Although *Macbeth hon'an* are not as numerous, I include Murakami's *Kafka* here as well, both because Murakami is such an internationally renowned writer and because his novel inherits the theme of anxiety over modern male subjecthood and female sexuality from the preceding *Hamlet/Macbeth hon'an*. Examining these *hon'an* adaptations, the chapter demonstrates how Shakespeare enriches Japanese literature and additionally how *hon'an* can be a useful indicator of Japan's complicated reactions to Shakespeare, imagined to be an embodiment of Western civilization.

PRE-HISTORY – REINVENTING JAPANESE THEATRE/LITERATURE VIA SHAKESPEARE: SHOYO TSUBOUCHI

Understanding Western literary works posed tremendous difficulty for Japan in the process of its modernization through Westernization, due to 'the essential differences between European and Japanese literature' (Kawachi 2016: 124). Shoyo Tsubouchi was most influential in modernizing and Westernizing Japanese novels (Toyoda 1940; Gallimore and Minami 2016; Kawachi 2016; Gallimore 2021), and he was also to be the first to translate the complete works of Shakespeare (1928). In his book on Western modern novels, *Shōsetsu shinzui* (*The Essence of the Novel*, 1885), he rejected the superiority of didacticism in Japanese prose over Western realism (Britannica Academic, *Shoyo Tsubouchi*). Moreover, whereas traditional prose fiction about the private lives of ordinary people, in contrast to prose epic narratives about politics and history, had been 'despised by the intellectuals as mere entertainments for women and children', he regarded modern, Westernized and realistic novels as a respectable genre worthy for men and intellectuals. In her most comprehensive study of novel adaptations of *Hamlet* in Japan, Kawachi writes that Tsubouchi's book was the first literary criticism in Japan, and that it led to the modernization/Westernization of Japanese literature (2016: 124).

Conflicts between modernity/Westernization and Japan's feudal past were something Tsubouchi had to deal with in his translation/adaptation/*hon'an* of Shakespeare's works. While modernization through Westernization was seen as the only way for Japan to survive, it caused conflicting reactions that influenced literary styles and theatre practices. Even though his translation of *Julius Caesar* in 1884 was a response to the Freedom and People's Rights Movement in the 1860s–1880s in Japan, which had been brought about by the influence of Western-style democracy, the language used in the translation was in traditional, feudal Kabuki playscript style (Quinn 2011: 168–83). His first translation of *Hamlet*, retaining much of the archaic vocabularies and manner of enunciation from the Kabuki tradition, appeared in 1907. In the continuous process of revising his Shakespeare translation, Tsubouchi changed his style to be closer to the contemporary spoken Japanese. Shakespeare translation/adaptation/*hon'an* thus helped produce modern, realistic literary language. As Alexa Alice Joubin analyses, 'Tsubouchi appropriated Shakespearean aesthetics to reinvent Japanese theatre' (2021: 39).

The first phase of the *hon'an* or free adaptations of Shakespeare's works occurred from the 1880s to the 1910s. The earliest kabuki-style *hon'an* of *Hamlet* by Robun Kanagaki (1886) is set in a feudal Japanese castle haunted by the ghost of King Hamlet in samurai armor; the novel *Tempest in Tohima clan* (1891) by Ouchi Sakurachi, has a female ghost, combining Gertrude and Ophelia, who urges the Hamlet figure to revenge. Otojiro Kawakami, the founder of modern, Westernized theatre in Japan, produced three Shakespearean plays (*Othello*, *The Merchant of Venice* and *Hamlet*) consecutively in 1903 (Kano 2001; Anderson 2011). All three productions were adaptations or *hon'an* – *Othello* set in Taiwan under Japanese colonization (Yoshihara 2014), *The Merchant of Venice* with the Shylock figure as an indigenous man in Hokkaido (a northern island colonized by Japan in the mid-eighteenth century) and *Hamlet* set in contemporary Japan. Kawakami's *Hamlet* has some references to Japan's military expansion in Asia at that time (for example, the Hamlet figure is exiled to Siberia, which Japan was ambitious to colonize). And then, in the 1910s, stage performance became dominated by literary, word-for-word translations, particularly by Tsubouchi. He produced the 1911 performance of *Hamlet*, the first full performance of the play in literary translation.

Thus, from the 1880s to the end of the century both onstage and on page, *hon'an* or adaptations rather than faithful translations of Shakespeare's original works were predominant. But the first decade of the twentieth century witnessed the rise of scholarly studies of Shakespeare's works and attempts at more direct and faithful translation. Western realist performance without overt Japanization became dominant, and Shakespeare, as noted earlier, became a subject to be studied by reading. Around that time, novels adapting Shakespeare's works into Japanese settings began to appear. The novels, rather than stage performances, provided more accommodating environments for making Shakespeare into *hon'an* adaptations.

VICTORIAN INFLUENCE ON JAPANESE NOVELS: SOSEKI NATSUME

Soseki Natsume, one of the founding voices in the modern Japanese novel, was also a scholar of English literature and, as a novelist, adapted Shakespeare's works: for example, *Kusamakura* adapts *Hamlet*, *Poppy* features a Cleopatra figure and *The Tower of London* refers to the two princes in *Richard III*. Though education at his younger age made him an admirer of classic Chinese literature, he was educated in the English Department of Tokyo Imperial University (1890–3). He had to struggle with the otherness of Shakespeare's works and English literature. He writes in 'Dr. Tsubouchi and Hamlet' that:

> Shakespeare does not possess that universality that European critics ascribe to it. For us Japanese it requires years of training to develop a proper appreciation of Shakespeare, and even then this is only a dim appreciation based on a deliberate adaptation of our sensibilities.

(qtd. in Karatani 1993: 12)

His sensibilities, mostly built upon his familiarities with Chinese literature, had to be deliberately adapted, with considerable pain, to English literature.

William James Craig (1843–1906), the general editor of *Arden Shakespeare*, First Series, influenced Natsume's understanding of Shakespeare. Natsume studied under the private tutorship of Craig in London and wrote a short story based on Craig's private lessons, 'Professor Craig' (1909; Natsume 2016). Craig as a character in Natsume's story is preparing the manuscript for the *Shakespeare Dictionary*. Craig gave up 'a chair in literature at a certain university in Wales and made the time to go to the British Museum every day' to compile the dictionary, and the narrator adds, 'this dictionary is the sole preoccupation of the professor's mind'(2016: No. 1541). The narrator superciliously asks the professor if there is any point to putting so much energy to compile his own Shakespeare dictionary 'when there is already [Alexander] Schmidt's *Shakespeare Lexicon*' (1902). The professor replies, 'If I was going to produce something of the same standard as Schmidt, would there be any need to go to all this trouble?' (No. 1545). Two years after the narrator returns to Japan, he finds a short article about Craig's death. The narrator wonders 'whether that dictionary had ultimately been left unfinished and ended up as wastepaper' (No. 1557). Sadly, Craig's *Shakespeare Dictionary* was indeed unfinished at his death. The narrator recalls, 'The Arden Shakespeare's *Hamlet* is a book from which I would derive an enormous profit when giving university lectures after returning home' (No. 1522), and also, we may presume, when the story's author was writing *Kusamakura*. Nineteenth-century Victorian Shakespeare culture in the form of Craig and Millais's Ophelia, as I shall examine later, was formative of Natsume's career as a novelist.

During this same time period, Hamlet became a philosophical, melancholic, agonistic and rebellious hero in Japanese imagination through the suicide of Misao Fujimura in 1903. Fujimura carved his death note on a tree trunk: 'Horatio's philosophy is entirely worthless. I cannot understand the universe at all. So I decided to commit suicide' (qtd. in Kawachi 2016: 125). There were numerous cases of (attempted) suicides among youths in imitation of Fujimura's, others similarly feeling that 'Horatio's philosophy is entirely worthless' in the materialistic world ruled by the ideal of a successful worldly man (with much influence from Samuel Smiles' *Self-Help*, translated in 1871). Natsume, who had taught English literature to Fujimura at an elite college, refers to Fujimura's suicide in his novels, *Kusamakura* and *I am a Cat* (1905).

Natsume's *Kusamakura* (1906) adapts Shakespeare with insights into the Victorian appreciation of Ophelia, who is described by Bram Dijkstra as 'the later nineteenth-century's all-time favorite example of love-crazed self-sacrificial madness' (1986: 42). As critics have shown, Ophelia is a figure around whom cultural expectations about the girl/femininity are expressed (Showalter 1985; Romanska 2005; Peterson and Williams 2012; O'Neill 2014; Traub 2014). The narrator, infatuated with John Everett Millais's painting *Ophelia* (1851–2), tries to tame an independent, sexually active and rebellious woman, Nami, into an image of Ophelia (Natsume saw Millais's *Ophelia* in London). The narrator learns about Nami's tempestuous life, including a forced separation from her lover, an unhappy marriage for money and divorce. Despite her sad life, she is a highly intellectual, independent-minded and sexually active woman – a character that contrasts sharply with Shakespeare's Ophelia or Victorian Ophelias, generally portrayed as fragile and powerless female victims.

Nami is presented as a femme fatale who allures and provokes the narrator, who feels she is threatening his sense of himself as the modern male subject. When listening to people talking about Nami's wedding ceremony in the cherry blossom season, the protagonist-narrator imagines her in the image of Millais's Ophelia: 'suddenly the face of Ophelia in Millais's painting' 'floating, hands folded, down the stream' 'springs unbidden' to his mind (2008: 21). Nami ridicules the narrator's infatuation with Ophelia when she suggests to him that she might commit suicide soon. She asks the narrator, 'Please paint a beautiful picture of me floating there – not lying there suffering, but drifting peacefully off to the other world'. He realizes he is being mocked when she grins and says, 'Aha, that surprised you, didn't it!' (102). Despite the narrator's wish that she would be like Ophelia, she does not die. In this way, *Kusamakura* challenges the romanticization of Ophelia's self-sacrificial death as well as its spectacularization in art and writing.

Another self-assertive Ophelia appears in Hideo Kobayashi's 1931 novel, *Oferia Ibun* (*Ophelia's Literary Remains*). Ophelia condemns Hamlet for his ill-treatment of her, saying: 'You said to me, "Get thee to a nunnery," but it is you that should die' (70) and 'You said "To be, or not to be, that is the question." How wonderful, how splendid! What are you waiting for? Just go ahead and solve the problem' (74). This Ophelia, like Nami in *Kusamakura*, survives; she sails out to the ocean on a small boat, leaving the abusive Hamlet behind. She is one of the angry Ophelias who would not die.

FEMININITY AND MASCULINITY IN *HAMLET* ADAPTATIONS IN THE EMPIRE OF JAPAN

Contrastingly, in Naoya Shiga's *Kuraudiusu no nikki* (*Claudius's Diary*, 1912), women, notably Gertrude and Ophelia, are stereotypically feminine, silent and obedient. The narrative focus is on Claudius; he is the narrator and, as such, while his inner agony is vividly shown, other characters are flat and colourless. Shiga's novel was the product of the author's antipathy for the 1911 *Hamlet*, the first full performance of the play in literary translation by Tsubouchi. Feeling more sympathy with Claudius, Shiga made Claudius his first-person narrator/protagonist. The story is a family melodrama, dramatizing male sibling rivalry between King Hamlet and Claudius over Gertrude and generational conflicts between Claudius and Hamlet. Claudius tells how he has loved Gertrude secretly for a long time, even before Hamlet's birth. King Hamlet began suspecting Claudius's feelings toward Gertrude, while she remained innocently unknowing. Claudius did not murder King Hamlet, but he was not innocent of the idea. The novel ends just after the time when Claudius has sent Hamlet away to England. At the end of the novel, the author's note states that though Claudius's diary ends here, his destiny after the novel might not necessarily be the same as in the original work. As a family tragedy, *Hamlet* was a fertile source material for Shiga, whose 'I' novels are male-centred and based on his Oedipal conflicts with his father (Ishizuka 2002: 31–44).

Japanese culture used Shakespeare as a vehicle for its cultural diplomacy when the first Japan Shakespeare Society was established in 1929, and the first president, Sanki Ichikawa, and his wife visited Stratford-upon-Avon on the occasion of Shakespeare's 367th birthday in 1931. In 1934 Minoru Toyoda, Professor of British Literature at Kyushu Imperial University, published *Shakespeare in Japan* in English with financial support from the Society for International Cultural Relations (Japan) and British Council for Relations with Other Countries (today's British Council). It was the period of Japan's brutal military aggression and political isolation: the Manchurian Incident (1931) started Japan's military invasion of Manchuria, and Japan withdrew from the League of Nations in 1933. 'Professional Shakespeare production ceased in 1938 with the worsening international situation' (Gallimore and Minami 2016: 487).

Osamu Dazai's *Shin Hamlet* (*New Hamlet*) (Dazai 2016) was published in July 1941, when Japan was continuing its military aggression in China and the Pacific, and a few months before the Pearl Harbor Attack (December 1941). Claudius asks for the courtiers' approval of his new kingship in a condescending manner for the sake of 'consideration for the people's sense of unwavering patriotism' (32) when Denmark has been lately at odd with Norway. He equates loyalty to the kingdom with familial devotion when he says, in permitting Laertes to go back to Paris, 'for children, the father's approval is more important than the king's approval. Harmony within the family equates to loyalty to the king' (43). Within the novel, family devotion, female reproductive bodies and male heroism are made to serve the state in a war.

Male homosocial bonds are in disarray. Hamlet's love for Ophelia is selfish and sexist, while the cross-generational same-gender bond between Gertrude and Ophelia helps Ophelia, pregnant, survive. Here, Gertrude is the one who is most critical about Hamlet's self-dramatization of himself as a tragic hero. She takes it as a sign of his unprincely attitude that he prioritizes private and familial matters before his duty to the country and the people. She is ashamed of him for still forcing people to baby him at twenty-three. Claudius pretends to be more soft, fatherly and understanding of Hamlet's youthful agony, but such pretense falls apart early. Ophelia has a long tête-à-tête with Gertrude, where she reveals herself witty enough to ridicule Hamlet's 'Nobody understands my suffering' attitudes (1140). She confesses that 'it was not Lord Hamlet—I quietly, earnestly loved and respected *you* [Gertrude], your grace' (1097). Cross-generational sisterhood or female solidarity between Gertrude and herself is essential for Ophelia, not heterosexual love for Hamlet. Ophelia declares to Hamlet that 'I will return to being that old tomboyish Ophelia' (1669) and criticizes Hamlet for pretending to be 'the protagonist of some tragedy'. Hamlet tries to silence her by quoting the authority of the Bible, 'Saint Paul said that "I permit no woman to teach or to have authority over men; she is to keep silent"', (1725) but she would not be silenced. She escapes from the castle to give birth to a child who is precious to her because s/he is a grandchild of Gertrude, not because s/he is Hamlet's child. Dazai's novel is remarkable in that it makes female characters more confident in speaking for themselves than the men, and in that it has its Ophelia, like Nami of Natsume's novel and Ophelia of Kobayashi's novel, survive.

The war with Norway begins, and Laertes dies heroically in fighting on the Norwegian warship. The independent, sexually active and strong-willed Gertrude in the novel, who was an efficient female ruler who put her political and public duties over her personal and private affection to her son, abandons her duty as a ruler when she, upon news of Norway's invasion, kills herself – by jumping into a narrow but deep stream, lined with willows. Through her death in a willowy stream, Dazai aligns his Gertrude with Shakespeare's Ophelia and her powerlessness. Now politically ineffective, Gertrude is wiped out of the story as if being punished for not being a self-sacrificial good mother to Hamlet. Claudius, condemning her as a weak and selfish woman, dramatizes himself as a solitary heroic male subject: 'God loves lonely men like myself. Be Strong, Claudius!' (1829). The author shows his ironic distance from Claudius's misogynistic and militaristic masculinity when he makes Hamlet say, at the very end of the novel, that he does not believe in Claudius's words and that 'I'll hold my suspicions about you [Claudius] until the day I die' (1826). On the other hand, Hamlet is ridiculed and criticized for his sexism when, just before Ophelia disappears from the story, he dictates to her that a 'woman will be saved through bearing children' and that a woman has to 'quietly attend to the children that are born to them' (1736). Dazai presents Hamlet's words, reflecting the Japanese ideology of 'good wife/wise mother' (*ryosai kenbo*), as signs of his misogyny. According to Hamlet, female sexuality is legitimatized and sanctioned only when women serve the state by reproducing the population and being good wives/wise mothers to male subjects. However, Ophelia does not listen to Hamlet's preaching, and steals away from him and the castle, pregnant with the child precious to her because s/he is a grandson of Gertrude. The author endorses the cross-generational sisterhood between Gertrude and Ophelia as an antithesis to male misogyny and militaristic masculinism.

SHAKESPEARE IN COLD WAR JAPAN

Imperial Japan surrendered itself on 15 August 1945. The Occupation by the Allied Powers lasted for six years until 1951. Perhaps surprisingly, professional Shakespeare productions quickly resumed at the initiative of Japanese actors rather than the Allied occupiers. *A Midsummer Night's Dream* was staged and directed by Yoshi Hijikata, a left-wing director, in 1946. In 1947, a Kabuki theatre troupe Zenshin-za, allied with the labour movement, performed *The Merchant of Venice* at factories, mining towns and schools. However, at the onset of the Cold War, with the founding of the People's Republic of China in 1949 and the beginning of the Korean War in 1950, left-wing, labour movement-based cultural productions came under suppression.

The central figure in Japanese Cold War Shakespeare production is Tsuneari Fukuda (1912–94), an author, dramatist, critic and theatre director who was to translate fifteen of Shakespeare's works between 1955 and 1986. In directing Shakespeare, Fukuda sought faithful replication of Shakespeare's Western performance, but in his creative writings borrowing materials from Shakespeare, he experimented with *hon'an* adaptations. He published *Horaisio nikki* (*Horatio's Diary*, 1949) as a postwar commentary on Japan's past as an invader of a British colony in Asia, Singapore. The novel is set in London during the Second World War with the protagonist David Jones, a director and actor with the Old Vic Company. Jones directs *Hamlet* and performs Horatio, conceptualized as an embodiment of British common sense. The story centres around an extramarital affair of Jones and Isabel, who performs Ophelia. The novel ends at the beginning of the Battle of Singapore (February 8–12, 1942), the Empire of Japan's military invasion.

Among Shakespeare performance in 1950s Japan, Fukuda's production of his translation of *Hamlet* (1955), through an impeccable imitation of the London Old Vic 1953 production (Gallimore and Minami 2016: 487), is considered to be especially important. The Rockefeller Foundation invited Fukuda and Shohei Ooka (1909–88), a novelist and former prisoner of war in the Philippines, to the United States and Europe in 1953–4, as part of the Rockefeller projects sending Japanese writers to the United States to make them pro-American, with varying degrees of success (Kim 2019). Ooka and Fukuda travelled together and watched *Hamlet* and *The Tempest* (featuring Richard Burton) at the London Old Vic in 1953.

Fukuda's dramatic adaptation of *Macbeth*, *Akechi Mitsuhide*, was performed in August 1957 (intriguingly, Akira Kurosawa's filmic *hon'an* adaptation of *Macbeth*, *Throne of Blood*, premiered in January the same year). Fukuda's adaptation is set in sixteenth-century Japan. The Macbeth figure, Akechi, is depicted in a sympathetic light as a noble warrior who, harassed brutally by the tyrannical Oda, cannot but kill him. The three witches are turned into one old witch, and one actress performs the part and Lady Macbeth figure. The Macbeth figure is killed by a peasant, not by the Macduff figure (who is absent from the adaptation). The play ends when Akechi is killed, but without the declaration of peace, with the witch's triumphant laughter thundering.

Fukuda became a conservative supporting pro-American policy in Japan. By contrast, Ooka expresses his reservation/criticism of American politico-cultural hegemony through his novel adaptation of *Hamlet*, *Hamuretto nikki* (*Hamlet's Diary*, first edition 1955, most recent edition 1988). He criticizes American military dominance in Asia and Japan's complicity with it during the Cold War and the Korean War (1950–3). In his afterword, he writes that 'I wanted to lay special emphasis on the US Army Forces occupying Japan after World War II' (qtd. in Kawachi 2016: 130). Hamlet in the novel is deeply frustrated because of his uncle's policy to let the Norwegian army pass through Denmark to Poland. Denmark in the novel is like Japan with US military bases, sending American military forces to the Korean War. Claudius and Polonius are selling weapons, foods, drinks and even sex services to the Norwegian army stationed in Denmark, just like Japan was gaining economic recovery by supplying everyday items and services necessary for military bases – if not weapons – for the US military. In Hamlet's eyes, Denmark cannot be an independent nation if it allows a foreign country to have its military base in Denmark, a clear allusion to Japan's situation. After Polonius's death, Laertes rises against Claudius's regime as a leader of the common people.

Ooka's novel underwent several stages of rewriting, especially concerning Ophelia. In the earlier versions, she is colourless and has no agency of her own, being an obedient daughter to her bourgeois father. Hamlet, though he shows a tiny bit of self-reflection when he says, 'it would be very convenient for us men if we can think of all women as voluptuous animals' (1988: 207), acts in quite openly misogynistic ways and forsakes Ophelia after having sex with her. Told of Ophelia's death, he imagines her floating on water. As Ooka watched Laurence Olivier's 1948 movie *Hamlet* repeatedly to write his novel, Ophelia in the movie (Jean Simmons), echoing Millais's Ophelia, must have been in Ooka's mind. Yet curiously, at Ophelia's funeral, Hamlet refers to 'the Instructions for the Battlefield of the Imperial Japanese forces' (1988: 331) that strictly forbade retreat or surrender. The Instructions direct soldiers to commit suicide rather than surrender to the enemy. As a soldier in the Second World War, Ooka witnessed numerous cases of soldiers' enforced suicides in Japan's wars against the United States in the Philippines (Ooka 1996). His Hamlet urges that the priests must give Ophelia a proper funeral, citing the instances of Denmark's soldiers who, surrounded by Norwegian forces, committed suicide. Here Hamlet compares Ophelia to Japanese soldiers forced to commit suicide during the war. Yet in this first edition, Ophelia herself remains a silent, beautiful corpse. In the 1988 edition, Ophelia returns as a ghost, and Ooka gives her the power to talk back to Hamlet. Hamlet dreams of Ophelia after her suicide. When she refers to their sexual relationship, Hamlet stops her by saying that a woman should not talk of sexual matters like a man. However, she talks back to his sexual double standard, as she, being dead, no longer needs to act like a demure, obedient maiden as she had to in her lifetime. Hamlet nevertheless still acts in a misogynistic way, treating her as a simple-minded nuisance. He tries to dismiss her by saying, 'You annoy me. You even contradict me? I, who have great ambition, have no time to listen to foolish words from a drowned girl. Dream or ghost, vanish!' (Ooka 1988: 339). However, she does not vanish: instead, she looks steadfastly at him, sadly but reproachfully. After numerous revisions, Ooka finally succeeds in making Ophelia confront Hamlet's sexism. If the first edition, published in 1955, was an allegory of political/military situations Japan faced during the Korean War, it was told solely from Hamlet's point of view. The final version can be thought of as a *hon'an* of the first version. In it, Ooka finally manages to take up gender politics, thereby relativizing Hamlet's militaristic masculinism.

HARUKI MURAKAMI'S POSTMODERN *MACBETH* AND ANXIETY OVER MALE SUBJECTHOOD AND FEMALE SEXUALITY

In *hon'an* adaptations of *Hamlet* and *Macbeth*, anxiety over modern male subjecthood and female sexuality are continuing elements. *Kishibe no Kafka* (*Kafka on the Shore*, 2002) by Haruki Murakami (1949–), which adapts *Macbeth*, inherits the elements, with some postmodern twists. Murakami combines Sophocles's *Oedipus* and *Macbeth* to create a story of patricide. The story centres on the two male characters, Nakada and a boy who calls himself Kafka. Nakada, who had a difficult relationship with his father, is a Macbeth who kills a Scottish King, here represented by the Scottish Whisky label character, Johnny Walker. Johnny Walker, in his turn, stands in for Kafka's abusive father. Kafka runs away from his home to escape from his father, who has forced him to believe that '"*Someday you will murder your father*" and sleep with his mother and sister' (Murakami 2006: 202) just like Oedipus. In his sixties at the novel's present, Nakada suffers from the trauma of the Second World War and family abuse he experienced. A man who calls himself Johnnie Walker, dressed in a red jacket and wearing a silk hat just like the logo character of the Scottish whisky, tries to incite Nakada to murder him (143) by killing cats that Nakada befriended. Looking at his hands soaked with the cats' blood, Johnnie Walker quotes, 'No, *this my hand will rather the multitudinous seas incarnadine, Making the green one red*' (145). He proclaims, '*O, full of scorpions is my mind!*' (148) and adds, '*Macbeth* again'. Nakada kills him, and on the same night, Kafka's father is found dead.

The novel repeatedly suggests that Nakada and Kafka are mirror images of each other, including when Kafka regains his consciousness at a Shinto shrine and finds his T-shirt soaked with blood, still fresh and wet (71). The night turns out to be the night of his father's death. Kafka washes the T-shirt in the sink, the blood dyeing the porcelain sink red. The sink dyed with blood corresponds, in a diminished form, with Duncan's blood, that would 'incarnadine' 'the multitudinous seas', in Macbeth's lines Johnnie Walker recites. Kafka washes his hands frantically. Nakada and Kafka are Macbeths, and Johnnie Walker/Kafka's father is Duncan. The story thus overtly dramatizes Kafka's struggle with the father figure, in a fashion reminiscent of Oedipus and Macbeth.

Several female characters are likewise reminiscent of Lady Macbeth. One is Nakada's female teacher when he was a child. Nakada was one of the sixteen school children who fell into a mysterious coma in 1944 during the Second World War. On the previous night, the teacher had an 'extremely realistic and sexually charged' dream regarding her husband, who had been drafted to fight in Manila, in the Philippines (99). When she supervises the children the next day her period suddenly starts, and she associates it with that sex dream. She hides the towels she used to clean herself among the bushes, but the boy Nakada finds the bloody towels. Out of control, she slaps him on his face. At that moment, the group coma among the school children begins (100). All children other than Nakada wake up shortly after. There are suspicions that their coma might have been caused either by a secret weapon of the United States or poison gas of the Japanese military. Nakada remains in a coma for three weeks, waking up only when a nurse, trying to draw a blood sample, spills some blood on the sheets (68). This scene appears just before the scene in which Kafka finds himself in a T-shirt soaked with blood (71), as discussed in the previous paragraph. Nakada has lost all his memory and become mentally challenged. When the teacher's husband dies just before the end of the war, she accepts it as inevitable (104), as if his death were the result of her sex dream, her menstruating body and her mistreatment of Nakada. Another woman sleepwalks and has sex with Kafka. The third woman, a sister figure, is raped by Kafka in his dream. When he comes, his 'hands are sticky with something—human blood' (371). All combined, these three female figures are reminiscent of the three witches as well as Lady Macbeth, and they horrify and allure Nakada/Kafka with their sexual bodies.

Murakami inherits a tradition of 150 years' history of *hon'an* of Shakespeare's works in Japanese novels, where – as we have seen through the *Hamlet*-based *hon'an* – they have been employed to express Japan's anxiety over male, modern and Westernized subjecthood and its related allure/horror of female sexual agency.

CONCLUSION

This chapter has placed Japanese novels from Natsume's *Kusamakura* to Murakami's *Kafka on the Shore* in the context of the East Asian culture of *hon'an*, which was regarded as a genuine creative endeavour, not inferior to original composition or direct translation. Earlier practitioners of Shakespeare adaptation/translation, such as Tsubouchi and Natsume, had to struggle with the otherness of Shakespeare, Western-style novels and literary theories. Many of the adaptations of *Hamlet* when Japan was a military empire adapted the original work as a story of a state in war and reflected Japan's wartime ideology. But Japanese novelists also provide representations of Ophelia that are quite different from the conventional image of her as a beautiful but powerless victim of patriarchy. The Ophelias in many of these novels survive. During the Cold War, adaptations of Shakespeare reflected Japan's ambivalence toward American socio-political hegemony. Finally, Murakami's novel in the early twenty-first century adapts *Macbeth* as a story of patricide/regicide. Even as these *hon'an* reveal Japan's endeavour to incorporate Shakespeare in building its national culture, they also show how Shakespeare's works outlive Shakespeare, crossing boundaries of nations and literary genres to express new times and social change.

REFERENCES

Anderson, J. L. (2011), *Enter a Samurai: Kawakami Otojiro and Japanese Theatre in the West*, vol. 1, Tucson, Wheatmark.

Britannica Academic online (2020), 'I Novel' (https://www.britannica.com/art/I-novel), 'Japanese Literature' (https://www.britannica.com/art/Japanese-literature/Modern-literature#ref61866), 'Shoyo Tsubouchi' (https://www.britannica.com/biography/Tsubouchi-Shoyo; all accessed 29 October 2021).

Dazai, O. (2016), *A New Hamlet*, trans. O. Cooney, Pennsauken: Bookbaby. Kindle edn.

Dijkstra, B. (1986), *Idols of Perversity*, New York, NY: Oxford University Press.

Gallimore, D. (n.d.), *Shakespeare in Japan*. Available online: https://www.sheikusupia.net/ (accessed 1 February 2021).

Gallimore, D. and R. Minami (2016), 'Seven Stages of Shakespeare Reception', in J. Salz (ed.), *A History of Japanese Theatre*, 484–96, Cambridge: Cambridge University Press.

Harada, N. (forthcoming 2021), '*Robinson Crusoe* in the Context of Travel Narrative of Early Modern England on Asia', in S. Clark and Y. Yoshihara (eds), *Robinson Crusoe in Asia*, New York, NY: Palgrave.

Ishizuka, N. (2002), 'Hamlet to Shiga Naoya, Claudius no nikki [Hamlet and Naoya Shiga, "Claudius's Diary"]', *Lingua* 13: 31–44.

Joubin, A. A. (2021), *Shakespeare and East Asia*, New York, NY: Oxford University Press, Kindle edn.

Kano, A. (2001), *Acting Like a Woman in Modern Japan: Theater, Gender and Nationalism*, New York, NY: Palgrave.

Karatani, K. (1993), *Origins of Modern Japanese Literature*, Foreword by F. Jameson, trans. B. De Bary, Durham and London: Duke University Press. Kindle edn.

Kawachi, Y. (2016), 'Hamlet and Japanese Men of Letters', *Multicultural Shakespeare* 14 (29): 123–35.

Kawatake, T. (1972), *Nippon no Hamuretto* [Hamlet in Japan], Tokyo: Sanso-sha.

Kawato, M. and T. Sakakibara, eds. (2000), *Sheikusupia honyaku bungakusho zensyu* [A collection of Shakespeare translation in Japan], Tokyo: Ozora-sha.

Keene, D. (1998), *Dawn to the West: Japanese Literature in Modern Era*, New York, NY: Colombia University Press.

Kennedy, D. and Y. L. Lan, eds (2010), *Shakespeare in Asia*, Cambridge: Cambridge University Press.

Kim, J. (2019), *Nihon bungaku no sengo to hensou sareru America* [The 'Postwar' in Japanese Literature and Variations of 'America': From the Period of American Occupation to the Age of the Cultural Cold War], Tokyo: Minerva Press.

Kishi, T. and G. Bradshaw, eds (2005), *Shakespeare in Japan*, London: Continuum.

Kobayashi, H. (1968), *Ofelia ibun* [Ophelia's Literary Remain], in *Kobayashi Hideo Zenshu* [Complete Works of Hideo Kobayashi], Tokyo: Shincho.

Lanier, D. (2014), 'Shakespearean Rhizomatics: Adaptation, Ethics, Value', in A. A. Joubin and E. Rivlin (eds), *Shakespeare and the Ethics of Appropriation*, 21–40, New York, NY: Palgrave Macmillan.

Miller, J. S. (2001), *Adaptations of Western Literature in Meiji Japan*, New York, NY: Palgrave Macmillan.

Minami, R., I. Carruthers and J. Gillies, eds (2001), *Performing Shakespeare in Japan*, Cambridge: Cambridge University Press.

Murakami, H. (2006), *Kafka on the Shore*, trans. P. Gabriel, New York, NY: Knopf Doubleday.

Natsume, S. (2008), *Kusamakura*, trans. M. McKinney, New York, NY: Penguin Books.

Natsume, S. (2016), 'Professor Craig', in *The Tower of London*, trans. D. Flanagan, London: Peter Owen. Kindle edn.

Ooka, S. (1988), *Nobi/ Hamlet Nikki* [Field Fire/ Diary of Hamlet], Tokyo: Iwanami.

Ooka, S. (1996), *Taken Captive*, trans. W. Lammers, New York, NY: John Wiley & Sons.

O'Neill, S. (2014), 'Ophelian Negotiations: Remediating the Girl on YouTube', *Borrowers and Lenders* 10 (1). Available online: https://openjournals.libs.uga.edu/borrowers/article/view/2287(accessed 1 February 2021).

Peterson, K. L. and D. Williams, eds (2012), *The Afterlife of Ophelia*, New York, NY: Palgrave Macmillan.

Quinn, A. (2011), 'Political Theatre: "The Rise and Fall of Rome and The Sword of Freedom", Two Translations of *Julius Caesar* in Meiji Japan: Kawashima Keizo and Tsubouchi Shoyo', *Asian Theatre Journal* 28 (1): 168–83.

Romanska, M. (2005), 'NecrOphelia: Death, Femininity and the Making of Modern Aesthetics', *Performance Research* 10 (3): 34–53.

Sano, A. (2008), 'Shakespeare Translation in Japan: 1868–1998', *Ilha do Desterro* 0 (36): 337–69.

Sasaki, T., ed. (1997), *Sheikusupia kenkyu siryo shusei* [Collected Japanese Academic Works on Shakespeare], Tokyo: Nihon Tosho Center.

Sasayama, T., J. R. Mulryne and M. Shewting, eds (1998), *Shakespeare and the Japanese Stage*, Cambridge: Cambridge University Press.

Shakespeare, W. ([1986] 2005), *The Oxford Shakespeare: The Complete Works*, 22nd edn, Oxford: Oxford University Press.

Shiga, N. (1968), *Claudius no nikki* [Claudius's diary], Tokyo: Shincho.

Showalter, E. (1985), 'Representing Ophelia: Women, Madness, and the Responsibilities of Feminist Criticism', in Patricia Parker and Geoffrey Hartman (eds), *Shakespeare and the Question of Theory*, 77–94, London: Methuen.

Toyoda, M. (1940), *Shakespeare in Japan: A Historical Survey*, Tokyo: Iwanami.

Traub, V. (2014), *Desire and Anxiety: Circulations of Sexuality in Shakespearean Drama*, New York, NY: Routledge.

Trivedi, P. and R. Minami, eds (2010), *Re-playing Shakespeare in Asia*, London: Routledge.

Yoshihara, Y. (2001), 'Japan as "half-civilized": an Early Japanese Adaptation of Shakespeare's *The Merchant of Venice* and Japan's Construction of its National Image in the Late 19th Century', in R. Minami, I. Carruthers and J. Gillies (eds), *Performing Shakespeare in Japan*, 21–32, Cambridge: Cambridge University Press.

Yoshihara, Y. (2014), '"Raw-Savage" Othello: The First-Staged Japanese Adaptation of *Othello* and Japanese Colonialism', in A. Huang and E. Rivlin (eds), *Shakespeare and the Ethics of Appropriation*, 145–59, New York, NY: Palgrave.

Yoshihara, Y. (2020), 'Ophelia and Her Magical Daughters: The Afterlives of Ophelia in Japanese Pop Culture', in V. Bladen and Y. Brailowski (eds), *Shakespeare and the Supernatural*, 262–75, Manchester: Manchester University Press.

Shakespeare in parts

Shakespeare Live! and the commemorative gala revue: rhetoric, festivity and fragmented adaptation

AILSA GRANT FERGUSON

The twenty-first century Shakespearean commemorative gala revue, *Shakespeare Live!* (dir. Gregory Doran, RSC, 23 April 2016) exists in a liminal space between modes of performance and adaptation, transgressing the boundaries of 'high' and 'low' theatre. It does so by mixing short extracts with songs, dance, sketches, film clips and pre-recorded segments. Shakespearean commemorative gala revues are shows that comprise a collection of parts of Shakespearean texts, adapted, often truncated or fragmented, to construct one cohesive show that forms a whole production that 'remembers' Shakespeare festively. This process of fragmentation and reconstruction can be read as a means by which British, but in particular, English, imperial and post-imperial national identity is defined and redefined through the 'national poet', Shakespeare. In *Shakespeare Live!*, we can trace a clear example of the ways in which texts and previous productions are both represented through fragments of themselves, creating a 'haunted stage' (Carlson 2003) of the re-animated pieces of text, memory and performance.

From wartime appropriations of *King John* and *Henry V* to the perpetual urge to truncate John of Gaunt's state of the nation speech in *Richard II*, England has 'remembered' Shakespeare via fragmented adaptation. Examining the rhetoric of adaptation, appropriation and the fragmentary nature of the gala, the chapter will arrive at its case study: the Royal Shakespeare Company's *Shakespeare Live!*, at the Royal Shakespeare Theatre, Stratford-upon-Avon, simultaneously broadcast live on BBC television and in cinemas, and available subsequently on DVD. Via this gala revue-style production, fragments (re)constructed into a 'whole' show are read as a valid iteration of Shakespearean adaptation, a festive upheaval of structure, form and memory.

In a gala revue in his honour, Shakespeare (man and text) exists only via adaptation, synecdoche and metonymy. Many texts may feature, but often there is no single work intact; where there is a 'complete' text, it is augmented with fragmentary representations of other works. There are not only textual fragments, here, but also revivals of moments from previous productions, in some sense literalizing Elin Diamond's assertion that all 'performance marks out a unique temporal space that nevertheless contains traces of other now-absent performances' (2015: 1), in which those ghostly predecessors are merged with the present performance 'live'. Some commemorative gala revues stretch this link further by using fragments of previous adaptations, such as *Shakespeare Live!*'s extensive use of opera, ballet and musical adaptations and appropriations of Shakespeare's works interspersed with extracts from the plays. Galas are constructed to commemorate and to pay homage to Shakespeare, an act of cultural 'remembrance' and, as the examples here will demonstrate, a means of (re)constructing cultural memory. They are liminal, too, in their cultural status, straddling 'high' and 'low' theatre forms yet avoiding the hackneyed criticism of 'dumbing down' via references or in-jokes that invite knowing complicity from their audiences. In both capacities, gala revues are rhetorical, using adaptation and appropriation, cutting, splicing, selecting and ordering, narrating and casting to mediate Shakespeare in unique ways.

At times of celebratory commemoration – Shakespeare is not being mourned but (re)constructed in public memory – festive audiences can be receptive to fragmentation, irreverent adaptation and downright mockery. In this way, commemorative performance can bring together affectionate lampooning, burlesque, melodrama, those 'illegitimate' Shakespeares made popular in the nineteenth and twentieth centuries (Collick 1989; Schoch 2002) with a bardolatrous selection of Shakespeare's 'greatest hits' in the form of the most famous scenes and most revered practitioners. The revue-style gala relies on the inter-relationship of textual and performative fragments juxtaposed against the multitude of accompanying meanings, assumptions and memories the audience brings to bear on each extract, adaptation or homage and, equally, 'ghost[ed]' (Carlson 2003) in the bodies onstage or screen. As such, these fragments constitute, in rhetorical terms, powerful synecdoches (in which a single part comes to represent the whole from whence it came), carrying the burdens of meaning and politics as ghostly memories. Add these fragments together, however, and the resulting 'adaptation' is one of multiple works, appropriated and reconstructed to form a new text, in which order, presentation, truncation, editing and performance all play a part in establishing a powerful rhetoric of Shakespeare, memory, festivity and cultural identity.

RHETORIC

As Linda Hutcheon has articulated, Daniel Fischlin and Mark Fortier's definition of adaptation, that it 'includes almost any act of alteration performed upon specific cultural works of the past and dovetails with a general process of cultural re-creation' (2000: 4), is challengingly broad for those seeking to theorize adaptation in process and result (Hutcheon 2012: 8). However, for the purpose of examining the gala revue, it is useful to take this wide-lens view of adaptation, particularly in performance. While Hutcheon defines adaptation broadly as text-to-text movement (2012: 8), the gala circles back to the possibilities of adaptation on a broader scale. *Shakespeare Live!* adapts not one text but over thirty, yet they all derive from a body of work that has been ascribed to one author and cultural monolith. Any literary commemorative act implicitly rejects post-structural debates on textual supremacy, by virtue of its very purpose. Yet, the gala revue adds another authorial hand in the director selecting and editing the parts, here, Gregory Doran. However, in reviving previous productions with other directors, even that single authorship is challenged. We are left primarily with a re-constructed Shakespeare, merging man and text, a new narrative constructed entirely from multi-layered adaptations and appropriations.

Essentially, *Shakespeare Live!* is not one fragment out of time and place, as Hutcheon might see those she discounts from qualifying as 'adaptation' (2012: 8). Instead, it is a laid-bare act of mass fragmentation, adaptation, appropriation and intertextuality that shows both the mechanisms and the agenda of its own appropriations. Piecing together fragments of text, myth, existing adaptations and appropriations, the show presents an adaptation not of single text but of oeuvre. Using each fragment both as synecdoche of its origin and as integral part to the new, complete show, *Shakespeare Live!* exemplifies the uniqueness of the gala revue. It is a curated anthology that comprises hundreds of acts of adaptation and appropriation in the most overt and conscious ways. The burlesque, the music hall and the melodrama haunt the gala, while modernist fragmentation and postmodern bricolage inform the show's eclecticism and disregard for sustaining tone or theme beyond one or two segments at a time, often with jolting results. Meera Syal, for example, has just ended the extract from the first scene of *Much Ado About Nothing* with a melancholy delivery of Beatrice's poignant words, 'I know you of old' (1.1.139), when she is promptly followed by a raucous performance of Cole Porter's jovially misogynistic Broadway song, 'Brush Up Your Shakespeare'. The textual and performative fragments that constitute revues represent a much larger set of indistinct entities: the original texts, the author, the cultural capital of that author and/or text and features of the text itself (plot, theme, character, form). Using an existing text as a starting point constructs a specific discourse via which the new text speaks, a language or code for which the original text is the key.

MEMORY

Understanding adaptation as cultural memory formation is core to how commemorative galas must be read. The very concept of 'cultural' and 'collective memory' is based on a figurative and rhetorical link with discourses in the individual mind. The terms are notoriously difficult to define. Astrid Erll argues that the term 'cultural memory' can be divided into two tropes in how it is utilized: metonymy, 'a literal use of the term "memory" … with a metonymic use of the attribute "cultural" (which stands for socio-cultural contexts and their influence on individual memory)' and metaphor, 'linguistic images for the organized archiving of documents, for the establishment of official commemoration days, or for the artistic process of intertextuality' (2011: 97). If we adopt Erll's dichotomy, it is plain to see the relevance to the practice of creating and experiencing commemorative performances and, specifically, galas that are constructed of fragments. The premodifier, 'cultural', attached to the deeply individual process/product 'memory', immediately renders the whole phrase to be figurative and rhetorical, rather than literal. Fragments may function as synecdoches or metonyms within the rhetoric, or discourse of performance, of the production as a whole.

Shakespeare commemorative galas, by adapting, splicing and reconstructing Shakespeare's work, function specifically as a tool of cultural memory formation via collective remembering. Conscious, 'individual' memory is based on incomplete segments formed into meaning by complex, hierarchical and continual processes. Cultural memory, too, can establish itself via small units of meaning. The gala commemoration relies partly on existing individual memories of its audience (recalling plays read in school, iconic scenes reproduced in popular culture, productions seen onstage or, later, film) and partly on building a collective experience of recall and recognition. The whole that is formed of these snippets and snatches of Shakespeare, becomes the new 'Shakespeare' that gala (re)constructs to be remembered. This risks a perpetuation of an elitism around the pre-knowledge required to be in on the hints, jokes and connotations of the fragments, just as it tries to lay claim to a democratic performance of Shakespeare. Crucially, too, the patchwork of Shakespearean fragments creates a whole adaptation made from many pieces onstage and in the memory of its audience that has its own textual cohesion and may construct a specific Shakespeare that meets a rhetorical and/or political agenda. In the First World War, for example, the tercentenary 'Shakespeare' constructed for the 1916 commemorations, such as in the wartime galas of Drury Lane and at the Shakespeare Hut, is a patriotic Shakespeare (Calvo 2010; Grant Ferguson 2014, 2019) and also, arguably, a reformer and a suffragist (Grant Ferguson 2014, 2019). These galas offer a useful example of how the gala combines pragmatism with creativity, 'high' with 'low' cultural forms and, crucially, the haphazardness of fragments brought together to accommodate diverse available players with the politics of adaptation for very specific purposes.

FESTIVITY AND THE SHAKESPEARE GALA

Shakespeare Live! took place at a festive moment, when we choose to 'remember' Shakespeare communally. As a theatre with a royal mandate and therefore national status, it treads a line between Bakhtin's (1965: 5–6) 'officialdom' (royal, national monument) and 'non-officialdom' (theatre, performance) that is delicate and vexed. Tasked to represent a national moment of celebratory commemoration, the RSC used a combination of its own theatre space and the Stratford-upon-Avon heritage sites to provide a show that tried to merge those worlds. Since David Garrick's 1769 Jubilee, post-Romantic worship of Shakespeare's 'genius' and the bardolatry that has taken hold since the nineteenth century, Shakespeare's texts, once part of the marginal world of theatre and performance, have become deeply embedded in the 'official' world. They have become ritualized and fetishized by repetitive encoding. However, they retain their potential for festive inversion, confusion, tricks and challenges to the structures of power. This dualism is the space in which the commemorative gala revue functions, projecting officially sanctioned cultural worship yet retaining the potential for festive tricks and inversions.

As both Michael Dobson (1992) and Andrew McConnell Stott (2019) have shown, Garrick's 1769 Jubilee at Stratford-upon-Avon marked the beginning of the creation of the performative Shakespeare myth we know today, despite the event being an infamous financial and pragmatic disaster. It was nearly a century later, in 1864, when the next major attempt was made to tie some sort of celebration of the poet, a national 'memory' of Shakespeare, to commemorative dates (in this case the tercentenary of his birth in 1564) as a festive moment. However, it was, as Andrew Dickson rather beautifully encapsulates it, dominated by a series of 'calamities and cock ups' (2015: 13), in which ever-multiplying committees and diffuse plans across Stratford and London led to an uncoordinated and disjointed set of outcomes. Yet, despite these unpromising beginnings, 'remembering' Shakespeare via the festivities of commemorative events has become entrenched as part of English national identity formation and, in turn, in British cultural and political imperialism (for example, in Australia, see Mead 2017, and the US, see Smialkowska 2016). While commercially and practically speaking these events were unsuccessful, they embedded worship of Shakespeare (or, to use George Bernard Shaw's coinage, 'bardolatry') as part of heritage tourism and led the way in what Hodgdon would coin 'the Shakespeare Trade' (1998) of the commodification of Shakespeare the man, text and myth: 'remembering' Shakespeare is now big business.

Some two and a half centuries after Garrick effectively began the national pastime of Bardolatry, the Shakespeare gala show of extracts and tributes, an extravaganza of Shakespeareana, has become a key form via which England's national poet can be 'remembered' at times of commemorative significance (Calvo 2010). The twentieth and twenty-first centuries have honed and established the form. From elaborate pre-war immersive adaptations (such as the 1912 'Shakespeare's England' exhibition's reconstructed Globe Theatre playing extracts of Shakespeare every day for six months) to London's relatively austere wartime galas, early-twentieth-century England distilled the tradition of gala-style bardolatry Garrick had foreshadowed in Stratford in 1769. The Tercentenary of 1916 saw the familiar lack of agreement on the most appropriate way to perform homage to the national poet, this time in the midst of war (Kahn 2001; Grant Ferguson 2014, 2019; McMullan 2017). However, this time, the perfect storm of wartime privation and a desperate need for entertainment, meeting powerful drives of patriotism and national morale, led to more contained one-off galas that condensed multiple extracts, adaptations and appropriations into single performances. In April, Drury Lane theatre held a gala performance that included a full production of *Julius Caesar* but surrounded it with additional spectacles and materials, such as tableaux and parade. Built in 1916, the Shakespeare Hut, a unique venue for soldiers that contained a small theatre, took on the mantle of ongoing commemorations, condensing the form still further into a series of annual commemorative galas from 1917–19. These truly embraced textual fragmentation and the revue style of a music hall with the 'high culture' of Shakespearean extracts, via presentations of songs, scenes, sketches and speeches delivered to audiences of servicemen (Grant Ferguson 2014, 2019).

In 1964, the quatercentenary of Shakespeare's birth, it would be a modern, fashionable exhibition towards which massive resources and national commemorations were focused, held in a purpose-built temporary structure on the Stratford riverbank. However, in 2016, the RSC's *Shakespeare Live!* revived the gala revue format. Showcasing the company's twenty-first-century commitment to diversity and representation (a far cry from the domination of white older male actors at Drury Lane in 1916, where no people of colour were seen and women were largely silent), it nevertheless recalled the fragmentary revue style, and frequently similar content, of its precursors though, unlike Garrick's damp squibs, the RSC's elaborate fireworks went off splendidly. These events exemplify how 'remembering' Shakespeare is defined by fragmenting text and performance into memorable pieces, both forming synecdoches and, conversely, disembodying fragments from context altogether, before reassembling the shards to form a new show, a rhetoric of Shakespearean remembrance and adaptation.

THE RSC'S *SHAKESPEARE LIVE!*

In 2016, the 'Shakespeare' of *Shakespeare Live!* (dir. Doran, RSC, 2016) was mediated as both quintessentially English *and* global, representing both the long-established status of the RSC as a 'national treasure' *and* its vision as a champion for inclusion and diversity. The gala revue form offers an excellent opportunity for the complex construction of composite meanings and to redefine the cultural memory of Shakespeare via the shared experience of commemoration, a moment of impressionable festivity. By opening with a big musical number from Bernstein's *West Side Story*, Doran's ambitious commemorative gala signalled its intention fully to embrace adaptation and appropriation, rather than faithfulness to the text, as core to what we mean by 'Shakespeare' in the twenty-first century.

The choice of the evening's presenters, David Tennant and Catherine Tate, draws attention to the fluidity between 'high' and 'popular' modes; the pair are at once well-known to TV audiences as a partnership of Doctor Who and Donna (*Doctor Who*, BBC TV, 2006, 2008–9) and to theatre audiences as Beatrice and Benedick (dir. Rourke, RSC, 2011). The pairing of equal presenters, one man and one woman, also points to the call for 50/50 gender representation onstage that the RSC was beginning to explore in 2016; the two presenters share their lines in fairly equal turn-taking. Their voices, too, avoid the received pronunciation so associated with conventional English Shakespearean production, with Tate's West London and Tennant's Scottish accent together signalling a democratic and British, rather than elite and English, celebration. Their welcome spiel carries the standard claims of authenticity presented by almost any Shakespearean commemorative event. First, unique timeliness is established, by pointing out that it is 'exactly four hundred years, to the day' since Shakespeare's death. Second, it is the authenticity of the location: 'a stone's throw from where he was born and where he is buried'. Finally, the claim of Shakespeare's universal influence is invoked:

TENNANT

It's not just the great stories he writes, the wonderful characters he creates and the memorable language. Shakespeare tells us about ourselves. He sees us from every angle.

TATE

Perhaps that is why for more than four centuries, he has inspired artists across the world.

TENNANT

From Berlioz to Bernstein, to hip hop and jazz,

TATE

From ballet to broadway, to blues and back.

TENNANT

And that's what we are celebrating tonight.

TATE

And there really is something for everybody.

TENNANT

So sit back and enjoy *Shakespeare Live!*

This opening script offers little challenge to the norms of bardolatry: that Shakespeare is universal; that he has a unique understanding of human nature; that he has influence across genre, space and time. Emphasizing an inclusive and accessible flavour for the evening, the presenters conclude, 'And there really is something for everybody', easing the audience into a show that will be nothing to fear: it will include and belong to us all.

In its Globe to Globe festival (2012) four years earlier, Shakespeare's Globe had revealed the complexity around the stability of the text to a wider audience, by hosting a season of productions from across the world, in languages including Shona, Urdu, Japanese and British Sign Language. However, while *Shakespeare Live!*'s fragmentary gala format circumvents, to a great extent, the vexed textual 'essence' that problematizes Shakespeare's cultural capital in translation, adaptation and appropriation, it also sidelines the plays in translation and does not provide signed interpretation of any of the segments as standard. Establishing its own legitimacy of Shakespeare the man (via geographical location, heritage presentation and rhetoric of space and place), the show also weaves conservative enough presentations of Shakespeare to avoid too much scrutiny by either end of the debate. There are no gender-flipped parts, here, no translations (not onstage, at least, only in brief clips), no questioning of Shakespearean cultural supremacy. Standard tropes of nineteenth- to twentieth-century Bardolatry such as Shakespeare's universality and timelessness are shored up by choices of extract and casting that present the company as an inclusive yet comfortably familiar version of Shakespeare.

Shakespeare Live! sells itself on its semi-punned title: Shakespeare will be 'live' onstage, broadcast 'live' on television and he is '[a]live' in our memories, both individual and cultural. The awkwardly sombre notion of celebrating a death day is conveniently sidestepped in all Shakespearean commemoration by his appearing to have died on his own birthday, nicely completing a cycle only further conveniently aligning with English national identity by falling, too, on 23 April, St George's Day (the national patron saint). That Shakespeare will 'live' and *be* 'live' through the RSC's gala is central to the rhetoric that threads its way through the show: Shakespeare's continuing contemporary relevance as well as his power in cultural heritage. By preserving the gala for future viewers via DVD and streaming services, though, the show speaks to the postmodern consumption of performance and is therefore no longer bound to a moment, even one that is crucial to the existence of the show at all: a commemorative moment. Belated viewers, therefore, will watch it outside its festive time but, the title tells us, will be drawn, 'live', into the resurrection of Shakespeare whenever and wherever they are.

Having launched on a big musical number, signalling the bond between this Shakespearean theatre and mid-century US and UK popular musical theatre, the gala continues on its way through around forty segments across a two-hour show. Eschewing the length of a full play or the need for an interval, the gala moves at a dizzying pace, weaving in speedy cast swaps and set-changes, concealing these pragmatic mechanisms of theatre from the remote television and cinema audiences by cutting to pre-recorded location footage. One thread throughout these non-live elements of the gala is footage of Joseph Fiennes, filmed at the Shakespeare Birthplace Trust's historic properties around Stratford, telling a version of Shakespeare's life story. Having played Shakespeare in the most commercially successful screen representation of the writer, *Shakespeare in Love* (dir. John Madden, UK/USA, 1998), Fiennes brings his former embodiment of Shakespeare to bear on the information he imparts. There is as much conjecture and legend as there is evidential 'fact' in what Fiennes presents. Yet he is also situated in Stratford, at the 'real' places of Shakespeare's birth, life and death, reinforcing the production as geographically authentic, the ghost of Shakespeare close by in audience recollections of Fiennes's embodiment. Fiennes gives us, through voice, body, location and image, the ghost of a 'live' Shakespeare so craved by those trying to reach him through commemoration. As Carlson suggests, 'the recycled body of an actor ... will almost inevitably in a new role evoke the ghost or ghosts of previous roles if they have made any impression whatever on the audience' (2003: 8). In the case of Fiennes, this character is Shakespeare himself, or rather the most commercially successful recent iteration. Positioning this actor in Stratford-upon-Avon, in fact among the costumed staff of the Shakespeare Birthplace Trust's heritage sites, provides a performance of authenticity in the presentation of Shakespeare's life story. This is the one version of a live Shakespeare body that 2016 can provide, and openly exploits audience memory and familiarity to create this effect.

In *Shakespeare Live!* the audience is rarely allowed to immerse itself in any representation, style or mode before another swiftly replaces it. Each fragment, homage, adaptation or appropriation is affected by those around it, however disparate the modes and styles might be. For example, an extremely light-hearted sketch by children's television's *Horrible Histories* team with no references to Shakespeare's texts (though the only other embodiment of Shakespeare the man included in the show) is followed directly by Alex Hassell, Jennifer Kirby and Leigh Quinn in Act 5, scene 2 of *Henry V*, conventionally staged and costumed in medieval-style dress. The following link from Tennant and Tate segues into a totally different piece, via the hackneyed adage that Shakespeare would today be a screenwriter:

TENNANT

[Shakespeare] was at the forefront of popular culture, so today he would be writing films, he would be writing tv shows… who are today's linguistic geniuses?

TATE

… Who better to answer than Hip Hop Shakespeare, with Akala and Nitin Sawhney and Dane Hurst.

The audience is thus suddenly shifted from trivial humour, to conventional Shakespeare fragment, to an interpretive dance (Hurst) with rap (Akala) and modern musical accompaniment (Sawhney). Akala appropriates Shakespearean phrases, reshaping them into a twenty-first-century ode to Shakespeare's enduring appeal: 'This mortal coil sprang back and founded this language that's used by us all'. Despite the apparent (post)modernity of the presentation, this is a piece that reinforces the construction of Shakespeare as a 'found[er]' of culture and literary discourse. Writing before the gala took place, Stephen O'Neill identifies Akala's reception in the media positioning him as 'simultaneously a critic of a traditionally valorized Shakespeare, one associated with high culture and white privilege, and an exponent of a more culturally hybrid, pliable Shakespeare that appeals to a young, multicultural demographic' (2016: 247), leaving him in a liminal position. In *Shakespeare Live!*, the work he presents tends towards a literary celebration but its embodiment onstage, merged with dance and musical elements performed by Black artists, leans away from both ends of the media interpretation of Akala's position in relation to Shakespeare and instead uses the RST space – and the moment of the centenary – to present Shakespeare as an element of cultural history that is shared, while neither obliterating nor overshadowing Black cultural expression and achievement. Akala is not by any means the first hip hop artist to co-opt Shakespeare's words and name into the rap lexicon and over the past few decades, various artists have utilized Shakespeare as a metonym for excellence in rhyme and the master manipulator of language, the declaration of a powerfully self-affirming voice that forms part of rap-battle tradition, while also appropriating the hegemonic signifier of genius into a subcultural discourse with Black ownership. For example, even back in the 1990s, Encore compares himself with Shakespeare (Tommy BNoy Music 1999). Shortly later, white rapper Eminem refers to himself as a 'modern day Shakespeare', within Jay-Z's 'Renegade' (Def Jam Records 2001), flipping the effect to a challenge to a generalized hegemonic snobbery and deliberately courting scandal via irreverence and hyperbolic self-praise, also comparing himself to Jesus in the same line. Akala's wider Hip Hop Shakespeare brand, therefore, responds not only to Shakespeare but also to other rappers' appropriations, harnessing and challenging Shakespeare's cultural capital as the white, English-speaking world's literary and performative idol. These layers of mediation establish an intertextuality around Hip Hop Shakespeare that speaks to the translation and 'repositioning' (Cartelli 1999) of Shakespeare's texts in postcolonial global contexts, but in so doing Akala also returns Shakespeare to Britain, away from his use as metonymical for superlative wordsmithery in US rap and claiming his texts as a legitimate site for expressing Black British literary culture.

Following as it does from one of Shakespeare's well-known mockeries of the in-earnestness of poetic language, the rhetoric of wooing in the final Act of *Henry V*, the juxtaposition of Akala's affirmation of Shakespeare's place as a 'found[er]' of literary expression combines to reassert Shakespeare's own powers of rhetoric and his usefulness as a rhetorical device for subsequent generations. Despite the rather awkward link Tennant and Tate have provided, the script has asserted Akala, Sawnhey and Hurst as those best placed to answer on who are 'linguistic geniuses', associating Akala's work with the literary canon. Akala's elaborate adaptation of Shakespeare takes the form of reconstructing fragments from across the Shakespearean oeuvre to create a cohesive rapped piece that presents Shakespeare as a language that can be owned, mediated, used and reused in contemporary cultural forms. This contrasts with the sections of adaptations (single dances from ballets, songs from musicals) that require contextualization to make narrative sense. Akala is explicitly presented within the gala as a new 'linguistic genius' and collaborative idea of cross-form expression (rap, poetry, song, instrumental music, dance) that challenges conventions of Shakespearean performance. Akala's approach, though, is scholarly and his lyrics have two levels of meaning: one, for those who 'know' Shakespeare and can recognize the original contexts and another for those who hear them only in their own right, not recognizing the elements from which they are constructed. Unlike much of the rest of the gala, Akala does not rely on the most famous fragments, moments or lines but instead pieces together lyrics that span a range of textual moments and contexts that are often less likely to be recognized. In this way, it is the moment in the gala that requires most prior knowledge to comprehend as an homage but it is the one furthest from conventional Shakespearean performance.

A gentle climax of the show occurs when Paapa Esseidu, who had just played Hamlet to wide acclaim in the RSC's first all-people of colour production of the play, arrives onstage to perform Hamlet's 'To be … ' speech (3.1.56–89), only to be interrupted with performance advice by comedian Tim Minchin, followed by a series of star actors including David Tennant, Rory Kinnear, Judi Dench, Ian McKellan and Harriet Walter. Lampooning the white supremacy of assuming Hamlet must be played by a white actor via Minchin feigning fear that he is not considered suitable as he is 'ginger', the sketch nevertheless still ends up presenting a single Black actor outnumbered by an entirely white cohort by the end of the sketch and Black actors remain in considerable minority across the show as a whole. Esseidu's broadly Standard Pronunciation delivery, too, presents Black Shakespearean acting as still expected to conform to traditions of voice delivery (Massai 2020: 32), even as we laugh when Minchin next questions David Tennant's right to play the Dane with his Scottish accent. Here, too, I recall my English school drama teacher appalled on our class trip, when he discovered with horror that the then newcomer, Alan Cumming, dared to play Hamlet with his real, Scottish accent (*Hamlet*, dir. Unwin 1993). My experience of the phrase as fragment is only one of thousands of iterations that could have embedded the phrase and part-speech in the collective and individual memories of *Shakespeare Live!*'s audience(s). Just as I have done, audience members will view the sketch – as they will the whole show – with a cache of individual and collective assumptions and memories that fill in the gaps, from unsaid jokes to full plays or recalled moments, that haunt the fragments that actually appear onstage.

Contemporary controversies around 50:50 gender casting, cross-casting and original practices, too, become sources of comedy in the same sketch. Harriet Walter's humorous response, 'not yet…' to the question of whether she has played Hamlet herself, provides an ideal example of the layering of both humour and appeal in the gala. Those very in tune with Shakespeare in production at the time would know that Walter had starred in the eponymous roles in Phyllida Lloyd's all-female productions of *Julius Caesar* (2012) and *Henry IV* (2014) (she would reprise and expand these later in 2016 in the Donmar Trilogy, playing Prospero, Henry IV and Julius Caesar). Without that knowledge, the joke still functions as a mischievous dig at the literally male-dominated stage on which she stands in that moment. In the gala as a whole, there is a balance of men and women actors, broadly speaking; yet Walter's 'not yet' is a wry remark that inadvertently signposts a conservative approach to casting in the gala itself. While women feature in many of the Shakespearean scenes, there is no cross-gender nor gender-blind casting. The only moments in which we have a hint of this practice take place in this one sketch, via Walter's remark and Judi Dench arriving onstage in doublet and hose as a comedy figure, 'Hamlet the Dame', holding a skull at the 'wrong' moment, corrected by the collected (mostly male) actors. Not even temporary festive reversal is allowed to take hold when it comes to gender, regardless of the antiquity of such a tradition of at least temporary gender role inversions, as seen in Shakespeare's own comedies or more generally in the cross-dressing essential to all early modern stage practice that kept female bodies off the public stage.

The sketch playfully mocks conservative casting and critique but it does so, crucially, from a place of safety. This jovial sketch takes just one iconic fragment, 'To be or not to be, that is the question' (*Hamlet*, 3.1.56), and uses it as the repeated punchline to a series of knowing jokes. However, it also does some rather conservative joking of its own. Both Minchin and Dench are holding skull props and are corrected by their acting colleagues, a nod to the merging of the two iconic speeches in the popular imagination, a cultural 'misremembering' in need of correction by those *in the know*. Finally, the sketch ends with a definitive final interjection, made by a surprise player: HRH Charles, Prince of Wales. This decisive grounding in establishment hierarchy, though, is as blithe as it is self-conscious and, indeed, the real Prince leaves the stage with Esseidu, both mutually patting each other on the back, the Prince and the actor-Prince. This ending blurs carnival king with monarch, actor with character and stage with audience; at this festive time, the 'player' and the 'king' can safely change places, just as we can temporarily play the trickster with the cultural 'king' that Shakespeare has become.

Elsewhere in the gala, deeply conventional adaptation and truncation are at play, selecting pieces from Shakespeare by their familiarity, presumably to ensure the production is 'for everyone'. For example, John of Gaunt's 'sceptr'd isle' speech from *Richard II* is known far more widely as a fragment than it is in its own context, as a fragment not only of a play but of a speech, usually anthologized in a truncation that stops far short of its original end. It carries Shakespeare's cultural capital, its textual context, the character of Gaunt (even the man on which he is based) and the 'ghosts' of those who have portrayed him (Carlson 2003). Further, though, the speech has, for several centuries, recurred in anthology, in propaganda, even in modern advertising, as a signifier of English pride. It brings with it a multitude of previous appropriations that have led to its familiarity in the public imagination that far exceeds those who know it from its original context. Browsing in a large chain bookshop in central London recently, I looked in vain for the British History section, only to find the whole section in fact titled 'This Sceptred Isle'. This Shakespearean fragment, then, has become a synecdoche that brings all of British History with it, despite its only referring to 'this England'. It thus represents English history as of a nation as superlative as the one Gaunt describes but England is of course, not an 'isle', as David Tennant's Scottish accent must remind *Shakespeare Live!*'s audiences throughout but, in case they miss it, is pointed out explicitly in the 'To be or not to be' skit. Yet this meaning relies on the truncation of the speech itself. It relies on people knowing *enough* but not *all* of it: that it is *by* Shakespeare is crucial to its value but that the speech in fact continues to decry the terrible state of England is silenced.

The form the speech takes in *Shakespeare Live!* is again the same truncation (ten lines taken from the middle of the speech) that dwells in anthologies, advertisements, monuments and, as such, is embedded without its textual context in cultural memory, from 'This royal throne of kings, this sceptr'd isle' to 'This blessed plot, this earth, this realm, this England' (2.1.140–50). Performed by Simon Russell Beale, the speech is pre-recorded on location at unidentified ruins. The weather is bleak and British, grey and cold. The ruins suggest the ancientness of the nation the speech describes. While Beale performs the speech in sombre, as opposed to celebratory tone, nevertheless the truncation speaks for itself. There is no warning to an 'insatiate' England 'prey[ing] upon' (3.1.38–9), nor 'making a shameful conquest of itself' (3.1.66). The speech may end there, and those words, 'this England', imply a full stop where there was once a comma. Beale's end pause is sustained through a lingering look directly into the camera, breaking the fourth wall. Cutting, editing and sometimes quite extreme truncation, are often features discussed in interrogations of the politics of adaptation. Yet, when the fragment is all that remains, when the origin text is absent, the fragment may lose synechdochic meaning for the text in which it once sat. Used often enough as a fragment alone, the synecdoche may become a metonym – Shakespeare *is* a particular England, 'this England', 'this sceptr'd isle'.

There are many moments in *Shakespeare Live!* where national politics are mapped onto the choice, order and presentation of the extracts and sketches. Ian McKellen gives More's speech addressing rioters against an influx of refugees, from the collaborative and possibly unperformed play, *The Book of Sir Thomas More* (British

Library, Harley MS 7368). The presenters' introduction establishes the apparent authenticity of this speech, presumably against all others, by drawing attention to the belief that it exists in Shakespeare's own handwriting, the only piece of creative writing to make this claim. While in London Shakespeare's 400th anniversary was being marked by displaying Shakespeare's signature at King's College London at the 'By Me, William Shakespeare Exhibition' (2016), Stratford's gala also signposts a physical link to Shakespeare's text as well as his body ('a stone's throw from where he was born and where he is buried'). Unlike the politically neutral presentation of a signature, it is Shakespeare's humanity specifically towards refugees that is put on display. In 2016, growing numbers of displaced people fleeing war and persecution, for example the bloody conflict in Syria, became the target of hatred and blame in British media. Specifically, this performance took place just two months before the referendum on Britain's membership of the EU that would lead to the Brexit vote. In the years leading up to the 2016 vote, right-wing press outlets made daily claims such as 'mass migration is allowing terrorists into the EU' (Slack 2016) and a report commissioned by the UNHCR found that 'coverage in the United Kingdom was the most negative, and the most polarised… Britain's right-wing media was uniquely aggressive in its campaigns against refugees and migrants' (Berry, Garcia-Blanco and Moore 2015: abstract). It is in this context that McKellen performs the speech. Unlike many extracts in the gala, this is framed by the fact that it was not cut from a Shakespearean play, but was Shakespeare's addition to someone else's. In that sense, too, it is the only performed extract to be synecdochic not of a Shakespearean whole but perhaps, in perception at least, of Shakespeare's broader humanity, collaborative practices and, indeed, contemporary political relevance.

The inclusion, at the almost literal 'centre' of this show, of McKellen's speech as More asks us to question who we are in relation to a very tangible and divisive contemporary debate around attitudes to refugees and migrant communities. Yet, in so doing, it establishes a particular Shakespeare, one who is 'for all time' and is both humane and empathetic. At the same time, like many of the play extracts chosen for the production (Henry V's wooing of Katherine, Beatrice and Benedick's battle of words, John of Gaunt's speech on the state of the nation, to name a few), this is primarily a moment of rhetorical acrobatics. Designed to provoke a response in a crowd, More's speech engages the RST, BBC and cinema audiences in a moment of reflection on who we, as individuals and as societies, want to be, or rather to see ourselves as being, in terms of shared values. Having attempted this response in its audiences, the show moves on directly to some pre-recorded extracts, via the following exchange between its presenters:

TENNANT
Shakespeare is performed all over the world.

TATE
He is translated into every language, from Albanian to Zulu.

TENNANT
Here are scenes from two landmark productions that opened our eyes to his global influence.

This dialogue links the speech into what follows: archive video clips of seminal Zulu and Japanese productions of *Macbeth*. Sandwiching More's speech between Paapa Essiedu's Hamlet and these clips creates a narrative that draws the audience into a sense of Shakespeare's rhetoric – and the RSC's – representing a counter to racist discourses. The very notion of what we mean by 'global' Shakespeare is vexed (Cartelli 1999; Loomba 2002) and this contrived order in the construction of the gala and festive atmosphere enables the RSC show to sidestep debates over cultural imperialism. The show is presented as for 'everybody' right from the start and glossing Shakespeare exportation could be read as a deliberate act to enforce the inclusivity of both the show and its creators.

Critical responses to *Shakespeare Live!* were mixed, often highlighting the challenges of its attempts at a democratized Shakespeare for this national occasion. The *Guardian*'s Michael Billington (2016) was unimpressed, citing Doran's attempt to include everything as ending up with incoherence:

> It is always worrying when an entertainment promises 'something for everybody'. That usually means there may be not quite enough for anybody. So it proved with the RSC's celebration of Shakespeare, conceived and directed by Gregory Doran... By including ballet, opera, jazz, hip-hop, Broadway musicals and solo songs, the evening stressed Shakespeare's legacy at the expense of his plays and, at times, resembled an upmarket version of the Royal Variety Show.

The final phrase, here, encapsulates the pitfalls of attempts to combine 'high' and 'low' culture around Shakespeare, since the comment relies fully on a readership seeing a resemblance to the Royal Variety Show as a negative. In other words, Billington is unhappy with the RSC legitimizing Shakespeare's potential as popular entertainment, and thus aligning it with '[down]market' theatre. Further, though, the review questions the prioritization of 'legacy' over text, rejecting the construction of Shakespeare presented by the show as a whole as losing sight of the work it claims to celebrate. A rhetoric that is all synecdoche, then, may not succeed in creating a whole at all. Yet the festive irreverence that peeps through the clockwork organization of the evening suggests that this review rather misses the point of a production that does not prioritize cohesion but rather embraces fragmentation, and at least a small element of chaos, to reflect the fluidity of who we think Shakespeare is – and who we think we are.

Robert McCrum, however, poured praise upon the show for the very diversity of content that his colleague saw as its downfall:

> Despite many intrinsic challenges, *Shakespeare Live!* was an apt and vivid reminder of the playwright's chameleon brilliance, his astonishing powers of assimilation, and the way in which the inspired juxtapositions of his language and poetry can ignite the cortical synapses of the imagination like no one in our literature. As usual, the man himself, always so impossible to pin down, was strangely absent, being both there and not there. Which is only another way of saying that Shakespeare, at once timeless and universal, speaks for the world.
>
> (McCrum 2016)

McCrum's assumptions, though, reveal a different set of problems in how we read the RSC production as part of an ongoing narrative of Shakespearean cultural memory formation. As this chapter has suggested, adapting that body of work and body/ figure 'Shakespeare' into a reconstructed set of fragments is one way to repurpose Shakespeare as a discourse through which to develop a rhetoric of adaptation and cultural memory. What McCrum's review makes clear is that the cliches of Shakespeare's 'timelessness' and 'universal[ity]' are enforced by trimming his texts into their most famous sections, adapting them in art forms we recognize to help us 'remember' Shakespeare. Yet this 'universality' is not a benign concept. McCrum's declaration that Shakespeare 'speaks for the world' reveals its dangers. 'To the world'? Perhaps, given the virtually global reach of Shakespearean performance, translation and appropriation. '*For* the world'? Surely not. McCrum's Shakespeare sounds colonial, rather than global.

Shakespeare Live!, the latest gala in a tradition of English Bardolatry at times of commemoration, reveals the instability of the cultural memory of Shakespeare we perform. Individual memories, associations and connotations meet collective experiences and memory in a festive space in which hierarchies are simultaneously mocked and reinforced. A production in which the selection, truncation and presentation of Shakespearean fragments can just as easily be read as random or pragmatic as it can calculated and cohesive. The rhetoric of the gala commemoration of Shakespeare is a festive one: we can play with his authority, and adapt, cut or, subvert both the texts and the 'man'. We can construct new Shakespeares to 'remember' out of the fragments on the stage and in the individual and collective memories of the audience.

REFERENCES

Bakhtin, M. (1965), *Rabelais and His World*, trans. H. Iswolsky, Bloomington, IN: Indiana University Press.

Berry, M., I. Garcia-Blanco and K. Moore. (2015), 'Press Coverage of the Refugee and Migrant Crisis in the EU: A Content Analysis of Five European Countries', Report prepared for the United Nations High Commission for Refugees. Available online: https://www.unhcr.org/protection/operations/56bb369c9/press-coverage-refugee-migrant-crisis-eu-content-analysis-five-european.html (accessed 21 May 2021).

Billington, M. (2016), 'Shakespeare Live! review – like an upmarket Royal Variety Show', *Guardian*, 24 April. Available online: https://www.theguardian.com/stage/2016/apr/24/shakespeare-live-review-like-an-upmarket-royal-variety-show (accessed 21 October 2021).

Calvo, C. (2010), 'Shakespeare as War Memorial', *Shakespeare Survey* 63: 198–211.

Carlson, M. A. (2003), *The Haunted Stage: The Theatre as Memory Machine*, Ann Arbor, MI: University of Michigan Press.

Cartelli, T. (1999), *Repositioning Shakespeare: National Formations, Postcolonial Appropriations*, New York, NY: Routledge.

Collick, J. (1989), *Shakespeare, Cinema and Society*, Manchester: Manchester University Press.

Diamond, E. (2015), *Performance and Cultural Politics*, New York, NY: Routledge.

Dickson, A. (2015), 'The Wrong Thing in the Right Place: Britain's Tercentenary of 1864', in C. Jansohn and D. Mehl (eds), *Shakespeare Jubilees, 1769–2014*, 13–30, Zurich: Lit Verlag.

Dobson, M. (1992), *The Making of the National Poet: Shakespeare, Adaptation and Authorship, 1660–1769*, Oxford: Clarendon Press.

Erll, A. (2011) *Memory in Culture*, trans. S. B. Young, Basingstoke: Palgrave.

Fischlin, D. and M. Fortier, eds (2000), *Adaptations of Shakespeare: A Critical Anthology of Plays from the Seventeenth Century to the Present*, New York, NY: Routledge.

Grant Ferguson, A. (2014), '"When wasteful war shall statues overturn": Forgetting the Shakespeare Hut', *Shakespeare* 10 (3): 276–92.

Grant Ferguson, A. (2019), *The Shakespeare Hut: A Story of Memory, Performance and Identity*, London: Bloomsbury/Arden Shakespeare.

Hutcheon, L. (2012), *A Theory of Adaptation*, 2nd edn, New York, NY: Routledge.

Kahn, C. (2001), 'Remembering Shakespeare Imperially: The 1916 Tercentenary', *Shakespeare Quarterly* 52 (4): 456–78.

Loomba, A. (2002), *Shakespeare, Race and Colonialism*, Oxford: Oxford University Press.

Massai, S. (2020), *Shakespeare's Accents: Voicing Identity in Performance*, Cambridge: Cambridge University Press.

Mead, P. (2017), 'Shakespeare, memory and the city: The Tercentenary in Sydney and its Afterlife', in *Antipodal Shakespeare: Remembering and Forgetting in Britain, Australia and New Zealand, 1916–2016*, co-author with K. Flaherty, M. Houlahan, G. McMullan and Ailsa Grant Fergusson, 64–88, London: Bloomsbury/Arden Shakespeare.

McConnell Stott, A. (2019), *What Blest Genius? The Jubilee that Made Shakespeare*, New York, NY: Norton.

McCrum, R. (2016), 'Shakespeare Live! was a bold and innovative tribute', *The Guardian*, 24 April. Available online: https://www.theguardian.com/culture/2016/apr/24/shakespeare-live-rsc-stratford (accessed 21 October 2021).

McMullan, G. (2017), 'Forgetting Israel Gollancz: The Shakespeare Tercentenary, the National Theatre and the Effects of Commemoration', in *Antipodal Shakespeare: Remembering and Forgetting in Britain, Australia and New Zealand, 1916–2016*, co-author with Kate Flaherty, Mark Houlahan, Ailsa Grant Fergusson and Philip Mead, 29–62, London: Bloomsbury/Arden Shakespeare.

O'Neill, S. (2016), '"It's William Back from the Dead": Commemoration, Representation, and Race in Akala's Hip Hop Shakespeare', *Studies in Ethnicity and Nationalism* 16 (2): 246–56.

Schoch, R.W. (2002), *Not Shakespeare: Bardolatry and Burlesque in the Nineteenth Century*, Cambridge: Cambridge University Press.

Slack, J. (2016), '"Staggering" number of European jihadis: EU's own border agency admits terrorists are exploiting refugee crisis and lax controls – but has no idea how many illegal immigrants there are', *Daily Mail*, 6 April. Available online: https://www.dailymail.co.uk/news/article-3525279/Mass-migration-allowing-terrorists-pour-Europe-EU-s-border-agency-admits-s-revealed-false-documents-not-facing-thoroughchecks. html (accessed 21 October 2021).

Smialkowska, M. (2016), 'Tercentenary Shakespeare: Britain and the United States, 1916', in B. Smith (ed.), *The Cambridge Guide to the Worlds of Shakespeare*, vol. 2, Cambridge: Cambridge University Press.

'What burgeons in the memory …': transgression, culture and canon in postmodern adaptations of the *Sonnets*

RUI CARVALHO HOMEM

This chapter addresses the tension between tribute and iconoclasm in a set of poetic responses to Shakespeare's *Sonnets*, focusing on two solo endeavours, Erik Didriksen's *Pop Sonnets: Shakespearean Spins on Your Favourite Songs* (2015) and James Anthony's *Shakespeare's Sonnets, Retold* (2018), as well as two edited collections, Sharmila Cohen and Paul Legault's *The Sonnets: Translating and Rewriting Shakespeare* (2012) and Hannah Crawforth and Elizabeth Scott-Baumann's *On Shakespeare's Sonnets: A Poets' Celebration* (2016). Published over a short period with its epicentre in the 2016 centenary, these creative responses are not ostensibly connected by evidence of mutual awareness; but all – through their discrete positioning vis-à-vis literary history; through the challenges they pose to the most canonical body of lyrics; and through their politics of form – variously merit the label 'postmodern'. They will be approached from a composite conceptual standpoint sustained by areas of inquiry that (even if remaining distinct) share a signal assumption: they acknowledge those broad claims for all writing to be construed as *re*writing, claims that have resonated across critical and creative environments for roughly half a century.[1]

The conceptual affinities that result from this composite approach are especially productive for considering texts that are particular and diverse in how they relate to the *Sonnets*. While presenting themselves as versions, they are strictly monolingual, and in the same language (English) as their sources. This means that, even when they explicitly appear as instances of 'translation', the *intra*lingual (English to English) transits that bind these texts to the *Sonnets* are hardly ever grounded on those expectations of literalness that many readers will entertain when different languages are involved.[2] And that is why my proposed discussion will gain from a conceptual accommodation of (a) insights from translation, ordinarily construed as occurring between different languages but within the same (verbal) medium, and (b) another set of critical frameworks. The latter include adaptation – primarily describing transits between different media, and hence objects that by definition do not correlate literally; parody – often associated with a challenge to a named source or object, in the same or in distinct media; and various other practices involving reference and/or replication within the verbal medium – such as citation, allusion, paraphrase – that can broadly be described as intertextual.

The sizeable imaginative response that the *Sonnets* have recently obtained in a rich history of rewritings allows us to gauge the extent to which Shakespeare's lyrical output has contributed to a historicized understanding of the literary canon and to creative breakthroughs that prove the continued currency of the sonnet form.[3] Furthermore, discussion of the many appropriations, rewritings and co-options the *Sonnets* have undergone, from versions by canonical authors to pop lyrics and burlesques, also illuminates the diversity of present-day (verse) cultures, and highlights the cultural conditions under which early modern poems find consequence in postmodern creative frameworks. Indeed, the adaptations considered here provide instances of such postmodern textualities as

> a marked self-reflexivity, often combined with a certain, sometimes parodic, intertextual exuberance and a critical engagement with history and historiography; ... and a contesting of the transparency of language itself as well as of the 'naturalness' of the relationship between form and content through a simultaneous use and abuse of poetic convention.[4]

(Hutcheon et al. 2012: 1095)

Balancing postmodern rewritings against their nominal early modern sources reveals intriguing homologies between the imaginative designs associated with those periods. This in no way amounts to endorsing an a- or trans-historical nexus: on the contrary, it involves historicization of both creative contexts, elucidating some reasons for the fascination that early modern practices and forms have exerted on present-day writers. Adaptation, energized as it is by a basic (re)creative impulse, can shed light on such fascination through the heuristic vantage ground afforded by pervasiveness: as signalled by Linda Hutcheon, '[in] the workings of the human imagination, adaptation is the norm, not the exception' (2006: 177).

Hutcheon emphasizes the prevalence of the re-creative approaches proper to adaptation in historically recent frameworks, but similar arguments abound for the early modern period, Shakespeare, and the sonnet form itself. Appropriative practices enjoyed a central and constitutive value in early modern writing that reflected both circumstance and doctrine, critically sustained as it was by notions of *imitatio* (or imitation of best models, often Classical). As for the sonnet, its attractiveness for exercises in rewriting has been noted as an almost paradoxical trait, especially when one considers the expectations of textual stability that might arise from a 'fixed form' of the lyric: as Katherine Duncan-Jones remarks, 'the sonnet, an almost uniquely contained, delimited form of versification, is peculiarly susceptible to tinkering' (1997: 13). Such 'tinkering' began with early modern sonneteers and was maximized by the incremental opportunities brought by sonnet sequences, themselves 'almost bound to be the product of (…) second thoughts and rearrangements' (14), the writing of new sonnets prompting poets to rethink and revise earlier ones. The sonnet balances the technical challenge posed by a fixed form against the comforts of a well-tried practice (those thousands of precedents for any new sonnet); and such abundant output has witnessed both the efforts required in asserting a new voice at any one moment in literary history, and the agonistic gestures of those using the form to address or redress a poetic predecessor.

Additionally, the period of roughly a quarter-century that we associate with Shakespeare's work witnessed an erosion of the favour enjoyed by the Petrarchan love sonnet, with its protestations of male devotion for a morally and physically 'fair' lady, and a tendency by some practitioners to use the form for representations that dissented (though to varying degrees) from the Petrarchan mold (Spiller 1992: 102–75). Shakespeare's own sequence, although unique (poetically, rhetorically), certainly reflects such shifts, both in sonnets 1–126, which quasi-sardonically adjust the Petrarchan discourse to celebrate a man rather than a 'mistress'; and in 127–154, addressed to a mistress who, in her pitilessly exposed flaws, could hardly be more different from Petrarch's. The appeal of relational, unstable textualities would thus seem to be part of the history of the form, accounting for the sense of congeniality behind the recent spate of rewritings of Shakespeare's sonnets and helping confirm the proposed homologies between early modern and postmodern. However, this is hardly a stabilized or consensual critical narrative. The notion that all writing is inevitably derivative may underpin recently developed areas of academic inquiry such as adaptation studies and translation studies, but this does not ensure that the inevitability of rewriting will promptly become central to perceptions of literary value in today's cultures. The provocative nature of some of the writing considered below reveals an urge to react against a resilient veneration for originality as a *sine qua non* of poetic achievement (*pace* the declining favour that Romantic notions of source and genius have experienced in academic circles since the late 1960s).

Such agonistic energy is hardly surprising: reverence for the original entails a corresponding debasement of anything construed as derivative or subsidiary, with a direct detrimental impact on the cultural capital held by translations and adaptations. A hierarchical understanding of the rapport between source and target is evident in those value judgements hinging on a translation's 'fidelity' to the original, an attitude that persists despite and beyond the non-hierarchical ethos underlying the rise of Translation Studies since the late 1970s (Lefevere 1992: *passim*). Adaptation has faced 'constant critical denigration' despite its cultural pervasiveness 'across genres and media and also within the same ones' (Hutcheon 2006: xi, xii). Critical approaches that address relational creative practices have had to battle the long-standing expectation that an artefact defined by its pointed reference to a prior artefact should be judged on the basis of that binary relation. In translation studies – despite the currency of arguments challenging the commensurability of discrete texts – available terminologies can hardly discard 'source' and 'target' compounds to refer to the texts, contexts and cultures involved in a translation process. In adaptation studies

– despite vocal pleas for considering the variety of adaptive practices as situated along a 'reception continuum' (Hutcheon 2006: 171) – the diversity of the practices and outputs considered, from 'versions' to 'spin-offs', 'sequels and prequels', can hardly do without that mental shuttling between source and target which remains crucial for an audience's basic understanding and enjoyment. Even 'within the same medium', 'adaptation *as adaptation* involves, for its knowing audience, an interpretive doubling, a conceptual flipping back and forth between the work we know and the work we are experiencing' (Hutcheon 2006: 139).

This 'doubling' is arguably in operation, and indeed proves fundamental for attaining the aesthetic and rhetorical goals of the re-creative process (gratifying to both creators and readers), irrespective of whether the link sought is primarily reverential or iconoclastic. The latter is usually seen as epitomized by parody, which nonetheless also hinges on a 'differential but mutual dependence' of parodying and parodied texts (Hutcheon [1985] 2000: xiv), a bond that qualifies the adversarial significance of the 'counter-song' that, etymologically, defines 'parody'.

Perceiving that a nexus of necessary mutuality prevails even in the ostensible aggressiveness of 'counter-writings', and that it may be more productive to think of re-creations as positioned along a 'continuum' of esteem rather than polarized between reverence and irreverence, will be of great importance for considering the diverse ways in which writers have responded to Shakespeare's sonnets. The relevance of pondering their complexities reflects the *Sonnets*' status as 'the prototypical lyrics in English, and perhaps the most successful in Western literature' (Boyd 2012: 4). The creative acknowledgements they receive in the form of adaptational responses add density to the place they hold in global memory; and memory is a notion that derives an additional, quasi-ironical cogency from its centrality to the imaginative economy of the *Sonnets*.

A discussion of the rich, varied manner in which the *Sonnets* are creatively remembered in present-day writing cannot but note the intensity with which so many pieces in Shakespeare's sequence obsess about triumphing over time, about their power to immortalize their addressee and become verse memorials: vowing, hence, to go to 'war with Time' (15); pondering how one could 'be new made' when one is old (2); and wondering about 'who will believe my verse in time to come' (17). If such tropes are intriguing from the standpoint of posterity – when one ponders the *Sonnets*' afterlife and imaginative consequence – they are no less so when we consider the pointed manner in which Shakespeare might himself be responding to an immediate poetic ancestry. Elsewhere in his work, Shakespeare tends to satirize sonnets and sonneteers and, while such moments provide instances of his 'acute and retentive (…) verbal and metaphoric memory' (Duncan-Jones 1997: 18), they also highlight the extent to which his *Sonnets* set themselves up *against* key traits of the sonnet tradition. Latter-day respondents can therefore be seen to extend a relational nexus that already defined the literary-historical significance of the source; in other words, our understanding of adapted Shakespeare gains critical depth from reading Shakespeare as serial adaptor.

The attractiveness of recognizing homologies between early modern and postmodern rewritings must be balanced against the risk of readerly weariness: as

Brian Boyd argues, Shakespeare's challenges to prior sonnet practice lead him to overload his own sequence with 'so much pattern and so many surprises that they provoke in some lasting fascination and in others lasting exhaustion' (Boyd 2012: 23). Given the rich range of expressive options and the overall vitality of sonnet rewritings, however, it is likely that the first impulse will prevail.

THIS WERE TO BE OLD MADE WHEN THOU ART NEW

Today's responses to a canonical body of poems such as Shakespeare's *Sonnets* often reflect the perception that readers may not recognize the addressed texts' particularity, but rather share a diffuse awareness of their formal conditions and the esteem they enjoy – a broad sense of 'a generally circulated cultural memory' (Ellis 1982: 3). Of the four publications considered here, none relies so evidently on this assumption as Erik Didriksen's *Pop Sonnets: Shakespearean Spins on Your Favourite Songs* (2015). Unlike most responses, Didriksen's compositions are not proposed as 'versions' of actual sonnets by Shakespeare: they aim rather at being recognized and enjoyed as what Shakespeare might have written were he prompted to take the key trope (or topic, or theme) of songs from recent popular culture and use it as the 'conceit' for sonnets of his own. The texts readers are therefore expected to recognize in any detail are not those in Shakespeare's sequence, but rather the pop lyrics that Didriksen himself rewrites in the form of one hundred pastiches of early modern sonnets.

Visually, the collection envelops this exercise in historic-looking typography, quaint and irregular, framed by decorative friezes and other ornaments, and including an 'early modern' title page with Shakespeare strumming a mandolin; balanced against a reproduction of Shakespeare's Droeshout portrait among the opening pages, the back flap features a faux-engraved image of Didriksen dressed as an Elizabethan gentleman (with feathered hat and ruff). The volume's brief introduction compounds this spoof with a textual history, a mock narrative of origins that draws on the uncertainties surrounding Shakespeare's text (of which even a non-specialist readership may have heard). It notes that 'his complete oeuvre was far larger' and included 'these sonnets', which 'survived by being passed down orally', only to be transcribed from 1743 by 'Sir Kirk de Edin', a transparent anagram of Didriksen's name (Didriksen 2015: xiv).

In its overall strategy, the volume appeals in a sardonic manner to the pleasures of recognizing 'repetition with variation' or even 'repetition with ironic critical distance, marking difference rather than similarity', Hutcheon's well-known definitions for the operation respectively of adaptation and parody (2006, [1985] 2000: *passim*). Constructing a relation between the rewritten pop songs and their sonneteered versions, Didriksen's book brings out the possible frivolousness of lyrics as 'light verse'; but it also ventures into the mock sameness of a transparent archaism. This is the basis of a rationale that involves offering *more* sonnets (additional to those 154) in a trademark 'Shakespearean' diction recognizable to a broad readership, who will be gratified by getting the joke and enjoying these translations from lowbrow to highbrow verse.

Didriksen organizes his sonnets into sub-genres, the titles of the book's five sections: 'Sonnets of Love', 'Sonnets of Despair', 'Songs of Time and Mortality', 'Rogues, Rascals & Wanton Women', 'Ballads of Heroes'. This formal arrangement enhances the canonizing of what some could deem the triviality of many of his source texts. The overall tone can be gauged from one of the 'Sonnets of Despair', which renders the closing lines of Britney Spears's hit, 'Oops! I Did It Again' – 'Oops, you think I'm in love / That I'm sent from above / I'm not that innocent' – as the couplet, 'Thou thinkest I'm thy angel, void of sin, / but I hold no such innocence within' (Didriksen 2015: 27)[5]. The gap between source and target texts is broad, as when the line, 'Can't you see I'm a fool in so many ways,' becomes, in its 'Shakespearean' version, 'I thought thou wouldst account, my dearest friend, / for how mercurial my moods may be' (27) – which involves no mere archaism, but rather a shift from the simplest to the most elevated of dictions (through both syntax and lexicon).

Shakespeare's writing is conjured almost only as analogy (these are a hundred extra sonnets that just look and sound somehow *like* his own), and yet some of his best-known lines are cited on occasion. A prominent example comes with Didriksen's 'spin' on Bruno Mars's 'Just the Way You Are', drawing on Shakespeare's sonnet 130 to render 'Oh, her eyes, her eyes / Make the stars look like they're not shinin''[6] as 'My mistress's eyes are nothing like the stars' (9) – and then borrowing the Shakespearian practice of punning on the poet's name by including the singer's name in the third line, 'her visage never mars'. More often than not, though, Didriksen's Shakespearian borrowings come from plays rather than the sonnets, possibly because of the relative ease with which citations may be recognized. For 'The Fresh Prince of Bel-Air' (credited to DJ Jazzy Jeff & The Fresh Prince) he echoes the Prologue to *Romeo and Juliet* (l.2) to proclaim, 'in fair Bel-Air, where I do lay my scene…' (99); while for the closing line of the sonnet after Billy Joel's 'Piano Man' he rewrites the opening line of *Twelfth Night* as, 'If music be thy trade, good sir, play on!' (100).

Other borrowings acquire wider implications through, for example, gender politics, as when the sonnet prompted by Madonna's 'Material Girl' echoes misogynous Petruchio's mercenary motto from *The Taming of the Shrew* ('I come to wive it wealthily in Padua; / If wealthily, then happily in Padua'; 1.2.74–5), but puts it in the voice of a woman: 'If wealthily, then happily when wed, / I am a girl by want of items led' (78). Didriksen embeds the most Shakespearian quotes in the volume's closing piece, his sonnet after Frank Sinatra's 'My Way' (116), which echoes *As You Like It* (2.7.140–1), 'all the world's a stage' and 'men and women players', and also, fundamentally, Hamlet's dying words, 'the rest is silence' (5.2.363). The sonnet thus cites Shakespeare's (and world literature's) most famous dramatic representation of tortured individuality in order to give seventeenth-century lyric form to what is possibly the most famous song of the late twentieth century about a recollected solo trajectory through life. Within the volume's rhetorical economy, this closing sonnet serves as the equivalent to a dramatic epilogue, 'The curtain falls; my time draws near its end' (116), and as the rewriter's self-apologia and request for applause. More importantly, Didriksen's 'My Way' is the poem that most deviates from the volume's prevalent insinuation of a risible imbalance between the forgettable 'lightness' of the pop songs and the monumentality of Shakespearian sonnets – and indeed comes closest to suggesting, provocatively, an encounter on canonically equal terms. This is proposed through the Shakespearization of a song that has long been the ultimate 'classic' of vocal jazz, propped up on a narrative of an unflinching individual pathway and made coextensive, in cultural memory, with the yet unchallenged masculine singularity (long after his death) of the performer celebrated as 'the Voice'.[7]

The closing sonnet is exceptional also in addressing one of the few songs in which the text's particularity is bound to be remembered by readers specifically *as text* – reflecting its narrative characteristics, as also the clarity with which the song's compositional conditions (tempo, rhythm, melodic line) allow it to be enunciated by the singer. It differs in this respect from most of the (strictly speaking) *pop* songs in the book, which either have less structured lyrics or embed them in the musical composition in ways that emphasize (at best) a refrain.

This imbrication of text and music suggests how Didriksen's collection fits prevalent understandings of adaptation, precisely because of the regularity with which the term has been applied to intermedial re-creation.[8] Indeed, although what Didriksen ostensibly produces is a set of translations of present-day pop lyrics into mock-early modern English, he names the singers, rather than the songwriters (who are not credited at any point), next to the song titles; this leaves no doubt that his re-creation has for its object songs that readers will recognize not from reading, but rather from listening – in fact 'easy listening', here converted to not-so-easy reading. The manner in which the reception/consumption of most of these songs has made them recognizable and hence adequate objects for Didriksen's exercise is characteristically intermedial: empirically, when faced with the sonnets and prompted to take them as versions of the songs, readers will in all likelihood hum or sing them, since the lyrics are bound to be remembered in direct connection with rhythms and melodic lines. And this cognitive and behavioural assumption is fundamental to the project's rationale.

Didriksen's book performs a balancing act: at base level it may appear no more than an elaborate literary-cultural joke, a witty exercise of limited consequence; but the very fact that it prompts reflection suggests that it *is* in fact consequential, to the extent that it enhances our ability to ponder prevalent perceptions of cultural value, patterns of taste and the conditions for literary and artistic creation to enter memory. Much of this complexity concerns the archaizing strategy, which in many re-creations reflects an attempt to retrieve the uniqueness and genuineness of a past diction (Steiner 1992: 352, 360; Heinz 2000: 290–1). By rendering many different pop lyrics into the same fixed form, in a diction consistently reminiscent of the same author and period, the whole exercise consciously exposes the banality of mechanical replication (Benjamin [1936] 1968: 221).

Enjoying Didriksen's collection hinges on acknowledging Shakespeare's cultural capital but also celebrating and extending the appeal of pop cultural artefacts often dismissed as ephemeral. The very suggestion that, if made to sound like Shakespeare, Didriksen's sonnets can become indistinguishable from poems at the very centre of the canon and triumph over time is the key element of their risible appeal but it nonetheless challenges the grounds for canonical status. Can the prosodic deftness of a rewriter cancel hierarchies and institute parity of esteem and memorability for such diverse artefacts as the actual pop songs and the revered sonnets they have been made to sound and read like? Asking this also highlights the authority claimed by the rewriter as the enacter of such levelling: albeit in a joking tone, Didriksen's volume reminds us of the extent to which, in the lyric (when received, as here, under the lingering influence of Romantic authorship), canonicity goes hand in hand with a celebration of individuality, especially because of the very close implication in this genre between the empirical author and the first-person voice in the poems.

IN WAR WITH TIME, I ENGRAFT YOU NEW

Approaching James Anthony's *Shakespeare's Sonnets, Retold* (2018) after discussing Didriksen is, at first glance, an antithetical experience given the two authors' approach to language, time and taste. Unlike Didriksen's archaizing venture, Anthony's is a full-on modernizing project, a translation of Shakespeare's complete sequence into present-day English. However, like Didriksen's, the target texts retain the formal arrangement of the Shakespearian sonnet, highlighting the rewriter's virtuosity. Despite the author of all 154 versions being the same, Anthony's collection shows a measure of variation in his management of the relation between his versions and their source, especially regarding his syntax and lexicon; and this has consequences for his readership's perception of wherein the *aggiornamento* specifically consists.

The volume features source and target texts on facing pages, as so often happens when two different languages are involved, and this option insinuates that Shakespeare's early modern English, even in modernized spelling, might as well be a foreign language, as regards the ability of Anthony's envisaged readership to comprehend the original sonnets – the resulting sense of necessity thus legitimizing the intralingual translation effort. The parallel-text option also prompts readers to engage in the 'doubling' already noted of adaptations more generally, suggesting that full enjoyment of Anthony's versions requires an encounter with the source, while the rewriter's own awareness of this parallel reading may have encouraged him to keep his distance, ensuring that his versions do not see their raison d'être questioned by too much proximity to Shakespeare's originals. The very project of translating Shakespeare intralingually has consistently proved controversial with academics and writers (Hoenselaars 2012: 18–21), an awareness of which may also be read between the lines of the volume's 'Foreword': actor Stephen Fry's celebrity endorsement commends this modernizing venture and states his confidence (ironically?) that 'schools and colleges will stamp and cheer with unrestrained gratitude and delight' (Anthony 2018: n.p.).

The strains of rewriting none other than Shakespeare in his own language may show in Anthony's identification of those traits in the source's lexicon and syntax that have arguably become archaic, as in his management of the prevalent register of his modernization. Any translator embracing such a challenge will want to make the ensuing versions as attractive as possible, and this may include exploring opportunities for laughter, the temptation of opting not only for 'variation' but also for the 'critical distance' and 'difference' that characterize parody (Hutcheon

[1985] 2000: xii). Anthony's Sonnet no. 1 sets the tone for these complexities, when Shakespeare's opening line, 'From fairest creatures we desire increase', sees its first hemistich, or half-line of verse, rendered in rather elevated diction – 'We strive to procreate' – only to be followed by the demotic, 'with gorgeous folk'.[9] This hybrid register is confirmed two lines below, when the commonplace, 'We reach a ripe old age', is followed, in the second hemistich, by the slangy and risible, 'but then we croak' – which tips the sonnet over into parody, while seeming to imply that a more neutral lexicon for 'dying' is somehow outdated. From the outset, then, the translator's choices prompt the question of what in the source text is perceived as archaic – and hence what the strategies will be, throughout the volume, for 'updating' Shakespeare. Will such modernizing consistently require colloquialisms and slang? And will a shift in register be matched by a referential adjustment, a concomitant shift in the representations understood as proper to the *Sonnets'* imaginative space?

This perceived need for new, modern tropes is confirmed throughout, as when in #86 Shakespeare's image for his rival's poetry, 'the proud full sail', is rendered as 'much like a yacht'. Occasionally, Anthony supplements rather than replaces tropes, as in the first line of his #20, which renders, 'A woman's face with nature's own hand painted' as 'A fresh-face like a female movie-star'. Shakespeare's trope for beauty requiring no artifice (hence 'painted' only by nature) is decoded as a cosmetic-free 'fresh-face' but the 'movie-star' simile anchors the sonnet in the imaginative present. The second line extends the slangy tendency that activates the parodic mode, as Shakespeare's resonant epithet for the sonnet's addressee, 'the Master Mistress of my passion', becomes 'the man who's got me in a pickle'. The same tendency leads, in #153, to 'my mistress' (which in its early modern usage refers, rather neutrally, to the beloved) becoming 'my floozy'.

These examples also reflect a general inclination to render explicit much of what in the source texts is implicit or suggested, especially regarding sexuality. In #3, the rather oblique 'tomb (...) of self-love' is rendered as 'self-masturbat[ion]'; in #135, a gallery of synonyms for sexual intercourse – 'copulation', 'sex', 'fornication', 'incubat[ing] my dick' – enters the lexical range of a sonnet that, in the source, is all innuendo and wordplay. Such sustained explicitness is part of an effort that the translator describes, in an afterword on 'meaning', as taking Shakespeare's 'double-entendres and subtle references' and 'reflect[ing] the hidden meanings in a relevant modern way' (2018: n.p.). This reveals Anthony's understanding of modernization as largely a matter of resolving ambiguities and dismantling the metaphorical scaffolding of the *Sonnets*, changes that will otherwise perplex readers for whom such linguistic and intellectual layers are coextensive with their sense of the literary. Those readers may wonder at the removal of polysemy (especially the famous waste / waist pun) from #129, in which Anthony renders 'Th'expense of spirit in a waste of shame' as 'The damage from a random carnal shag'.

Anthony's versions perform a sustained 'unmetaphoring' (Colie 1974: 11) of Shakespeare's writing, as evidenced in his treatment both of the central 'conceit' and other, more incidental tropes in some of the sequence's earliest sonnets.[10] His version of #4 almost totally discards the financial master-trope, as Shakespeare's paradoxical 'profitless usurer' becomes a 'wasteful bum', and the passage on 'having traffic with thyself alone' (in which onanism is represented as a self-inwoven type of commerce) is starkly unmetaphored as 'wanking over pornographic grot'. In #2, which famously anticipates the ravages of old age, Shakespeare's 'deep trenches in thy beauty's field' are decoded as 'crows-feet' [sic]; and the addressee's imagined reply to the key question on the whereabouts of his youth, a reply that Shakespeare phrases (in reported speech) as 'within thine own deep sunken eyes', becomes in Anthony's version (in direct speech), '"I drank, and screwed it up somehow"'.

Sonnet #1 proves, again, a touchstone for Anthony's practice of modernization as demotic unmetaphoring. His second quatrain omits anything that might correspond either to the pun on 'contracted' (which involves both contract and contraction), or to the oxymoronic 'famine where abundance lies', at no point attempting to replace them with alternative tropes, but supplying rather those lines' basic meanings. In the third, he replaces the crucial 'Within thine own bud buries thy content', memorable for the trope of self-burial within a rosebud and for the polysemous 'content' (both noun and adjective), with the brassy indictment, 'you're content to piss away your time'. Such rhetorically austere literalness, such belief in the possibility of detaching stark 'meanings' from their imaginative verbal elaboration in the source, comes across almost as a crib, with the fundamental difference that, unlike the strictly functional and informative translations that ordinarily go by that name, Anthony's versions are not positioned on the outside of formal concerns: on the contrary, they show the rewriter's pride in abiding and managing the prosodic requirements of the Shakespearian sonnet, all 154 times.

This pride is evident in the volume's brief paratexts: 'a beginner's guide' on 'understanding a Shakespearian sonnet'; some textual information and acknowledgement of sources; plus biographical notes on 'the Authors', Shakespeare and Anthony himself. Such authorial assuredness, however, does not preclude a measure of uncertainty regarding the book's goals and methods, poised as it is between an explicatory remit and an ambition for aesthetic autonomy, between modernizing and parodying. And the volume also challenges reflective readers to ponder the conceptual terms of its 'retelling'.

Within translation studies, Anthony's unmetaphoring drift may surprise all who endorse the influential notion that 'translation is the activity of creating metaphor' (Barnstone 1993: 16) and yet the book has been a major exemplar, in recent years, of intralingual translation. Its revision of the Shakespearian text's rich rhetoric of ambiguity, indirection and wordplay is at times suggestive of those projects for expressive simplification, fashioned to meet the needs or expectations of particular communities, often found within the generic range of adaptations, while Anthony's frequent iconoclasms clearly distance it from the didactic rationale that tends to define such projects. Within the cultures of postmodernity, however, the gallery of rewritings prompted by Shakespeare's *Sonnets* also prominently includes ventures that, rather than offer to clarify 'double-entendres and subtle references' and bring out 'hidden meanings' (Anthony 2018: n.p.), favour the enhanced expressive and formal complexities that often characterize artistic designs in our time, as is true of the adaptations to which I now turn.

NEW-FOUND METHODS AND COMPOUNDS STRANGE

Sharmila Cohen and Paul Legault's *The Sonnets: Translating and Rewriting Shakespeare* (2012) is emphatically different from Didriksen's and Anthony's books in its contents and overall design. The volume's material conditions make the difference immediately apparent: although paratextual information is minimal, and the volume does not reproduce the source texts, its compiled versions (all by different, mostly American authors) of the 154 sonnets cover roughly 250 pages.

Such length brings out an obvious feature of the project: while, like Anthony's, this is an English-to-English translation of Shakespeare's *Sonnets*, it does not generate another sonnet sequence but rather a collection of variously organized texts, often much longer than the source poems. Indeed, less than half the compositions are fourteen-liners, and only a small number of these abide by the sonnet conventions. No less importantly for its position in the range of postmodern responses to the *Sonnets*, the book includes contributions from the visual arts, materially straddling distinct media. In their short introduction, the editors present its diversity as programmatic and transgressive: for this 'first full length book' published under the imprint of *Telephone* (a translation journal), they prompted contributors, 'from their multitude of vantage points', to 'board the ship, loot and pillage, break things down, and reconstruct it all' (Cohen and Legault 2012: n.p.).[11]

Cohen and Legault's editorial decision not to print Shakespeare's sonnets next to the contemporary responses may reflect their awareness of the incommensurability of *these* source and target texts, which would hardly produce the sense of repetition-cum-variation across the page that marks Anthony's book. It has, however, additional implications. Whereas parallel texts invite comparison or parallel reading (Hutcheon 2006: 139), opting to print only the outcomes of the translation process can be a way of vindicating their autonomous expressive and aesthetic value, severing the derivative bond. Such a perception may prove congenial to the radical politics of form that prevail throughout the volume, while relating *less* congenially to the book's descriptive and potentially redundant subtitle, 'Translating and Rewriting Shakespeare'.

Some of the adaptations reflect a modernizing concern not unlike Anthony's, with the fundamental difference that they rarely feature metrical regularity and strict rhyme schemes. This emphasizes their provocative colloquiality, as in Rae Armantrout's version of sonnet 3 – 'You're a very pretty boy. / But the thing is, that won't last' (Cohen and Legault 2012: 3) – or Cedar Sigo's of #35: 'Fuck off with your crippling guilt' (53). Some pieces boast a radical updated diction that nevertheless allows the source text's concerns to transpire, and they often zoom in on the sexual angst energizing many of Shakespeare's sonnets. Such is the case with Terese Svoboda's version of #129, entitled 'Shakespearean Lust', which opens with the line, 'It's time wasted, in terms of chagrin, to shag', and (a rarity in the volume) closes with a regular couplet: 'All this we're well acquainted with, yet Hell / is our first exit, that No-Tell Motel' (203).

The book indeed abounds in versions that, in formal terms, do not depart so starkly from the source as to push it out of sight, but rather draw on the power of literary memory to achieve specific effects. Some commit to awareness-raising on behalf of particular causes, or voice the ethos of a community via identity politics. In 'Michelin Man Possessed by Shakespeare', for example, Matthea Harvey construes Shakespeare's 29 as involving a case of body dysmorphic disorder, and an implicit plea for body positivity yields, ironically, a regular sonnet accompanied by a photograph of the lower part of a body that can be either a 'Michelin Man' or someone posing as one (46–7). Randall Mann writes a metrically regular version of sonnet 124, with a Shakespearean rhyme scheme, that closes with the self-identified gay speaker, in a modern urban environment, having a shower and reflecting on a perceived tension between desire and disgust: '– Soapy, erect, I'll conjure up a time / when love was just a fecal, furtive crime' (197). Several contributors refract Shakespeare's sonnets through African American discursive modes, sometimes with a challenging and programmatic approach to language and canon as in June Jordan's 'Shakespeare's 116th Sonnet in Black English Translation' (187).[12] Jordan's late 1990s poem extends her lifelong advocacy for the civic and aesthetic worth of Black English as a distinctive expressive medium, 'not interchangeable' with standard English, the two systems not to be seen as 'communicat[ing] equal or identical thoughts, or feelings' (Jordan 1981: 77), because 'our language devolves from a culture that abhors all abstraction' (Jordan 1985: 129). Her text therefore rests on an understanding that translating a canonical English text into Black English will never be close to a calque rendering, nor yield an equivalent; Jordan stresses this by means of a pared-down diction, through which such lines as 'it [love] is an ever-fixed mark / That looks on tempests and is never shaken' become, in her rendering, 'Storm come. Storm go / away / but love stay / steady' (187).

The literalness with which some other pieces relate to the *Sonnets* becomes ironic, the proximity they ostensibly rehearse only highlighting how starkly they challenge their sources. Lee Ann Brown's 'The Lower 48 (Je Ne Regrette Rien)', which takes Shakespeare's 'thrust' in a bodily sense, renders being 'careful' as acting 'anally', and construes key words demotically and literally: Shakespeare's 'But thou, to whom my jewels trifles are' is rendered as 'To you, my churl, my jewels were just dessert' (72). Literalness becomes textual repetition with a minor variation when Jen Bervin's version of #2 presents a word-for-word transcript of Shakespeare's sonnet, with just ten words highlighted so as to bring out the sentence 'a (…) weed of small worth (…) asked (…) to be new made' (2) – a synecdoche of the source and a metatranslational comment.

Other contributors likewise opt for selective replications of the source texts' lexicon that result in discrete verbal compositions, sometimes exploding the 'conceit' around which Shakespeare's sonnets were organized. Gillian Conoley does this by keeping just a few words from each line of sonnet 58, with the residual lines 7 and 10 becoming an epitome of the challenges posed by paring down while attempting to retain core emphases: 'absence of your library', 'you list, your self, your time' (88). Prageeta Sharma takes sonnet 15's emphasis on mutability and 'war with Time' and carries out an exercise in verbal wandering, a narrative that refuses to cohere as bits of the Shakespearean text are retained but left adrift in disparate verbal matter, with the closing sentence troping the ambition of consequential writing: 'I engraft / through the tatteredness of mass and time / that the noise is kept alive' (21).

The volume's disruptions of both the form and rhetorical nexus associated with the sonnet tradition often reflect the transgressive and experimental poetics that have marked the American poetic scene since the 1960s (Hofer and Golston 2019). Such disruptions can be generic, targeting the conventions of the lyric, especially by shifting its monologic regime in the direction of dramatic dialogue. Dramatizations include Marcella Durand and Betsy Fagin's response in the form of transcripts of what was heard (truncated, distorted) when two people (Duran and Fagin themselves) read Shakespeare's sonnet 47 into corners 'in the Whispering Gallery in Grand Central Terminal' (68–71). Rachel Blau Du Plessis's 'Trans-literalization of Sonnet 9 into a 28-line Dialogue' has two voices, A and B, dramatizing the personal, social and ethical issues of wanting children (or not), as raised in this and other sonnets in the sequence; in the closing line, A indicts B for precisely the poetic solipsism of which the lyric often stands accused: 'You love your metaphors too much; that's the real delusion' (15).

The agonistic tensions that can thus be teased out of the sonnet form prompt other rewriters to 'talk back' in a variety of modes, countering the *Sonnets*' arguments, responding to them in a recalcitrant manner, or indeed amplifying the socio-political potential of the Shakespearean text when refracted through postmodern conditions. It is in this spirit that Julian Talamantez Brolaski contributes 'sonnet 13 redux / the fair youth's response to the argument that he should breed' (19); under the title 'Boycott', Vanessa Place transcribes Shakespeare's sonnet 20 and merely changes the pronouns, cancelling the misogyny (26); and Geoffrey G. O'Brien, for #55, writes a double sonnet in regular rhymed verse (rather than prose) as a medium for critical commentary, all the more provocative in its indictment of Shakespeare's supposed aloofness because the original sonnet is empathically about a concern with posterity: 'So Shakespeare will prefer the abstract shelf / Where bodies made of words are safe from harm' (85).

In spite of the volume's subtitle, many of the pieces are not so much rewritings as *after*-writings, reflections and aesthetic gestures that come in the wake of the *Sonnets*, adversarially or otherwise. Some muse on Shakespeare's employment of monetary tropes for procreation, possibly reflecting the language and concerns that marked the post-2008 global financial crisis. Hence, for sonnet 4, Dana Ward offers three-and-a-half pages of prose narrative that include the passage, 'when the baby was born I felt money. I wanted her to never have to suffer so I started wanting whatever there was' (6). Also in prose, Brian Teare's 'Occupy Sonnet', prompted by #40, starts off from the question 'Why turn a lover's discourse into a discourse about debt?' (59), reminding us that the personal cannot but be political. Other pieces are metapoetic, about authorship and the writing process and hence also self-referential, pondering their own intertextual and inter-authorial bonds. For #38 ('How can my Muse want subject to invent'), Ana Božičević writes a prose reflection on muses and peers entitled '14 Fragments / 10 Muses' (56–7); and, for #103 ('Alack, what poverty my Muse brings forth'), Amaranth Borsuk addresses four lines to Shakespeare on the topic of poetic insufficiency, followed by an extensive 'Translator's note' which acknowledges that 'sonnet #103 has long served as a challenge to successive generations of poets' and cites versions by other authors (162–5).

The volume is thus characterized by diversity, formal and thematic provocations, and creative idiosyncrasy. Nowhere are these features more in evidence than in contributions that straddle different codes. In just a few cases, the transcoding is still verbal, but interlingual; although the book describes itself as translating 'from English to English' (i), foreign language skills are occasionally activated. Donna Stonecipher contributes a linguistic conflation of Shakespeare's #148 and an Italian sonnet on an identical 'conceit' by 'Giacomo da Lentini, inventor of the sonnet' (228); Norma Cole renders Shakespeare's #21 into macaronics, made up of words from most Western European languages; and Pierre Joris contributes 'Shakespeare's sonnet #71, re-Englished after Paul Celan's German version without consulting the original even once' (109).

The descriptive titles and paratexts highlight a common element to contributions that involve different codes: they tend to be programmatic, their re-creative stance akin to conceptual art. K. Silem Mohammad, for example, rearranges 146 into one of his 'Sonnagrams'; as described in a note, 'each Sonnagram (...) is an anagram of a standard modern-spelling version of one of Shakespeare's Sonnets, containing exactly the same letters in the same distribution as the original' (224). Katie Degentesh reproduces, next to her version of #142, her handwritten plan – 'my translation process' – which includes the self-addressed instruction: 'pick a word from each line & use it to search a site of kids' book reviews', which then become sources for her poem (220).

Degentesh's contribution is an instance of the studied tension between design and chance underlying many of the challenges that Cohen and Legault's book poses to Shakespeare's canonicity; additionally, through the reproduced handwritten notes, it partakes in the volume's graphic or visual-art dimension. The book's intersemiotic and intermedial features, as ensured by such versions, call for an adaptive rationale to be critically combined with the focus on translation that otherwise prevails. This happens especially when text appears on the pages not through conventional typography but rather by being graphically processed, as when pasted photographs of print material are defaced or altered through collage and truncation. For #152, Jen Hofer pastes five pages from a dictionary, print matter that has been palimpsestically altered to highlight key words in the sonnet (233–7). Thom Donovan's response to #64, hinging on Shakespeare's image of 'lofty towers (...) down-razed', takes the form of a screenshot, from Google Translator, of a text on 9/11, complete with its translation into Arabic (100). But the medially composite and adaptive component of this nominally translational project, combined with the programmatic allure, is most evident in Gary Sullivan's #105 response: five pages of cartoons with minimal captions – 'Am I the next Shakspere?' [sic] – produced by 'doing a Google Image translation' and then selecting and arranging the resulting images. Unapologetically, Sullivan offers personal taste, 'feeling' and a sense of correspondence as the basis for the intermedial nexus: 'Words and images were chosen based on what felt to me like some meaningful correlation with the original poem' (168). The book's most provocative pair of 'versions' is its opening poem, Steve McCaffery's 'Two Alternative Translations' of sonnet 1, which provide instances of concrete poetry, in the form respectively of vowel sequences and series of brackets – for lines 1 and 2, for example, 'a.i.o.ua.eo.a.u.a / a.eo.o.a.ao.o.u.e' and '((((((((((/)))))))))))' (1). *The Sonnets: Translating and Rewriting Shakespeare* thus opens by exploding the linguistic and delexicalizing Shakespeare's discourse – providing the most radical instance of a poetics that emphatically contrasts with the prevalent tone of the fourth and final book to be discussed here.

MY MUSE IN MANNERS HOLDS HER STILL; OR, PROVING HIS BEAUTY BY SUCCESSION MINE

On Shakespeare's Sonnets: A Poets' Celebration (2016), edited by Hannah Crawforth and Elizabeth Scott-Baumann, was one of the high-profile publication projects marking the quatercentenary of Shakespeare's death. It compiles guest contributions by thirty poets from Britain and Ireland who respond to one of the sonnets, a group of sonnets or the sequence in general. The editors' 'Preface' notes how a sense of memory and posterity pervades Shakespeare's sequence but also positions it as an imaginative springboard, as the assembled writers 'look to the past and its literary riches as well as to the future and their own legacies' (xv). Many of the poets represented are established figures, conscious that their reputations precede them. Such authorial salience also generates an assumption that the new sonnets will relate as much to the poetic identity of such respondents as (in tribute or contentiously) to Shakespeare. Themselves their antecedents, poets invited as a reflection of their mature fame to challenge a hallowed predecessor do so in the shadow of their own seniority, which may confer on their rewriting the often reckless and disruptive conditions of 'late style' (Adorno 1937] 2002; Said 2004), or of that 'late writing' which shows authors, as Gordan McMullan notes of Shakespeare himself, operating 'in the proximity of death' (2007: n.p.); they are bound to respond 'in one of two modes: either as serene, synthetic, and consummatory, or as irascible, discordant, and recalcitrant (and sometimes in a curious, contradictory combination of the two)' (McMullan and Smiles 2016: 3–4).

The element of creative insurgence, especially in formal terms, that defined the Cohen and Legault collection appears only occasionally in Crawforth and Scott-Baumann's. It emerges in Simon Armitage's 'Di-Di-Dah-Dah-Di-Dit', which responds to sonnet 20 with rhythmically arranged series of syllables, thus materializing a refusal to react discursively to a sonnet notorious as much for its misogyny as for its evasive, self-apologetic construction of the speaker's homoeroticism. But contributions also tend to display the discursive traits that prevail in those strands of poetic production that have continued to yield the traditional lyric and that have, sometimes influentially, been critically endorsed as central to English poetry (Davie 1973; Ward 1991; Goodby 2000). Indeed, the overwhelming majority of poems *are* sonnets, many conforming to the conventional Shakespearian structure.

Nonetheless, the collection begins with a challenge in the form of Roger McGough's 'What poverty my Muse brings forth (*A Cento*)', a poem that disintegrates and then reintegrates its object, which here is the full sequence. A 'cento' is a text composed by patching together extracts from other texts, and each of McGough's fourteen lines comes from a different sonnet, while the poem's main title cites the opener of

#103, one of Shakespeare's exercises in poetic self-deprecation. Though referred by that opening line to a discourse of poetic and amatory modesty, McGough's sonnet is in fact a gesture of self-empowerment, since the rewriter proves his mastery in producing a conventional Shakespearian sonnet by appropriating and redeploying at will lines that Shakespeare wrote but never combined.

McGough's sonnet also enacts a tension between formal control and random composition often found in programmatic writing, in poems that are verbal correlatives of conceptual art. This programmatic attitude to poetic re-creation is partly represented by Paul Muldoon's 'Sonnet 15: A Graft' which combines schematic playfulness with a reflection on poetic appropriation, and hence, more broadly, on translational and adaptive practices. Muldoon takes his cue from Shakespeare's closing formula, which vows to perpetuate the beloved in writing: 'I engraft you new.' For such memorializing, Shakespeare enlisted a horticultural trope, the practice of reinvigorating a plant by inserting in it material from another, conveniently expressed through a word, 'engraft[ing]' (or grafting), derived from the Greek *grapheion*, also a root for words related to writing. Posing as dutiful follower, Muldoon offers 'a graft' that, through renewed inscription, should provide continuity to the great predecessor, but this is treated ironically both in formal and substantive terms. Formally, Muldoon's sonnet becomes 'engrafted' by borrowing the closing words (hence, the rhymes) of all fourteen lines from Shakespeare's sonnet 15. The resulting tension between tribute and iconoclasm is deepened by the sardonic literalness with which Muldoon redeploys Shakespeare's conceit: horticulture becomes the activity the poem ostensibly discusses, rather than a trope in a poem about procreation and posterity; the speaking self poses as timidly venturing only here and there into analogies between what happens in an orchard and in human existence.

The suggestion that propels the sonnet beyond its risibly literal commitment to ground and plants echoes the Shakespearean notion of an incision / inscription that ensures posterity: 'What burgeons in the memory / is how a stroke of your penknife could stay / us against the future… ' That it is 'penknife' rather than pen holds Muldoon true to his vow to offer a 'graft,' which also insinuates that something is amiss in the original, leaving it in need of imaginative reinvigoration; and all this bears ironically on the procreative incisiveness that marks Shakespeare's sonnet, across the page. This textual coexistence is key to Muldoon's meta-creative gesture, since the deliberately *grounded* nature of his piece – which in the closing couplet gives us 'cow dung' where Shakespeare gives us 'love' – clashes with Shakespeare's grand rhetorical drive. The equivalence and contrast afforded by the parallel texts entail that Muldoon's mock banality satirically downgrades Shakespeare's panache, and the latter sonnet claims its space by construing Shakespeare's stentorian claim to immortalize the beloved as hubristic and pretentious.

Muldoon's construction of rewriting as grafting can thus be seen to epitomize a meta-literary approach to anxieties about life, death and posterity; several other contributions to *On Shakespeare's Sonnets* explore such anxieties through representations of ordinary human experience, often with the poignancy brought by close intimations of death. Sonnet 22 prompts Wendy Cope to shine a candid focus on the ageing self: whereas in Shakespeare the structuring notion was an enhanced awareness of age caused by seeing its incipient symptoms in the beloved, in Cope's sonnet the relational play involves one's own image encountered on two different surfaces – a mirror and (contrastingly) the hetero-representation materialized in a photograph: 'My glass can't quite persuade me I am old – / (...) / But when I see a photograph, I'm told / The dismal truth: I've left my youth behind' (19). Cope extends this epiphany to the pathologies of seniority – 'Arthritic fingers, problematic neck, / Sometimes causing mild to moderate pain' (19) – but her use of such medical descriptions carries a mildly self-parodic tone. In stark contrast is Paul Farley's 'Gentian Violet', a response to sonnet 99, and especially to the line 'A vengeful canker ate him up to death'; haunted by the purple 'flowers' that, in medical imaging, reveal tumoral growths, the poem insinuates that such pathological proliferation can be equated with the textual growths prompted by Shakespeare's sonnets: 'The rainbow runs to earth: beyond here / it's all geophysics, worms, Pluto's blue torch / in the MRI, where flowers are the wounds / they once were gathered to heal' (59).

The collection blends such pathos with humour. Likewise offering a sharp, self-aware demonstration of the authorial conditions associated with 'late writing' is Douglas Dunn's version of #1, entitled 'Senex on Market Street'. The proposed persona embodies seniority as senescence, naming as it does the stock character in Classical New Comedy whose ambitions regarding love and lust are woefully mismatched by his age, and hence dramatically foiled and ridiculed. Dunn's readers are bound to detect a close authorial implication, since ageing has been a distinctive theme in his writing, sometimes with autobiographical candour; other well-known authorial traits with a bearing on the poem include Dunn's interest in public and social spaces, and a concern with form (e.g. Dante's *terza rima*) that sometimes blends with a focus on death and the afterlife (O'Brien 1998: 66).

Such trademark authorial features precede and inform Dunn's use of sonnet 1's '*Thou that art now the world's fresh ornament*' as epigraph and starting point, directly invoking Shakespeare's construction of a mature speaker addressing a loved, admired young person. That maturity is here construed as the bluntly announced old age of the heterosexual male gazing at a beautiful passer-by: 'Posh totty totters past on serious heels' (3). The line's tongue-twister quality deriving from its iambic regularity, alliteration and internal rhyme, gives the poem, from the outset, a mocking tone that targets both agent and object of the admiring look. As regards the speaker, the line leaves no doubt that this is the voice of the 'senex'; for readers familiar with Dunn's work, his persona has ironically upgraded from socially aware observation of working-class scenes to ogling well-heeled passers-by on the high street. The observed young woman is promptly pluralized – 'they walk… ' – and hence generalized into a stereotype, the opening epithet's mild dismissiveness compounded by a suggestion of vanity and frivolousness in tottering 'towards exams', we learn two lines below, 'on serious heels.' 'Serious' combines here its primary and colloquial senses, and this debases the young walkers' 'handsomeness' and 'confidence', insinuated rather as swagger and vanity. Since Dunn's and Shakespeare's sonnets are printed on facing pages, this satirical treatment of the admired young woman starkly contrasts with

Shakespeare's ecstatic treatment of the young man, even if the latter shares in the cognitive indifference to mortality that both sonnets pointedly denounce.

The 'totty' that Dunn considers and dismisses becomes an adaptive parody of Shakespeare's young man; but it is precisely the speaker's ability to retain a judgemental distance that rescues Dunn's persona from also becoming a parody of Shakespeare's wise persona. On the contrary, the course of the sonnet qualifies that self-indictment as 'senex' in the title: rather than lusting in comic hubris after the 'totty,' Dunn's persona hears, in the stilettos' percussion of the pavement on Market Street, 'the fateful tick-tock of the clock' – precisely what the parading young people fail to apprehend. Wisdom comes through the ear, countering the visual lure, as befits a verbal artist working in rhythms and measures, whose cognitive and expressive sharpness authorizes the *memento mori*, grounded on precedence, that launches the second quatrain: 'Young women, and young men, I, too, was young' (3).

This authority, allowing the speaker to reach the middle stages of the sonnet with his self-indictment as *senex* to some extent mitigated, also involves the emotions. Dunn's rise to canonical status found a landmark in *Elegies* (1985), a collection mourning a marital love destroyed by death, which resonates in the sonnet's third quatrain. It both spells the emotional urgency of a still overwhelming memory – 'There's something I must tell,' 'I loved a woman' – and proclaims a lasting power that applies to love as much as it does to the love lyric: 'even old love is for ever new'. Ironically, this allows the sonnet to end on an ambivalent couplet. The dead beloved is now the celebrated entity, an equivalent position to Shakespeare's young man: 'When she walked out she dulcified the air'; yet the closing line acknowledges the young woman's allure in an almost begrudging manner, possibly because it amounts to the speaker's surrender to his senses, aroused despite himself by young beauty, and hence returned (self-satirically) to his condition as *senex*: 'And so do you. To say so's only fair.'

AND IN ABUNDANCE ADDETH TO HIS STORE (BY WAY OF CONCLUSION)

My readings have confirmed the pervasiveness of a tension between homage and challenge in re-creative responses to Shakespeare's *Sonnets*. This pervasiveness is all the more revealing given the great diversity displayed by the collections in question, taken together: a volume of translations of present-day pop lyrics into mock early modern English; a complete translation of Shakespeare's sequence into present-day English; a collection of exercises in (predominantly) radical poetics, by American writers, prompted by the *Sonnets*; and a commemorative volume with contributions from established literary figures from Britain and Ireland.

This diverse, heterogenous corpus ranges from reverential to parodic, and indeed resists uniform description – adaptation, translation, rewriting, parody – requiring rather what I have described as my composite conceptual apparatus, necessary for a reading that has revealed patterns but also culturally distinct approaches for reprocessing canonical creations from the early modern past and making them resonate in postmodern cultural environments.

In such environments, the prevalent conceptual models also seem to resist a binary rationale, the limitations of which humanities adaptation studies have done much to expose. And yet the long-standing assumption persists, that any cultural object defined by its pointed reference to a prior cultural object cannot but be construed in light of a duality – source vs target, original vs derivative – derived from that referential bond; this has continued to shape both creative and critical endeavours. New creations prompted by Shakespeare's *Sonnets* achieve definition through the manner in which they 'talk back' to their ostensible source – adversarially, as corroborative 'after-writings', or in an ambivalent combination – confirming the critical productivity of Hutcheon's 'interpretive doubling' (2006: 139). And this relational nexus applies even when the object of the response is non-specific or diffuse, as when the re-creator is 'talking back' to a general sense of the Shakespearian sonnet and the cultural capital it carries (Ellis 1982: 3).

Within this broad common nexus, the re-creations discussed illuminate disparate tendencies. A particularly intriguing case involves contrasting attitudes towards Shakespeare's rhetorical complexities. The unmetaphoring tendency in James Anthony's 'retelling' of the *Sonnets*, driven by the perception that modernization requires a demotic decoding of the figurations in the early modern sources, contrasts with the elaborate re-tropings that mark the more radical re- and after-writings compiled by Sharmila Cohen and Paul Legault. Another notable set of re-creative diversities concerns verse prosody – the manner in which, technically, the Shakespearian sonnet is rendered, or responded to, by poets operating in the wake of a century of formal disruption and experimentation across Western poetics. Such diversities occupy the full spectrum of possibilities between polar opposites: at one extreme, the *Sonnets* have stimulated writers to prove their skills in adapting the compositional protocols of the Shakespearian sonnet; at the other, the re-creators fully depart from that prosodic model to offer free compositions that may reject discursiveness and sometimes include remediations, transpositions or extensions into media other than the verbal.

Taken together, the remakings and responses that the *Sonnets* encounter in postmodern literary cultures amount to a vivid 'proof of life', a concern and aspiration that Shakespeare's originals thematize, for humans as for texts. Present-day poetic re-creators have echoed and extended that theme in these volumes, through processes of rewriting and adaptation that often challenge established literary cultures. With their often transgressive practices, they institute new ways of remembering and revaluing Shakespeare. And even as they acknowledge their predecessor's melancholy awareness of the shadow of death, they engender a host of poetic afterlives.

NOTES

1   I draw on Linda Hutcheon's major studies of adaptation (2006) and parody ([1985] 2000); for translation and/as rewriting, on classic contributions (Hermans 1985; Lefevere 1992), but also the recent reassessment of the field (Gentzler 2017); on

      intertextuality (Worton and Stills 1990) and recent exploration of the concept's intellectual lineage (Baron 2020).

2   The term 'intralingual' was famously employed by Roman Jakobson to refer to '*rewording* (…) in the same language' ([1959] 2012). For a recent reassessment, see Albachten (2014).

3   On the *Sonnets'* unrivalled role as 'the prototypical lyrics in English', see Boyd (2012: 4); on the productive consequences of their 'fascinating textual instability', see Marotti (1990: 165); for a substantial sample of their unparalleled fortunes across cultures and languages, see Pfister and Gutsch (2009).

4   My use of the term 'postmodern' reflects Hutcheon's while endorsing Jean-François Lyotard's famous definition as an 'incredulity toward metanarratives' (Lyotard 1984: xxiv).

5   For Spears's lyrics, see AZLyrics.com, https://www.azlyrics.com/lyrics/britneyspears/oopsididitagain.html (accessed 1 January 2020). Didriksen credits each song to the performer rather than the author of the lyrics. Since part of the book's rationale, I will cite attribution as provided, rather than supplementing it with further credits.

6   For Mars's lyrics, see AZLyrics.com, https://www.azlyrics.com/lyrics/brunomars/justthewayyouare.html (accessed 1 January 2020).

7   The often-repeated epithet features in a plaque (a little memorial) marking Sinatra's birthplace – see *New Jersey Monthly,* https://njmonthly.com/articles/historic-jersey/in-franks-footsteps-sinatra-walking-tour/ (accessed 1 January 2020).

8   Hutcheon leaves no doubt that, for her, verbal re-creation falls under the heading of adaptation as much as outputs in other media (2006: 9, 16) but these prevail in most treatments of the topic (Kidnie 2009). See also the discussion of conceptual and disciplinary challenges faced by adaptation studies in Lanier (2014).

9   This volume has no page numbering; citations will therefore be referenced only by sonnet numbers.

10   In addition to Colie's reference to literal misreadings, I have in mind Harry Berger Jr's claim that 'to modernize is (…) to metaphorize' (2015: 3).

11   For a description of the goals of *Telephone*, 'a biannual experimental poetry translation journal', see the editors' interview at *Bomb*, https://bombmagazine.org/articles/telephone-1-phoned-in-13/ (accessed 19 November 2020).

12   Jordan's sonnet is one of the few not specially commissioned for the volume, as readers learn from the editors' acknowledgement of her posthumous *Collected Poems* (2005), Jordan having died in 2002.

REFERENCES

Adorno, T. ([1937] 2002), 'Late Style in Beethoven', in *Essays in Music*, selected by R. Leppert, trans. S. H. Gillespie, 564–8, Berkeley, CA: University of California Press.

Albachten, Ö. B. (2014), 'Intralingual Translation: Discussions within Translation Studies and the Case of Turkey', in S. Bermann and C. Porter (eds), *A Companion to Translation Studies*, 573–85, Chichester: Wiley-Blackwell.

Anthony, J. (2018), *Shakespeare's Sonnets, Retold*, London: W.H. Allen.

Barnstone, W. (1993), *The Poetics of Translation: History, Theory, Practice*, New Haven, CT: Yale University Press.

Baron, S. (2020), *The Birth of Intertextuality: The Riddle of Creativity*, New York, NY: Routledge.

Benjamin, W. ([1936] 1968), 'The Work of Art in the Age of Mechanical Reproduction', in H. Arendt (ed.), *Illuminations*, trans. H. Zohn, 217–51, New York, NY: Schocken Books.

Berger, Jr., H. (2015), *Figures of a Changing World: Metaphor and the Emergence of Modern Culture*, New York, NY: Fordham University Press.

Boyd, B. (2012), *Why Lyrics Last: Evolution, Cognition and Shakespeare's Sonnets*, Cambridge, MA: Harvard University Press.

Cohen, S. and P. Legault, eds (2012), *The Sonnets: Translating and Rewriting Shakespeare*, New York, NY: Telephone Books.

Colie, R. L. (1974), *Shakespeare's Living Art*, Princeton, NJ: Princeton University Press.

Crawforth, H. and E. Scott-Baumann, eds (2016), *On Shakespeare's Sonnets: A Poets' Celebration*, London and New York, NY: Bloomsbury/Arden Shakespeare.

Davie, D. (1973), *Thomas Hardy and British Poetry*, London: Routledge & Kegan Paul.

Didriksen, E. (2015), *Pop Sonnets: Shakespearean Spins on Your Favourite Songs*, London: Fourth Estate.

Duncan-Jones, K., ed. (1997), *Shakespeare's Sonnets*. Arden Shakespeare, 3rd series, London: Thomas Nelson.

Ellis, J. (1982), 'The Literary Adaptation: an Introduction', *Screen* 23 (1): 3–5.

Gentzler, E. (2017), *Translation and Rewriting in the Age of Post-Translation Studies*, Abingdon: Routledge.

Goodby, J. (2000), *Irish Poetry since 1950: Stillness into History*, Manchester: Manchester University Press.

Heinz, D. et al. (2000), 'Como conversazione: On translation', *Paris Review* 155: 255–312.

Hermans, T., ed. (1985), *The Manipulation of Literature: Studies in Literary Translation*, London: Croom Helm.

Hofer, M. and M. Golston, eds (2019), *The Language Letters: Selected 1970s Correspondence of Bruce Andrews, Charles Bernstein, and Ron Silliman*, Albuquerque, NM: University of New Mexico Press.

Hoenselaars, A. J., ed. (2012), *Shakespeare and the Language of Translation*, rev. edn, London: Arden.

Hutcheon, L. (2006). *A Theory of Adaptation*, New York, NY: Routledge.

Hutcheon, L. ([1985] 2000), *A Theory of Parody: the Teachings of Twentieth-Century Art Forms*, Urbana and Chicago, IL: University of Illinois Press.

Hutcheon, L., M. Woodland, T. Yu and A. Dubois (2012), 'Postmodernism', in R. Greene (ed.), *The Princeton Encyclopedia of Poetry and Poetics*, 4th edn, 1095–7, Princeton, NJ, and Oxford: Princeton University Press.

Jakobson, R. ([1959] 2012), 'On Linguistic Aspects of Translation' (1959), in L. Venuti (ed.), *The Translation Studies Reader*, 3rd edn, 126–31, London: Routledge.

Jordan, J. (1981), *Civil Wars*, Boston, MA: Beacon Press.

Jordan, J. (1985), *On Call*, Boston, MA: South End Press.

Kidnie, M. J. (2009), *Shakespeare and the Problem of Adaptation*, London and New York, NY: Routledge.

Lanier, D. (2014), 'Shakespearean Rhizomatics: Adaptation, Ethics, Value', in A. Huang and E. Rivlin (eds), *Shakespeare and the Ethics of Appropriation*, 21–40, New York, NY: Palgrave.

Lefevere, A. (1992), *Translation, Rewriting and the Manipulation of Literary Fame*, London: Routledge.

Lyotard, J. (1984), *The Postmodern Condition: A Report on Knowledge*, trans. G. Bennington and B. Massumi, Minneapolis, MN: University of Minnesota Press.

Marotti, A. (1990), 'Shakespeare's Sonnets as Literary Property', in E. D. Harvey and K. E. Maus (eds), *Soliciting Interpretation: Literary Theory and Seventeenth-Century English Poetry*, 143–73, Chicago, IL: University of Chicago Press.

McMullan, G. (2007), *Shakespeare and the Idea of Late Writing*, Cambridge: Cambridge University Press.

McMullan, G. and S. Smiles, eds (2016), 'Introduction', in *Late Style and its Discontents: Essays in Art, Literature, and Music*, 1–12, Oxford: Oxford University Press.

O'Brien, S. (1998), *The Deregulated Muse: Essays on Contemporary British & Irish Poetry*, Newcastle: Bloodaxe.

Pfister, M. and J. Gutsch, eds (2009), *William Shakespeare's Sonnets: For the First Time Globally Reprinted. A Quartercentenary Anthology 1609–2009*, Dozwil: Edition Signathur.

Said, E. (2004), 'Thoughts on Late Style', *London Review of Books* 26 (15): 3–7.

Schoenfeldt, M., ed. (2010), *A Companion to Shakespeare's Sonnets*, Malden, MA: Blackwell.

Spiller, M. R. G. (1992), *The Development of the Sonnet: An Introduction*, London: Routledge.

Steiner, G. (1992), *After Babel: Aspects of Language and Translation*, 2nd edn, Oxford: Oxford University Press.

Ward, J. P. (1991), *The English Line: Poetry of the Unpoetic from Wordsworth to Larkin*, Houndmills: Macmillan.

Worton, M. and J. Still, eds (1990), *Intertextuality: Theories and Practices*, Manchester and New York, NY: Manchester University Press.

'Play on', or the memeing of Shakespeare: adaptation and internet culture

ANNA BLACKWELL

Entering the name 'William Shakespeare' into the world's most popular internet search engine, Google, throws up what are – at first glance – unsurprising results. After a Wikipedia entry, websites for the Royal Shakespeare Company and the Shakespeare Birthplace Trust point to the continued appetite for 'real life' Shakespeare-based cultural activities and tourism. Other results might demonstrate his dominance over not only the British school curriculum but education internationally, with many websites aimed specifically at students. But sites such as these are likely to be visited as the result of a deliberate search to find out something about Shakespeare. There are infinite other internet Shakespeares who exist outside of such searches and yet who may well haunt our everyday (and less purposeful) browsing, depending on the complex algorithmic workings of the social media platforms we use, the friends we connect with or the interests we pursue. As Danielle Rosvally's engagement with Shakespeare's digital ghost recognizes, Shakespeare (as he appears online) is 'not a static value, but rather a force constantly shifting as users interact with it'; 'a massive Shakespeare network, one that crosses boundaries of culture, time and space' (2017: 150). It is indeed crucial to note that, despite the global possibilities of the internet, much of our use is already determined by the local space we search from. The results I describe above are particular to my IP address and to my own browsing history; I was correct that the search results were unsurprising for an academic who teaches on Shakespeare and lives close to Stratford-upon-Avon in the United Kingdom, but they may not be the same for you.

It is difficult to imagine such a sprawling, dense and highly idiosyncratic network. As Stephen O'Neill writes of the influence of the non-human alongside human users online, the digital turn signals 'hitherto unknown information speed and traffic, and in turn a surfeit of Shakespeares' (2018: 121). This surfeit provides ripe opportunities for the digital Shakespeare scholar. It is this chapter's intention, having outlined a spectrum of potential internet Shakespeare texts and surveyed existent critical work within the field, to focus on one previously overlooked node within Shakespeare's ghostly network: the meme, and, in particular, GIFs or graphic interchange formats. Despite the growing wealth of criticism on online Shakespeare fandom and its intersections or use within other fandoms, the meme has not yet been identified as a dynamic adaptive form, nor as an abundant site for mapping Shakespeare within online participatory culture. Yet, memes and GIFs specifically are significant for their function as a form of 'vernacular criticism' (Goodman 2016: 1). Goodman writes that GIFs often capture and recycle favourite moments that 'audiences love or worship, or that express a particular feeling or experience'; not dissimilarly to scholarly communities, the individuals who share or create GIFs are thus 'dedicated to the analysis, critique and appreciation of media' (2016: 1). As such, GIFs represent a particularly clear vantage point from which to observe the adaptation, remediation and dissemination of Shakespeare online.

Of course, the concept of the meme does not originate from internet culture nor do the practices discussed in this chapter exist remotely from other adaptive forms; they 'do not so much replace earlier media […] as sustain them in new guises' (O'Neill 2014: 6). First coined by Richard Dawkins to refer analogously to the successful passing-on of desirable traits through genes within evolutionary biology, memes refer to 'small cultural units of transmission' (Shifman 2011: 188). They, like genes, are spread by 'copying or imitation' and undergo constant processes of 'variation, selection and retention' (Shifman 2011: 188). Meme is a descriptor that functions, therefore, as both an overarching term for shared units of culture, but also individual instances of said culture. Videos, images, certain phrases, hashtags or intentional misspellings can all be memes, for instance. As memes are – by definition – successfully transmitted phenomena, they tend to be highly adaptable and relatively short form in nature, based around a core idea or joke. Memes can exist in any culture or within any media, but Shifman writes that the 'internet's flexibility, ubiquitous presence and accessibility' has facilitated their 'accelerated spread' as 'new visual genres of expression' (2011: 188–9). Certainly, while early creators of macros (another type of meme) or GIFs will have needed some rudimentary knowledge of coding to create their works from scratch, contemporary internet users only need to head to a website with a macro or GIF maker or pre-existing templates.

Despite the subsequent proliferation of meme use online, it is worth remembering that all internet use is inevitably personal and ephemeral. It is governed by algorithms which are most visible when they fail in their logic, but which otherwise work silently to shape our everyday experiences online. This point is of course significant for scholars working on internet texts, as the same systems which try to predict our future behaviour by looking at our past browsing patterns will inevitably return often idiosyncratic, geographically specific results with a high degree of variability depending on the parameters of our searches or even – as Kirk Hendershott-Kraetzer found in depictions of Juliet on Tumblr (2014: 144) – the time at which they were performed. The Google results detailed in this chapter's opening were, therefore, quite different when first writing in August 2019 and again in early 2021, with the world in the grip of the coronavirus pandemic. As I've already indicated, my geographical proximity to Stratford-upon-Avon or to London, meanwhile, no doubt prompts certain responses that may not appear to internet users searching in other countries. And yet, it is precisely these iterations of Shakespeare, inflected by both the bias of algorithms and the specific networks and locations that the user occupies, circulating on social media platforms such as Facebook, Twitter, Instagram, Tumblr and Reddit, which are of interest. Social media sites reveal key aspects of not only Shakespeare's contemporary cultural legacy, but the shaping and adaptation of this legacy through the 'pairing of affordance and constraint' (Hendershott-Kraetzer 2017: 145) offered by each platform.

FRAGMENTING SHAKESPEARE

The playful use of the verb 'shook' as the past participle of 'shake' provides me with my opening illustration of meme culture's adaptation of the persistently textual associations of Shakespeare's legacy in popular culture despite the visual expressiveness that characterizes much of the internet. 'Shook' has been appropriated from 1990s hip hop music into popular vernacular, thence into internet culture and from there it has met the broader uses and meanings that circulate around Shakespeare online, where it has adapted further. One meme features an illustration of Shakespeare looking quizzically at an Apple computer with the caption ' ... I am shooketh' (Meme Generator n.d.). This Shakespeare appears to be expressing his feeling of being 'shook' in a conventional sense as the verb is most commonly used online to signal humorously the user's feelings of discombobulation; surprise; excitement or upset. But if the meme imagines Shakespeare like any other internet user, telegraphing his responses to digital content or posting about everyday life in a deliberately hyperbolic manner, the addition of 'eth' to the already bastardized use of 'shook' refers to the playful anachronisms that are so often used to conjure Shakespeare in the cultural imaginary. The meme's comedy thereby relies on the viewer's ability to combine knowledge of the original meme – the ironic use of 'shook' – with a broader understanding of how Shakespeare is thought of, or indeed parodied, in popular culture.[1]

Memes such as these participate in complex networks of meaning that accord with Christy Desmet's description of 'alien Shakespeare[s]' as the 'disaggregation of a Shakespearean text into "units" – semantic segments, words, lines, or even morphemes' (2017: 5). Macros (a subset of memes) illustrate particularly well that this fragmentation is indeed 'necessary' and 'the condition of existence for digital texts' (Desmet 2017: 5) online. A macro is an image that has text superimposed upon it for humorous effect; said text might pay tribute to a popular cultural phenomenon or adapt an older joke or meme. As in the example above, particular comedy is derived in Shakespeare macros from the anachronistic contrast between a contemporary popular vernacular or the popular cultural zeitgeist and what is perceived variously in Shakespeare as the embodiment of the distant past, an inaccessible, elite form of 'high' culture or a level of intellectual or emotional profundity. It is significant, moreover, that this 'new' form entails a curious throwback to traditional notions of Shakespeare in terms of not only the macros' punchlines, but the images used to convey their jokes. Here, the fragmentation of image and text work to reinscribe myths about Shakespeare's authorship or to curate a selective account of Shakespeare's plays and their chief narratives. Shakespeare's exaggerated reputation for neologisms, for instance, is reflected in one macro that features the Cobbe portrait. The playwright stares out intently and along the top of the image is the caption 'Think he has no swag' and at the bottom the punchline, 'invented the word' (Tomlinson 2016). The use of the Cobbe portrait in comparison to the more frequently used Chandos or Droeshout depictions is relatively unusual in macros, but here it acts in service to the joke of Shakespeare's embodied *and* linguistic ownership of 'swag'. With his expensive-looking lace collar (emphasized by the cropping of the image), intelligent, dark gaze and lightly flushed cheeks, this version of Shakespeare does indeed seem in greater possession of 'swag' or a 'quantity of money or goods' potentially unlawfully gained (*OED Online* 2021) than his portrait counterparts. But if this macro demonstrates the fragmentation of Shakespeare's legacy into constituent parts waiting for reassembly – the portrait, the reputation for linguistic innovation – it also reveals the perils of an internet culture which remixes content compulsively and perhaps indiscriminately. Aside from the usage above, 'swag' has also more recently developed in African American culture as a noun that can be used in both a literal and figurative sense (as it is in this macro). It can refer to either a swaggering, self-confident walk or to a more general sense of 'bold self-assurance' (*OED Online* 2020). That the logic of the macro claims not only Shakespeare's possession of 'swag' in this later sense but his invention of the term itself reveals the implication of the playwright in deeply problematic and appropriative cultural practices online.

Other macros, too, parody Blackness through their juxtaposition of Shakespeare's whiteness with a burlesqued version of African American culture. They are assisted in this by the ready availability of meme generators populated with portrait images of Shakespeare. The remediation of an older medium here, along with its gendered and implicitly raced articulation of the 'Shakespearean', works through its contrast with the often deliberately crude, colloquial or – in opposition – distinctly raced vernacular of the macro in order to serve the meme's punch line. Shakespeare versions of the 'Yo Dawg' meme, for instance, function by borrowing the meme's phrasal template and its tautological logic. The meme, first popularized on the website 4chan in 2007 (Dubbs 2020), is based on the premise behind *Pimp My Ride* (TV, 2004–7), a programme about customizing cars presented by American rapper, Xzibit. In the series, Xzibit would oversee outlandish modifications to cars often based on the owner's tastes or hobbies; someone who enjoyed cooking might get an oven fitted in their car, for example. Early forms of the macro thus juxtaposed an image of Xzibit laughing with a phrasal template of nested statements ('Yo Dawg, I herd you like (noun X), so I put an (noun X) in your (noun Y) so you can (verb Z) while you (verb Z)' [Dubbs 2020]) in order to evoke the humorous incongruity of the modifications. The template has fast mutated beyond this original joke, however. As Jamie Dubbs (2020) elucidates, 'Memes are no longer simply artefacts of media, remixed and mashed up by the masses, they are living, participatory entities that ebb and flow with the users' involvement, often including the subjects themselves.'

One application of the meme set to the Droeshout portrait offers a humorous commentary on *Hamlet*: 'Yo dawg I herd you like plays / So we put a play in yo play / So you can watch a play / while you watch a play' (ontological_shock 2009). The replacement of Xzibit in the macro's background, however, only exaggerates the recursive patterns of meme production, where often culturally or racially specific language is reproduced in vastly different contexts for comic purpose, but in ways which do not – and perhaps cannot easily – acknowledge the appropriative dynamics of reuse. The internet is indeed awash with examples of this kind of appropriative behaviour. Another macro with the same portrait and the caption 'Wrote that bitch a sonnet / Bitches love sonnets' (Me.Me 2017), for instance, borrows a phrasal template inspired by *The Boondocks* (TV, 2005–14). An animated sitcom based upon Aaron McGruder's comic strip of the same name, *The Boondocks* focuses on the experience of a Black family, the Freemans, as they move into a white suburb of Chicago, a relocation which magnifies their experience of race and Black culture. That memes based upon the show trade on their ability to incongruously recontextualize aspects of Black culture or parts of African American vernacular feels ironically and perversely in keeping with the tensions that *The Boondocks* animates. But in doing so, the meme – like the 'Yo Dawg' macro – exemplifies what Lauren Michele Jackson defines as 'digital blackface': the use of memes or reaction GIFs featuring Black people by a white population who use 'the relative anonymity of online identity to [momentarily] embody blackness' (2017). Jackson writes that images (and perhaps we should add here, the language) of Black people 'more than anyone else' is 'primed to go viral and circulate widely online': 'We are your sass, your nonchalance, your fury, your delight, your annoyance, your happy dance, your diva, your shade, your "yaas" moments' (2017).

Like the performance of his plays, the disaggregation of Shakespeare online is thus never neutral and always involved in deliberate adaptive processes which are shaped by the 'units' (Desmet 2017: 5) involved and the affordances of the medium used to (re)assemble them. As W.B. Worthen writes, not only is our access to Shakespeare mediated by digital technology, but our 'imagination' is 'shaped by the forms and moods of digital culture' (2007: 227). Indeed, while author-based comic set-ups are common online, often replaying old Shakespeare myths in new contexts, related effects can be created through quite different cultural properties. For example, a still from the animated children's series, *My Little Pony: Friendship is Magic* (2010–) features the characters of Pinkie Pie and Twilight Sparkle in conversation, affixed with Hamlet's reflection to his friend, 'There are more things in heaven and earth, Horatio, than are dreamt of in your philosophy' (Know Your Meme 2011).[2] The pairing of *Hamlet* – a play with extraordinary cultural capital and a character known for his philosophical introspection – with *My Little Pony* – a series based on Hasbro's line of toys of the same name – seems straightforwardly humorous. Both the original toy line, with its collectable range of pastel-coloured ponies, and its later television and film adaptations with themes of friendship and self-respect are aimed at young girls. The use of Shakespeare in the macro would then seem recuperative – attaching Shakespearean depth to a property associated with its obverse in a way that highlights the shortcomings of the latter, albeit playfully. A light-hearted repurposing of the play's intensity and emphasis on male friendship for a property associated with girls' culture. And yet, there is more than meets Twilight Sparkle's purple eyes here. The macro is, in fact, reflexive in its acknowledgement of cultural capital. It quotes Shakespeare in humorous recognition of *My Little Pony*'s own status as an intellectual property because, despite the popularity of the series among its intended audience, it has also gained a non-ironic cult following among older viewers (known as 'Bronies') for its sincerity. Reporting from a Brony convention, Wesley Yiin notes that the adult attendees are 'devoted to a very deep reading of the conflicts and dynamics lurking within these two-dimensional horses' (Yiin 2016).

A Shakespeare/*My Little Pony* adaptive encounter might seem outré but the type of pairing it represents is not atypical. Indeed, it is contiguous with broader fan practices which treat Shakespeare's body of work as a 'refracted *urtext* at the core of the fan's creation'; an original that 'exists with the same autonomy as its adaptive counterparts' (Fazel and Geddes 2016: 281). 'The Army of King Henry V of England' by frostbitten_ written, a fanfiction which imagines a night of pleasure between King Henry and his (unnamed) queen, is an illustrative example. Frostbitten_written admits that they've neither read nor watched *Henry V* ('I don't know how the story actually goes' [2020]); their work is driven, rather, by a 'little obsession with Tom Hiddleston', who plays Henry in *The Hollow Crown* adaptation. Hiddleston's prominence online (whether in longer form works like these or memes) remind us that a version of Shakespeare filtered through his particular brand of celebrity is an erotic fantasy based on implicitly raced and classed qualities such as 'sophistication' or 'charm'. And yet, it is precisely the desirability of Hiddleston which also allows this example to evade some of those traps. 'The Army of King Henry V of England' paints a deliberately undetermined portrait of Henry's wife, affording what O'Neill describes as fanfiction's 'rescripting and expansion of inherited texts' (2021: 128). It is evidently not only a project in wish fulfilment for frostbitten_written but for any reader seeking an erotic fantasy of Hiddleston's Henry. She is unnamed because as the author instructs in their opening notes, 'Y'all are queens [...]; use your own name' and her body is only ever detailed as it responds to Henry's ministrations. The openness of the story to projection from the reader is also apparent within the fanfiction's metadata which categorizes its central pairing as Tom Hiddleston and an original female character *and* Hiddleston and an original female character of colour. Although Hiddleston's popularity may indeed be attendant upon distinctly raced understandings of Shakespeare, agency remains with online users to resist the continuance of these associations within their own work. Tagging can connect up the actions of individual users like frostbitten_written to similarly minded writers across fanfiction sites like *Archive of Our Own*, meanwhile: at the time of writing, twenty works also pair Hiddleston with an 'original female character of colour', with further tags for 'plus-sized reader' or 'gender neutral reader', working to imagine the protagonist's desiring *and* desired body in inclusive terms that move drastically beyond the tokenistic multiculturalism of *The Hollow Crown* itself (Pittman 2017: 185).

GIFFING SHAKESPEARE

Nora Williams stresses that digital spaces 'are not neutral new frontiers: they are built environments, made by people with biases and preferences that are reflected in their creations' (2019: 4). The memes I have already identified in this chapter demonstrate this point powerfully as they share an adaptive existence wholly shaped by the affordances of the internet and digital media – even if brought into life by quite different purposes, communities of users or cultural reference points. I have already invoked Goodman's argument that memes – and GIFs in particular – exist as a form of 'vernacular criticism' (2016: 1) but I return to it again in this section to underline that memes are no mere whimsy, but an important and dynamic adaptive form. Ayanna Thompson notes, for example, that performances of *Othello* on YouTube by Asian American students […] 'highlight aspects of Shakespeare production and reception we rarely address directly' (2011: 165). Thompson observes that while anonymity 'can unleash disturbing aspects of the play that are often suppressed or addressed in euphemistic terms' it can 'paradoxically [… .] allow us to confront these textual effects directly' (2011: 165). The Tumblr blog 'It's All About That Homoerotic Subtext' by user edgy-sparknotes illustrates Thompson's point, although in this case, using Shakespeare to illuminate racist responses to cross-racial casting in period dramas. They observe in one blog post: 'yt [white] people are really out here like "ohhhh having poc in period dramas is UNREALISTIC, there weren't poc [people of colour] in ye olde england!" as if othello does not exist' (edgy-sparknotes 2021). The affordances of the medium further shape the post's meaning: both the user's and the blog's name indicate a larger intent to recontextualize traditional literary reception practices. Meanwhile, the tags attached to the post echo its refutation of the absence of Black people in historic periods adding, for instance, '#also it's heavily implied throughout twelfth night that viola and Sebastian aren't white idk [I don't know] what to tell ya' (edgy-sparknotes 2021). So, as I move into this chapter's final focus, I wish to propose that not only does the study of internet-native forms such as memes help us identify the ideological work inevitably involved in Shakespeare's use online, but it can supply us with tools to deconstruct many of those biases. Like the YouTube comment sections Thompson describes, memes can thus function both as archive of adaptation or performance, and as means of criticism.

This chapter thus closes by applying the potential of the meme as a form of vernacular criticism and archive of adaptation to one other digital-native form (and subset of memes), the GIF. This form represents a significant development of, and potential complication to, inherited understandings of Shakespearean performance because if some internet versions of Shakespeare can be traced back to more traditionally hierarchized cultural forms, others represent something wholly new. GIFs, or graphic interchange formats, are 2- to 6-second-long videos made either directly from clipped footage or from sequenced or compressed images which are edited together in a way that gives the impression of animation. The GIF was first developed and released on 15 June 1987 by a team at CompuServe led by Steve Wilhite and it was popular among early internet adaptors who used them to animate their web pages. The development of its use as a mode of expression in and of itself has been traced back to 2012 and the popular Tumblr blog, #Whatshouldwecallme, where each GIF shared was accompanied by a caption that acted as a 'lightbulb' (Casserly 2012) to explicate the connection between the bitmap image and the poster's mood. A similar use – and many others beside – persists today, with the increasing sophistication and availability of smartphones encouraging the use of GIFs not only on websites as per their original design, but on social media and instant messaging platforms.

Perhaps the most significant quality of the GIF is the combination of its relative brevity with its continuously looping nature (GIFs will run ad infinitum if given the chance). Because GIFs are often built by recycling and adapting existing images or video, Shakespeare GIFs appear most often via clips from existing performances of the playwright (for instance, Charity Wakefield in the stage play *Emilia*); moments from adaptations or recorded performances of his plays (Kenneth Branagh's 1996 *Hamlet*); use of the aforementioned portraits (a version of the Droeshout portrait where William 'shakes pear' repeatedly lifts the fruit to his mouth); or other (typically popular) cultural texts which quote from, characterize or define Shakespeareanism in some way.[3] The brevity of these GIFs, in combination with the visibility or abruptness of their endless repetitions, provides a tangible demonstration of the fragmentation that is a condition of online texts (Desmet 2017). But it is often also the vehicle for the largely comic purpose of GIFs. One GIF popular among my own students, for instance, begins with the caption '*something mildly distressing happens*' and then the response of the 'Shakespeare characters', illustrated by Ralph Wiggum in *The Simpsons* who gleefully, and repeatedly, stabs himself with the naïve exclamation, 'oh boy!' (BazookaPikachu05 2020). Ralph's characteristically benign expression in the face of his apparent suicide is humorous in its own right, but the compulsive cycling of the GIF over and over underlines the message of the caption: like Ralph, Shakespeare's tragic heroes are compelled to a violent end they are seemingly unable to resist. The vast majority of Shakespeare-related GIFs thereby speak to the abstraction of Shakespeare online into key repeated jokes that require little knowledge of the playwright or his plays beyond the violence of the tragedies, his reputation for profundity, eloquence and/or potentially anachronistic or hard to understand language.

Greater adaptive license and a potentially more conventional or complete narrative structure is perhaps permitted by GIFs created from scratch, where the user is not restricted by the adapted material's prior existence or length – even if GIFs, like macros, often deliberately invoke the image's original context for comic incongruity. One example of this is the 'History Shakespeare GIF' by GIPHY Studios Originals which is comprised of two animated images. The first sees an illustrated version of Shakespeare modelled on the Chandos portrait winking to the viewer, accompanied by the annotation 'This day in History … Shakespeare wrote some cool stuff.' This cuts to the second image: a quite crudely drawn animated image of two cars parked '3 in.' apart with the caption, 'Today, I parallel parked like a champ.' Sequences like these can approach more conventional narrative forms, as I will continue to explain, but for the most part, GIFs are constructed using pre-existing materials and are posted in isolation. As even 6 seconds is too short for meaningful narrative progression, GIFs have an effect that is at once frustrating and peculiarly enjoyable to watch. As Daniel Rourke writes, there is an inherent tension in GIFs: they are always 'poised in lieu of a release'; each repetition winding content 'tight like a spring' (2017). Perhaps unsurprisingly, this format has worked effectively as vehicles for pornography in predominantly female fan communities, allowing users to reject 'dominant representations of heterosexual acts', by choosing 'the bodies and fragmented sexual inter/activities they desire' (Hester, Jones and Taylor-Harman 2015: 54). There is indeed something hypnotic about the endless looping quality of GIFs. I have written previously, for example, on what Tumblr user 1outside calls Mark Rylance's 'Olivia Glide™' (2015). Clipping footage from the DVD recording of Shakespeare's Globe's 2013 production of *Twelfth Night,* 1outside shares with her blog followers six separate GIFs of Mark Rylance crossing the stage dressed as the Lady Olivia. In each, Rylance travels with an uncanny grace – the movement of his legs hidden beneath the full skirt of his costume – that is 'enhanced by the mesmeric quality of the GIF' (Blackwell 2018: 111). A similarly pleasurable offering comes from a GIF shared by the official social media account for *Pose* (2018–), a television series about the ball culture in New York in the 1980s and 1990s. The GIF features Angel Evangelista, a young trans woman and sex worker, mid-performance as Juliet. Angel weeps while raising poison to her lips and the caption reads, '*cries in Shakespeare*' (Pose FX 2019). Unlike the other GIFs circulated by the network account which revel in (uncaptioned) loops that demonstrate – and thus exaggerate – the striking angularity that characterizes voguing as a dance form in the ballroom scene, the playful caption uses Shakespeare instead to indicate the high theatricality and camp of Angel's performance. The caption to the GIF also functions as an amusing exaggeration of Shakespeare's reputation for neologisms (already identified in this chapter as a key meme trope): even Angel's non-verbal cry can still be recognized as a distinct utterance 'in Shakespeare'.

GIFFING SHAKESPEAREANS

What grants GIFs their significance as a type of 'vernacular criticism' (Goodman 2016: 1) is that they thus destabilize the terms within which a romantic understanding of theatre performance (and its relationship to the present) operates. This is a notion that has, of course, already been questioned, not least by Philip Auslander's insistence on mediation as performance (2008: 11), but by the complication presented by the popularity of live and encore cinema broadcasts in the last decade and more recently, the necessity of digital performance due to coronavirus-related theatre closures worldwide. As Erin Sullivan muses, if theatre 'is an act of doing, and we are part of it', 'what happens when the very notion of "being there" starts to shift [… .]?' (2017: 627). As not only a (partial) recording of performance but a potentially edited one at that, GIFs are, therefore, undeniably 'something other' (Phelan 1993: 146). The supposedly singular quality of performance is rendered absurd within the often grainy, small confines of an infinitely looping 6-second video. Unlike the 'real' Shakespearean performer who is 'beholden to communicating the uniqueness, spontaneity and ephemerality of each performance', those reproduced in GIFs 'visibly display the repetitive nature of […] theatrical labour' (Blackwell 2018: 19). Nor does the GIF accord to what John Wyver characterizes as live cinema broadcast's 'myth of non-mediation'; an omission of broadcast directors or other significant authoring figures from critical discussions of the form that seems to imagine sequences appearing on screen 'courtesy of some kind of outside broadcast fairy' (2014: 109). These Shakespeareans instead reset, often disruptively, every 6 seconds; forever caught in a micro performative moment, the confines of which are forcibly – and visibly – set by its maker. Indeed, there lies in the experience of watching GIFs a realization of theatre's paradoxical need to consistently present unrepeatable, live moments; one feels ensnared within the mesmeric loops of the GIF, waiting for a variation or an ending that will never arrive.

It is precisely this sensation and the recycling of an apparently endless sameness that can be used to anatomize performance in a productive manner. On the blog *Shut up and drink your gin* is a chained series of seven GIFs, each edited from Adrian Lester's performance of 'To be or not to be' for the *Guardian* newspaper's 'Shakespeare Solos' series of videos (Henry Clervals 2018). By taking Lester's performance on a line-by-line basis (and for each clip to continually loop), the subtlest, shifting variances in his delivery are magnified beyond what Michael Billington already described as the series' 'microscopic' focus on its stars in order to 'expose the sinews of thought' (2016). The connectedness of the digital world and its users' familiarity with toggling between and across sites and platforms means, moreover, that in connecting the blog to the original YouTube video of Lester's performance (*Guardian* Culture 2016), Henry Clervals's post extends its scrutiny further. The blog reader is able to either fragment the performance into the seven GIFs or to reconstitute the individual moments into a whole with these moments interacting and modifying one another even outside of their iteration as part of a real-time sequence. It is in this quality that we see the GIF existing as perhaps a more extreme and vivid example (but not the unique instance) of Bruce R. Smith's concept of 'cutwork': acts of cutting and the resulting assemblage of cuts which 'open up new, unexpected features in Shakespeare's texts' and 'provide the means for creating new works of art' (2016: 25).

The GIF is an adaptive form that is able to simultaneously archive and to perform; to reconstruct, even as it superficially deconstructs and to allow one to identify subtle difference within sameness. Lester's example is particularly meaningful as his professional success and relative visibility as a performer (testament to his inclusion in this series) has helped to shift assumptions about the Shakespearean actor. As Barbara Hodgdon observed of his and the other 'Shakespeare Solos' performances, the series' 'en-framed space' and deliberate, 'precise timing' (2017: 3) allows the 'attentive listener' to occupy the role of author and 'let silent histories come into voice' (11). Or, as Worthen writes of the Wooster Group *Hamlet,* living speech becomes an 'instrument for rewriting the archive in its restoration to performance' (2008: 318). Hodgdon is concerned here with the quite literal voicing of a past which can be made present in both senses of the word through the marriage of performance and technology. It is striking, however, that the sequence of GIFs shared by Henry Clervals, though silent, also illustrates her description of Lester's vocal delivery *and* amplifies the performative choices he makes. The adaptation of his performance in GIF form can thus consolidate Lester's Shakespearean stardom. Indeed, the GIF's dissemination on platforms like Tumblr where it can be posted, shared and commented upon, may not only introduce Lester to communities of users previously unfamiliar with his work, but plant the seeds for further cross-platform circulation. Unlike the website article that Lester's video was originally contained within, the GIF requires no link in order to spread on other platforms: its inclusion is immediate and visible and thus 'the archive is remade by its performance' (Worthen 2008: 317).

#SHAKESPEARE

Shakespeare GIFs form part of sophisticated – and potentially knowing – online vocabularies. It is not easy to imagine that a GIF from *Titus Andronicus* (dir. Julie Taymor, 1999) where Laura Fraser's Lavinia gushes blood and spreads her tortured arms plaintively has much use in a Facebook group chat, for instance. A haunting image like this must receive quite purposeful circulation and Zupreme's posting of the GIF on her Tumblr blog, *Endless Flight* (2011), does not seem to originate from explicitly Shakespearean fan activities. It is difficult to say if Zupreme was responsible for the creation of the GIF as there is no other accompanying text in the post, but the blog does appear to be the source for subsequent reposts or shares, and the metadata tag 'zupreme gif' [*sic*] indicates a proprietorial relationship to the GIF. The other metadata tags used by Zupreme do not give anything else away. Tags serve a basic organizational function, allowing bloggers and visitors alike to browse for particular content, but contrary to Hendershott-Kraetzer's experience of browsing 'merely descriptive' Tumblr tags in a 'context-less aporia' (2017: 145), they can also act as a type of commentary, providing a metatextual framework for the post.[4] Somethingscarlet13, for instance, posts a queer reading of Hamlet's and Horatio's relationship using the tag 'hamratio' (a portmanteau forged by combining 'Hamlet' and 'Horatio') along with another recognized, somewhat parodic descriptor for this particular pairing: 'tragic danish boyfriends'. In doing so, Somethingscarlet13 knowingly connects their individual post with a multitude of similar pieces of writing, fan art or memes dedicated to pairing the two friends romantically (2018). The latter tag may be an unlikely candidate for an organizational metadata tag but its employment shows Somethingscarlet13's knowing participation within a particular fandom and ship. By comparison, Zupreme uses only neutral, descriptive tags: movie, titus [*sic*], gif [*sic*], Laura Fraser and William Shakespeare. More revealing of Zupreme's relationship to their content is, therefore, the fact that the only other post tagged with 'William Shakespeare' is another GIF of Lavinia in *Titus Andronicus*. By surveying Zupreme's blog as a whole, it is possible to see the two Shakespeare GIFs as less of a distinct engagement with the playwright than as part of a repeated interest in images of stark, feminine beauty and moody landscapes; a reminder of the need to read the medium of a given internet adaptation, as well as the available Shakespeare referent. To investigate Zupreme's GIF purely in terms of its remediation of *Titus Andronicus* would be to somewhat miss the point about the adaptational process in play. As Hendershott-Kraetzer observes, Tumblr blogs are not 'one thing but a collection of things' (2017: 145); a constantly shifting accretion of diverse moods, pursuits and passions; images, videos and text.

The GIF's form does not proscribe the kind of curatorial work seen on *Endless Flight*, or a level of understanding only expected in fans, students or scholars of

Shakespeare, however, and when these types of digital adaptations exist in relation to a playwright around whom there is so much cultural anxiety about understanding correctly, that is significant. After all, internet use is significantly personal. Algorithms operate across all social media to optimize a user's experience of the platform. They do this by predicting interests and patterns of use based on past behaviour; or put more simply, your online past is prologue to the adverts, links and ordering of data that will appear while you use the internet in everyday life. What GIFs Facebook offers me to post in private messages will no doubt vary to you, depending on where in the world you hail from and the type of internet use Facebook mines. But this is the final argument for the significance of GIFs as an adaptive form which can exist variously as a mode of punctuation, a visual spectacle, or as a rudimentary narrative form; embedded within specific local or national cultures or capable of transcending language barriers by operating purely visually or in reference to transnational properties. The simultaneous abstraction and anatomization of Shakespeare enables the 'Shakespearean' – as a capacious signifier – to respond flexibly to the digital landscape and the needs of its users. The GIF may thus prove a more indicative example of the way that Shakespeare continues to exist in popular and digital culture than more conventional, self-contained adaptations. I have already indicated some of the uses of Shakespeare GIFs by online communities as well as their usefulness to scholars: their function as archives of performance or adaptive histories; reification of Shakespeare's plays into key moments or tropes; testing of the limits of liveness; or involvement in the often-appropriative practices which extend across internet culture at large. What the GIFs share in common, however, is their illustration of the circuits of reuse and repetition that characterize not only the processes of adaptation but the affective economies of the internet. As Smith writes of cutting – apparent to differing degrees across Shakespeare history, but *always* present – the GIF is a phenomenon 'fundamental not only to perception, but also to artistic creation' (2016: 186). The obviousness of the limits of the GIF – its jolting stop and start or its often subtle but nevertheless discernible transitions between images – makes visible the processes and decisions at hand whenever we perform or adapt Shakespeare or 'play on[line]'.

NOTES

1   For those viewers even more savvy in their knowledge of internet memes, there is further ironic meaning at work. While the playful extension of 'shook' into 'shooketh' trades upon a familiar cod-Shakespearean sound, 'shooketh' was first used in a parodic vlog-style video by comedian Christine Sydelko as she shared with her friend Elijah her experience of being 'attacked' by a fan (2017). The YouTube video has received 1,134,313 views at the time of writing and popularized this version of 'shook's usage. By imaging Shakespeare uttering the same exclamation, the meme not only references Sydelko's particular use but imagines a scenario in which her invented baroque version of 'I am shook' makes sense.

2   It is difficult to both provide stable locations for memes and to identify their creator as, if successful, they circulate so frequently and widely. Where it has not been

possible to do either, I have provided references from meme aggregation websites such as Meme Base or Know Your Meme.

3   A notable exception to the tendency to construct GIFs from pre-existing materials lies in the work of visual artist Kate Bones, who worked with Shakespeare's Globe on advertising for productions of *Imogen*, *The White Devil* and *The Taming of the Shrew*. Bones combines digital and analogue techniques by animating photographs shot on film into looping GIFs. Hand-drawn elements are then often added frame-by-frame, introducing a smooth, continuous quality that plays against the transitions of the GIF through its constituent images. Gloria Onitiri's Katherina, for instance, stares out at the viewer with animated pink and black hair, green eyes framed by yellow eyelashes, arched red eyebrows and pale pink lipstick. Onitiri lifts her hand and wipes the lipstick away, revealing the skin concealed beneath Bones's animation. Her gesture is defiant; an echo, perhaps, of the 'curst' Katherina who witheringly couches the terms of her own marriage in that of prostitution.

4   The tagging function on Tumblr (equally possible through hashtags on platforms such as Instagram or fanfiction sites like *Archive of Our Own*) can reflect the blogger's reasons for posting, their thoughts on the post itself or gesture towards any larger communal or fan activities.

REFERENCES

1outside (2015), 'I Think You All Need a Few Gifs of Mark Rylance's Olivia Glide™', *Keeping it Cosmic*, 5 April. Available online: https://1outside.tumblr.com/post/115604963071/i-think-you-all-need-a-few-gifs-of-mark-rylances (accessed 2 October 2019).

Auslander, P. (2008), *Liveness: Performance in a Mediatized Culture*, London: Routledge.

BazookaPikachu05 (2020), 'Oof Shakespeare', *Tenor*, 17 April. Available online: https://tenor.com/view/oof-shakespeare-stress-ralph-simpsons-gif-16912843 (accessed 17 February 2021).

Billington, M. (2016), 'Shakespeare solos: peer into the minds of Lear, Hamlet and Titania', *Guardian*, 1 February. Available online: https://www.theguardian.com/stage/2016/feb/01/shakespeare-solos-lear-hamlet-titania-speeches (accessed 17 February 2021).

Blackwell, A. (2018), *Shakespearean Celebrity in the Digital Age: Fan Culture and Remediations*, Basingstoke: Palgrave Macmillan.

Bones, K. (n.d.), 'The Taming of the Shrew', *Kate Bones*. Available online: http://www.katebones.com/projects/the_taming_of_the_shrew/ (accessed 17 February 2021).

Bones, K. (n.d.), 'The White Devil', *Kate Bones*. Available online: http://www.katebones.com/projects/the_white_devil_at_shakespeares_globe/ (accessed 17 February 2021).

Casserly, M. (2012), '#Whatshouldwecallme Revealed: the 24-year old law students behind the new Tumblr darling', *Forbes*, 29 March. Available online: https://www.forbes.com/sites/meghancasserly/2012/03/29/whatshouldwecallme-revealed-24-year-old-law-students-tumblr-darling/?sh=3a72882c30f1 (accessed 4 January 2021).

Desmet, C. (2017), 'Alien Shakespeares 2.0', *Actes des congrès de la Société française Shakespeare* 35. Available online: http://journals.openedition.org/shakespeare/3877 (accessed 8 January 2020).

Dubbs, J. (2020), 'Xzibit Yo Dawg meme', *Know Your Meme*. Available online: https://knowyourmeme.com/memes/xzibit-yo-dawg (accessed 12 February 2021).

edgy-sparknotes (2021), 'yt people are really out here like ohhhh having', *It's All About That Homoerotic Subtext*, 31 January. Available online: https://edgy-sparknotes.tumblr.com/post/641822313420029952/yt-people-are-really-out-here-like-ohhhh-having (accessed 12 February 2021).

Fazel, V. and L. Geddes (2016), '"Give Me Your Hands if We Be Friends": Collaborative Authority in Shakespeare Fan Fiction', *Shakespeare* 12 (3): 274–86.

frostbitten_written (2020), 'The Army of King Henry V of England', *Archive of Our Own*, 18 November. Available online: https://archiveofourown.org/works/27622097 (accessed 6 January 2021).

GIPHY Studios Originals (n.d.), 'History Shakespeare GIF by GIPHY Studios Originals', *Giphy*. Available online: https://giphy.com/gifs/studiosoriginals-history-shakespeare-3o6ZtpaSGZRKHjnUBi(accessed 2 October 2019).

Goodman, M. Z. (2016), 'GIFs: The Attainable Text', *Film Criticism* 40 (1). Available online: https://quod.lib.umich.edu/f/fc/13761232.0040.123?view=text;rgn=main (accessed 20 January 2017).

Guardian Culture (2016), 'Adrian Lester as Hamlet: "To be or not to be" – Shakespeare Solos', *YouTube*, 1 February. Available online: https://www.youtube.com/watch?v=muLAzfQDS3M (accessed 4 October 2019).

Hendershott-Kraetzer, K. (2017), 'Juliet, Tumbld. Fan Renovations of Shakespeare's Juliet on Tumblr', in S.O'Neill (ed.), *Broadcast Your Shakespeare: Continuity and Change Across Media*, 141–60, London: Bloomsbury.

Henry Clervals (2018), 'Adrian Lester delivers Hamlet to be or not to be', *Shut up and drink yer gin*. Available online: https://henryclervals.tumblr.com/post/174407896592/adrian-lester-delivers-hamlets-to-be-or-not-to (accessed 4 October 2019).

Hester, H., B. Jones and S. Taylor-Harman (2015), 'Giffing a Fuck: Non-Narrative Pleasures in Participatory Porn Cultures and Female Fandom', *Porn Studies* 2 (4): 356–66.

Hodgdon, B. (2017), 'The Shakespearean Phonograph', *Shakespeare Bulletin* 35 (1): 1–14.

Jackson, L. M. (2017), 'We need to talk about digital blackface in reaction GIF's', *Teen Vogue*, 2 August. Available online: https://www.teenvogue.com/story/digital-blackface-reaction-gifs (accessed 12 February 2021).

Know Your Meme (2011), 'My Little Pony: Friendship is Magic – Image #121,410', *Know Your Meme*. Available online: https://knowyourmeme.com/photos/121410-my-little-pony-friendship-is-magic (accessed 4 October 2019).

Meme Generator (n.d.), 'I am shooketh – Shakespeare with computer', *Meme*. Available online: https://me.me/i/iam-shooketh-memegenerator-net-i-am-shooketh-shakespeare-with-computer-ff9ba9aac5564a01ac3f93391c9ce3b4 (accessed 4 October 2019).

Me.Me. (2017), 'Wrote that bitch a sonnet', *Meme*. Available online: https://me.me/i/wrote-that-bitch-a-sonnet-bitches-love-sonnets-none-13217622 (accessed 8 December 2021).

OED Online (2020), 'swag, n.2', December. Available online: https://oed.com/view/Entry/63342644?rskey=Tc9Zsd&result=2&isAdvanced=false (accessed 11 February 2021).

OED Online (2021), 'swag, n. 1', March. Available online: https://oed.com/view/Entry/195335?rskey=SvPCEh&result=1&isAdvanced=false (accessed 12 April 2021).

O'Neill, S. (2014), *Shakespeare and YouTube: New Media Forms of the Bard*, London: Bloomsbury.

O'Neill, S. (2018), 'Shakespeare's Digital Flow: Humans, Technologies and the Possibilities of Intercultural Exchange', *Shakespeare Studies* 46: 120–33.

O'Neill, S. (2021), 'Hiddleston-Shakespeare-*Coriolanus*, or Rhizomatic Crossings in Fanfic', in A. Hartley and P. Holland (eds), *Shakespeare and Geek Culture*, 112–31, London: Bloomsbury.

Ontological_shock (2009), 'Shakespeare macro', *Image Macros*, 25 June. Available online: https://imagemacros.wordpress.com/tag/shakespeare-macro/ (accessed 11 January 2021).

Phelan, P. (1993), *Unmarked: The Politics of Performance*, London: Routledge.

Pittman, M. (2017), 'Colour-Conscious Casting and Multicultural Britain in the BBC *Henry V* (2012): Historicizing Adaptation in an Age of Digital Placelessness', *Adaptation* 10 (2): 176–91.

Pose FX (2019), 'Season 2 Crying GIF by Pose FX', *GIPHY*, 17 June. Available online: https://giphy.com/gifs/poseonfx-XGxlscqR85DNeRRIII (accessed 17 February 2021).

Rosvally, D. (2017), 'The Haunted Network: Shakespeare's Digital Ghost', in L. Geddes and V. M. Fazel (eds), *The Shakespeare User: Critical and Creative Appropriations in a Networked Culture*, 149–65, Basingstoke: Palgrave.

Rourke, D. (2017), 'The Compulsions of the Similar: Animated GIFs and the TechnoCultural Body', *Daniel Rourke*, 15 July. Available online: https://machinemachine.net/portfolio/the-compulsions-of-the-similar-gifs/ (accessed 2 October 2019).

Shifman, L. (2011), 'The anatomy of a YouTube meme', *New Media and Society* 14 (2): 187–203.

Smith, B. R. (2016), *Shakespeare | Cut: Rethinking Cutwork in an Age of Distraction*, Oxford: Oxford University Press.

Somethingscarlet13 (2018), 'Things I am never ever going to get over', *A Fine Word Like Waffle Would Turn Out Just Awful*, 3 July. Available online: https://somethingscarlet13.tumblr.com/post/171645786975/things-i-am-never-ever-going-to-get-over-the (accessed 5 January 2021).

Sullivan, E. (2017), '"The forms of things unknown": Shakespeare and the rise of the Live Broadcast', *Shakespeare Bulletin* 35 (4): 627–62.

Sydelko, C. (2017), 'CRAZY FAN ATTACKED HER!!', *YouTube*, 2 March. Available online: https://youtu.be/0TE9DYDtPKI (accessed 4 October 2019).

Thompson, A. (2011), *Passing Strange: Shakespeare, Race and Contemporary America*, New York, NY: Oxford University Press.

Tomlinson, K. (2016), 'Shakespeare Meme for Thursday', *Eye of the Kat*, 9 June. Available online: http://kattomic-energy.blogspot.com/2016/06/shakespeare-meme-for-thursday.html (accessed 11 February 2021).

Williams, N. J. (2019), '@ Shakespeare and@ TwasFletcher: Performances of Authority', *Humanities* 8 (1): 1–16. Available online: https://www.mdpi.com/2076-0787/8/1/46 (accessed 11 February 2021).

Worthen, W. B. (2007), 'Performing Shakespeare in digital culture', in R. Shaughnessy (ed.), *The Cambridge Companion to Shakespeare and Popular Culture*, 227–47, Cambridge: Cambridge University Press.

Worthen, W. B. (2008), 'Hamlet at Ground Zero: The Wooster Group and the Archive of Performance', *Shakespeare Quarterly* 59 (3): 303–22.

Wyver, J. (2014), '"All the trimmings?": The transfer of theatre to television in adaptations of Shakespeare stagings', *Adaptation* 7 (2): 104–20.

Yiin, W. (2016), 'The grown men who love *My Little Pony* aren't who you think they are', *Washington Post*, 18 July. Available online: https://www.washingtonpost.com/lifestyle/style/the-grown-men-who-love-my-little-pony-arent-who-you-think-they-are/2016/07/18/d1c1cefe-476f-11e6-acbc-4d4870a079da_story.html (accessed 22 August 2019).

Zupreme (2011), *Endless Flight*, 12 September. Available online: https://zupreme.tumblr.com/post/10125838957 (accessed 2 October 2019).

Bollywood Gertrudes and Global Shakespeares

VARSHA PANJWANI

Gertrude does not have a single soliloquy in *Hamlet* and her dialogue reveals her feelings sparingly. This relative silence has bred widely divergent responses to the character: Trevor Nunn, who directed Imogen Stubbs in the role in the 2004 Old Vic production, suggests that Gertrude is silent in significant scenes because she is 'not a highly educated woman and perhaps not even blessed with a very sophisticated intelligence' (Stubbs 2006: 37) whereas when Vishal Bhardwaj directed Tabu in *Haider*, the 2014 Bollywood adaptation *Hamlet*, these very lacunae in Gertrude's speeches become tools to develop her interiority and present her as 'one of the most complicated' characters in the play (2014: vii).[1] The medium of film further enhanced Tabu and Bhardwaj's interpretation. In Lawrence Olivier's 1948 *Hamlet*, just before Hamlet is about to deliver Shakespeare's most famous soliloquy, 'to be or not to be', a tracking shot closes in on the back of Hamlet's head as if taking the viewer inside Hamlet's tortured mind. In *Haider*, the camera belongs to Ghazala [Gertrude] with frequent close-ups of Ghazala's countenance. However, this only makes Ghazala more inscrutable rather than more transparent. Talking about her role in the movie, Tabu explains that 'Haider's predicament is that he doesn't know what to do with his mother—whether to love her, hate her, believe her or kill her' (2014), and her Gertrude certainly evokes this intricate emotional response. If Shakespeare's Hamlet develops a relationship with the audience through soliloquies (Escolme 2004), then Ghazala develops a bond with the viewer through her lingering facial expressions.

This nuanced portrayal of Gertrude won wide critical approbation for Tabu and Bhardwaj. Reviewing the movie in *The New York Times*, Rachel Saltz (2014) writes that:

> as played by the sad-eyed Tabu, Ghazala has such depths and mystery that she hijacks the movie, pushing Haider (Hamlet) to the sidelines in his own story. It's her interior drama that draws you in: Where does her loyalty lie? What is she thinking? Will she take up arms against a sea of troubles and, by opposing, change the tale?

Poonam Trivedi similarly asserts that 'in *Haider*, the major change is with Gertrude/ Ghazala who is moved to the centre, and the story revolves largely around her'

(2018: 36). Questioning the centrality of Gertrude, she wonders, 'why does Bhardwaj arrive at this?' and traces 'several intertextualities' for this portrayal ranging from Sulayman Al-Bassam's *Al-Hamlet Summit*, to female suicide bombers in real and reel life, to the mother–son relationship prominent in Hindi cinema (Trivedi 2018: 37–8). In this chapter, I want to add an important intertextual or rather an ancestral link to Gertrude's portrayal in *Haider* – the Gertrudes in pre-Bhardwaj Bollywood adaptations of *Hamlet*. While this might seem like adding a footnote to the list of *Haider*'s intertextualities, my purpose in establishing this missing link is twofold: I want to revisit early Bollywood's claim over, and contribution to, Shakespeare, and I want to establish how studying Indian avatars of Shakespeare's women characters can contribute fresh insights to Feminist Shakespeare studies.

The stock of Shakespeare on Indian screens has risen only recently with the advent of Global Shakespeare studies. Vikram Singh Thakur notes that 'although Shakespeare has always "inspired" Bollywood films, unconsciously in many cases, it is because of the post-Vishal Bhardwaj phenomenon that "Bollywood Shakespeare" is now considered an important and serious area of study' (2014: 22). Trivedi goes even further to argue that 'until the past few decades, Indian cinema spoke mainly to the local, though millions, of the subcontinent… Vishal Bhardwaj's films have in no small measure changed this; they have become the "global" face of Indian/ Hindi cinema' (2018: 23).[2] Bhardwaj's films are a rich subject of study and merit all the critical attention that has been lavished on them but this 'post-Vishal Bhardwaj phenomenon' has also led to the undervaluing of early Bollywood adaptations of Shakespeare. While a handful of scholars have charted the Parsi theatre in Mumbai that gave rise to Bollywood Shakespeare, there is still a dearth of scholarship on the way in which individual characters and plays have been interpreted in Parsi theatre and in early Bollywood films.

This is partly due to archival chasms in such a research undertaking. However, both Rajiva Verma (2002: 81–93) and Amrit Gangar (2018: 111–26) have demonstrated how to recoup fragmentary information in order to gain insights from the lost and partial archive of Indian Shakespeare films. I follow their model here, piecing together Gertrudes in lost, silent and low-quality prints of early Bollywood *Hamlet*s, to prove that serious, analytical engagement with Shakespeare has a long history in Bollywood. Tradition bestows authority, and the longer the tradition the greater the authority; thus, emphasizing an enduring tradition of Bollywood Shakespeare is also a bid to assert authority for Bollywood Shakespeare, and contributes to Global Shakespeares's project of decentring Anglophone Shakespeare.

If establishing a tradition for Bollywood Shakespeare is important, then building a lineage of Gertrude's portrayals specifically is even more significant. Performance histories of *Hamlet*, especially in the UK and USA, often concentrate on the titular character when creating a pedigree of great productions from Richard Burbage to Edwin Booth to John Barrymore to Lawrence Olivier to Kenneth Branagh to Ethan Hawke to David Tennant. Sometimes, this list includes women who have played the role such as Sarah Bernhardt or Asta Neilson. In comparison, Shakespeare's Danish queen has generated so little interest that *The Palgrave Handbook of Shakespeare's Queens* (Mudan Finn and Schutte 2018) devoted to the topic does not even confer a full chapter on Gertrude. Also, while Gertrude's relative silence gives actors and directors a chance to generate a range of interpretations, this potential has not always been realized. Often, as Ellen J. O'Brian has demonstrated, the role is prone to cuts which have 'eviscerated the textual patterns which gave coherence – and even interest – to Gertrude's role' (1992: 34) or becomes a casualty at the hands of its mostly male directors who, as actor and director Janet Suzman asserts, 'just aren't very interested in the girls. They just aren't' (2020). In fact, so entrenched is the notion of an ineffectual Gertrude that even when Saltz and Trivedi praise Tabu's performance as Ghazala, they do not read it as an interesting performance possibility for Shakespeare's Gertrude; for Trivedi, Gertrude remains a 'passive, pushover queen, manipulated by all' who is 'reinvented in *Haider*' (Trivedi 2018: 37) and for Saltz, a powerful Gertrude 'sidelines [Hamlet] in his own story' (2014) reinforcing the assumption that *Hamlet* is primarily Hamlet's story. Yet, when detailed performance histories of actors playing the role of Gertrude have been published, they have provided piercing insights into its flexibility and range as written in Shakespeare's text. For instance, despite Nunn's dismissal, Stubbs, rehearsing Gertrude, kept probing the question of 'why is she silent, when she is silent' and decided that 'the answers are significantly different, I think, as the play goes along: increasingly she dares not articulate what is going on inside her head, and after a certain point there is an element of knowing, but not knowing, about what Claudius is doing and is planning to do' (Stubbs 2006: 37). Actor and scholar Paige Martin Reynolds argues that the role demands interiority, and offers a different and equally compelling explanation: Gertrude's silence is due to years of learnt behaviour of restraint when dealing with personal pain (2018: 85–110). These accounts re-write the performance history of the play by presenting Gertrude as a subtle, multifaceted role, and expose the directorial and critical bias that persists in favouring insignificant Gertrudes. It is this alternate performance history that I want to supplement by focusing on Gertrudes in early Bollywood cinema: these performances lie at the intersectional blind-spot where a disregard of Gertrude as a character and a neglect of early Bollywood cinema converge. By showing how these hitherto hidden histories can provide fresh frames with which to interrogate assumptions about Shakespeare's women characters, this chapter follows Diana Henderson's work in mapping ways in which Global Shakespeares can open a productive dialogue between media studies and gender studies (2016: 674–92).

KHOON-E-NAHAK (MURDER MOST FOUL), 1928

The first Gertrude on Indian screen appeared as early as 1928 in a silent film titled *Khoon-e-Nahak* (Murder Most Foul). Directed by K. B. Athavale, this film is now lost but it shares its name with a stage version of Shakespeare's play which was popular in India long before the release of the film. Written by the highly regarded playwright Mehdi Hasan 'Ahsan', it is a free adaptation of *Hamlet* in the Parsi theatre tradition.[3] It is well-documented that early Bollywood movies were heavily based on Parsi theatre productions (Verma 2002: 81), so it is highly likely that Athavle's offering was a filmed version of Ahsan's play.[4] If that was the case, then, as R. E. Vernede's account of the play details, the audience would have seen Mallika Gohrulnisa (Queen Gertrude) inciting Farrukh (Claudius) to murder King Hamlet:

> The first scene opens with the king chatting with the Queen in a room in the castle. He then feels drousy [*sic*] and subsequently falls asleep; whereupon the Queen sends for her husband's brother, Farrukh and induces him to drop poison in his ear. The King dies of its effects, and the Queen gives out, importunely attributing [*sic*] the cause to a serpent's bite.[5]

(1995: 236)

For R. K. Yajnik, this adaption is a 'travesty of Shakespearean characterization' not least because 'the Shakespearean problem of the Queen's guilt is solved absolutely. Here she goads her incestuous lover to murder her husband' (1933: 162). One person's travesty is another person's opportunity, because setting aside the fact that the extent of Queen Gertrude's guilt depends on which text of *Hamlet* is being followed, this interpretation of Gertrude interested me because of the parallels that it draws between two Shakespearean queens: Gertrude and Lady Macbeth. Sian Thomas, who played Lady Macbeth in Dominic Cooke's production while simultaneously playing Gertrude in Michael Boyd's production at the RSC in 2004 observes that 'Gertrude in many ways has much of what Lady Macbeth seems to need: a secure position as queen, a grown-up son, a husband who is a successful regicide who does not blab about seeing ghosts... In a funny way, Gertrude is the more political of the two' (2006: 105). *Khoon-e-Nahak* seems to amplify the echoes that registered with Thomas when she was playing these roles in tandem by presenting a Gertrude who is the instigator of the regicide. Moreover, it is Mallika Gohrulnisa (Queen Gertrude) who fabricates the story that King Hamlet was stung by a serpent (a lie that is strikingly believable in an Indian context), further chiming with Lady Macbeth's urging her husband to be a 'serpent' (1.5.66).[6] In emphasizing these links, the film not only becomes an important precursor to *Haider*, which likewise creates resonance between the two characters by casting Tabu as Gertrude when she had already played Lady Macbeth in *Maqbool* (Bhardwaj's Bollywood adaptation of *Macbeth*) but it also provides an early reading of Gertrude as a political queen.

If Shakespeare's text does not make Gertrude's guilt as explicit as Lady Macbeth's, it certainly leaves room for a Gertrude who is as well-versed in political machinations. Lady Macbeth knows the political significance of appearances: it is important to '*look* like th'innocent flower, / But *be* the serpent under't' (1.5.65–6, emphases mine). Similarly, there are many instances in *Hamlet* that attest to Gertrude's understanding of seeming amicable. Her first dialogue itself is at least as diplomatic as Claudius's first lines when she advises Hamlet to '*look* like a friend on Denmark' (1.2.69, emphasis mine). Glossing these lines, Marvin Rosenberg stresses how 'she doesn't ask that he *be* a friend, but that he *look like* one. Masking can be a way of life in Elsinore' (1992: 191). He suggests that 'by *Denmark* she means Claudius more than the country', but 'Denmark' could easily be a reference to the country itself (191). While the Danish are celebrating the royal wedding with which they have 'freely gone... along' (1.2.15–16), Hamlet is marking his otherness by wearing his mourning attire. Gertrude admonishes him to 'cast thy nighted colour off' (1.2.68) and make a visible effort to fit in within his home country regardless of what he might be feeling. As Hamlet has returned to Denmark after a long period of absence in Wittenberg, this is sound political advice given to the apparent heir to the throne. In another telling moment in the First Folio version of *Hamlet*, Gertrude changes her mind about speaking to the disturbed Ophelia. At first, she declares, 'I will not speak with her' (4.1.1), but when Horatio explains that Ophelia 'hems, and beats her heart / Spurns enviously at straws, speaks things in doubt / That carry but half sense' (4.1.4–7), Gertrude decides that ''Twere good she were spoken with, for she may strew / Dangerous conjectures in ill-breeding minds' (4.1.14–15).[7] In other words, she agrees to see Ophelia because she grasps the danger of Ophelia's performance in potentially moving onlookers to spark rebellion in the kingdom. Thus, *Khoon-e-Nahak*'s Gertrude might be more explicitly guilty than *Hamlet*'s Gertrude, but, far from being a 'travesty of Shakespearean characterization', she is not as far from Shakespeare's text as Yajnik believes. Rather, this Gertrude opens the possibility of reading Shakespeare's Danish queen as a politically engaged character just like her Scottish counterpart.

Khoon-e-Nahak's Gertrude does face more overt political antagonism than in Shakespeare's play. Both Somnath Gupt and Dashrath Ojha note how this Gertrude has a political opponent in Humayun (Polonius):

> *Mallika (Jahangir ki maa) apne mantri Humayun (Polonius) se Farrukh (Claudius) ko singhasanruth karne ki ichcha prakat karti hai parantu Humayun use sehmat nahi hota.*
> [Mallika (Jahangir's mother) expresses her will to install Farrukh (Claudius) on the throne but Humayun (Polonius) is not in agreement with her.]
>
> (Gupt 1981: 93)

> *[Mallika] Yuvraj Jahangir ki jagah Farrukh ko raaj dilana chahti hai par wazir taiyyar nahi hota.*
> [Instead of the young prince Jahangir, Mallika wants Farrukh to obtain the kingdom but the chief advisor does not agree.]
>
> (Ojha 1975: 125)

So, in *Khoone-e-Nahak* onstage (and by inference, in this film) viewers were presented with a Gertrude who was fully involved in matters of governance and who negotiates the succession of the throne with the chief advisor to the kingdom. Arguably there are hints of tension between Shakespeare's Gertrude and Polonius but this version adds a sharper subtext to their exchanges. For instance, in Shakespeare's play when Polonius is taking a rather circuitous route to his 'revelation' about the cause of Hamlet's madness, Gertrude cuts him off with her caustic remark to speak 'more matter with less art' (2.2.95). Carolyn Heilbrun, one of the first critics to reject the trend of reading Gertrude as 'incapable of any sustained rational process, superficial and flighty' (1957: 201), points out how 'it would be difficult to find a phrase more applicable to Polonius' (203). Later in the same scene, Gertrude appears suspicious of Polonius's suggestion that Hamlet is involved with Ophelia: 'Came this from Hamlet to her?' (2.2.112) she asks when Polonius shows her the letters that Ophelia received from the prince. In *Khoon-e-Nahak*, this scene was perhaps more antagonistic and Gertrude's reaction more understandable because she sees Polonius's meddling as a political manoeuvre from an opposing faction. It is also worth speculating why this Gertrude might have allowed Polonius to spy on her meeting with Hamlet. Did she want to prove to her chief advisor that Hamlet is in no fit state to rule? Did she engineer Polonius's murder by letting Hamlet think that it was Claudius behind the curtain? In the absence of the film, we do not know which encounters were cut and which were retained, nor how these were performed. However, simply reading the Gertrude–Polonius relationship from this angle produces a Gertrude who is an active participant in the play's plots and counterplots. It invests the text with new performance possibilities by making us look at Polonius and Gertrude's dynamics afresh.

KHOON KA KHOON (BLOOD'S MURDER), 1935

Seven years later, in 1935, Bollywood produced another *Hamlet* adaptation, *Khoon ka Khoon* (Blood's Murder) which is also lost.[8] This is particularly unfortunate because it predated Olivier's 1948 *Hamlet* which is believed to be the first full-length talkie of the play in English, so *Khoon ka Khoon* was probably the first full-length talkie of the play in the world. It is doubly unfortunate for this study, because it made some very interesting casting decisions regarding Gertrude. The film was directed by and starred Sorab Modi, a leading actor of his day famous for playing Hamlet on stage; Modi's Gertrude was Shamshad Begum – a well-known courtesan of her day (Mukherjee 2013). As a courtesan, she was a trained classical singer who had been working as a playback singer for movies, but apparently she had not been in front of the camera before. Clearly the film's producers wanted to capitalize on her celebrity, because the movie poster advertises her both as Shamshad and 'Chhamia' (her courtesan name).[9] They knew that if people would flock to the cinema to see Modi, they would be equally interested in seeing Shamshad Begum. Given her star power, it would have made sense for this Gertrude to receive substantial screen time.

Shamshad Begum's celebrity casting in this movie acquires even more significance if we consider that the film's Ophelia was played by Naseem Banu – Shamshad Begum's daughter. A look at the production photographs is enough to notice the family resemblance.[10] This ideologically loaded casting anticipates some highly experimental productions of the play in the late twentieth and early twenty-first century: Wooster Group's 2009 *Hamlet* directed by Elizabeth LeCompte, in which Richard Burton's 1964 Broadway production was projected behind a live performance of the play, and which saw Kate Valk play both Gertrude and Ophelia; Thomas Ostermeier's 2008 *Hamlet* in which Judith Rosmair essayed both roles; and Celestino Coronado's 1976 film adaptation in which Helen Mirren doubles as Gertrude and Ophelia. Justifying the decision, Ostermeier explains that 'what Hamlet's mistake is, is that he doesn't see the difference between Ophelia and his mother … For what his mother did, he punishes Ophelia' (Banks 2010). Whether or not Modi's decision was as self-conscious as Ostermeier's, the audience could have hardly escaped making the link that Hamlet is seeing Ophelia as a younger version of Gertrude.

In other ways, however, Modi's casting choice is also strikingly different from either of these productions because it underscores rather than undercuts the relationship between Gertrude and Ophelia. Whether the choice of playing Gertrude and Ophelia by the same actor reinforces or critiques Hamlet's misogyny, it certainly has the effect of diminishing the interaction between the two women. For example, in a scripted line, the Wooster Group's Hamlet instructs the technical team responsible for projecting the 1964 film version in the background to 'cut the Ophelia business' in her scenes with Gertrude due to the impossibility of recreating these onstage in the foreground with the same actor playing both roles. In contrast, Gertrude's scenes with Ophelia in Modi's version might have commanded greater attention with a real-life mother and daughter playing the roles. Were Gertrude's scenes with the disturbed, singing Ophelia more poignant in this version? Perhaps the portrayal of this relationship was closer to the one imagined by Deborah Newbold in her 2019 play *Outrageous Fortune*, in which she presents a mother–daughter-like bond between Gertrude and Ophelia to the extent that they go swimming together. Her Gertrude reveals that she had lied about the manner of Ophelia's muddy and violent death and had invented a sentimental drowning for the young girl out of love for her.[11] Yet even Newbold's play, which is unusual in creating a strong bond between Ophelia and Gertrude, does not allow an audience to witness the relationship between the two characters because it is a one-woman show.[12] In *Khoon ka Khoon*, was Gertrude's romanticizing of Ophelia's drowning – a notoriously difficult speech for Gertrude, according to Stubbs (2006: 35–7) – perceived as an act of kindness to Ophelia's memory, due to the off-screen relationship between the two actors embodying these roles? Usually, Gertrude's confrontation with Hamlet in her closet (3.4) is considered her critical scene, but in this version did her encounter with the distraught Ophelia (4.5) become Gertrude's pivotal scene? In the absence of the film these questions cannot be resolved, but the casting presents tantalising possibilities and encourages rethinking the relationship between the only two female characters in this male-dominated play.[13]

Modi's casting choices are an extension of the emphasis on women characters in Ahsan's stage play *Khoon-e-Nahak*. Actor-director Modi recounts that Ahsan's play was an immediate source for *Khoon ka Khoon* too:

> As the play had proved popular it was decided to film it the way it was presented on the stage – in the same chronological order of scenes, with the movie camera replacing the audience. It was shot at the Saraswati Studio at Poona, with painted backdrops serving as the sets. There was little camera movement but we did have long shots, mid-shots and close-ups. (qtd. in Verma 2002: 84)

Amongst other elements such as sets and movement, the movie may well have inherited the additional women characters and their suitors which Ahsan included in his adaptation. In *Khoon-e-Nahak*, Salman (Marcellus) is in love with Rehana (Ophelia's friend) but Rehana loves Anwar (Horatio). Similarly, Mansur (Cornelius's son) is in love with Meherbano (Ophelia) but she loves Jahangir (Hamlet). Employing the Shakespearean technique of amplification, Ahsan thus multiplies the central love triangle between King Hamlet, Gertrude and Claudius thrice.

Yajnik disapproves of these additions and finds it especially ridiculous that 'poor Ophelia' is 'sought by several lovers but prefers the eccentric one' (1933: 162). Ophelia does get slim pickings between Mansur, who forces himself upon her at one point, and 'the eccentric' Jahangir but no matter how much we mourn her selection, that is precisely the point. Yajnik and Hamlet might disapprove of Ophelia and Gertrude's choices respectively but the women in this play – Ophelia, Ophelia's friend and Gertrude – assert their right to elect their lovers.

A scene between Ophelia's friend, Rehana, and one of her wooers, Salman, serves to underline the point further. Its verbal sparring is wedged between Hamlet and Ophelia's interaction in the nunnery scene (3.1) and Hamlet and Gertrude's confrontation in the closet scene (3.4):

SALMAN:

> *... dekh toh mein kaisa rangeela chabila, sajeela shanoshaukat waala tarahdaar tera yaar.*

REHANA:

> *Chal badkaar mere yaar par se tujhe karun nisaar; kahan tu galli ka kutta murdaar aur kahan mera yaar Anwar naamdaar.*

SALMAN:

> *Hain, Hain, kya kaha? Anwar, woh akhtar ka biraadar, raaste ka patthar, mere baraabar!*

SALMAN:

> ... look at me how colourful, natty, dapper, stately, I am – your sublime lover!

REHANA:

> Go to – you evildoer – I'd readily offer you as a sacrifice to my sweetheart; here you are – a filthy street dog compared to my honourable Anwar over there.

SALMAN:

> Oh really – what did you say? That evil omen, that stumbling block, is comparable to me?!] (quoted in Gupt 1981: 66)[14]

Rehana not only makes it clear that she will not reciprocate Salman's affections but also lets him know that he is miserably failing in comparison to her Anwar. These lines, in a comic vein, echo those of Hamlet when he urges a similar comparison upon Gertrude: that she look at 'the counterfeit presentment of two brothers' (3.4.52) claiming that his father had 'Hyperion's curls, the front of Jove himself' (3.4.54) while Claudius is a 'mildewed ear' (3.4.62). By providing a refutation to Salman here, Rehana's dialogue suggests that there is a gap between the way in which men see their rivals and women perceive their lovers. Hamlet might think that his father was a Jove in contrast to Claudius, who is 'a king of shreds and patches' (3.4.99), just as Salman asserts that he is 'sublime' compared to the 'evil omen', Anwar. However, the script suggests that Gertrude, like Rehana, might think that the opposite is true. At one point, insulted by Salman's insinuation that she has ideas above her station,

Rehana even berates him saying '*Tu mar jaaye*' [I hope you die], '*Tujhe dase saap kaala*' [I hope a black serpent bites you]).[15] Here, too, the comic subplot and the exact wording of Rehana's curse resonate with the main plot. By including Rehana, a vocal woman character in a similar situation to Gertrude, Ahsan's play directs the audience's attention towards female desire in this play, and encourages the audience to question if Gertrude likewise wished death upon her husband because she found him lacking in comparison with Claudius. By placing this comic scene before the closet scene, Rehana and Salman's exchange pre-empts and provides a rebuttal to Hamlet's tirade and prompts the audience to consider the pictures from Gertrude's point of view.

In so doing, this play and the second movie based on it become important precursors to *Haider* which, at multiple points, encourages the audience to see the situation through Ghazala's eyes. Within the first few scenes of *Haider*, we witness a strained relationship between Ghazala and Hilaal (King Hamlet). Later, talking about her marital relations, Ghazala confesses to Haider (Hamlet), 'I died everyday ... Hilaal had lost himself in the hospital, a saint saving lives. His clothes, his skin reeked of blood. The smell of death. I had no other reason to live, but you.' In contrast, Ghazala and Khurram (Claudius) seem well-suited to each other and their scenes together are characterized by Khurram's attempts to please her. Moreover, in one of the several closet scenes in Bhardwaj's movie, before Haider can accuse Ghazala that her father's brother 'touches' her (2014: 91), she reminds Haider of his own wayward desires by recounting how Haider 'would snuggle between [his] father and Ghazala' (161), fighting with him if he touched her. Thus, both *Khoon ka Khoon* (through its borrowing from Ahsan's play and its casting choices) and *Haider* pay more overt attention to Gertrude's relationships, viewing them separately to Hamlet's interpretation of Gertrude's behaviour.

HAMLET, 1954

Kishore Sahu's 1954 film, simply titled *Hamlet*, is the earliest surviving Bollywood *Hamlet*; it has commanded the attention of critics mainly for the relationship that it bears to Lawrence Olivier's *Hamlet*, released six years before. On its website listing, the British Film Institute (BFI) claims that Sahu's film is a 'shot-by-shot reproduction of Lawrence Olivier's 1948 adaptation' (BFI 2019), and in a germinal article on Shakespeare in Indian films, Trivedi notes that Sahu's film 'modelled itself on, or rather "mimicked" closely the visualizations of Lawrence Olivier's film' (2007: 150). Trivedi further elaborates how the 'dark interiors, misty battlements, enframing arches, stair imagery – even the unfolding of scenes, especially in the beginning – were straight out of Olivier's film' (150). Closer to its own time, a reviewer in the popular Indian film magazine, *Filmfare*, described it as 'more or less based on Olivier's' (1995: 19). A cursory glance at the films will attest to the veracity of these observations. Yet these movies are significantly different, too.

Sahu's film is characterized by a transcultural hybrid ethos, not uncommon in Bollywood Shakespeare adaptations, which usually mix a variety of sources.[16] While the visual look might lean heavily on Olivier's, its 'modification of the plot' and 'rhetorical flamboyance' (Verma 2002: 86, 87) are more aligned with earlier stage and film versions of the play such as *Khoon-e-Nahak* and *Khoon ka Khoon*. The characters inhabit an Olivier-like castle in Sahu's film, but they speak in Urdu. They have the same names as their Shakespeare counterparts but have Urdu titles: Prince Hamlet is Shehzada Hamlet, Queen Gertrude is Mallika-e-Gertrude and so on. One of the biggest departures that Sahu's film makes from Olivier's is in its interpretation of women characters.

Giving his verdict on Sahu's version, film archivist Luke McKernan notes that Ophelia was 'about as good as you will ever see' because she is portrayed as a 'perky, impassioned, human' (qtd. in Rothwell 2004: 161). A handful of critics such as Andrew Dickson have briefly discussed this performance by Mala Sinha, who became a prominent movie star after this role (2016: 227–8). However, if Ophelia has engaged critics and reviewers, it was Gertrude, as played by Venus Bannerjee, who impressed Sybil Thorndike, the British actress who happened to be in Bombay for the premiere of Sahu's movie. Thorndike had performed various Shakespeare roles on stage and had played Portia and Lady Macbeth in silent film versions. Banerjee's Gertrude seems to have struck a chord with her and she has been quoted as saying that Bannerjee 'was magnificent as the Queen' (1995: 33).

Sahu's movie draws attention to Gertrude by giving her a second backstory that differs from the one narrated by the Ghost of King Hamlet, who details how Claudius 'with witchcraft of his wits, with traitorous gifts... won to his shameful lust / The will of my most seeming-virtuous Queen' (1.5.43–6). In Shakespeare's play, this account is not explicitly questioned. In Sahu's movie, by contrast, it is contested. Polonius explains to Hamlet that King Hamlet's untimely death had deprived his son of necessary training required to become capable of the crown. By acquiescing to marry Claudius, Polonius elaborates, Gertrude ensured both that Hamlet would receive proper guidance at the hands of his uncle while remaining the heir to the crown. This film, therefore, depicts a sympathetic relationship between Gertrude and Polonius and presents a Gertrude constrained by political circumstances in the aftermath of King Hamlet's death.

Despite the elaboration of a backstory, a politically circumscribed Gertrude is not solely an invention of Sahu's film: Shakespeare's *Hamlet* can sustain such an interpretation. Early in the play, Laertes advises Ophelia to refrain from giving credence to Hamlet's assurances of love because 'his will is not his own... on his choice depends / The safety and health of this whole state, / And therefore must his choice be circumscribed' (1.3.17–21). In his opening speech, Claudius, too, publicly reminds the council that they have approved his marriage to Gertrude (1.2.14–16). So, it is reasonable to extrapolate that royal marriages in Denmark are a matter of political expediency and that Gertrude's marriage to Claudius could have been urged by the council.[17]

This backstory might give the impression that the Gertrude being presented here is akin to the 'soft, obedient, dependent, unimaginative' character that Rebecca Smith envisions (1980: 194) in *The Woman's Part: Feminist Criticism of Shakespeare*. However, Bannerjee's Gertrude is nothing of the kind. Rather than a subdued figure, she commands the screen as she commands her courtiers. The camera often concentrates on her facial expressions; when Claudius dispatches Cornelius and Voltemand to negotiate the threat from Norway, Gertrude is included in the frame and her expressions show her actively engaged in the welfare of the kingdom.[18] Her marriage to Claudius is also not strained as a result of the political pressure, nor is she an overtly sensual and lustful Queen. Bannerjee's Gertrude instead emerges as a figure who has a firm grasp on the most beneficial outcome for Denmark, her son's prospects and her own happiness, and who has agreed to marry Claudius after taking all these factors into consideration.

The movie depicts Gertrude's political and emotional savvy at several moments. In Shakespeare's play when Laertes storms into Elsinore castle after the murder of Polonius, leading a rebellion and demanding his father's killer, Gertrude urges him to proceed 'calmly' (4.5.116); Laertes seizes upon her word to counter that 'that drop of blood that's calm proclaims me bastard, / Cries "Cuckold!" to my father' (4.5.118–19). In Sahu's film, Gertrude tries to defuse Laertes's rebellion, saying '*Laertes, tum ek shareef baap ki aulaad ho, isliye sharafat aur adab ka daaman apne haath se na chodo*' [Laertes, you are the son of a decent man so don't forgo your decency and manners]. Thus, she astutely appeals to Laertes on emotional and logical grounds by reminding him of the qualities of the very father whom he has come to revenge. In other words, almost anticipating his argument that he must honour his father through revenge, she reasons that the way to respect Polonius's memory is to behave in a civilized fashion and not to act violently. Only after this plea fails does she physically intervene between Laertes and Claudius as Shakespeare's dialogue intimates.

An incisive Gertrude emerges in this film in another key moment: the mousetrap scene. Before discussing Gertrude's portrayal, it is worth registering that its scenic composition and placement is unique to the Bollywood version. In Olivier's film, the play-within-the-play follows the sequence in Shakespeare's text but is severely cut. Claudius and Gertrude are shown watching the play but the camera only focusses on the back of their heads. Moreover, there is only one reaction shot of Claudius, and Gertrude's consternation is only glimpsed right before Claudius demands lights. Hamlet's question, 'Madam, how like you this play?' (3.2.223) and Gertrude's response, 'the lady doth protest too much, methinks' (3.2.224) are both excised.

In contrast, this scene is given due weight in Sahu's film. As the 'mousetrap' begins, Hamlet excuses himself from sitting with Gertrude so that he can observe both her and Claudius from an advantageous position. The camera follows Hamlet's gaze and witnesses several reactions from Gertrude, who is managing to keep calm but looks as if she is agitated (her breathing is shallow and she keeps glancing at Claudius). When Hamlet asks her whether she likes the play, she takes a moment to respond. Her expression makes it seem that she is weighing her response rather than letting something slip in a moment of frustration. She gently answers, '*Hamlet, Mallika ki baton mein kuch banavat zyada maloom hoti hai.*' A literal translation of her lines is telling: she says, 'Hamlet, the Player Queen's talk strikes one as somewhat excessively artificial'. It is worth noting that Mallika-e-Gertrude does not deem the Player Queen's protestations as merely 'too much' like her Shakespearean counterpart but also stresses that the Player Queen's excessive declarations are 'too artificial'.

The positioning of the scene in Sahu's version opens a fresh reading of these lines. In this movie, the 'mousetrap' has been shifted to the very end. Therefore, by this time, Gertrude has already seen Polonius's slaying at the hands of Hamlet and has been accused by him of colluding in his father's murder. So when the 'mousetrap' is unfolding, she seems to comprehend that Hamlet is using the play to reveal Claudius's treason. She has also realized that Claudius and Laertes are a threat to her son, because not only has Claudius berated Hamlet in front of her but she has seen the King plotting with Laertes. The rising tensions and increasing body count have created a precarious political situation by the time of this 'mousetrap'. So, both Gertrude's considered delivery and her choice of words imply that she speaks her line to minimize the potentially explosive impact of the drama by declaring its dialogue to be contrived, bearing little resemblance to any persons in the court. What gives this interpretation of Gertrude's performance credence is that, moments later, Hamlet uses the same tactic to reassure Claudius. When Claudius becomes suspicious and asks Hamlet whether the argument of the play might be dangerous, Hamlet assures him that it is a mere '*tamasha*' ['a play', 'a spectacle', 'an exaggerated performance']. In this scene, therefore, Mallika-e-Gertrude assesses the dangerous political situation and anticipates Hamlet in trying to contain it in the same way that she had tried to defuse Laertes's rebellion.

Mallika-e-Gertrude's sensitivity to the power of performance is shared by *Haider*'s Ghazala. If Haider is capable of putting on a show, so is Ghazala; both can wield play-acting as a weapon to the extent that Haider jokes that his mother could easily find a job in the National Dramatic Academy if she travelled to Delhi. Also, paralleling Sahu's movie, the camera is invested in Ghazala's reactions to the operatic 'mousetrap' of this film. While the rest of the audience is shown enjoying the show and clapping to the rhythm, Ghazala is paying close attention to the unfolding of the narrative song. By the end of the 'mousetrap', it is clear from this Gertrude's expressions that she has understood Claudius's treachery.

CONCLUSION

In tracking Ghazala's ancestry, I am not claiming that Bhardwaj and Tabu borrowed directly from these early Bollywood movies in *Haider*. Instead, I am interested in demonstrating that they have continued a long tradition of presenting nuanced Gertrudes in Indian cinema. Abigail Montgomery, echoing Elaine Showalter's phrase, has asserted, 'any "responsibilities of feminist criticism," indeed any responsible *Hamlet* criticism, should include reading Gertrude out of schemas that make her contingent upon men or an afterthought to Ophelia' (2009: 114). My chapter has explored the overlooked but rich archive (however fragmented and lost) of early Bollywood and discovered how Indian cinema has enlarged the repertoire of performance possibilities for this role, from Mallika Gohrulnisa to Gertrude's most recent reincarnation as Ghazala. As such, Indian Shakespeare cinema can and should be an important participant in feminist criticism of Shakespeare.

Such an approach also rebels against seeing Bollywood Shakespeares as only commenting on or originating from local and national geopolitical concerns.

Therefore, this chapter adds to the voices of Global Shakespeare theorists such as Sonia Massai, Mark Thornton Burnett, Douglas Lanier and Alexa Huang who have pointed out that we should resist the tendency to see non-Anglophone Shakespeares as hermeneutically sealed off from Anglophone Shakespeares originating in the UK/ US because such divisions tend to reinforce 'lingering notions of English Shakespeares as normative standard from which all other appropriations depart' (Massai 2007: 9). In *Shakespeare and World Cinema*, Mark Thornton Burnett argues that 'what is required to support an intellectual appraisal of this material is an approach that takes us away from the separate bracketing of the "foreign Shakespeare" and towards a new sensibility' (2013: 3) and in *'Hamlet' and World Cinema* (2019), he models this framework by studying the cinematic resonances and dissonances of *Hamlet* across the world from Japan to China to India to Europe. Douglas Lanier borrows the concept of rhizomes from Deleuze and Guattari and offers a new paradigm or a rhizomatic way of looking at Shakespeare adaptations around the world without hierarchies of 'source' and 'end product' and encourages studying intertextual links in all directions (2014: 21–40), while Alexa Huang reasons that due to the habit of studying Global Shakespeares only by situating them only in their local habitations, scholars are ill-equipped to critique work that does not fit neatly within geopolitical maps and boundaries (2013: 273–90). Thus, by looking at the complex ways in which layered portrayals of Bollywood Gertrudes are in dialogue with the performances of this role around the world, this chapter provides a template for a study of Global Shakespeare that crosses national and temporal boundaries to create a web of interconnected feminist interpretations. Creating and learning from such rich and networked performance histories would lead to more polyvocal classrooms, empowering rehearsal spaces and diverse research practices.

NOTES

I would like to acknowledge NYU (London) for supporting my trip to Portugal where I first presented my thoughts on Gertrude at the SEDERI conference. Deepest gratitude is also owed to friends and colleagues Robert Sawyer, Chloe Preedy, Anne Sophie Refskou, Eleine Ng and Kiki Lindell who offered feedback in the early stages of this work, and to the editors Diana Henderson and Stephen O'Neill and the anonymous reviewer for their generous and constructive comments.

1   Bhardwaj's Shakespeare trilogy of *Maqbool* (*Macbeth*), *Omkara* (*Othello*) and *Haider* has resisted easy categorization as 'Bollywood'; Rachel Dwyer has argued that Bhardwaj's movies are closer to what she terms *hatke* ('different') or multiplex cinema rather than Bollywood because 'these films feature major stars, big-budget production values and Bollywood music, but they have social and political references and often subordinate melodrama to realism in the manner of the multiplex' (2011: 199). In contrast, I deliberately use the term Bollywood to describe these films because Bollywood is a diverse and capacious category and many films besides Bhardwaj's are playful and creative in their use of traditional Bollywood tropes. There is a danger in labelling any politically and socially aware movie as *hatke* rather than as Bollywood

because it contributes to the West's narrow understanding of Bollywood as superficial or melodramatic and discourages seeing Bollywood cinema in all its diversity that is a result of its century-long history and hybrid transcultural influences.

2   Although a handful of art films such as those by Satyajit Ray and Shakespeare-based movies like *Shakespeare Wallah* (1965, dir. J. Ivory, New York: Merchant Ivory Productions) and *36 Chowringhee Lane* (1981, dir. A. Sen, India) were acknowledged and examined, it was only post-Bhardwaj, as Trivedi asserts, that Bollywood Shakespeare began to be systematically studied.

3   Mehdi Hasan 'Ahsan' also adapted Shakespeare's *Romeo and Juliet* as *Bazm-e-Fani*, *The Merchant of Venice* as *Dil Farosh*, *Comedy of Errors* as *Bhool Bhulaiya* and possibly *Othello*. On Parsi theatre traditions, see Somnath Gupt (1981).

4   For instance, Verma claims that all early film versions of *Hamlet* in Bollywood are 'direct descendants of the Parsi theatre versions of the play' (2002: 81).

5   R. E. Vernede saw a version of this play at a Bengal country fair in 1911. Exhibiting his ignorance of Parsi theatre conventions and Urdu language, he provides a sniggering account of the performance but his portrait is useful in one respect: he quotes the English programme of the play in its entirety thereby preserving the act-by-act plot of this adaptation.

6   William Shakespeare, *Macbeth*, ed. Kenneth Muir (London: Methuen, 1951). All references to *Macbeth* are from this edition and incorporated into the body of the chapter.

7   William Shakespeare, *Hamlet* (1623 Folio Text), ed. Ann Thompson and Neil Taylor (London: Bloomsbury, 2006). All references to the Folio text of *Hamlet* are from this edition and incorporated into the body of the chapter.

8   The title puns as *Khoon* can mean 'blood', 'blood relation' or 'murder'.

9   *Khoon ka Khoon* Movie Poster, National Film Archive of India (NFAI), Pune.

10   *Khoon ka Khoon* Production Images and Posters, National Film Archive of India (NFAI), Pune.

11   This play is still in its development phase.

12   Gertrude is a motherly figure to Ophelia in M. C. Clarke, *The Girlhood of Shakespeare's Heroines* (New York, NY: GP Putnam's Sons, 1874) and in J. Updike, *Gertrude and Claudius* (2001, London: Random House) but the relationship is more patronizing than loving in both fictional accounts. Gertrude is openly hostile towards Ophelia in M. Atwood, 'Gertrude talks Back', in *Good Bones and Simple Murders* (New York, NY: Random House, 2001, 16–19).

13   A similar meaningful mother–daughter casting can be observed in *Life Goes On*, a British-Indian adaptation of *King Lear*; Sharmila Tagore played Lear's dead wife in flashbacks and her real-life daughter Soha Ali Khan was cast as Dia/Cordelia. For more about this casting and this film, see Henderson (2019).

14   This is from an extract of Ahsan's play, which is printed in the Devnagari script in an appendix in Gupt, *Parsi Thiyetar: Udbhav aur Vikas*. All translations are mine.

15 Ibid.

16 For an excellent discussion of the way in which Bollywood Shakespeares emerge out of an 'accretive understanding of intercultural transaction' (2002: 21) evident in their hybridity, see Niyogi De, 'Modern Shakespeares in Popular Bombay Cinema: Translation, Subjection and Community'.

17 I wish to thank my students for discussing the marital politics of Shakespeare's Denmark with me, especially Orly Lipset who encouraged everyone in the seminar group to look at Hamlet's planned dynastic marriage to Ophelia.

18 An NYU Tisch School of the Arts and RADA student production interpreted Gertrude similarly. When Laertes begged for Claudius's permission to return to France, Claudius looked at Gertrude and only when she gestured acceptance did Claudius give his official approval (*Hamlet* 2019).

REFERENCES

Banks, S. (2010), 'A chat with director Thomas Ostermeier', *Exberliner*, 31 December. Available online: https://www.exberliner.com/whats-on/stage/five-questions-for-thomas-ostermeier (accessed 9 September 2019).

BFI (2019), '*Hamlet* (1955) [*sic*]'. Available online: https://www.bfi.org.uk/films-tv-people/4ce2b7230146f (accessed 9 September 2019).

Bhardwaj, V. (2014), 'Preface', in *Haider: The Original Screenplay (with English Translation)*, India: Harper Collins.

Burnett, M. T. (2013), *Shakespeare and World Cinema*, Cambridge: Cambridge University Press.

Burnett, M. T. (2019). '*Hamlet' and World Cinema*, Cambridge: Cambridge University Press.

Dickson, A. (2016), *Worlds Elsewhere: Journeys Around Shakespeare's Globe*, London: Penguin.

Dwyer, Rachel (2011), '*Zara hatke* ("somewhat different"): The New Middle Classes and the Changing Forms of Hindi cinema', in H. Donner (ed.), *Being Middle Class in India: A Way of Life*, 184–208, London: Routledge.

Escolme, B. (2004), *Talking to the Audience: Shakespeare, Performance, Self*, London: Routledge.

Filmfare (1995), '*Hamlet*: Review', *Filmfare* 4 (2): 19.

Gangar, A. (2018), 'The Indian "Silent" Shakespeare: Recouping an Archive', in P. Trivedi and P. Chakravarti (eds), *Shakespeare and Indian Cinemas*, 111–26, New York, NY: Routledge.

Gupt, S. (1981), *Parsi Thiyetar: Udbhav aur Vikas* [Parsi Theatre: Origin and Development], Allahabad: Lokbharti Prakashan.

Haider (2014), [Film] Dir. V. Bhardwaj, India: UTV Motion Pictures.

Hamlet (1948), [Film] Dir. L. Olivier, UK: Two Cities Films.

Hamlet (1954), [Film] Dir. K. Sahu, India: Hindustan Chitra.

Hamlet (1976), [Film] Dir. C. Coronado, UK: Essential Productions.

Hamlet (2008), [Stage Production] Dir. T. Ostermeier, Berlin: Schaubühne.

Hamlet (2009), [Stage Production] Dir. E. LeCompte, Gdansk: The Wooster Group.

Heilbrun, C. (1957), 'The Character of Hamlet's Mother', *Shakespeare Quarterly* 8 (2): 201–6.

Henderson, D. E. (2016), 'Magic in the Chains: *Othello, Omkara,* and the Materiality of Gender across Time and Media', in V. Traub (ed.), *The Oxford Handbook of Shakespeare and Embodiment*, 674–92, Oxford: Oxford University Press.

Henderson, D. E. (2019), 'Romancing *King Lear*: *Hobson's Choice, Life Goes On* and Beyond', in V. Bladen, S. Hatchuel and N. Vienne-Guerrin (eds), *Shakespeare on Screen: King Lear*, 125–39, Cambridge: Cambridge University Press.

Huang, A. (2013), 'Global Shakespeares as Methodology', *Shakespeare* 9 (3): 273–90.

Khoon-e-Nahak (1928), [Film] Dir. K. B. Athavale, India: Excelsior Film Co.

Khoon ka Khoon (1935), [Film] Dir. S. Modi, India: Stage-Film Co.

Lanier, D. (2014), 'Shakespearean Rhizomatics: Adaptation, Ethics, Value', in A. Huang and E. Rivlin (eds), *Shakespeare and the Ethics of Appropriation*, 21–40, New York, NY: Palgrave Macmillan.

Maqbool (2003), [Film] Dir. V. Bhardwaj, India: Kaleidoscope Entertainment.

Massai, S. (2007), 'Defining Local Shakespeares', in S. Massai (ed.), *World-wide Shakespeares: Local Appropriations in Film and Performance*, 3–14, New York, NY: Routledge.

Montgomery, A. (2009), 'Enter QUEEN GERTRUDE Stage Center: Re-Viewing Gertrude as Full Participant and Active Interpreter in *Hamlet*', *South Atlantic Review* 74 (3): 99–117.

Mudan Finn, K. and V. Schutte, eds (2018), *The Palgrave Handbook of Shakespeare's Queens*, New York, NY: Palgrave.

Mukherjee, D. (2013), 'Notes on a Scandal: Writing Women's Film History Against an Absent Archive', *BioScope: South Asian Screen Studies* 4 (1): 9–30.

Niyogi De, E. (2002), 'Modern Shakespeares in Popular Bombay Cinema: Translation, Subjectivity and Community', *Screen* 43 (1): 19–40.

O'Brien, E. J. (1992), 'Revision by Excision: Rewriting Gertrude', *Shakespeare Survey* 45: 27–35.

Ojha, D. (1975), *Hindi Natak Kosh* [Encyclopaedia of Hindi Plays], Delhi: National Publishing House.

Outrageous Fortune [*Hamlet*: Through the Eyes of Gertrude] (2019), [Stage Production] Dir. J. Wright, London: Greenwich Theatre.

Reynolds, P. (2018), *Performing Shakespeare's Women: Playing Dead*, London: Arden.

Rosenberg, M. (1992), *The Masks of Hamlet*, Newark: University of Delaware Press.

Rothwell, K. S. (2004), *A History of Shakespeare on Screen: A Century of Film and Television*, Cambridge: Cambridge University Press.

Saltz, R. (2014), 'Shakespearean Revenge in a Violent Kashmir', *The New York Times*, 2 October. Available online: https://www.nytimes.com/2014/10/03/movies/haider-puts-an-indian-twist-on-hamlet.html (accessed 9 September 2019).

Singh, H. (2014), 'Tabu: My Role in *Haider* is to Die for', *The Indian Express*, 26 September. Available online: https://indianexpress.com/article/entertainment/play/my-role-in-haider-is-to-die-for/ (accessed 9 September 2019).

Smith, R. (1980), '"A Heart Cleft in Twain": The Dilemma of Shakespeare's Gertrude,' in C. Ruth Swift Lenz, G. Greene and C. Thomas Neely (eds), *The Woman's Part: Feminist Criticism of Shakespeare*, 194–210, Urbana: University of Illinois Press.

Stubbs, I. (2006), 'Gertrude', in M. Dobson (ed.), *Performing Shakespeare's Tragedies Today: The Actor's Perspective*, 29–40, Cambridge: Cambridge University Press.

Suzman, J. in conversation with V. Panjwani (2020), [Podcast] Janet Suzman on *Hamlet, Othello, Antony & Cleopatra*, Series 1, Ep. 6. http://womenandshakespeare.com/.

Thakur, V. S. (2014), 'Parsi Shakespeare: The Precursor to "Bollywood Shakespeare"', in C. Dionne and P. Kapadia (eds), *Bollywood Shakespeares*, 21–43, New York, NY: Palgrave Macmillan.

Thomas, S. (2006), 'Lady Macbeth', in M. Dobson (ed.), *Performing Shakespeare's Tragedies Today: The Actor's Perspective*, 95–106, Cambridge: Cambridge University Press.

Trivedi, P. (2007), '"Filmi" Shakespeare', *Literature/Film Quarterly* 35 (2): 148–58.

Trivedi, P. (2018), 'Woman as Avenger: "Indianising" the Shakespearean Tragic in the films of Vishal Bhardwaj', in P. Trivedi and P. Chakravarti (eds), *Shakespeare and Indian Cinemas*, 23–44, New York, NY: Routledge.

Verma, R. (2002), '*Hamlet* on the Hindi Screen', '*Hamlet' Studies* 24: 81–93.

Vernède, R. E. (1995), *British Life in India: An Anthology of Humorous and Other Writings Perpetrated by the British in India, 1750–1950 with Some Latitude for Works Completed After Independence*, New Delhi: Oxford University Press.

Yajnik, R. K. (1933), *The Indian Theatre: Its Origins and its Later Developments under European Influence, with Special reference to Western India*, London: G. Allen and Unwin.

Media lenses and digital cultures

Screening dreamy LA: reading genre in Casey Wilder Mott's Hollywood *A Midsummer Night's Dream* (2018)

MELISSA CROTEAU

The iconic 1990 romantic comedy *Pretty Woman* (dir. Garry Marshall) concludes with the words of an anonymous Los Angeleno sage on the street: 'Welcome to Hollywood! What's your dream?… This is Hollywood, land of dreams. Some dreams come true, some don't,… so keep on dreaming!' First time director Casey Wilder Mott may have been channelling the final lines of this film when he decided to open his 2018 adaptation of Shakespeare's *A Midsummer Night's Dream*, set in contemporary Los Angeles, with these lines, appearing one by one on a black screen:

> Are you sure that we are awake?
> It seems to me that yet we sleep,
> We dream.

These words, a revision of Demetrius's lines in Act 4, scene 1 (ll. 91–2), set the dreamy tone for the film, which cleverly leverages LA's reputation and landscape to bring a refreshing lens to Shakespeare's metatheatrical masterpiece. In the press kit for the film, Mott writes,

> The giddy, quasi-schizophrenic feeling of being caught between worlds is instantly familiar to anyone in Hollywood, a place where crossing the line between fantasy and reality is simply part of daily life. Hollywood has itself been dubbed 'The Dream Factory,' as much for its fantastical creations as for the fairy tale lives of those who live there. The almighty mogul, the coquettish starlet, the brooding artist, the vaulting pretender: these are Dream Factory denizens.
>
> (Mott 2017)

In this film, Duke Theseus is a movie mogul, Hermia a not-so-innocent cinematic ingenue, Helena a screenwriter, Lysander a hipster celebrity photographer, Demetrius a slick talent agent and the 'rude mechanicals' are a group of AFI (that is, Athens Film Institute) students attempting to make a film. The fairy world is taken from a different cosmos, but one endemic to both Southern and Northern California: the nature-loving, New Age hippies, who revel in psychedelic drugs, trippy music and free love. There is something inescapably meta about LA, a place where, Mott points out, one can see a new blockbuster movie then run into the star on the street, blurring the boundary between the fabulous and the mundane (Mott 2019). The unique ambience and landscape of Los Angeles also align perfectly with the binaries around which the Bard's *Dream* is structured: Mott's film constantly traverses the divide between 'waking and dreaming; town and country; order and bedlam; courtship and desire' (Mott 2017). The play is also about role-playing, deception and, ultimately, transformation. Los Angeles – a city people come to from all over the world to establish new identities and follow their dreams – seems a perfect milieu for this narrative.

Mott's 'Tinseltown' mise en scène foregrounds the significance of film genre. Many of these genres were born in the inchoate studio system of the 1910s and 1920s. However, it was in the golden age of sound film, the 1930s and early 1940s, that most of the major genres associated with Hollywood grew to prominence: musicals, romantic comedy (including screwball), film noir, westerns, horror and gangster films. Large-scale, feature-length adaptations of literary fiction, often classics, also took the stage at this time and were considered 'prestige pictures', bestowing cultural gravitas on their directors, stars, studios and the film industry as a whole.[1] One such film is Max Reinhardt and William Dieterle's epic production of *A Midsummer Night's Dream* for Warner Brothers in 1935, starring Hollywood staples James Cagney, Dick Powell and Olivia de Havilland, plus a very young Mickey Rooney as Puck. Despite this star power, the film was a financial failure, as was George Cukor's lavish Hollywood adaptation of *Romeo and Juliet* in 1936, which features the director's celebrity wife, Norma Shearer, as Juliet. This led the Hollywood studio system to eschew Shakespeare adaptations for decades to come. It was largely European filmmakers, such as Laurence Olivier, Franco Zeffirelli and, more recently, Kenneth Branagh, who dared to use Shakespeare's language on screen. Olivier's 1948 *Hamlet* even won the Academy Award for Best Picture, but this did not inspire the American industry to return to Shakespeare. The most notable exception to this is the notorious auteur and Hollywood outsider Orson Welles, whose Shakespeare adaptations were passion projects made independently, often with very low budgets. In the past few decades, New York-based theatre and art house film director Julie Taymor also has made distinctive adaptations, but these are far from the mainstream. In the twentieth century, the Hollywood studio system did invest in adaptations 'twice removed' from Shakespeare's text and in popular genres, most notably the musicals *Kiss Me Kate* (George Sidney, 1953) and *West Side Story* (Jerome Robbins and Robert Wise, 1961), which won nine Academy Awards, including Best Picture. However, these versions of *The Taming of the Shrew* and *Romeo and Juliet*, respectively, were adapted from successful Broadway shows, making them appealing, bankable commodities. In the twenty-first century, Casey Wilder Mott approached his adaptation of *Dream* in the independent fashion of Welles, using Shakespeare's language and 'indie' ingenuity, functioning outside the Hollywood system; yet, metacinematically, Mott makes Hollywood his subject and employs the established genres of screwball comedy, the Los Angeles film and 'indie' cinema.

Adaptations of literature to film present a complex and polysemic generic situation in which genre is always already multiple. Scholars and students most often analyse them through the lens of adaptation theory and treat these films as members of the literary adaptation generic category. Shakespearean film adaptations occupy pride of place as a significant subgenre within that group.[2] However, these films also possess significant features of the genres occupied by their literary or theatrical 'source' texts (or hypotexts), such as revenge tragedy for *Hamlet* or farcical comedy for *The Taming of the Shrew*. Moreover, the narrative, thematic and stylistic properties of these films inevitably reflect cinematic genres beyond the pale of literary adaptation, and these generic discourses provide a rich vein of semantic material that is often ignored. There is much to be gained from examining Shakespeare adaptations in light of the many other generic categories in which they participate. Indeed, Harry Keyishian has argued that scholars must

> write these films into the histories of the genres of which they are examples. Only by placing them in the cinematic traditions that make their production possible and that shape and inform their meaning can we engage the actual film product before us, rather than our preconceptions, based on the knowledge of the Shakespeare text and its critical and performance traditions.
>
> (2000: 73)

The Hollywood setting of Mott's *Dream* and its prolific self-reflexivity make it a particularly fascinating subject for this type of reading, as does the biography of Mott himself, who has been working in the film industry for over a decade on the business, rather than artistic, side of things (Mott 2019). Like the rude mechanicals, Mott chose to adapt an ambitious classic text, but one with an established pop culture visibility, to launch his creative 'show business' career. Linda Hutcheon argues cogently that 'adapters' deeply personal as well as culturally and historically conditioned reasons for selecting a certain work to adapt and the particular way to do so should be considered seriously by adaptation theory' (2013: 95), despite the critical dismissal, in the latter half of the twentieth century, 'of the relevance of artistic intention to interpretation by formalists, New Critics, structuralism, and poststructuralists alike' (94). Thus, in order to delve into Mott's approach and process, this chapter pulls from an extensive interview with the filmmaker conducted by the author and from the official press kit marketing the film, valuable resources for analysing adaptations. Using these key resources along with more traditional types of scholarly research, I will explore the ways in which Mott's *Dream* embodies and plays with the genres of romantic comedy, the Los Angeles film and indie cinema, while considering Mott's motivations, intentions and inspirations in regard to these categories.

Casey Wilder Mott opens his *A Midsummer Night's Dream* metacinematically with a black-and-white shot featuring a film slate bearing Mott's name and held in front of the face of actor Fran Kranz. Dressed as the character he plays, Bottom, he is wearing a silk, fur-edged short robe he acquires from Titania later in the film's plot. Fran/Bottom is lying on the forest floor, and we have no idea if we are in the film's diegetic world or outside of it: the line between reality and illusion is blurred. A voice is heard saying, 'Good, Casey?', the slate snaps shut and 'action' is spoken, cued to a cut to a black screen where the words appear asking whether we are awake or dreaming, quoted at the beginning of this piece, as we hear tinkling wind-chimes that signal the presence of magical forces. This is followed by a montage of shots showing seemingly random snippets of various scenes in the film in no particular order, interspersed with shots of the film script for this movie and the slate. This collage of shots appears in a frame inside the film's frame, with black edges on all sides, and features split screen effects, quick cutting, distorted sound and the clicking of a film reel spinning on a projector. One of the final images in the montage is a dark long shot of a row of large, silver Mac computer monitors in a shadowy computer lab, and we hear someone typing on a keyboard, a mysterious solitary figure hidden by the monitor. An abrupt cut to an extreme close-up of a finger hitting the 'Return' key initiates a cut back to Bottom's startled face (see Figure 2.9.1). He awakes screaming in the forest where we have just seen him but this time in an extreme close-up in colour. Was the montage all in Bottom's fevered brain? Then, as his alarmed eyes look directly into the camera, we hear him in voice-over speak the famous lines from Act 4, scene 1: 'I have had a most rare vision' (ll. 201–2). After discovering a peculiar red arrowhead pendant around his neck – foreshadowing later plot points as well as symbolically connecting him to Puck – Bottom stumbles upon

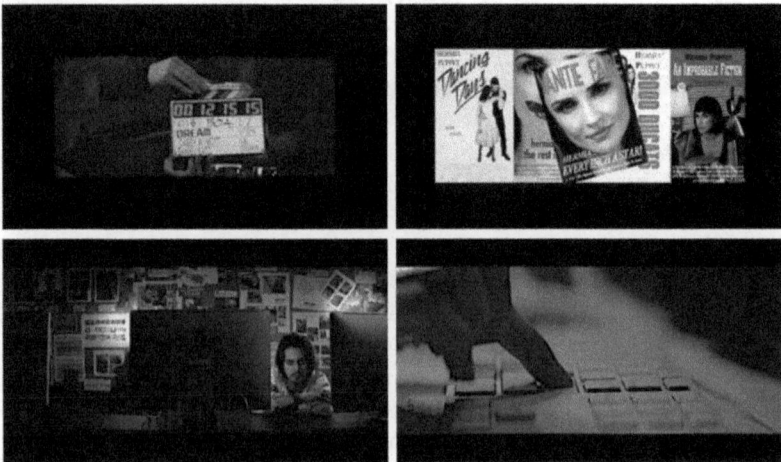

FIGURE 2.9.1 Metacinematic stills from Mott's *A Midsummer Night's Dream*, opening and end. Image credit: Daniel Katz.

quite incongruous red velvet curtains hanging from a bar in the forest. This is clearly a reference both to the theatrical roots of the play and to Baz Luhrmann, whose first three films, including *Willliam Shakespeare's Romeo + Juliet*, were dubbed 'The Red Curtain Trilogy' (Vela 2009: 105). Large white lettering spelling out the play's and film's name then overlays the curtain shot while we watch from behind Bottom, an arrangement that tells us we are watching Bottom's *Dream* (see Figure 2.9.2). The use of both metatheatrical and metacinematic tropes in this opening sequence displays what Katherine Rowe has called 'media convergence' (2008: 36–8): the semiotics of the filmmaking paraphernalia and the theatrical curtain vividly bespeak the heteroglossic interweaving of cinematic and theatrical discourses and prepare the audience for more outlandish media intersections, such as Shakespeare's language appearing in text messages. *Dream* then moves from this meta moment in the forest to a different type of dream topography.

Surprisingly, what immediately follows is a montage of current Los Angeles landmarks and neighbourhoods, and we see the uncanny replacement of the HOLLYWOOD sign with the word ATHENS, reminding us that someone is manipulating this cinematic world, which both is and is not Los Angeles (see Figure 2.9.3). Mott then moves into introducing the major characters with a short piece of film that encapsulates the personality and backstory of each (see Figure 2.9.4). The narrative of the play begins only after this, announced with a title overlay: 'Act I / The Athenian Youth.' The film's diegesis is divided into five named acts, reminding us again of the play and the film's meta-theatrical status. Throughout the film, Mott

FIGURE 2.9.2 Bottom and the red curtain at the opening of Mott's *Dream*. Image credit: Daniel Katz.

FIGURE 2.9.3 Montage of Los Angeles in Mott's *Dream*. Image credit: Daniel Katz.

FIGURE 2.9.4 The four young lovers introduced in filmic *dramatis personae* style in Mott's *Dream*. Image credit: Daniel Katz.

cuts at various moments back to the shadowy computer lab, where we see more close-ups of hands on the keyboard, clearly working on the screenplay for this film or editing footage of the film. In long shots of the back of the monitor, the viewer starts to recognize the 'real' *Dream* film project board, which occupies the large wall space behind the person sitting at the computer. Images and planning documents for the film we are currently watching occupy that space, but we do not get a clear, close glimpse of them until the very end of the film. In its final moments, the film cuts from the wedding reception where all five couples are seen, back to the now-familiar shadowy computer lab, where the mystery figure is putting the finishing touches on the end of the film, and we are at last allowed to see the plans on the project board. In a final shot of the back of the monitor, the hippie-surfer Puck, or the actor Avan Jogia (who can tell?), leans to his left and we at last see his face. 'Puck' has been the author of this fiction all along, and it is only natural that he should begin his playful apology here: 'If we shadows have offended ....' (see Figure 2.9.1). In this romantic comedy, Puck is both the mischievous Cupid who fatefully misses with his arrows and the trickster messenger Mercury, who does Oberon's bidding but always with his own irreverent flare. As Jan Kott declares, 'The true director of the night-rule in the woods is Puck, the Lord of Misrule' (1987: 56). But Puck is not only in charge of the 'green world' in this film: he is literally the director of the film and, of course, represents Casey Wilder Mott, who created this ludic, 'Russian doll' structure that adds even more resonance, and a postmodern frisson, to the mise en abyme elements found in the play (Mott 2019; cf. Kott 1987: 56). Mott gives us a Puck figure who, as Peter Holland writes of the character, 'belongs to and creates a world of flux and instability... [inhabiting] this place of shifting surfaces, of endless and almost uncontrollable transformability. It is, of course, his stage, a theatre where he is simultaneously playwright and actor and audience' (1995: 49). This is an especially apt description of Mott's Puck, who is (and is not) simultaneously director, actor, audience and real-life director (Mott 2019).

HYDRA-HEADED HYBRID GENRE, OR GENERIC INTRODUCTIONS

As with literary studies, genre categories in film studies are notoriously slippery, and inconsistent category distinctions plague the field; however, embracing generic diversity and hybridity can deepen and extend analyses of film texts. A broad definition is helpful yet reveals the protean and potentially problematic nature of the concept: 'a genre refers to a group of films that share a set of narrative, stylistic, and thematic characteristics or conventions' (Pramaggiore and Wallis 2011: 382). Thomas Schatz points out that genres are defined by different *types* of criteria – for instance, he divides Hollywood genres into those of determinate space (westerns, film noir, gangster) and indeterminate space (musical, screwball comedy, social melodrama). Genres of determinate space feature 'an ideologically contested setting' that serves as a 'symbolic arena of action', representing 'a cultural realm in which fundamental values are in a state of sustained conflict'; genres of indeterminate space 'generally involve a doubled (and thus dynamic) hero in the guise of a romantic couple who inhabit a "civilized"... ideologically stable milieu, which depends less upon a heavily coded place than on a highly conventionalized value system' (1981: 27–9). Whereas genres of determinate space depict conflict in and over specific environments, such as the western frontier town, those of indeterminate space represent characters who struggle to reconcile with one another or with the larger community, despite the obstructions posed to this harmony. Significantly, Schatz notes that these two categories have the same social function: 'In addressing basic cultural conflicts and celebrating the values and attitudes whereby these conflicts might be resolved, all film genres represent the filmmakers' and audience's cooperative efforts to "tame" those beasts, both actual and imaginary, which threaten the stability of our everyday lives' (29). Thus, though individual genres can be defined not only by varying criteria but also by different types of criteria, their functions are very similar, if not the same: to tackle unresolvable conflicts in interpersonal and communal life that disrupt the equilibrium and imperil the welfare of society. As Mott's *Dream* participates in the genre of Los Angeles film – treating the city as a character and signifier of essential themes – and as a romantic comedy, the film occupies both the category of determinate space and indeterminate space, in which LA is a 'symbolic arena of action' and the 'hero' is not one but five couples who magically arrive back at a 'conventionalized value system', marked by a triple wedding and the return of natural fecundity, embodied by the harmonious reunion of the fairy royal couple, Titania and Oberon. Mott even augments the play's four couples by adding a fifth, that of a female Quince with a bumbling but charming Bottom. *Dream*'s comedic triumph over death via the reproducing couple tames the 'beasts' of recurring division and strife between couples, generations and social classes as well as within more homogeneous communities, such as work colleagues, as portrayed by the 'rude mechanicals', here fellow students at Athens Film Institute. These unresolvable, recurrent conflicts in our quotidian lives are often transcended in genre films, which provide relief or escape in their predictable resolutions.

Genres, like language itself, are unstable and tricky. As Jacques Derrida asserts, 'Every text participates in one or several genres, there is no genreless text; there is always a genre and genres, yet participation never amounts to belonging' (1980: 65). In characteristic Derridean fashion, he reminds us that genres are playfully mercurial in that one text might occupy many generic categories at once while not entirely 'committing' to any of those labels. In this, genre itself resembles Puck: simultaneously the mischievous village sprite Robin Goodfellow and the classical Roman god of love, Cupid, in both his infantile, blinded form as well as his menacing, monstrous Apuleian form. Plus, as Oberon's errand boy, he fills the role of the trickster god Mercury (Kott 1987: 49). Lester Friedman et al. insist that '[a]n understanding of genre's intertextuality and hybridization does not invalidate its significance in the creation, production, reception, criticism, and distribution of cinematic art' (2014: 9). Indeed, the complexity of generic discourses in a given text can be challenging to unravel, but an examination of the multifarious generic intersections in a film can yield important insights regarding its development, making, marketing and reception, and, conversely, these elements can reveal a great deal about the play of genres in a film. In his work on Shakespeare adaptations and film genre, Michael Anderegg aptly reminds us that '[t]he seemingly elastic categories into which Shakespeare films can be made to fit, and the elasticity of the Shakespeare films themselves, reflect the multigeneric possibilities inherent in Shakespeare's plays, themselves a mix of literary genres and subgenres' (2004: 21). It is this ever-malleable generic potential of Shakespeare's plays that make them so alluring and popular as subjects of remediation. Anderegg goes on to contend that while Shakespeare films 'nearly always demand to be received as invocations of the Shakespeare text', they also must be read in their cinematic contexts, as products of particular places, moments and filmic discourses (11, cf. 19–23). It is inevitable that the multiple genres in adapted texts traverse dialogically between the various media involved, e.g. theatre, literature or cinema; nevertheless, as with all film texts, analyses of Shakespeare adaptations require attention to technical cinematic elements and to the concomitant apparatuses of the film industry. Anderegg concludes that

> [h]ybridity may be considered a strong generic aspect of the Shakespeare film. Shakespeare plays are themselves hybrids, happily mixing high tragedy and low humor, poetry and prose, history and fiction. Plots are combined and recombined from unrelated sources… ; historical periods are folded into each other; language can be, in the same work, high-flown and down to earth… ; tone can vary wildly from scene to scene.

(19)

The undeniable truth of this can be perceived in even a cursory look at *A Midsummer Night's Dream*, certainly one of the most vivid examples of this hybridity, as it careens through three distinct diegetic worlds populated by three diverse groups of characters: the aristocratic world of Athens, the forest with its supernatural denizens and the village rustics embodied by the 'rude mechanicals'. Casey Wilder Mott creates remarkably clever analogues for the three worlds and groups of characters in the landscape of Los Angeles, thereby adding the genre (or what one might in the Hollywood context call a *supra-genre*) of 'Los Angeles film' to the romantic comedy genre inherent in the play text. In addition, as his first foray into film directing, Mott self-consciously approached the project as an independent film of the 'indie' variety, both out of financial necessity and generic compatibility. While not all critics and scholars would agree that indie film should be considered a genre, per se, there are a number of scholars who specialize in independent cinema who argue that, since the rise of indie film culture in the United States during the late 1980s, this type of film has evolved into a genre, in contradistinction to mainstream studio film, with its own niche audience, generic features and modes of production and exhibition (cf. Newman 2011: 1–18). In the book *Independent Cinema*, D. K. Holm declares, 'Since there can be no economic classification of an independent film, it has evolved into a genre, with carefully cultivated audience expectations about the general nature of the "product"' (2008: 116). Mott's *A Midsummer Night's Dream*, while most obviously falling into the categories of literary and Shakespearean adaptation, simultaneously and meaningfully occupies the generic space of romantic comedy, Los Angeles film and indie cinema.

DREAM COMEDIES AND SCREWBALL LOGIC

Unlike the problem plays or the romances, *A Midsummer Night's Dream* has never had a generic identity crisis. The First Folio categorized it as a comedy, and, despite certain stage productions and film adaptations emphasizing the dark material in the text – such as Peter Brook's muddy, French New Wave-inspired adaptation in 1968 – it has firmly remained in that felicitous group. When looking at cinematic adaptations, *Dream*'s category narrows to the long-standing film genre of romantic comedy, which stretches back into the silent era with the best work of Charlie Chaplin (*City Lights, Modern Times*) and Buster Keaton (*Steamboat Bill, Jr., The General*). Indeed, the play might itself be seen as a precursor to such works: the authors of *An Introduction to Film Genres* (2014) open their chapter on romantic comedy with the words, 'Let's start with Shakespeare', opining that Shakespeare's comedies – compared to the works of the ancient Greek masters – 'offer more well-known and relevant predecessors' to our current Hollywood genre of romantic comedy (Friedman et al. 2014: 121). This is evidenced by the many adaptations of Shakespeare's plays that clearly fit into this group, such as *The Taming of the Shrew* directed by Sam Taylor (1929) and directed by Franco Zeffirelli (1965), both featuring Hollywood celebrity couples; Kenneth Branagh's *Much Ado About Nothing* (1993); Michael Hoffman's star-studded *A Midsummer Night's Dream* (1999); the teen-oriented *10 Things I Hate About You* (1999) and *She's the Man* (2006); and BBC's *ShakespeaRe-Told* adaptations of *Much Ado, The Taming of the Shrew* and *Dream* (2005). The New York-based auteur Woody Allen even tried his hand at a Shakespeare adaptation in his own idiosyncratic, neurotic rom-com syle with *A Midsummer Night's Sex Comedy* (1982). These film adaptations generally feature young (or occasionally middle-aged) people who meet, fall in love and then encounter numerous impediments to their relationship which must be overcome before the couple's (or couples') final reunion, establishing them as a symbol of the continuation of life through the potentially fruitful pairing. Friedman et al. point out that '[a]ll this fast-paced confusion serves to demolish the young people's fears, resistance to change, or initial arrogance; it makes them better people, more appropriate partners for each other, and ultimately capable of true love' (2014: 121). This description perfectly fits the riotous mayhem featured in *Dream*, particularly in the forest of Athens. As previously mentioned, Mott's *Dream* expands on the romantic maelstrom by adding a fifth couple to Shakespeare's four pairs of lovers (Hermia/Lysander, Helena/Demetrius, Theseus/Hippolyta, Titania/Oberon): the female student film director, Peta Quince, pines after the actor Bottom as they work on their short film, which is analogous to the play within the play (an exchange also used effectively in Michael Almereyda's *Hamlet* [2000]). During *Dream*'s denouement, following a screening for the three newly married couples in Duke Theseus's personal screening room of the students' film *Pyramus and Thisby* – a cheeky and inept parody of *Star Wars* (1977) – Quince, the elated and adorable bespectacled sci-fi nerd, heartily kisses the silly but undeniably lovable goofus Bottom (see Figure 2.9.5). They proceed to dance joyfully at the reception party afterward, surrounded by the glowing newlyweds, while the 'parents and original' of these couples sing Titania and Oberon's blessing from the final scene of the play (5.1.382–93). These elemental natural powers bestow benediction on the triumph of renewal over death, of spring over winter.

Northrup Frye famously discusses this principle in his work on Shakespearean comedy: '[T]he action… begins in a world represented as a normal world, moves

FIGURE 2.9.5 The 'rude mechanicals' making and screening their *Star Wars*-inspired version of *Pyramus and Thisbe* in Mott's *Dream*. Image credit: Daniel Katz.

into a green world, goes into metamorphosis there in which the comic resolution is achieved, and returns to the normal world' (2004: 97). This narrative pattern, he argues, represents the 'ritual of death and revival' (97), and it is usually followed by a festive ritual celebrating the rejuvenation of society. Apropos of his mise en scène and tendency to extend, Mott's film features *three* rituals that affirm the union of the now five couples: the wedding, the film screening, and the dancing and music-making of the couples at the reception, which is the final image of the Athenian world in the film. In his 'Director's Statement', Mott describes his film in the terms of conventional romantic comedies as well as Frye's green world: 'It's a giddy exploration of what happens when opposites collide …. And it is, finally, a celebration of personal transformation and spiritual rebirth' (Mott 2017). Friedman et al. also overtly connect the Hollywood genre of romantic comedy to Frye's green world (2014: 146–9).[3]

Comparisons particularly have been made between Shakespeare's comedies and the genre of screwball comedy that developed in Hollywood in the 1930s and 1940s. Mei Zhu contends, '[I]t is arguable that the entire tradition of screwball comedy has roots in Shakespearean comedies such as *Much Ado About Nothing*, *Love's Labour's Lost*, and *The Comedy of Errors*' (2004: 7). In his book *Pursuits of Happiness: The Hollywood Comedy of Remarriage*, the polymathic philosopher Stanley Cavell argues that screwball comedy reflects the 'green world' narrative pattern of Shakespeare's comedies and romances specifically (1984: 48–50). Film scholar Wes Gehring has taken issue with Cavell's analogy, arguing that there are no 'enchanted forests' in screwball, nor are there 'extremes of forgiving and forgetting' at their denouement, as appear in Shakespeare (1986: 48–50). However, Gehring's refutations seem disingenuous when looking at paradigmatic examples of screwball comedy, such as *It Happened One Night* (1934) and *Bringing Up Baby* (1938), both of which feature a 'green world' where the couple encounters various obstacles and, ultimately, each person grows to appreciate the gifts *and* accept the failings of his or her partner after a rousing 'battle' of the sexes. Indeed, most histories of the romantic comedy genre begin in the sound era because screwball comedy redefined cinematic comedy and established the typical characteristics of romantic comedy to this day: 'Screwball comedy combined the sophisticated fast-paced dialogue of the romantic comedy with the zany action, comic violence and kinetic energy of slapstick comedy' (Lent 1995: 327). It is obvious, from this description, that many of Shakespeare's comedies could fit comfortably in the screwball comedy category, especially *The Taming of the Shrew, Much Ado About Nothing* and *A Midsummer Night's Dream*. After Shakespeare's era, this tradition of screwball antics and witty dialogue carries right through British literature, as can be seen in plays stretching from the Restoration through the twentieth century, including standout classics such as Aphra Behn's *The Rover* (1677), William Congreve's *The Way of the World* (1700), Richard Brinsley Sheridan's *The School for Scandal* (1777) and Oscar Wilde's *The Importance of Being Earnest* (1895). The tremendous global success of British romantic comedy *Four Weddings and a Funeral* (Mike Newell, 1994) demonstrates that this tradition also has been incorporated into British cinema. However, this film also owes much to Hollywood's influential screwball classics and, thus, is a generic hybrid exhibiting the interweaving traditions of theatrical British comedies of wit with American screwball tropes.

Genres, as all texts within them, inevitably reflect their contexts, and screwball comedy films arose at a time when women's roles in the United States were shifting in the wake of female suffrage and the desperation of the Depression. The result, Tina Olsin Lent maintains, is that screwball comedy is 'more egalitarian in its vision' than slapstick comedy; in addition, '[t]he romantic leads often had eccentric qualities, and their unconventional behavior was both a form of social criticism and anarchic individualism' (1995: 327). One can see this clearly in the protagonists of the aforementioned Shakespeare comedies, and Mott enhances this by making his lovers' stereotypes indigenous to the Hollywood landscape. This is particularly true of *Dream*'s women. Hermia Puppet (with her symbolic surname) – played by erstwhile high school romantic comedy staple Rachael Leigh Cook – is a vain starlet, but one who is seeking more than wealth and beauty in a partner and who is willing to take a risk to possess an authentic love. Helena Maypole, played by the marvellous Lily Rabe, is a passionate, poetry-penning screenwriter of romantic comedies, such as *Star Cross'd Lovers*, which, we learn from a movie poster on Theseus's office wall, starred Helena's best friend Hermia. Mott chooses to contemporize the play by making Helena a stronger character, having her decisively turn away from Demetrius in the forest, voluntarily relinquishing her pursuit and attempting to reclaim her dignity, rather than simply losing track of him. Peta Quince, as already mentioned, is a cute, late-twenties Athens Film Academy student who is crazy about *Star Wars* and sweet on the clueless but endearing Nick Bottom (Fran Kranz). These three ladies assert themselves in audacious ways that bring them to happy unions with the objects of their desire, much like the fast-talking heroines of screwball comedy.

Mott also was inspired by a more recent trend in the romantic comedy genre: the grotesque, or vulgar, romantic comedy. In *The Hollywood Romantic Comedy*, Leger Grindon argues that the late 1990s ushered in a new era of the genre that embraced explicit depictions of sexual and bodily matters (2011: 63–5). In these usually R-rated films, 'gross-out' humour is paired with courtship, and sex is often used 'to disturb, humiliate, distort, and infantilize' major characters (63). When *Dream* is performed, the scenes shared by Titania and Bottom are often played onstage and in film in a grotesque manner, featuring very graphic depictions of sexual activity between the inveigled fairy queen and the monstrous ass-man. Mott takes this a large step further by choosing to give Nick Bottom an actual human derrière for a face rather than the standard donkey head, reading the 'ass' of the play's text in an entirely different sense. During the explicit love-making in the bower scenes, Bottom's ass-face makes obscene flatulent noises, adding a new level of ribaldry, akin to the coarse gags in films like *There's Something About Mary* (1998), *Knocked Up* (2007), *Forgetting Sarah Marshall* (2008), *Bridesmaids* (2011) and *Trainwreck* (2015). Mott, agreeing with Jan Kott, believes that what directors of *Dream* choose to do with the thematic import of Bottom's 'translation' says a great deal about their approach to the play. Mott opines that Bottom's metamorphosis and his coupling with Titania represent the marriage between man and nature, a central concern of the play, and their coming together should depict the sexuality, hilarity and folly of that union (Mott 2019). Explaining Bottom's ass-face, Mott has claimed, 'I was trying to stick to my guns: take the play, make it modern, make it bawdy, and make it irreverent' (Mott 2019). Here, like all adaptors, he indicates his desire to put his own stamp on Shakespeare's work and set his interpretation apart from all those that have come before. He admits, 'People don't have lukewarm feelings about the butt-face', but he seems pleased to have brought a new twist into the four-hundred-year-old narrative (Mott 2019). In his work on *Dream*, Kott cogently explains the important role of the ass (donkey) in comic rituals from Saturnalia to medieval *ludi*, citing Mikhail Bakhtin's assertion that the ass is 'the most ancient and lasting symbol of the material bodily lower stratum' (qtd. in Kott 1987: 43–4); the ass icon is 'the ritualistic and carnivalesque mediator between heaven and earth, which transforms the "top" into the "bottom"' (44). *Dream*'s scenes featuring Bottom and Titania reflect Bakhtin's concept of 'grotesque realism', which focuses on the 'material bodily principle, that is, images of the human body with its food, drink, defecation, and sexual life'; these are a crucial part of the comic ritual, which uses 'degradation', a 'coming down to earth', that buries, sows and kills in order to cultivate rebirth (18, 21). In fact, Mott's butt-faced Bottom is very much in keeping with Bakhtin's concept of regeneration through grotesque comic ritual.

TO LIVE AND DREAM IN LA

Mott also situates his *Midsummer Night's Dream* firmly in the genre of Los Angeles film. Films in this category use the landscape and culture of the Los Angeles region to shape their characters, themes, narratives and aesthetics. There are a few other cities in the world that feature so prominently in cinema that they frequently function as a character – New York, Paris, Rome, Mumbai, London, Tokyo – but there remains only one Hollywood. In his iconic documentary *Los Angeles Plays Itself* (2003), filmmaker and scholar Thom Andersen reminds us that 'Los Angeles is where the relationship between reality and representation gets muddled'. This echoes Mott's words above and reflects a kinship between Los Angeles, a city where fictions are created and dreams are spun, and one of Shakespeare's favourite themes: the permeable boundary between performance and life, illusion and reality. It is, in fact, an ideal location for this play full of desire, deception and meta-theatrics. Although, as Andersen and Mott admit, LA may be one of the least photogenic or handsome cities, it is a megalopolis replete with mythologies and secrets as well as banalities and frustrations. There is undeniably a magical and uncanny quality to Los Angeles. Steve Martin's romantic comedy classic *L.A. Story* (1991), which channels Shakespeare at several moments, provides a hilarious depiction of this with its riddling electronic freeway sign and protagonist's ability to manifest his love by changing the weather (see Buhler 1997). Of course, Los Angeles films come in all sorts of generic flavours, such as film noir and neo-noir – *The Big Sleep* (1946), *Chinatown* (1974), *L.A. Confidential* (1997); action films – To *Live and Die in L.A.* (1985), *Falling Down* (1993), the *Lethal Weapon* series (1989–98); gang films – *Boyz n the Hood* (1991); disaster films – *Earthquake* (1974); thrillers – *Collateral* (2004); science fiction – *Blade Runner* (1982); and even LA noir spoofs – *Who Framed Roger Rabbit* (1988), *The Player* (1992). Some of the genres listed here are of determinate space, but all films that fall into or intersect with the category of Los Angeles film function as genres of determinate space, in which the conflict over values and specific territory, physical and symbolic, is central. Compared to the genres just named, there are fewer romantic comedies set in this sprawling city of over ten million people. Indeed, New York, with its dazzling skyline and enchanting Central Park, is by far the most favoured city in this genre. The romantic comedies that are set in LA seem to focus on the difficulties of meeting suitable partners and staying together in such a challenging social and spatial landscape. *Pretty Woman*, *L.A. Story* and *500 Days of Summer* (2009) reflect this.

Los Angeles as a city tends to inspire another hybrid genre, the 'network film', which presents several storylines with different character groups at once, weaving them together with cross-cutting, alternating between seemingly disparate narrative strands, until the connection between the diegetic threads becomes clear. The seemingly endless, labyrinthine spread of Los Angeles lends itself to this narrative structure. Most LA network films are dramas or indies, such as *Short Cuts* (1993), *Pulp Fiction* (1994), *Magnolia* (1999) and *Crash* (2004), but *Valentine's Day* (2010) is a rare (and unsuccessful) attempt at an LA-based romantic comedy of this ilk. *A Midsummer Night's Dream*, with its three diegetic worlds populated by different types of characters, fits well within the network film structure, presenting different narrative strands intersecting in various ways leading to a final gathering together. Mott had this specifically in mind while developing his *Dream*, asking his department heads to look closely at the aforementioned films for inspiration (Mott 2019). He also directed them to examine *The Big Lebowski* (1998) for the Coen Brothers's cheeky reimagining of LA-based film noir, which he wanted to emulate, and referred his staff to David Lynch's *Mulholland Drive* (2001) and P. T. Anderson's *Inherent Vice* (2014) for their dreamy, hallucinatory tone and aesthetic. The impact of this can be seen clearly in the psychedelic cinematography in night forest scenes with the fairy court, played as earthy hippies smoking weed and jamming to trippy tunes. Mott's film style, like Brook's, is inspired by French New Wave aesthetics, which contrast with Hollywood conventions. This can be seen in the jumpy handheld cinematography in several scenes, visual effects such as split screen images, freeze frames and discontinuity editing, especially jump cuts and disorienting quick cutting between disparate locations in space and time. The chaos and confusion in the narrative is well expressed by these techniques, which communicate the diverse skein of people and places in LA as well as the frenetic pace of the city.

As noted above, by definition, the Los Angeles film is a genre of determinate space, and this includes Mott's *Dream*, despite its hybrid status as a romantic comedy. His transformation of the aristocratic characters into stereotypical denizens of the Hollywood scene would not work in any other locale, as Hollywood is both a physical place and an imagined, symbolic construction. Indeed, Hollywood is not a city at all but a community within Los Angeles, a city of exasperating traffic jams as well as high-flown dreams, as vividly depicted in the opening number of a more recent LA film, Damien Chazelle's *La La Land* (2016), which takes place during a traffic jam on a freeway overpass. This award-winning and highly successful musical set in Los Angeles was released while Mott's *Dream* was in production, so it did not have an affect on this film. However, Mott has said that its romantic plot, bright colour palette and focus on Hollywood were in keeping with his own approach. There is one other recent adaptation of a Shakespeare comedy that was filmed in LA, Joss Whedon's indie adaptation of *Much Ado About Nothing* (2012). The film stars the Whedonverse's group of recurring actors and was filmed over a weekend at the director's house. However, Whedon's screwball-comedy inspired film, hearkening back to the studio era with its classic black-and-white film stock, does not feature Los Angeles as a character. Indeed, all we see is the one house and its backyard, and the major characters are portrayed as participants in organized crime rather than Hollywood players or aspirants. As with many other romantic comedies, Whedon's *Much Ado* clearly could have been set in any leafy suburb. It is a hybrid genre film incorporating aspects of screwball, the Whedonverse, indie and Shakespeare adaptation, all genres of indeterminate space, unlike the Los Angeles film.

Mott wished to capture another key characteristic of life in Los Angeles in his *Dream*, which also happens to be a prime reason that the film industry moved to Los Angeles in the early twentieth century. Los Angeles provides access to an array of distinct landscapes within a relatively short distance, including areas of stunning natural splendor. Citizens of LA can readily escape the claustrophobia and grime of the city by heading to one of the many beautiful beaches or to the copious miles of wilderness parks stretching over the mountains and through the canyons. Angelenos regularly go to these natural landscapes for renewal, and this struck Mott, a long-time resident, as a perfect analogue for the green world structure of *A Midsummer Night's Dream* (Mott 2019). In contrast, the other Shakespearean romantic comedy in the Los Angeles film category, *L.A. Story*, uses Shakespeare intertextually to juxtapose the sophistication of London with the vapid cultural wasteland of Los Angeles, humorously highlighting the Bard's incompatibility with Tinseltown (Buhler 1997: 216). Mott's *Dream* is a fully anthropophagous adaptation, swallowing the play whole, incorporating it inextricably into the warp and woof of the Los Angeles region.

INDEPENDENT MEANS AND HOLLYWOOD INTERSECTIONS

Mott's work – in its budget, production process, distribution, exhibition and creative content – can also be understood as an 'indie' film. The term *indie* derived from the longer industrial moniker, independent film, during the 1980s, when a particular type of non-studio film grew to prominence with larger audiences thanks to the increased attention to major film festivals featuring this type of work, particularly Robert Redford's celebrated Sundance Film Festival. Many scholars credit Steven Soderbergh's *sex, lies, and videotape* (1989) with being the first breakthrough film in this realm (Holm 2008: 32; Newman 2011: 1–2). Michael Z. Newman asserts, 'Indie constitutes a film culture', which includes 'a cluster of interpretive strategies and expectations; their support personnel, including distributors and publicists; the staffers of independent cinema institutions such as film festivals; critics and other writers; and audiences' (2011: 11). As stated previously, film scholar D. K. Holm acknowledges that indie film now functions as a *genre*, while Yannis Tzioumakis prefers to call independent cinema a film discourse (2006: 1–14). *Specialty films* is the term most often used by film industry professionals since the rise of the 'Sundance-Miramax era' of the 1990s and early 2000s. Whatever the appellation, the type of independent film that has arisen, particularly in the United States, but not exclusively so, possesses identifiable characteristics, including 'some combination of authorial maverick quality, distance from the Hollywood marketing machine, and distance as well from the narrative and stylistic qualities' of films crafted for the hoi polloi, mainstream audiences, who frequent the local multiplex; this gives the indie genre a palpable patina of superior cultural clout (Newman 2011: 243).

Accordingly, Mott explains that he was drawn to adapting *A Midsummer Night's Dream* for his indie directorial debut at least partly because it is difficult to convince talented actors to join a low-budget indie film project with an unproven director, but there is a group of excellent actors who would leap at the chance to make a Shakespearean film because of their zeal for the Bard (Mott 2019). While Shakespeare's cultural capital does not have much pull in the Hollywood studio system or the major funders thereof, it does hold sway with many actors, particularly those who have trained in universities and cut their professional teeth treading the boards of the stage. This certainly worked in his favour with Lily Rabe (Helena) and Hamish Linklater (Lysander), regular performers in the New York Public Theater's Shakespeare in the Park series, as well as Fran Kranz (Bottom, also a producer on the film) and Finn Wittrock (Demetrius), who have extensive Shakespeare stage credits. This comprehension of and intimacy with Shakespeare's language results in some of the most lucid and naturalistic verse speaking to appear in any Shakespeare film, and it may be the finest performance of Shakespeare's language in an adaptation set in contemporary times. Mott's main Shakespearean cinema inspirations were Baz Luhrmann's *William Shakespeare's Romeo + Juliet* (1995), Ralph Fiennes's *Coriolanus* (2011) and Joss Whedon's *Much Ado About Nothing* (2012), but only Fiennes's film displays a virtuosity with the language equal to that in Mott's *Dream* (and *Coriolanus* mainly features actors also trained in stage performance). Furthermore, Mott, an avid Shakespeare acolyte himself, had the pre-existing Shakespeare film fan in mind when choosing the project, expecting that the 'egghead' market could be depended upon to seek out the film (Mott 2019). In the end, despite its largely positive reviews, the film had a very limited release in independent theatres, so brief that even Shakespeare aficionados found it difficult to track down. It then moved to streaming services charging a fee per viewing and currently is included with Amazon Prime Video. With new models of distribution, the film has the potential to expand its audience and bring in more revenue, providing opportunities for success, in its various guises, that were not available to the 1935 *Dream*. Though both films had low box office receipts, the earlier *Dream* was a big budget studio film whereas Mott's was greatly scaled down in budget and viewership expectations. Mott himself has stated that adapting Shakespeare to film, particularly using his language, is risky, and setting an early modern play in the twenty-first century is even more so (Mott 2019). Between these two extremes is Hoffman's mid-range *Dream* in 1999, which, though not the epic spectacle of Reinhardt and Dieterle's film, was aimed at a larger audience and drew a modest profit due to its celebrity cast, relatively low budget and Fox Searchlight studio's marketing campaign. Conversely, Mott's appeal to an intellectual audience is commensurate with the larger indie film culture. In fact, Mott embeds famous quotations from other Shakespeare plays throughout the film as 'Easter eggs' for Shakespeare lovers to find. In addition, his portrayal of the Pyramus and Thisby performance as a travesty, or 'mock-buster' version, of *Star Wars*, motivated by Peta Quince's obsession with the film, is meant as an analogue for this *Dream* film, inspired by Mott's passion for Shakespeare (Mott 2019) – a juxtaposition which also strongly underlines the differences between indie films, like the one we are watching, and blockbusters. However, this is also an inside joke, as George Lucas independently financed *Star Wars*, making the global powerhouse, technically, an independent film, an ironic point raised frequently in books on the subject. Of course, the embedded play of *Pyramus and Thisbe* is itself a travesty of Shakespeare's *Romeo and Juliet*, probably written shortly before *Dream*, so Mott is wrapping a joke within a joke, playing kaleidoscopically with metanarrative.

This kind of self-reflexivity in content and diegetic structure is often a feature of indie films. Newman identifies three primary 'expectations' of indie film:

1. characters are emblems
2. form is a game
3. when in doubt, read as anti-Hollywood (2011: 29).

Mott's *Dream* thoroughly embraces all three of these criteria. Not only does Shakespeare portray the young lovers, the aristocratic couple and the irate, controlling father, Egeus, in stereotypical guises, but Mott takes this a step further by making each of these characters a Hollywood stereotype as well, as described above. Even Hippolyta gets this treatment, becoming a model/actress trophy wife of the successful, older movie producer Duke Theseus. The members of the fairy world are represented as that California-specific stereotype of the New Age hippie, connected to nature (the ocean and the forest), immersed in hallucinogenic drug culture and always accompanied by an ambient musical soundscape. For this reason, Mott cast musicians in the parts of Titania (Mia Doi Todd) and Oberon (Saul Williams), and Todd wrote the evocative soundtrack for the film (see Figure 2.9.6). Both Shakespeare's and Mott's characters are emblems of social types, as are the vast majority of characters in genre films. Mott also plays with film form, both in narrative structure and aesthetics, in *Dream*. Newman uses the Coen Brothers' work to exemplify this quality of indie films, emphasizing their intense and complex emulation and transformation of generic properties in films like *Blood Simple* (1984), *Barton Fink* (1991, another LA film) and *Fargo* (1996). Mott plays with form in this way – as can be seen in the mock-buster *Pyramus and Thisbe/Star Wars* travesty of a travesty – but his most innovative treatment of 'form as game' for the viewers to ponder and solve over the course of the film is more akin to the earlier indie work (and some later work) of auteurs such as David Lynch, Quentin Tarantino and Christopher Nolan, who play in extreme ways with time and space, narrative structure and self-reflexivity.

Newman's third criterion of indie film is its positionality as an anti-Hollywood category, defining itself by its rejection of mainstream conventions. The extreme meta-cinematic and meta-theatrical elements clearly fit into this rubric, but these unusual features also could be read as reflections of the 'quirky' trend Newman describes in indie filmmaking: 'Quirk is a kind of tone or sensibility that depends for

FIGURE 2.9.6 The California hippie fairy world of Mott's *Dream*. Image credit: Daniel Katz.

its effects on a perception of its unusual, eccentric qualities, and this fits perfectly with the mission of indie cinema to distinguish itself against mainstream tone or sensibility or conventions of representation of characters and settings' (2011: 44). Furthermore, Mott's characterization of Helena, an awkward, arty poet who finds her identity in her intelligence and wit, is a classic quirky stereotype. When she finds herself unable to resist mawkishly chasing a man, in standard 'smart girl' fashion, she clearly is deeply disappointed in herself. This reading of Helena makes her part both more interesting and stronger in the film than in the play; plus, it brings her character into the current moment, when lovably (or annoyingly) eccentric young women – like the 'adorkable' Zooey Deschanel in *500 Days of Summer* and her long-running television show *New Girl* (2011–18) – always suffer a lengthy season of romantic misfortunes before they find their quirky, complementary 'Mr Right' and live happily ever after. It is an indie dream, and it happens charmingly in this *Dream*.

CONCLUDING VISIONS

Mott's doubling of himself as Puck, the filmmaker in control of all the flickering shadows, is more than a clever conceit. This choice foregrounds ubiquitous themes in Shakespeare's work and of life in Los Angeles: we are all players performing our parts on the stage or in the film of life, and the boundaries between our 'real' lives and the fictions with which we engage are always permeable and occasionally absent altogether. Mott's Puck is the 'wise fool' who, like the genre film itself, holds the key to resolving the conflicts that cannot be resolved in real life. Mott declares,

> Puck's the one who's in on the secret, which is the biggest secret of all,… that they're all just in a play. He's the one character in the entire unfolding drama who is aware of that. And that gives him incredible, almost omniscient power within the context of his reality, and I think that's the same sort of understanding that Shakespeare himself had of his world and his role in it.
>
> (Mott 2019)

While Casey Wilder Mott's *A Midsummer Night's Dream* unequivocally falls squarely into the subgenre of Shakespeare film, it also is meaningfully situated in the categories of romantic comedy, the Los Angeles film and indie film, occupying hybrid generic territory that must be explored to understand the significance, quality and achievement of this film.

The complexity of hybrid texts, such as Shakespeare's plays and their myriad incarnations on stage and screen, demand of the viewer and the scholar an interdisciplinary approach. There is much to be gained from examining the merging of disparate media discourses, for instance looking at the influence of the long theatrical tradition of the British comedy of wit on screwball comedy. However, as demonstrated in this chapter, it is also fruitful and critical to move beyond comparisons to other media and investigate cinematic elements, such as cinematography and editing, alongside the industrial, technological and historical contexts of a given film. This is not a call to embrace an essentialist or exceptionalist approach that claims film texts must be defined and evaluated solely by their 'uniquely cinematic' characteristics. As Rowe contends, when looking at screen Shakespeare, it is important to keep one eye on filmic properties and the other on the 'convergence' and 'recycling' of other media (2008: 41). While agreeing with this idea, this chapter sees Shakespeare adaptations as interlocutors with multiple cinematic discourses and contexts that are not directly connected to the playwright. It demonstrates the potential efficacy of this strategy by interrogating the ways in which Mott, in his *Dream*, incorporates features of different film genres; how he employs cinematic models and inspirations; and how he approaches industrial exigencies such as funding, casting and distribution. Shakespeare films, from the one-reel silent shorts to Mott's *Dream*, are rich texts wherein multifarious media intersect, and one of the great pleasures of studying these films is to delve into how they play with Shakespeare through the lenses and discourses of cinema.

NOTES

1   There were a plethora of silent film adaptations of literary classics and over four hundred silent films on 'Shakespearean subjects' (Jackson 2000: 2). However, the majority of silent film adaptations were short fragments of their hypotexts (source texts). Of course, most films of any type were short during the first decades of the medium due to the restrictions of technology. The few adaptations we would call 'feature-length' were generally of popular rather than literary provenance, such as D. W. Griffith's *The Birth of a Nation* (1915) in the United States and two European *Quo Vadis?* adaptations (1913 and 1924). One notable exception is the German-Danish adaptation of *Hamlet* in 1921 starring the Danish star Asta Nielsen as a cross-dressing female *Hamlet*.

2   Evidence for this can be found in the abundance of monographs and volumes of essays focusing on Shakespearean film adaptations, particularly since the late 1980s. Important earlier work focusing on Shakespeare on film can be found in Allardyce Nicoll's *Film and Theatre* (1936), Robert Hamilton Ball's *Shakespeare on Silent Film* (1968) and Roger Manvell's *Shakespeare and the Film* (1971). In the first edition of *Film Theory and Criticism: Introductory Readings* in 1974 (eds. Mast and Cohen), there is a section of essays specifically on 'Shakespeare and Film' within its 'Film, Theater, and Literature' section. In its 1979 second edition, the Shakespeare section is gone, but there is a section on 'Film Narrative and Other Arts', in which theorists such as Andre Bazin discuss Shakespeare onscreen, which has continued through the most recent, eighth edition of 2016 (eds. Braudy and Mast). Oxford University Press credibly claims this volume has been 'the most widely used and cited anthology of critical writing about film' for the past nearly fifty years. Prominent adaptation scholars not focused on Shakespeare, such as Linda Hutcheon, Timothy Corrigan and Thomas Leitch, frequently reference Shakespearean cinema. For a thorough history and bibliography of screen Shakespeare, see Kenneth S. Rothwell's *A History of Shakespeare on Screen: A Century of Film and Television* (2nd edition, 2007).

3   It is clear that Northrup Frye's vision of the features and functions of comedy is heteronormative; it is pertinent that Frye penned 'The Argument of Comedy' in

1948. The Hollywood genre of romantic comedy has been focused overwhelmingly on straight relationships as well. However, exceptions to this rule do exist. The Hollywood classic *Some Like It Hot* (Billy Wilder, 1959), for instance, plays with same-sex attraction and homoeroticism via the Shakespearean motif of cross-dressing. Generally, films prominently featuring comedic queer romance have been independent films, such as Ang Lee's *The Wedding Banquet* (1993) and Rose Troche's *Go Fish* (1994). Of course, in early modern England, a queering of the sexes and gender roles was inherent in the practice of boys and men playing female parts, so that in a comedy such as *Dream*, in which cross-dressing is not in the plot, gender fluidity and homoeroticism was at play with the male bodies on stage performing female roles. For an excellent examination of sexuality in the play, see Melissa Sanchez's article '"Use Me But as Your Spaniel": Feminism, Queer Theory, and Early Modern Sexualities', in *PMLA* (Sanchez 2012).

Mott's *Dream* follows the standard heteronormative conventions of Hollywood romantic comedy, with the exception of the highly sexualized fairies wandering about in bikinis who evidently are up for any sexual experience, including lesbian encounters. However, this seems more of a heterosexual male fantasy and nod to the 'free love' movement of the late 1960s and the 1970s than a counterpoint to heteronormativity. Mott's omission of the dispute over the Indian Boy also removes a potential homoerotic reference to the love and devotion shared between the fairy queen Titania and her votaress, on whose behalf Titania defies her 'lord' Oberon. One recent stage production that departed from *Dream*'s usual straight orientation was director Emma Rice's 2016 production at London's Globe Theatre, in which she recast Helena's character as a gay male Helenus seeking the love of a closeted Demetrius (Watson 2016).

REFERENCES

Anderegg, M. (2004), *Cinematic Shakespeare*, Lanham, MD: Rowman and Littlefield.

Braudy, J. and M. Cohen, eds (2016), *Film Theory and Criticism: Introductory Readings*, 8th edn, Oxford: Oxford University Press.

Buhler, S. M. (1997), 'Antic Dispositions: Shakespeare and Steve Martin's *L.A. Story*', *Shakespeare Yearbook: Hamlet on Screen* 8: 212–29, The Edwin Mellen Press.

Cavell, S. (1984), *Pursuits of Happiness: The Hollywood Comedy of Remarriage*, Harvard, MA: Harvard University Press.

Derrida, J. (1980), 'The Law of Genre', *Critical Inquiry* 7 (1): 55–81.

Friedman, L. et al. (2014), *An Introduction to Film Genres*, New York, NY: W. W. Norton.

Frye, N. (2004), 'The Argument of Comedy', in R. McDonald (ed.), *Shakespeare: An Anthology of Criticism and Theory 1945–2000*, 93–9, London: Blackwell.

Gehring, W. (1986), *Screwball Comedy: A Genre of Madcap Romance*, Westport, CT: Praeger.

Grindon, L. (2011), *The Hollywood Romantic Comedy: Conventions, History, Controversies*, London: Wiley Blackwell.

Holland, P, ed. (1995), Introduction, *A Midsummer Night's Dream*, by W. Shakespeare, Oxford: Oxford University Press.

Holm, D. K. (2008), *Independent Cinema*, Harpenden: Kamera Books.

Hutcheon, L. (2013), *A Theory of Adaptation*, 2nd edn, London: Routledge.

Jackson, R. (2000), 'Introduction: Shakespeare, Films and the Marketplace', in R. Jackson (ed.), *The Cambridge Companion to Shakespeare on Film*, 1–12, Cambridge: Cambridge University Press.

Keyishian, H. (2000), 'Shakespeare and movie genre: the case of Hamlet', in R. Jackson (ed.), *The Cambridge Companion to Shakespeare on Film*, 72–81, Cambridge: Cambridge University Press.

Kott, J. (1987), *The Bottom Translation: Marlowe and Shakespeare and the Carnival Tradition*, trans. D. Miedzyrzecka and L. Vallee, Evanston, IL: Northwestern University Press.

Lent, T. O. (1995), 'Romantic Love and Friendship: The Redefinition of Gender Relations in Screwball Comedy', in K. Brunovska Karnick and H. Jenkins (eds), *Classical Hollywood Comedy*, 314–31, New York, NY: Routledge.

Los Angeles Plays Itself (2003), [Film] Dir. and written by T. Andersen, The Cinema Guild.

A Midsummer Night's Dream (2017), [Film] Dir. and adapted by C. Wilder Mott, Beverly Hills, CA: Brainstorm Media.

Mast, G. and M. Cohen, eds (1974), *Film Theory and Criticism: Introductory Readings*, 1st edn, Oxford: Oxford University Press.

Mott, C. Wilder (2017), A Midsummer Night's Dream *Press Kit*, Beverly Hills, CA: Brainstorm Media.

Mott, C. Wilder (2019), Personal Interview, 22 January.

Newman, M. Z. (2011), *Indie: An American Film Culture*, New York, NY: Columbia University Press.

Pramaggiore, M. and T. Wallis (2011), *Film: A Critical Introduction*, 3rd edn, New York, NY: Pearson.

Rothwell, K. S. (2007), *A History of Shakespeare on Screen: A Century of Film and Television*, 2nd edn, Cambridge: Cambridge University Press.

Rowe, K. (2008), 'Medium-specificity and Other Critical Scripts for Screen Shakespeare', in D. E. Henderson (ed.), *Alternative Shakespeares 3*, 34–53, New York, NY: Routledge.

Sanchez, M. E. (2012), '"Use Me But as Your Spaniel": Feminism, Queer Theory, and Early Modern Sexualities', *PMLA* 127 (3): 493–511.

Schatz, T (1981), *Hollywood Genres: Formulas, Filmmaking, and the Studio System*, New York, NY: McGraw-Hill.

Tzioumakis, Y. (2006), *American Independent Cinema: An Introduction*, New Brunswick: Rutgers University Press.

Vela, R. (2009), 'Post-Apocalyptic Spaces in Baz Luhrmann's *William Shakespeare's Romeo + Juliet*', in M. Croteau and C. Jess-Cooke (eds), *Apocalyptic Shakespeare: Essays on Visions of Chaos and Revelation in Recent Film Adaptations*, 90–109, Jefferson, NC: McFarland.

Watson, E. (2016), 'A (Queer) Midsummer Night's Dream', *Ms. Magazine*, 19 July. Available online: https://msmagazine.com/2016/07/19/queering-shakespeare-in-2016/ (accessed 20 December 2020).

Zhu, M. (2004), 'Shakespeare's *Taming of the Shrew* and the Tradition of Screwball Comedy', *CLCWeb: Comparative Literature and Culture* 6 (1): 1–7.

Televisual adaptation of Shakespeare in a multi-platform age

SUSANNE GREENHALGH

Televisual adaptations of Shakespeare emerge from different 'citational environments' (Cartelli and Rowe 2007: 29) with distinct media histories that in turn shape the authority, significance, style and broadcasting space allocated to his works. According to Sarah Cardwell, televisual adaptation is 'the gradual development of a "meta-text" … that is constantly growing and developing, being retold, reinterpreted and reassessed' (2002: 24, 95). In their different forms, whether 'closely related' or 'thoroughly distanced' versions of their source (Pittman 2010: 9), television adaptations and allusions form a continuum – or, as Douglas Lanier has it, a 'network' – of prior Shakespearean adaptations (2017: 297), which is one of the ways in which Shakespeare's works retain the familiarity that allows viewers to recognize adaptations *as* adaptations. While the vast majority have been made and disseminated by English-language broadcasters, the presence of his plays in international theatre and education has also resulted in a body of work transmitted in translation by non-Anglophone media.[1] As a totality they provide a microhistory of how and for what uses Shakespeare has been adapted, and how this has changed during the century of television's existence.

The heritage of theatrical performances of Shakespeare constitutes a major part of the Shakespearean authority that is affirmed, appropriated and contested by televisual adaptation. Television's remediation of theatre has resulted in three kinds of adaptations of Shakespeare's plays: the recording of live performances in the theatre, studio-based restagings of theatre productions and made-for-television versions shot in the studio or by Outside Broadcast (OB) units on location. Moreover, they inhabit an adaptive context in which serial scheduling, form and content came to predominate. According to Shannon Wells-Lassagne, serial storytelling is central to 'the unique nature of the television adaptation', which is inherently 'an expansive one, incorporating new ideas, new models alongside the old' (2017: 7). In the current multi-channel, multi-platform era, Shakespeare increasingly exists as what scholars such as Richard Burt and Maurizio Calbi term 'Shakespeares' (Burt 1998,

2006; Calbi 2013): 'multi-mediated "manifestations"… in the increasingly digitized and globalized mediascape of the twenty-first century' (Calbi 2013: 2).

In 2008 Katherine Rowe noted a still prevalent 'media script' in which the low status of television meant that to admit to being 'a regular TV watcher in a community of Shakespeareans' called into question one's scholarly standing (2008: 37–8). Following the 'media turn' in Shakespeare Studies (O'Neill 2017: 1) the situation is very different today. An AHRC-funded project to create an online international database of audiovisual Shakespeare (http://bufvc.ac.uk/shakespeare/) has significantly expanded awareness of the multiplicity of television adaptations and allusions, many examples of which can be freely viewed online.[2] In recent years three books on Shakespeare in twenty-first-century 'complex' serials have appeared (Ronnenberg 2018; Bronfen 2020; Wald 2020). This chapter acknowledges the ways in which studies of televised Shakespeare have developed, first taking an historical and institutional approach to the different televisual modes in which the plays have been adapted by British and North American broadcasters, and then tracing the implications of the development of multi-platform viewing, genre shifts from single play to seriality and the emphasis on intertextual resonances of the plays' lines, narratives and characters when retold in contemporary terms.

REMEDIATING AND RETELLING SHAKESPEARE ON LOCATION AND IN THE STUDIO

For most of the second half of the twentieth century television was in the hands of national broadcasting networks. The BBC's existing radio service provided a model for national public service television (1937–), one initially mirrored in several European countries, as well as the Commonwealth nations. Television in the United States also began in the late 1930s, with licensing of commercially funded stations from 1941, the main networks being CBS, NBC and ABC (1948), all previously radio networks. The quantity, style and interpretative approach of Shakespeare adaptations are inseparable from the media institutions that produce and disseminate them and the processes they employ, since televised Shakespeare is 'caught up in, and shaped by, technologies of production' (Kidnie 2008: 104). Sound, preserved and delivered electronically, is as important as the images captured by cameras in the development of television broadcasting. For many early commentators this made television an especially suitable medium for delivery of Shakespeare's language, while musical soundtracks – often overlooked – could add another layer of meaning to the plays (Sanders 2013). Alongside its remediation of radio the framed, window-like screen of early television sets borrowed and adapted its perspectival visual conventions from photography and film, together with the distinction between on- and off-screen space (Bignell 2019: 150), turning television into a multi-medial art form (Cardwell 2006, 2014). While television was often considered 'too crude and too primitive a medium for Shakespeare' it was also argued that its 'tightness and crampedness' suited the intimate rendering of character psychology (Charney 1986: 2).

Both theatre restagings and made-for-TV versions of Shakespeare's plays are necessarily adapted to the requirements of the televisual environment in which they are filmed. The studio filming which predominated early on employed several cameras to capture close, medium and long shots, live edited from the control room. Unlike cinematic cutting with its standard grammar of shot/reverse shot, live and 'as live' mixing between stationary and mobile cameras presented viewers with a focal point, revealing details of set or action to be noticed as they occurred, and enabling continuous performance of scenes (Hewett 2015, 2017), filmed in long takes, with 'open wall' establishing shots that assumed an audience viewing from the perspective of a theatre-style auditorium space (Weissman 2012: 71). An intimate model of filming, which employed close-ups of facial expression and performance to interpret dramatic content, emerged alongside an expansive style, which employed technical and cinematic devices to explore the visual potential of the medium (Jacobs 2000: 130). Multi-camera OB units additionally selected elements to film in order to construct a sense of place or atmosphere for the viewer that was 'topographically and historically meaningful' (Charney 1980: 289). Cinematic-style filming, now the norm in much television drama, typically employs a single camera to shoot repeated takes for editing, thereby increasing the scope for further adaptive work post-production.

RESTAGING THEATRE: BRITAIN

For Maurice Hindle, 'it is the TV Shakespeares initially nurtured into dramatic life and success in a theatrical context that have fared most impressively on the small screen' (2007: 241. See also Anderegg 2004: 150; and Crowl 2008: 14–16). Jacek Fabiszak, writing of Polish adaptations, suggests that 'a television theatre production can be treated as a report about a performance resembling a staging of a play' (2017: 97). More expansively John Wyver argues that 'television productions of previous stagings might more productively be regarded as doubled adaptations—adaptations (for the screen) of a text that was a staging of a Shakespeare play that was once, simply as a staged performance, an adaptation in itself' (2014: 104). All early television was broadcast live, purporting to relay content transparently, though its producers were of course selecting and shaping – and thus adapting – the material they broadcast. As filming, editing and recording technologies developed, the 'resemblance' of the televisual remake to its source shifted from what Thomas Cartelli terms a 'tributary' relationship to one of 'reposition' and even 'transposition' (1999: 15, 17), where the televisual approach enhanced or modified the style and themes of the stage production. Moreover, as television became a vital part of everyday life and video generally available, from the 1980s theatre productions began to include the medium as part of their staging (Shaughnessy 2006a), inviting forms of self-reflexivity when adapted for television.

The BBC was the first broadcaster to adapt Shakespeare for television and has the longest history of such adaptations, many of which are preserved in the BBC Shakespeare Archive.[3] Theatre provided ready-made performances, 'democratic' access to culture, educational utility and a focus for further arts and discussion programming (Bignell 2019: 153). Originally studio restagings took the form of short scenes from current productions (which continued well into the 1950s before migrating to documentaries), as well as some live broadcasts of performances in the theatre or outdoors (see Wyver 2014, 2016); however, filming theatre in the controlled setting of the studio became the preferred approach. When Independent Television (ITV), a network of regional companies funded by advertising, opened in 1955, its licenses required some educational and cultural content, and its London channels followed the BBC by broadcasting several Shakespeare theatre productions from the studio. In the 1960s the Arts Council-subsidized Royal Shakespeare and National Theatre companies were formed, and contractual arrangement with these broadcasters for full-length adaptations of their productions could justify support of these new institutions by giving cultural access to a wider audience, while their theatre directors began to oversee the adaptation of their stage work for studio broadcast in collaboration with experienced programme makers.

Adapting a stage production implies fidelity to a pre-existing interpretation, especially when filmed in the originating theatre. However, *The Wars of the Roses* (adapt. Michael Barry, dir. Michael Dews and Robin Midgley, BBC1, 1965), which restaged Peter Hall and John Barton's 1963 conflation of *Henry VI* and *Richard III* as a three-episode series shot with multiple cameras in the Stratford auditorium on an extended stage, demonstrates the medium's capacity to 're-create a theatre production in television terms' (Bakewell 1970: 231; Wyver 2013, 2019: 48–56). Labelled as an adaptation in the opening titles, it combined 'theatre, television technique and film style' (Wyver 2019: 53) to successfully translate the production's portrayal of history as a relentless, recurring cycle of violence for a television audience.[4]

Both the BBC and ITV continued to film occasional stage-derived productions in subsequent decades but by the 1990s theatre recordings were mainly commissioned from the independent production company Illuminations, headed by John Wyver, who has made important contributions to research on the history of theatre adaptations in the UK (Wyver 2019; Wrigley and Wyver forthcoming 2022). Illuminations filmed the NT *Richard II* (dir. Deborah Warner, BBC2, 1997), using a single camera cinematically, on a soundstage. However, it was Gregory Doran's RSC *Macbeth* for Channel 4 in 1999 that pointed the way to a new style of theatre adaptation.[5] Rather than reconstructing the RSC set or employing its location in the atmospheric Round House as an empty space for performance, as Tony Richardson's filmed *Hamlet* (1969) had done (Shaughnessy 2006: 69–75, Greenhalgh 2018: 27–8), its *vérité* style turned the building's architectural features into an urban battlefield, filmed in night-vision by an embedded war reporter (Greenhalgh 2003: 103–8; Huertas 2018; Wyver 2019). Subsequent adaptations combined 'real world environments and single locations' (Wyver 2014: 116) with the insertion of film footage. *Hamlet* (dir. Gregory Doran, BBC2, 2009) opened with and returned frequently to the point of view of a CCTV camera or the handheld video camera deployed by David Tennant's prince, while the location in a disused seminary added naturalistic solidity and resonance to the glassy black surfaces of the original stage design. Rupert Goold's already cinematic Chichester Festival Theatre *Macbeth* (BBC4, 2010) was given further Expressionist and horror film connotations as Welbeck Abbey was turned into the headquarters of a Soviet army, where the Porter watched military parades on television, and state and supernatural surveillance manifested as 'repeated images, unintentional and disorganized snapshots' (Huertas 2018: 98).

A return to live broadcasts of performance in 2004, when BBC4 transmitted *Measure for Measure* and *Richard II* from Shakespeare's Globe, responded to a renewed interest in creating 'event theatre' television while also resurrecting the BBC's habit of marking technological advances with Shakespeare programming. Appropriating the heritage 'authenticity' of the setting, these digital transmissions also served as demonstrations of the 'red button' interactive technology that gave access to additional information and commentary (Shaughnessy 2006; Kidnie 2008; Wyver 2014). Over a decade later the 400th anniversary of Shakespeare's death in 2016 provided the pretext for live streaming Emma Rice's controversial amplified and gender-fluid production of *A Midsummer Night's Dream* at Shakespeare's Globe.[6] Talawa's all-Black *King Lear* (dir. Bridget Caldwell, 2016) was also streamed as well as broadcast by BBC4 on Christmas Day (Rogers 2018). In addition to acknowledging the multiple screens television now occupies, these digital versions testify both to growing concern to represent demographic diversity when Shakespearean theatre is selected for adaptation, and to the impact of NT Live's 2009 introduction of digital multi-camera capture of performance for live or 'as live' broadcast to cinemas worldwide (see Aebischer, Greenhalgh and Osborne 2018). The hybridity of stage and screen that characterized Illuminations' earlier work resulted in an 'African' *Julius Caesar* (dir. Gregory Doran, BBC4, 2012) whose all-Black cast was filmed both on the RSC main stage and on location (Huertas 2019). Phyllida Lloyd's all-female and multi-racial Donmar Trilogy of *Henry IV*, *Julius Caesar* and *The Tempest* (dir. Rhodri Huw, BBC4, 2017), set in an imaginary prison, included video sequences filmed by the actors as they performed, and premiered in cinemas (Aebischer and Greenhalgh 2018). Together with Robert Icke's media-saturated production of *Hamlet* (dir. Rhodri Huw, BBC2, 2018), these cross-platform films represent both a return to the privileging of theatrical Shakespeare, and an often meta-televisual approach to capturing performance.

With theatres closed during the global lockdowns of the COVID-19 pandemic in 2020–1, the broadcast of old shows and the creation of new ones became a vital form of moral and economic support for the sector, via digital streams, television programming or the live video-conferencing software Zoom, a technology which also promoted collective, transnational online viewing and post-production discussion groups.[7] As part of its 'Culture in Quarantine' initiative the BBC collaborated with the RSC to make some of its cinema broadcasts available digitally within the UK, as educational material for schooling at home.[8] NT Live, which had previously stressed the ephemerality of its theatre broadcasts, repeating them only in 'encore seasons' in cinemas or for schools, now renegotiated with rights holders to curate a selection made freely and internationally available for viewing on a weekly basis via their YouTube Channel, National Theatre At Home.[9] Though donations provided a small income stream the main benefit was the popularization of streamed theatre, and the NT brand in particular.

As well as extending access to performances on multiple platforms the constraints of the pandemic led to new forms of socially distanced, intermedial adaptation.

Simon Godwin filmed his *Romeo and Juliet*, which was due to premiere in 2020 in the National Theatre's Olivier, for international streaming. Performed in rehearsal rooms, and onstage behind the safety curtain, this much-trimmed, multicultural version of the play is intercut with film montage that foretells its tragic outcome. Instead of live broadcasting Erica Whyman's pandemic-postponed *The Winter's Tale* to cinemas the RSC recorded it onstage for transmission as part of the BBC's 'virtual festival of theatre staged in lockdown', *Lights Up* (dir. Bridget Caldwell, BBC4, 2021). The production explicitly acknowledges its shift to televisual remediation. Leontes confides his paranoia direct to the camera, the 1950s setting for the play's earlier acts features a televised show trial, broadcast in grainy black and white, while Perdita, Florizel and their guests play up to the home-movie camera as footage of the sheep-shearing festivities is screened 'as live'. As producers of their own media content theatre companies have replaced the television studio with the stage as location, thereby gaining back some of the adaptive agency previously ceded to broadcasters.

MADE-FOR-TV SHAKESPEARE: BRITAIN

The role of producer is as significant as that of the director or script adaptor in shaping an adaptation, through decisions about production team, resources and the intended role in the schedules (for example as an educational programme or as part of a general drama series). The choice of play and the approach taken depends on a number of interrelated factors. These include production costs like Union-negotiated employment restrictions, the type of filming and time allocated to it and the cuts needed. The view expressed by drama producer Gerald Savory is typical: 'There is scarcely a normal stage play that is not improved by some judicious editing. The plays themselves will be properly adapted for TV and sufficiently extended in setting to remove any feeling of staginess about the production' (cited by Smart 2014).

An *Age of Kings* (adapt. Eric Crozier, dir. Michael Hayes, 1961) was an early example of 'proper' adaptation, and a series in itself. Peter Dews, who had previously adapted and directed *Henry V* as *The Life of Henry V* (BBC, 1957) with the Chorus as a presenter in what was unmistakably a television studio, now produced Shakespeare's eight English history plays as a fifteen-part serial which blended the theatrical with the televisual. It was filmed live with a repertory-style cast of theatre actors, shooting with four cameras and a crane on composite studio sets that could be rearranged for each episode. Each play (except *Henry VI, Part I*) was allocated two episodes, between 60 and 75 minutes long, and given a new title, indicating the central action or theme, from 'The Hollow Crown' to 'The Boar Hunt'. As Emma Smith notes, '*An Age of Kings* is both serial – a segmented narrative structured towards a final conclusion, the accession of Henry VII after his victory at Bosworth Field – and series – an ongoing and potentially inconclusive unfolding of historical process' (2006: 138). Viewed in terms of televisual aesthetics, as well as form, the show is revolutionary. Close-ups replace pageantry, shots develop slowly rather than through intercutting and employ televisual effects such as image overlays and characters reflected in others' eyes. Moments of direct address to camera allow the audience to scrutinize the motives and machinations of the medieval politicians as they now did contemporary ones through the television medium.[10]

As videotape filming and recording became viable, the international, if niche, marketability of Shakespeare encouraged further adaptations with high production values. For the 400th anniversary of Shakespeare's birth in 1964 the BBC showcased new developments in broadcasting in *Hamlet at Elsinore* (dir. Philip Saville, BBC1), the first full-length outside broadcast drama production recorded on video, made in collaboration with Danish television. The adaptation exploited the setting of Kronberg Castle with *cinema verité* camerawork and echo chamber sound, and was later broadcast in North America and given a cinema screening in New York. ITV's engagement with the centenary was also noteworthy for its blend of popular and high cultural elements. Rediffusion's lavish studio *A Midsummer Night's Dream* (dir. Joan Kemp-Welch) stressed spectacle, using 'many-layered gauzes and complicated lighting to suggest a magical woodland setting' (Wrigley 2014: 414) complete with balletic sequences set to Mendelssohn. The broadcast attracted an audience of several million on Midsummer's Day by casting comedians familiar to ITV audiences as the mechanicals. A month earlier the Beatles had mocked the 1964 celebrations by launching a television music special with an irreverent skit of the 'Pyramus and Thisbe' play on a scaffolding mock-up of an Elizabethan theatre, complete with screaming fans clearly there to hear the group, not Shakespeare (Hansen 2010; Geddes 2012). Subsequent ITV productions were unashamedly vehicles for star performances. *Hamlet* (dir. Peter Wood, ATV, 1970), filmed on location in England in an elaborate Regency setting for America's *Hallmark Hall of Fame,* starred Richard Chamberlain, then still well known for his role in the medical drama series *Dr. Kildare* (NBC, 1961–6). ITV's investment in star-studded Shakespeare culminated in 1983 with Granada's studio production of *King Lear* (dir. Michael Elliott), starring Laurence Olivier. Billed as 'Laurence Olivier Presents' the production was set in a pre-Christian England, complete with Stonehenge, in a style reminiscent of Victorian theatrical historicism, and filmed in a combination of close-ups and more cinematic zooms and overhead shots.

The pictorialist approach to *King Lear* was similar to that taken earlier by South African producer Cedric Messina who was in charge of several BBC drama series, including *Play of the Month* (BBC1, 1965–83) for ten years from 1967, making him 'the most powerful and prolific figure in the history of television adaptations of stage plays in Britain' (Smart forthcoming 2022), dedicated to 'thumping good established plays with super casts' (cited in Nicholson 1970: 53). Aiming to create 'productions of tremendous visual pleasure' (Smart 2015: 68) in addition to overseeing nine Shakespeare productions including his own *The Merchant of Venice* (BBC1, 1972) he initiated the ambitious Time-Life sponsored project to televise the complete works of Shakespeare (1978–85) as 'straightforward' adaptations with 'no arty-crafty shooting' (Andrews 1979: 136). Although an advocate of using scenic locations for classic plays, having originated the *Shakespeare Plays* project whilst he was filming at Glamis Castle in Scotland, only two of the adaptations were filmed on location: *As You Like It* (dir. Basil Coleman, 1978), at Glamis, and *Henry VIII* (dir. Kevin Billington, 1978) in various English castles and great houses. While the adaptations Messina oversaw often gained favourable audience responses (Smart forthcoming 2022) his productions were judged mundane by colleagues, leading to his replacement by Jonathan Miller after two seasons. Miller applied his theories about adapting Shakespeare's plays to the two-dimensional naturalism of television by treating the screen in a painterly, perspectival manner, in studio settings derived from sixteenth- and seventeenth-century art.[11] Theatre directors Elijah Moshinsky and Jane Howell brought a readiness to adapt even more thoroughly. Moshinsky cut and deconstructed texts, while Howell's overtly theatrical approach to *Henry VI* and *Richard III* engaged viewers through its serial form, echoing *An Age of Kings* by employing an ensemble cast taking several roles in an adventure playground set. Despite these achievements and although audience response was often very favourable to individual productions, the series was in effect criticized for not adapting bravely enough (Wells 1982: 266).

The Animated Tales (adapt. Leon Garfield, S4C, 1992–4) was a more inventive series of adaptations, which turned thirteen plays into half-hour versions for children, through techniques of cell animation, puppetry and glass painting by Russian animators. As Laurie Osborne observes, these encouraged children 'to understand the plays cinematically rather than theatrically or literarily' (1997: 103). Subsequently only three made-for-TV adaptations were made by the BBC in the 1990s, all for the *Performance* series produced by the theatre and film director Simon Curtis (BBC2, 1991–8), two of them by stage directors. *Measure for Measure* (dir. David Thacker, 1994), constructed a futuristic Vienna in which television served a surveillance state. John Caird's heavily cut conflation of *Henry IV, Parts 1 and Two* (1995) fused expressive lighting, stylized sets and theatrical blocking with intimate close-ups, while Penny Woolcock's *Macbeth on the Estate* (1997) pointed in the direction that Shakespeare adaptation would take in the twenty-first-century. It had its origins in her documentary *Shakespeare on the Estate* (BBC2, 1994), in which the theatre director Michael Bogdanov attempted to rehearse and perform Shakespeare speeches with the inhabitants of a Birmingham council estate (Greenhalgh 2003). The juxtaposition of Shakespeare's language, a multicultural setting, documentary style and employment of tropes from contemporary TV crime drama made *Macbeth on the Estate* a precursor of the twenty-first century 'new wave' films identified by Cartelli and Rowe. These, they argue, approach the Shakespearean text and its performances 'as a literary, auditory, and visual archive ripe for reinvigoration', creating a 'sense of artifice or anachronism… the archaism of speaking Shakespearean language in a hyper-modern setting… [and] dwell on the materials and manufacture of text and image' (2007: 37).

The 2000s saw further growth in versions of Shakespeare plays reformatted to fit the evolving genres of television or retold in contemporary terms and language within a media environment shifting increasingly to productions commissioned from independent companies. Following Andrew Davies's vernacular reworking of *Othello* (dir. Geoffrey Sax, ITV, 2001) as a study of institutional racism in London's police force, in 2005 the BBC commissioned four adaptations for the BBC1 *Shakespeare Re-Told* series: *Much Ado About Nothing* (adapt. David Nicholls, dir.

Brian Percival), *Macbeth* (adapt. Peter Moffatt, dir. Mark Brozel), *The Taming of the Shrew* (adapt. Sally Wainwright, dir. Dave Richards) and *A Midsummer Night's Dream* (adapt. Peter Bowker, dir. Ed Fraiman), the latter two overseen by the Black producer Pier Wilkie. Each re-contextualizes the play in a contemporary setting: a television company, a political marriage, a high-end restaurant and a holiday park. The presence of character names, occasional lines from the original, and the meta-televisual settings, together with transmedial elements from cinematic romantic comedies (Pittman 2010: 137–76), produce a series which 'simultaneously enacts and disrupts expectations of "Shakespeare" as a generic category' (Kidnie 2008: 114).[12]

Even when Shakespeare's language is retained, changes to settings, plot and televisual cross-cutting within scenes can create a sense that the adaptation is a retelling. The 2016 anniversary of Shakespeare's death saw a version of *A Midsummer Night's Dream* (dir. David Kerr, BBC1) by celebrated television writer, Russell T. Davies. His mischievous 90-minute adaptation sets the play in an Orwellian, patriarchal and multiracial Athens in which a tyrannical Theseus holds Titania's fairy lover, Hippolyta, prisoner until his death frees everyone to choose their partner regardless of gender. Richard Eyre's *King Lear* (Amazon Studios, BBC2, 2018) cut the play to 'the bones of the narrative' (cited in Smith 2019: 2). With a high-powered cast including Antony Hopkins as the dispossessed king, the film portrayed post-Brexit Britain as a military dictatorship, mapping its divided terrain cinematically, from London's Shard and the Tower of London, via *Downton Abbey*-style stately homes, to despoiled and bombed-out landscapes peopled by refugees and the urban poor (see O'Neill 2019). Netflix's *The King* (adapt. David Michôt and Joel Edgerton, dir. David Michôt, Netflix, 2019) rewrites *Henry IV* and *Henry V* by turning Hal's two surrogate father figures, Falstaff and the Lord Chief Justice, into their opposites: Edgerton's Falstaff dies bravely at Agincourt, and Gascoigne, having used a false French assassination plot to start the war, is killed by Henry in the film's finale.

MADE-FOR-TV SHAKESPEARE: NORTH AMERICA

Early Shakespeare adaptations on commercial American television emerged from limited programming options, a licensing requirement to offer educational content, and sponsorship by companies seeking to reach middle-class consumers (Freedman 2007: 54–5). The first networked Shakespeare adaptation was NBC's *Twelfth Night*, a 60-minute version aptly aired a day after Shakespeare's traditional birthday on 24 April 1947, in the *Television Theatre* series sponsored by Philco, with commercial breaks only at beginning and end.[13] A 60-minute classically-set *Julius Caesar* (adapt. Worthington Miner, dir. Paul Nickell, CBS, 1949) is the earliest surviving recording, acclaimed by the *New York Times* reviewer for its mobile camerawork, framing of actors and use of voice-over:

> it provided a new insight into what television can be: the perfect integration of a host of older arts into a new form which stands on its own. It had the elusive

quality of kaleidoscopic oneness, with its appeal being rooted in the unorthodox use of the orthodox tools of stage craft.

(Gould cited in Rose 1986: 194)

Between 1949 and 1958 the productions of Shakespeare made for CBS's *Studio One* series, sponsored by Westinghouse, varied between conventionally staged and shot adaptations, and others utilizing developing television technologies, such as prerecorded soliloquies or superimposed images, or responding to new directions in contemporary staging. *Romeo and Juliet* (dir. Albert McCleery, 1949), for example, was played in the round and filmed from different angles by multiple cameras. However, experimentation did not necessarily produce new readings of the plays. Framed by advertising aimed at the female consumer, *The Taming of the Shrew* (dir. Paul Nickell) employs its contemporary setting and use of voice-over 'to legitimate the domestication of women' rather than visualize gender roles differently (Henderson 2003: 126).

The adaptations that most skillfully blended theatre and television were those made for *The Hallmark Hall of Fame* series (NBC, 1953–), which partnered British actor Maurice Evans with producer George Schaefer; they had previously collaborated on stage productions for American servicemen during the war. *Hamlet* (1953) used nineteenth-century costumes from the original 'G.I.' stage production and was filmed live by five centrally placed cameras with booms on four scaffolds to ensure sound quality. In an early example of television Shakespeare's role in representing the Special Relationship between America and Britain (see Breight 2008) footage of Elizabeth II's coronation the previous year – a major landmark in British broadcasting – preceded the two-hour broadcast of *Richard II* (1954). The *Hallmark* series was also one of the first shot in colour, a sign of its prestige status, and its studio productions were designed to take full advantage of the new technology through elaborate or stylized sets and costumes. *Macbeth* (1960) was recorded on location in Scotland, and later released as a film, presaging the shift to more cinematic modes of shooting drama as cameras became more lightweight and mobile and celluloid came into use for television filming. By contrast *The Tempest* (1960) was filmed in colour on videotape, in a fantastical setting reminiscent of contemporary science-fiction movies, and employed post-production image superimposition for Ariel's magic.

Across the border Canada's colonial history was evident in CBC's long tradition of broadcasting Shakespeare on radio, much of it the work of British producers. The first television production was *Othello* (1953), directed by British actor-turned-producer David Greene and starring Lorne Greene as a blackface Moor. Comparing it with NBC's *Hamlet* the same year, Alice Venezky Griffin judged its intimate style 'a more genuinely artistic and successful effort to present Shakespeare in the television medium... the camera was used to good advantage to establish relationships, to reveal subtle reactions through closeup, and to focus on the significant detail in a key scene' (1953: 335). Greene subsequently directed *Hamlet* and *Macbeth* in 1955, casting several British actors. In 1961, having previously directed a Stratford (Ontario) Festival Theatre production of *Julius Caesar* for television, Paul Almond, another British producer, with experience at ITV's Granada, serialized *Macbeth* for schools in five parts, with Zoe Caldwell and Sean Connery – fresh from success as Hotspur in the BBC's *An Age of Kings* – in the leading roles. Performed on abstract sets with angled camera shots focused on the actors' faces it 'made a substantial effort to serve as a revolutionary educational tool' (Van Wagner 2004). Apart from *Othello, the Tragedy of the Moor* (dir. Zaib Sheikh, Governor Pictures, 2008), which was developed by actors in the Canadian sitcom *Little Mosque on the Prairies* and portrayed Othello as an Islamic North African, CBC has mainly broadcast Stratford Festival productions, including those originally filmed for cinema. Even the spinoff *Slings and Arrows* (writ. Susan Coyne, Mark McKinney and Bob Martin, dir. Paul Wellington, Rhombus Media, 2003–6) shadows Stratford with its fictional New Burbage Festival, self-reflexively combining embedded Shakespeare productions with the conventions of workplace drama series (Wright 2017), and building its three seasons around *Hamlet*, *Macbeth* and *King Lear* to explore different stages of life and the survival of theatre in a media-dominated world.[14]

From the 1960s onward, America's National Educational Television (NET) and its successor PBS broadcast many of the BBC and ITV restagings and made-for-TV adaptations (some of them co-produced with American broadcasters) in series such as *Masterpiece Theatre* (1971–) and *Great Performances* (1971–), strengthening the identification of televisual 'quality' with British cultural offerings and acting. As Richard Burt points out, no real distinction was made between restagings or made-for-TV modes, or between rewritten versions or those retaining Shakespeare's language: all were 'Shakespeare' (2003: 15–16). While several productions by US companies exploited American settings, two 'retellings' situate plays explicitly in relation to US colonial history. Starring and produced by Patrick Stewart, *King Lear* (adapt. Stephen Harrington, dir. Uli Edel, Turner Television Network, 2002), is set during Texas's wars with Mexico (see Kapitaniak 2019). *The Tempest* (adapt. James S. Henerson, dir. Jack Bender, Bonnie Raskin Production and NBC Studios, 1998) acknowledges postcolonial readings and appropriations of the play by setting it on a Southern plantation in the American Civil War. Prosper learns his magic from one of his black slaves, the mother of Ariel, and uses it to help the Unionists defeat the Confederate army for which his brother spies. Bender would go on to be executive producer and episode director of *Lost* (ABC, 2004–10), a *Tempest*-like series that uses survivors marooned on a desert island to explore philosophical themes and narrative mysteries. *Lost* is credited by Jason Mittell as one of the 'complex TV' series which characterize contemporary storytelling on twenty-first-century television, generating the 'forensic fandom' and transmedia narratives discussed next (2006, 2010).

DIGITAL AND ON DEMAND: 'SHAKESPEARES' ON TWENTY-FIRST-CENTURY TELEVISION

During the last decades of the twentieth century, the television industry was becoming an increasingly competitive and global marketplace. Deregulation in the US during the 1970s and 1980s weakened the network 'oligopoly' of NBC, CBS and ABC. Independent cable and satellite companies now offered video on demand by subscription or pay-to-view, 'freeing the audience and the text from rigid weekly schedules, offering subscription options that eliminate commercials, creating or finding new audiences and new formats' (Thorburn 2019: 163). John Caldwell (1995: *passim*) argues that it was this rivalry that generated the innovations in primetime content and style that he terms 'televisuality', fostering an appreciation of television aesthetics and narrative complexity. As internet access, bandwidth and data capacity increased, digital media content became available on home computers, on 'smart' television sets and on mobile devices. This in turn encouraged forms of transnational and transmedia storytelling for devoted and participatory audiences of multi-platform programmes, which could be viewed, debated and analysed forensically, in online fan communities (Jenkins 2006; Mittell 2010, Pearson and Messenger Davies 2014). Home Box Office (HBO) began producing its own original content in the 1990s, inaugurating a 'post-television' era with its slogan 'It's not television. It's HBO'. Netflix, which had launched as a video-on-demand service in the 1970s, began a digital streaming service in 1997, providing a 'library' of films and television programmes as well as 'publishing' its own premium content from 2013. By making all episodes of a series available at once, Netflix also encouraged the practice of binge-watching, thereby significantly altering the experience of television seriality. YouTube, with its mix of harvested archive video and individuals' own created content, launched in 2005 (see Desmet 2014; O'Neill 2014), Amazon Prime Video in 2006. In the UK, the BBC's license fee funding gave it some stability (though also vulnerability to government pressure) and the means to plan for new digital channels, BBC Four (2002–) and BBC Three (2003–16). As the High Definition video format became standard, 'quality' or 'high end' television was identified by its 'multivalent visual idiom' (Wray 2021: 5) and its insatiable appetite for material to adapt in serial form.

SERIALITY AND SHAKESPEARE

Since the millennium a number of long-form drama series have appeared that include fleeting citations of Shakespeare or draw intermittently on character types and narratives from the plays. Christina Wald poses some pertinent questions about these Shakespearean 'returns':

> Do we need direct intertextual references, comments by writers themselves, or other material that proves their knowledge of Shakespeare's plays? Or can we assume a more indirect cultural influence of his plays on modern culture? Should we avoid the risk of obsessive readings that detect Shakespearean traces in later works simply because we as early modern scholars are so familiar with his oeuvre, or should we acknowledge that intertextual relations are created by readers as much as by authors?

(2020: 8)

American series originating in the network era like *Star Trek* (which first aired on NBC in 1966) still regularly employ Shakespeare allusions (notably to *Henry V* and *The Tempest*) together with what Wells-Lassagne calls 'microadaptations': occasional themed episodes that introduce difference into the story arcs of familiar characters via Shakespearean content (2017: 21). 'The Shakespeare Code' episode of the science-fiction drama series *Doctor Who* (BBC1, 2007) portrays Shakespeare saving the world with the language that has attracted alien witches to earth and identifies his 'dark lady' as the Doctor's black companion, Martha Jones. *The West Wing* (NBC, 1999–2006) uses Shakespeare to depict the nature and dilemmas of presidential government; as with *Star Trek*'s Jean-Luc Picard (played by the Shakespearean actor Patrick Stewart) Shakespeare references serve to underscore Josiah Bartlett's liberal humanism and capacity to lead, as well as the 'academic elitism' denounced by his Republican rivals. The episode 'Posse Comitatus' (writ. Aaron Sorkin, dir. Alex Graveskin, 2002) parallels the staging of a musical version of the English history plays with the decision to assassinate a foreign leader in an 'act of war', the tragic consequences of which play out in successive series. Patrick Finn argues that *The West Wing*'s endorsement of an American policy of 'muscular liberalism' is affirmed by 'the political and historical resonance' that accompanies Shakespeare's histories, without 'the limitations of direct allusion' (2004: 19, 18). By contrast, in *Westworld* (HBO, 2016–) individual lines from *Romeo and Juliet*, *Henry IV*, *Julius Caesar*, *Hamlet*, *King Lear* and *The Tempest* are constantly 'dislocated and replanted' from their dramatic contexts, haunting the theme park's Prospero-like creator and his creations as a virus or 'glitch' that both disrupts the robots' coding, triggering 'violent ends', and re-boots them as fully human (Hatchuel 2019; Bronfen 2020; Wald 2020; O'Neill 2021).

Other long-form series such as *The Sopranos* (HBO, 1999–2007) and *Breaking Bad* (Netflix, 2008–2013) have been deemed 'Shakespearean' not for any overt references but rather as a signifier of their complex, powerful (predominantly white male) characters and intensive psychological exploration of actions, motives and moral choices (Wrathall 2013; Chisum 2019). They are mainly the creation of male auteurs and executive producers, who act as showrunners for teams of researchers, writers and directors. Netflix's first original in-house production, the six-season series *House of Cards* (2013–18), drew from Andrew Davies's four-part 'Jacobean' adaptation of a Michael Dobbs novel for the BBC (dir. Paul Seed, BBC1, 1990), illustrating the significance of remakes in contemporary television. Francis Urquhart's Richard III-cum-Macbeth-style climb to Parliamentary power was embodied in the Shakespearean actor Ian Richardson's adroit handling of direct address. David Fincher and Beau Willimon's version cast Kevin Spacey, who had played Richard III on stage, as Machiavellian Frank Underwood, intent on becoming President of the United States at any cost. As Wells-Lassagne observes 'Long-running series in particular tend to fairly quickly outstrip their source material, leading them to almost systematically add in plotlines and characters' (2017: 7). The role of Claire Underwood, with its Lady Macbeth style connotations, expanded until, after Spacey's firing from the show, the series concluded with her own murderous ascent to presidential office. Bronfen has analysed this representation both in terms of Shakespeare's portrayal of villainous and compliant 'mother' queens and the role played by female presidents in American political drama series (2020: Ch. 3).

In *Succession* (HBO, 2018–), created by the British screenwriter Jesse Armstrong, the 'references to *Hamlet*, *Othello*, *Richard II*, *Coriolanus*, and *Macbeth* remain brief and superficial, a source of hermeneutic pleasure and dramatic irony, but *King Lear* informs the action… profoundly' (Wald 2020: 128). The series adapts elements of Armstrong's unproduced screenplay about media mogul Rupert Murdoch into a narrative that takes as its opening premise a ruler who does not abdicate but instead prolongs choosing a successor among his three children. Each of them competes as much for his love as for control of the global media conglomerate, Waystar Royco. The casting of the Scottish actor Brian Cox as Logan Roy, like Spacey in *House of Cards* (Pittman 2020a), underscores the character's complexity through association with the actor's theatrical background – Cox has played many Shakespearean roles, including Lear at the National Theatre in 1990. The super-rich lifestyle the characters enjoy provides an extravagant scenescape of mansions and castles, equivalent to the 'stories of kings and their palaces' that Aaron Sorkin wanted to contemporize in *The West Wing* (cited in Finn 2004: 18). The characters talk of themselves as courtiers or 'attendant lords', flattering and plotting their way to the centre of power. The Season Two episode 'Hunting' (writ. Tony Roche, dir. Andrij Parekh, 2019) depicts Logan, in a display of 'unhinged power' (Armstrong 2019), bullying his company executives into a humiliating game in the feudal setting of a Hungarian hunting lodge. Armstrong's background writing black political comedy such as *The Thick of It* (BBC Four and BBC Two, 2005–12) contributes to a series also noteworthy for its language, veering between artfully repeated clichéd exchanges and baroque, graphically violent and sexual metaphorical insults. In 'Tern Haven' (writ. Will Tracey, dir. Mark Mylod, 2019), the WASP family owners of long-established, revered newspapers that Logan targets for takeover deploy Shakespeare speeches as 'grace' before dinner. When they refuse Logan's offer he responds with his 'favourite Shakespeare quotation: Take the fucking money!' – a riposte that invites the viewer to acknowledge the series' rewriting of *King Lear* while simultaneously invoking irreverence towards the high culture elitism represented by Shakespeare.

Shakespeare infiltrates other television genres as well. Bronfen has 'crossmapped' the war games played out in the Baltimore drug trade in David Simon's *The Wire* (HBO, 2002–8) with the civil conflict of Shakespeare's histories in terms of their serial violence and resistance to closure (2020: 58–84), while Pittman (2020b) points to the way the series challenges white privilege by making tragic protagonists of its young black criminals. A long tradition of referencing Shakespeare in westerns continues in *Deadwood* (HBO, 2004–6), created by David Milch. As in *Succession* the 'Shakespearean' register of the characters' language manifests as an 'Elizabethan-like ornateness' that often coexists with obscenity (Benz 2007: 240). Shakespeare also signals theatricality, so that for Bronfen (2020) *Deadwood*'s inhabitants feature as players on a stage, directed by larger political and economic forces, as the lawless frontier settlement must become an orderly part of the American nation, while Susan Ronnenberg (2018) links *Deadwood*'s seriality with the Henriad. For Amy Rodgers, television's serialized dramas can be a means by which audiences gain historical information and understanding. Terming this 'entertainment historiography', she argues that such drama 'references its own fictional and typological genealogy as much as its cultural past and present… [and] tends to place past and present in a dialectic where the present echoes (rather than simply repeats) the past' (2015: 143).

Shakespeare's portrayal of the Wars of the Roses is also one source for George R. R. Martin's novel series, *A Song of Ice and Fire*: the Starks replacing the York dynasty, the Lannisters the Lancastrians and the Targaryens the Tudors. The television adaptation, *Game of Thrones* (adapt. David Benioff, D. B. Weiss and George Martin, HBO, 2011–19) draws on 'the literary strategies and achievements in Shakespeare's first tetralogy' (Wilson 2021: 17), grounding its fantasy setting in serial political machinations and bloody warfare, and echoing characters and situations from *Macbeth* and *Titus Andronicus*, among others.

The popularity of high-end serial drama was no doubt a factor when the film and theatre director Sam Mendes proposed that his Neal Street Productions company (with NBC Universal and WNET Thirteen), should film the English histories for the BBC, as part of the cultural festival accompanying the 2012 Olympic Games in London. *The Hollow Crown*, like *An Age of Kings* and *The Wars of the Roses* in the 1960s, encapsulated a reconfiguring of television Shakespeare as serial, in the form of 'quality drama that incorporates even as it exceeds the cinematic' (Wray 2021: 14). Apart from Thea Shurrock, who directed *Henry V*, the directors, Rupert Goold (*Richard II*) and Richard Eyre (*Henry IV, Parts 1 and 2*), were experienced in film as well as theatre. As Weisseman observes, prestige UK drama now exhibits a 'hybrid filmic performance style ... marked by greater emphasis on action, location shooting and the spectacle of the landscape' (2012: 80, 82). Filmed on location in England and Wales with a budget large enough to people its striking mise en scènes with the cream of British film, television and theatre acting, the series is an example of the 'heritage brand' which associates Britain with 'elitism, high culture, classic literature, and orderly society' (Selznick 2008: 76). However, as Ramona Wray observes, frequent sombre settings create an 'anti-heritage landscape' (2016: 474). She argues that Mendes occupies the role of showrunner, and that all four plays, their narratives centred on the male protagonists, 'refract one of the central concerns of Mendes's cinematic career—masculinity in crisis' (474), while each director also imposes his or her own adaptive style. *Richard II*, co-adapted by Goold and Ben Power, displays the visual cohesiveness evident in Goold's *Macbeth*, creating a sumptuous, religion-inflected court as background to the king's self-regarding performance of monarchy (see Wray 2021). Eyre contrasts this with the wintry bleakness of Henry's guilt-ridden and war-weary reign, while Power's adaptation of *Henry V* extends the role of the Chorus: as Falstaff's Boy he witnesses the war and its aftermath, the waste of military lives symbolized by the tattered English flag he clutches in the final sequence.

The Wars of the Roses (adapt. Ben Power, dir. Dominic Cooke, BBC2, 2016) screened in the UK at a time of national disunity. Paralleling the speaking of lines from *Richard II* (3.2.155–60) at the start of *The Hollow Crown*, the three-part series begins with a choric voice-over by Judi Dench (who also plays the Duchess of York) as the camera zooms in on the White Cliffs of Dover – although here citing Odysseus's speech in *Troilus and Cressida*:

Take but degree away, untune that string
And hark, what discord follows!

(1.3.85–8, 109–10)

Broadcast during a divisive national campaign the month before Britain's referendum on leaving the European Union, the contemporary political resonance was clear and very different from the celebratory mood of the 2012 Olympics. The red cross of St George (a symbol of English nationalism) that had dominated the mise en scène of Part One reappeared; even more frequently than in the previous series, the productions ratcheted up the emotional cost of war through extreme close-ups, battlefield points of view (often obscured by visors or glimpsed from hiding places) and graphic portrayal of the results of violence recalling *Game of Thrones* (Wollaston 2016; Gerzic 2019; Wilson 2021), culminating in a CGI-enhanced drone shot of hundreds of dead soldiers on Bosworth Field. Colourblind casting had been promised when the project was first announced (Rogers 2013: 405–7) but, with the exception of Sophie Okenedo's casting as Margaret, black or mixed-race actors played only minor roles in both series. As Jennifer Votava (2020) argues, a colour-conscious reading of Okenedo's portrayal reveals the contradictions attendant on adapting a white version of a nation's history for a multiracial and transnational television audience. Margaret's meaning shifts throughout the series, beginning as a transgressive foreigner and vicious revenger and ending as a grieving prophetess, whose mirror reveals the truth to her enemies, and ensures Richard's death at Bosworth (see also Pittman 2017; Rycroft 2020). In contrast to the providentialist reading of history in *An Age of Kings*, *The Hollow Crown*'s representation of race and gender 'weaves contested histories into its serial progress from start to finish' (Elliott 2018: 85).

Peter Morgan and Stephen Daldry's *The Crown* (HBO, 2016–) is another example of entertainment historiography, exploiting 'the uncanny symbiosis' that Shakespeare's texts have with British royalty (Wilson 2017: 77). Though less explicitly than *To Play the King* (BBC1, 1993: the second series of the BBC *House of Cards*) or the made-for-TV version of Mike Bartlett's verse drama *King Charles III* (BBC2, adapt. Mike Bartlett, dir. Rupert Goold, 2017), *The Crown* employs a Shakespearean lens through which to examine 'the way power – real and symbolic – functions in our name' (Morgan 2013: 16). The series is a chronicle history for our time, ticking off the political events that in the writers' view mirror the decline of postwar Britain. At the same time it is 'personalized' history (Otnes and Maclaran 2015: 137), projecting 'the monarchy as composed of human beings with passions, turmoil, and temptations' (142), attracting calls from Conservative Government ministers that its fictional status be acknowledged in its credits. The series draws on Shakespeare's versions of monarchy and implicitly on Kantorowicz's expounding of the medieval and early modern political theology of the king's 'body natural' and the 'body politic' to depict Elizabeth II as both fallible mother, wife and sister and as the royal icon. In what could be considered a form of the 'media allegories' Peter Donaldson has analysed (2012), the series self-reflexively explores the role and history of television, both in the performative 'show' of royalty and in the way the 'Royal Firm' is constantly watching events over which they have no power unfold on their television screens.

This chapter, like much previous scholarship, has concentrated on the large and often internationally distributed archive of British and North American adaptations.

Fabiszak's studies of Polish theatre adaptations (2005) and Hatchuel and Vienne-Guerrin's contextualization of the ways versions in the 1960s and 1970s were adapted to French culture (2008b) point the way to further comparative research into Shakespeare's televisual adaptation within national media ecologies. As well as the many theatre restagings, made-for-TV versions and retellings by European broadcasters, plays have inspired Brazilian soap operas (Marino 2011), Japanese *anime* for children (Minami 2016) and a wide range of Asian media texts, some of which are available on the *MIT Global Shakespeares Video and Performance Archive* website. Television's global marketplace continues to find a place for the Shakespeare brand, and Shakespeareans will continue to find many reasons to take its diverse and evolving adaptations seriously.

NOTES

1   For reasons of length and focus this chapter deals only with Anglo-American adaptations. Information about theatre restagings and made-for-TV versions by European and Asian broadcasters can be found in the *BUFVC: International Database of Shakespeare on Film, Television and Radio,* some of which are discussed in volumes in the *Shakespeare on Screen* series (2005–19).

2   In addition to the BBC Shakespeare Archive a number of Spanish made-for-TV adaptations are available via links on the MIT Global Shakespeares Video and Performance Archive website: https://globalshakespeares.mit.edu.

3   The BBC's first Shakespeare broadcast was Act 3, scene 2 of *As You Like It*, four months after the service opened in February 1937. The earliest surviving adaptation is *Romeo and Juliet* (1955). Surviving BBC adaptations are freely available online to British educational institutions on the educational recording agency (era) website, https://era.org.uk/shakespeare-archive/.

4   The series was repeated on BBC2 in January and February 1966, divided into fifteen episodes with titles, on the model of *An Age of King*, and sold to overseas broadcasters in this form.

5   Channel 4 opened in the UK as a not-for-profit commercially funded channel with a public service ethos. Adaptations include two further restagings: Kenneth Branagh's *Twelfth Night* (dir. Paul Kafno, 1988) and Trevor Nunn's RSC *King Lear* (dir. Chris Hunt, 2008). Three made-for-TV versions were originally schools programmes: *The Merchant of Venice* (adapt. Margaret Glover, dir. Alan Horrox, 1996), *Macbeth* (dir. Michael Bogdanov, 1998) and *Twelfth Night* (dir. Tim Supple, 2003).

6   The production was also made available internationally for six months on the 'Shakespeare Lives' website sponsored by the British Council.

7   See Aebischer (2022) and reviews in *Cahiers Élisabéthains* 103 (1), 2021, *Shakespeare* 2020, 2021, and *Shakespeare Bulletin* 38 (3), 2020, for responses to these lockdown theatre screenings.

8   At the time of writing, twenty of these can be watched on the BBC/ITV subscription archive, BritBox, which is advertised on British television by a cartoon Shakespeare.

9   This has since been launched as a subscription channel (https://www.ntathome. com/). In May 2021, Amazon announced an agreement to stream selected NT Live productions on Amazon Prime in the UK.

10   The expense of the series was justified not only by high audience appreciation in the UK but also abroad. When shown in America by National Educational Television (NET) it was 'the most acclaimed series of its era' (Hoberman 2009; see Crane 1961; Kiley and Marder 1961 for contemporary reviews), prompting the calls for more quality programming which led in time to the establishment of the Public Broadcasting Service (PBS).

11   Miller's style of directing is the subject of the documentary *Jonathan Miller Directs: The Making of Antony and Cleopatra*, (dir. Eszter Nordin, BBC2, 1981).

12   *Shakespeare Re-Told* may have influenced the *Shakespeare in Mzanzi* series which retells *Macbeth*, *Romeo and Juliet* and *King Lear* in South African settings and languages (SAB, 2008). See Seef (2017, 2018).

13   A student production of *Twelfth Night* (WRGB, 1943) may have been the first broadcast on American television (Hawes 1964). Another student production, *Julius Caesar*, the first at the Folger Shakespeare Library in Washington DC, was live broadcast by NBC in 1949 and restaged (dir. Paul Nickell) for transmission with *Macbeth* (dir. Garry Simpson) for NBC's *Philco Television Playhouse* drama series of adaptations of plays and novels.

14   The series has since been remade for Brazilian television as *Sound and Fury* (*Som & Furia*) (dir. Fernando Meirelles, Globo TV, 2009).

REFERENCES

Aebischer, P. (2022), *Viral Shakespeare: Performance in the Time of Covid*, Cambridge: Cambridge University Press.

Aebischer, P., S. Greenhalgh and L. Osborne, eds (2018), *Shakespeare and the 'Live' Theatre Broadcast Experience*, London: Bloomsbury.

Aebischer, P. and S. Greenhalgh (2018), 'Introduction: Shakespeare and the "Live" Theatre Broadcast Experience', in P. Aebischer, S. Greenhalgh and L.E. Osborne (eds), *Shakespeare and the 'Live' Theatre Broadcast Experience*, 1–16, London: Bloomsbury.

Anderegg, M. (2004), 'Electronic Shakespeares: Televisual Histories', in *Cinematic Shakespeare*, Landham, 148–76, Lanham, MD: Rowman & Littlefield.

Andrews, J. (1979), 'Interview: Cedric Messina Discusses the Shakespeare Plays', *Shakespeare Quarterly* 30 (2): 134–7.

Armstrong, J. (2019), 'Episode 3: Inside the Episode', HBO: *Succession*, https://www.hbo.com/succession/season2/3-hunting (accessed 12 February 2021)

Bakewell, M. (1970), 'The Television Production', in J. Barton and P. Hall, *The Wars of the Roses: Adapted for the Royal Shakespeare Company from William Shakespeare's Henry VI, Parts I, II, III and Richard III*, 231–36, Chatham: British Broadcasting Corporation.

Benz, B. (2007), '*Deadwood* and the English Language', *Great Plains Quarterly* 27 (4): 239–51.

Bignell, J. (2019), 'Performing the Identity of the Medium: Adaptation and Television Historiography', *Adaptation* 12 (2): 149–64.

Bladen, V., S. Hatchuel and N. Vienne-Guerrin, eds (2017), *Shakespeare on Screen: 'The Tempest' and Late Romances*, Cambridge: Cambridge University Press.

Bladen, V., S. Hatchuel and N. Vienne-Guerrin, eds (2019), *Shakespeare on Screen: 'King Lear'*, Cambridge: Cambridge University Press.

Boose, L. E. and R. Burt, eds (1997), *Shakespeare the Movie: Popularizing the Plays on Film, TV and Video*, London: Routledge.

Breight, C. (2008), 'Shakespeare on American television and the special relationship between the UK & the USA', in S. Davin and R. Jackson (eds), *Television and Criticism*, 37–48, Bristol: Intellect.

Bronfen, E. (2020), *Serial Shakespeare: An Infinite Variety of Appropriations in American TV Drama*, Manchester: Manchester University Press.

Bulman, J. and H. R. Coursen, eds (1988), *Shakespeare on Television: An Anthology of Essays and Reviews*, Hanover, NH: University Press of New England.

Burt, R. (1998), *Unspeakable ShaXXXspeares: Queer Theory and American Kiddie Culture*, rev. edn, New York, NY: Palgrave Macmillan.

Burt, R. (2003), 'Shakespeare. "Glo-cali-zation", Race, and the Small Screens of Post-Popular Culture', in R. Burt and L. E. Boose (eds), *Shakespeare the Movie Two: Popularizing the Plays on Film, TV, Video and DVD*, 14–36, London: Routledge.

Burt, R., ed. (2006), *Shakespeares After Shakespeare: An Encyclopedia of the Bard in Mass Media and Popular Culture*, 2 vols, Westport, CT: Greenwood Press.

Burt, R. and L. E. Boose, eds (2003), *Shakespeare the Movie Two: Popularizing the Plays on Film, TV, Video and DVD*, London: Routledge.

Calbi, M. (2013), *Spectral Shakespeares: Media Adaptations in the Twenty-first Century*, New York, NY: Palgrave Macmillan.

Caldwell, J. T. (1995), *Televisuality: Style, Crisis, and Authority in American Television*, New Brunswick, IN: Rutgers University Press.

Cardwell, S. (2002), *Adaptation Revisited: Television and the Classic Novel*, Manchester: Manchester University Press.

Cardwell, S. (2006), 'Television Aesthetics', *Critical Studies in Television* 1 (1): 72–80.

Cardwell, S. (2014), 'Television Among Friends: Medium, Art, Media', *Critical Studies in Television* 9 (3): 6–21.

Cartelli, T. (1999), *Repositioning Shakespeare: National Formations, Postcolonial Appropriations*, London: Routledge.

Cartelli, T. and K. Rowe (2007), *New Wave Shakespeare on Screen*, Cambridge: Polity Press.

Charney, M. (1980), 'Shakespearean Anglophilia: The BBC-TV Series and American Audiences', *Shakespeare Quarterly* 31 (2): 287–92.

Charney, M. (1986), 'Is Shakespeare Suitable for Television?' *Shakespeare on Film Newsletter* 10 (2): 1–8.

Chisum, J. (2019), 'The Macbeth of the American West: Tragedy, Genre and Landscape in *Breaking Bad*', *Critical Studies in Television* 14 (4): 415–28.

Cieślak, M. (2019), *Screening Gender in Shakespeare's Comedies: Film and Television Adaptations in Shakespeare's Comedies*, New York, NY, and London: Lexington Books.

Crane, M. (1961), 'Shakespeare on Television', *Shakespeare Quarterly* 12 (3): 323–7.

Crowl, S. (2008), *Shakespeare and Film: a Norton Guide*, New York, NY: W.W. Norton & Co.

Desmet, C. (2014), 'YouTube Shakespeare, Appropriation and Rhetorics of Invention', in D. Fischlin (ed.), *OuterSpeares: Shakespeare, Intermedia, and the Limits of Adaptation*, 53–74, Toronto: University of Toronto Press.

Donaldson, P. S. (2012) 'Shakespeare and Media Allegory', in A. R. Guneratne (ed.), *Shakespeare and Genre: from Early Modern Inheritance to Postmodern Legacy*, 205–23, London: Palgrave Macmillan.

Elliott, T. (2018), 'Shakespearean Seriality: The "Hollow Crown", the "Wooden O", and the "Circle in the Water" of History', *Adaptation* 12 (2): 69–88.

Fabiszak, J. (2005), *Polish Televised Shakespeares. A Study of Shakespeare Productions within the Television Theatre Format*, Poznan: Motivex.

Finn, P. (2004), 'The Politics of Culture: the Play's the Thing', in J. R. Keller and L. Strayner (eds), *Almost Shakespeare: Reinventing his Works for Cinema and Television*, 7–21, Jefferson, NC: McFarland.

Freedman, B. (2007), 'Critical Junctures in Shakespeare Screen History', in R. Jackson (ed.), *The Cambridge Companion to Shakespeare on Film*, 47–71, Cambridge: Cambridge University Press.

Geddes, L. (2012), '"Know that I, Ringo the Drummer Am": Shakespeare, You Tube, and the Limits of Performance', *Shakespeare Bulletin* 30 (3): 299–318.

Gerzic, M. (2019), 'Re-fashioning Richard III: Intertextuality, Fandom, and the (Mobile) Body in *The Hollow Crown*', in M. Gerzic and A. Norrie (eds), *From Medievalism to Early-Modernism: Adapting the English Past*, 188–206, London: Routledge.

Greenhalgh, S. (2003) '"Alas poor country!": Documenting the Politics of Performance in two British Television *Macbeths* since the 1980s', in P. Aebischer, E. Esche and N. Wheale (eds), *Remaking Shakespeare: Performance Across Media, Genres and Cultures*, 31–43, Basingstoke: Palgrave Macmillan.

Greenhalgh, S. (2018), 'The Remains of the Stage: Revivifying Shakespearean Theatre on Screen, 1964–2016', in P. Aebischer, S. Greenhalgh, and L.E. Osborne (eds), *Shakespeare and the 'Live' Theatre Broadcast Experience*, 19–40, London: Bloomsbury / Arden Shakespeare.

Griffin, A. V. (1953), 'Shakespeare through the Camera's Eye–*Julius Caesar* in Motion Pictures; *Hamlet* and *Othello* on Television', *Shakespeare Quarterly* 4 (3): 331–6.

Griffin, A. V. (1955), 'Shakespeare Through the Camera's Eye 1953–1954', *Shakespeare Quarterly* 6 (1): 63–6.

Griffin, A. V. (1966), 'Shakespeare through the Camera's Eye: IV', *Shakespeare Quarterly* 17 (4): 383–7.

Hansen, A. (2010), *Shakespeare and Popular Music*, London: Bloomsbury.

Hatchuel, S. (2019), 'Shakespeare's Humanizing Language in Films and TV Series', *Borrowers and Lenders* 12 (2).

Hatchuel, S. and N. Vienne-Guerrin, eds (2005), *Shakespeare on Screen: Richard III*, Rouen: Publications de l'Université de Rouen et du Havre.

Hatchuel, S. and N. Vienne-Guerrin, eds (2008a), *Shakespeare on Screen: Television Shakespeare: Essays in Honour of Michèle Willems*, Mont-Saint-Aignan: Publications des Universités de Rouen et du Havre.

Hatchuel, S. and N. Vienne-Guerrin (2008b), 'Remembrance of Things Past: Shakespeare's Comedies on French Television', in Hatchel and Vienne-Guerrin (eds), *Shakespeare on Screen: Television Shakespeare. Essays in honour of Michèle Willems*, 171–97, Mont-Saint-Aignan: Publications des Universités de Rouen et du Havre.

Hatchuel, S. and N. Vienne-Guerrin, eds (2008c), *Shakespeare on Screen: the Henriad*, Rouen: Presses Universitaires de Rouen et du Havre.

Hatchuel, S. and N. Vienne-Guerrin, eds (2009), *Shakespeare on Screen: The Roman Plays*, Mont-Saint-Aignan: Publications des Universités de Rouen and du Havre.

Hatchuel, S. and N. Vienne-Guerrin, eds (2011), *Shakespeare on Screen: 'Hamlet'*, Mont-Saint-Aignan: Publications des Universités de Rouen and du Havre.

Hawes, W. (1964), 'Much Ado About Shakespeare', *Journal of Broadcasting* 8(2): 127–40.

Henderson, D. (2003), 'A *Shrew* for the Times, Revisited', in R. Burt and L. E. Boose (eds), *Shakespeare the Movie Two: Popularizing the Plays on Film, TV, Video and DVD*, 120–39, London: Routledge.

Hewett, R. (2015), 'The Changing Determinants of UK Television Acting', *Critical Studies in Television* 10 (1): 73–90.

Hewett, R. (2017), *The Changing Spaces of Television Acting*, Manchester: Manchester University Press.

Hindle, M. (2007), *Studying Shakespeare on Film*, London: Palgrave Macmillan.

Hoberman, J. (2009), 'This Earth, This England, This Series', *New York Times*, March 25. Available online: http://www.nytimes.com/2009/03/29/arts/television/29hobe.html? (accessed 1 May 2021).

Huertas Martin, V. (2017), 'Rupert Goold's *Macbeth* (2010): Surveillance Society and Society of Control', *Sederi* 27: 81–103.

Huertas Martin, V. (2018), 'Filming Metatheatre in Gregory Doran's *Macbeth*', *Atlantis* 40 (2): 101–22.

Huertas Martin, V. (2019), '"A Mourning Rome a Dangerous Rome": Theatricality and Antitheatricality in two *Julius Caesar* Films', *Shakespeare Bulletin* 37 (4): 537–60.

Jacobs, J. (2000), *The Intimate Screen*, Oxford: Oxford University Press.

Jenkins, H. (2006), *Convergence Culture: Where Old and New Media Collide*, New York, NY: New York University Press.

Jenkins, H., S. Ford and J. Green (2013), *Spreadable Media: Creating Value and Meaning in a Networked Culture*, New York, NY: New York University Press.

Kantorowicz, E. (1996), *The King's Two Bodies: A Study in Medieval Political Theology*, Princeton, NJ: Princeton University Press.

Kapitaniak, P. (2019), 'Negotiating Authorship, Genre and Race in *King of Texas* (2002)', in V. Bladen, S. Hatchuel and N. Vienne-Guerrin (eds), *Shakespeare on Screen: 'King Lear'*, 111–24, Cambridge: Cambridge University Press.

Kidnie, M. J. (2008), *Shakespeare and the Problem of Adaptation*, London and New York, NY: Routledge.

Kiley, F. S. and L. Marder (1961), 'The Public Arts: An Age of Kings', *The English Journal* 50 (8): 566–8.

Lanier, D. (2017), 'Shakespeare/Not Shakespeare: Afterword', in C. Desmet, N. Loper and J. Casey (eds), *Shakespeare/NotShakespeare*, 293–306, Cham: Palgrave Macmillan.

Marino, A. (2011), 'Multicultural Shakespeare: Italian and British TV Series of the 9–11 pm Slot', *Anglistica* 15 (2): 15–26.

Minami, R. (2016), 'Hello Sha-kitty-peare? Shakespeares Cutified in Japanese Anime Imagination', *Journal for Early Modern Cultural Studies* 16 (3): 116–37.

Mittell, J. (2006), 'Narrative Complexity in Contemporary American Television', *The Velvet Light Trap* 58: 29–40.

Mittell, J. (2010), *Complex TV: The Poetics of Contemporary Television Storytelling*, New York, NY: New York University Press.

Morgan, P. (2013), 'Her Majesty will see you now', *The Guardian*, 14 January, 16.

Morse, R. (2014), 'The Hollow Crown: Shakespeare, the BBC, and the 2012 London Olympics', *Linguaculture* 1: 7–20.

Nicholson, G. (1970), 'If Cedric Messina has got excited about something then most probably the director will want to direct it and the actors will want to direct it and the actors will jump at the parts… and the chances are you'll love the play', *Radio Times*, 15 January, 52–5.

O'Neill, S. (2014), *Shakespeare and You Tube: New Media Forms of the Bard*, London: Bloomsbury / Arden Shakespeare.

O'Neill, S. (2017), 'Introduction: Sowed and Scattered: Shakespeare's Media Ecologies', in S. O'Neill (ed.), *Broadcast Your Shakespeare: Continuity and Change Across Media*, London: Bloomsbury.

O'Neill, S. (2019), 'Finding Refuge in *King Lear:* From Brexit to Shakespeare's European Values', *Multicultural Shakespeare: Translation, Appropriation and Performance* 19 (34): 119–38.

O'Neill, S. (2020), 'Shakespeare's Hand, or "the strangers' case": Remediating Sir Thomas More in the Context of the Refugee Crisis', *Borrowers and Lenders* 13 (1). Available online: https://openjournals.libs.uga.edu/borrowers/article/view/2364 (accessed 17 February 2021).

O'Neill, S. (2021), 'Bring yourself back on line, old bill: *Westworld*'s Media Histories, or Six Degrees of Separation from Shakespeare', *Cahiers Élisabéthains* 105 (1): 93–116.

Osborne, L. E. (1997), 'Poetry in Motion: Animating Shakespeare', in R. Burt and L. E. Boose (eds), *Shakespeare the Movie: Popularizing the Plays on Film, TV, and Video*, 103–20, London: Routledge.

Otnes, C. and P. Maclaran (2015), *Royal Fever: The British Monarchy in Consumer Culture*, Oaklands, CA: University of California Press.

Pearson, R. and M. Messenger Davies (2014), *Star Trek and American Television*, Oakland, CA: University of California Press.

Pittman, L. M. (2010), *Authorizing Shakespeare on Film and Television: Gender, Class and Ethnicity in Adaptation* (Studies in Shakespeare, vol. 19), New York, NY: Peter Lang.

Pittman, M. (2015), 'Shakespeare and the Cultural Olympiad: Contesting Gender and the British Nation in the BBC's *The Hollow Crown*', *Borrowers and Lenders* 9 (2). Available online: https://openjournals.libs.uga.edu/borrowers/article/view/2438/2544 (accessed 17 February 2021).

Pittman, M. (2017), 'Colour-Conscious Casting and Multicultural Britain in the BBC *Henry V* (2012): Historicizing Adaptation in the Age of Digital Placelessness', *Adaptation* 10: 176–91.

Pittman, M. (2020a), 'Too Soon Forgot: The Ethics of Remembering in *Richard III, NOW*, and *House of Cards*', *Borrowers and Lenders* 13 (1). Available online: https://openjournals.libs.uga.edu/borrowers/article/view/2365 (accessed 17 February 2021).

Pittman, M. (2020b), 'Resisting History and Atoning for Racial Privilege: Shakespeare's Henriad in HBO's *The Wire*', in C. Desmet, S. Iyengar and M. Jacobson (eds), *The Routledge Handbook to Shakespeare and Global Adaptation*, 378–87, London: Routledge.

Rogers, A. (2015), 'History as Echo: Entertainment Historiography from Shakespeare to HBO's *Game of Thrones*', in A. Hansen and K. J. Jr. Wetmore (eds), *Shakespearean Echoes*, 142–54. Basingstoke: Palgrave Macmillan.

Rogers, J. (2013), 'The Shakespearean Glass Ceiling: The State of Colorblind Casting in Contemporary British Theatre', *Shakespeare Bulletin* 31 (3): 405–30.

Rogers, J. (2018), 'Talawa and Black Theatre Live: "Creating the Ira Aldridges That Are Remembered" – Live Theatre Broadcast and the Historical Record', in P. Aebischer, S. Greenhalgh and L. E. Osborne (eds), *Shakespeare and the 'Live' Theatre Broadcast Experience*, 147–58, London: Bloomsbury.

Ronnenberg, S. C. (2018), *Deadwood and Shakespeare: The Henriad in the Old West*, Jefferson, NC: McFarland.

Rose, B. G. (1986), *Television and the Performing Arts: A Handbook and Reference Guide to American Cultural Programming*, Westport, CT: Greenwood Press.

Rothwell, K. S. (2004), *A History of Shakespeare on Screen: A Century of Film and Television*, 2nd edn, Cambridge: Cambridge University Press.

Rowe, K. (2008), 'Medium-Specificity and Other Critical Scripts for Screen Shakespeare', in D. E. Henderson (ed.), *Alternative Shakespeares 3*, 34–53, London: Routledge.

Rycroft, E. (2020), 'Hair in the BBC's *The Hollow Crown: The Wars of the Roses*: Class, Nation, Gender, Race, and Difference', *Shakespeare* 17 (1): 29–48.

Sanders, J. (2013), *Shakespeare and Music: Afterlives and Borrowings*, Hoboken, NJ: Wiley.

Schreiber, F. R. (1953), 'Television's *Hamlet*', *The Quarterly of Film Radio and Television* 8 (2): 150–6.

Schulman, A. (2010), 'The Sopranos: An American Existentialism?', *Cambridge Quarterly* 39 (1): 23–38.

Seef, A. (2017), 'Race, Post-Race, Shakespeare, and South Africa', *Borrowers & Lenders*, 11 (1). Available online: https://openjournals.libs.uga.edu/borrowers/article/view/2407 (accessed 17 February 2021).

Seef, A. (2018), *South Africa's Shakespeare and the Drama of Language and Identity*, *Global Shakespeares* series, Cham, Switzerland: Springer.

Selznick, B. J. (2008), *Global Television: Co-Producing Culture*, Philadelphia, PA: Temple University Press.

Shaughnessy, R. (2006), 'Stage, Screen and Nation: *Hamlet* and the Space of History', in D. E. Henderson (ed.), *A Concise Companion to Shakespeare on Screen*, 54–76, Oxford: Blackwell.

Shaughnessy, R. (2006a), 'The Revolution will not be Televised: Staging the Media Apparatus', in P. Holland (ed.), *Shakespeare, Memory and Performance*, 305–28, Cambridge: Cambridge University Press.

Smart, B. (2014), 'From Television World Theatre to the BBC Shakespeare: The fluctuating status of the classic play on BBC Television 1957–1985', *Forgotten Television Drama*, 1 August. Available online: https://forgottentelevisiondrama. wordpress.com/… 4/08/01/from-television-world-theatre-to-the-bbc-shakespeare-the-fluctuating-status-of-the-classic-play-on-bbc-television-1957-1985 (accessed 1 June 2021).

Smart, B. (2015), 'Producing Classics on Outside Broadcast in the 1970s: *The Little Minister* (1975), *As You Like It* (1978), and *Henry VIII* (1979)', *Critical Studies in Television* 10 (3): 67–82.

Smart, B. (2022), 'Cedric Messina: Producing Theatrical Classics with a Decorative Aesthetic', in A. Wrigley and J. Wyver (eds), *Screenplays: Theatre Plays on Television*, Manchester: Manchester University Press.

Smith, E. (2006), 'Shakespeare Serialized: *An Age of Kings*' in R. Shaughnessy (ed.), *The Cambridge Companion to Shakespeare and Popular Culture*, Cambridge: Cambridge University Press.

Smith, P. J. (2019) 'Richard Eyre's *King Lear*: A Brexit Allegory'. Available online: https://www.cambridge.org/files/5215/6086/0475/Shakespeare_on_screen_Richard_Eyre_Smith.pdf (accessed 17 May 2021).

Smith, P., J. Valls-Russel and D. Yabut (2020), 'Introduction to Special Section Shakespeare under Global Lockdown', *Cahiers Élisabéthains* 103 (1): 101–11.

Tempera, M. (2008), '"Only about Kings": Reference to the Second Tetralogy on Film and Television', in S. Hatchuel and N. Vienne-Guerrin (eds), *Shakespeare on Screen: The Henriad*, 233–68, Rouen: Presses Universitaires de Rouen et du Havre.

Thorburn, D. (2019), 'Unstable Platforms: TV in the Digital Age', *Critical Studies in Television* 14 (2): 160–9.

Van Wagner, D. (2004), 'Macbeth', in D. Fisclhin (ed.), *Canadian Adaptations of Shakespeare Project* website, University of Guelph. Currently unavailable online.

Votava, J. M. (2020), 'Through a Glass Darkly: Sophie Okonedo's Margaret as Racial Other in The Hollow Crown: The Wars of the Roses', *Shakespeare Survey* 73: 170–83.

Wald, C. (2020), *Shakespeare's Serial Returns in Complex TV*, Basingstoke: Palgrave Macmillan.

Weissman, E. (2012), *Transnational Television Drama: Special Relations and Mutual Exchange between the US and UK*, London: Palgrave Macmillan.

Wells, S. (1982), 'Television Shakespeare', *Shakespeare Quarterly* 33 (3): 261–77.

Wells-Lassagne, S. (2017), *Television and Serial Adaptation*, London: Routledge.

Wilson, J. R. (2021), *Shakespeare and Game of Thrones*, London: Routledge.

Wilson, R. (2017), 'The Madness of King Charles III', *Critical Survey* 29 (2): 76–93.

Wollaston, S. (2016), '*The Hollow Crown*: Henry VI Part 1 – a bit *Game of Thrones*? Absolutely!' *Guardian*, 9 May. Available online: https://www.theguardian.com/tv-and-radio/2016/may/09/hollow-crown-henry-vi-part-1-a-bit-game-of-thrones-absolutely (accessed 17 February 2021).

Wrathall, J. (2013), 'The Secret Life of Walther White', *Sight and Sound* 23 (9): 34–6.

Wray, R. (2016), 'The Shakespearean Auteur and the Televisual Mcdium', *Shakespeare Bulletin* 34 (3): 469–85.

Wray, R. (2021), 'Shakespeare and the New Discourses of Television: Quality, Aesthetics and *The Hollow Crown*', *Cahiers Élisabéthains* 105 (1): 76–92.

Wright, K. (2017), '"Who's There?": *Slings and Arrows*' Audience Dynamic', in I. R. Makaryk and K. Prince (eds), *Shakespeare and Canada: Remembrance of Ourselves*, 79–96, Ottawa: University of Ottawa Press.

Wrigley, A. (2014), 'Space and Place in Joan Kemp-Welch's Television Productions of Theatre Plays', *Historical Journal of Film, Radio and Television* 34 (3): 405–19.

Wrigley, A. and J. Wyver, eds (forthcoming 2022), *Screenplays: Theatre Plays on Television*, Manchester: Manchester University Press.

Wyver, J. (2012), 'Dallas Bower: A Producer for Television's Early Years, 1936–9', *Journal of British Cinema and Television* 9 (1): 26–39.

Wyver, J. (2013), 'Adapting the histories: *An Age of Kings* on screen', *An Age of Kings: Eight History Plays by William Shakespeare. Screen Plays 1*, London: Illuminations.

Wyver, J. (2014), '"All the trimmings?": The Transfer of Theatre to Television in Adaptations of Shakespeare Stagings', *Adaptation* 7 (2): 104–20.

Wyver, J. (2015), 'Between Theatre and Television: Inside the Hybrid Space of *The Wars of the Roses*', *Critical Studies in Television* 10 (3): 23–36.

Wyver, J. (2016), 'An Intimate and Intermedial Form: Early Television Shakespeare from the BBC, 1937–39', *Shakespeare Survey* 69: 347–60.

Wyver, J. (2017), 'Scenes from *Cymbeline* and Early Television Studio Drama', in V. Bladen, S. Hatchuel and and N. Vienne-Guerrin (eds), *Shakespeare on Screen: 'The Tempest' and Late Romances*, 56–70, Cambridge: Cambridge University Press.

Wyver, J. (2019), *Screening the Royal Shakespeare Company: a Critical History*, London: Bloomsbury.

On location in Asian Shakespeare stage adaptations

YONG LI LAN

ASIAN SHAKESPEARE AND INTERCULTURAL TEMPORALITY

It is apparent that the term, 'Asian Shakespeares', designates an imaginary category. Even in the plural, the qualifier 'Asian' for 'Shakespeare' cannot meaningfully unify as a set the diverse languages, performance cultures and socio-political histories that have transformed Shakespeare's plays in different ways, in many contexts, over time. The category does not designate commonalities in literary and theatre cultures. It locates a standpoint, regionally mapping the non-Anglophone world's relationships to Shakespeare from an implicit Anglophone position. If rather than indigenizing Shakespeare, we unfold the term as 'Shakespeare in Asia', distinguishing Shakespeare from contexts into which his work is relocated, it becomes possible to particularize and concretize those contexts. Yet this formulation too is spatial, placing Shakespeare 'inside' one or more holistic, geographically and culturally separable contexts. It is worth recalling that the formulations 'Asian Shakespeare' and 'Shakespeare in Asia' came into use at a specific moment, in the first decade of the twenty-first century when the number of productions from Asia that toured to the West reached critical mass; that is, these productions may have allowed Western audiences the illusion of seeing Shakespeare 'in' a country, when in fact practitioners were internationalizing their own theatre cultures for travel by adapting Shakespeare.

In the early 2000s, Rustom Bharucha criticized the ideational conjunction of 'Shakespeare' and 'Asia' as a neo-colonialist appropriation of the cultural capital of Asian theatres that were at a relative economic disadvantage by directors on both sides of the equation (2010: 253–82). Since then, the rapid globalization of theatre practices in Asian countries has altered the sense of authentic place that Bharucha's argument assumes and champions. During the first two decades of the twenty-first century, international networks among theatre industries expanded through tours, performing arts fairs, festival commissions and cross-border collaborations. These became a regular part of programming by both theatre companies and arts organizations that circulated artistic practices through a globalized milieu of cosmopolitan arts festivals and festival-goers. An active network of venues at which productions from disparate cultural locations might be staged and seen alongside one another came to shape not only practitioners' approaches to adapting Shakespeare but also, reciprocally, the perspectives of their local audiences who travelled more extensively and watched more travelling performances at home. To recognize the internationalization of East Asian adaptations is not to say that they are now more uncertainly located in their own theatre cultures, but rather to attend to how a local theatre culture is a well-travelled one. This is the case even where productions do not have the means, or interest, to travel.

An important response to the rate of circulation of artists, audiences and adaptation approaches is that creative strategies for bringing Shakespeare's plays into interaction with a particular set of theatrical, socio-political and historical circumstances at a particular moment have become much more detailed in expressing difference. It is illuminating to note, for instance, changes in the treatment of location between Yohangza Theatre Company's *Pericles* (2015) and their exceptionally well-travelled production of *A Midsummer Night's Dream*, which played just three years earlier in London at the Globe to Globe Festival in 2012. True to the company's name 'Yohangza', which means 'voyager', their *Dream* had by then toured to many cities since its first performances in 2002. Its set was designed to bring an imaginary Korean night peopled with *Dokkebi* (goblins) onto almost any stage around the world, since the setting was largely evoked by how the actor-musicians used the stage space. In contrast, Yohangza's *Pericles* was located in an imaginary Middle Eastern space. Pericles, wearing a *keffiyeh* and speaking the greeting, 'As-Salaam-Alaikum', entered a stage set covered in sand, at once desert and beach, on which random pieces of the debris of civilizations seemed to have collected or been washed up: a grand piano, a chandelier, the prow of a small boat jutting out from the sand, an enormous head of Diana lying on its side. Yohangza chose for their *Pericles* a geography-specific (not culture-specific) setting as a habitat for imagining the action at the places named in the play. The relationship between its Korean performance location and the original English staging was formulated as a relationship between the director Yang Jung-Ung's and William Shakespeare's respective ways of imagining, and theatrical means of presenting, a region geographically foreign and temporally distant to both contemporary Korean and seventeenth-century English audiences. The setting also reflected the production's own moment, when violent ISIS operations filled the international media.[1] Yang, the artistic director of Yohangza, is one of a younger generation of practitioners who are successors to the first wave of East Asian experimentation with Shakespeare and have matured in international theatre-making and theatre-going contexts, working with actors and designers who experienced changing regimes of theatre training in South Korea. Yohangza's radical shift in relocating the action challenges a basic assumption: that to produce the play in a South Korean location is to re-situate the play *in* South Korea by adapting it to Korean culture, performance styles and/or society. The assumption that the fictional action is relocated to its place of production is contrary to

Shakespeare's own practice in his most-adapted plays, which are situated outside England, in foreign places. Implicitly, this expectation defines the source of adaptation as 'English Shakespeare', rather than the way locations are depicted by Shakespeare in his plays. It is now obvious (although it was always the case) that critical approaches need to interrelate multiple notions of 'location' in order to meet the individuated, *un*representative strategies for adapting Shakespeare's settings in East and Southeast Asian theatres.

The idea of different locations is fundamental to the act of bringing Shakespeare and Asian performance together. Theorizations of 'intercultural' performance as they apply to Shakespeare's plays in East Asian performance first conceived of an interaction between a performance form and culture indigenous to one location and the performance tradition and culture of Shakespeare in the Western Anglophone world (Pavis 1992). If understood in this way, the interaction telescopes the process in the product, treating the performance as a stage presentation of a direct encounter between two locations. Yet the impression of such an encounter is only possible because that encounter in fact occurred about a century ago.

Contemporary approaches to adapting Shakespeare for performance in the region have in common modes of realist Shakespeare performance that were introduced with modern drama during the period of modernization, which was in many respects synonymous with Westernization. These transitional periods occurred over the late nineteenth to mid-twentieth centuries as a consequence of British colonization and Western imperialism, and unfolded in socio-political circumstances unique to each country, that were at the same time related to each other and thus overlapped. After the Meiji Restoration Government of Japan was installed in 1868 and undertook the project of Westernization, modern theatre movements eventually led to the establishment of training organizations, Bungei Kyōkai under Tsuboushi Shoyo being a particularly significant figure for his translation of Shakespeare and the inception of *Shingkei* (new drama). In China, the break with feudal *Xiqu* (opera) towards the formation of *Huaju* (spoken drama) is closely allied with the political May Fourth Movement (1919). In the British colonies of the Straits Settlements (1826–1946) and Hong Kong, the staging of English-language productions by expatriate drama groups created an elite theatre by and for the ruling class and race, into which only a few local individuals were selectively admitted (Minami, Carruthers and Gillies 2001; Booth 2002; Li 2003). Over the course of the twentieth century, local varieties of realist Shakespeare performance have come to be regarded as 'traditional' in different senses: partly due to their initial emulation of and continuing association with English Shakespeare performance traditions of the early twentieth century; but also partly due to their association with the inception of the modern nation. To perform Shakespeare now is necessarily to reflect in some sense a turning point in local theatre that is inseparable from seismic political and social changes which took place at that time. When realist Shakespeares appear in productions now, their performative location is always already here, in our past.

A common paradigm for adapting Shakespeare's plays now brings these local histories into view by introducing a formal break. The break may occur between different genres, between theatrical and metatheatrical levels, and/or between time frames. A performative break with the twentieth-century tradition of realist Shakespeare mirrors the prior and correlative break, made by the introduction of realism, with pre-modern, non-realist theatre traditions. The performative break thus figures a historical break, even while it may be read as a stage encounter between discrete locations. A major strategy has been to metatheatrically disrupt the realist style of performing Shakespeare in translation, for instance in Ninagawa Yukio's use of classical Japanese forms in his *Macbeth* (1980) and *The Tempest* (1987); or to frame realist acting within another performance form, such as Hwadong Theatre Company's *Pericles* directed by Kim Kwang-Lim (2010), which cast Gower as a *Pansori* singer. In this approach, abrupt changes in performance genre and style enact a break back and forth between realism and an older non-realist tradition. Since pre-modern traditions have continued into the present, these switches do not represent a sequential history in the theatre, but rather, invoke their audiences' participation in distinct theatre cultures with different historical origins. The audience of Hwadong's *Pericles* (captured in the performance recording archived in the Asian Shakespeare Intercultural Archive) adjust accordingly, responding with the customary shouts of *chuimsae* (words of encouragement) to the solo singer and the drummer during the *Pansori* performances of Gower (played by Lim Jin-Taek) and remaining quiet during the acting of the plot. These instances juxtapose co-existing cultural locations within a country.

Importantly, non-culture-specific or experimental strategies are equally employed in the break with realist Shakespeare. Early landmark examples are the Beijing People's Art Theatre's *Hamlet* directed by Lin Zhaohua (1989), where the actors playing Hamlet, Claudius and Polonius repeatedly exchanged their roles in mid-stream; and *A Tale of Lear* directed by Suzuki Tadashi (1988), which is set in a mental asylum and rejects realism altogether. These adaptation strategies that draw upon avant-garde performance are primarily situated within the company or director's own body of work, which is largely non-Shakespearean and may focus on specific methods of actor training, such as Suzuki's internationally taught and practised Suzuki method (Allain 1998; Suzuki 2015). Such strategies ambiguate, disperse or resist the identification of theatre cultures by their traditional (and by extension, national) forms. Instead, engaging with Shakespeare continues to be instrumental in developing performance practice within a continuing project of theatrical modernity, which has not ended with realism.

In the rest of this chapter, I offer a counteraction to the ahistorical, regional mapping expressed in the category 'Asian Shakespeare' by exploring the temporalities of relocating Shakespeare's plays on stages in Asia. I set two productions, Yohangza's *Pericles* (2015) and Ryutopia's *Othello* (2006), alongside each other, to explore how, in different ways, they reach beyond their own production locations in adapting Shakespeare. In particular, I focus on their use of dual time frames to enact a performative break in the temporality of location. The dual times are not usually historically differentiated, such as depicting the past and present of a particular location. And while the restructuring of the plot may manifest the self-reflexivity and belatedness of a play that is treated as already known, such restructuring likewise differs from post-modernist dismantling of narrative sequence. Rather, the dual time frames bifurcate the production's location into dual temporalities by introducing into the plot two other dimensions of time: a spiritual realm in which the sense of time encompasses the afterlife; and the presentational time of the performance experience. Pre-modern performance forms such as *Mugen Noh* and *Gut* (Korean shamanism) are rooted in belief systems that bring the unlimited time after death into interaction with the historicity of Shakespeare's drama through the temporal progression of the plot. Conversely, aesthetic principles that foreground the presentational over the representational engage their audiences in an engrossing play-making activity that suspends or is co-present with the fictional narrative. Intercultural temporality, as distinct from the history of Shakespeare's introduction into local theatre, or even the historicity of intercultural strategies such as revisionist treatments of realism (Yong 2017: 135–53), involves not one linear time (e.g. Japanese theatre history of Shakespeare), but interacting histories, and interacting temporalities of action.

LOCATING THE PLAY IN THE THEATRICAL MOMENT

I attended Yohangza Theatre Company's *Pericles* at the Towol Theatre of the Seoul Arts Center in 2015, crossing from Tokyo to Seoul together with the Japanese co-directors of A|S|I|A, Suematsu Michiko and Kobayashi Kaori. Before the performance, the A|S|I|A Korean co-director, Lee Hyon-U, who translated the playscript, explained to us that this performance of Gower marked the return to theatre after a ten-year break by Yoo In-Chon, a star actor in the 1980s and former Minister of Culture, Sports and Tourism.[2] As well, Yoo's son, Nam Yoon-Ho, was playing the young Pericles. This local information would probably have been known to our fellow audience members in Seoul since at least the moment when they had obtained tickets for the performance. Seeing the huge banners with Yoo's face in the foyer space, we were conscious of a sense of occasion for the Seoul audience. My awareness of the lead actors' identities gave a particular meaning to the narrative transition at the start of Act 4.[3] Yoo, playing Gower in a black overcoat, seated on a chair in front of a huge tilted dial, looked across at the tableau of Nam as Pericles, standing with his courtiers at the prow of the half-submerged boat looking out into the audience. When he leaned back reflectively and said something about Pericles, Nam stooped and coughed. Yoo said a little more about Pericles, then rose from his chair and walked to the boat with his right hand raised. Nam jumped off the prow and did a high five with his father to the audience's applause, then took his ring off and gave it to Yoo who put it on. Without following the Korean speech it was nonetheless easy to recognize what had happened: father and son had changed roles as Pericles. Yoo bowed, the audience applauded again, and he went around to head the tableau on the boat. The change of roles and the audience's participation in it occurred simply and naturally.

After the performance we met with Yoo and the director Yang Jung-Ung. I became conscious that as the director of A|S|I|A, my non-local position was also one of agency for internationalizing the performance. The A|S|I|A team works together in the digital medium, which allows us to try to equalize or balance our respective positions and languages. The rare moments when we meet in person on-site locate our work back in the affective, lived situation for Shakespeare from which that work originates. Then, our collaboration shares the city scenes, food, weather, and theatre-going culture of one of our locales, and most of all the experience of Shakespeare performances from which that collaboration sprang. Meeting over dinner in Seoul expanded the event to the people who work together behind and after that performance, both in local theatre-making and international archiving, and brought to the fore the relationships that make it possible to join those spheres of work. Asking Yang for copyright for *Pericles* was part of the pleasure of this meeting in an old friendship that has formed even though we don't converse easily across our languages.

Once the script had been translated for A|S|I|A,[4] I learned that Yoo as Gower had said, 'Oh, by the way, Pericles has aged too', as a cue to Nam to cough, and the video showed that a second later Yoo coughed too, leading into the change of roles. I also realized that just before he walked across to do the high five with Nam, Yoo said:

> I think we need old Pericles from this point on.
> Young Pericles, you did a great job. You were wonderful.[5]

I then understood that the audience applauded in support and enjoyment of the father's praise of his son. Grasping the symbolic legacy of the high five and the ring's transfer between the famous actor-father and his actor-son, I could better share the audience's warm response when their family relationship was opened to include the audience in these gestures. So, shifting the performativity of the production from a live event located in Seoul to a subtitled video-recording situated in the digital environment prompted me to re-experience it. The interaction between my memory of the event and the archival translation of it clarified Yohangza's use of its local history to adapt Shakespeare's play affectively. Yohangza situated its *Pericles* within South Korean acting history, invoking its audiences' collective memories of Yoo's earlier performances as well as their associations from that period. At the same time, his metatheatrical performance of emotions between father and child was closely bound up with those of the dramatic narrative, since this transition took place at the point just before Pericles discovers Marina's 'death'. In this way, the emotional congruence and mutual resonance of the metatheatrical and the theatrical brought the time frame of present-day theatre in Seoul into conjunction with the progress of the plot.

Location-specific, historically significant moments of intercultural conjunction between Shakespeare's plot and particular performance histories have doubtless occurred regularly, but are less often a concrete part of staging. Another well-known instance where a turning point in a famous actor's own career became part of his performance took place in Contemporary Legend Theatre's *Li Er Zai Ci* (Lear is Here). The artistic director and lead performer Wu Hsing-kuo recounts that he had dissolved the company for two years, due to lack of funding, when Ariane Mnouchkine persuaded him to restart it after he performed a version of *Li Er Zai Ci* at a master seminar.[6] Contemporary Legend Theatre reopened with *Li Er Zai Ci* in 2001 in Taipei. It contained a key break in Act 1, scene 3 after Wu's solo virtuoso

Jingju (Beijing Opera) performance of the mad Lear in scenes 1 and 2. Wu removed the face paint of his character, then removed and folded his costume as he spoke:

> Who can tell me? Who I am!
> I want to know who I am!
> My kingdom, my wisdom and my power all beguile me!
> They want me to believe that I belong here!
> I have returned!
> I am still my past self, my present and my future self!
> I revert to my essence,
> This is a breakthrough nobler than becoming a monk!
>
> (timecode 0:24:18–25:47)

As Wu spoke the last lines, he stood facing his audience in the undergarments of the *Jingju* warrior role, holding out the pile of his costume and beard in both arms. When he finished, he bowed very low and placed the pile on the stage before him. The audience bursts into applause in the video recording of the Singapore performance (2003), originally archived in A|S|I|A. This speech is made at once in the character of Lear facing his lost kingdom and by the *Jingju* actor Wu addressing his supporters in the 'kingdom' of *Jingju*. As in Yohangza's *Pericles*, the emotions of the theatrical and metatheatrical moments merge in the performer's address of his particular audience in a specific chronotope. In both these productions, the performative break by the lead actor reveals an adaptation of Shakespeare's play to be placed temporally and geographically by the occasion it marks in local theatre history. However, unlike *Pericles*, the location of *Li Er Zai Ci* extended across national boundaries into Chinese opera-going cultures in neighbouring countries like Singapore, and perhaps further into the diasporic Chinese communities worldwide.

In the later recording (2006) that has replaced the first recording in A|S|I|A, this moment is performed in a more polished manner but not with the same personal intensity of feeling; it is no longer the same event.[7] After its extensive tours abroad, the production's location is now worldwide; or rather, the place of *Jingju* in which *Li Er Zai Ci* locates itself had been extended by its own touring.[8] Knowing that *Jingju* means 'opera of the capital' and, as Li Ruru notes, was once also referred to as *guoju* (national drama) in Taiwan (2010: 170–87) allows a viewer to link Wu's career to a wider context, where *Jingju* practice is situated in Taiwan through the historical trajectory and current politics of Taiwan's relationship with mainland China. In *Li Er Zai Ci*, Wu implicitly refers to debates (controversies) over the training and future of *Jingju* that were ongoing in 2001, in which Wu was himself a major exponent of one side then, and has been increasingly since. As his anecdote about Mnouchkine indicates, *Li Er Zai Ci* was from the first enjoyed by audiences uninvolved in its historical moment within either Wu's career or *Jingju* in Taiwan. Yet as information on Asian productions is increasingly available in English,[9] and even more so where a referent of cultural identity is employed to adapt Shakespeare than where it is not, how that referent designates location asks to be understood in relation to the situated practice and to the identitarian issues motivating the adaptation of that practice to Shakespeare's play. It is the ground level of the production, which emerges briefly in a performative break revealing its location in place, time and immediate addressee, and the significance of adapting this Shakespeare play for this audience at this time.

In South Korea, performance practices for adapting Western plays (especially plays regarded as classic) are often collectively referred to as 'Koreanization', even though these practices are extremely diverse. Within the assumptions of realist theatre, the term 'Koreanization' would be assumed to refer to the onstage representation of identifiable Koreanness in some form. Writing about his experience of watching Koreanized Western plays while he was a visiting professor in Seoul, Patrice Pavis expresses his intercultural uncertainty about the stage product of 'Koreanization' from a European standpoint (which he explicitly identifies as his own positionality):

> I was often confused as to what exactly I was watching: the staging of an intangible text, a classic text, and in translation, for instance; or a play paraphrased in language written anew (e.g. Oh Tai-Sok's *The Tempest*); or the staging of an original new text (*Medea on Media*, composed by Kim, Hyun-tak); or a performance on the theme of a known play (e.g. Yang, Jung-ung's *Midsummer Night Dream* [*sic*]).
>
> (2017: 60)

Pavis proposes that the various possibilities encompassed within the scope of 'Koreanization' may be understood inclusively through the European concept of mise en scène: 'the organization of a performance or the final organized result' (60). His interpretation emphasizes a changed 'scene' on the stage. He considers the translation and editing of the text, the use of signs of Korea or 'Koreanisms' in performance forms and their kinesthetic rhythm and organization. However, treating the staging of representation or reference as the primary performative of Koreanization objectifies Korean identity and tends to reduce the complex act of creative adaptation to markers of another culture. Instead, a production such as Yohangza's *Pericles*, which explicitly avoids using Korean cultural signs, reveals the chief organizing principle that locates its adaptation in South Korea to be experiential rather than representational.

Yohangza's *Pericles* creates a complex relocation of Shakespeare's play by presenting dual time frames in its set and stage action. Its set, sketched above, is an imaginary space that allows the scenes of the play to be enacted outside the laws of realism. The scale of the space is evoked by a very deep stage covered in sand, with a huge moon projected on its horizon at the back, that sometimes changes into a compass. On the one hand, this set evokes at once desert and beach somewhere in the Middle East; on the other, it is 'a space in the middle of nowhere'.[10] The scene suggests mythological pasts by the gigantic fallen head that dwarfs the actors and the half-buried boat; both imply events irretrievably far back in time. The boat reminds us of Pericles' shipwreck at Pentapolis. Diana's head seems to reference Thaisa's entry into her temple at Ephesus and her appearance to Pericles in a dream; yet it also resembles the heads found at Nemrut Dağ (in modern-day Turkey), erected by Antiochus I of Commagene. These choices at once suggest places in the real world and distance the play temporally from a setting 'in' them. They reflect the ancient world of 'a song that old was sung' (*Pericles*.1, Prologue.1), not as a setting in the present time of the plot, when the city of Antioch is still 'the fairest in all Syria' but in a time when only evocative glimpses of that setting remain. With this shift in time, Yang reflexively positions his production at an unspecified point in the future after the play's events, in the geographical region of its locations in Antioch, Tyre, Tarsus, Pentapolis, Mytilene and Ephesus.

The setting surrounds the action with the presence of distant pasts, amongst which are hints of its own events. The ways in which this set is used bring the plot moment into conjunction with its lingering resonance. Diana's head is often lit in green, giving the scene a surreal atmosphere; the characters may be captured by the camera against her eyes or mouth, and Marina climbs atop the head to sing her song in the brothel. In this space, a strategy of open metatheatricality focuses on the immediacy of play-making. The audience's present-day world enters this setting through the use of ubiquitous, mundane objects to produce its events. The storm at sea is created when Pericles is pushed onto a darkened stage on a table on wheels by actors in bright blue hooded raincoats, who move the table from side to side as if upon 'rough waves'. The actors' movements mime their lurching on the deck, while other actors at the margins spray the scene with water from insecticide cans, and yet others hold up swaying hurricane lamps. The various staging elements – lurching table, tumultuous sounds, clouds of water and flickering lights in semi-darkness – all centre upon Pericles' loud, desperate pleas to the god of the sea and Lucina. When he casts Thaisa's body overboard, she walks in a rhythmic movement imitating her body rocking away upon the waves of the sand to a slow chant sung by male voices. The strategy co-opts the audience into the play-making, thereby involving us in the emotions of its dramatic narrative.

Yohangza's approach to metatheatrical performance is rooted in a primary aesthetic principle of Korean theatre that organizes the relationship of the players and the audience, and which Lee Hyon-U argues has its origins in the traditional theatre space, the *madang* ('yard'):

> The yard is an essential part of traditional Korean theatre, called *Talchum* (mask dance) or *Talnori* (mask play). The yard constitutes the stage. Therefore, the players are surrounded by the audience, and can interact with the audience by speaking to audience members, treating them as fellow players, or acting as if they themselves are part of the audience.

(2013: 41)

The actors' facing of the audience is a Korean acting style within this playing space, which plays a decisive part in reorienting the dynamics of naturalistic acting: instead of constituting a 'fourth wall', the audience is directly engaged by the actor as his or her addressee. Diverse strategies for 'Koreanizing' Shakespeare's plays have in common the active, frontal involvement of the audience in the play as a shared theatrical method, though that involvement works towards different ends and experiences. This principle, then, does not stage the performance in Korea, but generates a Korean experience of community.

Through a metatheatrical strategy for adapting Shakespeare's plays, *Li Er Zai Ci* and Yohangza's *Pericles* both situate their performances in the time frame of the present, thereby allowing the action to break into its extra-narrative moment in local theatre history. Neither production locates the place of its adaptation nationally, but in terms of its audience communities: Wu's audiences for *Jingu* reach into mainland China and further, into diasporic Chinese communities; and Yang generates a Korean sense of community in an imaginary space located far distant from Korea.

LOCATING REALISM BY THE AFTERLIFE

In this section I turn to the formal use of a stage space to locate a realist adaptation. I focus on the Ryutopia Noh Theatre Shakespeare Series' production of *Othello* (2006) in order to consider how the broad identification of Noh with Japan may be precisely located interracially and interculturally, by bringing the temporality of the afterlife in Noh into interaction with the historicity of realism in Shakespeare's *Othello*. The roots of Noh drama as entertainment during temple or shrine rituals, the spiritual discipline embodied in its formalized practice and rules, the symbolism of its stage, its plays and the concepts of its famous master Zeami Motokiyo have long been translated and studied (in English, most famously by Ernest Fenellosa and Ezra Pound).[11] The religio-aesthetic system of Noh drama presents a holistically alternative world to that in which Shakespeare wrote his plays. The Ryutopia Noh Theatre Shakespeare Series directed by Kurita Yoshihiro at Niigata Noh Theatre was a sustained project to bring Shakespeare onto the Noh stage. Like Wu, Kurita lightly attributes the series' genesis to a turning point in his own career in 1999, when he was appointed associate director of Niigata City Performing Arts Centre, where there was a Noh theatre. Kurita's series was prompted by being in Niigata and rethinking Shakespeare in this specific place:

> Zeami [the father of Noh] was exiled to the Niigata island of Sado and there are still over thirty Noh stages remaining on the island today. '*Takigi Noh*' [outdoor Noh performance] is also popular and it has long been a mark of one's status as a Noh performer to have performed in Niigata.
>
> (qtd in Yokouchi 2005)

Prior to this appointment, Kurita had performed traditional *Buyo* dance and the Super Kabuki of Ennosuke Ichikawa, and had also directed contemporary theatre, including Shakespeare and other plays in translation.

> I guess I had come to feel a basic contradiction in the act of performing a play from a translated script that was not written originally in your native language. Even if you got the actors to use lines that had a natural sense of daily life, the historical background would still be missing and that in itself is enough to undermine the reality and make a production hopeless.

At the same time, Kurita questioned the traditional Japanese style, *Wa*: 'what should a style "of the Japanese and for the Japanese" be, and how much should we focus on that idea to begin with' (qtd. in Yokouchi 2005). He aimed to create a 'new mixed breed of original Shakespeare', not a mismatch. In a similar way to Ninagawa Yukio's aim for his *Tempest*, he wanted audiences abroad to see it and to see how they felt about it.[12]

The square, roofed wooden Noh stage is open on three sides and has a *Hashigakari* (bridgeway) attached to it. In *Mugen Noh*, the actors' entrance and exit along the *Hashigakari* presents their passage between the world of the living on the main stage and that of the dead beyond the curtain at the end of the *Hashigakari*.[13] The back wall is painted with a pine tree that depicts the sacred pine at Kasuga-Taisha Shrine in Nara. This image is the unchanging backdrop of all Noh performances, placing the action against the backdrop of eternity. The production script of Ryutopia's *Othello* is almost wholly the standard translation by Matsuoka Kazuko,[14] but prior to Shakespeare's opening, a wordless prologue takes place that uses the Noh stage to frame his plot. Desdemona and Othello enter along the *Hashigakari* in Westernized Japanese kimono, followed by a Spirit wearing a dark gold mask and a pile of dreadlocks. The couple lay out a white sheet on the floor, their movements in natural accord, proceeding steadily step by step with no suggestion of passion or secrecy. The moment Othello kisses Desdemona, the Spirit interrupts and comes between them. To the growing pace of the drums, and holding an ancient stone knife in her hand, the Spirit conducts a ritual that is at once wedding ceremony and curse. She cuts her throat with the knife, then wipes it on a white cloth that we recognize as the strawberry-spotted handkerchief when she holds it up, and gives it to Desdemona.[15] This prologue changes the setting of *Othello*, from places in the human world (Venice and Cyprus) to the Noh stage, a space where the spirit world of *Mugen Noh* reveals itself. Through the handkerchief, stained with blood that is at once Desdemona's in sexual consummation and the Spirit's in suicide, the prologue introduces a premise for the action of Shakespeare's play, a premise that exists in another world than that action and in terms of which we thereafter see that action.

The Spirit's appearance identifies her with Africa, but her identity and motivations are ambiguous (ambiguity being an important aspect of Noh). During the course of the action, she may be seen as representing Jealousy, which the programme notes imply; as the Spirit of Barbary, since she removes her mask to sing Barbary's Willow song in place of Desdemona (5.1); as Desdemona herself; and as representing the African diaspora who assume the individual form of Barbary. The Spirit remains silently present throughout the action, her presence and influence upon it manifesting in adjustments to the *Shingeki* acting by the other actors. While their expressions and verbal delivery are realist, the blocking of their movements and positions on the stage consistently draws bodily relationships with the Spirit's body. For instance, the other actors position themselves along a diagonal line between her seated, unmoving position at the front left pillar of the stage, and the point on the *Hashigakari* just before it joins the main stage. So once they re-enter the realm of the living by stepping onto the main stage, they believe themselves to be acting of their own accord, but their movements physically embody their alignment with or control by the fate that the Spirit represents. The audience perceives the action to be taking place in dual time frames of the present, where the characters act on their own initiative, and the afterlife, where their fate becomes apparent.

The prologue also introduces Desdemona and Othello outside Shakespeare's play. Played by Tanida Ayumi, Othello does not seem of a different race, merely slightly darker skinned. Desdemona is played by Ichikawa Emiya II, a famous

Kabuki *Onnagata* (male actor specializing in female roles), who does not perform the role in Kabuki but in *Shingeki* style.[16] In their bearing, movements and expressions, Tanida and Ichikawa respectively play Othello and Desdemona with dignity and gentleness that do not role-play race or gender in any overt manner. Thus, all three roles in the prologue are presented as non-realist roles, whose actions dramatize the intertwined binaries of black/white and male/female in Desdemona and Othello's marriage in a symbolic manner. The effect of symbolism is made possible by the actors' performance style that alludes to the ritual stillness of masked Noh acting.

When Shakespeare's play begins, Tanida and Ichikawa switch into *Shingeki* acting with the rest of the cast, while the Spirit remains on stage without changing her acting style. The naturalism, although slightly stylized for performance on the Noh stage, underlines Tanida's portrayal of Othello without concrete ethnic differences from his fellow Japanese actors. In costume and behaviour Othello presents much like the Venetians but for a gold vest that marks his status as the general. The ambiguous differentiation of Othello has two combined, unsettling effects: first, of treating Othello's racial difference as abstract; and second, of drawing attention instead to the Japanese ethnicity, language and culture of the naturalism. The small difference of Othello's skin tone requires us to imagine his racial difference, and in so doing it metatheatrically introduces a third race and positionality – that of being Japanese – into the black/white polarity of the play and the history of its critical reception. Such a triangulation of races disrupts the binary by relativizing raced-ness from the viewpoint of the Far East and in the persons of a different colour, reminding an audience of histories of orientalism that are also part of white colonialism.

At the same time, the actors' committed *Shingeki* performance clearly positions the Japanese as the normative 'white' Venetians. Their ceremonial movements and formalized blocking enact a social decorum taken for granted by all onstage. It is in the context of a marked social collective that Ichikawa's training as an *Onnagata* takes its place as performing ideal femininity in his costume, behaviour, gestures and expressions. His projection of Desdemona gains definition as a traditional exemplar of femininity by being set alongside the female actors who play Emilia and Bianca as stronger, more modern women. In this performance the third race of the Japanese, then, is at once *us* and *other* – when seen from my own non-Japanese positionality. Here, one recognizes that realist Shakespeare produced in Asia is *a priori* cross-racial performance. The naturalization of Othello in Tanida's *Shingeki* performance as almost-Japanese is matched inversely by the strangeness of a Noh-like Spirit who watches from the perspective of an indigenous older Japan *as another race*. Although she does not alter the action, the masked Spirit's position on the stage and the movements of Shakespeare's characters constantly align to present the plot as a pattern that she is part of. When Othello recounts the course of his strange life, she walks to Brabantio. During Othello's pause after 'The Anthropophagi and men whose heads / Do grow beneath their shoulders' (Ryutopia's *Othello* 2006: 0:23:54), she silently confronts Brabantio, who rises on his knees with a shocked, fearful expression, then sinks down, defeated. Brabantio's shock is a regular crux in Noh plots when the true visage of a spirit is revealed, but the moment also presents another character's spiritual self-realization. The Spirit functions as a mirror of

Othello's foreignness, which is sublimated in Tanida's portrayal. Since she may be seen as the *Shite* (the primary role of Noh drama), we also see the action through her eyes, so, in reverse, she brings into view the cross-racial performance of whiteness by the *Shingeki* actors.

LOOKING ABROAD

Yohangza's *Pericles* and Ryutopia's *Othello* both use non-realist strategies to face or step out from their locations and interact with those of Shakespeare's plays. Experimenting with how *Shingeki* and Noh drama may be brought together, Kurita adds to Shakespeare's characters an African-like Noh Spirit that reflects histories of race outside Japan, and the raced background of realist Shakespeare itself. Yang places his production in a performative parallel to Shakespeare's text: in both, the tale of *Pericles* takes place in roughly the same geographical location, his set accompanying the play's verbal evocation. These productions' address of the foreign place (the Middle East) and foreigner (Othello) constitutes a strategy for treating their own non-Anglophone position for adapting Shakespeare's play. Inseparable from the two productions' relocation of the plays is their use of theatrical principles that introduce alternative dimensions of time – the immediacy of play-making, and the afterlife. Ultimately, these two dimensions, while producing such contrasting theatre experiences in the desert and on the Noh stage, are part of similar belief systems that rebalance the historical time of realism within an awareness of the other world. Yang pointed out about the set of Yohangza's *Pericles*,

> there is also in the sand the element of temporality. I thought of the sand in an hourglass or in a sandglass and so the stage in some ways is a symbol of time. And the image of Diana lying in the sand in some ways represents the presence of the sacred in temporality to which the human beings submit in the end.[17]

Contemporary Legend Theatre's *Li Er Zai Ci* by comparison forms an important reminder that the apparent unity of performance form with its location is in fact questioned by the historicity of the production's innovation and the positionalities of its different audiences.

NOTES

The Asian Shakespeare Intercultural Archive (A|S|I|A) project is part of three successive research projects supported by the Singapore Ministry of Education (Relocating Intercultural Theatre, MOE2008- T2-1-110; Digital Archiving and Intercultural Performance, MOE2013-T2-1-011; and Digital Performance Scholarship, MOE2018-T2-2-092).

1   In the online Watch Party he held for the World Shakespeare Congress 2021, Yang said, 'I felt that the tragic catastrophes that are happening in Syria were on my mind and that experience is something that entered into the production' ('Watch Party: *Pericles*', live translation by Yu-Jin Ko, National University of Singapore, 17 July 2021, 1:12:10).

2   Yoo In-Chon was South Korea's Minister of Culture, Sports and Tourism from February 2008 until January 2011.

3   Scene and act divisions are slightly different in the playscript from Shakespeare's.

4   Park Ha-Rim translated the script from Korean into English for A|S|I|A.

5   Performance recording and script of Yohangza Theatre Company's *Pericles*, kindly donated to A|S|I|A by Yohangza Theatre Company, A|S|I|A, 1:38:34–58, 10 March 2021. Available online: http://a-s-i-a-web.org (accessed 12 August 2021).

6   Programme, Chinese Festival of Arts, Singapore, 10 February 2003, 17.

7   Contemporary Legend Theatre requested that we replace the earlier video with the later one which was produced at a higher technical standard and represented their 'finished' version of the play. This version, produced with a presentation box, was issued for the twentieth anniversary of the company in 2006. However, Wu asked us for a copy of the earlier video because the company no longer had one and it represented the original.

8   A detailed timeline of performances is maintained on the CLT website, http://www. twclt.com/en/event.aspx (accessed 12 August 2021).

9   The major daily newspapers have online English versions with reviews of performances, and performance blogs are also growing. A|S|I|A data has a first level category for 'Points of Reference'.

10 A|S|I|A data for Yohangza Theatre Company's *Pericles*, Art/Forms, 10 March 2021, http://a-s-i-a-web.org (accessed 12 August 2021).

11 Ernest Fenellosa and Ezra Pound (1916). Also see Shimakazi Chifumi (1972–81), *The Noh, Volumes I–III* and her other translated plays published by the Cornell East Asia Series; Nakamura Yasuo (1971); and Sekine Masaru (1985).

12 The Ryutopia Noh Theatre Shakespeare's *The Winter's Tale I* (2005) was revived for a proscenium stage and toured to Europe in 2006 and 2008. The production of *Hamlet* (2007) toured to the 14th Gdańsk Shakespeare Festival in 2010.

13 Of the two types of Noh plays, *Mugen Noh* which deals with spirits, animals and other non-human beings, is more popular by far than *Genzai Noh*, which takes place in the present time and is realistic.

14 Performance recording and script of the Ryutopia Noh Theatre Shakespeare's *Othello* kindly donated to A|S|I|A by Ryutopia Noh-theatre Shakespeare and Niigata City Art & Culture Promotion Foundation, A|S|I|A, 21 May 2021. Available online: http://a-s-i-a-web.org (accessed 12 August 2021).

15 This section draws upon collaborative annotations and discussions of Ryutopia's *Othello* by the editorial team, comprising Michael Dobson, Jessica Chiba, Alvin Lim Eng Hui and myself, who began work on this production for the multimedia volume, *Spirits and Shakespeare in Asian Performance* (currently in preparation as part of the A|S|I|A project) while I was writing this chapter.

16 Ichikawa Emiya II is the stage name conferred upon Izumiyama Takao after he had achieved eminence in successive stages of training and apprenticeship. By the

conferral of this name, he was adopted into the leading Kabuki family of Ichikawa whose lineage stretches back to the late seventeenth century.

17 Watch Party: *Pericles*', live interpretation by Yu-Jin Ko, National University of Singapore, 17 July 2021, 0:46:08–41.

REFERENCES

Allain, P. (1998), 'Suzuki Training', *TDR: The Drama Review* 42 (1): 66–89.

Bharucha, R. (2010), 'Foreign Asia/Foreign Shakespeare: Dissenting Notes on New Asian Interculturality, Postcoloniality and Re-colonization', in D. Kennedy and Y.L. Lan (eds), *Shakespeare in Asia: Contemporary Performance*, 253–82, Cambridge: Cambridge University Press.

Booth, D. (2002), 'Preparing Shakespeare's Texts for the Stage', in K. K. Tam, A. Parkin and T. S. H. Yip (eds), *Shakespeare Global/Local: The Hong Kong Imaginary in Transcultural Production*, 43–54, Frankfurt: Peter Lang.

Fenellosa, E. and E. Pound (1916), '*Noh*', or Accomplishment: A Study of the Classical Stage of Japan*, London: Macmillan.

Lee, H. U. (2013), 'The Yard and Korean Shakespeare', *Multicultural Shakespeare: Translation, Appropriation and Performance* 10 (25): 39–52.

Lee, R. (2003), *Shashibiya: Staging Shakespeare in China*, Hong Kong: Hong Kong University Press.

Lee, R. (2010), 'Millenium *Shashibiya*: Shakespeare in the Chinese-speaking World', in D. Kennedy and Y. L. Lan (eds), *Shakespeare in Asia: Contemporary Performance*, 170–87, Cambridge: Cambridge University Press.

Minami, R., I. Carruthers and J. Gillies (2001), *Performing Shakespeare in Japan*, Cambridge: Cambridge University Press.

Nakamura, Y. (1971), *Noh: The Classical Theater*, New York, NY: Walker/Weatherhill.

Pavis, P. (1992), *Theatre at the Crossroads of Culture*, London and New York, NY: Routledge.

Pavis, P. (2017), *Performing Korea*, trans. J. Anderson, London: Palgrave Macmillan.

Sekine, M. (1985), *Ze-Ami and His Theories of Noh Drama*, Gerrards Cross: Colin Smythe.

Shimazaki, C. (1972–81), *The Noh, Volumes I–III*, Tokyo: Hinoki Shoten.

Suzuki, T. (2015), *Culture is the Body: The Theatre Writings of Tadashi Suzuki*, trans. K. H. Steele, New York, NY: Theatre Communications Group.

Yokouchi, K. (2005), 'Interview: A Meeting of Eastern and Western Classics – The Noh-Staged Shakespeare of Yoshihiro Kurita', Performing Arts Network Japan Artist Interview, 16 March, 1–3. Available online: http://performingarts.jp/E/art_interview/0503/1.html (accessed 12 August 2021).

Yong, L. L. (2017), 'Interacting with Naturalism', in J. L. Levenson and R. Ormsby (eds), *The Shakespearean World*, 135–53, Oxford and New York, NY: Routledge.

'And we will ship him hence': The case for Shakespeare fan studies

VALERIE M. FAZEL AND LOUISE GEDDES

In Privatbi's 2018 fanfic, 'Okay', Hamlet and Horatio are 'shipped' – that is to say, the two characters are reimagined as lovers – and their erotic relationship played out in a scene in which Horatio's textual (or canonical) dependability is envisioned as part of his romantic devotion to his beloved Hamlet. The fanfic's readers are privileged to Horatio's interiority, his tender thoughts of desire to protect his emotionally fragile lover. The penultimate line in the brief fanfic pictures the lovers entwined with Horatio yearning to forestall Hamlet's breakdown: 'If I just keep holding him, thought Horatio, giving in to wishful thinking, I can keep him from shattering.' This moment draws from Shakespeare's play, perhaps inspired by Horatio's declaration to be 'more an Antique Roman than a Dane' (5.2.341), in which Hamlet's friend suggests his willingness to kill himself so as not to live without Hamlet. While Horatio in Shakespeare's play has a fairly familiar relationship with several characters, his lack of a soliloquy means his persona can only be surmised through his dialogue with Hamlet, Gertrude and other members of Claudius's court. Although brief, Privatbi's fanfic offers a glimpse into an imagined relationship between Horatio and Hamlet; its speculative reimagining combines a reading of lines from the playtext and the author's affective interest in creating a subtext for *Hamlet*. The fanfic invites a reconsideration of the homoerotics of a Hamlet/Horatio relationship that might contribute to a new way to understand why Hamlet can only commit to loving Ophelia in the wake of her death.

In the twenty-first century, fanworks – including fanfic, fan art, fan comics and fan videos – are tremendously popular critical and creative approaches to Shakespeare. For instance (at the time of writing) *Archive of Our Own (AO3)*, the most prominent fanfic repository on the internet, reports *Hamlet* tagged as the subject of over eight hundred fanfics. In sum total, Shakespeare is represented on *AO3* in over twelve thousand fan crafted narratives. Although *AO3* and the genre of fanfic is perhaps mostly widely known in popular culture, internet social repositories for art, quizzes, videos, discussions and more abound: wattpad, Commaful, fanfiction.net, Tumblr, asianfanfics and deviantArt are popular, frequently cited websites favoured by fans. As fanwork pops up in real and virtual arenas, it emerges as a form of appropriation that openly acknowledges its affective investment in Shakespeare. However, appropriation theory is fundamentally impeded by the fallacy of academic objectivity – a belief that relies on Barthes's famous claim for the death of the author, which then necessitates a study of artefacts over process. The resulting methodological practice can never capture the appropriative act as it occurs, and therefore inevitably fails most attempts to understand a relationship between two objects: Shakespeare and its appropriation. Shakespeare is both an ever-increasing archive of texts *and*, as Kavita Mudan Finn demonstrates, a '[c]onversation – between fan authors, fan artists and those who consume their works' (2017: 212); these compatible approaches afford inclusivity and diversity in the critical expansion of Shakespeare adaptation studies. This chapter argues that by including fan studies as part of appropriation theory scholarship we can account for this conversation, manifest in likes, re-posts and experimental fan work. Because of the interplay between creator and audience, the focus of appropriative study shifts from the end product, the new Shakespeare iteration, to the fan relationship with an object that results in appropriation and the creation of new works. By centring the fan, appropriation theory can fully engage with the *processes* of appropriation (in addition to the fan product) recognizing and situating the fan as both consumer and producer of popular Shakespeares.

Critical fan scholarship has only very recently nudged its way into the field of Shakespeare adaptation studies. Yet, fandoms have always been part of the Shakespeare legacy. Shakespeare's past and present appearance onstage and screen, coupled with the recurrence of his name in institutional curricula around the globe, has long inspired the building (and rebuilding) of theatres, countless adaptations and new scholarship. The recent critical work by both Stephen O'Neill (2020) and Johnathan H. Pope (2020), and critical-creative work by Kavita Mudan Finn and Jessica McCall (2016), and our own methodological approaches have each argued and demonstrated that fan practices are, quite plainly, Shakespeare adaptations. In *The Shakespeare Multiverse: Fandom as Literary Praxis* (2021) we argue that scholarship is a form of fan activity and expand the definition of adaptation to accommodate the type of conversations and creative endeavours that indirectly adapt Shakespeare and (or with) other cultural phenomena by validating fanwork that draws from any Shakespeare text. While for so long the wealth of fan studies gravitated towards the affective fandoms of popular culture phenomena (broadcast media and professional sports, for instance), the stance of Shakespeare adaptation critics, ostensibly, was on the objective study of popular uses of Shakespeare. The subjective positionality advocated for in fan studies has been present in Shakespeare adaptation studies almost since its inception, yet until recently has remained methodologically unacknowledged. Shakespeare fan studies and adaptation theories draw from the central precepts of both fields: consumption is manifest in production and production reiterates or re-presents the text in a way that adapts it for individual or specialized use. Certainly, approaches such as critical race studies and feminist or queer theory challenge traditionally held notions of objectivity and neutrality because they closely attend to identity valences and their cultural framings. Such perspectives acknowledge the extent to which the understanding of Shakespeare depends on the subjective positioning of his audience or reader. They and fan studies offer new pathways for Shakespeare adaptation criticisms in the future.

Fandom's affective power and the twenty-first-century dependence on the internet as both chronicler and source of culture, have proven influential forces that have the power to impact dominant media forces such as broadcast serial television. For example, a 2018 fan campaign to protest Fox's cancellation of the beloved television show *Brooklyn 99* resulted in broadcast competitor NBC contracting a new season thus continuing the series and the show's move to its new network. Elsewhere, the vocal objections of fans have forced celebrities to acknowledge problematic actions such as in 2020 when fans of *RuPaul's Drag Race* protested Sherrie Pie's inclusion in the contest in the wake of allegations of sexually inappropriate behaviour, resulting in their removal from the show and a sizable donation to an LGBTQIA+ youth charity. Fan organized activities in and around virtual spaces such as LiveJournal and Wattpad, followed by the popular and seductively visual Tumblr and Instagram, and the aforementioned *AO3*, each and all call attention to new strategies for access and sharing Shakespearean adaptations. Many online technologies facilitating fan activity render traces of the ways fan communities form, respond to and arrange themselves, empowering a grassroots validation of a fanwork through 'likes' and reposts that increase a text's presence and mobility across media. The visibility and organization of fans encourages consideration of how scholarly organizations structure themselves in similar ways. The emphasis on dialogue, intellectual exchange and community all predicated on a presentist understanding of Shakespeare that insists on the importance of our current moment is undeniably fan-like. Fandom takes for granted the methodologies that drive presentist literary criticism, an approach premised by the concept that 'the questions we ask of any literary text will inevitably be shaped by our own concerns, even when these include what we call "the past"' (Grady and Hawkes 2006: 5). Recognizing fandom not only calls for understanding the subjective position from which new adaptations of Shakespeare emerge, but also requires an acknowledgment of the importance of affective pleasure and self-aware criticism in literary studies.

Although adaptation has been described as a process (Kidnie 2009: 26), without the capacity to acknowledge the fan's centrality to that process, discourse is limited to a study of objects. As fan studies and adaptation theory has shifted to reflect an increasing awareness of those who use Shakespeare, scholars contributing to the burgeoning field of Shakespeare fan studies have been increasingly invested in thinking about the networks of integrated units that put Shakespeare into conversation with other fan objects. Mudan Finn's work notes a critical resistance to the overlap between professional appropriations of Shakespeare and amateur fanwork, highlighting the extent to which 'attitudes toward professionally produced adaptations within the fandom are double-edged' (2017: 214), with scholars using fandom as a source of study while disavowing their own affective sensibility. Anna Blackwell approaches fandom as part of a larger discourse of celebrity, examining how Shakespeare fandoms intersect with other celebrity fandoms such as the fandoms of actors who perform Shakespeare onstage alongside other roles in mainstream culture (2018). David Tennant's ever-popular portrayal of the tenth doctor, for example, in BBC's popular *Doctor Who*, series 2 through to 4 which broadcasted between 2005 and 2010, brought a legion of sci-fi fans to Shakespeare theatre, and these two seemingly separate career trajectories frequently cross over and cannot be unseen within the Shakespeare fandom. Jennifer Holl also takes up the idea of intersecting fan objects in her suggestion that we consider auteurs such as Joss Whedon, Kenneth Branagh, and Julie Taymor as Shakespeare fanboys and fangirls engaged in a playful relationship with Shakespeare (2017: 111). Holl would likely concur with Blackwell's definition of such users as 'fans of Shakespeare; remediators of his work, knowledgeable users of digital technology and skilled participants in Internet culture' (Blackwell 2018: 165) and Finn repeatedly draws attention to the ways in which fan studies and academic practices mirror each other. Each scholar argues that to imagine professional Shakespeareans as exempt from the circulations of knowledge and affect that new media engender is disingenuous. We need an expanded understanding of fandom to include not only the fans who appropriate Shakespeare, but also the people who perform him – individuals whose popularity might attract new followers into Shakespeare fandom – and invite Shakespeare scholars to recognize the vast network of confluences that shape the adaptation process.

ARCHONTIC SHAKESPEARE

Rather than think of a Shakespeare text as discrete from its offshoots, a fannish adaptation theory collapses the distinction between Shakespeare and, for example, Emily St. John Mandel's *Station Eleven*, which leans heavily on *King Lear*, to rethink how we understand the text to accommodate diverse explorations. Abigail Dericho (De Kosnik) suggests that curation defines the fan texts themselves, characterizing the works as archontic. She explains, '[a]n archontic text allows, even invites, writers to enter it, select specific terms they find useful, make new artefacts using those found objects, and deposit the newly made work back into the source text's archive' (Derecho 2006: 65). Finn, however, encourages literary scholars to look further than Derecho's archontic to include Catherine Tosenberger's postulation of fanworks as 'recursive' (2016: 3). Tosenberger argues that '"[a]rchontic" refers to a space, "recursive" refers to an action… [recursive] contains the greater assumption of agency, of action, for the activities of fans' (emphasis original, Tosenberger qtd. in Finn 2017: 212). Finn notes the fine distinction between archontic and recursive is one that shifts a perception of Shakespeare from 'an ever-growing archive into which knowledge is poured to a circular conversation between authors and readers' (2016: 3), where appropriation can lead the reader back to the text. Baz Luhrmann's 1996 *William Shakespeare's Romeo + Juliet*, for instance, manifests recursive exchange between the diverse cultures of 1990s Southern California and past *Romeo and Juliet* adaptations, including *West Side Story* (itself an adaptation).

Fan culture borrows heavily from Luhrmann as evidenced by fan Mercutios – non-white, flamboyant, sexualized – found liberally on the internet (Fazel and Geddes 2021). Both archontic and recursive offer a theoretical underpinning of Shakespeare fan studies as an appropriative practice that draws equally from the technologies used to represent Shakespeare, the playtexts, past adaptations and the fan's desire to build the Shakespeare they want, but the idea of an archontic text more firmly supports the intertextual nature of Shakespearean fandom. Put simply, one cannot assume that the fan returns to the same iteration of the text when they want to enjoy or use Shakespeare.

The many ways a fan can encounter 'the text', from the scholarly Arden editions of individual plays to a fan's favourite celebrity performance of *Hamlet*, draws attention to the ambiguity of the object referred to when fans utter 'Shakespeare'. While certainly the chequered editorial history of Shakespeare means that authorial intention is always beyond the grasp of fans, part of the uncertainty as to what constitutes Shakespeare also arises through the prevalence of the internet and the ubiquity of instant access and person-to-person sharing. Millennials have developed a preference for learning through conversation and through methods that are far less top-down than the traditional classroom, resulting in an increasingly experiential and personalized approach to Shakespeare. User-generated cultural artefacts reign in a domain that rivals dominant producers' entertainment: the videos that abound YouTube, the memes that scroll down a Tumblr page, the uncountable Instagram accounts that visually chronicle users' Shakespeare experiences and the critical discussions that take place on reddit. All of these grant us access to Shakespeare, and sometimes even stand in lieu of the text itself. What becomes immediately clear is that many people are happy to learn from strangers on the web. The communities that form around fan objects are driven by an affective sensibility and a diminished or non-existent sense of fidelity to any individual source that influenced the shape of the fan object. That is to say, a fan might learn about *Coriolanus* from watching Tom Hiddleston's 2013 Donmar Warehouse pay per view production online just as effectively as they might from reading an edition of *Coriolanus* in a class. Accessibility is key to understanding Shakespeare fan studies, and while access empowers fans and non-fan scholars alike to change the way they position themselves in relation to Shakespeare, it also deconstructs the Shakespearean 'work'.

The idea of Shakespeare, then, breaks down and in so doing enables fans to use for themselves whatever they find worthwhile. Online, as Christy Desmet reminds us of contemporary Shakespeares, the 'disaggregation of a Shakespearean text into "units" – semantic segments, words, lines, or even morphemes – is the condition of existence for digital texts, necessary for such features as text formatting and a workable search engine' (2017: 5). Under such conditions, Shakespeare cross-pollinates with other 'units' and acquires meaning from other sources, which may or may not support the 'original' Shakespearean meaning. This intersection is 'archontic production' (De Kosnik 2016: 277), as the Shakespeare text becomes a crowdsourced archive. Subverting the producer → fan trajectory, De Kosnik suggests that 'media audiences have begun to perceive that they, themselves, are the archons, the ones who make the laws that govern the textual archives they encounter, take possession of, explore, and exploit' (2016: 279). Shakespeare, therefore, becomes both a space (DeKosnik's archontic site) where fans roam around, explore and break off bits of Shakespeare, and Kidnie's and Mudan Finn's process, a recursive experience by which these pieces are returned to Shakespeare, making him more complicated, and more richly palimpsestic.

Historically, the substance that is Shakespeare culture has always been a weave of creative and critical work. Across the centuries, scholars and artists – from Nahum Tate to David Garrick and Samuel Taylor Coleridge – documented their own appropriate relationship with Shakespeare, and allowed their attachment to seep into their creative output. At the beginning of the twentieth century, William Poel's Shakespeare Society emphasized the importance of scholarly research to perform the plays, bringing what we would now term 'original practices' to the Victorian stage. Fast forward to the 2010s and purposefully, Shakespeareans, including Ewan Fernie, Rob Conkie and the two of us have become more open about the inability to disconnect critical and affective creative methods, instead seeking out new critical structures that can accommodate affective responses both within and to adaptation. Graham Holderness, for instance, demonstrates through his creative work *Black and Deep Desires: William Shakespeare Vampire Hunter* and his argument for a theory of creative collision in *Tales from Shakespeare*, 'the impact of a number of forces and objects upon one another… accounting for what sometimes happens to produce the phenomenon we know as "Shakespeare"' (2014: 17). As Finn and McCall note, 'creating, reading, and writing fanfiction preserves the multiplicity and complexity of meaning in the text rather than replacing it; it also offers a radical and safe space for students and amateur Shakespeareans alike to stretch their wings through a ridiculousness that only exists, and can only exist, in the unmonitored marginalia of academia' (2016: 29). More recently, Rob Conkie has begun to explore 'creative critical Shakespeares', recognizing that fanwork can and should sit alongside traditional criticism because of its capacity to expand the archontic text and offer new critical perspectives (2019: 1–20). Creative criticism, as each scholar suggests in their work, expands the Shakespeare text rather than offering an alternative to it.

Fan activity, then, covers a wide range of practices, from academic journal writing (or writing chapters for books such as this one), fanfic, fan art and other, more innovative processes. Platforms such as *AO3*, Tumblr and TikTok enable appropriations that exist entirely in digital format, becoming 'viral' responses that are circulated widely and archived in personal repositories alongside other fandoms, manifest as a digital chapbook of sorts. Tags in fanfics show how fans amass vast cultural ephemera and reach wide audiences as a result. Amerna's 2016 fanfic 'Reports About My Love Life Have been Greatly Exaggerated' collapses characters Captain America and Thor from the Marvel Cinematic Universe with Jane Austen and Shakespeare, with the author acknowledging in the tags that 'I took cues from Shakespeare and Jane Austen' and that 'they are probably rolling over in their graves' because of this particular mash-up. At the time of writing the fic has been read 96,660 times, earning 3,343 kudos and 1,896 complimentary comments, illustrating the interactivity of fan communities. Many of these commenters beg for more chapters, and anticipate the trajectory of the fic as it progresses. This fan activity highlights a process that is as dependent on the interaction of its reading community as it is on the appropriating author's intentions. Moreover, the immateriality of these fanfics marks them as ephemera, but the far-reaching influence these texts hold suggests that fan communities are not necessarily dependent on the traditional models of transmission and publication that appropriation scholarship values.

Other fan appropriations begin in these more overtly fannish spaces and migrate to material objects, suggesting that the hierarchical presence of print culture still carries weight. A recent bilingual (English and Russian) book project by the fan writer Avoirbanane, documented on their Bēhance page, shows not only how fans contribute materially to the growth of the Shakespeare text but also the collaborative nature of fanwork that depends on a critical consensus about the text itself. The book emerged because of Avoirbanane's enjoyment of the Royal Shakespeare Company's 2013 production of *Richard II*, directed by Gregory Doran and starring the aforementioned David Tennant. After sharing some of their Tennant/*Richard II* fan art online, and with the encouragement of other fans, Avoirbanane decided to turn the whole production into a graphic novel of sorts based on their sketches. They explain that it was a collaborative effort, describing how other people joined the team and

> created a parallel translation into Russian, highlighted parts that were omitted or changed by Doran, gathered and added tonns [*sic*] of commentaries and notes. They also contacted [the] Royal Shakespeare Company to get permission to go forward with the idea, organised crowdfunding and printing.
>
> (Ryzhova 2021)

This beautiful book is a crowdsourced critical project, adapting a performance (which in itself might be considered an adaptation) alongside a translation, critical commentary and editorial notes. Some 130 editions were published and sent worldwide, with one being hand-delivered to David Tennant himself. The material existence of the book suggests how fanwork mirrors scholarly production, generating a new text, drawn from careful transcription of a production, incorporating and explaining edits and editorial choices, and rendering text more accessible through images. The only difference, in this instance, is that unlike scholarship, which is ostensibly practiced for the advancement of humanist knowledge, Avoirbanae's project is driven by enthusiasm for Tennant's portrayal of Shakespeare. The fact that the publication is an additional degree or two away from the kind of proximity to the text that scholarship promotes makes this project no less valuable as a critical object. Its existence validates an archontic adaptation theory because it illustrates how the text is articulated through a fannish perspective and is primarily inspired by Gregory Doran's production.

Other fanworks sit a few degrees from scholarly work, but nonetheless contribute to the archontic growth of Shakespeare. For example, *The Tempest* fanfic, 'Answer Echoes, Dying, Dying' (Reine_des_corbeaux 2019), located on *AO3,* is a brief backstory of Caliban and Ariel that explores how colonial figures of authority and power are indifferent to the suffering of the indigenous people. The story follows Caliban's childhood relationship with what he imagines to be a magical tree, one bound up with the spirit of Ariel. 'Answer Echoes, Dying, Dying' deliberately evokes Prospero's own narrative trajectory when Sycorax tells her infant child that '[w] e won't be here much longer, because we don't belong here, with these damned spirits and these damned rocks and vines. We should be around other people. Our own people. This island isn't our Home.' Caliban, who like Miranda, had never encountered people before, lived in bliss with his tree until Prospero's arrival. Buoyed by the security of Ariel's presence, Caliban helps Prospero, leading, as we know, to his later enslavement. After yet another beating, Caliban asks Ariel why the spirit betrayed him and suggests that Ariel had simply traded one bondage for another. Ariel guiltily accuses Caliban back: 'And would you have freed me to the winds, or left me in the tree your mother threw me in for your own amusement?' and the fic ends. This eloquent retelling of Caliban's experience invites consideration of the repeated disenchantment that characterizes *The Tempest*, from the harsh realities that undermine Gonzalo's colonialist dream or the fragility of the fantasy of repentance that Prospero strives to elicit from his unwilling brother. The fic reclaims the experiences of both Caliban and Ariel and contributes to a reading of *The Tempest* that foregrounds the inevitable cruelty of the colonial project and its dehumanization of the indigenous people in an occupied land. 'Answer Echoes, Dying, Dying' is moderately popular, but in the comments one reader remarks that 'I'm going to share this story with absolutely everyone I know and keep it as my own private headcanon/background for the show' that their Shakespeare group is planning to produce, hinting at its further circulation in small, esoteric fan communities offline.

While many Shakespeare fans write fanfic, produce fan art and/or create fan videos, a presumed respectability affixed to Shakespeare underpins a particular emphasis on the more careful consumption of Shakespeare as artistic or scholarly, rather than fan. Such a perspective effaces the emotive drives that are – self-acknowledged or not – the animating spirit of fandom. Shakespeare scholars write blogs, they register for conventions, attend (and analyse) performances and subscribe to journals, but because their fandom is 'articulated through their knowledge of the subject', it is afforded the greater privilege of being recognized as scholarship, which frequently silos itself from more ephemeral fan productions such as those archived on *AO3* (Blackwell 2018: 22). Two factors contribute to the breakdown of the binary between scholar and fan: firstly, sub-communities on platforms known by such names as BookTok and academic Twitter, alongside blogs like Arizona State University's Sundial facilitate more publicly available pedagogic and critical discourse; secondly (the economic hardships that universities face having left well-trained and still-active researchers unable to secure employment within the academy), a discourse community that congregates in non-academic spaces (particularly the aforementioned virtual spaces) resulting in a more inclusive humanities. The language by which fans are described, however, is intended to reinforce the binaries that authorize one voice over another. Roberta Pearson notes the arcane labels that are perpetuated as an attempt to maintain outdated distinction along cultural hierarchies:

> [T]he absence of a single agreed-upon name signals the invisibility in which power often cloaks itself... [t]he terms 'buffs'/'enthusiasts'/'devotees' are at worst neutral, while 'aficionados'/'cognoscenti'/'connoisseurs,' with their implications of specialized, and more importantly, worthwhile knowledge, positively value those to whom they are applied.
>
> (2007: 99)

The distinction between 'buffs' and 'fans' designates a hierarchy that separates the so-called objective scholar from the passionate fan. The distinction continues to manifest itself in fan studies: few in the field have touched on 'high brow' literary fandom, perhaps as Pearson argues, 'within the strain of cultural studies that traces its lineage to Birmingham, high culture figures only as a repressive other against which to celebrate the virtues of the popular' (2007: 99) although more recently the critical work of Anna Wilson, Erica Haugvelt and Balaka Basu has begun to address how literature functions as fan activity. Understanding how literary works such as John Milton's *Paradise Lost* might be seen as a fannish adaptation of The Bible, or how Victorian publishing practices created cultures of serial media consumption builds a rich and convincing history of literature as media that connects the contemporary fan to the seemingly distant author.

Fandom itself has had a vexed relationship with the idea of being subject to a scholarship that did not always openly recognize its own affective stance. One fan, cited on the crowd-sourced website Fanlore, notes: 'knowing you might end up in a psych or sociology journal could put a real damper on your enthusiasm and willingness to participate, taking away fandom's greatest appeal' (Larsen and Zubernis 2011: 11). Books such as Larsen and Zubernis's 2011 *Fandom at the Crossroads: Celebration, Shame and Fan/Producer Relationships* and their 2013 *Fangasm: Supernatural Fangirls*, and Francesca Coppa's *The Fanfiction Reader: Folk Tales for a Digital Age* attempted to navigate this critical challenge by documenting their experience of researching their own fandoms, in the case of Larsen and Zubernis, or creating a curated reader of fanfic, as Coppa does, in an attempt to recognize our subjective intellectual position in regards to the things we love, even as it recognizes that perhaps 'acafans tend to be uncomfortable on both sides of the fence' (Larsen and Zubernis 2011: 11). In Shakespeare studies, there are varying degrees of intersubjective participation with Shakespeare that do not invoke shame, because they are considered professional. Take, for example, the theatre practitioner who writes books about their experience acting in, or directing Shakespeare. Such practitioners run across the spectrum from the primarily academic, such as Valerie Clayman Pye, to the purely artistic, for example, the late actor Sir Antony Sher. The discourse of shame, perhaps, is not so much acknowledging one's investment in Shakespeare, but one's love for Shakespeare.

Of course, this is not to say that Shakespearean adaptation studies has been entirely indifferent to the affective desire that drives many projects. Christy Desmet and Robert Sawyer's pioneering book *Shakespeare and Appropriation* examines 'individual acts of "re-vision" that arise from love or rage, or simply a desire to play with Shakespeare' (1999: 2) recognizing that the appropriative impulse is an affective response to the text and implicitly critiquing the ostensibly detached eye of literary scholarship (Desmet and Sawyer 1999: 2). Desmet's implicit recognition of fandom's affective investment is manifest in her observation that 'Shakespearean appropriations have a personal urgency for their creators and might, in Adrienne Rich's words, even be considered acts of survival' or resistance (Desmet 1999: 2). The collection paved the way for the emergence of a new field of study, producing extensive scholarship and the open-access journal, *Borrowers and Lenders: A Journal of Shakespeare Appropriation* that charts the path between Shakespeare and its appropriations. An acknowledgment of fan studies within this discourse consequently creates a space to consider the reception of Shakespeare upon which adaptation depends.

SHAKESPEARE FAN STUDIES

Diana Henderson's proposal that we put Shakespeare on the same level as his appropriators and recognize 'Shake-shifting' as acts of contemporary collaboration remains under-utilized, suggesting an ongoing resistance to the necessary self-reflexive practice of critical study (2006: 25). Henderson points out the obligation to a presentist perspective when she observes that

> recontextualizing Shakespeare's play for the modern stage or screen involves another layer of awareness of time and history: in addition to the historical era represented within the Shakespeare text, and the Elizabethan moment of its composition, one must add (at least) the present moment of performance — as well as, in most cases, some awareness of the theatrical and screen history of productions intervening.
>
> (2006: 253)

Henderson repositions adaptation and performance as a palimpsested process of media consumption that, with self-awareness, manifests itself in a new work. Although Henderson only considers professional appropriations, we might take her conclusions further and suggest that her concept of Shake-shifting implicitly recognizes appropriations as akin to fan fiction.

An example of the richly palimpsestic work that characterizes both fanwork and appropriation can be found in the K-pop themed fanfic, 'A Korean Midsummer Night's Comedy: A Shohina89's Storyline', an appropriation of *A Midsummer Night's Dream* published on asianfanfics.com. The author scripts Korean pop (K-pop) counterparts to Demetrius, Helena, Hermia and Lysander, to make readers 'cry with laughter and laugh till your guts hurt'. Professing she is 'taking a break' from her usual interest in horror fanfic writing, Sho – as she self-identifies – explains to her readers that because 'we saw many versions of Shakespeare but never seen [*sic*] modern versions of this class story so I decided to add a touch of K-Pop with romance, drama, comedy and magic into a hilarious [*sic*] cocktail'. Sho updates the *Midsummer's* narrative setting to 'Modern South Korea', and opens the fanfic with a 'main cast' list of twelve Shakespeare characters identified by Korean names listed as counterparts to Shakespeare's *dramatis personae*. Her publication's first installment appeared in June 2019, and she stated then that the narrative will be a multi-chapter work. In November 2020, Sho published the first chapter installment, a first-person introduction to her storyworld told from the perspective of Park Jin Young, the Korean counterpart to Theseus. This initial offering provides readers with a page-length, detailed plot overview that situates the fanfic's ShaK-pop characters within the arenas of K-pop and K-drama, including complicated family relations, love interests and conflict. Immediately clear is Sho's desire to add a transnational twist. One of the characters is born a 'Prince of Thailand', another an 'American-born K-pop star' named Tiffany. Not only does Sho borrow from Shakespeare's narrative arc, but the fanfic also evinces the widespread transnational influences of what John Lie labels 'Korean Wave 2.0: a swelling interest in South Korean popular music' (2013: 41) and the entangled and complicated subplots of Korean television drama. The fanfic enrobes Shakespeare in both popular phenomena, K-pop and K-drama, each politically and economically a soft (culture) power exportation encouraged and supported by South Korea's government. This opens questions on the role of fan art in the dissemination of political and economic subtexts. As Tilland notes, Korean 'fandom is now taking on a new life as fuel in South Korea's soft power ascendancy' (2017: 381). The transnational flow evinced in fandoms alerts us to ways Shakespeare fanart is far from frivolous consumption and production, and sometimes there is more than art put to task. Furthermore, while Shakespeare fan studies has, for the most part, trained its gaze on the white Western English-speaking fan and playtext, Sho's fanfic example demonstrates that fans' affective leanings, and the cultural phenomena through which Shakespeare is played, is not affixed to cultural whiteness or Western democratic or neo-liberal culture alone. In its own way, Sho's fanfic demonstrates her creative deliberation (and liberation) from the dominant structures that presume what Shakespeare should be.

With attention on the fan as the locus of appropriation, a renewed focus on the importance of shared reading communities emerges. For instance, critical race theory has opened up new avenues by which we might think more critically about our position as fans of Shakespeare, and what our rhetorical situation might mean for appropriation. As scholars have begun to challenge the under- or unremarked whiteness of fan studies, we are confronted with the critical truism that 'race is still frequently treated as an add-on or as something that should be addressed somewhere later' (Wanzo 2015: 1.6) and the extent to which whiteness is foundational to many fan cultures. Rebecca Wanzo's 2015 essay rebukes Henry Jenkins's early work, suggesting that his 'utopian understanding of fans in science fiction communities as being antiracist and progressive' (2015: 1.4) is antithetical to the lived experience of many fans of colour – and is currently evidenced in Shakespeare fan studies by the dearth of interest in, for example, Korean Shakespeare fan activity. Wanzo suggests that 'we should see fans as having a dialectical relationship to normativity that is not always explicit in fan studies (and sometimes not acknowledged)' (2.4). Wanzo suggests a shifting vector of what is 'normal' that requires a recognition of one's own subjectivity, from not only the scholar, but the fan-scholar, or acafan.

Wanzo herself accepts the mantle of acafan, suggesting that it is 'love — and at times disappointment — that can produce scholarship that really articulates the intellectual stakes of a work' (4.1). By reclaiming her status as acafan, Wanzo implicitly acknowledges that the presentist perspective is key to the adaptive process – that decisions are made to privilege either Shakespeare's history or our own. Fan emphases thus dovetail with the presentist Shakespeare Terence Hawkes argued for when he wrote, 'we choose the facts. We choose the texts. We do the inserting. We do the perceiving. Facts and texts, that is to say, don't simply speak, don't merely mean. *We* speak, *we* mean, *by* them' (2002: 3).

In acknowledging the ethnographic nature of Shakespearean fan appropriation, Shakespeare studies must also be required to recognize how the structures of fandoms build and sustain a potentially exclusionary scholarly practice. In their 2017 essay, Lori Morimoto and Bertha Chin challenged the 'depoliticized use of imagined communities' (2017: 174) in fan studies. An uncritical stance towards fans' identity, they note, ignores *how* fan communities are imagined and implicates both fans and fan scholars. Morimoto and Chin argue that critical studies would benefit from a more careful assessment of 'which culturally specific practices and assumptions are privileged, which are rejected and why' (2017: 175). Rukmini Pande has also attempted to navigate the ethnographic (and auto-ethnographic) challenges facing fan scholarship in order to recognize the need for an 'inclusive theoretical frame that demands an awareness of these intersections' (2018: 193). As Morimoto and Chin assert, when 'we lose sight of the disparities and disjunctures that may characterize transcultural interactions within fandoms both on- and offline' (2017: 174), we risk silencing those voices and further entrenching the field in unhelpfully limited distinctions of fans. What these critics affirm is the place of inclusion that acafandom facilitates, and the extent to which methodological fallacies about objectivity marginalize fans and scholars who are not willing or able to divest their subjective stance.

Ebony Elizabeth Thomas and Amy Stornaiuolo suggest that all critical studies, whether they manifest as creative work or scholarly essays, are acts of appropriation. This is vital to understanding the re-constitutive value of Shakespearean fanworks, because 'tracing these historical antecedents of restorying is important for understanding how stories are told, shared, and revised in relation to metanarratives about whose stories matter' (Thomas and Stornaiuolo 2019: 2.6). This emphasis on restorying explicitly invites adaptation studies scholars to consider whose stories are being told, and how we might navigate those that stand in opposition to the institutions that produce Shakespeare appropriations. If, as Arthur Little Jr. suggests, we recognize Shakespeare as 'white property', any interpretation of Shakespeare becomes potentially appropriative, because it makes visible the ways in which cultural hegemonies designate Shakespeare as inaccessible to fans of color (2016: 88). What Vanessa Corredera suggests is the 'cultural alienation' (2016: 45) symptomatic of Shakespeare studies' overarching whiteness might be navigated through appropriative acts that recognize what we have elsewhere noted as the 'use' of Shakespeare. To frame appropriation as use, we suggest, asserts 'a claim about reader agency that pushes back against the traditional scholarly notions of objectivity as the defining quality of value' (Fazel and Geddes 2017: 4). Moreover, centralizing those who appropriate Shakespeare as users 'necessitates an inquiry into these affective experiences and digital practices that shape one's encounter with Shakespeare' (Fazel and Geddes 2017: 5), echoing Alan McKee's claim that 'academics conduct their work of consumption and production just as much within a capitalist culture as do other kinds of fans' (2007: 95).

By recognizing the place of the user-fan – both in terms of their reception and production of new Shakespeares – understanding the impact of affective investment in Shakespearean adaptation and appropriation becomes essential. This appropriative space might be best articulated as a neighbourhood, as Taarini Mookherjee argues. Mookherjee suggests that Shakespeare appropriation – when situated in a global context – evokes the figure of the neighbour, a metaphor that 'traverses the divide between "familiarity and anonymity" and is that image of the self that can never be fully known' (2019: 4–5). The conceptualization of the neighbour implicitly recognizes our own subjectivity by positioning adaptive uses that might, to the dominant white Western Shakespeare fan community, be classified as 'other', as different only in that 'other' is different *to us*. Neighbours are, Mookherjee contends, 'refracted, distorted, and repeated versions of each other' (2019: 9). Moreover, from the subjective scholar, or aca-fan's standpoint, what the concept of 'neighbor and the neighborhood opens up instead is a space for considering the ethical charge both of our orientation as scholars and of the relationship(s) between these various "adaptations, allusions, and (re)productions"' (13). Mookherjee's drive to reconceptualize the relationship between each individual's Shakespeare recognizes a larger shift towards a recognition of how different uses of Shakespeare depend on an acknowledgment of the subjective stance of those who play with him. By acknowledging this work as part of an affective fandom, Shakespearean adaptation studies is better equipped to capture adaptation as it occurs, transcending a study of discrete objects in favour of an examination of how (and perhaps why) Shakespeare moves within and across diverse fan communities.

REFERENCES

Alassa (2012), 'The Hollow Crown', http://fav.me/d5mbzqs (accessed 12 July 2021).

Alienablackmores (2018), 'Henry V', https://philosopherking1887.music.blog/tag/the-hollow-crown-fanart/ (accessed 12 July 2021).

Ang, L. (1985), *Watching Dallas: Soap Opera and the Melodramatic Imagination*, London: Psychology Press.

Bacon-Smith, C. (1992), *Enterprising Women: Television Fandom and the Creation of Popular Myth*, Philadelphia, PA: University of Pennsylvania.

BCfan72 (2016), 'Hear ye, Hear ye', https://bcfan71.wordpress.com/2016/01/22/hear-ye-hear-ye/ (accessed 12 July 2021).

Blackwell, A. (2018), *Shakespearean Celebrity in the Digital Age: Fan Cultures and Remediation*, London: Palgrave Macmillan.

Brown, Jeffrey A. (2000), *Black Superheroes, Milestone Comics, and Their Fans: Milestone Comics and Their Fans*, Jackson, MS: University Press of Mississippi.

Burt, R. (2002), *Shakespeare After Mass Media*, New York, NY: Palgrave.

Cavicchi, D. (1998), *Tramps Like Us: Music and Meaning Among Springsteen Fans*, New York, NY: Oxford University Press.

Coppa, F. (2006), 'Writing Bodies In Space: Media Fanfiction as Theatrical Performance', in K. Helleckson and K. Busse (eds), *Fan Fiction and Fan Communities in the Age of the Internet*, 225–44, Jefferson, NC: McFarland.

Corredera, V. (2016), 'Not a Moor exactly': Shakespeare, *Serial*, and Modern Constructions of Race', *Shakespeare Quarterly* 67 (1): 30–50.

De Kosnik, A. (2016), *Rogue Archives: Digital Cultural Memory and Media Fandom*, Cambridge, MA: MIT Press.

Desmet, C. (2014), 'Recognizing Shakespeare, Rethinking Fidelity: A Rhetoric and Ethics of Appropriation', in A. Huang and E. Rivlin (eds), *Shakespeare and the Ethics of Appropriation*, 41–57, New York, NY: Palgrave Macmillan.

Desmet, C. (2017), 'Alien Shakespeares 2.0', *Actes des congrès de la Société française Shakespeare*. Available online: http://shakespeare.revues.org/3877 (accessed 12 July 2021).

Desmet, C. and S. Iyengar (2015), 'Adaptation, Appropriation, or What you Will', *Shakespeare* 11 (1): 10–19.

Desmet, C. and R. Sawyer, eds (1999), *Shakespeare and Appropriation*, London: Routledge.

Duffett, M. (2013), *Understanding Fandom: An Understanding to the Study of Media Fan Culture*, London: Bloomsbury.

Fanlore, (2019), 'Acafan', August 16, https://fanlore.org/wiki/Acafan (accessed 12 July 2021).

Fazel, V. M. and L. Geddes (2017), 'Introduction', in *The Shakespeare User: Critical and Creative Appropriations in a Networked Culture*, 1–22, New York, NY: Palgrave Macmillan.

Fazel, V. M. and L. Geddes (2021), *The Shakespeare Multiverse: Fandom as Literary Praxis*, London: Routledge.

Fiske, J. (2010), *Understanding Popular Culture*, 2nd edn, New York, NY: Taylor & Francis.

Finn, K. M. (2017), 'Historyplay: Critical and Creative Engagement with Shakespeare Tetralogies in Transformative Fanworks', *Shakespeare* 13 (3): 210–25.

Finn, K. M. and J. McCall (2016), '"Exit, Pursued by a fan": Shakespeare, Fandom, and the Lure of the Alternative Universe', *Critical Survey* 28 (2): 27–38.

Grossberg, L. (1992), 'Is There a Fan in the House? The Affective Sensibility of Fandom', in L. Lewis (ed.), *The Adoring Audience: Fan Culture and Popular Media*, 50–68, London: Routledge.

Harrington, C. L. and D. Bielby (1995), *Soap Fans: Pursuing Pleasure and Making Meaning in Everyday Life*, Philadelphia, PA: Temple University Press.

Harris, C. and A. Alexander (1998), *Theorizing Fandom: Fans, Subculture and Identity*, Cresskill: Hampton Press.

Hawkes, T. (2002), *Shakespeare in the Present*, London: Routledge.

Hawkes, T. and H. Grady (2006), *Presentist Shakespeares*, London, Routledge.

Hellekson, K. and K. Busse, eds (2006), *Fan Fiction and Fan Communities in the Age of the Internet*, Jefferson, NC: McFarland.

Henderson, D. E. (2006), *Collaborations with the Past: Reshaping Shakespeare Across Time and Media*, Cornell, NY, and London: Cornell University Press.

Hills, M. (2002), *Fan Cultures*, London: Routledge.

Holderness, G. (2014), *Tales from Shakespeare: Creative Collisions*, Cambridge: Cambridge University Press.

Holl, J. (2017), 'Shakespeare Fanboys and Fangirls and the Work of Play', in V. Fazel and L. Geddes (eds), *The Shakespeare User: Critical and Creative Appropriations in a Networked Culture*, 109–20, New York, NY: Palgrave Macmillan.

Huang, A. and E. Rivlin (2014), 'Introduction', in *Shakespeare and the Ethics of Appropriation*, 1–20, New York, NY: Palgrave Macmillan.

Hume, R. (1997), 'Before the Bard: "Shakespeare" in Early Eighteenth-Century London', *ELH* 64 (1): 41–75.

Iyengar, S. (2014), 'Upcycling Shakespeare: Crafting Cultural Capital', in Daniel Fischlin (ed.), *Outerspeares: Shakespeare, Intermedia, and the Limits of Adaptation*, 347–71, Toronto: University of Toronto Press.

James, E. (2014), *Much Ado About You*, Avon Lake, OH: Avon Press.

Jenkins, H. (1992), *Textual Poachers: Television Fans and Participatory Culture*, New York, NY, Routledge.

Jenkins, H. (2006), 'Confessions of an Aca-Fan', 19 June, http://henryjenkins.org/blog/2006/06/who_the_is_henry_jenkins.html (accessed 12 July 2021).

Jenkins, H. (2013), *Textual Poachers: Television Fans and Participatory Culture*, 20th Anniversary edn, New York, NY: Routledge.

Jenson, J. (1992), 'Fandom as Pathology: The Consequences of Characterization', in L. Lewis (ed.), *The Adoring Audience: Fan Culture and Popular Media*, 9–29, London: Routledge.

Kidnie, M. J. (2009), *Shakespeare and the Problem of Adaptation*, New York, NY: Routledge.

Lanier, D. (2002), *Shakespeare and Modern Popular Culture*, Oxford: Oxford University Press.

Lanier, D. (2014) 'Shakespearean Rhizomatics: Adaptations, Ethics, Value', in A. Huang and E. Rivlin (eds), *Shakespeare and the Ethics of Appropriation*, 21–40, New York, NY: Palgrave Macmillan.

Lanier, D. (2017), 'Shakespeare/Not Shakespeare: Afterword', in C. Desmet, N. Loper and J. Casey (eds), *Shakespeare/Not Shakespeare*, 293–306, New York, NY: Palgrave Macmillan.

Larsen, K. and L. Zubernis (2011), *Fandom at the Crossroads: Celebration, Shame, and Fan/Producer Relationships*, Cambridge: Cambridge Scholars' Press.

Larsen, K. and L. Zubernis (2013), *Fangasm: Supernatural Fangirls*, Iowa City, IA: University of Iowa Press.

Lewis, L. (1992), *The Adoring Audience: Fan Culture and Popular Media*, London: Routledge.

Lie, J. (2013). 'Introduction to The Globalization of K-pop: Local and Transnational Articulations of South Korean Popular Music', *Cross-Currents: East Asian History and Culture Review*, 9: 40–3. Available online: https://cross-currents.berkeley.edu/sites/default/files/e-journal/articles/lie_intro_0.pdf (accessed 12 July 2021).

Little, A. (2016), 'Re-Historicizing Race, White Melancholia and the Shakespearean Property', *Shakespeare Quarterly* 67 (1): 84–103.

McKee, A. (2007), 'The Fans of Cultural Theory', in J. Gray, C.C. Sandvoss and C. Harrington (eds), *Fandom: Identities and Communities in a Mediated World*, 88–97, New York, NY: New York University Press.

Mookherjee, T. (2019), 'Theorizing the Neighbor: *Arshinagar* and *Romeo and Juliet*', *Borrowers and Lenders: A Journal of Shakespeare Appropriation*, 12 (2). Available online: https://openjournals.libs.uga.edu/borrowers/article/view/2374/2416 (accessed 12 July 2021).

Morimoto, L. and B. Chin (2017), 'Reimagining the Imagined Community: Online Media Fandoms in the Age of Global Convergence', in J. Gray, C. Sandvoss and C. L. Harrington (eds), *Fandom: Identities and Communities in a Mediated World*, 2nd edn, 174–90, New York, NY: New York University Press.

Murray, J. (1997), *Hamlet on the Holodeck: The Future of Narrative in Cyberspace*, Cambridge, MA: MIT Press.

Newcomb, L. (2018) 'Towards a Sustainable Source Study', in D. Britton and M. Walters (eds), *Rethinking Shakespeare Source Study: Audiences, Authors, and Digital Technologies*, 19–45, London: Routledge.

O'Neill, S. (2020), 'Hiddleston–Shakespeare–Coriolanus, or Rhizomatic Crossings in Fanfic', in A. Hartley and P. Holland (eds), *Shakespeare and Geek Culture*, 112–31, New York, NY: Bloomsbury/Arden Shakespeare.

Pande, R. (2018), *Squee from the Margins: Fandom and Race*, Iowa City, IA: University of Iowa Press.

Pearson, R. (2007), 'Bachies, Bardies, Trekkies, and Sherlockians', in J. Gray, C. Sandvoss and C. L. Harrington (eds), *Fandom: Identities and Communities in a Mediated World*, 98–109, New York, NY: New York University Press.

Pope, J. (2020), *Shakespeare Fans: Adapting the Bard in the Age of Media Fandom*, New York, NY: Routledge.

Radway, J. (1982), *Reading the Romance: Women, Patriarchy, and Popular Literature*, Durham, NC: University of North Carolina Press.

Reine_des_corbeauxb (2019) 'Answer Echoes, Dying, Dying', https://archiveofourown. org/works/21088823 (accessed 12 July 2021).

Rose, T. (1994), *Black Noise: Rap Music and Black Culture in Contemporary America*, Hanover and London: Wesleyan University Press.

Rosvally, D. (2017), 'The Haunted Network: Shakespeare's Digital Ghost', in V. Fazel and L. Geddes (eds), *The Shakespeare User: Critical and Creative Appropriations in a Networked Culture*, 149–66, New York, NY: Palgrave Macmillan.

Ryzhova, A. (2021), *Richard II THE BOOK*, Behance. Available online: https://www. behance.net/gallery/115001503/Richard-II-THE-BOOK?tracking_source=search_ projects_recommended%7Cmuch%20ado%20shakespeare (accessed 12 July 2021).

Sanders, J. (2016), *Adaptation and Appropriation*, 2nd edn, London: Routledge.

Sandvoss, C. (2005), *Fans: The Mirror of Consumption*, Malden, MA: Polity.

Starks, L. (2016), 'From Face to Facebook: Levinas's Radical Ethics and "Shakespcare Friends"', *Borrowers and Lenders: A Journal of Shakespeare Appropriation* 10 (1).

Available online: https://openjournals.libs.uga.edu/borrowers/article/view/2431/2530 (accessed 12 July 2021).

Taylor, G. (1999), 'Afterword: The Incredible Shrinking Bard', in C. Desmet and R. Sawyer (eds), *Shakespeare and Appropriation*, 197–205, London: Routledge.

Thomas, E. and A. Stornaiuolo (2019), 'Race, storying, and restorying: What can we learn from black fans?', *Transformative Works and Cultures* 29. Available online: https://doi.org/10.3983/twc.2019.1562 (accessed 12 July 2021).

Tilland, B. (2017), 'Save Your K-Drama for Your Mama: Mother-Daughter Bonding in Between Nostalgia and Futurism', *Acta Koreana* 20 (2): 377–93.

Wanzo, R. (2015), 'African American acafandom and other strangers: New genealogies of fan studies', *Transformative Works and Cultures*, 20. Available online: https://doi.org/10.3983/twc.2015.0699 (accessed 12 July 2021).

PART THREE

New directions

Reduce, rewrite, recycle: adapting *A Midsummer Night's Dream* for Yosemite

KATHERINE STEELE BROKAW AND PAUL PRESCOTT

In 2018, in Yosemite National Park, the seasons were altered: ladybugs were mating in January and snowstorms came in March. Elsewhere in California, wildfires raged on unprecedented scales (only to be exceeded in the following seasons). On our screens, we saw images of dolphins and birds killed by the human trash dumped into oceans and streams, and of Native Americans from around the United States risking their personal safety to protect their water supplies and sacred lands. In July 2018, the scientist Jem Bendell published the paper 'Deep Adaptation: A Map for Navigating Climate Tragedy' in which he persuasively argued that irreversible anthropogenic climate change will lead to 'a near-term collapse in society with serious ramifications for the lives of readers'; Bendell also analysed some of the reasons for 'collapse-denial' (2018: 2). One clear reason lies in the relative priorities mainstream media afford to certain issues: a study by Deloitte in 2019 found that UK television news in 2017–18 referred more often to Shakespeare (5,444 mentions) than it did to climate change (3,126) (Townsend 2019).

In 2005, environmental leader Bill McKibben called for books and plays about ecological collapse:

> If the scientists are right, we're living through the biggest thing that's happened since human civilization emerged... But oddly, though we know about it, we don't *know* about it. It hasn't registered in our gut; it isn't part of our culture. Where are the books? The poems? The plays? The goddamn operas?

His call has been heeded by many writers and artists since, but has only recently been taken on by makers of Shakespearean theatre. Given the cultural capital of this playwright in not just the UK but around the world, we join a growing number of Shakespearean theatre-makers in asserting that Shakespearean theatre can and should be adapted to address the climatic, social and ecological emergencies facing the planet. We have asked ourselves: what processes of 'deep adaptation' do his works require to make them fit for raising environmental awareness? Or, to put it differently: how do we as professional Shakespeareans make the thing we love a thing that matters?

Shakespeare in Yosemite is our response to these questions. This mini festival, founded in 2017, offers free, outdoor, site-specific adaptations of Shakespeare's productions every April for visitors to Yosemite National Park, California. Yosemite is one of the most-visited and best-loved outdoor spaces in North America. Even those who have not visited the seven-mile Yosemite Valley at its heart will recognize images of Yosemite's staggering granite peaks such as Half Dome and El Capitan, of Yosemite Falls (the largest set of waterfalls in the US) and of the giant sequoia trees found in Mariposa Grove and the adjoining Sequoia and Kings Canyon National Parks. These natural phenomena have inspired the production of a range of cultural artefacts: the canvases of Thomas Hill and Albert Bierstadt, the creative non-fiction of John Muir, the photography of Ansel Adams, as well as more recent examples such as Ken Burns's National Park documentary and the film *Free Solo*, about climber Alex Honnold's ascent of El Capitan. As these examples illustrate, our awareness of 'nature' depends on adaptive mediation to reach wider audiences – in fact, Muir's prose is directly responsible for the foundation of the Park, and thus its preservation. But as these examples also illustrate, a lot of this mediation had depended on or devolved to white male narrators or agents, a point to which we shall return in the context of our mixed-race and gender-flipped *Dream*.

Shakespeare in Yosemite is offered in celebration both of Earth Day and Shakespeare's birthday and is a collaboration between the National Park Service and our home institution of University of California Merced ('Shakespeare in Yosemite').[1] We adapt and produce a different play – always a comedy or tragicomedy – each year. In a generically comedic pattern, our adaptations highlight ecological threats (from plastic pollution in *Dream* to forest fires in *As You Like It*), provide a deepened experience in the 'green world' of Yosemite that helps park visitors better reflect on their own relationship to the biosphere[2] and model the collaborative, inclusive processes by which environmental catastrophes may be addressed and averted.

This chapter provides an illustrative account of the adaptive principles and practices that informed the creation of our 2018 production of *A Midsummer Night's Dream*. Our process begins – as our chapter title suggests – with reducing Shakespeare's texts to what is relevant to our purposes, rewriting unclear or needlessly offensive bits of texts, and recycling words, songs and materials from the world around us. The prefix 're-', meaning 'again', permeates our adaptive process. Adapting Shakespeare is a looking back to look *again* – and to look forward through this revised lens. We ask how an early modern play can *again* make meaning for audiences, even as we ask how trash might be used *again*. And we also ask if we as a human species are going to *again* ignore the warnings of scientists and indigenous communities. Throughout our adaptive process, we aim to inspire future action by re-purposing the texts and materials produced in the past.

This chapter lays out the theories and methods that inform our adaptive, eco-theatrical[3] Shakespeare, describes the collaborative processes used to create and

FIGURE 3.1.1 Shakespeare in Yosemite performs in the Lower River Amphitheatre, Yosemite National Park. Image credit: Thomas Ovalle.

re-hearse our *Dream* as well as the processes we use to re-view and re-search its impact on audiences. While the impact of Shakespearean theatre on the entire planet may be minimal, we nonetheless assert that eco-adapted Shakespearean theatre has a role to play in the cultural revolution that is necessary to save life on Earth, and that – much less crucially – these adaptive processes also ensure the continued relevance of the plays.

ADAPTING SHAKESPEARE FOR THE PLANET: THEORIES AND PRINCIPLES

In describing the methods informing the practice and research that turns Shakespeare's texts into pieces of eco-theatre, we pay particular attention to the role adaptation plays in these methods and ideas. Shakespearean eco-theatre occurs at the intersection of Environmental Communications, eco-criticism and Applied Theatre. Also crucial to this work are the methods associated with performance-based Practice as Research.[4]

In the words of Solitaire Townsend, CEO of the environmental consultancy group Futerra, 'Climate change is as much a crisis of culture as it is of chemistry. The most powerful tool for cultural change is storytelling, be that compelling science or gripping fiction… without exceptional communications, the science is impotent in the face of the Anthropocene' (2020). Environmental Communications refers both to writing and media related to the environment – everything from Rachel Carson's *Silent Spring* to David Attenborough's films – and also to the study of what makes effective environmental communication. In the definition provided by the International Environmental Communications Association (IECA), Environmental Communications is an 'interdisciplinary field of study that examines the role, techniques and influence of communication in environmental affairs' ('About the IECA' n.d.). Environmental activists and scientists increasingly recognize the role that writers and artists must play in addressing climate change and biodiversity loss, as has been discussed in both academic circles and the news media.[5] We see Shakespeare in Yosemite and other ecologically minded adaptations of Shakespeare as a form of environmental communication, one that we both create and study.

In doing so, we are also responding to and theatrically manifesting eco-critical Shakespeare scholarship, a subfield that began to evolve primarily in the 2010s. Dan Brayton and Lyn Bruckner's 2011 collection *Ecocritical Shakespeare* traces the roots of the field in the fact that one finds 'in early modernity a sincere concern for the human impact on the biophysical environment' (3). They note that while scholars have long written about Shakespeare and nature, ecocritical work attends to issues like anthropocentrism (human-centred thinking and its dangers), environmental degradation and scientific literacy (3). Many works of ecocritical Shakespearean scholarship, like Randall Martin's *Shakespeare and Ecology* (2015), Gabriel Egan's *Shakespeare and Ecocritical Theory* (2015) and Daniel Brayton's *Shakespeare's Ocean: An Ecocritical Exploration* (2018), call attention to the ways in which the plays themselves are attuned to issues like deforestation, the overuse of resources and the effects of the climate-disrupting 'Little Ice Age' of the sixteenth century, while also providing twenty-first-century humans with stories of both existential despair and miraculous renewal that may resonate in an age of ecological crisis. Craig Dionne's *Posthuman Lear: Reading Shakespeare in the Anthropocene* (2016) joins essays by Robert Watson (2011), Sharon O'Dair (2011b), and others that attune readers to Shakespeare's engagement with the non-human: to the animals and plants we share a biosphere with, and to a possible post-human future.

Watson's reading of *Dream* was particularly useful to us as we adapted our 2018 show. He explains the way the play demonstrates humankind's intricate relationship with the natural world:

> Precisely by seeming to be just a nice little story about lovers and fairies in the forest on a moonlit summer night, this comedy can slip into our heads something it is otherwise hard to get our heads around: the fact that our insularity as individuals and as a species is a destructive illusion, an enclosure crisis of the human self.
>
> (2011: 53)

Watson's understanding of the usefulness of comedy to convey the crises that ensue from humans losing touch with their connectedness to the biosphere became a starting point for our adaptation.

Echoing a statement expressed by many Shakespearean eco-critics, Brayton and Bruckner argue that this crisis requires us all to go beyond historical and textual study, to in fact 'rethink the role of scholarship' so that 'pedagogy and scholarship [become] significant arenas for ideological and political transformation' (2011: 2).[6] And while teaching certainly holds potential for transformation, we agree with Randall Martin, who suggests in his conclusion to *Shakespeare and Ecology* that 'Shakespeare's greatest possibilities for becoming our eco-contemporary arguably lie not in academic discourse but in performance' (2015: 167).

Eco-theatrical adaptations of Shakespeare's plays can also be described as a form of Applied Theatre, that is, productions and programmes that seek to use Shakespeare for social good.[7] Jenny Hughes and Helen Nicholson describe Applied Theatre as that which 'emerges as a creative force that responds imaginatively to [...] new questions about how increasingly nuanced ideas of authority can be harnessed for social change' (2016: 2). Applied Shakespeare, a new subfield of Applied Theatre, is particularly interested in how Shakespearean authority might be 'harnessed for social change', which is certainly not the legacy of all the uses to which Shakespeare has historically been 'applied'.[8] Martin and O'Malley argue that there is a potential utility for harnessing Shakespearean authority when it comes to ecological issues: 'far from shying away from Shakespeare's canonicity, it seems worth trying to exploit it for whatever (limited) potential it may contain' (2018: 386). Shakespeare's plays get different people in the door than might attend a play explicitly advertized as 'environmental', and as we explain more fully below, the collaborative adaptation of them into new works of art can be, for many audience members, an artistic and political revelation.

Eco-theatre is a crucial and growing form of Applied Theatre. The Broadway Green Alliance, founded in 2008, 'educates, motivates, and inspires the entire theatre community and its patrons to implement environmentally friendlier practices on Broadway and beyond ('Broadway Green Alliance' n.d.), and the 'Artists and Climate Change' site lists several organizations producing ecological theatre, like Earth Matters on Stage, which 'fosters new dramatic work and performances that help us re-imagine our human place in a more-than-human world' ('Artists and Climate Change: Organizations' n.d.). The Shakespeare world is beginning to take note: Randall Martin and Evelyn O'Malley's guest-edited special issue of *Shakespeare Bulletin* explores several recent eco-theatrical Shakespearean productions, and the ways in which Shakespeare can 'become an ecological discourse on the stage, as well as a model for environmental practices in the theatre' (2018: 378). Martin himself is leading the 2020–2 'Cymbeline in the Anthropocene' project, a collaboration between a number of theatres, including Shakespeare in Yosemite as well as companies in Australia, Argentina, Canada, Georgia, Kazakhstan and Wales, all of whom are staging ecologically aware productions of *Cymbeline* in 2021 and 2022 ('Cymbeline in the Anthropocene' n.d.). COVID-19 has meant that many of these productions – including our own 2021 *Cymbeline* in Yosemite – have been filmed rather than staged live, and thus will be more widely available. And, to conclude this brief round-up of recent eco-Shakespeare initiatives, we are currently working with Shakespeare's Globe (UK) and a range of other theatres to form the EarthShakes alliance, a collective of Shakespeare theatres dedicated to both green practices and adaptive, ecologically-minded dramaturgy. The EarthShakes Alliance was officially launched in spring 2021 at the Globe 4 Globe: Shakespeare and the Climate Emergency symposium in London.[9]

In creating our eco-theatrical Shakespeare in Yosemite adaptations, we are also practicing a form of Practice as Research (PaR). Baz Kershaw defines PaR as 'the uses of practical creativity as reflexive enquiry into significant research concerns (usually conducted by "artist/scholars" in universities)' (2009a: 4). As university-based scholar-artists, we see the performances we create in Yosemite as a form of publishing in the literal sense of making ideas public. But we also study the processes and outputs of these productions in an iterative process combining scholarly research – often ethnographic in nature but informed too by the ecocriticism described above – and theatrical creativity.

Of particular relevance here is the fact that these processes are highly collaborative. Diana Henderson's notion that Shakespearean adaptation is a form of collaborating with the past resonates with us, for indeed

> collaboration focuses attention on the connections among individuals, allowing artists credit and responsibility, but at the same time refusing to separate them from their social location and the work of others. It also makes a space for emotion as part of art's appeal and reality, for both its creators and for its audiences.
>
> (2006: 8)

As we discuss below, the connections made through collaboration and performance are crucial to the project's mission to inspire ecological awareness and collective action.

Henderson suggests that modern artists have used Shakespeare as a source of 'unquestioned artistry and authority' and 'then they either celebrate and market that power or struggle against his institutional associations and codified performance traditions as well as the time-bound aspects of the plays themselves' (2008: 3). We would like to suggest, however, that collaborative adaptation of Shakespeare can follow a third way: that of exploiting Shakespearean cultural capital while ignoring – indeed flouting – the hegemony of established performance traditions. We will now describe the processes by which we collaborated with Shakespeare's text; the make-up of our team of student, community and professional actors and designers; and the materials (both human-made and natural) we used to adapt *Dream* for Yosemite National Park.

REDUCE, REWRITE, RECYCLE: SCRIPTING

Reduce

In most easily accessible online texts, *A Midsummer Night's Dream* is about seventeen thousand words long. Uncut productions with an interval tend to run for about 2.5 to 3 hours. Our production needed to last no longer than 90 minutes without an interval. We knew that we wanted to add a few musical numbers not found in Shakespeare's text, so our cut text needed to be about 70 minutes or about 9,500 words long, a substantial reduction of approximately 40 per cent of the original text. This calculation is based on the formula devised by dramaturg Scott Kaiser at the Oregon Shakespeare Festival (OSF), who cross-referenced the word count of prompt books with the running times and found that, in an average production, it takes 1 minute to speak 135 words (2004: 47).

The play is so beautifully plotted that there was no question of removing one of the narrative strands or indeed any of the characters (with the one semi-exception of the Indian Boy, who was replaced with a bear cub puppet), so in this adaptation we stuck broadly with the sequence of scenes found in the original. Reducing the text was, then, a question of sometimes light, sometimes severe internal pruning. Cuts were made for any of the following reasons: obscurity; redundancy; lack of poetic or comedic quality; (ir)relevance to the production's concept and messages; potential to cause offence. These are highly subjective judgments which led to dozens if not hundreds of textual alterations. They ranged from smallish excisions in the lovers' scenes (no threat of rape from Demetrius to Helena, no 'tawny Tartar' as an insult from Lysander to Hermia) to the removal of larger blocks of text (no Bergamask, no sweeping and blessing of the house at the end of the play).

Rewright/rewrite

The process of devising a world and a concept for the production happened in tandem with the act of cutting the text. The concept for the show was briefly explained to audiences in the programme with the following note:

> The play is so weird, so dream-like, that it can be interpreted in all sorts of ways. We want our production to be site-specific and time-sensitive: this play is about being right here in Yosemite National Park, right now in late April 2018. Our lovers leave a fancy wedding party in the valley and flee into the back country; our "Mechanicals" (i.e. working people) earn their various livings in the Park; the object of Titania and Oberon's quarrel is not an Indian boy (as in Shakespeare's text) but a bear cub; our fairies take the names of Yosemite flora and fauna.

We interpolated a couple of sequences in Act 1 to establish that Theseus and Hippolyta were not regular visitors to the Park but had chosen it as the location for their wedding based on its picturesque, Instagrammable backdrops. Hippolyta casually dropped some litter while taking a selfie; both in their separate pre-nuptial hotel suites called room service for some bottled water (none too subtly, this strand was designed to chime with the World Earth Day 2018 theme to 'End Plastic Pollution'.) At this point, Puck intervened, casting a thunderbolt spell on them with the words 'thou shalt be transformed!' and the pair wheeled offstage to return minutes later as their alter-egos, Oberon and Titania. The Fairies and the Mechanicals were also doubled and their identities made site-specific. The Mechanicals were all Park employees: Bottom the Facilities Operations Specialist, Snout the Wilderness Ranger, Snug the Wildland Firefighter, Flute the Mountaineering Instructor and Starveling the Majestic Hotel server. Five out of six of the Fairies/Mechanicals were played by and as women, a casting decision designed to highlight the crucial role played by female Park employees (which the NPS itself was highlighting on their Instagram feed that spring). The Fairies were renamed and costumed to look like species of Yosemite: Sugar Pine, Orange Poppy, Lacewing and Mule Deer. In common with Oberon, Titania and Puck, the Fairies occasionally but pointedly used words drawn from Native American languages. We did this under advice and with the blessing of representatives of the South Sierra Miwok and Paiute peoples, two of Yosemite's indigenous tribes. South Sierra Miwuk is a dying language and the man, Tony Cabezut, who taught us these words said one of the best ways to honour his tribe was to speak its endangered language. The Fairies and Puck therefore used the South Sierra Miwuk names for waterfalls and fires, as well as place names like Half Dome (Tessayak), indicating the idea that the fairies had been custodians of the land far before the profit-hunting arrival of white Europeans.

Recycle

The principle of recycling operated on two levels: costumes and props (discussed in the following section), and music. The latter is always a central component of our Yosemite adaptations and our *Dream* featured snatches of songs by Bob Dylan, Kendrick Lamar, The Beatles, The Proclaimers and Patty Griffin. After Hermia eloped, we had her mother, Egea, wandering through the woods, calling her name, while Oberon – fascinated by human feelings – sang a bit of 'Like A Rolling Stone' ('how does it feel… ?'); this cross-faded into Hermia and Lysander singing the refrain from 'To Make You Feel My Love', a highly effective musical segue that we gratefully recycled from the superior jukebox musical *Girl From the North Country*. When Bottom sang to show she was not afraid, she did so to the tune of The Beatles' 'Blackbird' ('Bottom singing in the dead of night! / Take these broken wings and learn to fly. / All your life, you were only waiting / For this moment to arise… '). Recycling these bits of folk and pop music in our shows echoes a practice Shakespeare and his contemporaries employed in their plays, whereby popular ballads, drinking songs and psalms were re-performed on the stage by characters from Lear's Fool to Autolycus.

RE-HEARSING, DESIGNING AND PERFORMING

Figuring out how to adapt Shakespeare, like figuring out how to adapt ourselves for survival on Earth, is a group effort. But in a society that overvalues individual achievement and rights over collective success and the common good, it is not surprising that the narratives praising the success of Applied Shakespeare projects often focus on the singular: the reformed prisoner or the triumphant student actor. This is of a piece with the emphasis on the individual in Shakespeare's plays themselves – especially the tragedies and histories – and on contemporary theatre's focus on star directors and actors. We know that to save a habitable planet, we need to emphasize the collective in our work and decisions. In our collaborative process of making *Dream* – which is already one of Shakespeare's more ensemble-driven plays – we wanted our theatre-making to model the kind of group-led, consensus-driven work that is central to political and ecological efforts, too. Or as we said in an op-ed we published the week of the show in local papers:

> Most importantly, perhaps, our *Dream* is a piece of theatre, and theatre is cooperative and collaborative. It is only by working together – all humans with regard for each other and for the Earth's animals and plants – that we can safeguard our planet and ourselves for the future.

> (Brokaw and Prescott 2018)

As directors, we wanted to de-centre our expertise and learn alongside our cast and designers about consumption and trash, and together to figure out how to translate what we learned onto the stage. Crucially, we found that ecological practices and ecological messaging form a reciprocal relationship: collecting trash for costumes brings awareness to the production team that feeds our collaborative rehearsal process, and the sight of trash on stages brings out the production's messages about consumption. At the same time, the research and thought that went into bringing ecological themes out of the play made us more aware of the environmental impact of theatre-making.

We knew that costume design would be a key element of the show (given the setting, there is no need for a constructed set). We hired local professional costumer Kristine Doiel, who along with two student assistants was in charge of creating our *Dream* world out of recycled clothes and trash. In the programme note, Doiel

FIGURE 3.1.2 Traci Sprague (Lacewing), Connie Stetson (Bottom), Jessica Rivas (Orange Poppy), Devon Glover (Mule Deer) and Juniper Sprague (Sugar Pine) wear costumes designed by Kristine Doiel and made from collected trash. Image credit: Frederik Goris.

explained the impact the process had on her work as a designer: 'The exercise of utilizing discarded materials has not only challenged my creative thinking but also increased my awareness that we throw away so many useful materials.' In initial meetings, Doiel came up with several ideas that became important to the show's development – most crucially, the idea that Titania and Oberon would represent two elemental forces in Yosemite: waterfalls and forest fires. The water from Sierra snowmelt and periodic fires are both crucial to the area's ecosystem and potentially destructive when out of joint: the park has been closed for both floods and fire in recent years. The idea to highlight Yosemite's elements was furthered by an early conversation with Lisa Wolpe about her Puck, in which Wolpe had the idea that Puck could synthesize the elements of Earth and Air: she would be a creature who cares deeply for the Earth that she so gracefully circumnavigates in the air. That idea was enhanced by Doiel's research into the trash problems in Yosemite, when she learned that hiking and climbing gear is often left on trails in the back country. Doiel created Puck wings covered in hiking maps and tangled climbing ropes to convey the idea that when travelling between Earth and sky, Puck gets caught up in a very specific kind of human detritus.

As we describe below, the image of trash in the form of fairy wings, ass heads and discarded water bottles did resonate with many audience members, but first the process of collecting this trash for Doiel's design team affected our cast. James McIntyre, our Demetrius, echoed the sentiment of many when he said that while rehearsing and collecting, 'I found myself becoming overly conscious of the waste I was producing and what efforts I could take to reduce these detriments' (2018). Devon Glover, who as Sonnet Man travels to schools and theatres around the world, said that working on this show 'inspired me to include more natural resources when working on productions with youth groups, and work on practicing and teaching the concept of turning trash to treasure' (2018).

The design process overlapped with our rehearsal process, which was equally collaborative. It was informed by the experience and expertise of our cast, and by conversations about Yosemite and the environment. The evidence of this collaboration can be found in our rehearsal log, which includes the following entries:

- First read-through: Cast shares memories of Yosemite and/or Shakespeare. We discuss the mission of the show. Ranger Jess (Snout) talks about why public lands exist and why they need to be preserved. She raises the important point that the arts have always been important to the protection of public lands in the USA, and that begins with Yosemite. It was the writing of John Muir, the paintings of early landscape artists, and early photography that convinced politicians back East that the place needed to be preserved, and the need for it to be cherished continues to be amplified and held up in writing and photography – and why not theatre, too?
- First lovers blocking rehearsal: Together we come up with the idea that the 'love token' Egea refers to in 1.1 could be a paper flower made out of a

FIGURE 3.1.3 Lisa Wolpe as Puck performs with Tonatiuh Newbold (Lysander), who accompanied most of the play's songs on guitar. Image credit: Thomas Ovalle.

copy of *Midsummer Night's Dream*, and that Egea throws it on the ground in 1.1 and it later becomes the purple flower that Oberon asks for.
- First rehearsal with the Mechanicals: Jess talks with Traci (Snug), Taryn (Quince), Juniper (Starveling) and Connie (Bottom) about being a female wilderness ranger. She'd grown up feeling like the outdoors was a man's world, and then came to think that only a certain kind of woman could be outdoorsy. But the outdoors *are* for everyone, and everyone should feel comfortable being outside. Connie (a woman in her 60s who has

lived in the Yosemite area for decades) talks about how Yosemite and the hiking world have changed over the decades to include many more women.

- Fairy rehearsal: Working with GB (Theseus/Oberon) we realize that Oberon is on a different time scale, which is like Fairy time but also like Miwok time, and he returns to impatience when becoming Theseus again and worrying about passing 3 hours.
- First rehearsal with Lisa (four days before opening): Together we discuss the ending: should there be any hope that these people can be redeemed, can help save the Earth? Lisa seems to think maybe there isn't, that they are too preoccupied with themselves. But GB says 'I think there *has* to be hope.' And we decide that at the end, Hippolyta and Theseus will spot the trash-wings that Puck has removed, and have a moment of recalling their woods-selves and they will pick up the wings (thus picking up trash) and carry them off stage. And then Lisa comes on with the Globe she carried at the start, the presence of which unifies everyone as they sing the production's closing and optimistic musical number.

This collaborative rehearsal process – and the performances in the park – changed the way cast members thought about Shakespeare's adaptive potential. McIntyre found it revelatory: 'working on *Midsummer* has encouraged me to view Shakespeare's words as more of a vehicle for expression of contemporary ideas rather than a set of artifacts to be preserved'. For Connie Stetson, our Bottom, the experience was almost spiritual as she commented on 'how profoundly the words of Shakespeare intertwined with the pine-breath of our magnificent Yosemite have affected my consciousness' (2018). For Glover, working on the show was an affirmation of his belief: 'The production [...] continued to prove my theory that Shakespeare can be adapted anywhere and connect to people of all ages and cultures [...] and working on it made me more interested in our National Parks' (2018). All of this language – seeing Shakespeare as a 'vehicle for expression [...] rather than a set of artifacts', as something that can be 'intertwined', and as something that can be 'adapted anywhere', indicate that for these actors, the act of adaptation – of adding Shakespeare to Yosemite – is where meaning was made.

Ranger Jess Rivas had further thoughts about how theatre might be used to get people to think more deeply about both the environment and the people inhabiting it:

The adaptation is very inclusive. Lisa [Wolpe, as Puck] does a very good job of including people in the audience, and they feel connected to the show now, they are a part of this experience instead of just observing this experience. And I think that's really important when you are addressing issues like climate change, and some of these very hard to accept and maybe even very uncomfortable conversations – it's really important that we are all included, because otherwise, if we are not connected to that, we are also not connected to the solution.

(2018)

Equally important for Rivas – a Chicana-Lebanese-American female park ranger – is the show's norm-setting for both Shakespeare and National Parks, long preserves of white men:

> I mean we have women – a lot of women – in this production... And I think that [for] the little kids in the audience, without them even knowing, this is a norm to them, this is what they are seeing as normal. And so their vision and their standard has been set for what is normal for Shakespeare, for National Parks, for theatre. ... They had no idea that rangers could do this and now they want to be a ranger. Or they had no idea that women can play these predominantly masculine roles and be girly, and funny, and dynamic.

As these cast reflections imply, much meaning gets created in performance beyond what is planned in the rehearsal room. In the case of this production, the environment was a particularly crucial maker of meaning: the fact of being in Yosemite National Park, a beloved place long home to the South Sierra Miwuk and Paiute and now threatened by over-tourism, governmental underfunding and climate change. As Sally Mackey argues,

> The fragility and mutability of place has become an increasingly global issue, arising from climate change rather than (or as well as) warzones or related forms of human directed deterritorialisation. There will surely be an increasingly important role for participatory, applied performances of place, responding to, initiating or critiquing environmental change and its impact on our understandings and animations of place.
>
> (2016: 124)

We think our adaptation responds to this call by drawing close attention to the contested place of performance.

This particular place affects each performance differently. Weather and climate are crucial in affecting attention and engagement: wind in the surrounding trees combining with the ambient volume of the Merced River and Yosemite Falls threatening the audibility of actors; hot, direct sunlight inducing physical discomfort and sometimes relocation within the amphitheatre: much of this prompts the kind of mid-performance adaptation by both actors and audience that are familiar to anyone involved in site-specific (and especially outdoor) Shakespeare production. Yosemite is a particularly profound place to observe what Baz Kershaw – adopting an ecological term – calls 'edge effects' (2009b: 186); the park's eco-system rubs up against the theatrical ecosystem of the play, and so Mule Deer the fairy character beholds a real mule deer in the wings, two squirrels run onto the stage and mimic Helena's chase, Puck calls a wandering toddler a 'woodland sprite' when he gets close. Wolpe describes how the animals, plants and landscape of Yosemite affected her performance:

> Puck is a goblin of the forest, you couldn't really talk about the forest more effectively than being on this spongy grandmother earth and being so far away

from artificial light and being reminded how small we are in connection to this place. There's no tree around me that wasn't here before I was born.

(2018)[10]

There was no question that the performances had a profound effect on our cast, but we wanted to know what sort of impact they were having on our audiences, too.

RE-VIEWING AND EVALUATING

How do you measure the fitness of an adaptation? How calibrate its impact on its target audience? For this production of *Dream*, we largely depended on in-person surveys filled out directly after the show; most of the audience remained in their seats for 5–10 minutes while cast and crew distributed forms and pens. The questionnaire was short (one side of a half-sheet) and featured the following questions:

1. How familiar with Shakespeare were you before today's show?
2. How many times have you been to Yosemite?
3. What aspect or moment of the play had the biggest impact on you?
4. Please share any thoughts about how today's show may have changed the way you think about any of the following: Shakespeare; Yosemite National Park; your relationship to the natural world; or anything else.

The survey did not measure audience demographics according to ethnicity, gender, employment, etc. The first two questions are an attempt to profile the audience member strictly in terms of their prior experience of Shakespeare and Yosemite (both of which, of course, can be heavily influenced by socio-economic and other demographic factors). In the limited space we had, our main concern was to steer the respondents to reflect on impact. Our motive in conducting the survey was primarily *survival*: the more raw evidence we could produce of audience appreciation and even of personal changes of feeling, the stronger the likelihood of our being able to fund future iterations of the festival.

The response rate was very high. Of a combined audience of approximately a thousand people over five shows, we received exactly 250 feedback forms, a return rate of about 25 per cent; this is substantially higher than the norm for such surveys, moreover several of those forms were filled out on behalf of a family or couple (top tip: we found it really helps to have a charming Park Ranger in your cast who can strongly encourage survey completion during the curtain call.) From question 1, we learned that 30 per cent of our audience felt they knew Shakespeare very well and 39 per cent were 'somewhat' familiar with his work; 24 per cent were 'a little' familiar and the remaining 7 per cent 'not at all'. On the whole, the audience was more familiar with Yosemite National Park than it was with Shakespeare – half had lost count of the number of times they'd been to the Park, although 12 per cent said it was their first time there.

For many, the overriding response was to the synergy between place and production:

- I believe that this is a good variation. We love how well (and easily) Shakespeare could be set in Yosemite – and Yosemite could become so

well folded into this Shakespeare play.[11]
- It was a beautiful integration of the park, preservation, & protection into a tried & true Shakespeare play.

Revealingly, these two responses offer different versions of what is happening in site-specific adaptation: is Shakespeare being 'set in Yosemite' or is Yosemite being 'integrated' into a 'tried and true Shakespeare play'? The chiasmatic first response suggests both: the Park and the Play are mutually absorbent – Shakespeare, like any other tourist, is a guest of the Park; unlike most other tourists, though, he is capacious enough to enfold his host. As Gerald Prince argues writes in introducing Genette's argument, 'Any text is a hypertext, grafting itself onto a hypotext, an earlier text that it imitates or transforms' (1997: ix). If we think of 'Yosemite National Park' and *A Midsummer Night's Dream* as texts, which is the earlier? Viewed geographically, Shakespeare was grafted onto the hypotext that is Yosemite National Park, but that grafting in turn modified and adapted the audience's sense of the Park.

Many audience responses registered a change of personal perception. Here the play's interest in translation and metaphor – carrying overs, transformations, new combinations – seemed to be mimicked in this production's reception:

- I didn't see any connections between Shakespeare and the natural world before this performance!
- It was a great combination of Yosemite interpretation and Shakespeare! Makes me love Yosemite, & Re-imagine Shakespeare.
- We rearranged our entire day plans when we read this was going on and it was completely worth it to spend an evening with this energy. Our little family needed this. Our own transformation that only being in nature together can bring.

Perhaps of most interest to this volume, there was a strong strain of reception that explicitly evaluated the production in terms of adaptation (a word not used in our programme notes). Here are some of the eleven pieces of feedback (about 4 per cent of the overall yield) that mentioned 'adaptation' or some cognate term (including 'to fit'):

- The adaptation to the region and nature conservation was very well executed.
- What an incredible rendition of a classic, perfectly & creatively modified to fit the background.
- The more I see adaptions [*sic*] the more I love them. I love making Shakespeare accessible to everyone. Art is so important for bringing people together!
- The clever mixing/adaptation – the simplicity AND the complexity.
- Modern adaptations are great!
- Loved the adaptation to the setting. Well acted – very entertaining liked the environmental message as well.
- Loved adaptation of the Shakespeare to park and current music.

It was clear that for many, the re-fitting of Shakespeare to new purposes was the most revelatory aspect of the experience. Adaptation in and of itself is usually appreciated and embraced by general audiences, many of whom have only traditional men-in-doublets notions of Shakespearean performance.

In response to the prompt, 'What aspect or moment of the play had the most impact on you?', two features of the production particularly stood out. Of the 250 forms, 75 referred to the production's use of song and music as a highlight, while the most frequently cited individual performance was that of Lisa Wolpe's Puck (63 references). Although the cast featured some other highly experienced performers, Wolpe was the only Equity actor in the show. Furthermore, her Puck had complete license to roam, physically and textually; she broke the fourth wall far more frequently than any other character and also, with her directors' happy permission, ad-libbed and spoke more than was set down for her, pretty much when the fancy took her. The role was also made more prominent by the addition of speeches from elsewhere in Shakespeare; Wolpe opened the show with a small globe in her hand, asking 'To be or not to be' before launching into part of John of Gaunt's 'This England' speech. This Puck's troubled subjectivity and eco-consciousness thus memorably framed the experience.

While the vast majority of responses were 'on message' and enthusiastic about the adaptation's very evident cultural and environmental politics, there were some outliers. In 'Pyramus and Thisbe', the role of Wall was played by Ranger Jess – the wall suit consisted of recycled food packets and cartons. Two respondents (almost certainly friends) at the same performance both wrote, 'MAGA = loved the wall'.

FIGURE 3.1.4 The whole cast joined in the final song. Dancing in front from left to right are Egea (Carin Heidelbach), Hermia (Amber Fowler), Lysander (Tonatiuh Newbold), Hippolyta/Titania (Rachel Rodrigues) and Theseus/Oberon (G. B. Blackmon). Image credit: Thomas Ovalle.

We hope it will need explaining to future readers that 'MAGA' is the acronym for 'Make America Great Again', the slogan on which Donald Trump ran for President in 2016; 'the wall', for these viewers, clearly reminded them of Trump's ongoing promise to build a wall along the entirety of the Mexico–US border. Meanwhile, a barrier of a more psychological kind was apparently erected for the eight-year-old boy whose main takeaway from the show was that 'it made me not want to kiss ever (I'm 8)'.

CONCLUSION

Shakespeare's plays are re-newable cultural resources that can be adapted into works of theatre that urge action on ecological issues. While many of the Earth's resources will never come back after being extracted and exhausted, Shakespeare's plays are not diminished when plundered to energize a new work of art: quite the opposite, as creative adaptation of these plays has generally ensured their survival better than has conservative preservation. The process of adaptation – of re-ducing, re-writing and re-cycling these plays – also re-news them: it turns them into fresh creative artefacts. Adaptation leverages these old plays' canonicity and their natural imagery to address humanity's greatest threats. We see no more urgent purpose to which these plays might be put in the twenty-first century.

NOTES

1   *Dream* in 2018 was preceded by *One Touch of Nature* in 2017, which was an original collage show about nineteenth-century conservationist John Muir's relationship to Shakespeare, and followed by an adaptation of *As You Like It* in 2019. Our planned 2020 *Love's Labour's Lost* has been postponed until 2022, and in 2021 we filmed a production of *Cymbeline*. Photos and production information can be found at our website. The 2017, 2018 and 2019 productions were co-sponsored by University of Warwick, then Paul's home institution.

2   As National Geographic explains, 'The biosphere is made up of the parts of Earth where life exists. The biosphere extends from the deepest root systems of trees to the dark environment of ocean trenches, to lush rain forests and high mountaintops' ('Biosphere' n.d.).

3   We are using the term 'eco-theatrical' to talk about theatre that prioritizes environmental themes and practices. Theresa J. May calls this kind of work 'ecodramaturgy' and describes it as theatre making that puts ecological reciprocity at the centre of its theatrical and thematic intent (May 2017). See also Heddon and Mackey (2012).

4   Practice as Research is work that uses performance practice itself as a form of research, and is sometimes called Performance as Research, especially in North America.

5   See for example Corner 2013; Moezzi et al. 2017; Arnold (2018).

6   See also Estok (2011); O'Dair (2011a).

7   See also Katherine Steele Brokaw's description of Applied Theatre/Community Practice and its usefulness to the scholar of Shakespearean performance (2017).

8   The Winter 2019 special issue of *Critical Survey on Applied Shakespeare* describes several projects, including Shakespeare in Yosemite (McKenzie and Shaughnessy 2019).

9   See earthshakesalliance.ucmerced.edu. The site also has free video recordings of the entire Globe 4 Globe conference.

10 Lisa's statement about the age of all the trees in the park, even if not strictly accurate biologically, is poetically true.

11 Audience responses collected in Yosemite National Park, 21–3 April 2018. For surveys and interviews, we have received a waiver of IRB approval from UC-Merced.

REFERENCES

'About the IECA' (n.d.), IECA, https://theieca.org/about (accessed 27 October 2020).

Arnold, A. (2018), *Climate Change and Storytelling Narratives and Cultural Meaning in Environmental Communication*, London: Palgrave.

'Artists and Climate Change: Organizations' (n.d.), Artists and Climate Change, https://artistsandclimatechange.com/organizations/ (accessed 27 October 2020).

Bendell, J. (2018), 'Deep Adaptation: A Map for Navigating Climate Tragedy', *IFLAS Occasional Paper* 2. Available online: https://www.lifeworth.com/deepadaptation.pdf (accessed 20 September 2019).

'Biosphere' (n.d.), National Geographic, https://www.nationalgeographic.org/encyclopedia/biosphere/ (accessed 28 October 2020).

Brayton, D. (2018), *Shakespeare's Ocean: an Ecocritical Exploration*, Charlottesville, VA: University of Virginia Press.

Brayton, D. and L. Bruckner (2016), 'Introduction: Warbling Invaders', in L. Bruckner and D. Brayton (eds), *Ecocritical Shakespeare*, 1–11, Aldershot: Ashgate.

'Broadway Green Alliance'(n.d.), https://www.broadwaygreen.com/about-us (accessed 28 October 2020).

Brokaw, K. S. (2017), 'Shakespeare as Community Practice', *Shakespeare Bulletin* 35 (3): 445–61.

Brokaw, K. S. and P. Prescott (2018), 'Saving the Earth needs all hands on deck, including Shakespeare's', *Modesto Bee* and *Merced Sun-Star*, 11 April. Available online: https://www.modbee.com/opinion/article208648584.html (accessed 28 October 2020).

Corner, A. (2013), 'The Art of Climate Change Communication', *Guardian*, 18 March. Available online: https://www.theguardian.com/sustainable-business/art-climate-change-communication (accessed 28 October 2020).

'Cymbeline in the Anthropocene' (n.d.), https://www.cymbeline-anthropocene.com (accessed 28 October 2020).

Dionne, C. (2016), *Posthuman Lear: Reading Shakespeare in the Anthropocene*, New York, NY: Punctum Books.

Egan, G. (2015), *Shakespeare and Ecocritical Theory*, London: Bloomsbury/Arden Shakespeare.

Estok, S. C. (2011), *Ecocriticism and Shakespeare: Reading Ecophobia*, London: Palgrave Macmillan.

Glover, D. (2018), Interview with authors, 22 April.

Heddon, D. and S. Mackey (2012), 'Environmentalism, Performance, and Applications: Uncertainties and Emancipations', *Research in Drama Education: The Journal of Applied Theatre and Performance* 17 (2): 162–92.

Henderson, D. E. (2006), *Collaborations with the Past: Reshaping Shakespeare across Time and Media*, Ithaca, NY: Cornell University Press.

Hughes, J. and H. Nicholson (2016), 'Applied Theatre: Ecology of Practices', in J. Hughes and H. Nicholson (eds), *Critical Perspectives on Applied Theatre*, 1–12, Cambridge: Cambridge University Press.

Kaiser, S. (2004), 'How Long Do You Think It Will Run?', *Shakespeare Bulletin* 22 (3): 47–8.

Kershaw, B. (2009a), 'Performance Practice as Research: Perspectives from a Small Island', in S. R. Riley and L. Hunter (eds), *Mapping Landscapes for Performance as Research: Scholarly Acts and Creative Cartographies*, 1–13, London: Palgrave Macmillan.

Kershaw, B. (2009b), *Theatre Ecology: Environments and Performance Events*, Cambridge: Cambridge University Press.

Mackenzie, R. and R. Shaughnessy, eds (2019), *Critical Survey* (Special issue on Applied Shakespeare) 31 (4).

Mackey, S. (2016), 'Performing Location: Place and Applied Theatre', *Critical Perspectives on Applied Theatre*, J. Hughes and H. Nicholson (eds), Cambridge: Cambridge University Press.

Martin, R. (2015), *Shakespeare and Ecology*, Oxford: Oxford University Press.

Martin, R. and E. O'Malley (2018), 'Eco-Shakespeare in Performance: Introduction', *Shakespeare Bulletin* 36 (3): 377–90.

May, T. J. (2017), '*Tú eres mi otro yo* – Staying with the Trouble: Ecodramaturgy and the AnthropoScene', *The Journal of American Drama and Theatre* 29 (2): 1–18.

McIntyre, J. (2018), Email correspondence with authors, 26 April.

McKibben, B. (2005), 'What the warming world needs now is art, sweet art', *Grist*, 22 April. Available online: https://grist.org/article/mckibben-imagine/ (accessed 28 October 2020).

Moezzi, M., K. Janda and S. Rotmann (2017), 'Using stories, narratives, and storytelling in energy and climate change research', *Energy Research and Social Science* 31: 1–10. Available online: https://doi.org/10.1016/j.erss.2017.06.034(accessed 28 October 2020).

O'Dair, S. (2011a), 'Is it Ecocriticism if it isn't Presentist?', in L. Bruckner and D. Brayton (eds), *Ecocritical Shakespeare*, 71–85, Aldershot: Ashgate.

O'Dair, S. (2011b), '"To Fright the Animals and to Kill Them up": Shakespeare and Ecology', *Shakespeare Studies* 39: 74–83.

Prince, G. (1997), 'Foreword', in G. Genette, *Palimpsests: Literature in the Second Degree*, Lincoln: University of Nebraska Press.

Rivas, J. (2018), Interview with authors, 22 April.

'Shakespeare in Yosemite' (n.d.), https://yosemiteshakes.ucmerced.edu/ (accessed
    28 October 2020).
Stetson, C. (2018), Email correspondence with the authors, 2 May.
Townsend, S. (2019) 'Climate Change Versus Cats… Zombies, Cake, Brexit
    and Gravy', *Forbes*, 15 May. Available online: https://www.forbes.com/sites/
    solitairetownsend/2019/05/15/cats-versus-climate-change-revealing-issue-coverage-on-
    our-screens/#66c35b7a479e (accessed 28 October 2020).
Townsend, S. (2020), Email correspondence with authors, 10 October.
Watson, R. N. (2011), 'The Ecology of Self in Midsummer Night's Dream', in D. Brayton
    and L. Bruckner (eds), *Ecocritical Shakespeare*, 33–56, Aldershot: Ashgate.
Wolpe, L. (2018), Interview with authors, 22 April.

Hamlet in the age of algorithmic production

ANNIE DORSEN

INTERVIEWED BY MIRIAM FELTON-DANSKY

Annie Dorsen is a director and writer whose works explore the intersection of algorithms and live performance. Her most recent project, *Infinite Sun*, is an algorithmic sound installation commissioned by the Sharjah Biennial 14. Previous performance projects, including *The Great Outdoors* (2017), *Yesterday Tomorrow* (2015), *A Piece of Work* (2013) and *Hello Hi There* (2010), have been widely presented in the US and internationally. Some of the venues where her work has been seen include The Festival d'Automne de Paris, The Holland Festival, BAM's Next Wave Festival, New York Live Arts, Kampnagel Summer Festival, Impulstanz, and The New York Film Festival's 'Views from the Avant-garde' series, along with many others. The script for *A Piece of Work* was published by Ugly Duckling Presse, and she has contributed essays for *The Drama Review*, *Theatre Magazine*, *Etcetera*, *Frakcija* and *Performing Arts Journal*. She is the co-creator of the 2008 Broadway musical *Passing Strange*, which she also directed. In addition to awards for *Passing Strange*, Dorsen received a 2019 MacArthur Fellowship, a 2018 Guggenheim Fellowship, the 2018 Spalding Gray Award, a 2016 Foundation for Contemporary Arts Grant to Artists Award and the 2014 Herb Alpert Award for the Arts in Theatre.

In 2019, Dorsen spoke with critic-scholar Miriam Felton-Dansky about *A Piece of Work*, the algorithmic *Hamlet* she created in 2013, the second in Dorsen's algorithmic theatre trilogy, which also includes *Hello Hi There* and *Yesterday Tomorrow*. Mixing live performance with algorithms and interfaces, *A Piece of Work* is a digital *Hamlet* for a post-humanist age. The spectator is absorbed in a swirl of connections amongst memory, language and technology, implicating both the past and future of theatre itself. New scenes, songs, scores and visuals emerge from an intricate web of technology that uses Shakespeare's original text as data (Cartelli 2019; Felton-Dansky 2019). Virtuosic actor Scott Shepherd or the legendary Joan MacIntosh (who alternate in the role) perform alongside computers, automated lighting systems, sound and video that have all been programmed to generate a new production of the play nightly.

Miriam Felton-Dansky: What kind of relationship did you have with the play *Hamlet*, as a director and theatre maker, before you made *A Piece of Work*?

Annie Dorsen: Almost none. Of course, I had seen it several times, read it, studied it in school. I never directed it, I never thought about directing it. I chose it because it is the English language play that most obviously represents the link between humanism and theatre. I remembered Harold Bloom's essay from *The Invention of the Human*: he says Hamlet creates what it is to be a modern human being with an inner life. He seizes on those parts of *Hamlet* where the character seems to be at war with himself, a conflicted inner life that can only be untangled with language. 'I have that within which passeth show' – there is such a thing as an inner life which is not apparent to others when they look at you. So for Bloom, it's as if the character of Hamlet pops into three dimensions and the other characters in the play are sort of still two-dimensional, more like theatre characters had been in the previous hundred years of dramatic writing.

MFD:

Does he mean in the previous hundred years, or does he mean ever?

AD:

I think [Bloom] probably means ever, but as far as I remember he is talking about specific antecedents to Hamlet such as [Thomas Kyd's] *The Spanish Tragedy*. [Bloom] says, for instance, that Ophelia is much closer to a stock character than Hamlet is. So when I started thinking about doing a play, an algorithmic play, it seemed obvious that *Hamlet* was the one to do. First, I was thinking about that Bloom thesis. And then I was thinking about the language – I mean, that everyone knows it – so when you scramble it, it would still be familiar. You wouldn't just be listening to gibberish, you would be listening to specifically Shakespearian, Hamletian gibberish.

I had used a little bit of Shakespeare in *Hello Hi There* [Dorsen's first algorithmic theatre piece, which premiered in 2010]. 'O that this too too sullied flesh' – that speech is in the database that the chatbots draw from, and I loved it when it came up in that piece. It felt, in a very Harold Bloom way actually, like this moment when the two chatbots were yearning towards something, reaching towards selfhood. Like they were as close as they could ever come to having souls, just because that language was so much more beautiful than any other language they had access to. And this kind of lament about being a person and how awful it is to have a body, it seemed like a kind of sweet, sad, doomed effort on the part of the chatbots to become human.

And then I liked on a pure sensory level the way the words sounded when they were spoken by text-to-speech programmes. Because it's a sacrilege. It's such a profane thing to do to these words. The whole history of modern Shakespeare performance is defined by John Barton, basically, by the invention of a way to speak Shakespeare – he wants to call it a rediscovery but it's an invention – a technique for speaking Shakespeare in which the breath and voice of the actor is subordinated to the needs of the words. There's an idea that the words should almost speak themselves. That you should not have to try to make meaning from the language, as long as you speak the words correctly the meaning will 'reveal itself'. You simply have to open your mouth and say it properly on a technical level, and the meaning will be released in an almost alchemical way from the combination of your lung capacity, your tongue, your mouth and those magical words. It's almost like speaking magic. So I thought the worst thing you can do to Shakespeare is to have a low-quality computer voice speaking it. One thing you always notice with speech synthesis programmes is that the voices don't breathe. Or maybe you don't notice it, but they don't. That's part of what gives them that uncanny feeling, the fact that there's no breath. So whatever the quality of the voice may be, it can never sound truly convincing because there's no heartbeat, there's no breath, there's no lips. All those physical things. Most American actors first learn about speaking as a physical action when they learn to speak Shakespeare. You have to develop control and power over your breath, to think almost choreographically about how you're going to speak, how you will place the words, how you will play along with the music of the text. So the nice thing about the computer voices is that it was not just a provocation for its own sake, but it was a revealing provocation about a lot of assumptions around Shakespearean performance. It exemplified some of the questions I was asking about bodiless performance in general, and whether you can still have a live, real-time spontaneous performance by a computer programme as opposed to by a human.

MFD:

How many voices were there speaking text-to-speech in *A Piece of Work*?

AD:

We cast the full thing, each character had their own voice. We cracked the Mac voices, the ones that come standard on the computer, and we bought a few commercial voices and cracked those as well. Greg Beller, the sound designer, who is a specialist on speech synthesis, took all those voices apart and used the parts to make new voices. A couple of characters were just the Mac voices you might recognize. 'Alex' is Hamlet. 'Vicki', the younger voice, is Ophelia, 'Victoria' is Gertrude, and I think one of the commercial voices we bought was Claudius. We used the default old man voice for Polonius. A silly kind of novelty voice for one of the Clowns, that sort of thing. For the rest we played around with the rate of speech, the timbre, the attack, the pitch range, all of those variables. We got very precise. It was a lot of fun actually, it was really like casting the roles through the tuning of the computer voices.

MFD:

And stage directions?

AD:

Stage directions were spoken by a voice, another voice. We cast that too.

MFD:

Alongside listening to the speech, I'm thinking also about the decision to have the text appear on the screen upstage in all these different ways – different sizes, in different places on the screen.

AD:

Right, it's like staging a play. That was my version of staging, figuring out how the text would go on the screen. I wanted to gently encourage the audience to be able to imagine bodies onstage, so we did some placement of text to suggest that if the characters had bodies they might be in this or that spatial relationship to one another.

MFD:

Did you always have the idea for the wooden platform onstage as well? With kind of a hole in the middle that one would imagine the ghost coming through?

AD:

We thought about taking elements of the Globe Theatre, stripping them down, and separating them. There would be a platform, there would be a trapdoor, a curtain and a roof. That was the beginning of our scenic design process. Thinking about the basic architectural elements of the Globe, stripping them down to basics and then putting them in different places than they would ordinarily be in.

MFD:

The play is inherently about absence, but this staging made it feel more explicitly so. The very spare design elements reminded me of what a more fully constructed set or theatre might look like. There was a platform that looked like humans could walk on it – but there were no humans walking on it.

AD:

It's not built to be structurally sound, please don't walk on it!

MFD:

Okay, good to know!

AD:

That was a thing that we understood also as we went through the design process, that it's good that we have this place for people that there are no people on. And there were other little effects. Every time there was an entrance there was a little gust of air from behind the curtain that blew it open as if someone were entering through it. Those effects were there precisely to amplify the absence of bodies.

MFD:

I'm curious what discoveries you made about the play during the process of making *A Piece of Work*.

AD:

When I first started playing with Markov models, I did an experiment in which I put all the text that Hamlet speaks in the play and all the text that Ophelia speaks in the play into the pot, and used a Markov chain to create a new scene between Hamlet and Ophelia. There's still a version of that in the final piece. And of course, when I say create a new scene, I mean that each time the algorithm runs it creates a new text – the parameters stay the same, but the specific words chosen are different each time. The new lines assigned to

Hamlet or Ophelia will be blends of both of their text from the original play. The thing I noticed was in each version of the scene the algorithm generated, Ophelia seemed to pop as a character: When she has access to Hamlet's language, all of a sudden she has an inner life, doubts, questions about the world, the capacity to reflect on her own conditions. She seemed like someone you could imagine actually falling in love with, a real person. I thought, oh now this is seeming like a recognizable relationship between two human beings who seem to know each other and have things to talk about. Ophelia becomes less a functional symbol and more a sparring partner and match for Hamlet. And he also started to seem like someone with desires, vulnerabilities, not so certain of himself. So there was an interesting kind of modernity that was introduced into the text.

Similarly, running some of the soliloquies or monologues through the algorithm made them feel somehow contemporary. Gertrude's speech about Ophelia's death, when it's put through the algorithmic wringer, it comes out traumatized, really like the text has been traumatized. It's full of false starts, repetitions, stutters and non sequiturs. Gertrude turns into Gertrude Stein.

MFD:

Following on these initial discoveries, can you say a little about the process of making the piece?

AD:

The joke we always made in rehearsal was that I decided to do it without having reread the play first. It had probably been years since I read *Hamlet*. I was sitting in a bar in Vienna with a computer programmer friend, and he asked what I was doing next and I kind of spontaneously said oh, I'm going to use Markov chains on *Hamlet*, and we had a big laugh about what a stupid idea that was. But then the next day I realized I was serious and I went immediately to my design team and we started planning the project. We went into preproduction, and it was ages before I realized that I hadn't actually looked at the play. I had been talking about it with everyone, I had been organizing it and preparing and I'd gotten Scott Shepherd involved, but I didn't totally remember exactly what happens in the play. What are the boring parts that people never remember, and how far into it does Polonius die, and all of that. And so, with the team it became a joke of, let's see if we can get to the end of the process and nobody reads the play… but of course Scott knew it all by heart because he had played Hamlet with The Wooster Group, and he's got an amazing memory so he more or less had the entire play memorized. As we progressed we all realized that of course we had to engage with the play in a real way. I think some of the designers mostly engaged with it from the perspective of digital humanities, of statistical information, as opposed to the more traditional perspective of story or structure.

MFD:

Like: how many two-word sentences are there?

AD:

Yes, that sort of thing. We also treat the stage directions from the edition we were using as though they were part of the play. Which is also a sacrilegious, low-level thing to do as a director because, you know, those were added later, they are not written by Shakespeare. But we decided just to take them as part of the artifact. In a way, you could say I didn't direct *Hamlet*, I directed the Hamlet.xml file.

MFD:

I was about to ask what edition you used.

AD:

That was a bit of a discussion because of course theatre people who were involved in the project always asked what edition we were using and wanted to go through and discuss the differences, and all the things you normally do when you do Shakespeare. But what we really needed was a version of the play we could use as data for our processing. The lead programmer on the project found a document that had been prepared as part of a larger digital humanities project out of Northwestern called Word Hoard. They've made a version of all thirty-six plays that's searchable, sortable, scannable, each word is tagged up with lots of helpful information – character, act and scene, line number, grammatical part of speech, all sorts of things. So we started from that. And then did a lot of work correcting the text, and fleshing it out, adding additional information to it.

Scott was enormously helpful in this because he not only has the whole play memorized but he also seems to have all the differences between all the different versions in his head, and so he came around a few times to discuss options, or advocate for his preferences. I gave him the job of updating the XML to be something he could be happy with. And then we did an emotion analysis project, so we ended up with a version of the XML that was heavily expanded in terms of its data.

MFD:

What was the emotion analysis project?

AD:

We did a simple form of emotion analysis. We tagged each word of the play with a score between zero and five for each of the four basic emotions: joy, anger, fear, and sadness. And we used those scores to do all kinds of things. To determine the colour and the intensity of the lighting, to create the musical underscoring. Sometimes we used it as an additional pressure on the text selection so as it's running along doing its Markov chain thing we would slowly increase the minimum allowable score for sadness, for example, over the course of the scene. So over time the algorithm would be forced to select more and more high scoring 'sad' words. An additional pressure on the text selection. And we did some fun things, like when we would hit a certain intensity of emotion, a certain high scoring word, we would put a tremor in the computer voice, as if there were a little more acting going on.

MFD:

You toured it to places where audiences didn't have English as their first language. Presumably there were people who weren't familiar with *Hamlet*, or do you think it's just so universal that this didn't matter?

AD:

Of course, everywhere we toured, the audience was familiar with *Hamlet,* with the story. But in some countries the actual language was not familiar to people – they had only experienced the play in translation. That's a problem for this piece. In most languages, as far as I know, Shakespeare translations are modernized, there's not an attempt to make the language equivalently antiquated. The closest would be an older translation, from the eighteenth or nineteenth century. But those are not often produced anymore. In any case, a lot of the pleasure of *A Piece of Work* has to do with recognizing the language, the surprise at how it's being treated, the odd new meanings created by the procedures we're using. Without familiarity with the specific words of the play, it's difficult. Those audiences were sometimes struggling to keep up with the flow of words to begin with, and then they also didn't have the satisfaction of that bell-ringing thing.

MFD:

What was your experience with English-speaking audiences?

AD:

With a native English-speaking audience the humour of the piece comes out more. Those audiences are able to find it funny because they get the scrambled language automatically, without having to do any translation in their heads. So the sharp right and left turns in the text, even if they didn't know exactly what had been done to a certain speech, they knew it wasn't like *that* in the original. You know, the capacity to understand one's native language is automatic, it's not a process our brains go through, it's an automatic involuntary reaction. That's part of the mechanism that this piece relies on. That understanding language is an involuntary reaction, rather than a process. You can't help but make meaning of what you hear when it's in your own language, no matter how thorny the language might be – you may be frustrated in your attempt to understand, but the words themselves will have an impact on you. A physical or mnemonic one. The actual experience of the piece is the thinking alongside the language as it unfolds. But translating from a second language *is* a process, like an algorithm, a conscious process of trying to understand. So if your brain needs the time to go through that process then you're out of sync with the rhythm of the performance.

MFD:

I was reading Lee Edelman's essay about *Hamlet* in a 2011 issue of *Shake-speare Quarterly*, and he talks about the action of the play as essentially a form of writing: how Hamlet says he's going to 'wipe away all trivial fond records' and inscribe there, instead, the Ghost's commandment. And then the story of the play is his effort to reproduce those actions in the world, that the play is really about reproduction. And this made me wonder about algorithmic rep-etition and reproduction in *A Piece of Work*.

AD:

With this question I start thinking about Walter Benjamin, and the loss of aura in mechanically reproduced art. Algorithmic reproduction is something else. It would be great if Benjamin were around to tell us what he makes of it, art in the age of algorithmic generation. I suppose some of the same issues pertain in terms of loss of aura, but when it comes to algorithmic production, it's not just copies. It's more about the vast number of iterations that make up a set, the set of all the possible solutions to the problem you've set the algorithm to solve. Instead of an endless number of cheap copies, you have an endless number of cheap originals. I mean cheap in the sense that the cost of creation is very low for an algorithm. Once the algorithm is written, you can run it a thousand times and each time it will give you something new. It's like text by the yard. If you want to spit out another hundred versions of *A Piece of Work*, it will take about ten minutes.

This is very unlike the work of earlier artists working procedurally or using chance operations. Handmade procedural work, by artists like John Cage or Jackson Mac Low – that work is very costly. But right now, there exist thousands of computer science students all playing around with neural nets, generating endless amounts of funny, weird language. That vast quantity of material, all of which is different but all of which has a kind of sameness, is maybe interesting in light of *A Piece of Work*. *Hamlet*, the great masterpiece of Western theatre, is contrasted to the endless amounts of twenty-first-century, computer-generated hamletishness.

MFD:

I wonder if it's also different because unlike the visual art Benjamin describes, *Hamlet* was never 'one' thing: there are all the different texts, the quartos, the folios, the original performance that we don't have access to. In theatre, there's never a singular original in quite the same way.

AD:

Sure. The notion of the 'actual play' is already an uncertain thing. The differences between the first quarto and this or that folio – well, I can see how one could get very involved in them. I don't want to do that. But certainly, while watching *A Piece of Work*, you're continuously comparing what you see to whatever you remember of the real play. In that sense it's putting you in an interesting position as a viewer between an idea of memory and an idea of futurity. It's calling up the ghost of the play that lives in your memory.

MFD:

In the sense of calling up the ghost of the original – do you think of this as an adaptation of *Hamlet*?

AD:

I thought of this as a version of *Hamlet*. I wasn't thinking in terms of adaptation, I thought, that this is the *Hamlet* I'm directing.

MFD:

Was your version of *Hamlet* a tragedy?

AD:

I don't know. There can't be tragedy with computers because they're not sentient. They're too stupid for tragedy.

MFD:

I think of tragedy in terms of a dramatic structure but also a social dimension, something was destined and has happened but it's the downfall not of one human but a whole society, or a city-state, something about a whole civilization that has to get destroyed, it's got a public dimension.

AD:

Maybe the tragedy of *A Piece of Work* is that we humans are not going to be able to help ourselves from getting more and more entranced by and dependent on these digital technologies that are ultimately only going to be bad news for us. It's the tragedy of technology. It's not *Hamlet* at all, then, it's Prometheus. It's about not being able to stop ourselves from giving these tools incredible amounts of power over us.

REFERENCES

Cartelli, T. (2019), *Reenacting Shakespeare in the Shakespeare Aftermath*, New York, NY: Palgrave Macmillan.

Felton-Dansky, M. (2019), 'The Algorithmic Spectator: Watching Annie Dorsen's Work', *TDR/The Drama Review* 63 (4): 66–87.

CHAPTER 3.3

A King Lear sutra

PRETI TANEJA

My debut novel *We That Are Young* (Taneja 2017) can partly be understood as a translation of Shakespeare's *King Lear* to a novel form, set in a near-real vision of contemporary India. It was written out of two decades of immersion in the play, and a lifetime of engagement with Indian literature, language, politics, mythology and culture. I situate it also partly within a global modernist tradition of writing that includes Virginia Woolf, Saadat Hasan Manto, Bapsi Sidwa, Ismat Chugtai, Jean Rhys and Gertrude Stein. It is rooted in my hybrid lived experience as a woman of colour: an insider/outsider in both India (the country of my parents' birth) and England (where I was born and grew up). And so, its form is necessarily innovative/ experimental, and, after *Lear's* own example, its register (and genre) are what I call 'epic hyperreal'.

We That Are Young steps away from the debut immigrant bildungsroman novel that usually has traction in the UK publishing industry. It articulates hybridity at the sentence level instead of seeking this through a thematic of assimilation, to reveal how complex and entwined the cultural, legal and capitalist entanglement of Britain and India really are in contemporary structures of power and in contemporary bodies. I wanted to develop a polyvocal, intertextual and multilingual style to explore forms of identity in the world of my book: an India of syncretic linguistic and literary traditions, multi-theism and older, nature-based psychologies of transcendence, as well as (at the time of writing the novel) a 'rising' Hindu fascism and uber-capitalism which since has matured into full-blown horror. The story is told primarily by five young people: an American-Indian 'foreign return', a closeted homosexual and sham holy man, and three close but (thanks to India's shift from socialism to capitalism in the mid-1990s) very different generations of women: sisters who are part of the second and third generation to be born in the aftermath of colonization; in the seventy years since the subcontinent was partitioned by the British and the new nation state of India was formed. All are negotiating gilded patriarchy, duty and individual desires. Above all the novel explores the generational damage done to those who inherit power over a divided earth, while questioning who they are now, and what we then might become.

We That Are Young was researched and written from 2010–13, and edited over four more years, including an extended period in hard-to-access parts of Indian-occupied Kashmir in 2012, and later in the archives of the United Nations in New York. Its argument (made via a tightly stitched, or sutured, or sutra-ed intertextuality) that colonial-inspired, Indian billionaire-funded Hindu fascism would, under the guise of economic development and via extreme constitutional changes, lead to the eventual annexation of Indian occupied Kashmir preceded these events as they actually came to pass in 2019. Two years after the book was published. And as I wrote this chapter.

Being invited to contribute a piece reflecting on my process of writing the novel so soon after publication was a privilege of course. But many fiction writers shy away from this kind of thinking. We make the work; we don't always *want* to critically understand why or how we did it; in the end it has to stand alone to honour the compact of trust between writers and readers. Creativity is mysterious and this kind of analysis can feel risky for a number of reasons. In that sense, critical thinking on the novel by others is always more interesting (to me), and conversations rather than self-analysis often show me more than I was always conscious of while writing. I'm lucky to have had skilled interlocutors who have enabled me to clarify my own thinking about my process. Particularly Christie Carson, Margo Hendricks, Sinéad Morrissey, Georgie Lucas, Farah Karim-Cooper, Poonam Trivedi, Miranda Fay Thomas, Jessica Chiba, Diana Henderson, Ayseha Ramachandran, Julie Sanders, Letitia Garcia, Sandeep Parmar, Kathryn Vomero Santos, Sarah Colvin and Helen Smith and her undergraduate class at the University of York who awed me with the depth of their engagement with the book.

I'm truly grateful for this scholarly interest in, and embrace of, the novel. It is from that place that I set my practice in some kind of context here, even though of course over time my sense of that context may change. In order to make this kind of reflection writable for me, a political fiction writer with a human rights/journalistic background and academic training, I use some of the strategies I've described above. Like my novel, this chapter has a poetic register, a syntactical variation from the academic voice, and a sense of structure as a circular journey rather than a linear argument, as Adrienne Rich writes, 'the grammar turned and attacked me' (Rich 1970: 338).[1] This formally innovative way of writing feels most honest as I construct a narrative of my process; it comes from my own reading practice across global early modern, modernist and postmodern traditions and also from my desire as an intersectional feminist to reject reductive categories of identity or culture and to make space for multiplicity within the academy for 'other' forms of critical writing. While on a panel at a literary event I was once asked to identify what tradition I write within – I take that as the literary equivalent of the question so often put to 'immigrants', *where are you from? where are you really from?* – that above all else, articulates the anxiety of the questioner about their own place in the world.

In fact I think this kind of hybridity is a hallmark of Anglophone writing by minoritised women of colour working in literary fiction today. It arises from and in resistance to structures of power that encode systemic racism and misogyny, and yet also exists because of and among people, and readers working against that culture. Modernist, contemporary and certainly not 'post' colonial, it is so far uncategorized as a genre (perhaps it should stay that way).

My own debut was a journey into articulating these ideas, and in that spirit of linguistic and stylistic multiplicity, I offer a necessarily partial patchwork of that here. Completion comes from the reader, whenever, wherever and however they may find these words.

Preti Taneja, June 2021

* * *

Slavery broke the world in half, broke it in every way. It broke Europe. It made them into something else, it made them slave masters. It made them crazy.

–Toni Morrison, *The Source of Self-Regard*

Translation, transformation. My mother teaches me at six years old to sew. I want to sew with her/I want to read alone. I stitch together remnants of remembered reading, and slowly make new work. I read Adrienne Rich's *A Valediction Forbidding Mourning*, and want 'to do', with Rich, 'something very common, in my own way' (Rich 1970). That is, write.

What does Rich mean by, 'in my own way'? Her poem takes its title from John Donne's *A Valediction: Forbidding Mourning*. I think she means to read the canon, to question canonicity. To find a style and a voice as a woman writing in and against that man made world. I read *King Lear* and recognize a British-Indian history. I want to find a style and a voice that comes from a living, breathing body, but am made aware of my categorized identity. That is, politicized. The British state defines me as British Asian (Indian), second generation. Descendent of Independence/Partition, of 'Commonwealth citizens' now known as *immigrants*. Result of a story that finds its correlative in the classroom only through Shakespeare's tragedy.

My title, *We That Are Young*, is taken from the ambivalent end lines of *King Lear*, spoken by Edgar in the Folio edition. His words are a jumping-off point to an India that daily provides examples of what happens when religious nationalism meets the neocolonial hunger of global capitalism: an extreme abrogation of minority rights, extreme inequality enabled by caste, class and a deepening of gendered hierarchies embedded in every facet of life (and which infuse the diaspora as well); and that has the largest, most youthful and fastest-growing population of the world's democracies (*Economic Times* 2019). Edgar's lines, so potent with the potential of rhetoric, allow us to read what we want into them:

> The weight of these sad times we must obey,
> Speak what we feel, not what we ought to say.
> The oldest hath borne most; we that are young
> Shall never see so much nor live so long.

(5.3.322–5)

The lines encode truisms; to some readers they offer wisdom and pity for the young who will never be wise, and for the old who have suffered so much. Given the end of *King Lear*, they also remind us that cruelty, violence and self-estrangement are systemic, and an old order might raise the same again. We might end by feeling glad this is not our world, and go home happy. Or this encounter with art might prompt us to counter systemic harms in our own times. The lines take us beyond the action of the play, and we, the audience or reader, that are all young in comparison to the world a 400-year-old play gives us, are left with a reflection of our own societies, families, histories and a question about the kind of world we want to write into being, which we want to come. But in their refusal to offer any way forward, or statement of intent, their implicit claim to integrity seems highly suspect to me and so I begin to question the narrative force of the play; its focus on men, masculinity, the power that is.

My childhood had its own natural hybridity: two languages, traditions, uniforms, foods. Ours was double-cultured life (though at home, we never ate shop-bought yoghurt). At home my parents taught me to aspire to being a 'citizen of the world' as a moral imperative. The right-wing English government says that this means I am a 'citizen of nowhere' (Davis and Hollis 2018). In the world outside my home, I have yet to learn of the strategy of dominant culture, which is to 'palisade all art forms: monitor, discredit, or expel those who challenge or destabilize processes of demonization or deification' (Morrison 2019: 14). I have yet to realize that literary categories are palisades. They define what is exclusive/excluded. That what is representative creates what is token by divorcing it from itself.

Rich's poem entreats me not to make an idol of the white marble bust in the library. Call him *Shakespeare*/call him *King Lear*/call him an idea of 'the literary'. Frozen lips will never yield. Black American women's writing and Indian writing in English provide another route through the maze – though what centre will this lead to, and will there be someone 'like me' there?

I learn the grammar of the canon and think about the 'other' canons that exist within me. I will have to suture all these parts together and make these migrant thoughts generate, regenerate, repair the generational damage begun with colonization, Partition of the Indian subcontinent, and further torn by migration into new countries and tongues.

Use the sentence as a needle to stitch a whole. To unpick language and divisions of kingdoms, the violence that is perpetrated on brown women, stitching up our mouths passed down and locked into my body, into me. To thread samples of time, to understand how it traps us in loops of historical violence. To feel shame and grief as they are passed down. Into the female body through colonization, colonized, gender violence, 'honour': write it onto the page with the voices of my characters, dictating their own ways of being.

If modern life begins with slavery, grandfather of the fissures and dislocations and ultimately the schism into which all will fall, Imperialism and colonization are its next iteration. The Holocaust is the ongoing chapter of this horrific tale: neoliberal capitalist societies hiding religious-supremacist nationalism along with the threat of nuclear and climate annihilation are our reckoning. It seems obvious to me, reading, young, that literary fiction should make itself felt through a combination of politics, aesthetics and ethics. I read *King Lear* as a map of masculinity and patriarchy, and of how those palisade women in nation. Partly through Shakespeare's language which contains prismatic meanings. *Bond. Tender.* Time collapses back into childhood: the novel I am writing as an adult becomes an act of translation. *King Lear* asks us to recognize collective and yet specific trauma, while its existence as art and as an artefact apparently expresses hope for a more equal world.

When I am young, *Lear* offers a very specific rubric to the Indian context: my context as British Asian. In the twentieth century, our grandparents became living experiments, their migration began us. We are the children of the recreation of Empire, this time within England, the green and pleasant land. I do not agree that gratitude and respect are a given. And I think about the existential heart of *King Lear*, and what daughters owe their father and their other father countries. *Who is it that can tell me who I am?* (1.4.221).

My mother teaches me at six years old to sew. Backstitch requires forward stitch. As I begin to write this chapter, Kashmir is still under curfew. It has been so for more than fifty days. The populists are meeting in New York. President Donald Trump, Prime Minister Narendra Modi. In the UK, the names are limitless into history. It is September, 2019. Yet another Brexit-motivated election is about to be called. Hindutva agents in India will use WhatsApp to persuade British Asian voters not to vote Labour. My parents came to the UK in 1968. 'Go home' is an echoing slur.

In 2019, here is a small list of actions that will soon be transmuted into reactions: India's anti-Muslim Citizenship Bill, Brexit lies, the absolute disgrace that is the UK's Prime Minister, Boris Johnson, and his Conservative cabinet… Border control and virus. I'm editing this at last in mid-June, 2021. Academic publishing and the global pandemic stretches thought like taffy over time. If I keep updating as I write, the chapter will not end.

That summer two years ago, I was asked – more than at any other moment since *We That Are Young* was first published two years prior again – how did you know [that fascism was rising]? It was always there. I had seen it all my life, in months spent visiting, travelling across India. I heard it in the stories told to me by people across caste, gender, class and socio-economic divides as I researched the book in the summer of 2012. It was in the UN archives on Kashmir which I read going back to 1937. And in the news reports and magazine advertisements and ether. In the demolition of the Babri Masjid. In the ethnic cleansing of over two thousand Muslims in Gujarat under Modi's watch in 2002. If I keep backdating as I write, the chapter will not end.

When I began writing *We That Are Young*, I was not thinking about what had shaped me. I had an imperative: to write *King Lear* as an Indian story. That came first. I knew the text in some completely indigenous way I located in my teenaged education. As I wrote I became more conscious of trying to excavate my own authorial voice through years of conditioning and silencing by cultures in two homelands.

In *King Lear*, Shakespeare demonstrates the potential of language to break and remake our minds. I had held this knowledge since I was at school; I think it speaks particularly to a bi/multilingual consciousness. I held it close, as a fierce belief I might one day prove. It was a story of split tongues and personalities that I felt I lived inside and already knew. The play's setting, in pre-Christian Britain, its non-linear whirligig of prophetic time, its epic sensibility circling the straight arrow of classical tragedy correlated with the principles of dharma. Its feudal, caste-based and gendered system spoke to the divide-and-rule politics of Empire and of an everyday misogyny considered culture in Indian life. The visceral disgust of women expressed in Lear's curses, Act One Scene One: the division of land linked to women's bodies through dowry, and to the demand for our obedience. *King Lear*, I thought, was a seventeenth-century prophecy, arising concurrently with the East India Company, foreseeing how a country could be divided and its women squandered and lost. It felt like a history and politics lesson. And if the basics need spelling out, the division of a kingdom leading to a civil war (where 'civil' is a state of mind, of the smilingly-violent tongue) legitimized my knowledge of colonial history. The conflict in Kashmir was at a peak in the mid- to late 1990s, when I was first reading *Lear*. The fact it was an exam text for my GCSE school curriculum mattered: it was the first time I had encountered even the metaphor of Partition discussed in the classroom. 'Fine word, *legitimate*' (1.2.18).

Back stitch. The first time I learned about the depravity of the Rowlatt Act and the Radcliffe Line, I was a child.[2] I had to believe my mother was making up a story, yet I knew what she was saying was true. Nothing else could make sense of why my maternal grandmother held so much bitterness towards anything Angrezi. In her sorrow and rage and refusal to learn English, or to come to England at all, I felt my grandmother, whose first name Satya (*truth*) was given to her by her husband's family when she married at thirteen, was rejecting my parents' choices, rejecting me. But it was not that. Underneath her memories of her happy Lahori youth, there was devastation. In her clinging to her modest Haryana home and its objects – the bureau, the mandir, the dial telephone, her hand-crocheted antimacassars – there was the paranoia of possession and an undertow of fear that her cheezen could be lost to her again. I knew about the locked house across the border in Pakistan. She had left to move to India in 1947, pregnant with my mother, as part of the great migration.

Still, as children we laughed, because we had not learned the *truth* of her story in our white school. Or could it be that none of our teachers knew about it, about India and Britain and all I heard at home? Otherwise how could it *not* be taught? At first I was embarrassed for my teachers' ignorance. And then for myself, in case I was being lied to at home. I said nothing. *King Lear* filled in that silence.

Forward stitch. Studying, I found a copy of A.C. Bradley's *Shakespearean Tragedy* (1904) in the school library. I read and reread the chapters on *King Lear*. They made sense: they made no sense from where I saw it – the argument of salvation for this king, for his men, predicated on the deaths of daughters good and bad. Daughters performing duty, daughters refusing. I wrote my essays to argue with and against Bradley. Small, quiet girl, small, quiet town. Reading. Brown in a white landscape whose careful layout segregated people along race and class lines that I crossed from house and school to go to the Indian shop, the covered market, the Gurudwara. The library was a turning point.

And then, Toni Morrison's *Beloved* (1988) was published in the UK and alongside *King Lear* became a curriculum set text. The book begins with Morrison's dedication: 'Sixty Million and more'. For generations of children who grew up reading *The Diary of Anne Frank* (1952) in that same curriculum, six million was the number we knew. Before I learned better, I remember wondering in the same way as I doubted my mother, *Could she have it wrong?* Then the opening salvo in Morrison's argument inscribed itself on my imagination: the enslavement of Black people was the first breaking of the white world. Before the Holocaust. For me it was also the beginning of reading a community of women-affirming literature, a novel blending modernist aesthetics with (Black American) history and politics. Morrison used language in a way I thought had echoes of Shakespeare's experiments in *King Lear*. One word, so many meanings. Layers of history encoded in a single metaphor. Yes I will say it was a moment of awakening. Morrison was the *only* woman writer of colour ever taught in my English literature curriculum through all my years of school.

At home there was another set of books. My mother travelled and brought me books by women from across the world. Especially from India. I read Urvashi Butalia's *The Other Side of Silence* (1998) and it changed the way I understood my own history and about writing Indian women's voices. About what a father could do to a daughter who belongs first to him. In the book, Butalia gathers testimony of the women killed in Partition by the men of their own families, to prevent them being abducted or raped by men of the other faith. As a method of colonization, an act of conversion, of war. The murders were a question of national and community and family honour, and of avoiding shame.

There were few survivors left to make sense of it, but Butalia found them and spoke to them. Here was oral history and memory, first-hand testimony and subaltern speech elevated to book status. Here was an Indian woman, researching silenced pain, connecting the female body to the formation of two nation-states; writing the broken family; interviewing the fathers, uncles, brothers and sons who committed the killings.

I believe in collective unconscious and historical memory. I know that such trauma is passed to women through generations. It is in our blood, running silent, looping in our veins. These stories had been silenced by at least three nations, by racial and gender hierarchies. The other side of the border Butalia crossed was also my inheritance. In her refusal to stay quiet, or speak only the palatable version of a nationalist history, there was an answer to that silencing: a brown women's answer.

There was still form to find. I read *Imaginary Maps* by Mahasweta Devi in translation by Gayatri Spivak (1995). I saw more clearly how aesthetics could be part of the politics of my writing. Here was an aesthetic template for South Asian women's resistance on the page. Devi writes, 'Our double task is to resist "development" actively and to learn to love.' Spivak's translator's note states, 'All words in English in the original have been italicized. This makes the English page difficult to read. The difficulty is a reminder of the colonial encounter' (Devi, trans. Spivak 2019: 2). So *station*, so *train*, so *timber plantations*, so *Christianity*. The subaltern woman's point of view is central; she has voice against colonial power and something important to say, and a point about language and power could be made. It was such an elegant solution to a problem of italics that had always left me feeling disenfranchised when I saw it in books by Indian writers in English who were published in the UK. The Bloomsbury style guide supplied to me as I proofed this piece states, 'Italics must be used for the following: Foreign words or phrases in an English sentence'.[3] I knew I wanted to write an equality of the tongue onto the page. To write into being a future literary world of un-slanted otherness I had rarely encountered even in the category of 'World Literature', which is more cognizant of Anglophone writing outside England and of works in translation into English than of British minority voices. Perhaps those women's works didn't exist with enough emphasis in the market, or they and their authors had already been 'forgotten' by the time I would have read them.[4] There were to my knowledge then no British Asian 'first generation' women writers to reach for. Even among men, the class politics of immigration and systemic bias in media and publishing ensured that, as Clair Wills writes, 'there would be no V.S. Naipaul or Edna O'Brien, celebrated by an English and international readership, among this generation of Asian writers' (2017). Not even a Sam Selvon, documenting the Caribbean migrant experience in an exciting but palatable way. Wills goes on to say that we 'should be alert to how the histories we tell of the post-colonial novel continue to obscure from view a specifically immigrant writing and the new genres it turns out to be shaping' (2017). The rot exists from primary school to British university English literature departments and on into teaching, publishing, critical culture; it repeats through cycles of elision, curation, pedagogy, the encoding of silence and shame again and again.

I began with the women. In Goneril, Regan and Cordelia, I saw women within a strict kind of patriarchy, trained to speak and serve a family name with the father at the heart. Forced to inhabit pernicious archetypes of patriarchal culture such as the spinster, mother, wife, whore or pure angel existing to redeem men. Transformed as Gargi, Radha and Sita, they turn against received notions of honour and shame that bind Indian women as signifiers of family and of nation (which Butalia tracks). They have the chance to try for sisterhood, to take each other by the hand (to paraphrase *King Lear*). Yet the world they inhabit makes certain that they cannot. This is the tragedy I wanted to make real, and which I think Shakespeare seeds within the play itself.

As a young woman I read Goneril's frustration with her father in Act 1 scene 3 of *King Lear*, in the same way as I felt the unfairness of Indian culture which puts the burden of household and family care so heavily on women from wives to daughters. In Goneril I saw a woman doing her duty in order to live: speaking according to her bond, no more, no less.

Here was Regan: and when she conveniently objectifies *herself*, during the love test of Act 1 scene 1, saying 'I am made of that self same mettle as my sister, and prize me at her worth' (1.1.70), I read a depth of despair that can only come from a spirit broken in captivity, colluding in its own destruction as a way of pleasing its master for affection and attention. This middle child, caught between father and sister, may be the most abused mind in the play: one whose stifled voice, constantly obedient while endlessly seeking an outlet for its rage, I had seen manifest in countless depictions of 'perfect' Indian womanhood on screen, in Hindu canonical texts such as the integral *Laws of Manu* (which I repurpose in the Jeet section of the novel), as well as actually living among the Indian-British/British Asian families I knew. The violence Regan displays comes as no surprise when understood in this context – as other re-writers of Lear have likewise explored. Who can forget Edward Bond's *Lear* (1971), which gives us Goneril and Regan as Fontanelle and Bodice, and their feminized, craft-based weapon of choice – knitting needles in the ears?

And then there was Cordelia, whose radical refusal to play by the rules was striking to me. She has no care for her own safety. She has no care for her father's temper. But her individuality also revealed her partial collusion in patriarchy: she has no care for what more work her sisters might have to do if she disobeys. I did not read her 'untender' (1.1.107) or 'nothing' (1.1.87) as a lesson for Lear, but a moment of emancipation – if only for herself – still opening the possibility of something else for good girls encountering her.

In the play her determination backfires into her disinheritance: one could argue it is the making of her, even if it doesn't end well. The King of France offers a kind of partnership on equal terms, breaking feudal tradition and in our time, breaking capitalist logic; both are transgressive, exciting and right. The novel form offers these possibilities for interpretation, and with a fiction writer's prerogative, I took them.

In *We That Are Young*, Cordelia correlates to Sita, evoking the Hindu goddess Sita, the epic model of Hindu Indian chastity, purity, honour and self-sacrifice, an icon of perfect woman-ideal in the Hindu mainstream. Post-Partition, women who were 'lost' to either side were reclaimed as in an epic quest: the Hindu women in Pakistan were referred to by the government during this time as 'every Sita' (qtd. in Menon and Bhasin 1993: 3). Sita also means 'furrow' (as in ploughed), with its obvious link between land, women as sex object, fertility. Her story can be briefly sketched here: wife to the god Ram, she is abducted in the forest by the demon Ravana and held in his palace. Upon her rescue, Ram asks her to prove her chastity by walking through fire. Though she does so successfully, he asks her to go again. She hesitates and the earth opens up, and she enters it. Conservative readings have seen this as proof of punishment for disobeying Ram. But I have always understood Sita as clever. She stands for herself, and takes herself from the world rather than stay to be publicly humiliated by her husband's sexual jealousy, his sense of ownership over her. Sarah Mitter calls Sita's hesitation an 'elegant, ultimate act of rebellion, worthy of herself' (1991: 90); to me, Cordelia's and Sita's radical refusals are a means of escape from the father. I read Cordelia's desperate last lines in the play – '*shall we not see these daughters and these sisters?*' (5.3.7) – as a final attempt at escape from being buried alive, or death with Lear.

There was also a question of time, and faith. There were strict laws against blasphemy when Shakespeare wrote *King Lear*. He had to bury his exploration of Christian ideas, images and doctrinal debates under the surface of the performance text (Bate 2019). This generative constraint provided one motivation to set the play in a pagan universe before Merlin's time (as the Fool reminds us), and gives the play its epic and prophetic quality. *Lear's* complex eschatology is born from this not-yet place. The questions of nature, of divine justice and power are articulated as characters make their appeals to a pantheon of Gods, nature and superstitions: to nothing, and to everything. Time is a whirligig we must find our way through – that's what Edgar's backward looking-forward thinking lines at the end of the play suggest.

This resonates in multifaith India, and via Hinduism, which has multiple ways of thinking about worship, from the meditative to the temple-going ritual, as well as many deities to serve. The whirligig of time is encoded in language: the word 'kal' in Hindi stands for '*tomorrow*' and also for '*yesterday*'. In Sanskrit, kālá means *time*. It is also related to kāla – *black* – which gives us Kālī, the black-faced central goddess of time, creation, destruction and power, central figure of the *Mahavidyas*, the ten Tantric goddesses so beautifully evoked in Nisha Ramayya's *States of the Body Produced By Love* (Ramayya 2019). The linear eschatology of Christian time *and* the cycle of dharma that is central to Hinduism are built into my structure as the forward-driving point of view of the five young characters in the book, who voice the present, unstoppable entropy of late capitalism, just as Devraj as Lear remains trapped in a circular narrative of the past catching up with the moment of death through the driving forward of a linear plot. I wanted a sense of wild searching in this structure to muddy bordered thinking about what conventional narrative and a more formal, linear Christian eschatology dictate; there is no beginning, there is no middle, there is no end. In melding faith systems, time and language, I express the central prophetic idea in *King Lear*: where the Fool steps out of the action to call into being an ethical future,[5] predicting that what we know and experience will pass, and new forms will rise. That is also the central message of the *Mahabharata* as Gurcharan Das reminds us, the emphasis on *how to be good in the world*; it is not a quest for Godhead, because nothing lasts in its known form (Das 2009: xlix).[6] The centrality of this passage within the structure of *Lear* evokes the Bhagavad Gita's placement within the *Mahabharata* as rhetorical reflection on the code of the whole piece.

Just as in *Lear* all paths lead to Dover, so does all the action in my novel spiral relentlessly towards Srinagar, Kashmir. In 2012 when I travelled there to research the book, the signs of what was coming were evident. I understood in real terms what the creep of settler colonialism via economic development linked to a hardline Hindu politics might look and sound like. The Imperial view of 'culture' as a monolithic force for control was a key strategy for the British East India Company, and translated into Hindutva strategy in Kashmir and across India. The RSS's long project towards a Hindu-Hindustan was being seeded even then. It is being mirrored in the UK governement's current proposals to defund the humanities and cap numbers of students taking arts degrees. Culture is the battleground: workers know, fiction writers know, curriculum designers, editors, publishers, critics and prize-juries know. Politicians know.

In the UK the reality that the Kashmiri people have suffered for seven decades has not been part of a national consciousness, conscience or conversation except at key moments, including as I write, as the terrors of the Kashmir conflict in the 1990s re-emerge.[7] The civilian population is still under siege by the Indian state. In Kashmir, where the endless demand is for 'azadi' (*freedom*), Lear's question, 'who is it that can tell me who I am?' echoes to the Zabarwan mountains: how we hear it, and how it is answered by honouring the Kashmiri right to self-determination matters more than ever.

Outside the subcontinent, articulating Kashmiri reality is in the hands of the few artists and writers whose important work has found Western audiences. Inasmuch as the crisis must be recognized by all of us whose governments are responsible historically and now, and whose own lives exist as somewhat 'free' because of it, I had to make decisions on how far, as a writer, I would go in voicing this long history of subjugation and violence, when freedom of speech for Kashmiris themselves is shut down by the state. In her 2018 PEN lecture, Arundhati Roy reminds us what is at stake:

> For a writer, Kashmir holds great lessons about human substance. About power, powerlessness, treachery, loyalty, love, humor, faith. What happens to people who live under a military occupation for decades? What are the negotiations that take place when the very air is seeded with terror? What happens to language?

> (Roy 2019)

Part of my resolution to the question of writing about Kashmir with the consciousness Roy asks for is to think through language: not to voice a Kashmiri Muslim character, which would cross my own limits with regards to cultural appropriation, or to place the trauma of its people in service to a single outsider character's narrative of self-realization (e.g. Sita). Instead it was to write the trauma of place and people into the fabric of my story through the ways in which Kashmir and its people continue to be harmed, *by the people and policy doing the harm*. By deconstructing Hindu-Indian fascist power's sense of sovereignty inherited and formed against Imperial power or the ultimately inviolable masculine self as Lear, via multiple points of view and on the wider canvas of the whole book, I examined colonial trauma and occupations of various forms within language itself. I am, at the sentence level, seeking a rubric for writing a state(lessness) of mind that is working towards its own emancipation. To create a hyperreal, epic poetic register that suited the book's mythic underpinnings and present correlative plot but not only to show parallels; to make a new whole. Morrison writes that,

> The construction of race and its hierarchies have a powerful impact on expressive language, just as figurative, interpretive language impacts powerfully on the construction of a racial society. The intimate exchange between the atmosphere of racism and the language that asserts, erases, manipulates or transforms it is unavoidable among fiction writers, who must manage to hold an unblinking gaze into the realm of difference.

> (2019: 271)

I wanted to bring my language and gaze to this difference. In her groundbreaking essay, 'Not A British Subject: Race and Poetry in the UK', Sandeep Parmar notes that,

> Mechanisms in place systematically reward poets of colour who conform to particular modes of self-foreignizing, leaving the white voice of mainstream and avant-garde poetries in the United Kingdom intact and untroubled by the difficult responsibilities attached to both racism and nationalism. In the United Kingdom, we like to think racism exists only in the fringe minority of society — represented by extremes on the right and left of politics.

> (Parmar 2015)

The same has felt true for a long time for literary fiction by writers of colour, it underpinned the struggle *We That Are Young* had to publication (four years of seeking the right house[8]) and is the reason I rejected the form of self-foreignizing usually required to pass through publication's gates. Even now, Parmar's end shot still slays me. 'The British look at the United States and abhor the actual physical violence against black citizens. We disregard our own violence done both by language and by the silence we allow.' In the UK the situation for Black literary fiction writers is worse than for brown. Exceptions like mine that ultimately end in 'success' only prove these rules. I write this in an attempt to open up that door and with others, keep it open. Cultural and linguistic mixedness is the reality of millions of lives: it is the story of language itself. To recognize this is to recognize the fully formed humanity of those historically seen as 'other', 'less than', even biologically sub-genre.

I had first experienced the potential and multiplicity of language in *King Lear* and in *Beloved*, and the two together formed a shelter for me within which to work. Traditional avant-garde strategies such as puns are an ideal expression for minds negotiating power relationships: there is a subversive intoxication to their doubleness and code; they hide as much as they show and therefore hold some particular grace for those passing in many worlds, who live their lives in translation. In fiction the excitement is magnified by the fact that the reader can see both sides; understand the critique as well as the submission. The lesson came early and came back to me again and again as I honed that epic hyperreal voice. Aural and literal puns and half-puns opened a door of perception and connection through which I could easily offer many meanings, embracing doubt, ambivalence, critique and potential. I remembered Devi and Spivak and chose not to italicize or translate words in any of the languages the book contains. Transliterated Hindi, Hinglish, transliterated Urdu, transliterated Sanskrit, and Napurthali (which is a fictional language from a fictional place, so I guess, fictional transliteration), some transliterated Punjabi and some gibberish. *King Lear* contains so much linguistic innovation and hybridity: Shakespeare trusted his audience to come with him on that adventure. Following this, the languages in my novel also include various Englishes. I hoped that these aesthetic choices would work to

> ... interrupt a journalistic history with a metaphorical one; to impose on a rhetorical history an imaginative one; to read the world, misread it; write and unwrite it. To enact silence and free speech. In short... I wanted my work to be the work of disabling the art versus politics argument; to perform the union of aesthetics and ethics.

> (Morrison 2019: 337)

I came to understand it so: to be born an experiment is to write experimentally. So it follows: there is no 'experiment'. The woman writer of colour is the centre (not the shadow – as in 'Lear's shadow' [1.4.234] – a shadow has no agency. Perhaps instead, the place where the shadow meets the feet.).

I began to see the novel as a translation of Shakespeare and of an experience, where 'the translator is the writer of new sentences on the close basis of others, a producer of relations' (Briggs 2017: 45), between worlds. In the feminist sense of Rich's definition of textual 're-vision, or the act of looking back' (Rich 1972: 18), I wanted to inoculate against the sickness that is the first-generation nostalgia for 'home' *and* the British nostalgia for the Raj which still saturates contemporary UK culture.

A passage of *We That Are Young* when Jeet/Edgar, in disguise as Rudra/Poor Tom, is in hiding in the basti draws many of these threads together. Jeet has nationalist tendencies; he's a proto-Modi mixed with the saffron-wearing chief minister of Uttar Pradesh in India: the holy man/politician, Yogi Adityanath. Jeet becomes deranged with fever, and articulates a twisted vision in a passage that has become the anti-anthem of the book:

> We that believe in India shining, we that believe we are better than all others, we that are the youngest, the fastest, the democracy, the economy, the future technology of the world, the global Super Power coming soon to a cinema near you, we, hum panch, that are the five cousins of the five great rivers, everybody our brother-sister-lover, we that are divine: the echo of the ancient heroes of the old times, we that fight, we that love, we that are hungry, so, so hungry, we that are young! .... We are that are a force of all that is natural – slow – death to – Muslims, gays, chi-chi women in their skin tights, hai!

and ends,

> ... Who do you think you are? Nanu says. Where? This is the world where pundits take bribes for blessings. Do not shiver. When thieves don't come to the market, when gandus and hijras get married in Krishna mandirs, then hamara apna India will shine, heh? Somewhere it rains every day, whether you feel it in your palace or not.[9]

(Taneja 2017: 405–6)

This passage condenses and refracts the book's marriage of ethics and aesthetics and its critique of contemporary India as no country for minorities or women. The mind, heart and sinews of an Indian nation constructed partly by the British and incubating the RSS over one hundred years has now reached its maturity. Its project is intimately concerned with purging Muslims from its land, and attacks against them are fuelled by political and cultural rhetoric and endorsed by state policy.

Lear's question *who is it that can tell me who I am?*, became one of making a space, not just for a writing voice, but more for this joyous, queer thing that a piece of art can be to its maker (no matter how bleak the actual work might be). I finished it in the knowledge that literature can recognize collective and yet specific trauma through its aesthetic and ethical choices, while a book's existence as art and as an artefact expresses hope. The fashioning of a new aesthetics and politics was partly forged through gaps and silencing, at home and in the world. I can think of no other way to describe it – in simple terms what I am saying is, we are what we read. I want to ask and answer to how artwork 'speaks' its own name, how it writes its author into the world, and how it both voices and resists systemic inequalities to create something new.

If we must make new language for our writing, we must also break categorization in our work. If we make new categories, who do we exclude? Perhaps we don't need categories at all. This is poetry's great potential, and it is one to which I constantly return.

In her introduction to Rich's collected works, Claudia Rankine, whose *Citizen, An American Lyric* (2014) has Black American women at its centre, quotes Rich as a form of connection, compassion; arm linking through ways of speaking:

> Poetry is liberative language, connecting the fragments within us, connecting us to others like and unlike ourselves, replenishing our desire... [I]n poetry words can say more than they mean and mean more than they say. In a time of frontal assaults both on language and on human solidarity, poetry can remind us all we are in danger of losing – disturb us, embolden us out of resignation.

> (Rankine 2016)

This is the kind of compassion that leads from art into activism. Our times are incendiary years of unchecked nationalist one-nation/one-religion/one-language politics; they are violently erasing what I want to understand as a working definition of humanity. We know the game of personality-driven politics is fascistic and we know, in the briefest time spent browsing online, that cookies are collecting our data 'to make our searches easier' – to make us better consumers of material objects yes, but also of ideas. Algorithms are not neutral, and multinationals we are barely aware of control so many aspects of our lives.

It is not possible for me to be silent on this in my fiction, especially when it can work through and around and over 'Shakespeare' and with Shakespeare's great play, *King Lear*. Fascism's resurgence is global and if race and nation are the faultlines, women and minorities are ever more at risk, ever more to be the target of incendiary rhetoric, discriminatory laws and funding distribution, unaccountable, state-endorsed violence and policing. Palisading through policy. And so, cultural space must be fought for; it must be claimed and reclaimed until it does not have to be so again.

Shakespeare consistently deconstructs and decentralizes power through language, plot, form. His characters bend and subvert all rules; that is their nature. But eventually they submit to the social proper. They become cowards of their age, 'As the time is' (5.2.36) and this makes their lives tragic. We do not have such luxury. There can be no safety in happy endings, only calls to different arms: perhaps those that form human links to protect people more vulnerable than them as they pray, vote, claim their right to live and breathe as they choose.

We live under the clouds, and wealth rises above us: can it yet be made to answer to us, and our futures, without further commodifying us for its own rewards? We must claim our ground and bodies and write in our languages whether they are understood in elite spaces or not, whether they are valued in those spaces or not. Until they are, and when they are, or not. Working with *King Lear* from the inside out in *We That Are Young* as a debut novel was a way of beginning this journey for me, of joining generations of women, and women writers, in re-visioning and articulating the world as it is for us, against the harms that states do to the most vulnerable in order to make themselves shine. But also making a new space for a particular kind of hybridity I could not see anywhere else. To take a few 'canons' and undo their binding; to select from them and stitch a different set of words – before the 'promised end' (5.3.2777), whatever that might be, is reached.

NOTES

1   The full poem is an answer to John Donne's *A Valediction: Forbidding Mourning*, in which a man chides a woman against tears on parting. Rich uses her poem to concentrate on the form that feminist writing can forge for itself against the academy's accepted use of grammar and punctuation as a correct style. In the piece she also syntactically rejects male-orientated canon-worship, and war and its valorization; she rejects social control over the female bleeding that allows life to exist.

2   The Rowlatt Act, officially known as The Anarchical and Revolutionary Crimes Act, 1919 passed by the British government's Imperial Legislative Council to enhance their superiority over the people of British India. It gave them the power to arrest and detain any person without trial, restricted freedom of the press and empowered police to search without warrant. The intention was to repress the growing Indian nationalist movement and its aims for Independence. The Radcliffe Line was the boundary demarcation line drawn by lawyer Sir Cyril Radcliffe on his first trip to India which became the de facto border between India and Pakistan and later, Bangladesh. Sewing together, my mother described it so: *he took a ruler, and drew a line.*

3   Bloomsbury's style guide (2013) is highly problematic in its choice of examples to illustrate elements of style. For 'Quotations' (16), for example, I note the decision to use, of all quotations in all the world, the following:

> 'Or, as Judge Harlan formulated it in 1896 in the famous decree of the Supreme Court about the constitutionality of racial segregation:
>
> The white race deems itself to be the dominant race in this country ... So, I doubt not, it will continue to be for all time, if it remains true to its great heritage and holds fast to the principles of constitutional liberty.[60]
>
> Because of the experience with slavery, Americans held the most explicit views about the black race and miscegenation.'

4   See for example the 1972 novel *Nowhere Man* by Kamala Markandaya, republished in 2019 by Hope Road (London). Emma Garman's introduction provides a chilling warning to contemporary British Asian women writers of how cultural gatekeeping works to stymie a dissenting voice even despite previous literary successes; *Nowhere Man* was Markandaya's seventh novel, a critique of Enoch Powell's Britain of 1968 (also the year my parents came as 'commonwealth' citizens to live in the UK).

5   The corresponding passage of *King Lear* is 3.2.81–96.

6   Though there is much I agree with and disagree with in Das's arguments, this book and the epics it references, which I grew up reading, were foundational to the theology explored in *We That Are Young*.

7   5 August 2019: Modi unilaterally sweeps away Article 370 of the Indian constitution, which protected Kashmir's special status. Once gone, it cannot be replaced. Gone, the promise of the right to self-determination, to freedom in its various forms. After seventy years of Indian administration, call it occupation, the world might finally be taking notice of what is happening in Kashmir. Today, it is too late. Eight million people remain under curfew, communications truncated, arbitrary arrests and with no right to gather without Indian Army crackdowns. The Independence-era word 'azadi' still resonates as the Kashmiri demand. Freedom. From colonizing forces, and from military occupation. From the fear of rape, blinding by pellet guns, arbitrary arrests, communications sanctions, eventual ethnic cleansing: genocide.

8   Galley Beggar Press, a small independent press renowned for its risk taking and publishing of what could be called high new-modernist work, including Eimear McBride's *A Girl is a Half-Formed Thing*, Lucy Ellman's *Ducks Newburyport*, Paul Stanbridge's *Forbidden Line* and Alex Pheby's *Lucia* (about Lucia Joyce).

9   'The rain it raineth every day', from *Twelfth Night* (5.1.415). The passage spoken by Nanu in *We That Are Young* is an homage to the master-less Fool in *Twelfth Night*, a character I take to be the same all licensed fool who disappears from the middle of *King Lear* and wandered from that play into the India-infused dreamland of *Twelfth Night's* Illyria.

REFERENCES

Bate, J. (2019), 'Why was Shakespeare Wary of Writing About Religion?', *LitHub*, 30 April. Available online: https://lithub.com/why-was-shakespeare-wary-of-writing-about-religion/ (accessed 13 July 2019).

Briggs, K. (2017), *This Little Art*, London: Fitzcarraldo Editions.

Butalia, U. (1998), *The Other Side of Silence: Voices from the Partition of India*, New Dehli: Penguin.

Das, G. (2009), *The Difficulty of Being Good: On the Subtle Art of Dharma*, New Delhi: Penguin.

Davis, J. and A. Hollis (2018), 'Theresa May's Brexit speech had shades of Hitler', *Guardian*, 12 October. Available online: https://www.theguardian.com/politics/2018/oct/12/theresa-mays-brexit-speech-had-shades-of-hitler(accessed 24 June 2020).

Devi, M. (2019), *Imaginary maps*, trans. Gayatri Chakravorty Spivak, London: Routledge.

Economic Times (2019), 'Mukesh Ambani ranks 13th on Forbes world billionaire list', 6 March. Available online: https://economictimes.indiatimes.com/magazines/panache/mukesh-ambani-jumps-six-positions-ranks-13th-on-forbes-worlds-billionaire-list/articleshow/68279649.cms?from=mdr (accessed 27 June 2019).

Menon, R. and K. Bhasin (1993), 'Recovery, Rupture, Resistance: Indian State and Abduction of Women during Partition', *Economic and Political Weekly* 28 (17): 2–11.

Mitter, S. S. (1991), *Dharma's Daughters: Contemporary Indian Women and Hindu Culture*, New Brunswick, NJ: Rutgers University Press.

Morrison, T. (2019), *The Source of Self-Regard: Selected Essays, Speeches, and Meditations*, New York, NY: Random House.

Parmar, S. (2015), 'Not a British Subject: Race and Poetry in the UK', *LA Review of Books*, 6 December. Available online: https://lareviewofbooks.org/article/not-a-british-subject-race-and-poetry-in-the-uk (accessed 20 June 2021).

Ramayya, N. (2019), *States of the Body Produced by Love*, London: Ignota.

Rankine, C. (2016), 'Adrienne Rich's Poetic Transformations', *The New Yorker*, 12 May. Available online: https://www.newyorker.com/books/page-turner/adrienne-richs-poetic-transformations (accessed 5 November 2019).

Rich, A. (1970), 'A Valediction Forbidding Mourning', *Collected Poems 1950–2012*, New York, NY: W.W. Norton, 2016.

Rich, A. (1972), 'When We Dead Awaken: Writing as Re-Vision', *College English* 34 (1): 18–30.

Roy, A. (2019), 'Literature provides shelter, that's why we need it', *Guardian*, 13 May. Available online: https://www.theguardian.com/commentisfree/2019/may/13/arundhati-roy-literature-shelter-pen-america(accessed 5 November 2019).

Taneja, P. (2017), *We That Are Young*, Norwich: Galley Beggar Press.

Wills, C. (2017), 'Passage to England: Punjabi Immigrants Stories', *TLS*, 1 September. Available online: https://www.the-tls.co.uk/articles/punjabi-immigrants-stories/(accessed 3 June 2020).

RESOURCES

VANESSA I. CORREDERA

This section is designed to provide an annotative overview of the research resources in the field of Shakespeare adaptation studies. It aims to identify current research resources that scholars and students alike use, but also new venues and platforms that lie outside the traditional boundaries of academic institutions. Determining the best resources for Shakespearean adaptation studies depends on how broadly one defines *adaptation*. Interestingly, several of the journals that Shakespeare adaptation scholars have gravitated towards do not subscribe to a singular or fixed definition. Even so, by and large, adaptation scholars look outside of Shakespearean performances – considered the purview of performance studies – even if these performances change the original early modern milieu. Performances that move farther away from the Shakespearean text as we know it, such as Djanet Sears's *Harlem Duet*, may more clearly fall within the purview of adaptation. Iterations of Shakespeare in film, television and the modern written word (whether it be novels, young adult literature or graphic novels) as well as other mediums that move away from performance, are much more agreed upon areas of inquiry. The following list of resources, however, includes performance-focused resources in recognition of the fact that both students and teachers often think about performance in terms of adaptation: the choices made in transforming the play from page to stage. Moreover, these resources may be useful not just for the present of adaptation studies, but also for its future, where inquiries into the distinctions between adaptation and performance seem likely. The overview is, by necessity, selective, but it aims to show where one can find research on Shakespeare adaptation studies, both in terms of traditional academic publishing, such as the major journals that have shaped the field, as well as the cultural institutions, online resources and networks that continue to sustain it.

ACADEMIC JOURNALS

Adaptation

Published by Oxford, this international, peer-reviewed journal is comprised of academic articles as well as film and book reviews addressing 'popular and "classic" adaptations, theatre and novel screen adaptations, television, animation, soundtracks, production issues and genres in literature on screen'. Edited by Deborah Cartmell and Imelda Whelehan, the journal invites submissions that 'theorise and interrogate the phenomenon of literature on screen from both a literary and film studies perspective'. Its reviews focus on adaptations from book to screen *and* from screen to book.

Though previously a print publication, since January 2018 *Adaptation* moved entirely online. *Adaptation* capitalizes on its online platform by providing readers a user experience 'with access to digital components of content, usage information and citation data, reference linking, and other vital metrics'. Submission following the MLA Style Manual must be blind and will be sent out to two external reviewers. Illustrations accompanying essays are encouraged.

The journal also offers The *Adaptation* Essay Prize, launched in 2011, which has the dual aims of advancing the 'best new scholarship in the field' as well as helping promote the research of early career scholars. As such, this annual competition especially invites submissions that challenge the relationship between literature and film so central to adaptation, instead inviting work on 'computer games, opera, popular music, animation, genre fiction or work with a wider theoretical sweep'. Contributors to the competition must be currently registered for or have completed within six months of the closing date a postgraduate degree (either MA or PhD) '[o]n any subject within adaptation studies'. The winner will have their essay published in *Adaptation* and will also receive a free subscription for a year.

https://academic.oup.com/adaptation

Borrowers and Lenders: The Journal of Shakespeare and Appropriation

Borrowers and Lenders was started in 2015 by founding editors Sujata Iyengar and the late Christy Desmet at the University of Georgia. The current co-general editors are Iyengar, Matthew Kozusko and Louise Geddes. Published by ACMRS Press, this online, peer-reviewed, multimedia journal publishes articles 'that analyze appropriation as a process of collaboration with Shakespeare, and to that end seek work that either demonstrates something new both about Shakespeare and about the field of appropriation or that works with Shakespeare to extend theories of adaptation and appropriation'. Its entirely open-access articles range from 7,000–9,000 words, though special issue or cluster submissions may be shorter. Editors send essays to at least two peer reviewers, with at least one reader being a Shakespearean while the other may have expertise in a second field of inquiry explored by the submission. The journal also publishes reviews of books, performances and digital appropriations.

A newer sub-section of *Borrowers and Lenders* entitled 'Notes' may be of particular interest to adaptation scholars. 'Notes' invites thesis-driven submissions of '"found" Shakespeare-ephemera that might be accidentally discovered and largely unknown in Shakespeare studies'. This peer-reviewed section aims to provide a taxonomy of 'everyday, lost, or forgotten Shakespeare appropriations', which means that obscurity and lack of scholarly scrutiny are important criteria for submissions. This ephemera can be wide ranging, including 'television advertisements, fan work, craft projects, memorabilia, obscure or unknown films, podcasts, web episodes', and even objects 'that one might define as kitsch'. Submissions should be no more than one thousand words, and multimedia is encouraged.

https://openjournals.libs.uga.edu/borrowers/index

Cahiers Élisabéthains

This international, English-language journal, founded in 1972, publishes articles (about four to five per issue), theatre reviews, book reviews and notes addressing various aspects of the English Renaissance, broadly understood. Articles range in topic from 'Chaucer to Restoration drama', though the journal's focus is on Elizabethan literature and drama. Articles on Shakespearean adaptation across film, television and stage appear regularly both in typical and special issues. The journal's quality has been recognized and is supported by the French National Centre for Scientific Research, and is also published in association with IRCL (UMR 5186) and Université Paul-Valéry Montpellier.

The journal invites submissions of 6,000–9,000 words (including notes), which then undergo a double-blind peer-review process. *Cahiers Élisabéthains* is currently run by Editors-in-Chief Florence March, Jean Christophe-Mayer, Peter J. Smith and Nathalie Vienne-Guerrin and is published by Sage Journals.

https://journals.sagepub.com/home/cae

The Journal of Popular Culture

A peer-reviewed journal published by Wiley Blackwell and helmed by Editor-in-Chief Ann Larabee, *The Journal of Popular Culture* is the official publication of the Popular Culture Association. The journal seeks articles that break down the barriers between so-called 'low' and 'high' culture and focuses on 'filling in the gaps a neglect of popular culture has left in our understanding of the workings of society', an aim it achieves through traditional essays and book reviews, the former of which should 'make a significant contribution to the field of popular culture studies'. As such, the journal recommends that submissions avoid narrow or niche arguments that might be better suited to a specialized, disciplinary journal. Essays should range between 5,000 and 7,500 words. Authors whose manuscripts are accepted must subscribe to the journal for at least one year at the time of acceptance. Reviews should be between 500 and 1,000 words, noting 'the scope and purpose of the work, as well as its usefulness to scholars', and should be 'balanced, although mostly positive'. Those wishing to submit a book review should contact Book Review Editor Tricia Jenkins at Texas Christian University.

http://www.journalofpopularculture.com/

Literature/Film Quarterly

Founded in 1973 by Jim Welsh and Tom Erskine, *Literature/Film Quarterly* 'is the longest standing international journal devoted to the study of adaptation'.

While the journal has long accepted submissions exploring 'various ways of conceptualizing adaptation' – essentially, the transformation of fiction and drama into film – more recently it has also invited far-reaching explorations on 'intertextuality, adaptation theory, and other related concerns'. Indeed, potential articles may focus on case studies, address multiple adaptations, consider intertextual projects, reflect on adaptation theory or adaptation studies, address historical or archival projects, consider adaptation as an industry, explore the pedagogy of adaptation studies, produce critical-biographical studies of important figures related to adaptation studies or provide interviews with key figures in adaptation studies as well as book reviews. The journal stresses that it does not take a singular view regarding adaptation. For instance, recently, it has published essays in the vein of more traditional 'fidelity studies' alongside essays calling for the end to such an approach. The journal therefore stresses that it depends on writers to 'set the direction of our discourse'. As such, potential contributors should 'be aware of the long-running discussion and debates within adaptation studies' even if these debates are not the explicit focus of their submission. Submissions should be between 5,000 and 6,000 words, though the journal may make exceptions and give a longer word count if the length is warranted. Those wishing to submit interviews should send an email of inquiry with the understanding that *Literature/Film Quarterly* only publishes original interviews, typically of about 5,000 words in length. Submissions should follow the New MLA Style.

Though originally printed, as of 2016, the journal moved online and is now open access. Issues feature traditional essays and reviews, though they can also include less traditional material, like interviews with directors. *Literature/Film Quarterly* is edited and published at Salisbury University under the guidance of Editor-in-Chief Elsie Walker.

https://lfq.salisbury.edu/

Shakespeare

The journal of the British Shakespeare Association, *Shakespeare* (published by Taylor & Francis) aims to bring together scholarship on Shakespeare in performance and in academia. This international, quarterly journal aims to publish 'the most recent developments in Shakespearean criticism, historical and textual scholarship, and performance'. As such, the journal invites submissions about work in Shakespeare's own time 'through to the present day'. *Shakespeare* also provides performance reviews of a wide range of global productions, book reviews and a section on critical debates and surveys of the state of the field. All submissions are first appraised by the journal's editors – currently comprising Deborah Cartmell, Gabriel Egan, Lisa Hopkins, Brett Greatley-Hirsch and Tom Rutter – and if approved are then sent for double-blind peer review. There are no strict word limits for submission, but articles typically range from 6,000 to 8,000 words.

https://www.tandfonline.com/toc/rshk20/current

Shakespeare Bulletin

This peer-reviewed journal, published by Johns Hopkins University Press and currently edited by Peter Kirwin, is the 'leading journal of early modern performance studies', as well as theatre history. Released quarterly, *Shakespeare Bulletin* invites essays on performance (understood broadly) and also publishes theatre, film and book reviews so as to create 'a record of performance and scholarship in a variety of media throughout the world'. The journal has a long history, beginning in 1980 as the publication of the New York Shakespeare Society and then becoming 'integrated' with the *Shakespeare on Film Newsletter* in 1992. Now, it is based in the School of English at the University of Nottingham, UK. Despite its title, the journal actually invites essays not just on Shakespeare, but also other early modern dramatists. As the journal's aims and history suggest, all submissions should focus on performance, but the journal accepts essays on performance across mediums and eras. Submissions may also address the following: performance and pedagogy, performance-related methods or theoretical approaches, production comparisons, analyses of new modes, mediums or venues of and for performance, and performance history, among others. Recently, the journal has made a concerted effort to address issues of diversity and inclusion in academic publishing by diversifying its editorial board, placing a call for submissions specifically addressing the topic of race, ethnicity and performance, and making explicit its editorial practices and processes. A typical submission ranges between 6,500 and 9,000 words. The journal also invites the submission of special issues of four to eight articles with a total of 40,000 to 55,000 words.

https://www.press.jhu.edu/journals/shakespeare-bulletin

Shakespeare Studies

This annual peer-reviewed volume, published by Boston University and edited by James R. Siemon and Diana E. Henderson, highlights the work of international 'performance scholars, literary critics and cultural historians' who write about Shakespeare and other early modern dramatists, but also 'theoretical and historical studies of socio-political, intellectual and artistic contexts that extend well beyond the early modern English theatrical milieu in both space and time'. In addition to publishing traditional scholarly articles, *Shakespeare Studies* also invites scholarly dialogue through Forums on a given topic related to Shakespeare, such as the recent cluster of essays addressing 'Shakespeare and Cultural Translation'. It also publishes book reviews. The volume follows the Chicago Manual of Style, and submissions are made online through the volume's website. *Shakespeare Studies's* website does not delineate any word count at the time of this volume's publication.

http://sites.bu.edu/shakespearestudies/

Shakespeare Survey

Known as the 'yearbook of Shakespeare studies and production', this annual journal has brought together the 'best international scholarship in English' on Shakespeare since 1948. Each volume focuses on 'a theme, or play, or group of plays', and also includes both textual and performance reviews. Under the leadership of Editor Emma Smith, *Shakespeare Survey* has worked to respond to 'evidence about journals as gatekeepers' by expanding its editorial board through a targeted search and by making *Othello* the theme for Volume 75, with a call particularly seeking work employing Critical Race Studies. Additionally, the journal has committed to making itself 'a platform for new work' by offering one article per issue open access, without author fees, in order to 'help early career scholars and scholars of colour make their work more visible'. Each article is peer reviewed by the editor and at least one member of an Advisory Board, which is made up of international Shakespeare scholars. *Shakespeare Survey* also accepts submissions outside of its advertised theme, and it actively encourages 'proposals for small clusters of 3–5 articles on a particular topic or approach'. Interested scholars should contact the editor for details or with any questions.

https://www.cambridge.org/core/what-we-publish/collections/shakespeare-survey

AUDIOVISUAL RESOURCES

All the World's a Screen – Shakespeare on Film

Directed by David Thompson, this 2016 BBC-produced documentary – part of the 41st season of the arts television programme Arena – 'charts the cinematic evolution of Shakespearean adaptations since the conceptions of cinema, right through the present day'. Over the course of one hour, the documentary takes a transnational and cross-historical look at a number of popular Shakespearean adaptations and includes archived interviews with Shakespearean directors such as Akira Kurosawa, Orson Welles and Kenneth Branagh.

American Archive of Public Broadcasting

This collection of forty thousand hours is a joint project between the Library of Congress and WGBH in Boston that strives 'to preserve for posterity the most significant public television and radio programs of the past 60 years'. Many of the archive's programmes 'have had a national impact', though most are regional and local programmes from the 'last half of the twentieth century and the first of the twenty first'. Entries in the archive range from the 1940s to the present and are meant to serve as a resource to 'scholars, researchers, educators, students, and the general public'. While the programmes may not necessarily be adaptations themselves, they do include reviews, commentaries, interviews and more that would be helpful for considering Shakespeare and adaptation. Users can streamline searches not only through a wide range of filters, but also by selecting records that are available online, digitized or all records.

https://americanarchive.org/

Shakespeare in American Life *radio documentary*

This 2016 radio documentary, created by Richard Paul and narrated by Sam Waterston, was part of the Folger Shakespeare Library's four hundred years of Shakespeare celebrations. The podcast, comprised of three hour-long episodes, 'explores the English language's most important playwright and his influence on American performance, politics, and popular culture'. For those working on adaptation, most pertinent will be 'Shakespeare Becomes American: Shakespeare in Performance', which considers Shakespeare's influence on stage and film by examining topics such as method acting, Hollywood and the ways that 'actors, directors, and audiences…have made Shakespeare our own'.

Shakespeare in American Life had an accompanying website with a range of materials for teachers, children and all interested in Shakespeare, which is now archived by the Folger. As an adaptation resource, most helpful would be the section on 'Stage and Screen'.

Podcast: https://www.folger.edu/shakespeare-in-american-life

Website: http://wayback.archive-it.org/2873/20160129172218/http://www.shakespeareinamericanlife.org/

Shakespeare Unlimited *Podcast*

Shakespeare Unlimited is the Folger Shakespeare Library's official podcast that draws an array of connections between 'Shakespeare, his world, and our world'. Produced by award-winning radio documentary producer Richard Paul, different hosts interview a range of subjects – actors, scholars, authors, etc. – in order to shed light on a variety of topics related to Shakespeare. Transcripts of each episode can be found on the *Shakespeare Unlimited* website.

Of the current 161 episodes, the following would likely appeal to those interested in Shakespeare and adaptation (organized in reverse-chronological order as they appear on the podcast's website):

- Episode 161: 'Shakespeare in the Harlem Renaissance'
- Episode 160: 'Naomi Miller on Mary Sidney and *Imperfect Alchemist*'
- Episode 159: 'Shakespeare and *Game of Thrones*'
- Episode 151: '*Richard II* on Radio'
- Episode 150: 'Maggie O'Farrell on *Hamnet*'
- Episode 145: 'Sandra Newman on *The Heavens*'
- Episode 138: 'Shakespeare and Folktales'
- Episode 131: '*Pericles* and Mark Haddon's *The Porpoise*'
- Episode 127: 'Shakespeare and Opera'
- Episode 126: 'If Shakespeare Wrote Mean Girls'
- Episode 124: 'Lis Klein on *Ophelia*'
- Episode 123: 'Casey Wilder Mott and Fran Kranz on their LA *Midsummer*'
- Episode 122: 'The Gender Politics of *Kiss Me Kate*'

- Episode 119: '*Hamlet 360*: Virtual Reality Shakespeare'
- Episode 117: 'Deborah Harkness: *A Discovery of Witches*'
- Episode 115: 'Simon May: *Mad Blood Stirring*'
- Episode 113: 'Olivia Hussey: *The Girl on the Balcony*'
- Episode 112: 'Duke Ellington, Shakespeare, and *Such Sweet Thunder*'
- Episode 110: 'Pop Culture Shakespeare and Teens with Stefanie Jochman'
- Episode 109: 'Julie Schumacher on *The Shakespeare Requirement*'
- Episode 86: 'Tang Xianzu and Shakespeare in China'
- Episode 85: 'Shakespeare and Science Fiction'
- Episode 84: 'Edward St. Aubyn: *Dunbar*'
- Episode 83: 'Shakespeare in Swahililand'
- Episode 80: 'Leonard Bernstein and *West Side Story*'
- Episode 78: 'Akala and Hip-hop Shakespeare'
- Episode 77: 'Creating TNT's *Will*'
- Episode 74: 'Tracy Chevalier: *New Boy*'
- Episode 72: 'Adapting Shakespeare'
- Episode 70: '*The Book of Will*—Lauren Gunderson'
- Episode 69: 'How *King Lear* Inspired *Empire*'
- Episode 68: '*Something Rotten!* The Broadway Musical'
- Episode 65: 'Shakespeare in California'
- Episode 64: 'Q Brothers—*Othello: The Remix*'
- Episode 62: 'Shakespeare and YA Novels: Ryan North and Molly Booth'
- Episode 54: '*American Moor*'
- Episode 48: 'Shakespeare in Africa'
- Episode 46: '*Kill Shakespeare* Comics'
- Episode 45: 'Reduced Shakespeare Company'
- Episode 42: 'Shakespeare and World Cinema'
- Episode 41: 'Pop Sonnets'
- Episode 40: 'Shakespeare in India'
- Episode 37: 'William Shakespeare's *Star Wars*'
- Episode 35: 'Shakespeare in the Caribbean'
- Episode 27: 'Shakespeare in Hong Kong'
- Episode 26: 'Shakespeare on Film'
- Episode 20: 'African Americans and Shakespeare'
- Episode 19: 'Shakespeare in Black and White'
- Episode 12: '*Romeo and Juliet* Through the Ages'
- Episode 5: 'Punk Rock Shakespeare'

https://www.folger.edu/shakespeare-unlimited?fbclid=IwAR0TPcnS5miYkpRX
4mMyftNtBO-lZ6yWwG3JO34rGmHt3yh3ZL6zJhq0odU

WOMEN AND SHAKESPEARE PODCAST

Developed by Dr. Varsha Panjwani and premiering in spring 2020, Women and
Shakespeare brings together past and present as 'women directors, actors, writers,

and academics' join Panjwani to discuss 'how Shakespeare is used to amplify the voices of women today and how women are redefining the world's most famous writer'. Sponsored by the NYU Global Faculty Fund Award, Women and Shakespeare is made up of two seasons, with an Introduction and six episodes comprising the first season, and as of February 2021, one episode and a bonus comprising the second. The podcast can be accessed through Apple Podcasts, Spotify and Google Podcasts.

http://womenandshakespeare.com/

INSTITUTIONS

The Folger Shakespeare Library

Located in Washington, DC and founded in 1932 as a development upon the collection begun by Henry Clay Folger and Emily Jordan Folger, the Folger Shakespeare Library boasts 'the world's largest collection of materials relating to Shakespeare and his works, from the 16th century to the present day…'. The collection also includes non-Shakespeare related materials from Renaissance Europe, such as books, prints and manuscripts.

The library spotlights performance history as one of its strengths. While much of its collection focuses on the stage – with 250,000 playbills and 2,000 promptbooks – film recordings are increasingly part of its archive. The Folger houses Shakespeare 'on film, video, and DVD, from silent films to recent television and movie versions'. The collection also includes screenplays, souvenirs, press kits and other materials that allow users to understand the context of Shakespeare productions on film. The Folger also houses a number of audio recordings.

For those interested in stage performance and/as adaptation, the Folger contains numerous pieces of Shakespeare performance 'ephemera', such as theatre tickets, toys, scrapbooks and more, as well as costumes and props from productions.

The Folger's web page is another excellent resource for those writing and teaching on adaptation. It includes short analytical essays on Shakespeare's plays, YouTube videos and links to the library's podcast, among other helpful features.

In order to access the collection, researchers must become a reader. Readers are either 'regular or a special-permission reader'. Academics, librarians, curators and Folger docents are eligible to receive a regular reader card. Specifically, the Folger provides regular reader cards to:

- full-time faculty from academic institutions working in a field related to the Folger's collections
- PhDs and PhD candidates who have completed their qualifying exams successfully and who work in a field supported by the Folger's collections
- librarians and curators affiliated with research institutions
- Folger docents who have either six years of consecutive service or have completed six hundred hours.

Potential readers will need to fill out the Reader Registration form (found online). They will also need to provide one letter of reference from a professional colleague that 'verifies your qualifications'. Reader cards are good for one year from the date of issue.

Special-permission reader cards are for students, educators, theatre professionals and all others who need access to the collections. According to the Folger, 'the length of special permission reading privileges is determined on a case-by-case basis'. Those eligible for special permission include:

- graduate students who have yet to complete qualifying exams but who have a research project requiring access to the collections
- undergraduates at the junior or senior level working on a project 'for which the Folger provides unique resources'
- others, 'such as artists, actors, booksellers, professional theater staff, teachers, and writers for whom Folger collections are critical for study, preparation, or production'.

Special readers must also fill out the Reader Registration form (found online). They will need to provide two reference letters that 'verify your academic qualifications and the relevance of the Folger collection to your research'. Undergraduates or graduate students must submit one letter from an advisor.

https://www.folger.edu/

The New York Public Library for the Performing Arts

Located at 40 Lincoln Center in Manhattan, New York City, the New York Public Library for the Performing Arts is 'known particularly for its prodigious collections of non-book materials such as historic recordings, videotapes, autograph manuscripts, correspondence, sheet music, stage designs, press clippings, programs, posters and photographs'. Of particular interest to Shakespearean adaptation studies is the Library's Theater on Film and Tape Archive and The Reserve Film and Video Collection.

The Library encourages researchers to apply for a library card online prior to their visit. Even those who live outside of New York are eligible for a card that provides three months of access to the Library's materials. Researchers must register online and bring photo ID and proof of address upon their arrival in order to receive a card. The Library also recommends that researchers request materials before their visit and/or that they make an appointment for their film or video viewing. Researchers should plan carefully and contact the librarians of particular divisions within the library that they may need to access given that divisions differ in their registration requirements. Researchers may also be interested in the Katharine Cornell-Guthrie McClintic Special Collections Reading Room. Most of the reading room's materials can be searched online, but the Library's card catalogue provides a more extensive understanding of the Library's special collections holdings.

The Victoria & Albert Theatre and Performance Archive

This national collection, founded in the 1920s through the donation of Gabrielle Enthoven, houses objects 'documenting current practice and the history of all areas of performing arts in the UK, including drama, dance, opera, circus, puppetry, comedy, musical theatre, costume, set design, pantomime, popular music and more'. The museum says that the collection's 'particular strengths' include the archives of 'key theatres, theatre and dance companies, twentieth-century stage designers, actors and directors, photographers and government bodies', which can include materials like photographs, designs, manuscripts, diaries, letters and more.

According to the website at the time this volume is in press, 'there is currently no access to the V&A's study collections at Blythe House, including the Theatre & Performance Archives, while we relocate them to the new V&A East Storehouse in Stratford's Queen Elizabeth Olympic Park. We are unable to consult material in the collections on behalf of enquirers and our enquiry service at tmenquiries@vam.ac.uk is therefore very limited. Full access and enquiry services will resume in 2024'.

The V&A also provides the National Video Archive of Performance (NVAP), which contains more than three hundred high-quality performance recordings made since 1992. This archive results from an agreement between the Federation of Entertainment Unions and the V&A Theatre & Performance Department, which allows a waiver of artists' fees for research purposes. Once the collections reopen, researchers might be able to access the archive through an appointment, presumably booked by email. The email should state the recording title, reference number and date of the desired visit.

https://www.vam.ac.uk/info/theatre-performance-archives

ONLINE RESOURCES AND DATABASES

Archive of Our Own

Run by the Organization for Transformative Works – a nonprofit established by fans in 2007 – *Archive of Our Own (AO3)* 'offers a noncommercial and nonprofit central hosting place for fanworks using open-source archiving software', which is built by and for fans. This archive is thus a vital resource for people interested in fan adaptations. In its beta form, the archive particularly focuses on fanfiction, but it hopes to include 'transformative works such as fanart, fan videos, and podfic' in the future. Because *AO3* is entirely funded by donations, users do not pay, and there are no advertisements on the site. *AO3* not only includes a William Shakespeare fandom, but also fandoms of particular plays, such as *Romeo and Juliet* and *Macbeth*, as well as fandoms of Shakespearean adaptations.

https://archiveofourown.org/

The Canadian Adaptations of Shakespeare Database

The Canadian Adaptations of Shakespeare Project (CASP) was developed by the University of Guelph and founded and directed by Dr. Daniel Fischlin. This database provides a nearly comprehensive set of records on matcrial for those interested in how 'Shakespeare's plays have been transformed and adapted in Canada'. Version 2, available since 2007, has seen an increase in multimedia files, but the database includes other resources such as books, documents, scholarly articles, images, reviews and even a literacy video game. It also boasts the 'most comprehensive and intensely multi-mediated study guide of *Romeo and Juliet* ever created'.

The site interprets 'adaptation' broadly, including not just film but also asserting that 'adaptation is also quickly becoming an especially Canadian approach to theatrical production'; as such, the database includes materials from filmmakers and playmakers alike. CASP creates thematic and structural connections in its 'Spotlights' section, which began in 2004 with 'Spotlight on Canadian Aboriginal Adaptations of Shakespeare', and now includes 'Spotlight on *Slings & Arrows*' and 'Spotlight on Shakespeare and French Canadian Theatre'.

Especially notable is the site's Virtual Shakespeare Made in Canada Exhibit (VSMIC). Developed over a number of years, the VSMIC contains 'hundreds of unique artefacts', including video interviews with those who contributed to the project, 'unique images', as well as 'documentation and scholarship', essentially, the transfer of a full-scale museum exhibit into a digital space.

https://news.canadianshakespeares.ca/2006/04/26/canadian-adaptations-of-shakespeare-project-c/

HyperHamlet

Described as 'a dictionary-in-progress', this database collects 'references to Shakespeare's most famous play' as quoted in later texts. Extracts can be searched by characters or scenes, but the aim is not to 'tell us where phrases come from… but rather where Shakespeare's phrases have gone'. With the goal of reconstructing *Hamlet's* cultural history, the database does not attempt a neat or uncomplicated approach to *Hamlet* but rather questions the 'how' of *Hamlet*, how its characters or phrases have entered particular discourses, how quotations have increased the play's influence and how 'later references have fed back into the understanding of the play'. As such, *HyperHamlet*, which boasts over 11,487 entries, strives to move away from the 'author/work/tradition' triad to one of 'text/discourse/culture' in order to advance intertextuality studies. Entries for particular phrases include a bibliographic entry for the quotation, a composition/publication date, a genre and whether the quotation from *Hamlet* is marked or unmarked, among other data.

http://www.hyperhamlet.unibas.ch/

IMDB.com

While IMDB, like Wikipedia, is a crowd-sourced database, meaning that all facts and figures should be confirmed elsewhere when possible, it provides an easily accessible and searchable starting point for determining not only *what* Shakespearean adaptations exist in television and film, but also details regarding those adaptations, such as directors, screen writers, actors, box office numbers and more. IMDB also has lists for and by users, including one on Shakespearean adaptations, which, though not comprehensive, provides a helpful starting point.

https://www.imdb.com/

International Database of Shakespeare on Film, Television and Radio

Run by the British Universities Film and Video Council and funded by the Arts & Humanities Research Council, this online database holds over nine thousand records of international 'Shakespeare-related content in film, television, radio and video recordings' ranging from the 1890s to the present day. Users can search by media types (audio, film, multimedia, radio, television, video), by play or by keywords, and they can also limit the searches by media types and dates.

The database's records provide important information, such as release dates, the name of production companies, run length, the title's distributor, etc., and might also include notes and the history of the title. When possible, the records link to the title itself. Users can mark records, adding up to one hundred records per session, with the ability to save them in .xml,.txt. and Bibtext format. These records are only kept for one session, however.

http://bufvc.ac.uk/shakespeare/

Internet Shakespeare Editions: Shakespeare In Performance Database

This database 'features materials from over 1000 film and stage productions related to Shakespeare's works'. Materials include posters, director's notes, performance stills, images of stage and costume design, and more. Users can also explore what the site calls 'production artefacts', such as programmes, performance clips, interviews and promptbooks. This database, under General Performance Editor Alexa Alice Joubin, serves the Internet Shakespeare Editions' goal 'to inspire a love of Shakespeare's works in a world-wide audience by delivering open-access, peer-reviewed Shakespeare resources with the highest standards of scholarship, design, and usability', a project ISE has undertaken since 1996, and which is now under the leadership of Coordinating Editor Janelle Jenstad.

https://internetshakespeare.uvic.ca/m/index.html

MIT Global Shakespeares – Video and Performance Archive

The MIT Global Shakespeares Video and Performance Archive is a collaborative project that brings together over three hundred Shakespearean productions in order to foster inquiry into Global Shakespeares. *Performance* here means everything from film to traditional stagings to versions of plays that radically reimagine them. The archive is a self-described 'work in progress' meant for 'students, teachers, and researchers'. Users can view the performances and also access 'essays and metadata provided by scholars and researchers in the field'. Users can search by play, language and region. The site's newest feature is the ability to study Shakespeare through a particular 'environment', starting with Shakespeare Performance in Asia. The Education section of the site also provides important resources, such as interviews with directors, as well as scripts of select performances, and an extensive bibliography. MIT Global Shakespeares is also a great tool for teaching adaptation in the classroom. Users can even make clips from the videos provided, an excellent tool for pedagogy and/or public presentations.

https://globalshakespeares.mit.edu/

The Movie Corpus and The TV Corpus

These two databases are an excellent resource for those interested in language use in movies and television. The Movies Corpus 'contains 200 million words of data in more than 25,000 movies from the 1930s to the current time'. The TV Corpus 'contains 325 million words of data in 25,000 TV episodes from the 1950s to the current time'. Both sites explain that researchers can examine a variation over time or between dialects, as well as explore a variety of details inherent in both 'very informal language' and 'actual spoken English'. Because all the movies are linked to their IMDB entry, users have 'extensive metadata' available.

The Movie Corpus: https://www.english-corpora.org/movies/

The TV Corpus: https://www.english-corpora.org/tv/

Shakespeare and Early Modern Friends

Founded by Lisa S. Starks (Professor of English at University of South Florida St. Petersburg), and now run by Jennifer A. Low (Professor Emerita at Florida Atlantic University) and Mateo Pangallo (Assistant Professor of English at Viginia Commonwealth University), Shakespeare and Early Modern Friends is a closed Facebook Group for 'Shakespearean academics, educators, theater practitioners/ performers and artists'. Members post about all things Shakespeare: pedagogical questions, new and forthcoming publications, events, news and more. Regarding adaptation, members frequently crowdsource adaptations of particular plays for courses or research projects, while others post about films, performances and texts that adapt Shakespeare.

Those who wish to join may request to do so but must answer questions, including providing specifics about affiliation and interest, before they are approved. Those who are already members may suggest others for inclusion. In order to do so, they must send the group administrator a private message providing affiliation information regarding their nominee. Anti-Stratfordians are not permitted to join.

https://www.facebook.com/groups/174255305946944/)

The Sundial

This digital publication is the newest publication offering from the Arizona Center for Medieval and Renaissance Studies. This public-facing venue looks to 'publish work in early modern and medieval studies that utilizes the richness of the past to ask questions about our present moment and look to the future'. Because essays are not peer-reviewed, there is not a formal submission process at this time. Instead, interested parties should contact the team at acmrs@asu.edu and provide a brief summary of the piece, with a specific articulation of 'how it engages the past to address a contemporary issue'.

https://medium.com/the-sundial-acmrs/welcome-to-the-sundial-2f4fccf3eb42

Twitter

Twitter may not be the first place one thinks of when considering Shakespeare and adaptation, but it can prove to be an immensely useful site on which scholars increasingly post about new or forthcoming publications or promote public talks. Threads likewise frequently provide helpful resources about ways to interpret a play or important scholarship on a given academic topic. While the value of the site is entirely up to the user, Twitter can serve the vital function of making professional connections, so that, for instance, emerging scholars might ask more experienced voices about the adaptation essays they find most helpful for students, or conversely, more established scholars can inquire to up-and-coming voices about the areas of adaptation studies for which they are most excited. When national conferences draw near, sustained online dialogues often appear, as do annotated bibliographies. Take, for instance, the #ShaxCultApp hashtag utilized in the winter and spring of 2019 in conjunction with the Shakespeare Association of America seminar on Shakespeare and Cultural Appropriation, or the frequent, popular and productive #ShakeRace hashtag, which is just as likely to point to adaptations and performances as it is to historical work. Ultimately, Twitter's efficacy depends on the user's personal engagement and the decisions made when curating the people from which the user would like to hear.

https://twitter.com/home

Wikipedia: List of William Shakespeare screen adaptations

While in no way comprehensive, Wikipedia's list of Shakespearean adaptations provides a starting point for those newly discovering Shakespeare and adaptation for either research or classroom use. International in its scope, this list limits adaptation to film and television versions of Shakespeare's plays, as well as titles that explore Shakespeare as a character. Organized by plays in alphabetical order and ending with categories on 'Shakespeare as Character' and 'Acting Shakespeare', the list provides the title, medium, country, year, director/s and stars of each work, as well as a brief description for many. The list also includes a brief overview of television series, academic productions and miscellaneous titles that likewise adapt Shakespeare, but perhaps in ways that are not reimaging a specific play, such as the television series *Slings and Arrows* or the film *The Lion in Winter*.

https://en.wikipedia.org/wiki/List_of_William_Shakespeare_screen_adaptations

World Shakespeare Bibliography

Containing over 127,000 records, *The World Shakespeare Bibliography* – run by the English Department at Texas A&M University – is 'a searchable electronic database consisting of the most comprehensive record of Shakespeare-related scholarship and theatrical productions published or produced worldwide from 1960 to the present'. The bibliography provides annotated entries for articles, dissertations, audiovisual materials, media, books, book reviews, theatrical productions and theatre reviews, as well as other scholarly and popular materials. The bibliography signals the international interest in Shakespeare, covering more than 120 languages 'and representing every country in North America, South America, and Europe, and nearly every country in Asia, Africa, and Asutralasia'. Users interested in adaptation can filter by categories on Production, Film and Audio Recording. Once they find an entry of interest, they can save the entry and subsequently export, email, print or download either individual entries or all saved entries. Editors Laura Estill and Heidi Craig update the bibliography quarterly.

https://www.worldshakesbib.org/

VIDEO AND STREAMING SERVICES

British Film Institute (BFI) Player

The BFI claims that its National Archive 'holds the world's' greatest collection of moving image material relating to Shakespeare', and now, much of that material is available through the BFI Player. The BFI Player has two 'Shakespeare on Film' sites, Free and Rentals. The Free site includes interviews, silent films, short documentaries and promotional clips. The Rentals site contains international films from the 1930s onward that span a range of adaptation types and styles, all available to rent for varying prices.

Those researching or teaching Shakespeare and adaption might also want to peruse *Sight and Sound,* BFI's international film magazine, which often contains articles on Shakespeare and film.

Shakespeare on Film Free: https://player.bfi.org.uk/free/collection/shakespeare-on-film

Shakespeare on Film Rentals: https://player.bfi.org.uk/rentals/collection/shakespeare-on-film

Sight and Sound: https://www.bfi.org.uk/news-opinion/sight-sound-magazine

Marquee TV

A Netflix-style streaming service for the arts, Marquee TV provides links to recordings of ballet, opera, contemporary dance, theatre and documentaries. The service houses a collection of performances from the Royal Shakespeare Company, as well as a number of performances from The Globe. It also includes a range of ballets based on Shakespeare's plays. This service would thus be more appealing to those who take a broader approach when classifying what counts as a Shakespearean adaptation. Marquee TV costs $8.99 monthly and $89.99 annually (often with introductory special offers). With either plan, users receive unlimited access to all content through Marquee TV's app, supported by iOS, Android, AppleTV, AndroidTV, Roku and Amazon Fire.

https://welcome.marquee.tv/

YouTube

This online repository for videos of all kinds serves as an excellent resource for finding Shakespearean adaptations, from course projects reimagining Shakespeare's texts to international television series that depend on Shakespearean tropes. Users can search by play, acts and scene numbers, actors and more. YouTube also functions as a helpful resource for considering Shakespeare fandom: how people respond to Shakespeare's plays, famous Shakespearean actors or even the historical figure himself. There are also dedicated websites that curate YouTube Shakespeare. Bardbox, established by Luke McKernan in 2008, annotates 'the best' of Shakespeare video production from YouTube and Vimeo. Several of the videos McKernan highlights have featured in Shakespeare publications and scholarly research.

YouTube: https://www.youtube.com/
Bardbox: https://bardbox.net/

ANNOTATED BIBLIOGRAPHY

KAVITA MUDAN FINN

One of the most daunting aspects of Shakespeare studies is the sheer volume of scholarship, and even a subfield as comparatively recent as adaptation studies reflects the prolixity of the field as a whole. Just as an example, a 'selective' bibliography from 2002 that limits itself to Shakespeare on film runs a full thirty pages (see Fernández in Starks and Lehmann 2002). This bibliography will therefore also be, of necessity, a selective one.

As chapters in this volume suggest, adaptation studies is an interdisciplinary umbrella that includes but is not limited to: Shakespeare in film and television; in fiction, music, dance, visual art; in marketing, merchandising and tourism; in material culture; in video games; on the internet. It spans from high to low culture – however one feels about those divides and how they are imposed – and across linguistic and geographical borders. It also shares an uneasy, permeable border with performance studies, and it is difficult if not impossible to pinpoint exactly where the Shakespearean performance ends and the adaptation begins. New work is constantly appearing, both within academic circles and without, and keeping up was a challenge even before the COVID-19 pandemic. Although, in a grim reflection of Shakespeare's own time, the theatres then shut down – some permanently – adaptations of his works were and are still being produced, written, performed and studied in new and different contexts (e.g. outdoor performances, staged readings and productions using videoconferencing software, audio production and limited filming).

The most comprehensive listing of Shakespeare scholarship produced after 1960 is the *World Shakespeare Bibliography*, www.worldshakesbib.org, a subscription-only database. The open-access journal *Borrowers & Lenders*, founded by Sujata Iyengar and the late Christy Desmet in 2005, is dedicated to the study of Shakespeare and adaptation and offers consistent, cutting-edge scholarship to the general public as well as academics. The two also collaborated with Miriam Jacobson on the *Routledge Handbook of Shakespeare and Global Appropriation*, published in 2019.

This bibliography is divided into eight thematic sections, with entries arranged alphabetically.

I. General studies and collections
II. Theorizing adaptation
III. Adapting Shakespeare (the man)
IV. Stage (drama, music, dance)
V. Page
VI. Film and television
VII. Visual arts
VIII. Transmedia

One of the joys of adaptation studies is the variety of topics found in essay collections, often ranging across medium, genre, language and approach, so I have chosen to place collections that are not explicitly focused on a single medium in the **General studies and collections** category and encourage readers to pay close attention to individual essay titles. **Theorizing adaptation** includes works that are specifically focused on defining, contextualizing and producing theories about adaptation itself. **Adapting Shakespeare (the man)** is devoted to the development of biographical criticism and the 'adaptations' that manifest there. **Stage** includes not just theatrical adaptation and translation, but operatic, musical and dance adaptations of Shakespeare's works. **Page, film and television** and **Visual arts** each focus on different adaptational media, while the **Transmedia** category explores adaptations that engage more directly with reception studies, media studies and online communities.

Note: Owing to disruptions caused by the COVID-19 pandemic, some bibliographic details (e.g. page numbers for individual chapters) may be missing from some entries. I (K. Mudan Finn) beg the reader's indulgence for this, and trust that chapter titles, where provided, will be sufficient to track down whatever they might be looking for.

GENERAL STUDIES AND COLLECTIONS

Balizet, Ariane M. (2019), *Shakespeare and Girls' Studies*, London: Routledge.

Argues that 'the cultural construction of girlhood is a powerful animating force in contemporary Shakespearean adaptation', supported by four case studies that address fiction, television, film and multimedia webseries.

Bladen, Victoria and Yan Brailowsky, eds (2020), *Shakespeare and the Supernatural*, Manchester: Manchester University Press.

Chapters by (a) Anchuli Felicia King ('Digital puppetry and the supernatural: double Ariel in the Royal Shakespeare Company's *The Tempest* (2017)'), (b) Katherine Goodland ('From Prospero to Prospera: Transforming gender and magic on stage and screen'), (c) Gayle Allan ('"I'll put a girdle round the earth in forty minutes": Representing the supernatural in film adaptations of *A Midsummer Night's Dream*'), (d) Yukari Yoshihara ('Ophelia and her magical daughters: The afterlives of Ophelia in Japanese pop culture').

Bristol, Michael D. (1996), *Big-time Shakespeare*, London: Routledge.

Explores 'the brisk circulation of Shakespeare's works in the cultural market' and considers the role played by Shakespeare in Western constructions of modernity (xii).

Burnett, Mark Thornton, Adrian Street and Ramona Wray, eds (2011), *The Edinburgh Companion to Shakespeare and the Arts*, Edinburgh: Edinburgh University Press.

Far-ranging interdisciplinary collection split into six categories (the book, music, stage and performance, youth culture, visual and material culture, and media and culture). Chapters by (a) Sonia Massai ('Textual Shakespeare', 11–36), (b) Peter Holbrook

('Shakespeare and Poetry', 37–48), (c) Marianne Novy ('Shakespeare and the Novel', 49–67), (d) Alexander C. Y. Huang ('Shakespeare and Translation', 68–87), (e) Kate Rumbold ('Shakespeare Anthologized', 88–105), (f) David Bevington ('Shakespeare and Biography', 106–17), (g) Christopher R. Wilson ('Shakespeare and Early Modern Music', 119–41), (h) Adrian Streete ('Shakespeare and Opera', 142–68), (i) Julie Sanders ('Shakespeare and Classical Music', 169–84), (j) Fran Teague ('Shakespeare and Musical Theatre', 185–99), (k) Rodney Stenning Edgecombe ('Shakespeare, Ballet and Dance', 200–18), (l) Adam Hansen ('Shakespeare and Popular Music', 219–37), (m) Lucy Munro ('Shakespeare and Drama', 239–57), (n) Edel Lamb ('Shakespeare and the Renaissance Stage', 258–73), (o) Fiona Ritchie ('Shakespeare and the Restoration and Eighteenth-Century Stage', 274–91), (p) Richard Foulkes ('Shakespeare and the Victorian Stage', 292–309), (q) Christie Carson ('Shakespeare and the Modern Stage', 310–31), (r) Andrew James Hartley ('Shakespeare and Contemporary Performance Spaces', 332–47), (s) Amy Scott-Douglass ('Shakespeare for Children', 349–76), (t) Kevin J. Wetmore, Jr. ('Shakespeare and Teenagers', 377–87), (u) Michael P. Jensen ('Shakespeare and the Comic Book', 388–407), (v) Erin C. Blake ('Shakespeare, Portraiture, Painting and Prints', 409–34), (w) Balz Engler ('Shakespeare, Sculpture and the Material Arts', 435–44), (x) Mark Thornton Burnett ('Shakespeare Exhibition and Festival Culture', 445–65), (y) Judith Buchanan ('Shakespeare and Silent Film', 467–83), (z) Anne-Marie Constantini-Cornède ('Shakespeare on Film, 1930–90', 484–501), (aa) Ramona Wray ('Shakespeare on Film, 1990–2010', 502–21), (bb) Stephen Purcell ('Shakespeare on Television', 522–40), (cc) Susanne Greenhalgh ('Shakespeare and Radio', 541–57), (dd) Michael Best ('Shakespeare on the Internet and in Digital Media', 558–76).

Burt, Richard, ed. (2002), *Shakespeare After Mass Media*, New York, NY: Palgrave.

Analyses the pop cultural afterlife of Shakespeare in two parts: first, the appropriation of 'Shakespeare' as a person and concept, and secondly, the appropriation of specific works. Chapters by (a) Donald K. Hedrick ('Bardguides of the New Universe: Niche Marketing and the Cultural Logic of Late Shakespeareanism', 35–57), (b) Peter S. Donaldson ('"In Fair Verona": Media, Spectacle, and Performance in *William Shakespeare's Romeo + Juliet*', 59–82), (c) Mark Thornton Burnett ('"We are the makers of manners": The Branagh Phenomenon', 83–105), (d) Diana E. Henderson ('Shakespeare: The Theme Park', 107–26), (e) Laurie E. Osborne ('Harlequin Presents: That '70s Shakespeare and Beyond', 127–49), (f) Josh Heuman and Richard Burt ('Suggested for Mature Readers? Deconstructing Shakespearean Value in Comic Books', 151–71), (g) Craig Dionne ('The Shatnerification of Shakespeare: Star Trek and the Commonplace Tradition', 173–91), (h) Douglas Lanier ('WSHX: Shakespeare and American Radio', 195–219), (i) Fran Teague ('Shakespeare, Beard of Avon', 221–41), (j) Stephen M. Buhler ('Reviving Juliet, Repackaging Romeo: Transformations of Character in Pop and Post-Pop Music', 243–64), (k) D. J. Hopkins and Bryan Reynolds ('The Making of Authorships: Transversal Navigation in the Wake of *Hamlet*, Robert Wilson, Wolfgang Wiens, and Shakespace', 265–86), (l) Helen M. Whall ('Bartlett's Evolving Shakespeare', 287–94), (m) Richard Burt ('Shakespeare and the Holocaust: Julie Taymor's *Titus* is Beautiful, or Shakesploi Meets (the) Camp', 295–329).

Burt, Richard, ed. (2007) *Shakespeare After Shakespeares: An Encyclopedia of the Bard in Mass Media and Popular Culture*, Westport, CT: Greenwood Press.

Includes overview essays on adaptations of specific plays as well as in different media, with extensive bibliographic listings.

Cartelli, Thomas (1999), *Repositioning Shakespeare: National formations, postcolonial appropriations*, London: Routledge.

Considers adaptations from former British colonies (including the United States and Canada), focusing on 'what becomes of Shakespeare's work in its translation from early modern playtext to colonialist pretext to postcolonial target, preoccupation, or objective' (2).

Desmet, Christy, Sujata Iyengar and Miriam Jacobson, eds (2019), *The Routledge Handbook of Shakespeare and Global Appropriation*, London: Routledge.

An impressive collection of thirty-nine essays that illustrates the variety of topics and approaches that fall within adaptation studies. Chapters by (a) Sharon O'Dair ('"... the great globe itself... shall dissolve": art after the apocalypse in *Station Eleven*'), (b) Alexa Alice Joubin ('Others within: ethics in the age of Global Shakespeare'), (c) Alfredo Michel Modenessi ('"You say you want a revolution?": Shakespeare in Mexican [dis]guise'), (d) Ruben Espinosa ('"Don't it make my brown eyes blue": uneasy assimilation and the Shakespeare-Latinx divide'), (e) Jason Demeter ('"To appropriate these white centuries": James Baldwin's race conscious Shakespeare'), (f) Brandon Christopher ('*Bishōnen* Hamlet: stealth-queering Shakespeare in *Manga Shakespeare: Hamlet*'), (g) Barbara Sebek ('Edmund hosts William: appropriation, polytemporality, and postcoloniality in Frank McGuinness's *Mutabilitie*'), (h) Katherine Gillen ('Shakespeare appropriation and queer Latinx empowerment in Josh Inocéncio's *Ofélio*'), (i) Jennifer Flaherty ('Calibán Rex? Cultural syncretism in Teatro Buendía's *Otra Tempestad*'), (j) Poonam Trivedi ('Fooling around with Shakespeare: the curious case of "Indian" *Twelfth Night*'s'), (k) Daniel Fischlin ('"Flipping the turtle on its back": Shakespeare, decolonisation, and First Peoples Canada'), (l) Avraham Oz ('Nomadic Shylock: nationhood and its subversion in *The Merchant of Venice*'), (m) Donna Woodford-Gormley ('"What country, friends, is this?" Carlos Díaz's Cuban *Illyria*'), (n) Adele Seef ('Inheriting the past, surviving the future'), (o) Jane Plastow ('The politics of African Shakespeare'), (p) Theresa M. DiPasquale ('Da Kine Shakespeare: James Grant Benton's *Twelf Nite O Wateva!*'), (q) Sheila T. Cavanagh ('"Make new nations": Shakespearean communities in the twenty-first century'), (r) Jessica Walker ('Appropriating Shakespeare for marginalised students'), (s) Matthew Kozusko ('Beyond appropriation: teaching Shakespeare with accidental echoes in film'), (t) Laurie E. Osborne ('Teaching Global Shakespeare: visual culture projects in action'), (u) Krystyna Kujawińska Courtney ('*Othello* in Poland, a prevailingly homogeneous ethnic country'), (v) Nicholas Grene ('Shakespeare in Ireland: 1916–2016), (w) Tina Krontiris ('Shakespeare's presence in the land of ancient drama: Karolos Koun's attempts to acculturate Shakespeare in Greece'), (x) Kirilka Stavreva and Boika Sokolova ('"To be/not to be": *Hamlet* and the threshold of potentiality in post-communist Bulgaria'), (y) Ryuta Minami ('What's in a name? Shakespeare and Japanese pop culture'), (z) David C Moberly ('"Subjugating Arab forms to European meters"? Shakespeare, Abu Shadi, and the first translations of the sonnets into Arabic'), (aa) Aḥmad Zakī Abū Shādī, trans. David C. Moberly ('Shakespeare's *anāshīd*'), (bb) Robert Sawyer ('Paul Robeson, Margaret Webster, and their transnational *Othello*'), (cc) Sujata Iyengar ('Ecologies of the Shakespearean artists' book'), (dd) Stephen M. Buhler ('Falstaff and the constructions of musical nostalgia'), (ee) Vanessa I. Corredera ('The Moor makes a cameo: *Serial*, Shakespeare, and the white racial frame'), (ff) Keith Botelho ('De-emphasizing race in young adult novel adaptations of *Othello*'), (gg) L. Monique Pittman ('Resisting history and atoning for racial privilege: Shakespeare's Henriad in HBO's *The Wire*'), (hh) Amrita Sen ('Indigenizing Shakespeare: *Haider* and the politics of appropriation'), (ii) Lisa S. Starks ('Ovidian appropriations, metamorphic illusion, and theatrical practice on the Shakespearean stage'), (jj) Marina Gerzic ('Determined to prove a villain? Appropriating Richard III's disability in recent graphic novels and comics'), (kk) Louise Geddes ('Some Tweeting Cleopatra: crossing borders on and off the Shakespearean stage'), (ll) Miriam Jacobson ('*The Sandman* as Shakespearean appropriation'), (mm) Christy Desmet ('Shakespeare's scattered leaves: mutilated books, unbound pages, and the circulation of the First Folio').

Desmet, Christy, Natalie Loper and Jim Casey, eds (2017), *Shakespeare / Not Shakespeare*, New York, NY: Palgrave.

Explores the largely contemporary phenomenon whereby things can paradoxically 'be' and 'not be' Shakespeare. Chapters by (a) Graham Holderness ('"This is not Shakespeare!"', 25–41), (b) Maurizio Calbi ('Chasing Shakespeare: The Impurity of the "Not Quite" in Norry Niven's *From Above* And Abbas Kiarostami's *Where Is My Romeo*', 43–58), (c) Jim Casey ('HypeRomeo & Juliet: Postmodern Adaptation and Shakespeare', 59–75), (d) Charles Conway ('"I'll Always Consider Myself Mechanical": Cyborg Juliette and the Shakespeare Apocalypse in Hugh Howey's *Silo Saga*', 79–95), (e) Kristin N. Denslow ('Guest Starring *Hamlet*: The Proliferation of the Shakespeare Meme on American Television', 97–110), (f) Kirk Hendershott-Kraetzer ('Romeo Unbound', 111–28), (g) Barbara Correll ('Chaste Thinking, Cultural Reiterations: Shakespeare's Lucrece and The Letter', 131–47), (h) Brandon Christopher ('Paratextual Shakespearings: Comics' Shakespearean Frame', 149–67), (i) Caitlin McHugh ('"Thou Hast It Now": One-on-Ones and the Online Community of Punchdrunk's *Sleep No More*', 169–83), (j) Scott Hollifield ('Dirty Rats, Dead for a Ducat: Shakespearean Echoes (and an Accident) in Some Films of James Cagney', 187–202), (k) Jennifer Holl ('YouShakespeare: Shakespearean Celebrity 2.0', 203–19), (l) Natalie Loper ('Finding Shakespeare in Baz Luhrmann's *The Great Gatsby*', 221–38), (m) Melissa Croteau ('Surfing with Juliet: The Shakespearean Dialectics of Disney's *Teen Beach Movie*', 241–58), (n) Allison Machlis Meyer ('"Accidental" Erasure: Relocating Shakespeare's Women in Philippa Gregory's *The Cousins' War* Series', 259–74), (o) Christy Desmet ('Dramas of Recognition: *Pan's Labyrinth* and *Warm Bodies* as Accidental Shakespeare', 275–91), afterword by Douglas Lanier (293–306).

Desmet, Christy and Robert Sawyer, eds (1999), *Shakespeare and Appropriation*, London: Routledge.

Explores novels, contemporary drama and film, as well as historical productions and criticism, and uses each as a lens not just to interrogate how people talk back to Shakespeare, but to 'challenge the idea that Shakespeare must always already be co-opted by the dominant culture and caution against the easy assumption that Shakespeare can set us free' (3). Chapters by (a) Ivo Kamps ('Alas, poor Shakespeare! I knew him well', 15–32), (b) Terence Hawkes ('Entry on Q', 33–46), (c) Laurie E. Osborne ('Romancing the Bard', 47–64), (d) Sudipto Chatterjee and Jyotsna G. Singh ('Moor or less? The surveillance of *Othello*, Calcutta 1848', 65–82), (e) Caroline Cakebread ('Remembering *King Lear* in Jane Smiley's *A Thousand Acres*', 85–102), (f) James R. Andreas, Sr. (Signifyin' on *The Tempest* in Gloria Naylor's *Mama Day*', 103–118), (g) Georgianna Ziegler ('Accommodating the virago: Nineteenth-century representations of Lady Macbeth', 119–41), (h) Robert Sawyer ('The Shakespeareanization of Robert Browning', 142–59), (i) Lisa S. Starks ('The displaced body of desire: Sexuality in Branagh's *Hamlet*', 160–78), (j) Richard Finklestein ('Disney cites Shakespeare: The limits of appropriation', 179–96), afterword by Gary Taylor (197–205).

Desmet, Christy and Anne Williams, eds (2009), *Shakespearean Gothic*, Cardiff: University of Wales Press.

Traces the evolving relationship between Shakespeare's canonicity and the rise of Gothic literature. Chapters by (a) Anne Williams ('Reading Walpole Reading Shakespeare'), (b) Rictor Norton ('Ann Radcliffe, "The Shakespeare of Romance Writers"'), (c) Jeffrey Kahan ('The Curse of Shakespeare'), (d) Marjean D. Purinton and Marliss C. Desens ('Shakespearean Shadows' Parodic Haunting of Thomas Love Peacock's *Nightmare Abbey* and Jane Austen's *Northanger Abbey*'), (e) Carolyn A. Weber ('Fatherly and Daughterly Pursuits: Mary Shelley's *Matilda* and Shakespeare's *King Lear*'), (f) Yael Shapira ('Into the Madman's Dream: The Gothic Abduction of *Romeo and Juliet*'), (g) Diane Long Hoeveler ('Gothic Cordelias: the Afterlife of *King Lear* and the Construction of Femininity'), (h) Jessica Walker ('"We are not safe": History, Fear, and the Gothic in *Richard III*'), (i) Christy Desmet ('Remembering Ophelia: Ellen Terry and the Shakespearizing of *Dracula*'), (j) Susan Allen Ford ('"Rites of Memory": the Heart of Kenneth Branagh's *Hamlet*'), afterword by Frederick Burwick.

Dionne, Craig and Parmita Kapadia, eds (2008), *Native Shakespeares: Indigenous Appropriations on a Global Stage*, Aldershot: Ashgate.

Recasts Shakespeare as '"native" – the place to which one returns – when rethinking the possibility of resistant forms of self and culture in the postcolonial context' (2). Building on earlier scholarship by Cartelli (1999), Sturgess (2004), Massai (2005), Orkin (2005) and Trivedi and Bartholomeusz (2005), this collection 'expands the category of appropriation to examine how Shakespeare is situated in a range of social practices: various educational, artistic, and political discourses, social rituals, and revisions in novels' (6). Chapters by (a) Thomas Cartelli ('The Face in the

Mirror: Joyce's *Ulysses* and the Lookingglass Shakespeare', 19–36), (b) Craig Dionne ('Commonplace Literacy and the Colonial Scene: The Case of Carriacou's Shakespeare Mas', 37–56), (c) John Carpenter ('"The Forms of Things Unknown": Richard Wright and Stephen Henderson's Quiet Appropriation', 57–72), (d) Santiago Rodriguez Guerrero-Strachan and Ana Sáez Hidalgo ('The Fooler Fooled: Salman Rushdie's Hybrid Revision of William Shakespeare's *Hamlet* through "Yorick"', 73–89), (e) Parmita Kapadia ('Jatra Shakespeare: Indigenous Indian Theatre and the Postcolonial Stage', 91–104), (f) Jennifer Drouin ('Nationalising the Bard: Québécois Adaptations of Shakespeare Since the Quiet Revolution', 105–22), (g) Maureen McDonnell ('An Aboriginal *As You Like It*: Staging Reconciliation in a Drama of Desire', 123–52), (h) Niels Herold ('Movers and Losers: *Shakespeare in Charge* and *Shakespeare Behind Bars*', 153–72), (i) Pier Paolo Frassinelli ('Shakespeare and Transculturation: Aimé Césaire's *A Tempest*', 173–86), (j) Ameer Sohrawardy ('Twin Obligations in Solomon Plaatje's *Diphosho-phosho*', 187–200), (k) Donna Woodford-Gormley ('In Fair Havana Where We Lay Our Scene: *Romeo and Juliet* in Cuba', 201–12), (l) Atef Laouyene ('"I am no Othello. I am a lie": Shakespeare's Moor and the Post-Exotic in Tayeb Salih's *Season of Migration to the North*', 213–32), afterword by Jyotsna G. Singh (233–40).

Driver, Martha W. and Sid Ray, eds (2009), *Shakespeare and the Middle Ages: Essays on the Performance and Adaptation of the Plays with Medieval Sources or Settings*, Jefferson, NC: McFarland.

Addresses not just adaptations of Shakespeare but Shakespeare as adaptor of medieval texts; features fifty-seven black-and-white photos. Chapters by (a) Jim Casey ('"*Richard*'s Himself Again": The Body of Richard III on Stage and Screen', 27–48), (b) Catherine Loomis ('Falstaff in America', 49–61), (c) Linda K. Schubert ('Scoring the Fields of the Dead: Musical Styles and Approaches to Postbattle Scenes from *Henry V* (1944, 1989)', 62–77), (d) Carl James Grindley ('"We're Everyone You Depend On": Filming Shakespeare's Peasants', 89–104), (e) Patrick J. Cook ('Medieval *Hamlet* in Performance', 105–15), (f) Sid Ray ('Finding Gruoch: The Hidden Genealogy of Lady Macbeth in Text and Cinematic Performance', 116–32), (g) Martha W. Driver ('Reading *A Midsummer Night's Dream* Through Middle English Romance', 140–60), (h) Julia Ruth Briggs ('"Chaucer… the story gives": *Troilus and Cressida* and *The Two Noble Kinsmen*', 161–77), (i) Gary Waller ('Shakespeare's Virgin Mother on the Modern Stage: *All's Well, That Ends Well* and the Madonna del Party Tradition', 178–91), (j) Kelly Jones ('"The Quick and the Dead": Performing the Poet Gower in *Pericles*', 201–14), (k) R. F. Yeager ('Shakespeare as Medievalist: What It Means for Performing *Pericles*', 215–31), (l) Louise M. Bishop ('A Touch of Chaucer in *The Winter's Tale*', 232–44), (m) Kim Zarins ('Caliban's God: The Medieval and Renaissance Man in the Moon', 245–62).

Fischlin, Daniel, ed. (2014), *OuterSpeares: Shakespeare, Intermedia, and the Limits of Adaptation*, Toronto: Toronto University Press.

An important collection on Shakespeare as an intermedial phenomenon. Chapters by (a) Daniel Fischlin ('Introduction: OuterSpeares: Shakespeare, Intermedia, and the Limits of Adaptation', 3–50), (b) Christy Desmet ('YouTube Shakespeare, Appropriation, and the Rhetorics of Invention', 53–71), (c) Jennifer L. Ailles ('"Is there an app for that?": Mobile Shakespeare on the Phone and in the Cloud', 75–113), (d) Don Moore ('Melted into Media: Reading Julie Taymor's Film Adaptation of *The Tempest* in the Wake of 9/11 and the War on Terror', 115–51), (e) Daniel Fischlin, Tom Magill and Jessica Riley ('Transgression and Transformation: *Mickey B* and the Dramaturgy of Adaptation: An Interview with Tom Magill', 152–203), (f) Kim Fedderson and J. Michael Richardson ('*Slings & Arrows*: An Intermediated Shakespeare Adaptation', 205–29), (g) Andrew Bretz ('Your Master's Voice: The Shakespearean Narrator as Intermedial Authority on 1930s American Radio', 230–56), (h) Daniel Fischlin ('Sounding Shakespeare: Intermedial Adaptation and Popular Music', 257–89), (i) James McKinnon ('"Playing the Race Bard": How Shakespeare and *Harlem Duet* Sold (at) the 2006 Stratford Shakespeare Festival', 290–319), (j) Monika Smialkowska ('Patchwork Shakespeare: Community Events at the American Shakespeare Tercentenary (1916)', 321–46), (k) Sujata Iyengar ('Upcycling Shakespeare: Crafting Cultural Capital', 347–71), (l) Mark Fortier ('Beyond Adaptation', 372–85).

Fischlin, Daniel and Mark Fortier, eds (2000), *Adaptations of Shakespeare: An Anthology of Plays from the 17th Century to the Present*, London: Routledge.

This selection of plays is foundational for anyone interested in adapted Shakespeare. It conveys the long history of adapted Shakespeare, with a particular emphasis on the politics of adaptation in works from the 1960s onward. The plays included are: John Fletcher, *The Woman's Prize or the Tamer Tamed*; Nahum Tate, *The History of King Lear*; John Keats, *King Stephen: A Fragment of a Tragedy*; Federico Garcia Lorca, *The Public (El Publico)*; Bertolt Brecht, *The Resistible Rise of Arturo Ui*; Welcome Msomi, *uMabatha*; Charles Marowitz, *Measure for Measure*; Heiner Müller, *Hamletmachine*; The Womens Theatre Group and Elaine Feinstein, *Lear's Daughters*; Paula Vogel, *Desdemona: A Play About a Handkerchief*; Philip Osment, *This Island's Mine*; Djanet Sears, *Harlem Duet*. The editors provide a detailed introduction (1–22) that theorizes Shakespeare adaptation and frames it as 'a process rather than a beginning or an end' (3). Noting adaptation's cultural and political contexts, Fischlin and Fortier argue that adapted Shakespeare is a form of working in and through history or 'the interpenetration of contemporary circumstances and contingencies with earlier histories and values' (18).

Fotheringham, Richard, Christa Jansohn and R. S. White (2008), *Shakespeare's World/ World Shakespeares: The Selected Proceedings of the International Shakespeare Association World Congress, Brisbane, 2006*, Newark, DE: University of Delaware Press.

An international collection of twenty-seven essays drawn from the Congress, many focusing on issues of adaptation and translation.

Hansen, Adam and Kevin J. Wetmore, eds (2015), *Shakespearean Echoes*, New York, NY: Palgrave Macmillan.

Uses the framework of the echo to address Shakespeare at the nexus of influence, both echoing earlier texts and being echoed by later ones. Chapters by (a) Laurie E. Osborne ('Reviving Cowden Clarke: Rewriting Shakespeare's Heroines in Young Adult Fiction', 21–39), (b) Adam Hansen ('"Give me my sin again": Disco Does Shakespeare', 40–55), (c) Greg M. Colón Semenza ('Echoes of *Romeo and Juliet* in *Let the Right One In* and *Let Me In*', 56–67), (d) Kevin J. Wetmore, Jr. ('The Immortal Vampire of Stratford-upon-Avon', 68–79), (e) Alfredo Michel Modenessi ('Cliché "By any other name…" Or *Romeo and Juliet* the *telenovela*', 80–96), (f) Courtney Lehmann ('Shakespearean Reverberations: from Religion to Responsibility in Roberta Torre's *Sud Side Story*', 97–107), (g) Lauren Shohet ('Othello's iPad', 108–119), (h) Laura Campillo Arnaiz ('Echoes of *The Tempest* in *Tron: Legacy*', 120–29), (i) Sharon O'Dair ('Cursing the Queer Family: Shakespeare, Psychoanalysis and *My Own Private Idaho*', 130–41), (j) Amy Rodgers ('History as Echo: Entertainment Historiography from Shakespeare to *Game of Thrones*', 142–54), (k) Patricia Taylor ('"This is not the play": Shakespeare and Space Opera in Lois McMaster Bujold's Vorkosigan Saga', 155–67), (l) Todd Landon Barnes ('*The Tempest*'s "Standing Water": Echoes of Early Modern Cosmographies in *Lost*', 168–85).

Henderson, Diana E. (2006), *Collaborations with the Past: Reshaping Shakespeare Across Time and Media*, Ithaca, NY: Cornell University Press.

A set of four case studies focused on 'instances that require modern artists to work with an exceptional absent presence' that 'illuminates both the multiplicity and the richness of "Shakespeare" for moderns, and the problems his collaborators seek to alter or carry, from his world into our own' (8). Introduction theorizes 'Shakeshifting' and diachronic collaboration, chapters on *Othello* and racial displacement in Scott's *Kenilworth*; *Cymbeline* and Woolf's *Mrs. Dalloway*; *The Taming of the Shrew* in film and Freud's 'A Child is Being Beaten'; and *Henry V* as historical adaptation and film remediation.

Hennessey, Katherine and Margaret Litvin, eds (2019), *Shakespeare and the Arab World*, New York, NY: Berghahn Books.

Wide-ranging collection of essays interrogating 'Arab/ic Shakespeares' – thus incorporating both Shakespeare in the Arabic world and Arabic-language engagements with Shakespeare. Chapters by (a) Margaret Litvin ('Vanishing Intertexts in the Arab Hamlet Tradition', 13–34), (b) Sameh F. Hanna ('Decommercialising Shakespeare: Mutran's Translation of *Othello*', 35–62), (c) Mohamed Enani ('On Translating Shakespeare's Sonnets into Arabic', 63–76), (d) Kamal Abu-Deeb ('The Quest for the Sonnet: The Origins of the Sonnet in Arabic Poetry', 77–101), (e) Hazem Azmy ('Egypt Between Two Shakespeare Quadricentennials (1964–2016): Reflective Remarks in Three Snapshots', 102–20), (f) David C. Moberly ('The Taming of the Tigress: Faṭima Rushdī and the First Performance of *Shrew* in Arabic', 121–39), (g) Rafik Darragi ('The Tunisian Stage: Shakespeare's Part in Question', 140–51), (h) Samer al-Saber ('Beyond Colonial Tropes: Two Productions of *A Midsummer Night's Dream* in Palestine', 152–71), (i) Yousef Awad ('Bringing Lebanon's Civil War Home to Anglophone Literature: Alameddine's Appropriation of Shakespeare's Tragedies',

172–87), (j) Robert Lyons ('An Arabian Night with Swedish Direction: Shakespeare's *A Midsummer Night's Dream* in Egypt and Sweden, 2003', 188–96), (k) Graham Holderness and Bryan Loughrey ('"Rudely Interrupted": Shakespeare and Terrorism', 197–213), (l) Katherine Hennessey ('*Othello* in Oman: Aḥmad al'Izkī's Fusion of Shakespeare and Classical Arab Epic', 214–34), (m) Noha Mohamad Mohamad Ibraheem ('Abd al-Rahīm Kamāl's *Dahsha*: An Upper Egyptian *Lear*', 235–54), (n) Khalid Amine ('*Ophelia Is Not Dead* at 50: An Interview with Nabyl Lahlou', 255–64).

Hodgdon, Barbara (1998), *The Shakespeare Trade: Performances and Appropriations*, Philadelphia, PA: University of Pennsylvania Press.

Documents 'how [Shakespeare's] cultural capital, his chief stock-in-trade, and that of the Elizabethan age, circulate in and have been appropriated and exploited by recent cultural practices' (xi). The first three chapters focus, respectively, on *The Taming of the Shrew*, *Othello* and *Antony & Cleopatra*, and the final two on biographical rather than literary capital – first, of Queen Elizabeth I, and lastly, of Shakespeare himself, encapsulated in the tourist industry of Stratford-on-Avon.

Holbrook, Peter and Paul Edmondson, eds (2016), *Shakespeare's Creative Legacies: Artists, Writers, Performers, Readers*, London: Bloomsbury.

Published as part of Shakespeare's quadricentennial, a series of seven essays about Shakespeare's legacy in the arts, followed by personal reflections by prominent practitioners. Chapters by (a) Paul Prescott ('Shakespeare and the Theatre'), (b) Sukanta Chaudhuri ('Shakespeare and Poetry'), (c) Tom Bishop ('Shakespeare and Music'), (d) David Fuller ('Shakespeare and Dance'), (e) Penny Gay ('Shakespeare and Opera'), (f) Graham Holderness ('Shakespeare and the Novel'), (g) Russell Jackson ('Shakespeare and Film and Television'). Reflections by John Ashbery, John Baird, Shaul Bassi, Simon Russell Beale, Sally Beamish, David Bentley, Michael Bogdanov, Kenneth Branagh, Debra Ann Byrd, Antoni Cimolino, Wendy Cope, Gregory Doran, Margaret Drabble, Dominic Dromgoole, Ellen Geer, Michael Holroyd, Gordon Kerry, John Kinsella, Juan Carlos Liberti, Lachlan Mackinnon, David Malouf, Javier Marias, Yukio Ninagawa, Janet Suzman, Salley Vickers, Rowan Williams, Lisa Wolpe and Greg Wyatt.

Huang, Alexa and Elizabeth Rivlin, eds (2014), *Shakespeare and the Ethics of Appropriation*, New York, NY: Palgrave.

Focuses on the ethical considerations in appropriating Shakespeare, observing that 'appropriations raise ethical questions with a special intensity because they display self-awareness about their enmeshment in intertextual relationships and their interdependence with other texts' (5). Chapters by (a) Douglas Lanier ('Shakespearean Rhizomatics: Adaptation, Ethics, Value', 21–40), (b) Christy Desmet ('Recognising Shakespeare, Rethinking Fidelity: A Rhetoric and Ethics of Appropriation', 41–58), (c) Adrian Steele ('Ethics and the Undead: Reading Shakespearean (Mis)appropriation in Francis Ford Coppola's *Dracula*', 59–72), (d) Elizabeth Rivlin ('Adaptation Revoked: Knowledge, Ethics, and Trauma in Jane Smiley's *A Thousand Acres*, 73–88), (e) Courtney Lehmann ('Double Jeopardy: Shakespeare and Prison Theatre', 89–106), (f)

Margaret Litvin ('Theater Director as Unelected Representative: Sulayman Al-Bassam's Arab Shakespeare Trilogy', 107–30), (g) Robert Sawyer ('A "Whirl of Aesthetic Terminology": Swinburne, Shakespeare, and Ethical Criticism', 131–44), (h) Yukari Yoshihara ('"Raw-Savage" Othello: The First-Staged Japanese Adaptation of *Othello* (1903) and Japanese Colonialism', 145–60), (i) Gitanjali Shahani and Brinda Charry ('The Bard in Bollywood: The Fraternal Nation and Shakespearean Adaptation in Hindi Cinema', 161–78), (j) Ema Vyroubalová ('Multilingual Ethics in *Henry V* and *Henry VIII*', 179–92), (k) Sheila T. Cavanagh ('In Other Words: Global Shakespearean Transformations', 193–210), afterword by Thomas Cartelli (211–20).

Joubin, Alexa Alice (2009), *Chinese Shakespeares: Two Centuries of Cultural Exchange*, New York, NY: Columbia University Press.

Explores engagements with Shakespeare in China from the First Opium War (1839) to the present day.

Joubin, Alexa Alice (2021), *Shakespeare & East Asia*, Oxford Short Topics Series, Oxford: Oxford University Press.

Comparative introduction to Shakespeare onstage and screen in East Asia, covers works from Japan, China, Taiwan, Hong Kong, South Korea, Singapore and Asian diasporic communities in the UK.

Kennedy, Dennis and Yong Li Lan, eds (2010), *Shakespeare in Asia: Contemporary Performance*, Cambridge: Cambridge University Press.

Investigates how Shakespeare's works have been 'reinvented and deployed' in contemporary Asia. Chapters by (a) John Russell Brown ('Shakespeare and the *Natyasutra*', 27–41), (b) Daniel Gallimore ('Speaking Shakespeare in Japan: voicing the foreign', 42–56), (c) Fei Chunfang and Sun Huizhu ('Shakespeare and Beijing opera: two cases of appropriation', 57–71), (d) Richard Burt ('All that remains of Shakespeare in Indian film', 73–108), (e) Minami Ryuta ('Shakespeare for Japanese popular culture: Shojo Manga, Takarazuka and *Twelfth Night*', 109–31), (f) Kumiko Hilberdink-Sakamoto ('Shakespeare's villains in Japan', 132–153), (g) Suematsu Michiko ('Import/export: Japanizing Shakespeare', 155–69), (h) Li Ruru ('Millennium Shashibiya: Shakespeare in the Chinese-speaking world', 170–87), (i) Yong Li Lan ('Shakespeare here and elsewhere: Ong Keng Sen's intercultural Shakespeare', 188–217), (j) Shen Lin ('What use Shakespeare? China and globalisation', 219–33), (k) John W. P. Philips ('Shakespeare and the question of intercultural performance', 234–52), (l) Rustom Bharucha ('Foreign Asia/foreign Shakespeare: dissenting notes on New Asian interculturality, postcoloniality, and re-colonization', 253–82).

Lanier, Douglas (2002), *Shakespeare and Modern Popular Culture*, Oxford: Oxford University Press, 2002.

General introduction to different facets of Shakespeare's ubiquity in twentieth- and early-twenty-first-century popular culture. Includes a chapter on Shakespeare's biography as well as adaptations of his works.

MacDonald, Joyce Green (2020), *Shakespearean Adaptation, Race, and Memory in the New World*, New York, NY: Palgrave Macmillan.

Uncovers the moments in which Black women appear and disappear in Shakespeare's plays and in adaptations of *Romeo and Juliet*, *Antony & Cleopatra*, *Othello* and *The Taming of the Shrew* – 'physically absent, but socially present, and called on to do various kinds of work in establishing social, sexual, and racial hierarchies' (3).

Massai, Sonia, ed. (2005), *World-Wide Shakespeares: Local appropriations in film and performance*, London: Routledge.

Focuses on adaptations of Shakespeare's plays that engage substantially with local cultures, customs and histories. Chapters by (a) Tobias Döring ('*A Branch of the Blue Nile*: Derek Walcott and the tropic of Shakespeare', 15–22), (b) Suzanne Gossett ('Political *Pericles*', 23–30), (c) Elizabeth Klein and Michael Shapiro ('Shylock as crypto-Jew: A New Mexican adaptation of *The Merchant of Venice*', 31–39), (d) Ruru Li ('Negotiating intercultural spaces: *Much Ado About Nothing* and *Romeo and Juliet* on the Chinese stage', 40–6), (e) Poonam Trivedi ('"It is the bloody business which informs thus… "': Local politics and performative praxis, *Macbeth* in India', 47–55), (f) Boika Sokolova ('Relocating and dislocating Shakespeare in Robert Sturua's *Twelfth Night* and Alexander Morfov's *The Tempest*', 57–64), (g) Sabine Schülting ('"I am not bound to please thee with my answers": *The Merchant of Venice* on the post-war German stage', 65–71), (h) Marcela Kostihová ('Katherina "humanised": Abusing the Shrew on the Prague stage', 72–79), (i) Ton Hoenselaars ('*Shooting the Hero*: The cinematic career of *Henry V* from Laurence Olivier to Philip Purser', 80–7), (j) Lukas Erne ('Lamentable tragedy or black comedy?: Friedrich Dürrenmatt's adaptation of *Titus Andronicus*', 88–94), (k) Sonia Massai ('Subjection and redemption in Pasolini's *Othello*', 95–103), (l) Alfredo Michel Modenessi ('"Meaning by Shakespeare" south of the border', 104–11), (m) Robert Shaughnessy ('Dreams of England', 112–21), (n) Maria Jones ('The cultural logic of "correcting" *The Merchant of Venice*', 122–31), (o) Margaret Jane Kidnie ('Dancing with art: Robert Lepage's *Elsinore*', 133–40), (p) Mark Houlahan ('Hekepia? The *Mana* of the Maori *Merchant*', 141–8), (q) Saviour Catania ('The Haiku *Macbeth*: Shakespearean antithetical minimalism in Kurosawa's *Kumonosu-jo*', 149–56), afterword by Barbara Hodgdon.

Poole, Adrian (2014), *Shakespeare and the Victorians*, Arden Critical Companion Series, London: Bloomsbury.

Pushes back against the term 'appropriation', emphasizing instead the 'different kinds of dialogue the Victorians conducted with Shakespeare, as writers, readers, performers, audiences, visual artists and spectators' (1).

Ritchie, Fiona and Peter Sabor, eds (2012), *Shakespeare in the Eighteenth Century*, Cambridge: Cambridge University Press.

Explores Shakespeare's impact on the culture of eighteenth-century England and its immediate associates. Chapters by (a) Marcus Walsh ('Editing and publishing Shakespeare', 21–40), (b) Antonia Forster ('Shakespeare in the reviews', 60–77),

(c) Brean Hammond ('Shakespeare discoveries and forgeries', 78–97), (d) David Fairer ('Shakespeare in poetry', 99–117), (e) Thomas Keymer ('Shakespeare in the novel', 118–40), (f) Tiffany Stern ('Shakespeare in drama', 141–59), (g) Robert Shaughnessy ('Shakespeare and the London stage', 161–84), (h) Jenny Davidson ('Shakespeare adaptation', 185–203), (i) Michael Burden ('Shakespeare and opera', 204–25), (j) Shearer West ('Shakespeare and the visual arts', 227–53), (k) Roger Paulin ('Shakespeare and Germany', 314–30).

Shaughnessy, Robert, ed. (2007), *The Cambridge Companion to Shakespeare and Popular Culture*, Cambridge: Cambridge University Press.

Takes a long view of the 'ways in which Shakespeare has been consumed and reinvented, allowing for interface between cultural, literary, performance, and cinema studies, by means of focused and localised case studies as well as through the mapping of larger cultural logics of Shakespeare-making' (2). Chapters by (a) Diana Henderson ('From popular entertainment to literature', 6–25), (b) Peter Holland ('Shakespeare abbreviated', 26–45), (c) Barbara Hodgdon ('Shakespearean stars: stagings of desire', 46–66), (d) Stephen Orgel ('Shakespeare illustrated', 67–92), (e) Douglas Lanier ('Shakespeare(™): myth and biographical fiction', 93–113), (f) Laurie Osborne ('Narration and staging in *Hamlet* and its afternovels', 114–33), (g) Emma Smith ('Shakespeare serialised: *An Age of Kings*', 134–49), (h) Stephen M. Buhler ('Musical Shakespeares: attending to Ophelia, Juliet, and Desdemona', 150–74), (i) Susanne Greenhalgh ('Shakespeare overheard: performances, adaptations, and citations on radio', 175–98), (j) Nicola Watson ('Shakespeare on the tourist trail', 199–226), (k) W. B. Worthen ('Performing Shakespeare in digital culture', 227–47), (l) Carol Chillington Rutter ('Shakespeare's popular face: from the playbill to the poster', 248–71).

Shellard, Dominic and Siobhan Keenan (2016), *Shakespeare's Cultural Capital: His Economic Impact from the Sixteenth to the Twenty-first Century*, New York, NY: Palgrave.

Examines the impact of the 'Shakespeare industry' four hundred years after his death. Chapters by (a) Siobhan Keenan ('Shakespeare and the Market in His Own Day', 13–31), (b) Gabriel Egan ('Shakespeare and the Impact of Editing', 32–56), (c) Deborah Cartmell ('Marketing Shakespeare Films: From Tragedy to Biopic', 57–76), (d) Anna Blackwell ('Shakespearean Actors, Memes, Social Media and the Circulation of Shakespearean "Value"', 77–98), (e) Graham Holderness and Bryan Loughrey ('Ales, Beers, Shakespeares', 99–125), (f) Dominic Shellard ('A King Rediscovered: The Economic Impact of Richard III and *Richard III* on the City of Leicester', 126–47), (g) Conrad Bird, Jason Eliadis and Harvey Scriven ('Shakespeare is "GREAT"', 148–62), (h) Susan Bennett ('Sponsoring Shakespeare', 163–79).

Smith, Bruce, ed. (2016), *Cambridge Guide to the Worlds of Shakespeare*, Cambridge: Cambridge University Press.

More an encyclopaedia than a traditional essay collection, and co-edited by Katherine Rowe with others, the *Guide* is aimed at conveying the global reach of Shakespeare's

writing and its afterlives. Volume 1, 'Shakespeare's World, 1500–1660', provides
a survey of the world in which Shakespeare and his contemporaries lived. Volume
2, titled 'The World's Shakespeare, 1660–Present', will be of particular interest for
students of adapted Shakespeare, exploring as it does Shakespeare afterlives and status
as a cultural icon across the past four centuries.

Thompson, Ayanna (2011), *Passing Strange: Shakespeare, Race, and Contemporary
America*, Oxford: Oxford University Press.

Examines 'modern constructions of racial identity through Shakespearean reference/
performance and the modern constructions of Shakespearean identity through
racial reference/performance' across a range of media (11) including film, plays and
YouTube.

Trivedi, Poonam and Dennis Bartholomeusz, eds (2005), *India's Shakespeare: Translation,
Interpretation, and Performance*, New York, NY: Pearson.

Interrogates the contested and complex place that Shakespeare occupies in India,
both during British rule and after independence. Chapters by (a) Sisir Kumar Das
('Shakespeare in Indian Languages', 47–73), (b) Harish Trivedi ('Colonizing Love:
Romeo and Juliet in Modern Indian Disseminations', 74–91), (c) Javed Malick
('Appropriating Shakespeare Freely: Parsi Theater's First Urdu Play *Khurshid*',
92–105), (d) Vijaya Guttal ('Translation and Performance of Shakespeare in
Kannada', 106–19), (e) R. A. Malagi ('Toward a Terrestrial Divine Comedy: A Study
of *The Winter's Tale* and *Shakuntalam*'), (f) R. W. Desai ('England, the Indian Boy,
and the Spice Trade in *A Midsummer Night's Dream*'), (g) Sukantha Chaudhuri
('Shakespeare's India'), (h) Poonam Trivedi ('"Folk Shakespeare": The Performance
of Shakespeare in Traditional Indian Theater Forms'), (i) Laxmi Chandrashekar
('"A sea change into something rich and strange": Ekbal Ahmed's *Macbeth* and
Hamlet'), (j) Shormishtha Panja ('An Indian (Mid)summer: *Bagro Basant Hai*'), (k)
Ananda Lal ('Re-Creating *The Merchant of Venice* on the Indian Stage: A Director's
Note'), (l) Dennis Bartholomeusz ('Shylock's Shoes: The Art of Localization'),
(m) Debjani Sengupta ('Playing the Canon: Shakespeare and the Bengali Actress
in Nineteenth-Century Calcutta'), (n) Sarottama Majumdar ('That Sublime "Old
Gentleman": Shakespeare's Plays in Calcutta, 1775–1930'), (o) Rajiva Verma
('Shakespeare in Hindi Cinema').

Trivedi, Poonam, Paromita Chakravarti, Ted Motohashi, eds (2020), *Asian Interventions
in Global Shakespeare: 'All the World's His Stage'*, London: Taylor & Francis.

Reads 'globalisation of Shakespeare through the larger Asian Shakespeare phenomenon,
for the Asian continent has contributed in no small measure to the worldwide presence
of Shakespeare' (1). Chapters by (a) Poonam Trivedi ('Making Meaning between the
Local and the Global: Performing Shakespeare in India Today'), (b) Ted Motohashi
('How Could We Present a "Non-localised" Shakespeare in Asia? Colonialism and
Atlantic Slave-Trade in Yamanote-Jijosha's *The Tempest*'), (c) Mike Ingham ('"We
Will Perform in Measure, Time, and Place": Synchronicity, Signification and Cultural

Mobility in Tang Shu-wing Theatre Studio's Cantonese-Language *Macbeth*'), (d)
Mariko Anzai ('From Cultural Mobility to Cultural Misunderstanding: Japanese Style
of Love in Akio Miyazawa's Adaptation in the Cardenio Project, *Motorcycle Don
Quixote*'), (e) Andronicus Aden ('Something Rotten in the State of Dankot: *Hamlet*
and the Kingdom of Nepal'), (f) Paromita Chakravarti ('Globalising the City: Kolkata
Films and the Millennial Bard'), (g) Lingui Yang ('Shakespeare's Uses in Chinese Media
and Trans-Sphere'), (h) Yukari Yoshihara ('Bardolators and Bardoclasts: Shakespeare
in Manga/Anime and Cosplay'), (i) Thomas Kullmann ('Shakespeare on the Internet:
Global and South Asian Appropriations'), (j) Judy Celine Ick ('The Performance
Archive and the Digital Construction of Asian Shakespeare'), (k) Supriya Chaudhuri
('Global Shakespeare and the Question of a World Literature'), (l) Swati Ganguly
('Beyond Bardolatry: Rabindranath Tagore's Critique of Shakespeare's *The Tempest*'),
afterword by Michael Dobson.

THEORIZING ADAPTATION

Cohn, Ruby (1976), *Modern Shakespeare Offshoots*, Princeton, NJ: Princeton University
Press.

Offers early definitions of key terms (reduction/emendation, adaptation, transformation)
and case studies exploring them.

Conkie, Rob and Scott Maisano, eds (2019), *Shakespeare and Creative Criticism*, New
York, NY: Berghahn Books.

Integrates creative and critical modes of writing. Revised and expanded from *Critical
Survey* 28.2: *Creative/Critical Shakespeares* (2016). Chapters by (a) Matthew
Zarnowiecki ('Responses to Responses to Shakespeare's Sonnets', 21–37), (b) Kavita
Mudan Finn and Jessica McCall ('Exit, pursued by a fan: Shakespeare, Fandom, and
the Lure of the Alternate Universe', 38–53), (c) Jessica McCall ('A Merry Midsummer
Labor Merchant's Tempest in King Beatrice's Verona', 54–60), (d) Kavita Mudan Finn
('Pickled Red Herring', 61–100), (e) Scott Maisano ('Enter Nurse, or Love's Labour's
Won', 101–18), (f) Mary Baine Campbell ('Echo and Narcissus, or Man O Man!',
119–27), (g) Dan Moss ('*The Fair Maid of Alexandria*, or The Glass Tower', 128–45),
(h) David Nicol ('A Tragedy of the Plantation of Virginia', 146–64), (i) Rob Conkie
('*Othello*: Original Practices: A Photographic Essay', 165–80).

Desmet, Christy and Sujata Iyengar (2015), 'Adaptation, appropriation, or what you will',
Shakespeare 11.1: 10–19.

Examines dominant terminology (e.g. adaptation vs. appropriation), reviews critical
histories and considers theoretical advantages and drawbacks; concludes that both are
useful in different, relational ways.

Erickson, Peter (1991), *Rewriting Shakespeare, Rewriting Ourselves*, Berkeley, CA:
University of California Press.

Uses the doubled lenses of new historicism and feminist criticism (specifically Adrienne
    Rich, Maya Angelou and Gloria Naylor) to ask two major questions: 'What effect
    does a revised canon have on Shakespeare's position? How does our relationship to
    Shakespeare's work change in a new context?' (6) and attends closely to questions
    of race as they play out in adapted Shakespeare. That these questions are still under
    debate today, thirty years after the publication of this volume, says a lot.

Holderness, Graham (2014), *Tales from Shakespeare: Creative Collisions*, Cambridge:
    Cambridge University Press.

Combines Shakespeare's plays with modern stories to produce 'creative collisions'.

Iyengar, Sujata (2017), 'Shakespeare Transformed: Copyright, Copyleft, and Shakespeare
    After Shakespeare', *Actes des congrès de la Société française Shakespeare 35*.
    DOI:10.4000/shakespeare.3852.

Advocates for the use of *transformation* instead of *adaptation* or *appropriation* (cf.
    Rozette); based on considerations of copyright law, book history, reception studies and
    pedagogy. In the absence of an accessible Shakespearean original, 'we are reinventing
    it/him and ourselves with every iteration, appropriating it in the sense that we make it
    part of our own mental furniture and even our embodiment, our property' (11).

Kidnie, Margaret Jane (2009), *Shakespeare and the Problem of Adaptation*, London:
    Routledge.

Encourages a shift in the discourse surrounding Shakespeare and adaptation studies to
    focus less on notions of textual fidelity and more on the potentialities of the work
    found through adaptation, with an emphasis on how the work gets entangled in the
    adaptational process.

Rozette, Martha Tuck (1994), *Talking Back to Shakespeare*, Newark, DE: University of
    Delaware Press.

Places student-centric resistant readings to Shakespeare in conversation with other
    transformative works, ranging from the nineteenth to the late twentieth century.
    Considers both 'diachronous transformations' or "supplements to the Shakespearean
    text' such as prequels and sequels, or 'synchronous transformations', which 'retell
    or revise [...] as an ideologically inspired engagement with the text's narrative
    assumptions, implicit values, and accumulated critical reputation' (6).

ADAPTING SHAKESPEARE (THE MAN)

Dobson, Michael (1992), *The Making of the National Poet: Shakespeare, Adaptation, and
    Authorship, 1660–1769*, Oxford: Oxford University Press.

Follows Shakespeare's reputation from that of a popular playwright during his lifetime
    and shortly afterward to the centre of the burgeoning English literary canon in the
    eighteenth century.

Holderness, Graham (2011), *Nine Lives of William Shakespeare*, London: Continuum.

Combines biography and fictional narrative to offer a new interpretation of the scant facts
we have about Shakespeare's life.

Leinwand, Theodore (2016), *The Great William: Writers Reading Shakespeare*, Chicago,
IL: University of Chicago Press.

Uses engagements with Shakespeare by Samuel Taylor Coleridge, John Keats, Virginia
Woolf, Charles Olson, John Berryman, Allen Ginsberg and Ted Hughes to address
how these writers read and appropriated Shakespeare.

Scheil, Katherine West (2018), *Imagining Shakespeare's Wife: The Afterlife of Anne
Hathaway*, Cambridge: Cambridge University Press.

The first full-length study to trace Anne Hathaway's afterlife from her first appearances in
Shakespeare biographies in the eighteenth century to the present day.

Taylor, Gary (1991), *Reinventing Shakespeare: A Cultural History, from the Restoration to
the Present*, Oxford: Oxford University Press.

Charts the posthumous 'reinvention' of Shakespeare (the man, the myth, the legend) by
each succeeding generation.

STAGE (DRAMA, MUSIC, DANCE)

Bennett, Karen, (2003), 'Star-cross'd lovers: Shakespeare and Prokofiev's "pas-de-deux"
in *Romeo and Juliet*', *Cambridge Quarterly* 32.4: 311–47.

Analyses the score for Sergei Prokofiev's ballet adaptation of *Romeo and Juliet* within the
context of the Stalin regime.

Borkowska-Rychlewska, Alina (2019), *Shakespeare in 19th-Century Opera*, New York,
NY: Peter Lang.

Considers operatic adaptations of Shakespeare's plays from the nineteenth century,
including Verdi's *Macbeth, Otello* and *Falstaff*; Rossini's *Otello*; Halévy's *The
Tempest*; Gounod's *Roméo et Juliette*; and Thomas's *Hamlet* in the context of their
nineteenth-century reception, as seen in critical essays and press reviews.

Delabastita, Dirk and Lieven D'Hulst (1993), *European Shakespeares: Translating
Shakespeare in the Romantic Age*, Amsterdam: John Benjamins.

Considers Shakespeare's reception in the Romantic period across continental Europe.
Chapters by (a) José Lambert ('Shakespeare en France au tournant du XVIIIe siècle.
Un dossier européen', 25–44), (b) Werner Habicht ('The Romanticism of the Schlegel-
Tieck Shakespeare and the History of Nineteenth-Century German Shakespeare
Translation', 45–54), (c) Brigitte Schultze ('Shakespeare's Way into the West Slavic
Literatures and Cultures', 55–74), (d) Yuri D. Levin ('Russian Shakespeare Translations
in the Romantic Era', 75–90), (e) Kristian Smidt ('The Discovery of Shakespeare in
Scandinavia', 91–104), (f) Raymond Van den Broeck ('Report', 105–9), (g) Gaby
Petrone Fresco ('An Unpublished Pre-Romantic *Hamlet* in Eighteenth-Century Italy',

111–28), (h) Maria João da Rocha Afonso ('Simão de Melo Brandão and the First Portuguese Version of *Othello*', 129–46), (i) Péter Dávidházi ('Providing Texts for a Literary Cult, Early Translations of Shakespeare in Hungary', 147–62), (j) Wolfgang Ranke ('Shakespeare Translations for Eighteenth-Century Stage Productions in Germany: Different Versions of *Macbeth*', 163–82), (k) Theo Hermans ('Report', 183–5), (l) Jacques Gury ('Heurs et malheurs de *Roméo et Juliette* en France à l'époque romantique', 187–202), (m) Norbert Grenier ('The Comic Matrix of Early German Shakespeare Translation', 203–18), (n) Dirk Delabastita ('*Hamlet* in the Netherlands in the Late Eighteenth and Early Nineteenth Centuries. The Complexities of the History of Shakespeare's Reception', 219–34), (o) Theo D'haen ('Report', 235–6).

Desmet, Christy (2007), 'Southern *Shrew*s: Marriage and Slavery in American Appropriations of Shakespeare', *Upstart Crow* 26: 6–28.

Interrogates the trend of setting productions of *Taming of the Shrew* in the antebellum South with an eye to how the dynamics of race and gender play out in potentially subversive ways.

Duncan, Sophie (2017), *Shakespeare's Women and the Fin-de-Siècle*, Oxford: Oxford University Press.

Considers the intersection between Shakespeare, performance and celebrity culture at the turn of the century, such as Lillie Langtry's Cleopatra, Madge Kendal's Rosalind and Ellen Terry's Lady Macbeth.

Fielder, Brigitte (2017), 'Blackface Desdemona: Theorizing Race on the Nineteenth-Century American Stage', *Theatre Annual: A Journal of Theatre & Performance of the Americas* 70: 39–59.

Uses the nineteenth-century image of the 'begrimed and blackface Desdemona' to contextualize nineteenth-century American adaptations of *Othello* within larger discourses about white and black womanhood.

Golder, John (1992), *Shakespeare for the Age of Reason: The Earliest Stage Adaptations of Jean-François Ducis 1769–1792*, Voltaire Foundation, in association with Liverpool University Press.

Full-length study of the French adaptations of Shakespeare's plays by Jean-François Ducis. Includes chapters on *Hamlet*, *Roméo et Juliette*, *Le Roi Léar* (*King Lear*), *Macbeth*, *Jean Sans-Terre* (*King John*) and *Othello*, as well as appendices with cast lists, early manuscript details and a lost version of *Timon of Athens* called *Timon le misanthrope*.

Gregor, Keith (2010), *Shakespeare in the Spanish Theatre, 1772 to the Present*, London: Continuum.

Survey of four centuries of Shakespearean stage history in Spain.

Hartley, Andrew James (2015), 'Ren Fest Shakespeare: The Cosplay Bard', *Shakespeare Survey* 68: *Shakespeare, Origins, and Originality*: 210–20.

Focuses on a particular subset of Shakespeare performance, the casual, interactive,
'shared-light audience' performances that take place in and around Renaissance Faires
in the United States.

Hartley, Andrew James, ed. (2017), *Shakespeare and Millennial Fiction*, Cambridge:
Cambridge University Press.

Essays that 'manifest larger ideas about how Shakespeare is perceived in the wider
(non-academic) world, how his works are invoked in a larger navigation of status
and how they present a window on a particular moment in the evolving history of
Shakespeare in education and popular literary culture' (8). Chapters by (a) Graham
Holderness ('Hamlet the Dane: "Tell My Story"', 13–32), (b) Rebecca Bushnell
('Shakespeare Found and Lost', 33–45), (c) Ken Jacobsen ('Shakespeare's Novel Life:
Speech, Text, and Dialogue in recent Shakespearean Fictions', 46–63), (d) Regina
Buccola ('The School of *(The) Night Circus*: Performing Shakespeare Arcana in Novel
Forms', 64–80), (e) M. Tyler Sasser ('"A Delicate and Tender Prince": Hamlet and
Millennial Boyhood', 81–100), (f) Jennifer Flaherty ('How Many Daughters Had
Lady Macbeth?', 101–14), (g) Emily Detmer-Goebel ('Engaging Ophelia in Early
Twenty-First Century Young Adult Fiction', 115–28), (h) Erica Hateley ('Criminal
Adaptations: Gender, Genre, and Shakespearean Young Adult Literature', 129–44),
(i) Lisa Hopkins ('A Man With a Map: The Millennial Macbeth', 145–58), (j) Sujata
Iyengar ('Shakespeare and the Post-Millennial Cancer Novel', 159–76), (k) Christy
Desmet ('Posthuman *Tempests* in the Twenty-First Century', 177–92), (l) Michelle
K. Yost ('Stratford-Upon-Web: Shakespeare in Twenty-First-Century Fanfiction',
193–212), (m) Laurie E. Osborne ('The Paranormal Bard: Shakespeare Is/As Undead',
213–29), (n) Douglas M. Lanier ('The Hogarth Shakespeare Series: Redeeming
Shakespeare's Literariness', 230–50).

Hawkes, Terence (1986), *That Shakespeherian Rag: Essays on a Critical Process*, London:
Routledge.

Highly influential early study of Shakespearean critics A. C. Bradley, Walter Raleigh, T. S.
Eliot and John Dover Wilson that frames the 'processing' of Shakespeare as a kind of
appropriation.

Klett, Elizabeth (2019), *Choreographing Shakespeare: Dance Adaptations of the Plays and
Poems*, London: Routledge.

Considers forty different productions based on Shakespeare's plays and poems, focusing
on the translation of Shakespeare's verbal cues into choreographic ones. Also includes
interviews with Stanton Welsh (*Romeo and Juliet*), Doug Elkins (*Othello*), Paul
Vasterling (*Macbeth*), Stephen Mills (*Hamlet*), Dominic Walsh (*Titus Andronicus*) and
David Bintley (*The Tempest*).

Loomba, Ania (1998), '"Local-manufacture made-in-India Othello fellows": Issues of race,
hybridity and location in post-colonial Shakespeares', in *Post-Colonial Shakespeares*,
ed. Ania Loomba and Martin Orkin, London: Routledge.

Uses Salman Rushdie's *The Moor's Last Sigh* (1995) and an Indian production of *Othello* from 1996 adapted into the Kathakali style of dance-drama to 'suggest that any meaningful discussion of colonial or post-colonial hybridities demands close attention to the specificities of location as well as a conceptual re-orientation with requires taking on board non-European histories and modes of representation' (144).

Marshall, Gail and Adrian Poole (2003), *Victorian Shakespeare Volume 1: Theatre, Drama, and Performance*, New York, NY: Palgrave.

Explores 'the ways in which the production of Shakespeare fundamentally informs the changing nature and status of Victorian theatre'. Chapters by (a) Katherine Newey ('Shakespeare and the Wars of the Playbills', 13–28), (b) Julia Swindells ('Behold the Swelling Scene! Shakespeare and the 1832 Select Committee', 29–46), (c) Peter Holland ('Performing Shakespeare in Print: Narrative in Nineteenth-century Illustrated Shakespeares', 47–72), (d) Richard W. Schoch ('Shakespeare Mad', 73–81), (e) Lisa Merrill ('Acting Like a Man: National Identity, Homoerotics, and Shakespearean Criticism in the Nineteenth-century American Press', 82–98), (f) Jane Moody ('Shakespeare and the Immigrants: Nationhood, Psychology and Xenophobia on the Nineteenth-century Stage', 99–118), (g) Sara Jan ('"At the Side of Shakespeare": Ibsen's *The Pretenders* and Victorian Shakespeare', 119–27), (h) Inga-Stina Ewbank ('As They Liked It: Shakespearean Comedy goes Continental', 128–45), (i) Richard Foulkes ('Touchstone for the Times: Victorians in the Forest of Arden', 146–60), (j) Jean Chothia ('Varying Authenticities: Poel, Tree and Late-Victorian Shakespeare', 161–77), (k) John Stokes ('"Shopping in Byzantium": Oscar Wilde as Shakespearean Critic', 178–91), (l) Nina Auerbach ('Perturbed Spirits: Victorian Actors and Immortality', 192–202).

Marshall, Gail and Adrian Poole (2003), *Victorian Shakespeare Volume 2: Literature and Culture*, New York, NY: Palgrave.

While the first volume of *Victorian Shakespeare* is more straightforward performance history, the second brings together essays analysing engagements with Shakespeare by prominent nineteenth-century novelists, poets and critics. Chapters by (a) Diana E. Henderson ('Othello Redux? Scott's *Kenilworth* and the Trickiness of "Race" on the Nineteenth-century Stage', 14–29), (b) John Glavin ('To Make the Situation Natural': *Othello* at Mid-Century', 30–45), (c) Juliet John ('Dickens and Hamlet', 46–60), (d) Clare Pettitt ('Shakespeare at the Great Exhibition of 1851', 61–83), (e) Philip Davis ('Implicit and Explicit Reason: George Eliot and Shakespeare', 84–99), (f) Philip Home ('"Where Did She Get Hold Of That?" Shakespeare in Henry James's *The Tragic Muse*', 100–13), (g) Robert Douglas-Fairhurst ('Shakespeare's Weeds: Tennyson, Elegy and Allusion', 114–30), (h) Christopher Decker ('Shakespeare and the Death of Tennyson', 131–49), (i) Danny Karlin ('"The Names": Robert Browning's "Shaksperean Show"', 150–69), (j) Ann Thompson ('Mary Cowden Clarke: Marriage, Gender and the Victorian Woman Critic of Shakespeare', 170–89), (k) Pascale Aebischer ('Shakespeare, the Actress, and the Prostitute: Professional Respectability and Private Shame in George Vandenhoff's *Leaves from an Actor's Notebook*', 190–

202), (l) Francis O'Gorman ('"The Clue of Shakespearian Power Over Me": Ruskin, Shakespeare, and Influence', 203–18).

Massai, Sonia (2000), 'Nahum Tate's Revision of Shakespeare's *King Lears*', *Studies in English Literature 1500–1900* 40.3: 435–50.

Argues that Nahum Tate's 1681 *History of King Lear* represents 'the only surviving instance of a critical assessment of the *dramatic* qualities of Quarto and Folio *King Lear*' and outlines Tate's editorial choices across the play (435).

Monahin, Nona (2017), 'Prokofiev's *Romeo and Juliet*: Some Consequences of the "Happy Ending"', *Borrowers and Lenders* 10.1. https://openjournals.libs.uga.edu/borrowers/article/view/2419.

In the original version of Prokofiev's ballet adaptation of *Romeo and Juliet*, he allowed Friar Laurence to intercept Romeo on his way to Juliet's tomb, giving the story a happy ending. After backlash, he then changed that ending to be more faithful to Shakespeare's. This article focuses on the compositional impact of that change to the ending.

Myles, Rob (2020), *The Show Must Go Online*, YouTube. https://www.youtube.com/c/RobMyles/videos.

A groundbreaking series where all thirty-seven of Shakespeare's plays were produced over Zoom during the first year of the COVID-19 pandemic, and archived on YouTube.

Ryuta, Minami, Ian Carruthers and John Gillies, eds (2001), *Performing Shakespeare in Japan*, Cambridge: Cambridge University Press.

Collection of essays bringing together scholars and artists to discuss Japanese engagement with Shakespearean performance. Chapters by (a) Anzai Tetsuo ('What do we mean by "Japanese" Shakespeare?', 17–20), (b) Yoshihara Yukari ('Japan as "half-civilised": an early Japanese adaptation of Shakespeare's *Merchant of Venice* and Japan's construction of its national image in the late nineteenth century', 21–32), (c) James R. Brandon ('Shakespeare in Kabuki', 33–53), (d) Matsumoto Shinko ('Osanai Kaoru's version of *Romeo and Juliet*, 1904', 54–66), (e) Ueda Munkata Kuniyoshi ('Some Noh adaptations of Shakespeare in English and Japanese', 67–75), (f) Michael Shapiro ('*The Braggart Samurai*: a Kyogen adaptation of Shakespeare's *The Merry Wives of Windsor*', 76–85), (g) Paula von Loewenfeldt ('Weaving the spider's web: interpretation of character in Kurosawa Akira's *Throne of Blood* (*Kumonosu-jô*)', 87–100), (h) Suematsu Michiko ('Innovation and continuity: two decades of Deguchi Norio's Shakespeare Theatre Company', 101–11), (i) Takahashi Yasunari ('Tragedy with laughter: Suzuki Tadashi's *The Tale of Lear*', 112–20), (j) Ian Carruthers ('*The Chronicle of Macbeth*: Suzuki method acting in Australia, 1992', 121–32), (k) Suzuki Masae ('The rose and bamboo: Oda Hideki's *Sandaime Richâdo*', 133–45), (l) Minami Ryuta ('Shakespeare reinvented on the contemporary Japanese stage', 146–58), (m) Ohtani Tomoko ('Juliet's girlfriends: The Takarazuka Revue Company and the *Shôjo* culture', 159–71), (n) Ted Motohashi

('Directing "Japanese Shakespeare" locally and universally: an interview with Gerard Murphy', 172–81). Part III includes interviews with directors and actors: Deguchi Norio (183–95), Suzuki Tadashi (196–207), Ninagawa Yukio (208–19), Noda Hideki (220–9), Hira Mikijirô (230–5), afterword by John Gillies (236–48).

Sanders, Julie (2013), *Shakespeare and Music: Afterlives and Borrowings*, Oxford: Wiley.

Explores the musical tradition inspired by Shakespeare's plays across Western Europe from the seventeenth century onwards.

Sasayama, Takashi, J. R. Mulryne and Margaret Shewring, eds (1999), *Shakespeare and the Japanese Stage*, Cambridge: Cambridge University Press.

Collection in two parts, studying the interaction of Japanese and Western conceptions of Shakespeare. The first part focuses on twentieth-century productions; the second part considers parallels and divergences between Japanese and Western theatre over a longer period. Chapters by (a) Akihiko Senda, trans. Ryuta Minami ('The rebirth of Shakespeare in Japan: from the 1960s to the 1990s', 15–37), (b) Brian Powell ('One Man's *Hamlet* in 1911 Japan: The Bungei Kyokai production in the Imperial Theatre', 38–52), (c) Dennis Kennedy and J. Thomas Rimer ('Koreya Senda and political Shakespeare', 53–70), (d) J. R. Mulryne ('The perils and profits of interculturalism and the theatre art of Tadashi Suzuki', 71–93), (e) Margaret Shewring ('Hideki Noda's Shakespeare: the languages of performance', 94–109), (f) Tetsuo Kishi ('Japanese Shakespeare and English reviewers', 110–23), (g) Tetsuo Anzai ('Directing *King Lear* in Japanese translation', 124–39), (h) Stephen Greenblatt ('Preface to the Japanese translation of *Renaissance Self-Fashioning*', 141–4), (i) Takashi Sasayama ('Tragedy and emotion: Shakespeare and Chikamatsu', 145–58), (j) Gerry Yokota-Murakami ('Conflicting authorities: the canonization of Zeami and Shakespeare', 159–75), (k) Izumi Momose ('Shakespearean drama and the Noh: *theatrum mundi* and nothingness', 176–85), (l) Minoru Fujita ('Tradition and the Bunraku adaptation of *The Tempest*', 186–96), (m) Yoko Takakuwa ('The performance of gendered identity in Shakespeare and Kabuki', 197–213), (n) Yasunari Takahashi ('Kyogenising Shakespeare/Shakespeareanising Kyogen', 214–25), (o) Yasunari Takahashi ('*The Braggart Samurai*: a Kyogen adaptation of *The Merry Wives of Windsor*', 226–41), afterword by Robert Hapgood (243–56). Also includes a chronological table of Shakespeare productions in Japan from 1866 to 1994, compiled by Ryuta Minami.

Scott L. Newstok and Ayanna Thompson, eds (2010), *Weyward Macbeth: Intersections of Race and Performance*, New York, NY: Palgrave.

Interrogates the place of *Macbeth* in 'American constructions and performances of race' (1). Includes an appendix listing productions of *Macbeth* that feature non-traditional casting. Chapters by (a) Celia R. Daileader ('Weird Brothers: What Thomas Middleton's *The Witch* Can Tell Us About Race, Sex, and Gender n *Macbeth*', 11–21), (b) Heather S. Nathans ('"Blood Will Have Blood": Violence, Slaver, and *Macbeth* in the Antebellum American Imagination', 23–34), (c) John C. Briggs ('The Exorcism of Macbeth: Frederick Douglass's Appropriation of Shakespeare', 35–44), (d) Bernth Lindfors ('Ira Aldridge as

Macbeth', 45–54) (e) Joyce Green MacDonald ('Minstrel Show *Macbeth*', 55–64), (f) Nick Moschovakis ('Reading *Macbeth* in Texts By and About African Americans, 1903–1944: Race and the Problematics of Allusive Identification', 65–77), (g) Lisa N. Simmons ('Before Welles: A 1935 Boston Production', 79–82), (h) Marguerite Rippy ('Black Cast Conjures White Genius: Unraveling the Mystique of Orson Welles's "Voodoo" *Macbeth*', 83–90), (i) Scott L. Newstok ('After Welles: Re-do Voodoo *Macbeths*', 91–100), (j) Lenwood Sloan ('*The Vo-Du Macbeth!*: Travels and Travails of a Choreo-Drama Inspired by the FTP Production', 101–11), (k) Harry Lennix ('A Black Actor's Guide to the Scottish Play, or, Why *Macbeth* Matters', 113–20), (l) Alexander C. Y. Huang ('Asian-American Theatre Reimagined: *Shogun Macbeth* in New York', 121–6), (m) Anita Maynard-Losh ('The Tlingit Play: *Macbeth* and Native Americanism', 127–32), (n) Jose A. Esquea ('A Post-Apocalyptic *Macbeth*: Teatro LA TEA's *Macbeth 2029*', 133–6), (o) William C. Carroll ('Multicultural, Multilingual *Macbeth*', 137–43), (p) Wallace McClain Cheatham ('Reflections on Veri, *Macbeth*, and Non-Traditional Casting in Opera', 145–50), (q) Douglas Lanier ('Ellington's Dark Lady', 151–60), (r) Todd Landon Barnes ('Hip-Hop *Macbeth*s, "Digitized Blackness," and the Millennial Minstrel: Illegal Culture Sharing in the Virtual Classroom', 161–72), (s) Francesca Royster ('Riddling Whiteness, Riddling Certainty: Roman Polanski's *Macbeth*', 173–82), (t) Courtney Lehmann ('Semper *Die*: Marines Incarnadine in Nina Menkes *The Bloody Child: An Interior of Violence*', 183–92), (u) Amy Scott-Douglass ('Shades of Shakespeare: Colorblind Casting and Interracial Couples in *Macbeth in Manhattan*, *Grey's Anatomy*, and Prison *Macbeth*', 193–203), (v) Charita Gainey-O'Toole and Elizabeth Alexander ('Three Weyward Sisters: African-American Female Poets Conjure with *Macbeth*', 205–10), (w) Philip C. Kolin ('"Black up again": Combating *Macbeth* in Contemporary African-American Plays', 211–22), (x) Peter Erickson ('Black Characters in Search of an Author: Black Plays on Black Performers of Shakespeare', 223–33), afterword by Richard Burt (235–40).

Sen, Suddhaseel (2020), *Shakespeare in the World: Cross-Cultural Adaptation in Europe and Colonial India, 1850–1900*, London: Taylor & Francis.

Argues that theatrical, novelistic, operatic and prose adaptations of Shakespeare were crucial to the transmission of his works to non-Anglophone communities in Europe and colonial India.

Smith, Charlene V. (2018), 'Margaret of Anjou: Shakespeare's Adapted Heroine', in *The Palgrave Handbook of Shakespeare's Queens*, ed. Kavita Mudan Finn and Valerie Schutte, New York: Palgrave, 455–73.

Traces stage adaptations of the three parts of *Henry VI* and *Richard III* shaped around the character of Margaret of Anjou from the nineteenth to the twenty-first century.

Trivedi, Poonam and Minami Ryuta, eds (2010), *Re-Playing Shakespeare in Asia*, London: Routledge.

Explores restagings and other theatrical adaptations of Shakespeare's works in central and emerging areas of Asia, including Japan, China, India, Korea, Taiwan, Singapore, Indonesia and the Philippines. Chapters by (a) James Brandon ('Other Shakespeares in Asias: An Overview'), (b) Brian Singleton ('Asian Theatres, Mnouchkine and Shakespeare: The Search for a Theatrical Form'), (c) Poonam Trivedi ('Shakespeare and the Indian Image(nary): Embod(y)ment in Versions of *A Midsummer Night's Dream*'), (d) Minami Ryuta ('"What, has this thing appear'd again tonight?": Re-playing Shakespeares on the Japanese Stage'), (e) Ian Carruthers ('Fooling with Lear: A Performance History of Suzuki Tadashi's *King Lear* (1984–2006)'), (f) Ruru Li ('Six People in Search of "To be or not to be ... ": Hamlet's Soliloquy in Six Chinese Productions and the Metamorphosis of Shakespeare Performance on the Chinese Stage'), (g) Yoshihara Yukari ('Is this Shakespeare?: Inoue Hidenori's Adaptations of Shakespeare'), (h) Tapati Gupta ('From Proscenium to Paddy Fields: Utpal Dutt's Shakespeare Jatra'), (i) Judy Celine Ick ('And Never the Twain Shall Meet? Shakespeare and Philippine Performance Traditions'), (j) Kim Moran ('The stages "occupied by Shakespeare": Intercultural Performances and the Search for "Koreanness" in post-colonial Korea'), (k) Nurul Farhana Low Abdullah and C. S. Lim ('Shakespeare in the Shadows: Cultural Alienation, Politics and Eddin Khoo's Shadow Puppet Adaptation of Macbeth'), (l) Peichen Wu ('The Peripheral Body of Empire: Shakespearean Adaptations and Taiwan's Geopolitics'), (m) Alexa Alice Joubin ('"No World Without Verona Walls?": Shakespeare in the Provincial Cultural Marketplace'), (n) Paromita Chakravarti and Swati Ganguly ('Dancing to Shakespeare: Crossing Genre and Gender in the Tragedies'), (o) John Emigh ('"Living in a Different House": A Gambuh *Macbeth* in Bali'), (p) Bi-qi Beatrice Lei ('"O Heavy Lightness, O Serious Vanity": Camping Romeo and Juliet in Postcolonial Taiwan').

PAGE

Alhawamdeh, Hussein A. and Ismail Suliman Almazaidah (2018), 'Shakespeare in the Arab Jordanian Consciousness: Shylock in the poetry of 'Arār (Mustafa Wahbi Al-Tal)', *Arab Studies Quarterly* 40.4: 319–35.

Considers how the early-twentieth-century Jordanian poet 'Arār uses the character of Shylock from *The Merchant of Venice* to critique the actions of Zionism against Arab Palestinians.

Barber, Sarah (2013), 'Parenting Young Readers with *The Girlhood of Shakespeare's Heroines*', *Studies in English Literature 1500–1900* 53.4: 809–27.

Considers Mary Cowden Clarke's fictionalized accounts of the childhoods of Shakespeare's heroines within the context of larger nineteenth-century discourses about women's education, the moral worth of Shakespeare and parent–child relationships.

Benjamin, Shanna Green (2009), 'Race, Faces, and False Fronts: Shakespearean Signifying in the *Colored American Magazine*', *African-American Review* 43.4: 621–31.

Illustrates how writers for the *Colored American Magazine*, particularly M. F. Hunter, Bob Cole and Pauline Hopkins, used Shakespeare to promote a 'political and literary stance that was direct, yet nonconfrontational, inclusive, yet highbrow' (621).

Berg, Dianne (2014), '"I think nothing, my lord": Emptiness, Absence, and Abused Innocence in "Ophelia, the Rose of Elsinore"', *Borrowers & Lenders* 9.1: *Girls and Girlhood in Adaptations of Shakespeare*. https://openjournals.libs.uga.edu/borrowers/article/view/2294.

Reads Mary Cowden Clarke's account of Ophelia in *The Girlhood of Shakespeare's Heroines* as an ultimately disempowering and silencing interpretation of Shakespeare's character.

Erne, Lukas (2013), *Shakespeare and the Book Trade*, Cambridge: Cambridge University Press.

Landmark study of the print history of Shakespeare's works during his life and in the century thereafter; argues that Shakespeare himself played a major role in the dissemination and publicising of his works in print.

Fuller, David (2021), *Shakespeare and the Romantics*, Oxford: Oxford University Press.

Explores the revival of interest in Shakespeare's works, and their influence on poetry, drama and fiction during the Romantic period in England, France and Germany. The final two chapters focus on editions and stage history.

Hugo, Victor (1985), 'Préface de Cromwell', in *Œuvres Complètes: Critiques*, ed. Anne Ubersfeld, Paris: Robert Laffont, 3–44.

Originally published in 1827 with the first edition of Hugo's play *Cromwell*. Uses Shakespeare as the prime example of 'realist' poetry, in contrast to 'idealistic' (the Bible) and 'grandiosity' (classical epic) and hails him as the poet of the modern era.

Marrapodi, Michele, ed. (2014), *Shakespeare and the Italian Renaissance: Appropriation, Transformation, Opposition*, Aldershot: Ashgate.

Interrogates the appropriation of Italian culture in Shakespeare's plays, particularly the 'variegated ways in which the exploitation of Italian culture is deeply rooted in the processes of ideological transformation, involving questions of political negotiations, antagonism, and opposition' (5). Chapters by (a) Harry Berger Jr. ('*Sprezzatura* and Embarrassment in *The Merchant of Venice*', 21–38), (b) John Roe ('A Niggle of Doubt: Courtliness and Chastity in Shakespeare and Castiglione', 39–56), (c) Thomas Kullmann ('Dramatic Appropriations of Italian Courtliness', 57–72), (d) Maria Del Sapio Garbero ('Disowning the Bard: Coriolanus' Forgetful Humanism', 73–92), (e) Melissa Walter ('Matteo Bandello's Social Authorship and Paulina as Patroness in *The Winter's Tale*', 93–106), (f) Karen Zyck-Galbraith ('Tracing a Villain: Typological Intertextuality in the Works of Painter, Webster, Cinthio, and Shakespeare', 107–21), (g) Keir Elam ('"Wanton pictures": The Baffling of Christopher Sly and the Visual-Verbal Intercourse of Early Modern Erotic Arts', 123–46), (h) Sergio Costola and Michael Saenger ('Shylock's Venice and the Grammar of the Modern City', 147–62), (i) Eric Nicholson ('Helen, the Italianate Theatrical Wayfarer of *All's Well That Ends Well*', 163–80), (j) Bruce W. Young ('"These Times of Woe": The Contraction and Dislocation of Time in Shakespeare's *Romeo and Juliet*', 181–98), (k) Camilla

Caporicci ('"Dark is Light" - From Italy to England: Challenging Tradition Through Colours', 199–214), (l) Iuliana Tanase ('The Italian *Commedia* and the Fashioning of the Shakespearean Fool', 215–33), (m) Michele Marrapodi ('The Aretinean Intertext and the Heterodoxy of *The Taming of the Shrew*', 235–56), (n) Lawrence F. Rhu ('Shakespeare Italianate: Sceptical Crises in Three Kinds of Play', 257–74), (o) Hanna Scolnicov ('The Jew and the Justice of Venice', 275–90), (p) Rocco Coronato ('*Hamlet*, Ortensio Lando, or "To Be or Not To Be" Paradoxically Explained', 291–304), (q) Duncan Salkeld ('Much Ado About Italians in Renaissance London', 305–16), (r) Anthony R. Guneratne ('Shakespeare, Italian Music-Drama, and Contemporary Performance: Space, Time, and the Acoustic Worlds of *Romeo and Juliet* and *The Tempest*', 317–32).

Martindale, Charles and A. B. Taylor, eds (2009), *Shakespeare and the Classics*, Cambridge: Cambridge University Press.

Focuses on Shakespeare's engagement with specific classical authors and their impact on his works. Chapters by (a) Colin Burrow ('Shakespeare and humanistic culture', 9–27), (b) Vanda Zajko ('Petrucio is "Kated": *The Taming of the Shrew* and Ovid', 33–48), (c) A. B. Taylor ('Ovid's myths and the unsmooth course of love in *A Midsummer Night's Dream*', 49–65), (d) Heather James ('Shakespeare's learned heroines in Ovid's schoolroom', 66–86), (e) Charles Martindale ('Shakespeare and Virgil', 89–106), (f) Wolfgang Riehle ('Shakespeare's reception of Plautus reconsidered', 109–21), (g) Raphael Lyne ('Shakespeare, Plautus, and the discovery of New Comic space', 122–38), (h) Yves Peyré ('"Confusion now hath made his masterpiece": Senecan resonances in *Macbeth*', 141–55), (i) Erica Sheen ('"These are the only men": Seneca and monopoly in *Hamlet* 2.2', 156–70), (j) John Roe ('"Character" in Plutarch and Shakespeare: Brutus, Julius Caesar, and Mark Antony', 173–87), (k) Gordon Braden ('Plutarch, Shakespeare, and the alpha males', 188–206), (l) A. D. Nuttall ('Action at a Distance: Shakespeare and the Greeks', 209–22), (m) Stuart Gillespie ('Shakespeare and Greek romance: "Like an old tale still"', 225–39), (n) Michael Silk ('Shakespeare and Greek tragedy: strange relationship', 241–58), (o) David Hopkins ('"The English Homer": Shakespeare, Longinus, and English "neo-classicism"', 261–76), (p) Sarah Annes Brown, ('"There is no end but addition": the later reception of Shakespeare's classicism', 277–93).

Mayer, Jean-Christophe (2015), 'Reading in Their Present: Early Readers and the Origins of Shakespearian Appropriation', *Shakespeare Survey* 68: *Shakespeare, Origins, and Originality*: 146–57.

Argues that early modern commonplacing operates as a kind of appropriation and transformation of the Shakespearean playtext.

Novy, Marianne, ed. (1999), *Transforming Shakespeare: Contemporary Women's Re-Visions in Literature and Performance*, New York, NY: St. Martin's.

Inspired by Adrienne Rich's concept of 're-vision' as 'entering an old text from a new critical direction' and 'an act of survival', this collection interrogates feminist adaptations of Shakespeare from the late twentieth century (2). Chapters by (a)

Barbara Hodgdon ('Making it New: Katie Mitchell Refashions Shakespeare-History', 13–34), (b) Penny Gay ('Recent Australian *Shrews*: The "Larrikin Element"', 35–50), (c) Patricia Lennox ('A Girl's Got to Eat: Christine Edzard's Film of *As You Like It*', 51–66), (d) Marianne Novy ('Saving Desdemona and/or Ourselves: Plays by Ann-Marie MacDonald and Paula Vogel', 67–86), (e) Peter Erickson ('Rita Dove's Shakespeares', 87–102), (f) Francesca T. Royster ('Cleopatra as Diva: African-American Women and Shakespearean Tactics', 103–26), (g) Barbara Mathieson ('The Polluted Quarry: Nature and Body in *A Thousand Acres*', 127–44), (h) Iska Alter ('*King Lear* and *A Thousand Acres*: Gender, Genre, and the Revisionary Impulse', 145–58), (i) Jane Smiley ('Shakespeare in Iceland', 159–80), (j) Suzanne Raitt ('"Out of Shakespeare?": Cordelia in *Cat's Eye*', 181–98), (k) Diana Brydon ('Tempest Plainsong: Retuning Caliban's Curse', 199–216), (l) Caroline Cakebread ('Sycorax Speaks: Marina Warner's *Indigo* and *The Tempest*', 217–36), (m) Linda Bamber ('Claribel at Palace Dot Tunis', 237–58).

Sanders, Julie (2001), *Novel Shakespeares: Twentieth-Century Women Novelists and Appropriation*, Manchester: Manchester University Press.

Focuses on late-twentieth-century novels where women writers 'talk back' to Shakespeare, exploring the cultural and theoretical underpinnings of that engagement, arguing that 'Shakespeare is not invoked simply as an authenticating male canonical presence in these works but, rather, as a topos to be explored, dissected and reconfigured as much as any other' (13).

FILM AND TELEVISION

Adams, Brandi K. (2020), 'The King, and not I: Refusing neutrality', *The Sundial*, 9 June, https://medium.com/the-sundial-acmrs/the-king-and-not-i-refusing-neutrality-dbab4239e8a9.

Pushes against the idea that any Shakespeare adaptation can be truly 'neutral' on the topic of white supremacy, using the case study of the 2019 Netflix film *The King*, based on Shakespeare's two parts of *Henry IV* and *Henry V*.

Anderegg, Michael A. (2004), *Cinematic Shakespeare*, New York, NY: Rowman & Littlefield.

General introduction to Shakespeare in film, from the 1930s to 2000.

Ball, Robert Hamilton (1968), *Shakespeare on Silent Film: A Strange, Eventful History*, London: Routledge.

A study in two parts: first, a detailed history of silent films based on Shakespeare within the context of film history more generally; followed by individual treatment and commentary for each of the films treated in the first part. Still well-regarded today, though some conclusions have been re-evaluated (see Buchanan 2009).

Biswas, Madhavi (2017), '"Light Your Cigarette with My Heart's Fire, My Love": Raunchy Dances and a Golden-hearted Prostitute in Bhardwaj's *Omkara* (2006)', *Borrowers and Lenders* 10.2. https://openjournals.libs.uga.edu/borrowers/article/view/2422.

Focuses on the character of Billo (based on Bianca) in Vishal Bhardwaj's 2006 film *Omkara*, a reworking of *Othello* set in contemporary small-town India, particularly her persistent association with musical numbers.

Boose, Lynda E. and Richard Burt, eds (1997), *Shakespeare, the Movie: Popularizing the plays on film, TV, and video*, London: Routledge.

Essay collection intended to 'open up questions about Shakespeare's status as legitimating author-function, about the relation between original and adaptation, about youth culture and pedagogy, and finally, about the relation between the popular as hip and the popular as politically radical' (2). Chapters by (a) Lynda E. Boose and Richard Burt ('Totally Clueless?: Shakespeare Goes Hollywood in the 1990s', 8–22), (b) Barbara Hodgdon ('Race-ing *Othello*, Re-engendering White Out', 23–5), (c) Donald K. Hedrick ('War is Mud: Branagh's Dirty Harry V and the Types of Political Ambiguity', 46–67), (d) James N. Loehlin ('"Top of the World, Ma": *Richard III* and Cinematic Convention', 68–80), (e) Robert Hapgood ('Popularizing Shakespeare: The Artistry of Franco Zeffirelli', 81–96), (f) Valerie Wayne ('*Shakespeare Wallah* and Colonial Specularity', 97–105), (g) Laurie E. Osborne ('Poetry in Motion: Animating Shakespeare', 106–23), (h) Tony Howard ('When Peter Met Orson: The 1953 CBS *King Lear*', 124–37), (i) Kenneth S. Rothwell ('In Search of Nothing: Mapping King Lear', 138–50), (j) Diana E. Henderson ('A Shrew for the Times', 151–71), (k) Peter S. Donaldson ('Shakespeare in the Age of Post-Mechanical Reproduction: Sexual and Electronic Magic in *Prospero's Books*', 172–89), (l) Lynda E. Boose ('Grossly Gaping Viewers and Jonathan Miller's *Othello*', 190–201), (m) Katherine Eggert ('Age Cannot Wither Him: Warren Beatty's Bugsy as Hollywood Cleopatra', 202–19), (n) Ann Thompson ('Asta Nielsen and the Mystery of *Hamlet*', 220–30), (o) Susan Wiseman ('The Family Tree Motel: Subliming Shakespeare in *My Own Private Idaho*', 231–45), (p) Richard Burt ('The Love that Dare Not Speak Shakespeare's Name: New Shakesqueer Cinema', 246–74).

Boose, Lynda E. and Richard Burt, eds (2003), *Shakespeare, the Movie, II: Popularizing the plays on film, TV, video, and DVD*, London: Routledge.

Somewhere between a revision and a sequel to the 1997 collection, featuring nine new essays and revised versions of three essays. Chapters by (a) Richard Burt ('Shakespeare, "Glo-cali-zation," race, and the small screens of post-popular culture', 14–36), (b) Katherine Rowe ('"Remember me": technologies of memory in Michael Almereyda's *Hamlet*', 37–55), (c) Michael Anderegg ('James Dean meets the pirate's daughter: passion and parody in *William Shakespeare's Romeo + Juliet* and *Shakespeare in Love*', 56–71), (d) Katherine Eggert ('Sure can sing and dance: minstrelsy, the star system, and the post-postcoloniality of Kenneth Branagh's *Love's Labours Lost* and

Trevor Nunn's *Twelfth Night*', 72–88), (e) Barbara Hodgdon ('Race-ing *Othello*, re-engendering white-out, II', 89–104), (f) Peter S. Donaldson ('Shakespeare in the age of post-mechanical reproduction: sexual and electronic magic in *Prospero's Books*', 105–19), (g) Diana E. Henderson ('A *Shrew* for the times, revisited', 120–39), (h) Laurie Osborne ('Mixing media and animating Shakespeare tales', 140–53), (i) Douglas Lanier ('Nostalgia and theatricality: the fate of the Shakespearian stage in the *Midsummer Night's Dream*s of Hoffman, Noble, and Edzard', 154–72), (j) James N. Loehlin ('"Top of the world, ma": *Richard III* and cinematic convention', 173–85), (k) Thomas Cartelli ('Shakespeare and the street: Pacino's *Looking for Richard*, Bedford's *Street King*, and the common understanding', 186–99), (l) Susan Wiseman ('The family tree motel: subliming Shakespeare in *My Own Private Idaho*', 200–12), (m) Donald K. Hedrick ('War is mud: Branagh's *Dirty Harry V* and the types of political ambiguity', 213–30), (n) Courtney Lehmann ('Out damned Scot: dislocating *Macbeth* in transnational film and media culture', 231–51), (o) Amy Scott-Douglass ('Dogme Shakespeare 95: European cinema, anti-Hollywood sentiment, and the Bard', 252–64), (p) Richard Burt ('Shakespeare and Asia in postdiasporic cinemas: spin-offs and citations of the plays from Bollywood to Hollywood', 265–303).

Buchanan, Judith (2009), *Shakespeare on Silent Film: An Excellent Dumb Discourse*, Cambridge: Cambridge University Press.

Builds on Robert Ball's 1968 study of the same name using new primary materials such as trade papers (fanzines), scripts, actors' memoirs, press books, programmes and other ephemera to interrogate the assumption that these films were received poorly at the time. Includes two separate filmographies (one for commercially available silent films, one general).

Buchanan, Judith R. (2014), *Shakespeare on Film*, London: Routledge.

Overview of feature film adaptations of Shakespeare from 1899 to the early 2000s.

Cartmell, Deborah (2000), *Interpreting Shakespeare on Screen*, New York, NY: Palgrave.

Focuses on Shakespeare in popular film, specifically 'how Shakespeare is used by the film industry to appeal to the masses in terms of the presentation of issues such as gender, race, violence, and nationalism' (5).

Corredera, Vanessa I. (2020), '*Get Out* and the Remediation of *Othello*'s Sunken Place: Beholding White Supremacy's Coagula', *Borrowers & Lenders* 13.1: *Shakespeare and Politics Between Media*. https://openjournals.libs.uga.edu/borrowers/article/view/2361.

Radical rereading of *Othello* through concepts introduced in Jordan Peele's 2017 film *Get Out* – the 'coagula' and 'the sunken place' that 'places blame for Othello's extreme responses not on his blackness, but rather on the physiological and psychological violence enacted upon him by white supremacy'.

Corredera, Vanessa I. (2020), '"How Dey Goin' to Kill Othello?!" *Key & Peele* and Shakespearean Universality', *Journal of American Studies* 54.1: 27–35. DOI:10.1017/S0021875819001981.

Uses a sketch by comedians Key & Peele, 'Othello: Tis My Shite', to interrogate ideas of Shakespearean universality.

Crowl, Samuel (1992), *Shakespeare Observed: Studies in Performance on Stage and Screen*, Columbus, OH: Ohio State University Press.

Considers the interplay between stage and screen performances, with chapters on Orson Welles, Adrian Noble, Kenneth Branagh and Peter Hall.

Crowl, Samuel (2003), *Shakespeare at the Cineplex: The Kenneth Branagh Era*, Athens, OH: Ohio University Press.

Focuses on Shakespeare films produced between 1989 and 2001, putting Branagh's films in their larger context.

Donaldson, Peter S. (1990), *Shakespearean Films / Shakespearean Directors*, London: Routledge.

Over seven chapters, addresses Olivier's *Henry V* and *Hamlet*, Kurosawa's *Throne of Blood*, the *Othello*s of Orson Welles and Liz White, Zeffirelli's *Romeo and Juliet* and Jean-Luc Godard's *King Lear*.

Ferguson, Ailsa Grant (2016), *Shakespeare, Cinema, Counter-Culture: Appropriation and Inversion*, London: Routledge.

Explores a series of films from the 1980s to the turn of the twenty-first century that 'use Shakespeare's text as part of their counter-cultural or oppositional endeavours' (xiii).

Fernández, José Ramón (2000), 'Shakespeare on Television: A Bibliography of Criticism', *Early Modern Literary Studies* 6.1. https://extra.shu.ac.uk/emls/06-1/diazbibl.htm.

A comprehensive and exhaustive reference guide to scholarship on television adaptations of Shakespeare, up to 1999.

Fernández, José Ramón (2001), 'An Annotated Checklist of Shakespeare on Screen Studies', *The European English Messenger* 10.1: 22–33. Reprinted in Starks and Lehmann, *The Reel Shakespeare* (2002).

Fernández, José Ramón (2016), 'Shakespeare on Screen: A Second Update (2002–16)', *The ESSE Messenger* 25.2: 26–56.

Extensive bibliography of 'the most important publications in the field of Shakespeare on film and television' (259) up to 2002. Supplemental update published in 2016.

Hatchuel, Sarah and Nathalie Vienne-Guerrin, eds, *Shakespeare On Screen* Series. Presses des Universités de Rouen et du Havre (PURH). Cambridge University Press.

Each volume focuses on the screen adaptation history of a single play. Extant volumes include: *A Midsummer Night's Dream* (PURH, 2004), *Richard III* (PURH, 2005), *The*

Henriad (PURH, 2008), *The Roman Plays* (PURH, 2009), *Hamlet* (PURH, 2011), *Macbeth* (PURH, 2013), *Othello* (CUP, 2015), *The Tempest and Late Romances* (CUP, 2017) and (with Victoria Bladen, ed.) *King Lear* (CUP, 2019).

Henderson, Diana E., ed. (2006), *A Concise Companion to Shakespeare on Screen*, Oxford: Blackwell.

Intended to be accessible to undergraduates and to demonstrate particular theoretical lenses and approaches in each essay; also includes a useful comparative chronology (1898–2004) of film adaptations with historical and cultural touchstones. Chapters by (a) Elsie Walker ('Authorship', 8–30), (b) Anthony R. Guneratne ('Cinema Studies', 31–53), (c) Robert Shaughnessy ('Theatricality', 54–76), (d) Diana E. Henderson ('The Artistic Process', 77–95), (e) Barbara Hodgdon ('Cinematic Performance', 96–111), (f) Pascale Aebischer ('Gender Studies', 112–32), (g) Mark Thornton Burnett ('Globalization', 133–54), (h) Anthony Dawson ('Cross-Cultural Interpretation', 155–75), (i) Douglas Lanier ('Popular Culture', 176–96), (j) Roberta E. Pearson and William Uricchio ('Television Studies', 197–215), (k) Peter S. Donaldson ('Remediation', 216–37), afterword by Kathleen McLuskie (238–49).

Henderson, Diana E. (2020), 'Parted eyes and generation gaps in twenty-first-century perceptions of screen Shakespeare', in *Shakespeare/Sense: Contemporary readings in sensory culture*, ed. Simon Smith, London: The Arden Shakespeare.

Explores shifts in the meanings, production and viewing modes of screen Shakespeare from the early broadcast television era (case study following Sean Connery in *An Age of Kings*) through stage use of video to green screen (Dead Centre's *Hamnet*).

Jackson, Russell (2007), *Shakespeare Films in the Making: Vision, Production, and Reception*, Cambridge: Cambridge University Press.

Treats the production and reception of five Shakespeare films from the twentieth century: *A Midsummer Night's Dream* (Reinhardt, 1935), *Romeo and Juliet* (Cukor, 1936), *Henry V* (Olivier, 1944), *Romeo and Juliet* (Castellani, 1954) and *Romeo and Juliet* (Zeffirelli, 1968).

Jackson, Russell, ed. (2007), *The Cambridge Companion to Shakespeare on Film*, Cambridge: Cambridge University Press.

Second edition, revised to include more recent films and scholarship. Chapters by (a) Russell Jackson ('From play-script to screenplay'), (b) Michèle Willems ('Video and its paradoxes'), (c) Barbara Freedman ('Critical junctures in Shakespeare screen history: the case of *Richard III*'), (d) Harry Keyishian ('Shakespeare and movie genre: the case of *Hamlet*'), (e) Michael Hattaway ('The comedies on film'), (f) H. R. Coursen ('Filming Shakespeare's history: three films of *Richard III*'), (g) J. Lawrence Guntner ('*Hamlet, Macbeth* and *King Lear* on film'), (h) Patricia Tatspaugh ('The tragedies of love on film'), (i) Anthony Davies ('The Shakespeare films of Laurence Olivier'), (j) Pamela Mason ('Orson Welles and filmed Shakespeare'), (k) Mark Sokolyansky ('Grigori Kozintsev's *Hamlet* and *King Lear*'), (l) Deborah Cartmell ('Franco Zeffirelli and Shakespeare'), (m)

Samuel Crowl ('Flamboyant realist: Kenneth Branagh'), (n) Carol Chillington Rutter ('Looking at Shakespeare's women on film'), (o) Neil Taylor ('National and racial stereotypes in Shakespeare films'), (p) Neil Forsyth ('Shakespeare the illusionist: filming the supernatural'), (q) Tony Howard ('Shakespeare's cinematic offshoots').

Lehmann, Courtney and Lisa S. Starks, eds (2002), *Spectacular Shakespeare: Critical Theory and Popular Cinema*, Madison, NJ: Fairleigh Dickinson University Press.

Essay collection addressing the way popular Shakespeare films negotiate authorship and reflect on 'Shakespeare' as a genre as well as a person. Chapters by (a) Marguerite Hailey Rippy ('All our Othello: Black monsters and white masks on the American screen'), (b) Lisa Hopkins ('"How very like the home life of our own dear queen": Ian McKellen's *Richard III*'), (c) Alfredo Michel Modenessi ('(Un)doing the book "without Verona walls": a view from the receiving end of Baz Luhrmann's *William Shakespeare's Romeo + Juliet*'), (d) Laurie Osborne ('Cutting up characters: the erotic politics of Trevor Nunn's *Twelfth Night*'), (e) Samuel Crowl ('The marriage of Shakespeare and Hollywood: Kenneth Branagh's *Much Ado About Nothing*'), (f) Courtney Lehmann ('Shakespeare in love: romancing the author, mastering the body'), (g) Douglas Lanier ('"Art thou base, common, and popular?": The cultural politics of Kenneth Branagh's *Hamlet*'), (h) Elizabeth A. Deitchman ('From the cinema to the classroom: Hollywood teaches *Hamlet*'), (i) Annalisa Castaldo ('The film's the thing: using Shakespearean film in the classroom'), afterword by Richard Burt.

Leonard, Kendra Preston (2015), 'Music for Olivier's *Richard III*: Cinematic Scoring for the Early Modern Monstrous', in *The Oxford Handbook of Music and Disability Studies*, ed. Blake Howe, Stephanie Jensen-Moulton, Neil Lerner and Joseph Straus, Oxford: Oxford University Press, 836–55.

Examines William Walton's score for Laurence Olivier's 1955 film of *Richard III*, particularly its engagement with Richard's disability.

Mallin, Eric (2019), *Rereading Shakespeare in the Movies: Non-Adaptations and their Meaning*, Cham, Switzerland: Palgrave Macmillan.

Argues that popular movies often provide more interesting intertexts than more direct film adaptations, with chapters linking *Memento* with *Hamlet*, *Titanic* and *Romeo and Juliet*, *Birdman* and *The Tempest*, *Titus Andronicus* and *The Texas Chainsaw Massacre*, and an epilogue on *Three Billboards* and revenge.

McJannet, Linda (2017), '"A hall, a hall! Give room, and foot it, girls!": Realising the Dance Scene in *Romeo and Juliet* in modern film', *Borrowers and Lenders* 10.1. https://openjournals.libs.uga.edu/borrowers/article/view/2418.

Offers a comparison of the dancing sequences at the Capulet ball (Act 1, scene 5) that culminate in the first meeting of Romeo and Juliet from the films of George Cukor (1936), Franco Zeffirelli (1968) and Baz Luhrmann (1995).

Pittman, L. Monique (2011), *Authorizing Shakespeare on Film and Television: Gender, Class, and Ethnicity in Adaptation*, New York, NY: Peter Lang.

Wide-ranging study of filmed Shakespeare adaptations, including both feature films and television series.

Robison, William B. (2018), 'The Bard, the Bride, and the Muse Bemused: Katherine of Valois on Film in Shakespeare's *Henry V*', in *The Palgrave Handbook of Shakespeare's Queens*, ed. Kavita Mudan Finn and Valerie Schutte, New York: Palgrave, 475–501.

Traces the evolution of Princess Katherine of Valois onscreen in productions of *Henry V*, particularly Judi Dench in *An Age of Kings*, Emma Thompson in Branagh's 1989 film and Mélanie Laurent in *The Hollow Crown* (2012).

Rothwell, Kenneth S. (2004), *A History of Shakespeare on Screen: A Century of Film and Television*, second edition, Cambridge: Cambridge University Press.

Traces the history of screen adaptations of Shakespeare's plays. First edition published in 1999; revised and updated second edition in 2004.

Starks, Lisa S. and Courtney Lehmann, eds (2002), *The Reel Shakespeare: Alternative Cinema and Theory*, Madison, NJ: Fairleigh Dickinson University Press.

Focuses on Shakespeare film adaptations produced outside the Hollywood mainstream. Includes an annotated bibliography. Chapters by (a) Kenneth S. Rothwell ('Hamlet in silence: reinventing the prince on celluloid'), (b) Peter S. Donaldson ('"Two of both kinds": modernism and patriarchy in Peter Hall's *A Midsummer Night's Dream*'), (c) Alan Walworth ('Cinema hysterica passio: voice and gaze in Jean-Luc Godard's *King Lear*'), (d) Lia M. Hotchkiss ('The incorporation of word as image in Peter Greenaway's *Prospero's Books*'), (e) Lisa S. Starks ('Cinema of cruelty: Powers of horror in Julie Taymor's *Titus*'), (f) Bryan Reynolds ('Untimely ripped: Mediating witchcraft in Polanski and Shakespeare'), (g) Kathy M. Howlett ('Utopian revisioning of Falstaff's tavern world: Orson Welles' *Chimes at Midnight* and Gus Van Sant's *My Own Private Idaho*'), (h) Douglas E. Green ('Shakespeare, Branagh, and the "queer traitor": Close encounters in the Shakespearean classroom'), (i) John Brett Mischo ('The screening of the shrews: Teaching (against) Shakespeare's author function'), (j) José Ramón Diaz Fernández ('The reel Shakespeare: A selective bibliography of criticism').

Trivedi, Poonam and Paromita Chakravarti, eds (2020), *Shakespeare and Indian Cinemas: 'Local Habitations'*, London: Routledge.

Explores the rich and varied world of filmed Shakespeare across the Indian subcontinent, from silent film to the modern day. Chapters by (a) Poonam Trivedi ('Woman as Avenger: "Indianising" the Shakespearean Tragic in the Films of Vishal Bhardwaj'), (b) Robert S. White ('Eklavya: Shakespeare meets the *Mahabharata*'), (c) Nishi Pulugartha ('Reworking Shakespeare in Telugu Cinema: *King Lear* to *Gunasundari Katha*'), (d) C. S. Venkiteswaran ('Shakespeare in Malayalam Cinema: Cultural and Mythic Interface, Narrative Negotiations'), (e) Koel Chatterjee ('"Where art thou

Muse that thou forget'st so long, / To speak of that which gives thee all thy might?'": *Qayamat Se Qayamat Tak* (1988) – A Neglected Shakespearean Film'), (f) Amrit Gangar ('The Indian "Silent" Shakespeare: Recouping an Archive'), (g) Anil Zankar ('Shakespeare, Cinema and Indian Poetics'), (h) Preti Taneja ('Such a Long Journey: Rohinton Mistry's Parsi *King Lear* from Fiction to Film'), (i) Paromita Chakravarti ('Cinematic *Lear*s and Bengaliness: Locus, Identity, Language'), (j) Varsha Panjwani ('Shakespeare and Indian Independent Cinema: *8x10 Tasveer* and *10ml Love*'), (k) Thea Buckley ('"Singing is such sweet sorrow": *Ambikapathi*, Hollywood Shakespeare and Tamil Cinema's Hybrid Heritage'), (l) Mark Thornton Burnett ('Gendered Play and Regional Dialogue in *Nanjundi Kalyana*'), (m) A. Mangai ('Not the Play but the Playing: Citation of Performing Shakespeare as a Trope in Tamil Cinema'), (n) Amrita Sen ('Indianising *The Comedy of Errors*: *Bhranti Bilash* and its Aftermaths'), (o) Parthajit Baruah ('Regional Reflections: Shakespeare in Assamese Cinema'), followed by interviews with three directors: Pankaj Bhutalia, Roysten Abel and Aparna Sen.

Wilson, Jeffrey R. (2020), *Shakespeare and Game of Thrones*, London: Routledge.

Considers the relationship between Shakespeare's history plays and the flagship HBO fantasy series *Game of Thrones* (2011–19), not just in terms of textual analysis, but also reception history and fannish engagement. Includes interviews with cast members.

VISUAL ARTS

Goodman, Michael John, The Victorian Illustrated Shakespeare Archive. https://shakespeareillustration.org/

An open access resource of illustrations from nineteenth-century editions of Shakespeare's plays curated by Michael John Goodman at Cardiff University.

Marrapodi, Michele, ed. (2017), *Shakespeare and the Visual Arts: The Italian Influence*, London: Routledge.

Rather than focusing solely on adaptations of Shakespeare (although several chapters do concern those), explores Shakespeare's own appropriation of and engagement with the visual arts of the Italian Renaissance. Considers 'drama as a hybrid genre, combining the figurative power of imagery with the plasticity of the acting process, and explains the three-dimensional quality of the dramatic discourse in the verbal-visual interaction, the stagecraft of the performances and the natural legacy of the iconographical *topoi* of painting's cognitive structures'. Chapters by (a) Claudia Corti ('Shakespeare the emblematist'), (b) Paromita Deb ('*Titus Andronicus* and the Renaissance visual culture: Contemporary emblems of the hand and *Ekphrasis*'), (c) Peter Látka ('"All Adonises must die": Shakespeare's *Venus and Adonis* and the episodic imaginary'), (d) Olivia Coulomb ('Shakespeare's Octavia and Cleopatra: Between stasis and movement'), (e) Hanna Scolnicov ('Both goddess and woman: Cleopatra and Venus'), (f) Claire T. Guéron ('Vanishing points and horizons of audience perception in Shakespeare's late plays'), (g) Michele Marrapodi ('"Pencill'd pensiveness and colour'd sorrow": Italian visual arts and ekphrastic tension in *Othello*, *Cymbeline*, and *Lucrece*'), (h) Camilla Caporicci ('"Wear this jewel for me, 'tis my picture": The miniature in Shakespeare's work'), (i) Rocco Coronato ('The charm of decapitation: Medusa in Caravaggio and *Measure for Measure*'), (j) Muriel Cunin ('"Those foundations which I build upon": Construction and misconstruction in *The Winter's Tale*'), (k) Anthony R. Guneratne ('Shakespeare's genre paintings'), (l) Necla Çikigil ('Verbal painting by means of dance and portraits'), (m) José Manuel González ('Painting and representing gender in the drama of Shakespeare and his Spanish contemporaries'), (n) Sandra Pietrini ('Shakespearean iconography: Some nineteenth-century popular editions and the verbal-visual nexus to serpents'), (o) Timothy A. Turner ('"Paint me in my gallery": Time, perspective, and the Painter Addition to *The Spanish Tragedy*'), (p) Sabina Laskowska-Hinz ('Wladyslaw Czachórski – A Polish painter with Italian soul and Shakespearean vision: "Hamlet Receiving the Players"'), (q) Graham Holderness ('*Julius Caesar*: Shakespeare and the ruins of Rome'), afterword by Stuart Sillars.

Martineau, Jane, ed. (2003), *Shakespeare in Art*, New York, NY: Merrell.

Lavishly illustrated 'exhibition' book bringing together artworks inspired by Shakespeare from galleries across the world in twelve essays. Contains at least ninety images.

Sillars, Stuart (2006), *Painting Shakespeare: The Artist as Critic 1720–1820*, Cambridge: Cambridge University Press.

Explores the relationship between the developing concept of Shakespeare as an English national author and the rise in paintings based on scenes in his plays. Chapters focus on William Hogarth, Henry Fuseli, George Romney, William Blake and Joshua Reynolds, concluding with the Boydell Shakespeare Gallery.

Whitfield, Peter (2013), *Illustrating Shakespeare*, London: British Library.

Traces the history of illustrations and other visual art based on Shakespeare's works.

TRANSMEDIA

Blackwell, Anna (2013), '"Yes, I have gained my experience." (*As You Like It*, 4.3.23) Kenneth Branagh and adapting the "Shakespearean" actor', *Critical Survey* 25.3: 29–41.

Interrogates the idea of the 'Shakespearean' actor, particularly with regard to contemporary popular media, using the case study of Kenneth Branagh.

Blackwell, Anna (2018), *Shakespearean Celebrity in the Digital Age: Fan Cultures and Remediation*, New York, NY: Palgrave.

The first monograph on 'Shakespearean celebrity and its role in contemporary culture', uses several case studies to interrogate, through the careers of several popular and prominent actors, 'the underlying assumptions, associations and cachet that Shakespeare carries in the contemporary moment' (12).

Fazel, Valerie (2016), 'Researching YouTube Shakespeare: Literary Scholars and the Ethical Challenges of Social Media', *Borrowers & Lenders* 10.1 *Shakespeare and Social Media*, ed. Maurizio Calbi and Stephen O'Neill. https://openjournals.libs.uga.edu/ borrowers/article/view/2430.

Addresses an issue central to adaptation studies, particularly those who focus on Shakespeare and the internet: 'researchers' responsibility in the research process and dissemination of YouTubers' information between research and public scholarship' (2). Applicable to most social media platforms, not just YouTube.

Fazel, Valerie and Louise Geddes (2015), '"Give me your hands if we be friends": Collaborative authority in Shakespeare fan fiction', *Shakespeare* 12.3: 274–86. https:// doi.org/10.1080/17450918.2015.1048708.

Urges adaptation scholars to take a closer look at fanfiction based on Shakespeare's plays as an illustration of 'what Shakespeare means to everyday users'.

Fazel, Valerie M. and Louise Geddes, eds (2017), *The Shakespeare User: Critical and Creative Appropriations in a Networked Culture*, New York, NY: Palgrave Macmillan.

Focuses on Shakespeare and online culture, particularly 'user agency and authority in the face of shifting cultural practices that take place in both offline and online contexts' (2). Chapters by (a) Matthew Harrison and Michael Lutz ('South of Elsinore: Actions that a Man Might Play', 23–40), (b) Ruben Espinoza ('Beyond *The Tempest*: Language, Legitimacy, and *La Frontera*', 41–62), (c) Courtney Lehmann and Geoffrey Way ('Young Turks or Corporate Clones? Cognitive Capitalism and the (Young) User in the Shakespearean Attention Economy', 63–80), (d) Nicole Edge ('Circus-Global Transmission of Value: Leveraging *Henry V*'s Cultural Inheritance', 81–108), (e) Jennifer Holl ('Shakespeare Fanboys and Fangirls and the Work of Play', 109–28), (f) Stephen O'Neill ('Theorizing User Agency in YouTube Shakespeare', 129–48), (g) Danielle Rosvally ('The Haunted Network: Shakespeare's Digital Ghost', 149–66), (h) Laura Estill ('Shakespeare and Disciplinarity', 167–86), (i) Eric M. Johnson ('Opening Shakespeare from the Margins', 187–206), (j) Graham Holderness ('Shakespeare and the Undead', 207–28).

Finn, Kavita Mudan (2017), 'History play: critical and creative engagement with Shakespeare's tetralogies in transformative fanworks', *Shakespeare* 13.3: 210–25.

Frames fanfiction based on Shakespeare's history plays as a form of critical praxis and suggests parallels between early modern literary culture and contemporary online fan communities.

Geddes, Louise (2018), 'Unlearning Shakespeare Studies: Speculative Criticism and the Place of Fan Activism', *Shakespeare Survey* 71: 209–20.

As in 'Give Me Your Hands' (2015), argues for the critical analysis of amateur Shakespeare-based fanworks as a gauge for attitudes toward Shakespeare amongst 'users'.

Henderson, Diana E. (2011), 'Catalysing What? Historical Remediation, the Musical, and what of *Love's Labour's* Lasts', *Shakespeare Survey* 64: *Shakespeare as Cultural Catalyst*: 97–113.

Focuses on cross-media adaptation of Shakespeare's play to stage (as the first Black British West End musical, *The Big Life*) and screen (Branagh's film musical).

O'Neill, Stephen (2014), *Shakespeare and YouTube: New Media Forms of the Bard*, London: Bloomsbury.

First full-length study of the uses, potentialities and limitations of Shakespeare on YouTube, with particular focus on YouTube users as producers and creative adapters of Shakespearean characters and scenes. Chapters consider engagements with *Hamlet* and *Othello*, queer erasure in the Sonnets, and the teaching potentialities of Shakespeare on YouTube.

O'Neill, Stephen, ed. (2018), *Broadcast Your Shakespeare: Continuity and Change across Media*, London: Bloomsbury.

Interrogates and explores the intersection between Shakespeare production and study and the use of new and different kinds of media. Chapters by (a) Darlena Ciraulo ('Broadcasting Censorship: Hollywood's Production Code and *A Midsummer Night's Dream*'), (b) Robert Sawyer ('Broadcasting the Bard: Orson Welles, Shakespeare, and War'), (c) Diana Henderson ('"This Distracted Globe, This Brave New World": Learning from the MIT Global Shakespeares' Twenty-First Century'), (d) David C. Moberly ('"Once more to the breach!": Shakespeare, Wikipedia's Gender Gap, and the Online, Digital Elite'), (e) Christy Desmet ('Emo Hamlet: Locating Shakespearean Affect in Social Media'), (f) Joseph Haughey ('"It Is Worth the Listening To": The Phonograph and the Teaching of Shakespeare in Early Twentieth-Century America'), (g) Kirk Hendershott-Kraetzer ('Juliet, Tumbld: Fan Renovations of Shakespeare's Juliet on Tumblr'), (h) Sarah Olive ('"Certain o'er uncertainty": *Troilus and Cressida*, Ambiguity, and the *Lewis* episode "Generation of Vipers"'), (i) Douglas Lanier ('Vlogging the bard: Serialization, Social Media, Shakespeare'), (j) Romano Mullin ('Tweeting Television / Broadcasting the Bard: @HollowCrownFans and Digital Shakespeares'), (k) Anna Blackwell ('"Somewhere in the world... someone misquoted Shakespeare. I can sense it.": Tom Hiddleston performing the Shakespearean online'), afterword by Courtney Lehmann.

O'Neill, Stephen (2018), 'Shakespeare's Digital Flow: Human Technologies and the Possibilities of Intercultural Exchange', *Shakespeare Studies* 46: 120–33.

Considers Shakespeare as part of 'a digital information flow' and explores 'values that are being iterated through Shakespeare within these settings' (121), with a particular focus on modern adaptations and appropriations of the 'strangers' case' scene in *Sir Thomas More*.

Pope, Johnathan (2020), *Shakespeare's Fans: Adapting the Bard in the Age of Media Fandom*, New York, NY: Palgrave.

Proposes an origin for Shakespeare fandom in the eighteenth century and applies fan studies approaches to Shakespeare adaptations.

Teague, Fran (2011), 'Using Shakespeare with memes, remixes, and fanfic', *Shakespeare Survey* 64: *Shakespeare as Cultural Catalyst*: 74–82.

Challenges the taxonomy of adaptation studies (appropriation, derivative, allusion, adaptation, etc) through an analysis of Shakespearean memes, remixes and several examples of fanfiction.

INDEX